The Domestic Context of Soviet Foreign Policy

Studies of the Research Institute on International Change, Columbia University

Radicalism in the Contemporary Age, edited by Seweryn Bialer and Sophia Sluzar
    Volume 1: Sources of Contemporary Radicalism
    Volume 2: Radical Visions of the Future
    Volume 3: Strategies and Impact of Contemporary Radicalism

The Relevance of Liberalism, edited by the Research Institute on International Change

Asia's Nuclear Future, edited by William H. Overholt

Also of Interest

The Soviet Union in World Politics, edited by Kurt London

The Soviet Union in the Third World: Successes and Failures, edited by Robert H. Donaldson

Studies of the Research Institute on International Change, Columbia University
Seweryn Bialer, Series Editor

The Domestic Context of Soviet Foreign Policy
edited by Seweryn Bialer

This collective volume highlights those aspects of Soviet internal dynamics that influence foreign policy and international relationships. The authors almost uniformly reflect a growing awareness of the importance of internal factors as a critical determinant shaping not only the Soviet Union's position in the international arena, but also the making and effectiveness of Soviet foreign policy. A central premise of this volume is that both the range of options in Soviet foreign policymaking and the predispositions among the policymakers toward the selection of particular options are influenced and circumscribed by the dynamics of Soviet social, economic, and political development.

Seweryn Bialer is a professor of political science and director of the Research Institute on International Change at Columbia University. He is a specialist in Soviet domestic politics, with emphasis on contemporary Soviet elites. His publications include *Stalin and His Generals: Soviet Military Memoirs of World War II* and *Stalin's Successors: Leadership, Stability, and Change in the Soviet Union.*

The Domestic Context of Soviet Foreign Policy

edited by Seweryn Bialer

Westview Press • Boulder, Colorado

Croom Helm • London, England

∞ The paper used in this publication meets the requirements of the American National Standard for Permanence of Paper for Printed Library Materials Z39.48-1984.

Studies of the Research Institute on International Change, Columbia University

This volume is included in Westview's Special Studies on the Soviet Union and Eastern Europe.

Published in 1981 in the United States of America by
  Westview Press, Inc.
  5500 Central Avenue
  Boulder, Colorado 80301
  Frederick A. Praeger, Publisher

Second printing, 1982

Published in 1981 in Great Britain by
  Croom Helm Ltd.
  2-10 St John's Road
  London SW11

Library of Congress Catalog Card No. 80-11877
ISBN (U.S.): 0-89158-783-7; 0-89158-891-4 pb
ISBN (U.K.): 0-7099-0623-4

10 9 8 7 6 5 4

Printed and bound in the United States of America

Contents

Part 1. Culture and Ideology

Part 2. Politics and Society

Part 3. Economics

Part 4. Eastern Europe

Part 5. Domestic Context: An Overview

Figures and Tables

Preface

This volume grew out of a project that the Research Institute on International Change at Columbia University undertook for the Department of State. I hereby acknowledge the help received from the State Department in making this volume possible.

Because of space limitations, a number of original papers prepared for the State Department project could not be included. I gratefully acknowledge the contributions of the authors of these papers: Abraham Brumberg, "Dissent and Soviet Foreign Policy"; Ben Fischer, "The Soviet Political System and Foreign Policy-Making in the Brezhnev Era"; Edward Keenan, "Muscovite Political Folkways: Some Prolegomena to the Study of Great Russian Political Culture"; Robbin Laird, "The Scientific-Technical Revolution and Soviet Ideology"; and Boris Rabbot, "Soviet Travelling Professionals: An Inside View." I also acknowledge the advice and contributions of those who participated in two meetings organized for the project: Vernon Aspaturian, Coit Blacker, George Breslauer, Lawrence Caldwell, Paul Cocks, Arnold Horelick, Jerry Hough, Gail Lapidus, Robert Legvold, Harry Rigby, Alvin Rubinstein, Morton Schwartz, Dimitri Simes, Helmut Sonnenfeldt, Jan Triska, Jiri Valenta, and Donald Zagoria.

Throughout the preparation of this volume I received invaluable help from Alexander Dallin, who, aside from contributing one of the summary chapters, always offered sound advice and counsel. Finally, I thank those whose roles were crucial in editing this volume: Richard Coffman, Michael Klecheski, Cynthia Roberts, and Penny Yee, without whose efforts, hard work, and patience this volume would never have been finished. Cynthia Roberts and Michael Klecheski did the bulk of the original editing of the chapters; Richard Coffman and Michael Klecheski reviewed all of the copy editing and the page proofs of the book. Their work is deeply appreciated and their expertise and solidness in Soviet affairs is deeply admired. I am quite fortunate to be able to rely on the help of students of such caliber.

Seweryn Bialer

Contributors

Hannes Adomeit, of the Siftung Wissenschaft und Politik, specializes in Soviet foreign policy.

Jeremy Azrael, professor of political science at the University of Chicago, specializes in Soviet politics and comparative Communism.

Seweryn Bialer is director of the Research Institute on International Change, Columbia University. He is a specialist in Soviet domestic policies, with emphasis on contemporary Soviet elites.

Morris Bornstein, professor of economics at the University of Michigan, specializes in the Soviet and East European economies.

Timothy J. Colton is a professor in the Department of Political Economy at the University of Toronto, whose field of specialty is Soviet military developments.

Walter D. Connor, professor of sociology at the University of Pennsylvania, is also affiliated with the East European–USSR Studies of the Foreign Service Institute in the State Department. He has written on social stratification and political change.

Alexander Dallin, professor of political science and history at Stanford University, specializes in Soviet and Russian foreign policy.

Warren W. Eason is professor of economics at Ohio State University. His specialties are the Soviet economy and Soviet population and manpower.

Franklyn Griffiths, professor in the Department of Political Economy at the University of Toronto, specializes in Soviet politics.

Grey Hodnett, professor of political science at York University, Canada, is on leave at the Central Intelligence Agency. His fields of specialty are current Soviet politics and nationality policies.

Arcadius Kahan, professor of economics at the University of Chicago, specializes in agricultural economics and the economic history of Russia and Europe.

Andrzej Korbonski, professor of political science at the University of California, Los Angeles, specializes in comparative politics of East Central Europe.

Herbert S. Levine, professor of economics at the University of Pennsylvania, specializes in economic planning and technology transfer to the Soviet Union.

Paul Marer is professor of international business at the Graduate School of Business, Indiana University. His field of specialty is the East European economy.

Adam Ulam is professor of government and member of the Russian Research Center at Harvard University. His specialty is nineteenth- and twentieth-century Russian history.

Acronyms

CC	Central Committee
CIA	Central Intelligence Agency
CMEA/	
COMECON	Council for Mutual Economic Assistance
CPSU	Communist Party of the Soviet Union
CSCE	Conference on Security and Cooperation in Europe
DOSAAF	Voluntary Society for Assistance of the Army, Air Force, and Navy
EEC	European Economic Community
FRG	Federal Republic of Germany
GATT	General Agreement on Trade and Tariffs
GDR	German Democratic Republic
GNP	Gross National Product
GRU	State Investigation Administration
IIB	International Investment Bank
IMF	International Monetary Fund
KGB	Committee of State Security
KPC	Communist Party of Czechoslovakia
MBFR	Mutual Balanced Force Reduction
MFN	Most Favored Nation
MID	Ministry of Foreign Affairs
MPA	Main Political Administration
MPLA	Popular Movement for the Liberation of Angola
MTS	Machine Tractor Stations
MVD	Ministry of Internal Affairs
NEM	New Economic Mechanism
NEP	New Economic Policy
NKVD	People's Commissariat of Internal Affairs
NMP	Net Material Product
OAU	Organization of African Unity

PLO   Palestine Liberation Organization
PRC   People's Republic of China
SALT   Strategic Arms Limitation Talks
SMA   Soviet Military Administration (in postwar Germany)
SPD   Social Democratic Party
SRI/WEFA
 SOVMOD   Stanford Research Institute/Wharton Econometric
                 Forecasting Associates Soviet Econometric
                 Model

PART 1

Culture and Ideology

1
Russian Nationalism

Adam Ulam

One hundred years ago Dostoyevsky wrote: "Every great people believes, and must believe if it intends to live long, that in it alone resides the salvation of the world; that it lives in order to stand at the head of the nations, . . . to lead them in a concordant choir toward the final goal preordained for them."[1] This, to be sure, was meant in an existentialist rather than a literal sense: the great writer did not propose that Russia should conquer the world, but he wanted his countrymen to develop a new sense of national pride and to rid themselves of the perennial feeling of inferiority vis-à-vis "Europe." Like many Russians, practically into our own day, he was envious of the British for their alleged superb self-confidence: " . . . lord or worker, every Englishman strives above all to be English in every facet of his activity, social or political, and even his love of mankind is expressed in a specifically English way." Of what we would today call "consumer-oriented states," Dostoyevsky's tone was contemptuous: "Those prudent, honest, peaceful nations which eschew exorbitant ambitions, nations of traders and industrialists with their riches and tidiness . . . God be with them, but they will not amount to much, they represent mediocrity which is of no use to mankind."

This was not a very original sentiment—statements similar to Dostoyevsky's were at the time forthcoming from many thinkers and politicians throughout Europe. But the point is that while in the West this view became unfashionable after World War I (and is now extinct), in Russia it still provides the psychological underpinning of the official ideology. Marxism, the most internationalist of nineteenth century ideologies, has merged with Russian nationalism, their synthesis being Soviet Communism, which is internationalist in form and nationalist in essence. Consider the ritualistic phrases: the USSR is "the fatherland of socialism" or of "the world proletariat," and the Russians "the leading nationality of the Soviet Union." While Dostoyevsky would not approve because of his intensely religious mentality, he would in all likelihood be impressed by the achievement of the Communist rulers of his country. How skillfully they have harnessed a worldwide movement and ideology to the interests of their state, or, to be more blunt, to those of the Soviet power elite! How puny that Pan-Slavism in which many of Dostoyevsky's contemporaries sought to find a surrogate of universalist appeal for Russian nationalism, when compared with the reality of the "camp of socialism" of today — the countries of East and Central Europe, and not merely those peopled by Slavs, are being led by Russia "in a concordant choir toward (mankind's) final goal." And as for other Communist movements, while it is no longer quite true that, as a perceptive French Socialist said: "They are neither on the left nor on the right, they are in the east," the fact remains that with one huge and a few minor exceptions, they remain in various degrees dependent on Moscow. It has become fashionable to challenge this conclusion and talk about "Eurocommunism." Yet, while it is undeniable that the Italian, French, and other parties are no longer as slavishly obedient to the Kremlin as they were in Stalin's time, they remain, let us say, deferential to their Soviet colleagues.

What has enabled Russian nationalism to transmute itself into Soviet Communism and as such to grip and exploit a worldwide movement? Suppose that following World War I militant Marxism had triumphed in Germany rather than in Russia. Could Berlin have controlled world Communism to the same extent that Moscow has? Most unlikely.

First, it is well to recognize certain peculiar characteristics of Russian nationalism before the Revolution. This nationalism contained many traits typical of the psychology of what might be called underprivileged nations, such as Poland or Ireland, which had to struggle for independent statehood or even for national survival. And yet, for most of the modern period, Russia was already a great power and territorially the world's largest state. The feeling of vulnerability and constant threat to the national community has accompanied Russia's almost continuous expansion. National security in the popular mind has become associated with the expansion of the state's power and frontiers, perhaps a legacy of those distant days when old Russia lay open to frequent invasions both from east and west. The necessity of imperialism and of Russianization has been argued not only by spokesmen for the Right, but also by some leading representatives of the revolutionary tradition. The Decembrist Paul Pestel wanted Russia to be nationally homogeneous after tsarism had been overthrown; most of the non-Russians would have had to be assimilated and the Jews expelled. Few major figures in Russian history were as free of chauvinism as Alexander Herzen, yet even he held Kiev to be a Russian city and is on record as saying, "Sometime Constantinople will be Russia's capital."[2] Those Russian revolutionaries who, like Herzen, supported the Polish insurrection of 1863 soon found themselves isolated, denounced even by the most radical elements of the intelligentsia at home.

Nationalism in this peculiar, partly defensive, and partly aggressive form has thus been the strongest element in Russian political culture, permeating the radical as well as the liberal and conservative camps. This situation seemed to be drastically altered with the entrance of Marxism on the political scene. Disciples of the new ideology were bound to heed its founder's words that workers have no country. Officially and no doubt sincerely both major branches of the Russian Social Democratic Party adhered to internationalism and condemned Great Russian chauvinism as it affected both domestic and foreign policy. And yet, a perceptive observer wrote of the father of Russian Marxism: "In his heart he ([Georgi] Plekhanov) has remained an unflinching patriot. . . . He sees Russia as the giant socialist state of the future and will not concede a foot of her soil. "[3] This could not have been said of Plekhanov's pupil and protagonist, Lenin, who characterized tsarist Russia as "the prison house of nations" and who, before the Revolution, was a staunch advocate of every nationality's right to self-determination up to and including full separation from the socialist Russia of the future. By the same token it is grotesquely incorrect to present Lenin, as in Solzhenitsyn's *Lenin in Zurich,* as militantly anti-Russian. Whatever his convictions, the logic of his views on power and centralization would, after the Revolution, make him the father of that Soviet nationalism which under Stalin would become mainly Russian in context.

The Bolsheviks' nationality policy served them well during the civil war and during the first years of the Soviet regime. Yet it became clear very early that Communism represented what might be called political assimilation and that whatever the ethnic composition of the party leadership at the time, the psychological meaning of this assimilation implied, even in those earliest and most internationally oriented years of Soviet power, a degree of Russianization. The struggle for power and against foreign intervention made it easy to rationalize departures from strict Marxist orthodoxy. If the policy of "all land to the peasants" could be excused by the circumstances of the moment, then why not appeal in a moment of danger to good old-fashioned nationalism? Already when the Brest-Litovsk negotiations broke down, Lenin's government proclaimed in a broadside that "the Socialist Fatherland was in danger." Later, during the Soviet-Polish war, more uninhibited language was used. In 1920 a Communist journal spoke in tones reminiscent of 1863 when it contrasted "the perfidious Jesuitism of the Poles" with "the open and honest nature" of the Russians.[4] As it emerged in 1921 the Soviet state claimed to be the legitimate heir to all the territories, except ethnic Poland and Finland, which composed the tsar's empire.

The crucial step in the final emergence of Soviet nationalism and in its symbiosis with world Communism was marked by Stalin's concept of "Socialism in one country." The security and power of the Soviet Union were proclaimed to be the first priority and obligation not only for the Soviets, but also for foreign Communists. And another step in the Russianization of the concept of Soviet nationalism was taken when a whispering campaign during Stalin's struggle against the New Opposition stressed the predominantly Jewish character of the leadership of the latter.

Most of the studies of Soviet foreign policy of the early and middle 1920s emphasize that it was organized along two parallel lines: the policy of the Comintern designed to foment revolutions and that of the Narkomindel attuned to the state interests of the USSR. From the beginning each line slanted toward the other, and they finally merged by the end of the decade. The Comintern's policy was heavily oriented toward attacking Britain's imperial interests. To be sure this reflected the ideological-tactical precepts of Lenin: Britain is the linchpin of the world's capitalist system and colonialism is its Achilles heel. But as one studies Soviet moves in regard to India, southern China, Afghanistan, or Turkey, one is forcibly reminded of the nineteenth century imperialist rivalry between the tsar and Great Britain. For all of the Comintern's alliance with the Kuomintang, the Soviet government hastened to reclaim its imperial predecessor's rights and properties in Manchuria, negotiating over them with the local warlord. One of the most cherished ambitions of Russian nationalists had been to unite within their state all of the territories inhabited by the East Slavs. The persistence of these aspirations under the Soviets was demonstrated by the fact that the Comintern's branch in the southeastern portion of the interwar Polish state was named the Communist Party of Western Ukraine and was organizationally separate from the corresponding Polish body.

In fact it would be difficult at any stage to point to a single case where the policy of the Comintern ran counter to the interests of the Soviet state or for that matter to the age-long aspirations of old Russia. The accoutrements of the Socialist Fatherland concealed but imperfectly the traditional figure of Mother Russia. Foreign Communists were required to be and soon became Soviet nationalists. Said Stalin: "He is a revolutionary, who without a reservation, unconditionally, openly . . . is ready to protect and defend the USSR. . . . He who thinks to defend the world revolutionary movement apart and against the USSR is going against the revolution and will certainly slide into the camp of the enemies of the revolution."[5]

By the end of the 1920s, the relationship between the national interest of the Soviet Union and activities of world Communists was thus defined, even if not fully articulated publicly: the primary task of foreign Communism was not to advance the cause of world revolution, but to defend and support the USSR. In turn, the latter (or more properly its ruler) saw the first priority of its foreign policy as the defense of the territorial integrity and of the sociopolitical system of the Soviet state. As interpreted in the late 1920s and early 1930s, this implied the preservation of European peace, for Stalin and his associates did not believe that Russia could afford to be dragged into a general European war at a time when it embarked on an ambitious program of rapid industrialization and collectivization. By 1932 Stalin's analysis of the world situation was already different from the prevailing Soviet view following the end of the civil war. From both the ideological and state interest points of view, the Soviet leaders expected and hoped that the "inherent contradictions" of capitalism would erupt into another imperialist war. General peace had been seen as a danger to the Soviet state, for the capitalists might settle their differences in order to launch a joint offensive against the homeland of Communism. Any step toward restoration of international stability was thus viewed as a potential threat. The League of Nations was a "league of imperialist robbers." The Dawes Plan, by contributing economic stabilization in Europe, was aimed against Communism in general and the Soviet Union in particular. Weak and isolated, the USSR welcomed any sign of internal or interstate conflict in the capitalist camp and feared and opposed any step that would shore up the system damaged by World War I or assuage the national passions aroused by the war and by the settlement of Versailles.

By 1930 this somewhat primitive analysis was supplanted by a more sober and realistic appraisal of the realities of the world situation. The Soviet regime, in the midst of a life and death struggle to conquer its peasantry, had a stake in avoiding the kind of international chaos that would lead to war. But while Soviet nationalism was now in complete ascendance as the guiding principle of Soviet-Comintern policies, ideological considerations still colored Stalin's perceptions as to what policies the interest of the Soviet state required. It was difficult for Moscow to see that it had a vital stake in the preservation of the Weimar Republic. Hitler, it was thought, was a lesser evil than a victory of conservative and center forces in Germany might be. The latter might effect a final reconciliation of German nationalism with France and Britain, while the National Socialists, quite apart from their anti-Western tendencies, could not conceivably retain power very long; their collapse, after they had destroyed what remained of democratic institutions in their country, would almost inevitably clear the path for the Communists. Even when the character and aspirations of National Socialism became better understood, and there was no thought of the Nazi-Soviet pact, Moscow refused to throw its full weight on the side of the Western democracies. What is known as the collective security or, almost equally fatuously, the Litvinov period of Soviet foreign policy was not designed to mount a crusade against Hitler, but simply to prevent any accommodation he might make with Britain and France. Soviet national interest, Stalin believed, required a stalemate, whether in peace or war, between Germany and the West and would suffer were one or the other to get the upper hand. This belief found its logical culmination in the 1939 pact.

The 1930s revealed more clearly the Russian character of Soviet nationalism. Domestically this was exemplified by the condemnation of the Pokrovsky school of historiography, the introduction of the Cyrillic alphabet for the Central Asian languages, and so forth. But above all, with an unerring instinct, Stalin labored to present the Soviet state (more specifically his own regime) as the heir to eternal Russia. "Aside from reactionary Russia, revolutionary Russia always existed. . . . All this fills (and must fill!) the hearts of Russian workers with the feeling of revolutionary national pride capable of moving mountains, of forging miracles."[6] In fact, the Soviet regime was presented as the culmination and the highest stage of Russia's historical development; it was only under Communism-Stalinism that the nation could reach its destined greatness. "The history of Old Russia shows . . . that because of her backwardness, she was constantly being defeated, by the Mongol Khans, by the Polish Lithuanian noblemen, by the Anglo-French capitalists. . . . We are behind the leading nations by fifty to one hundred years. We must make up this distance in ten years. Either that or we go under."[7]

Stalinism marked a further attenuation of the distinction between Soviet domestic and foreign policies. Every repressive policy at home had been long rationalized in terms of the foreign danger. Now the task of social engineering, so hideously costly in human lives and suffering, was carried out. Forcible collectivization and industrialization were justified as necessitated by defense needs of the Soviet state ("Either that or we go under"). Thus by definition any manifestation of political dissent became treason, pure and simple. The main function of the great purge trials, 1936–1938, was to make this lesson clear to the masses of the Soviet people. To oppose any of Stalin's policies—whether by refusing to deliver the scheduled quota of grain to the state or by questioning the guilt of any of the countless victims of the purges—meant to be working for the benefit of the foreign enemy, trying to bring down the Soviet state, to destroy Russia. Had there not been a widespread acceptance of this rationale by the Soviet people, and especially by its Russian component, it is difficult to see how the regime could have survived the bloodbath of the 1930s. His success in exploiting the emotional power of Russian nationalism was to astound Stalin himself. He had been almost sure (and his nervous breakdown at the beginning of the war in 1941 is a vivid demonstration of this fact) that the regime, or at least his personal power, could not survive a major defeat and foreign occupation of a sizeable area of the country. And yet, even at the height of Soviet defeats during the war, Stalin's power was not challenged. On the contrary, the man whose sins of commission and omission caused the greatest disaster in Russian military history in terms of human casualties emerged as the national leader, with even the Russian political exiles acclaiming his rule and supporting his territorial claims at the end of the war. Russian nationalism was proven to be the strongest psychological prop of Soviet Communism. Stalin acknowledged this in his famous toast to the Russian nation at the victory banquet in the Kremlin following VE Day. And after Japan's defeat the dictator's language was unabashedly chauvinistic. Men of his generation, he said, had long awaited this moment of revenge for the perfidious Japanese attack on Russia in 1904. "Long live and flourish our Fatherland."

In light of the preceding, it might appear paradoxical to assert that considerations of national greatness (to use a slightly antiquated term) were, from the political point of view, less important for Stalin than they have become for his successors. Certainly, following World War II his power could not be jeopardized by any, even serious, setback in the Soviet Union's foreign policy or a demonstration that its power and worldwide influence were still considerably inferior to that of the United States. It is difficult to imagine any post-1953 leader being able to remain in power after one of the satellites had slipped the Soviet leash, but the defection of Yugoslavia (which resulted mainly from the despot's senile suspiciousness and megalomania) did not in the slightest affect his position. Khrushchev's downfall was undoubtedly hastened by the Cuban fiasco of 1962 and his inability to avoid revelations of how intense the Sino-Soviet quarrel had become. Yet Stalin could shrug off both the diplomatic defeat over the Berlin blockade and the very serious miscalculation of the Korean venture of 1950. Once the most threatening part of World War II was over, Stalin was in the pleasant position of being able to exploit Soviet-Russian nationalism without being unduly constrained by it. His position was so secure that he could afford to jest on the subject. He told Roosevelt with a straight face at Yalta that were he to allow any Ukrainians to revert to Polish rule, he might incur considerable political trouble.

Why then the frantic Russian chauvinism of his last years, the denunciation of cosmopolitanism, the crackdown on anything that even vaguely suggested cultural (never mind political) self-assertiveness among the non-Russian nationalism, and the undercurrent of anti-Semitism? This undoubtedly represented the final state of Stalin's own Russian chauvinism rather than a response to specific political needs or apprehensions. To be sure, in the so-called Zhdanov campaign there was also an element of historical caution: the USSR had to be immunized against Western ideas so that such ideas would not corrupt Russia's intellectual elite as they had after another victorious war, that of 1812–1815. But these precautions were not connected to any fear for his own power, which at the time was threatened by only one enemy — old age.

Stalin's death was followed by crisis in the political system he had created. One of the most interesting aspects of this crisis was a temporary breakdown of the synthesis of Communism and Russian nationalism or, to paraphrase the official semantics, the revelation of inherent contradictions within Soviet nationalism. Needless to say, we have little concrete evidence, as official intimations of the crisis were tendentious and colored by the struggle for succession. Domestic nationality policy was shifted away from the extreme Russianization measures of Stalin's last years. We do not know whether — as officially charged — L. P. Beria made a bid for power, one element of which could have been his attempt to exploit the grievances of the non-Russian elements of the party apparatus. Also far from being firmly established is the version that Beria's proposed policies envisaged a degree of retrenchment in Soviet foreign policy. Communist Germany was to become a negotiable item in any settlement with the West. But the mere fact that such rumors were circulated, along with the changes actually effected by the winning faction, both at home and in connection with foreign policy, suggests strongly that there had been considerable argument and disagreement within the ruling elite on the need to redefine the relationship of Soviet national interest to world Communism.

This reexamination touched primarily on the question of what to do about China. Throughout the Khrushchev period the Chinese problem weighed heavily on all aspects of Soviet foreign policy, and it undoubtedly influenced domestic politics as well. It must have been clear to the Soviet leaders as early as 1953, if not before, that a China united under Communist rule would in the long run present the greatest danger to the vital interests of the Soviet state — especially to what might be called the Russian side of its national interest. Why then did the Soviet Union not take any steps to counter this threat? Why, on the contrary, did it appease China until 1959–1960 through economic help on a scale unimaginable in Stalin's time, including assistance to Peking's nuclear program, diplomatic support, and so on? The answer clearly is that Moscow believed any public intimation of the fictitious nature of the "unbreakable unity of the Chinese and Soviet people" would have handed a ready weapon to U.S. diplomacy, perhaps emboldening it to go beyond mere rhetoric in exploiting the Soviet Union's troubles in Germany and Eastern Europe. The logic of the Soviets' fears would have required the USSR to seek an accommodation, if not an alliance, with the United States as early as the mid-1950s in order to contain China and especially to prevent her from acquiring the one thing both Moscow and Washington feared most—nuclear capability. Yet to pursue such a policy openly would have damaged, perhaps irreparably, Soviet domination of world Communism and, in view of the Americans' organic inability to practice realpolitik, might have turned China into an open enemy without securing the United States as an ally. What then could be done to resolve this dilemma? The only way out, Khrushchev believed, was to pursue a much more ambitious and militant foreign policy. China's fears might be allayed and her nuclear ambitions postponed in the recognition of Soviet militancy vis-à-vis the West, while the latter, confronted with Soviet pressure in the Middle East, over Berlin, and in the Caribbean, would be forced to seek an overall accommodation.[8] The Cuban missile crisis of 1962 exposed the bankruptcy of this policy. The Sino-Soviet conflict, which had been public knowledge since 1960, now entered its sharpest phase.

In retrospect, Khrushchev's last two years in power can be seen as the period of the greatest strain on the Soviet nationalism–world Communism nexus. Recognition that it was a fellow Communist state, rather than capitalism, which presented the greatest threat to the USSR now reached beyond the ruling elite and penetrated the Soviet masses. On 2 September 1964, *Pravda* published an interview Mao held with some visiting Japanese in which he unabashedly advanced Chinese claims not only to Manchuria, but also to huge areas in Siberia. He characterized the Soviet Union as an imperialist state, devoted to constant expansion: "The Russians took everything they could."[9] The manner of the Chinese taunting of the USSR implied considerable confidence, possibly exaggerated, that the Soviet leaders could not launch any outright hostilities against China without threatening the rule of the Communist system in their own country. For some time past, Moscow had hinted that Mao's tactics—his "leftist sectarianism" and Chinese encouragement of "wars of national liberation" —were ultimately designed to embroil the United States and the Soviet Union in a war. The Sino-Soviet break illustrated in vivid relief the fact that the perfect symbiosis between Soviet nationalism and world Communism had been possible only because of the peculiar historical circumstances attending the Stalin era and the absence until the very end of that era of another large Communist state. Without Stalin, and with China growing in power and acquiring rudimentary nuclear capability, the non-ideological premises of Soviet foreign policy were bound to clash with the ideological ones.

On 14 February 1964, at a meeting of the Central Committee, Suslov declared: "The Chinese leaders, and not only they, should get it through their thick skulls that our Central Commitee, headed by this faithful

Leninist, Nikita Sergeievich Khrushchev, is more than ever united and monolithic."[10] The propagation of hostility toward the USSR, Suslov charged, had become the main concern of Mao's regime. He tried to expose Peking's double game: "With a stubbornness worthy of a better cause, the Chinese leaders attempted to prevent the improvement of Soviet-American relations, representing it as 'plotting with the imperialists.' Yet it is clear that they themselves would not refuse to improve relations with the United States but as yet do not see favorable circumstances for such an endeavor."[11]

Had he stayed in power, it is quite possible that Khrushchev would have tried to draw closer to the West with the ultimate objective of obtaining a free hand vis-à-vis China. Even his removal, (though among its immediate effects was a certain relaxation of tension between the two Communist giants) might not have affected his successors' determination to pursue the same policy. But then came Vietnam. The massive involvement of the United States in Southeast Asia did not bring Moscow and Peking any closer, but it made immediate détente with the United States both impractical and unnecessary. Impractical because it would not have been within the Brezhnev-Kosygin team's power (as it would have been for Stalin) to make a deal with the United States that would sacrifice the interests of North Vietnam. Such a move might have dealt a decisive blow to Soviet domination of the Communist camp. Unnecessary because by 1967 two things became clear. The United States, because of the domestic repercussions of the war, would not be able to secure its objectives in Southeast Asia and the West would in all likelihood have to come to Moscow seeking détente rather than vice versa. Furthermore, the Cultural Revolution and the consequent internal turmoil in China made the settling of the Chinese problem less urgent. China's challenge to Soviet domination of world Communism suffered a decisive setback. Soviet influence again became predominant in Hanoi. The pro-Peking Indonesian Communist party, on the threshold of attaining power, was shattered in 1965 and the news was greeted in Moscow with poorly concealed satisfaction. America's foreign and China's domestic foolishness thus spared or at least postponed for the Soviet leadership the necessity of making a clear-cut choice between foreign policies attuned mainly to either matters of national interest or ideology. In fact, the Brezhnev regime can claim that it has achieved a new synthesis of the two: the Soviet Union has grown much stronger during the past thirteen years, and so has the influence of Communist parties and national liberation movements directed by or allied to Moscow. There is no reason, the official view would hold, for a Soviet citizen to feel that there is any conflict between his country's security and greatness and its obligations to "fraternal parties" and national liberation movements. In fact, the two reinforce each other; the citizen ought to feel a surge of national pride when—as at the last Party Congress—103 delegations of Communist and allied organizations from 96 countries appeared to congratulate the Soviet regime on its achievements and to express their support and gratitude to it. What other state in history has had as numerous and widespread a body of supporters and sympathizers throughout the world?

How convincing this argument is to the mass of the Soviet people is, of course, something we cannot gauge with any degree of precision. But it is important that we separate the question of the emotional appeal of Soviet nationalism as linked with the worldwide Communist movement from that of the belief in Marxism-Leninism. The latter, as almost everybody agrees, has simply lost any meaning and relevance in the lives of the vast majority of the citizens of the Soviet Union. But can the same be said about worldwide power and influence of the Soviet Union? The "man in the street" will shrug off the news of the Soviet successes in Angola or of the Communist prospects in Italy. He may have grown sophisticated enough to discount much of the official party line about the West. He may feel acutely his deprivations as a citizen and as a consumer and blame them on the system under which he lives. But is he, consciously or unconsciously, impervious to the argument that the course of events during the past twenty years or so indicates that history has already rendered its verdict regarding which side must prevail in the competition between the Soviet Union and the West? It can be argued that for the ruling elite, success in foreign policy and growth in external power of the Soviet state has become the principal means of legitimizing its policy system. Even as resolute an enemy of Communism as Solzhenitsyn has been constrained to recognize this fact: "No less an achievement than Stalin's have been the successes of Soviet diplomacy in recent years; for the Western world as a single united force no longer counterbalances the Soviet Union."[12]

Solzhenitsyn goes on to argue that this apparent harmony between the national interest and Communist expansionism is a delusion that in the long run will prove fatal because of a huge fly in the ointment—China. Communism as a world movement cannot tolerate two centers of power, according to Solzhenitsyn. The only way for the Soviet Union, for the Russian nation, to avoid a cataclysmic war is to shed this false and ultimately self-destructive ideology. Then "ideological dissension will melt away and there will probably never be a Sino-Soviet war. And if there should be, then it will be in the remote future and a truly defensive, truly patriotic one."[13] Of late it has become fashionable in certain Western circles to deride Solzhenitsyn for his allegedly reactionary "Slavophile" views. But, whatever his politics, the great writer has one very perceptive insight: the hold of Soviet Communism can be loosened only if it is shown to be incompatible with Russian nationalism. "And the whole of this letter that I am putting before you is patriotism which means rejection of Marxism."[14] Let the Soviet Union's present rulers retain their authoritarian system — Solzhenitsyn is not optimistic about prospects for democracy in the foreseeable future — provided they shake off the incubus of the ideology that, though no longer believed in even by the rulers, requires the USSR to pursue a dangerous and ultimately disastrous foreign policy of conquest and expansion. "The demands of internal growth are incomparably more important to us, as a people, than the need for any external extension of our power."[15]

Alas, the problem, as one suspects even Solzhenitsyn knows, is not that simple. Cynical though they undoubtedly are, the Soviet leaders, like politicians elsewhere, are not immune to their own rhetoric. And quite apart from that, it is their self-interest that makes it impossible for them to explicitly renounce their ideology. It is naive to suppose that the ruling elite could "secularize" the Soviet state and still preserve its own power and privileges. The Communist party certainly could not survive such a step.

Yet there is another and much more fundamental difficulty. "Soviet patriotism" today is an ideological veneer over good old-fashioned Russian nationalism. But rub off this veneer and the problem of preserving the territorial integrity of what is now the Soviet Union becomes well-nigh impossible, or so at least it must appear not only to the rulers but to a great majority of Russians who have no use for the ideological trappings of the state. With Communist authoritarianism discarded, what other system could keep the major non-Russian nationalities within the Russian state? The nationalist in Solzhenitsyn is clearly ambivalent on this subject. He grants that Soviet "protective surveillance" of Eastern Europe would have to be given up. He would not keep any "peripheral nation" forcibly within the bounds of his non-Communist Russian state of the future. But how about the Ukraine, certainly a "peripheral nation"? Reading between the lines, one can see that for him, as for his fellow countrymen throughout the ages, it is almost impossible to accept the idea of an independent Ukraine.

Solzhenitsyn's position illustrates the difficulty faced by those who would break the nexus between Soviet Communism and Russian nationalism. The ideology has become a servant of nationalism, but after sixty years of Soviet power this servant cannot be dismissed without gravely imperiling the position of the master. Furthermore, the only dimension in which this ideology remains relevant is that of foreign relations. The West is in retreat; the power and influence of the Soviet Union is advancing. Is that not, for all the real and alleged injustices and shortcomings of Soviet society, a palpable proof of the superiority of the Communist system?

In 1826 Thaddeus Bulharin, a reactionary journalist, wrote a memorandum for the tsarist authorities, advising them on policies that would prevent the spread of subversive Western ideas and enable the autocratic regime to secure the loyalty of the various classes of Russian society. The intelligentsia, he counseled, could best be rendered harmless and submissive if they were employed by the government. "In Russia it is easier to deal with this class than one might think. The main thing is to keep their minds occupied by employing the educated class in fields of activity chosen by the government itself." As for the middle class — corresponding to what today would be the main body of Soviet officialdom — the ingenious toady's advice was to provide it with the illusion of sharing in policymaking, but in fact to have it thoroughly indoctrinated with the official point of view. "Our public can be rendered submissive . . . loyal to the throne by the mere shadow of freedom. . . . Having formed public opinion, it would be easy [for the government] to manipulate it like a piece of machinery." As for the lower classes — what today would be described as "the Soviet working masses" — it is also very simple to manipulate them, for one thing can always sway them like a magic wand: an appeal in the name of Mother Russia. People in that social stratum are ruled by emotion rather than reason. The renegade Pole was certainly ahead of his time. He anticipated the main lines of the current propaganda techniques of the Soviet regime.[16]

Has the traditional role of Russian-Soviet nationalism been affected by such recent phenomena as the emergence of consumerism in the USSR, the new importance of the nationality problem, and political dissent? Undoubtedly, but in the sense quite opposite to that postulated by those who believe that Soviet internal troubles act as a brake on expansionist foreign policies. Domestic pressures and difficulties increase the leaders' need for spectacular successes abroad.

There is no reason to believe that the people of the Soviet Union are immune to those changes in social psychology that have affected other highly industrialized countries. Soviet advances in Africa or Communist successes in France and Italy do not make an average citizen less disgruntled over his difficulties in procuring meat and fresh vegetables or a young intellectual less bitter over his lack of freedom. But the sum of impressions of what goes on beyond the borders of his country must inculcate in many a malcontent's mind a passive — if not positive — acceptance of the system under which he lives.

To be sure, there is another side to this picture. The danger and expense of an overassertive foreign policy must occasionally give rise to serious misgivings within the elite and among the public at large. This was certainly true under Khrushchev and contributed to his downfall. But the present regime has been very successful in allaying fears and discontent concerning the Soviet Union's world role. Though it does not wish its subjects to lapse into complacence concerning the capitalist danger, the

Kremlin can claim that détente has made the possibility of a confrontation like the 1962 Cuban missile crisis very remote. This is indeed the best of all possible worlds, where the power of the USSR is steadily advancing with practically no danger of a shooting war. Those within the elite who realize the costs of supporting the Cuban economy, of courting Mrs. Gandhi's India, and of salvage operations in satellites such as those that took place in Poland in 1970–1971 must be reassured by the fact that in the last few years the West has been induced to launch a virtual Marshall Plan for the benefit of the Communist camp, with Western credits and technology shoring up the shaky economies. To quote Solzhenitsyn again, Soviet diplomacy "in terms of its actual achievements . . . might even be regarded as brilliant . . . it knows how to make demands, exact concessions, in ways that Tsarism never knew."[17] If this is the verdict of the leading dissenter, the man who loathes Communism and everything it represents, how can one expect the mass of his fellow Russians, constantly propagandized, to be unimpressed by their country's apparent grandeur and mounting power?

Many years ago Walter Lippmann entitled a book *American Foreign Policy — The Shield of the Republic.* Alas, in the case of the United States, foreign policy has proved a very porous shield. But for the USSR, Soviet nationalism and foreign policies based on it, as developed over sixty years, are the first and most important line of defense of the Communist system. Until this line is breached, it is unlikely that the Soviet Union will undergo a fundamental change.

Notes

1. Feodor Dostoyevsky, *The Diary of a Writer* (New York: George Braziller, 1954), p. 575.

2. N. A. Tuchkova-Ogareva, *Vospominaniia* (Moscow, 1959), p. 234.

3. Lev Tikhomirov, *Vospominaniia* (Moscow, 1927), p. 327.

4. Leon Trotsky, *Kak vooruzhilas revolutsiia*, vol. 2, pt. 2 (Moscow, 1924), p. 153.

5. Jane Degras, ed., *Soviet Documents on Foreign Policy*, vol. 2, 1925–1932 (London: Oxford University Press, 1952), p. 243.

6. Joseph Stalin, *Sochineniia*, vol. 13 (Moscow, 1951), p. 25.

7. Ibid., pp. 38–39.

8. This would have included a German peace treaty and possibly also (to mollify Peking) the removal of U.S. protection from Taiwan.

9. *Pravda*, 2 September 1964, p. 2.

10. *Plenum tsentral'nogo komiteta kommunisticheskoi partii sovet'skogo soiuza* (Moscow, 1964), p. 551.

11. Ibid., p. 495.

12. Alexander Solzhenitsyn, *Letter to the Soviet Leaders* (New York: Harper & Row, 1974), p. 11.

13. Ibid., p. 19.

14. Ibid., p. 45.

15. Ibid., p. 41.

16. Michael Lemke, *Nikolaevskie zhandarmy i literatura, 1826–1855* (St. Petersburg, 1908), pp. 239–240.

17. Solzhenitsyn, *Letter to the Soviet Leaders,* p. 10.

2
Ideological Development and Foreign Policy

Franklyn Griffiths

In the international relations sections of the last three Central Committee reports to congresses of the Communist Party of the Soviet Union (CPSU), four concepts are notable: the self-image of the CPSU, the party's image of its adversaries, its conception of the international situation, and its view of its own foreign policy. Elements of change as well as persistence in what was said are of interest in surveying these most authoritative pronouncements of the CPSU on external affairs in the Brezhnev era.

Nominally it is the task of the international report of the Central Committee to summarize external developments and Soviet foreign relations since the preceding congress, to account for the party's activity in this sphere, and to chart a course for the interval to come. The reporting is, however, sufficiently selective and the mode of presentation sufficiently repetitive from one congress to the next to suggest that functions in addition to the communication of information are being performed. These seem to include the legitimization of the regime and its actions, the maintenance of a preferred state of awareness among the mass of inadequately informed party members and the population at large, the presentation of an appropriate stance in relation to various foreign audiences, and, perhaps most important, the guidance of officialdom by the issuance of binding assertions as to the character of the current context and Soviet policies. All of this means these documents must be read with care. They are not to be taken literally, nor are they to be disregarded as merely chaff. Certainly they are prepared with considerable care in the formulation employed, the ordering of subject matter, and in any major deviation from one report to the next.

Conversations with recent Soviet emigrés indicate that compilation of the international reports is a complex procedure subject to change.[1] Brezhnev's personal secretariat is said now to be responsible for preparation of the Central Committee report. Officials in this office work through appropriate

departments of the Central Committee Secretariat in the construction of a
draft that is presumably reviewed and finalized by the general secretary and
the Politburo. Responsibility for preliminary drafting of the international
report is evidently assigned to the International Department of the Central
Committee Secretariat, headed by B. N. Ponomarev, a party secretary and
candidate member of the Politburo. Brezhnev's personal advisors are also
in a position to commission special contributions that may be incorporated
at some point in the drafting process. The bulk of the initial working papers
is, however, reported to come to the International Department from the
Foreign Ministry, the Institute of the World Economy and International
Relations of the USSR Academy of Sciences, the Institute of the United
States and Canada, and other sources. These papers are shaped into draft
form by working groups under the supervision of the International Department. Such groups are likely to include individuals with various political
orientations if not institutional affiliations as well. The same applies to
special ad hoc working groups set up to deal with specific problems such as
the preparation of the Peace Programmes presented to recent CPSU congresses. The whole process begins a year or more before a forthcoming congress. It may occupy a sizeable portion of the time of Central Committee
officials, consultants, lecturers, and individuals in the various academic
and ministerial institutions concerned.

The access of institutions to the drafting process evidently alters from one
congress to the next. The Institute of the World Economy and International Relations is said to have made a major contribution to the international report presented to the Twenty-fourth Congress in 1971. Among
other things, it apparently wrote substantial portions of the Peace Programme that appeared that year. In 1976, however, it was the Department
of General International Relations of the Ministry of Foreign Affairs that
seems to have had a lead role, with the Institute of the World Economy being relegated to a primary concern with economic matters. Such a change
in participation would be quite in line with the growth of the Foreign
Ministry's authority following the elevation of A. A. Gromyko to the Politburo in 1973 and with the failure of the director of the Institute of the
World Economy to advance from candidate membership in the Central
Committee at the Twenty-fifth Congress. The probability that the Foreign
Ministry, an element of the state apparatus, played an enhanced role in the
formulation of the Central Committee's report on external affairs in 1976 is
rather incongruous and should be considered in assessing any changes of
inflection that may be observed in the most recent reports.

From the foregoing it should be apparent that the documents on external
affairs read by the general secretary on behalf of the CPSU Central Committee are negotiated and not dictated texts. They are elaborated in an ex-

tended interaction that includes a variety of personalities and institutions and offers an opportunity for the expression of divergent points of view. Their main operational significance for Soviet external behavior would seem to lie in their capacity to endow certain foreign-policy orientations and actors with the highest approbation and to deny approbation to others. Participants in the drafting process are determined to secure the adoption of language that states their preferred definitions of the situation and preferred policy options and that consequently allows them to argue, "As the Report of the Central Committee to the Twenty-fifth Congress makes clear. . . ." This sanction may lose force as the underlying political coalition that brought it into existence comes under stress and as external developments alter the character of Soviet constraints and opportunities. An authorship role is nevertheless much sought after. It lends the prevailing institutions greater stature and envelops them in a "cloud of power." And within institutions, prestige accrues to those who had a hand in writing the winning words.

At the same time, even a quick look at the international reports reveals that no single viewpoint prevails to the exclusion of all others where major issues are concerned. The negotiation that produces these documents is only partially successful. From the perspective of the participants, a point won in one paragraph or under one subheading may be offset by adverse wording elsewhere. And from the perspective of the overall direction or general line of party policy in international affairs, unity invariably yields to a conflict of tendencies whose relative influence may vary from one congress report to the next. In preparing the Central Committee reports on foreign policy, the Soviets negotiate among themselves over the major issues of the day. In view of the subsequent significance of these reports in stacking the deck in favor of certain tendencies in the Soviet foreign policy process, Western diplomats should consider the possibility of exercising influence on the negotiations that take place during the preparation of the reports. This assumes, at the very minimum, that the Central Committee's international reports are indeed internally contradictory and that there has been some development from one report to the next since the beginning of the Brezhnev era.

Self-image

Table 2.1 presents the titles and subheadings of the foreign reports delivered by L. I. Brezhnev on behalf of the Central Committee to the Twenty-third (March–April 1966), Twenty-fourth (March–April 1971), and Twenty-fifth (February–March 1976) CPSU Congresses. Aside from the immediate impression of repetition and, indeed, ritual that would

TABLE 2.1   Structure of the International Relations Section
CC Reports to CPSU Congresses (1966-1976)

XXV Congress I. The World Situation and the CPSU's International Activity.
(1976)

1. Further Strengthening of Friendship and Cooperation with the Socialist
   Countries. Historic Successes of the Socialist World and the Growth of
   Its Might and Influence.
2. Strengthening Cooperation with the Developing Countries. Increasing Their
   Role in World Development.
3. The Development of Relations with the Capitalist States.
4. Programme of Further Struggle for Peace and International Cooperation and
   for the Freedom and Independence of the Peoples.
5. The CPSU and the World Revolutionary Process.

XXIV Congress I. The International Position of the USSR. The CPSU's Foreign Policy Activity.
(1971)

1. For Further Development of the Friendship and Cooperation of the Socialist
   Countries.
2. Imperialism Is the Enemy of the Peoples and of Social Progress. The
   Peoples Against Imperialism.
3. The Soviet Union's Struggle for Peace and the Security of the Peoples.
   Rebuffing the Imperialist Policy of Aggression.

XXIII Congress I. The USSR's International Position. The Foreign Policy Activity of the CPSU.
(1966)

1. The World System of Socialism, the CPSU's Struggle for the Strengthening
   of Its Unity and Might.
2. The Deepening of the Contradictions of the Capitalist System. Development
   of the Class Struggle of the Proletariat.
3. The CPSU in the Struggle for the Solidarity of the World Communist Movement.
4. Development of the National-liberation Movement. Our Party's Support of
   the National-liberation Struggle of the Peoples.
5. The Soviet Union's Struggle Against the Aggressive Policies of Imperialism
   and for Peace and International Security.

Source: The Current Digest of the Soviet Press, Vol. XVIII, No. 12 (Part I), April 13, 1966;
         Vol. XXIII, No. 12, April 20, 1971; and Vol. XXVIII, No. 8, March 24, 1976.

become even more evident if earlier outlines were added (how long can the contradictions of capitalism go on increasing?), certain differences in the titling of these documents are evident at once. The Twenty-third and Twenty-fourth Congresses heard reports on "The International Position of the USSR," as had party congresses since soon after Lenin's day. But in 1976, the party received a report on "The World Situation and the CPSU's International Activity." Rather than continuing to agree with wording that suggested the Soviet Union was the object of others' actions, someone in a position of authority preferred to address the topic from the viewpoint of the Soviet Union as actor rather than object. The retitling of the foreign affairs section suggests a greater measure of assertiveness and self-assurance in the official Soviet view of self. On the other hand, every subheading of the 1966 report continued a reference to "struggle," whereas this notion was scarcely highlighted in the two subsequent reports. Similarly, where "imperialism" was headlined in the 1966 and 1971 reports, it did not figure in the 1976 titling. This last point squares with a comment made to me in 1977 by a Soviet economist, who observed that the concept of imperialism was now rarely employed in professional analysis in the USSR. The self-image presented in the headings of the three reports is one of declining combativeness and militance combined with greater self-confidence.

The impression of change in the Soviet self-image is reinforced by changes of tone in the three reports on external affairs. All congress reports are, of course, obliged to strike a triumphant note and all did emphasize that progress was being made on a variety of fronts. But the relatively militant antiimperialist orientation that predominated at the Twenty-third Congress seemed increasingly difficult to sustain by the early 1970s, as was suggested by the report to the Twenty-fourth Congress. The 1966 statement emphasized mobilization in the face of an increasingly aggressive imperialism in an international context that presented the growing danger of world war. In this situation the CPSU, the Soviet government, and their allies were depicted as marching in close formation and with a clear sense of purpose marred only by the existence of "serious difficulties" within the international Communist movement.[2] By 1971, however, the international report had struck a rather fretful and uncertain note. Certain "difficulties and complications" had arisen in the world system of socialism, which was nevertheless designated as "the decisive force in the antiimperialist struggle."[3] Unity within the Communist movement remained "a complicated task," because of Chinese splitting activities, nationalistic self-isolation, and the revival of both left- and right-wing opportunism.[4] These and other considerations obliged Brezhnev to declare, "We have not everywhere advanced toward our outlined goals as swiftly as we might have wished."[5] But by 1976 the tone had changed to one of marked satisfaction and perhaps even surprise at the Soviet achievements.[6] Major victories had been recorded in Vietnam, Laos, and Cambodia.[7] The Soviet bloc had become "the most dynamic economic force in the world."[8] Postwar European frontiers had been ratified.[9] A "major shift" had occurred in relations with West Germany, making the latter one of the USSR's major economic partners.[10] An "important fundamental mutual understanding" had been reached with the United States, raising the possibility of further cooperation and improvements in the international atmosphere.[11] In sum, the mood of the congress reports on foreign affairs had changed from combativeness and resolve, through uncertainty and a degree of irresolution, to self-congratulation and enhanced confidence.

Given these variations in mood, certain continuities in the Soviet presentation of self must be stressed. The first is that the might of the Soviet Union and the world socialist system was seen to have become steadily greater. In 1966 the Soviet bloc was reported to have "grown considerably stronger" and in 1971 Soviet defense might was seen to have experienced "substantial strengthening."[12] As of 1976 Soviet might had grown substantially once again.[13] All of this was reported with mounting satisfaction, so much so that it would appear entirely legitimate in intraparty discussion to support increased Soviet might. Moreover, it was pointed out repeatedly that Soviet influence and prestige had also grown.[14] By 1976 it was being claimed with gratification that the USSR enjoyed the "respect and support" and exerted an "enormous influence on the thoughts and feelings" of hundreds of millions of people the world over.[15] The foregoing suggests the existence within the party of a readiness to experience a sense of satisfaction and greater self-worth arising from increased military and political power.

On the other hand, it was repeatedly asserted that the CPSU had been "compelled" to expend resources on defense. In 1966 "imperialist military production" was cited as the factor forcing the USSR and other countries to "spend considerable sums to strengthen their own defenses."[16] According to the Twenty-fifth Congress, mankind was "tired of living on top of mountains of weapons."[17] Moreover, if new arms limitation agreements were enacted, there was the expectation that substantial amounts would be saved for "productive purposes, for improving peoples' lives."[18] Evidently it was also quite appropriate for party members to assert that increases in Soviet military might and its attendant benefits were not entirely desirable. This thought merges with another persistent theme that stressed the attractive force of socialist ideas and the revolutionary contribution of Communist construction in the Soviet Union.[19] In addition, the Central Committee reports, of course, consistently projected a peace-loving Soviet self-image, according to which the CPSU was seeking to ensure peaceful conditions for socialist and Communist construction,[20] threatened no one,[21] and by implication was not properly in the business of amassing "a mountain of weapons." When added to the assertion that the Soviet bloc and primarily the USSR was the principal revolutionary and antiimperialist force,[22] the foregoing aspects of the Soviet self-depiction suggest an interest in emphasizing more "productive" economic development and arms limitation negotiations, as opposed to the continual accumulation of military might and other assets required to outweigh the opponent in the world correlation of forces. Either way, the objective was greater prestige and respect. But force of example, as opposed to greater might, remained the weaker element in the self-image expressed in the Central Committee reports of the Brezhnev era.

To further the point, a dualistic self-conception emerges at various points in the three accounts. The 1971 report said, "Our policy invariably combined a firm rebuff to aggression with a constructive line."[23] At the Twenty-third Congress similar language had been employed: "In exposing the aggressive policy of imperialism, we at the same time consistently and unswervingly pursue a course of the peaceful coexistence of states with different social systems."[24] Similarly, in regard to China, the 1971 report noted that whereas the CPSU had "resolutely opposed attempts to distort the teaching of Marxism-Leninism, to split the international Communist movement," the party and the Soviet government had been "displaying restraint and not yielding to provocation" in doing everything possible "to bring about a normalization" of Sino-Soviet relations.[25] Equivalent language, emphasizing rebuff and normalization, was used in 1976 regarding Soviet conduct toward China.[26] And with respect to the United States, the 1976 report asserted that the Soviet Union, while opposing certain aspects of U.S. policy, would firmly pursue "a course aimed at the further improvement of Soviet-American relations."[27] In effect, the Soviet self-image as projected in reports to recent party congresses suggests an awareness that Soviet behavior is internally inconsistent, composed of alternate tendencies whose relative influence varies with the requirements of the moment.

In sum, the stated Soviet self-image as it emerges from these documents is one of being better off — slowly at first, after 1966, then more rapidly better off and more appealing to more people. As Brezhnev summed it up in 1976, "This is the fourth decade in which we have lived in conditions of peace. The positions of socialism have grown stronger. The easing of tensions has become the leading trend."[28] This state of affairs was attributed primarily to the growing might of the USSR and the world socialist system. On the other hand, there seems throughout to have been an awareness of dualism in Soviet external behavior, dualism that reflected differences over methods (military might and the ability to "rebuff" vs. economic development and the force of example) in achieving broadly similar "revolutionary" and security goals.

The Adversaries

Turning to the image of the capitalist system generally, to the United States in particular, and then to China, we find that as the stated Soviet self-image after 1966 was one of faring increasingly well, the capitalist world was seen as being in an increasingly precipitous decline. At all three congresses the Central Committee report asserted that the general crisis of capitalism was deepening.[29] This crisis was first said to be manifested in recurring recessions and other economic difficulties including inflation, in combination with growing divisions among the United States, the Common Market countries, and Japan.[30] By 1971 mention was being made of "serious economic convulsions," monetary and fiscal crises, the simultaneous growth of inflation and unemployment, and the existence of "increasingly acute" economic and political struggles among the United States, Western Europe, and Japan.[31] In 1976, however, the report noted the onset of "a crisis whose sharpness and depth . . . can be compared only with the crisis of the early 1930s."[32] Now the "crisis" was manifested in sharp production cuts; increased unemployment; currency, energy, and raw materials crises; and inflation unprecedented in peacetime.[33] In addition, inter-imperialist rivalries had intensified, as had the working class struggle and the "ideological-political crisis of bourgeois society."[34] Although the 1976 report disclaimed any prediction of the "automatic collapse" of capitalism, its instability and lack of prospects were said to be increasingly obvious and, by contrast, the attractive force of socialism had become still greater.[35]

This picture of steadily declining capitalist economic and political capabilities was qualified, however, both tacitly and explicitly. In the international report to the Twenty-fifth Congress, the discussion of the general crisis of capitalism was placed in the section dealing with the CPSU and the world revolutionary process and not among the passages concerned specifically with Soviet relations with capitalist states, as had been the case with the two previous reports. The intensification of crisis phenomena in the West was thus by implication to be regarded as primarily affecting Western Europe. This was because, as every Soviet schoolchild knows, the world revolutionary process had yet to reach into the United States to bring a significant Communist party to life there as it had in Western Europe.

More interesting was the stated perception that "reserves" were available to assist the capitalist system.[36] These reserves consisted, inter alia (Maoist China was also a "reserve" of imperialism),[37] of state regulation of the economy, the "wide use" of scientific and technological achievements, and the introduction of partial political reforms.[38] Such measures, it was acknowledged, had assisted in the stimulation of capitalist economic growth and efficiency.[39] The language of the three reports suggested that capitalist use of these economic reserves to promote growth and assure class peace was most evident in 1971, when it was recognized that capitalism had succeeded within limits in "adapting itself to new conditions."[40] The implication was that by the early 1970s the opposing social system was doing sufficiently well in the economic and technological competition to justify a greater Soviet commitment to East-West economic cooperation and technological transfer to compete more efficiently in areas in which the USSR was threatened with being left behind. By 1976, however, the reserve clauses in the Soviet concept of the "reserves" of capitalism were being stressed: state economic regulation could not work, crises could not be averted, and promises to create general prosperity had failed. The outlook was one of political unrest and economic instability in Western Europe and possibly short-term moves toward recovery in the United States—all within a long-term framework of diminishing economic and political capabilities of the opposing social system.

Noteworthy were some comments *not* being made about capitalism in the three reports. Mention was not made of the fact that mature capitalism is subject to progressive inner modification (expressed, for example, in state economic regulation, the growth of economic planning capabilities, the increasing socialization of production, etc.) that represents the development of material and organizational preconditions for socialism. As pointed out, capitalism was certainly seen to be capable of adaptation. But there was nothing admittedly "progressive" about this. On the contrary, adaptation reflected the efforts of the monopolists to strengthen their positions, to intensify their exploitation, and to ward off the development of mass revolutionary movements.[41] The nature of contemporary capitalism thus remained essentially unchanged. If there were to be progressive transformations within the developed nonsocialist countries, they would evidently have to come through "collapse," or as the result of political action represented by the advent to power of the antiimperialist forces in Western Europe. Such transformations would not develop spontaneously under the aegis of monopoly capitalism. Applied to the United States, these considerations suggested a bias of official perception or belief against the notion of relying on or supporting the evolution of relatively progressive social forces in the United States. Instead, if the United States were to be transformed, it would be the result of economic and social catastrophe or, more likely, the application of superior external counterpressure. In effect, the United States was the way it was, would remain so for the foreseeable future, and could not be modified internally or substantially "mellowed" until the distant day when socialism took over.

This brings us to the question of the "aggressiveness" of imperialism as communicated in the three reports. Here, too, we encounter a degree of uncertainty in stated Soviet assessments. At any given moment imperialism was characterized as being aggressive, but the degree varied with the immediate situation, so that by 1976 it was seen to be considerably less warlike than a decade earlier. At the time of the Twenty-third Congress imperialism was said to have become "increasingly aggressive," insolent, and provocative, as exemplified primarily by the U.S. intervention in Vietnam.[42] By the Twenty-fourth Congress a somewhat more moderate reference was made to the "unchanging reactionary and aggressive nature" of imperialism.[43] And, at the Twenty-fifth Congress, the word was that "although imperialism's possibilities for aggressive actions are substantially curtailed now, its nature remains the same."[44] In effect, the reported belligerence of the Soviet Union's principal capitalist adversaries diminished notably and with it the estimated danger of war.[45] On the other hand, it was asserted in 1971 that imperialism had sought to overthrow one socialist system in Czechoslovakia[46] and in 1976 that an attempt had been made to destroy another socialist state by armed force in Vietnam.[47] Not very reassuring for those predisposed to believe.

As to the long term, imperialism evidently remained quite aggressive subjectively, but objectively it was less and less able to act on this basis. The Twenty-third Congress had been told that the worse things went for imperialism, the more dangerous and warlike it would become.[48] A decade later it was being said that favorable changes in the world correlation of forces — and thus a deterioration in the world position of capitalism — were substantially reducing the capacity of imperialist powers to take aggressive action. Instead, the 1976 report seemed to say, the belligerent nature of imperialism would receive expression primarily in efforts to intensify the arms race.[49]

In sum, imperialism was depicted as a permanent but increasingly manageable threat. Further improvements in the world correlation of forces would, on balance, stimulate not increased aggressiveness but a continued reduction in the danger of war. Correspondingly, arms limitation would become an increasingly important issue in the further bridling of imperialism. Once again, however, it was largely external pressure and the weakening of imperialist positions combined with negotiation, rather than inner modifications in the nature of the opposing system, that were expected to do the job.

And yet there were obvious problems with negotiation, arising again in part from the perceived character of the opponent. First, "the nature of imperialism is such that each country strives to obtain advantages at the expense of others, to impose its own will."[50] If this was how imperialists negotiated with one another, there was a good deal more than met the eye in the 1976 report's favorable reference to the prospect of "the development of mutually advantageous cooperation" between the USSR and the United States.[51] Unable to relinquish the pursuit of unilateral advantage, the United States would presumably engage in negotiation with little more than tactical, unilateral objectives in mind. Second, in all three reports references to the arms race included assertions that it was the imperialists who were conducting the race or "whipping" it along,[52] so much so that it was not presented as a "race" in the sense of a competition, but rather as a situation in which the other side was doing all the "racing" while the USSR was looking to the improvement of its defenses. Indeed, one can almost hear the reports referring to "their arms race," as though the USSR were not a part of it at all. This is a long-standing and obviously more primitive Soviet counterpart to Albert Wohlstetter's view that it is only the other side that is racing, if there is a "race" in the first place.

Finally, there was the question of the "Soviet threat." In all three reports mention was made of the use of a threatening image of the USSR by supporters of NATO and increased Western armaments.[53] This theme, together with that of checking the arms race, seems to have acquired greater significance by the time of the Twenty-fifth Congress, if frequency of mention was any indication. Especially interesting here is the repeated assertion that references to the Soviet threat by Western politicians and others were "lies."[54] This assertion suggested it was not absurd for members of the CPSU to believe that even the most aggressive of knowledgeable Soviet opponents recognized that the USSR had in fact "no intention of attacking anyone."[55] Imperialism was thus even more aggressive than might otherwise have been thought, since its military activities were governed not by fear but by viciousness. And where arms negotiations were concerned, this outlook suggested there was no way of reasoning with the exponents of defense preparedness in the West; they already knew the truth about the Soviet Union and were determined to engage in deceit to achieve their objectives.

All of this indicates a bias in official activity against thinking in terms of interaction and mutual dependence between the USSR and imperialism, particularly the United States. The drafters of the reports seem to have assumed, or to have wished others to assume, that both sides behaved autonomously. The argument runs: We act. They act. But we are in no way responsible for their bad behavior. They arm up, pointing to a Soviet threat they do not believe in. We look to our own defense needs. No real problem of perception or misperception exists on either side. Everyone seriously concerned knows fairly well what is going on. They, by their nature, will employ negotiations to achieve gains at the expense of socialism. If they use negotiations as a form of conflict, socialism itself can hardly avoid regarding negotiation in a tactical and instrumental light. Since the arms race is caused by the imperialists, it is they who must make more of the concessions. And so on.

On the other hand, the Central Committee reports also implicitly recognized the existence of dualism in the foreign behavior of the United States. For example, in 1971, reference was made to "frequent zig-zags in American foreign policy" evidently connected to "short-term domestic political maneuvers."[56] And whereas U.S. imperialism was described in 1966 as a "rapacious, plundering strangler of the peoples, hated by all,"[57] a decade later it was said to be capable of developing relations with the Soviet Union on a "realistic basis," while also being subject to internal pressure from "influential forces . . . interested neither in the improvement of relations with the USSR nor in the easing of international tension in general."[58] Realism in 1976 was described as a view in which "given the obvious differences in the class nature of the two states and in their ideologies, there is a firm intention to settle disagreements and disputes not by force, not by threats or saber rattling, but by peaceful political means."[59] Just how the U.S. capacity for being reasonable was to be explained in the light of everything else reported about imperialism by the Central Committee was not made clear. The interested party member was left to draw his own conclusions, as in the case of an oblique reference to the U.S. interest in saving funds through strategic arms limitation.[60]

Nevertheless, within the United States there evidently existed a base of support that was perceived to offer a real prospect of lessening the danger of war and improving the outlook for Soviet-U.S. relations. The image of the United States presented in the various Central Committee reports was thus one in which domestic political conflict did have a role in shaping the relative influence of aggressive and realistic tendencies in U.S. conduct. But this remained a weakly developed theme, so much so that the notion of Moscow attempting by its own behavior to influence the politics of U.S. foreign policy was barely evident even between the lines. The image of the United States presented in the three reports accordingly suggested that arguments to this effect — and similar views drawing attention to the possible adverse impact of Soviet military developments and other moves on Western behavior — would have to be made with greater circumspection than was the case for the more primitive assessment presented by the Central Committee.

As regards China, the stated Soviet image of the Chinese deteriorated as the image of the United States became somewhat more benign. Increasing but still relatively little space was allocated to the discussion of China and Sino-Soviet relations in the three reports. In each case, China was considered largely under the heading of "socialist countries." At the Twenty-third Congress there was no explicit criticism, merely a statement of regret that relations remained unsatisfactory.[61] The attention paid to China in the 1966 report was about equivalent to that granted the United Nations. By 1971, the CPSU had rather more to say: the Chinese leaders' ideological platform was "incompatible with Leninism."[62] They were directing hostile propaganda against the Soviet Communist party and state and had made territorial claims and brought matters to the point of armed border incidents.[63] By 1976 the CPSU was saying, "It is no longer adequate to say Maoist ideology and policy are incompatible with Marxist-Leninist teaching. They are openly hostile to it."[64] The actions of the Chinese leaders were now seen to be directed against socialist states and in accord with the positions of the "most extreme reactionaries."[65] Indeed, as mentioned above, Chinese policy was seen to have become a new "reserve" for imperialism. Accordingly, the CPSU for the first time officially stated its readiness to normalize relations with China "on the principles of peaceful coexistence"[66] — a term hitherto employed in Central Committee reports to refer to relations between states with different social systems. In effect, the deterioration in the stated Soviet image of the Chinese leadership was nearing the point where revision of a major doctrinal precept was approaching. At the same time, the modest amount of space given to China in the three reports (peaking at five paragraphs in 1976) and the virtually complete lack of comment on the military dimension of Sino-Soviet relations suggested that China was not a preoccupation equivalent to the Soviet bloc, the United States, or Western Europe — or that it was so sensitive and rancorous a subject that the less said the better.

The International Situation

As documents purporting to assess the international situation and the position of the Soviet Union in the world, the three Central Committee reports had remarkably little to say about the international situation as such. Aside from a few general observations, it was left to the listener or reader to piece together an overview.

By and large, stated perceptions of the international situation improved in phase with improvements in the Soviet self-image. The four years leading up to the Twenty-third Congress were described as a period of "constant increase in the international influence of the Soviet Union," together with mounting international tension and danger of war reflecting the "increased difficulties and contradictions" said to beset the world capitalist system.[67] The years preceding the Twenty-fourth Congress were depicted as years of "great social and political changes," in which the Soviet international position had become "still more secure" and the "great alliance of three main revolutionary forces" (socialism, the workers' movement, and the national liberation struggle) had continued to acquire strength and depth.[68] Nevertheless, a corner had not been turned and improvements, it was acknowledged, had not come as fast as they should.[69] By 1976, however, the global outlook had improved considerably. Now Brezhnev was able to report that "The world is changing before our eyes, and it is changing for the better."[70] The change Brezhnev referred to was a favorable shift in the world correlation of forces, composed apparently — for this was not spelled out in so many words — of increases in the might of the world socialist system, crisis and disarray in the capitalist world, and a greater assertiveness in the activity of the new states and national liberation movements.[71] It found its expression primarily in an easing of tension with the capitalist world and the United States in particular.[72]

Whereas Western perceptions of the international situation after 1971 would likely have cited the onset of multilateral diplomacy and a reordering of world power relationships, the stated Soviet perception remained essentially one of a persisting bipolar or two-camp world, in which the socialist system had the superior dynamism and more rapidly growing ability to determine the future course of events. China remained a secondary presence throughout the three reports and Japan was evidently quite distant from central Soviet calculations and concerns. Nor, aside from an indicated interest in preventing nuclear proliferation, was there any real sign that global issues in the form of poverty, population, pollution, or the exhaustion of nonrenewable energy sources had begun to penetrate the consciousness of the Central Committee. As Table 2.1 indicates, international developments did little to disrupt the stated concerns of the party throughout the period under review.

Where East-West relations were concerned, the situation was seen to have altered from one of confrontation, tension, and increased danger of war to one of peaceful coexistence, diminished tension, and a somewhat lowered threat of nuclear war.[73] To the Twenty-third and Twenty-fourth Congresses the Central Committee reported that there was a sharp "confrontation" under way between the two world social systems.[74] Indeed, the language used in 1966 suggested that this was an appropriate state of affairs. By 1976, however, confrontation seemed to have been left behind: "The transition from the cold war and the explosive confrontation of two worlds to the easing of tension was connected above all with changes in the alignment of forces in the world arena."[75] Confrontation, too, had ceased to be an appropriate expression of relations between opposing social systems.

The correlation of forces in Europe was described as being "essentially one of equilibrium"[76] and it was in the European context that the notion of making détente irreversible was put forward as the goal of an extended struggle.[77] As it was, various positive developments were said to have occurred in Europe by 1971, including improved relations with West Germany and France, the signing of treaties between West Germany and the USSR and Poland, and other actions.[78] By the Twenty-fifth Congress, bilateral relations with Western European countries in general could be "appraised as positive," as could the 1971 Berlin agreement and the Conference on Security and Cooperation in Europe (CSCE).[79]

More important, there had also been "a turn for the better" in Soviet dealings with the United States, a factor that had "unquestionably contributed to the improvement of the international climate as a whole, including the climate in Europe."[80] At the 1976 talks in Moscow, Washington, Vladivostok, and Helsinki, an "important fundamental mutual understanding" was said to have been reached between the leaders of the United States and the Soviet Union.[81] This had led to "a whole system" of Soviet-American treaties, agreements, and other measures, the most important of which seemed to be not the 1972 strategic arms limitation accords, but the agreement on "basic principles" to govern the Soviet-American relationship.[82] Despite the activities of those in the United States who opposed the improvement of relations with the Soviet Union, the 1976 report endorsed a view of the situation in which the prospects vis-á-vis the principal adversary were good.[83] And yet, it was noted that an agreement with Washington implementing the 1974 Vladivostok understanding had yet to be achieved and that Soviet proposals for banning new strategic weaponry had "unfortunately" not been accepted by the U.S. side.[84] Clearly the CPSU had come a long way since 1966 in its dealings with the United States, but despite favorable developments in the world distribution of forces, there remained a considerable distance to go before the idea of détente as an irreversible policy could properly be applied to Soviet-American as well as Soviet-European relations.

The stated situation in the developing areas also altered in the course of the three Central Committee presentations. The Twenty-third and Twenty-fourth Congresses both heard reports that characterized the Third World broadly as an arena of East-West competition: the imperialists did their evil works (which were itemized in some detail), and the CPSU and Soviet government assisted the national liberation movements and newly independent states to resist and to affirm their economic and political independence. In both reports primary attention was given to the more radical — and therefore to the minority — of Third World actors in the form of states pursuing the noncapitalist path and national liberation movements. A lack of social progress was acknowledged to exist in many former colonies, and the reports noted the existence of "capitalist monopolies, still to a great extent in control of the economies and resources of many countries in Asia, Africa, and Latin America."[85] In effect, a large part of the Third World was written off as inaccessible and the CPSU seemed to have neither a developed understanding of the situation nor a policy to deal with it in toto. Instead the Central Committee was inclined to proffer narrow and self-defeating notions, for example the observation that "the struggle for national liberation in many countries has in practice developed into a struggle against exploitative relations, both feudal and capitalist"[86] — a formulation that, if acted upon, would hardly assist the rapid development of Soviet-Third World intergovernmental relations.

By 1976, however, the outlook had evidently altered quite significantly. Where previous Central Committee reports had considered the developing countries under the headings of the national liberation struggle or "Imperialism is the Enemy of the Peoples," the Twenty-fifth Congress evaluation was gathered for the most part under a new subtitle, "Strengthening Cooperation with the Developing Countries. Increasing Their   Role in World Development." For the first time in the decade under review, the process of social development in the new countries was acknowledged to be "complicated" and "complex."[87] More interesting, though, was "the important fact that the influence of [the new] states . . . has grown considerably."[88] Most of them were said to be defending their economic and political rights more vigorously in a "confrontation with imperialism."[89] This confrontation was to be seen in changes in the political orientation of the nonaligned movement, in the activities of the Organization for African Unity (which rated a mention for the first time), and of "various economic associations" set up by the developing countries.[90] These changes suggested "that given the present alignment of class forces in the world, the liberated countries are fully capable of standing up to imperialist diktat and achieving just — i.e., equal — economic relations."[91] In addition, it appeared as though the Third World's "contribution to the common struggle for peace and security of peoples, already quite significant, may very well become even more substantial."[92] Taken together, these remarks indicated a change in Soviet perspective on Third World affairs between the Twenty-fourth and Twenty-fifth Congresses. Where previously — under the slogans of national liberation and antiimperialist struggle — the CPSU and the Soviet state had sought to make a few new states and movements their own, or as nearly so as possible, under the slogan of greater cooperation the Soviets seemed to be moving to support the governments of many new states in a sharpening confrontation with imperialism.

Turning briefly to specific difficulties and problem areas, in an effort to round out the stated picture of the international situation, it may be noted that some problems dropped off the agenda while others remained throughout the decade. Vietnam, Cambodia, and Laos all came off the active list, as did Chile, the former Portuguese colonies in Africa, Portugal, Greece, Czechoslovakia, Poland, recognition of the East German regime, regulation of the Berlin question, affirmation of postwar European frontiers, the nuclear nonproliferation treaty, and so on. On the other hand, there remained Societ bloc integration, strife with China, disagreements with Japan, difficulties in the international Communist movement, human rights and the freer flow of information in the CSCE and Soviet-American bilateral contexts, the Middle East, intensification of the arms competition, and the general future of East-West cooperation. Since several of these subjects have already been commented upon, the discussion here will be confined to a few remarks on stated Soviet perceptions of the situation in the Middle East and the Communist movement.

Coverage of the Middle East can be considered fairly quickly, since there was nothing to report in 1966 and subsequent commentary was quite bland. The weakening of the Soviet position in recent times is evident from a comparison of the Twenty-fourth and Twenty-fifth Congress reports. Whereas in 1971 the Soviet Union was depicted as seeking — in conjunction with the major Arab states — to weaken "Israeli extremists" and to appeal to those in Tel Aviv who might "take a sober view of things, "[93] five years later it was a matter of acting with Syria, Iraq, and the Palestine Liberation Organization (PLO) against Egypt as well as Israel.[94] Certain unspecified "forces" were said to have succeeded in undermining Soviet-Egyptian relations and were turning a Middle East settlement into a political game in which separate agreements were being negotiated rather than the overall guaranteed settlement apparently desired by Moscow. In this context, the Soviet Union was now looking further afield to Libya and Algeria and was seeking support at a resumed Geneva negotiation for the concept of a Palestinian national state as well as Israeli withdrawals from the West Bank. The situation was clearly an unfavorable one in which Moscow had lost political ground.

Where the international Communist movement was concerned, the 1966–1976 period also witnessed a deterioration of the stated Soviet position. As of the Twenty-third Congress "serious difficulties" in the international movement were acknowledged without, however, the Chinese party's being cited as the main source of the problem. By 1971, difficulties had become "negative phenomena" in the form of "nationalistic tendencies" and "right-wing and left-wing revisionism," as well as "opportunistic elements in the Communist Parties."[95] Chinese activities were criticized openly and there was implied criticism of other parties in that the task of strengthening the unity of the international movement was said to be a "complicated" one.[96] The 1976 report, recognizing a further erosion of support within the movement, launched a sharp but indirect criticism of Eurocommunism. Emphasizing that certain general laws of Marxism-Leninism governed the revolutionary process and the activities of Leninist parties, the Central Committee characterized proletarian internationalism as "one of the main principles of Marxism-Leninism" and went on to say, "Unfortunately, some people have begun to interpret it in such a way that in fact little remains of internationalism. There are even people who openly suggest that internationalism be renounced. In their opinion [it] has become outmoded."[97]

This, in the view of the CPSU, would be to "do a good turn for the class enemy."[98] For the Soviets to be expressing pointed disapproval of West European parties on matters of principle was an indication of continued worsening of the outlook where the international movement was concerned.

In sum, the overall international situation was seen definitely to have improved in the course of the three Central Committee reports. Stripped to the essentials, however, the improvement seemed to be based on the increased might of the Soviet bloc — mainly of the USSR — and on disarray in the West. Significant future obstacles, if not loss of the progress achieved, were suggested by acknowledged difficulties with the United States over strategic arms limitation, with China, with COMECON members over the implementation of agreed measures, with West European Communist parties, and in the Middle East. On the other hand, there did seem to be an opening in the Third World for action designed to stiffen the resistance of developing countries to the principal Western adversaries and presumably to Chinese influence as well. Indeed, if the tone of various sections of the 1976 Central Committee Report are considered, the CPSU is most venomous in regard to China and most avuncular in regard to the prospect for better relations with an increasingly self-assertive developing world. In short, the international situation seemed to have become one in which very significant but now diminishing progress had been made bilaterally in regard to the developed capitalist world. Correspondingly, the developing areas seemed to offer greater prospects for further positive movement in the correlation of world forces.

View of Soviet Policies

Whereas recent Central Committee reports provided relatively sketchy accounts of the international situation as such, they were replete with characterization of Soviet foreign policy and with general specific foreign policy commitments. Among the central points discussed were stated Soviet conceptions of the nature of their own foreign policy, activity in regard to the Soviet bloc, conduct toward the developing countries, peaceful coexistence with the capitalist states and China, and the "Peace Programmes" presented to the Twenty-fourth and Twenty-fifth Congresses.

Perhaps the simplest manner of conveying the Central Committee's stated image of its foreign policy activity is to list some of the modifiers used to describe it in 1976: Marxist-Leninist, peaceloving, realistic, tension-reducing, antiimperialist, global in reach,[99] principled, correct, respected, practical, effective, timely, resolute, steadfast, consistent, patient, vigilant, loyal, noninterfering, and nonthreatening. Note that Soviet foreign behavior was not specifically described as "revolutionary," although the CPSU was said to be guided by a "revolutionary conscience."[100] Nor, on the other hand, was foreign policy depicted as being "flexible" or ready to "compromise" except in principled relations among Communist parties. On balance, the attributes presented were those of a pragmatic and cautious policy concerned more with the achievement of results than with a sense of mission.

Consideration of the stated purposes of Soviet foreign policy suggests that the CPSU conceived itself as being guided first by a desire to ensure favorable external conditions for Communist construction within the USSR.[101] This persistent goal would appear to have been defensive in nature and was to be met by the assignment of priority to strengthening the unity and might of the world socialist system.[102] Socialist might was implicitly seen as essential to a successful foreign policy. Without increasing strength, there was evidently no backing for diplomacy, less likelihood of prestige, and a diminished prospect of significant change in the world correlation of forces. Throughout the decade there seemed to be no hesitation whatsoever on these points. On the other hand, it is appropriate indirectly to ask, "How much is enough?" by citing the opportunity costs of defense. My guess is that one would have found virtually complete unanimity within the party on the need for a strong defense throughout the period. Permissible differences of opinion would very likely have arisen over matters of proportion and degree in the defense effort.

At the same time, by 1976 Soviet relations with other bloc members were said to have received "primary attention" in the foreign policy activity of the leadership.[103] Compared with this, the task of improving relations with the principal opponent had apparently received only "a great deal of attention."[104] In other words, unlike U.S. policy during the decade, Soviet foreign relations were said to have been constructed with a primary concern for the improvement of alliance relations as opposed to relations with the main adversary.

Where the developing areas were concerned, Soviet policy was presented in decreasingly radical and more realistic terms. This was done first by redefining the situation in the developing countries in a manner that suggested new policy options and, second, by directly restating Soviet goals and commitments. Consider, for example, the following general assessments of the situation in the new states:

- The new life in the liberated countries is being born in . . . sharp struggle between the forces of progress and the forces of reaction within these countries. (1966)[105]

- The main thing is that *the struggle for national liberation in many countries has in practice developed into a struggle against exploitative relations, both feudal and capitalist.*(1971)[106]

- A complicated process of the delimitation of class forces is taking place in many liberated countries, and the class struggle is building up. (1976)[107]

In 1966 the class struggle was said to be widespread and acute, in 1971 the action was located only in many countries, and by 1976 it was only beginning to take shape in many new states. All of this was another way of saying that more was to be gained from a realistic and accommodating policy toward existing regimes than from self-isolation or minimal involvement prompted by an excessively radical perception of the situation.

Doctrinal modification in regard to Third World affairs, as indicated by the failure of the Twenty-fifth Congress report to mention the "noncapitalist path," also suggested policy change. The noncapitalist path had been emphasized in the 1966 and 1971 reports, which devoted special attention to those developing countries that were said to have embarked on "the long-term construction of socialist society"[108] and the implementation of "profound social changes"[109] or "serious social transformations."[110] Where these earlier reports had stressed the significance of "young states that [had] adopted a course toward socialism,"[111] the 1976 assessment relaxed the criteria for Soviet approval. This was done by omitting reference to the noncapitalist path altogether and by speaking instead of "Arab, African and Asian states having a socialist orientation" and being engaged in the implementation of "profound progressive [*sic*] changes."[112] The implication again was that the CPSU would thereafter be more inclusive in its approach to Third World states and that the concept of the noncapitalist path had been found wanting in view of both the actual pace of Third World social change and the opportunity to exploit the rising potential of developing states in world politics.[113] How could the Soviet Union seek to enlarge its cooperation with new states if it remained wedded to "the radical reconstruction of backward [*sic*] social relations on a non-capitalist basis?"[114]

Correspondingly, the Central Committee's presentations of Soviet policy vis-à-vis the developing areas displayed a shift of emphasis away from support for national liberation struggles and toward intergovernmental relations. The Twenty-third Congress report was emphatic in promising "all possible support" to popular struggles against colonialism and "all-round cooperation" with the liberated states.[115] By 1971, the Soviet Union was said merely to be supporting liberation struggles "wholly" and to be developing relations with new states on a basis of "mutual interest."[116] As of 1976, however, the Soviet Union was described as being "united with the overwhelming majority" of new states in a "community of fundamental aspirations."[117] The CPSU had given "support" to Angola and would continue to assist "peoples fighting for their freedom" as a consequence of "revolutionary conscience and . . . Communist convictions."[118] In the same breath, the Soviet Union committed itself to lend "full support" to the developing countries' efforts to eliminate imperialist exploitation and to control their own national wealth. Given the perceived increase in actual and potential influence of the new states in international politics and economic affairs, the changes of inflection in stated Soviet policy objectives suggested the Central Committee was thinking of broader state-to-state cooperation and increased world roles for the developing countries at the expense of the West. This presumably meant facing the West with the possibility of higher prices for less secure "national wealth" in the Third World. It also indicated the Central Committee was anxious to avoid having the Soviet Union and its allies grouped with the rest of the "North" in a sharpening North-South confrontation. At the same time, a more vigorous and pragmatic Soviet involvement in the affairs of the developing areas promised to include continued support for armed national liberation struggles.

This brings us to developments in the stated Soviet image of policy toward the principal adversaries, as considered under the heading of "peaceful coexistence." A comparison of the three Central Committee reports shows changes of formulation and, indeed, an innovation of doctrinal significance. As of the Twenty-third Congress, the CPSU regarded coexistence "as a form of the class struggle between socialism and capitalism," while at the same time "consistently advocat[ing] the maintenance of normal, peaceful relations with the capitalist countries."[119] What this meant in practice was that the CPSU's prosecution of the class struggle in the developing and developed countries was not to be inhibited unduly by Soviet ties with capitalist states and that for these latter ties to develop the

United States would first have to cease its prosecution of the Vietnam War.[120] By the time of the Twenty-fourth Congress, when the Soviet Union was negotiating with the United States on matters of strategic arms limitation as the Vietnam War continued, peaceful coexistence was being treated exclusively as a matter of "principles" to be applied in relations between states with different social systems. [121] Official insistence on an interpretation of peaceful coexistence as a form of class struggle had been dropped, replaced by a comparatively narrow and noncommittal conception of the term more suited to East-West negotiations. By 1976, however, the Twenty-third Congress definition had been reversed. The Central Committee now stated flatly that "detente and peaceful coexistence refer to relations between states" and therefore could not "abolish or alter the laws of class struggle."[122] Where the 1966 definition had made peaceful coexistence subordinate to considerations of the class struggle, the party's preference a decade later was to limit coexistence to state relations and to attempt to decouple these from the effects of persisting Soviet involvement in antiimperialist operations in the developing and developed countries. Moreover, the Central Committee was not saying, as it might have, that East-West coexistence facilitated the class struggle in the First and Third worlds. It was saying that East-West interstate cooperation and Soviet anti-imperialism would have to proceed in tandem — a point not made in 1971.

At the same time, the Twenty-fifth Congress report authorized the application of the concept of peaceful coexistence to Soviet relations with China.[123] This doctrinal innovation can only be interpreted as a belated and partial acknowledgment of a setback of historic proportions for the Soviet Union. The doctrine of coexistence had hitherto described the relations of socialist and capitalist systems in an epoch of the transition to socialism on a world scale. Now a step was being taken toward doctrinal recognition that the transition could involve major reversals, placing one-time socialist states on an equal footing with capitalist polities in relation to the USSR. China was being declared not merely a momentary aberration from the proper course of historical development — and susceptible to reintegration into the socialist system — but an alien force now seemingly in fixed enmity toward the USSR. A fundamental assessment of this kind, which seemed to rule out any restoration of the Sino-Soviet alliance, was quite in line with the immediate state of affairs that saw China accused of cooperation with "the world's most extreme reactionaries."[124]

This brings us to the CPSU's approach to the Peace Programme, with which it evidently sought to tie together the different strands of policy relating to the West, the developing areas, and China. The Twenty-third Congress, it should be noted, had been proferred a marginal program of peace action, but it was only in 1971 that the Central Committee report delivered what remained on paper a rather narrow mandate for practical moves connected largely with security in East-West relations. Now, at the Twenty-fifth Congress, a "Programme for Further Struggle for Peace" was advanced. It stressed measures to limit and reduce the arms race, to eliminate all remnants of colonialism, and to remove all vestiges of inequality in international economic relations. That the 1976 program wove together the competing strands or broad options in Soviet policy presumably was recognized. Depending on the response it received, it could stabilize and otherwise improve Soviet relations with the United States and Western Europe, while stiffening the developing countries' economic and political demands on the capitalist world, thereby on both counts reducing Chinese influence and prospects. Or it could result in incremental successes in the Third World at the expense of China and at the cost of an increasingly belligerent West. Or—and this seemed least likely—it could lead to more far-reaching Soviet-American cooperation, serving to constrain China and to limit East-West rivalry in the developing areas.

Ideological Development and Foreign Policy

From the foregoing it should be clear that the international reports of the Central Committee to CPSU congresses are internally contradictory and that there is development in the positions taken from one report to the next. The inner inconsistency that characterizes a given report may be described in various ways. It is preferable to distinguish between conflicting tendencies that in this case reflect and also form part of persistent patterns in Soviet foreign conduct more generally—in the total volume of communication through which the behavior of Soviet policy on external matters is formulated, decided upon, and implemented.[125] There are three such patterns or tendencies—sectarian, activist, and reformative. They, and potentially a fourth and properly reformist tendency, coexist uneasily in Soviet foreign conduct.[126] Their relative influence alters as a consequence of developments in the external environment and within the USSR, which produce changes in inflection and sometimes more marked shifts of emphasis and mood in Soviet behavior. Soviet foreign policy is not unilinear. This is not the place to describe these tendencies fully, nor to demonstrate their persistence as alternate responses of the Soviet system virtually irrespective of leadership changes, nor to illustrate them in any great detail by employing the words of Central Committee foreign reports (as could readily be done). A brief account is, however, necessary if we are to speak systematically of ideological development as represented by the Central Committee reports on foreign affairs in the Brezhnev period.

The sectarian tendency is exhibited in a propensity to divide the world into two counterposed camps with the USSR heading the tightly organized forces of socialism and peace in an irreconcilable struggle against imperialism and all its dependents. This is the line of conduct that would ensue if the CPSU were monolithic in its commitment to the 1966 report's assessment of U.S. imperialism as a "rapacious, plundering strangler of the peoples, hated by all." Intermediate political actors and forces (nationalism, neutralism, nonalignment, bourgeois reformism, pacifism, anti-Americanism, etc.) would disappear from view in a stark confrontation resulting in the self-isolation of the CPSU and in the reduction of its influence in a manner similar to that experienced by an increasingly militant sect when no one is prepared to listen. This orientation to the external world, which clearly favors massive military preparations and extreme political vigilance and control, meshes readily with a tendency to revert to Stalinist practices and priorities within the Soviet Union.

Activism, on the other hand, is expressed in a preference for the use of intermediate political forces under conditions of limited relaxation of international tension aimed at securing sustained advances of the Soviet bloc on all fronts at the expense of its adversaries, principally the United States. Itself dualistic, activism is reflected in statements that assert the need simultaneously to "expose the aggressive policy of imperialism" and to "pursue a course of peaceful coexistence with different social systems." It indicates an awareness that if the risks of nuclear war and the self-defeating political consequences of sectarianism are to be avoided, and if favorable conditions are to be created for the advance of Soviet influence in Western Europe and the Third World, a limited reduction of international tension and tactical agreements with principal adversaries are required. It also entails a fixation on the accumulation of military might and other assets required to outweigh the Western states in the world alignment of forces. It exhibits a propensity to marshal external counterforce against the adversary, as opposed to creating a still more relaxed international setting that would permit a more rapid acceleration of evolutionary forces within the capitalist system. As such, activism corresponds externally to the requirements for a limited departure from the internal priorities and practices of the Stalin era.

The reformative tendency consists of a propensity to manipulate differences within opposing elites, to negotiate with the principal opponent, and — through a combination of conflict and cooperative behavior — to further a transition of East-West rivalry from the military-political to the political-ideological and economic plane to improve Soviet security, influence, and well-being more rapidly. The foreign policy that would result if this was the sole tendency in Soviet conduct would be guided by notions of "force of example" as opposed to an emphasis on the political utility of military force; the use of economic resources for "productive purposes" as opposed to wasteful military spending ("tired of living on mountains of weapons"); and, above all, the development of cooperative relations with the United States on a "realistic" basis involving stabilizing agreements and mutual avoidance of conflict in local areas. Not only would the Soviet system be permitted to evolve more properly and rapidly in such a context, but the most "reactionary" elements in Western ruling classes would be increasingly isolated, thereby speeding up the process of favorable social change in the nonsocialist world.

Although China, Japan, regional conflict, and other considerations could be factored into this account of conflicting tendencies in Soviet foreign behavior, the foregoing should suffice to illustrate that each of the international reports under consideration here offers a different blend of the sectarian, activist, and reformative tendencies. The Twenty-third Congress, partly in reaction to the reformative emphasis of the last years of the Khrushchev regime, received a foreign report that was virtually devoid of reformative language. Sectarianism and activism predominated in a militant and quite forbidding view of the world situation in 1966. By 1971, however, the reformative tendency had surfaced once again, evidenced primarily by the Peace Programme and a variety of formulations imparting a modest awareness of the need for negotiation with the principal adversary. Correspondingly, sectarianism had suffered something of a setback. Although activism had become more clearly the principal burden of the Central Committee's message to the Twenty-fourth Congress, the fact that it was offset by sectarianism on the one hand and a reformative tendency on the other imparted a somewhat irresolute quality to the foreign report that year. At the Twenty-fifth Congress, however, sectarianism had been further diluted and the reformative tendency had been strengthened. Although the reformative tendency had by no means acquired parity with activism, the diminution of sectarianism by comparison with the report of 1966 markedly altered the substance and tone of the 1976 account and suggested a certain readiness to resume the process of cooperation with the United States. The predominance of activism supported by the reformative tendency as opposed to sectarianism was reflected in the 1976 report's articulation of a substantially more secure and successful self-image, a less menacing image of the adversaries, a more relaxed and optimistic view of the international situation, and a less militant conception of Soviet foreign policy than had been the case a decade earlier.

Though activism remained the leading tendency in all three Central Committee reports—and, indeed, in Soviet external behavior generally during the period under consideration—the essential point here is that the relative influence of the sectarian and reformative tendencies altered in favor of the latter. In effect, a process of deradicalization[127] may be discerned in the three Central Committee reports of the Brezhnev years. A limited process, it consisted of the erosion of sectarianism, the assertion of activism, and a strengthening of the reformative tendency. Stated somewhat differently, the comparatively militant and mobilized leadership that authorized the report of 1966 moved with increasing success to manipulate rather than transform the world about them in the decade that followed. By 1976, the party seemed on the whole to be more at ease and somewhat more inclined to accept the world about it than had been the case ten years earlier. In so doing it succeeded in posing an increasingly potent threat to the interests of its opponents, since a deradicalizing party in a nonrevolutionary situation is bound to exert greater influence than one that persists with an unworkable policy line.

The deradicalization process appears, however, to have been limited. Activism, of course, retained elements of the sectarian emphasis on the transformational struggle. Moreover, deradicalization appeared to represent the trajectory of the party leadership rather than the political system as a whole, as had been the case in the Khrushchev era. Particularly on matters of East-West cooperation, changes of outlook and orientation seemed to occur near the peak of the system, without being allowed to seep down to the lower reaches. This was perhaps because in East-West cooperation the real danger to the stability of the Soviet system lies not in the insinuation of Western ideas, but in the effects of a Soviet endeavor to penetrate and manipulate the politics of Western foreign and military policies. Reformism could be stimulated within the regime by placing a higher priority on no-nonsense perceptions of the opponent, by greater acceptance of the need for unilateral restraint required to influence the opponent's internal processes, by further blurring of the external threat, and so on. Hence the continued utility of refraining from doctrinal modifications on key issues even as policy and presumably informal opinion diverged from doctrine during the course of the decade. This was to be seen most clearly in the rigidity of the Central Committee's ultimate assessment of imperialism and of the lack of prospect for progressive evolutionary transformations within the capitalist system. This attested to an intention to minimize the deradicalizing effects within the USSR of a foreign policy orientation that represented the leadership's partial coming to terms with its varied environments.

This ideological development seems ultimately to reflect the workings of what might be termed a deradicalization cycle, in which a new leadership group comes to power with a comparatively militant sense of purpose that is then subject to erosion under the flow of domestic and international circumstance. A broadly similar process could surely be documented from Central Committee reports in the course of the Khrushchev era; it could be found in the personal trajectories of early Soviet leaders, including Lenin and Bukharin; and it could well be repeated once the present leadership leaves office.

Notes

1. The author is grateful to Mr. I. S. Glagolev, now of Washington, D. C., and to Mr. Dimitri K. Simes of the Georgetown University Center for Strategic and International Studies, Washington, D. C., for their valuable comments on the drafting of Central Committee reports.

2. *Current Digest of the Soviet Press,* 18, no. 12 (Part 1)(13 April 1966): 9, col. 1. International reports to the Twenty-fourth and Twenty-fifth CPSU Congresses are to be found in the same series in 23, no. 12 (20 April 1971) and 28, no. 8 (24 March 1976) respectively. For the sake of brevity these sources will hereafter be cited by year to indicate the congress in question, by page number, and by column number (there are two columns per page). Thus the citation given above may be rendered as follows: 66/9,1.

3. 71/5,1. Reference was also made to "difficulties of an objective and subjective order" (71/4,2). These difficulties evidently included "political crisis in Czechoslovakia" (71/7,2), "difficulties" in Poland (ibid.), and unspecified shortcomings in the work of "officials of our planning and economic agencies" (71/6,2). Nevertheless, "with its successes and prospects, with all its problems," the Soviet bloc was "on the whole" gaining in strength and cooperation (71/8,1 and 5,1).

4. 71/10,1; 7,1; 10,2.

5. 71/13,2.

6. Surprise or a tacit acknowledgment of prior opposition was suggested by the repeated observation that in retrospect a "correct" or "accurate" course had been chosen at the Twenty-fourth Congress (76/3,1 and 8,2).

7. 76/5,1.

8. 76/6,1.

9. 76/9,2.

10. 76/9,1.

11. 76/10,1.

12. 66/5,2 and 11,1; 71/3,1.

13. 76/3,2 and 4,2.

14. 66/5,2; 76/4,2; 71/13,2.

15. 76/4,1 and 6,2.

16. 66/7,2.

17. 76/10,2.

18. 76/11,1.

19. 66/8,1; 76/12,2.

20. 66/5,2; 71/11,1 and 13,2.

21. 66/7,1; 71/13,l; 76/10,2.
22. 66/5,2; to a lesser extent 71/4,2.
23. 71/11,1.
24. 66/12,2.
25. 71/7,1.
26. 76/7,1.
27. 76/10,1.
28. 76/14,2.
29. 66/5,1; 71/8,2; 76/12,2.
30. 66/7,1.
31. 71/8,2.
32. 76/12,2.
33. 76/12,2 and 13,1.
34. 76/13,1.
35. 76/13,1 and 12,2.
36. 76/13,1.
37. 76/7,1.
38. 66/7,1; 71/8,2; 76/12,2.
39. Ibid.
40. 71/8,2.
41. 66/6,1 and 7,2; 71/8,2; also 76/13,1, which is less emphatic.
42. 66/5,1 and 11,1.
43. 71/8,2.
44. 76/11,2.
45. On this last point see 76/8,2; 9,2; 10,1.
46. 71/7,2.
47. 76/5,1.
48. 66/5,1 and 1,2.
49. 76/10,1 and 10,2; 76/11,1 and 11,2.
50. 76/13,1.
51. 76/10,1.
52. For example, 76/10,2.
53. 66/7,1; 71/13,1; 76/10,1 and 10,2.
54. Ibid., but especially 76/10,2.
55. 76/10,2.
56. 71/12,2.
57. 66/7,2.
58. 76/10,1.
59. Ibid.
60. 76/11,1.
61. 66/6,2.
62. 71/7,1.
63. 71/7,1 and 7,2.
64. 76/7,1.
65. 76/6,2 and 7,1.
66. 76/7,1.

66. 76/7,1.
67. 66/5,1 and 5,2.
68. 71/3,1 and 3,2.
69. 71/3,2.
70. 76/3,1.
71. 76/12,2.
72. 76/4,1; 8,2; 10,2.
73. Compare, for example, 66/11,1 and 11,2 with 76/9,2 and 10,1.
74. 66/7,1; 71/4,2; 3,1; 8,2.
75. 76/8,2. "Ideological confrontation" did, however, continue. See, for example, 76/6,2.
76. 76/11,2.
77. 76/9,2.
78. 71/12,1.
79. 76/9,1 and 9,2.
80. 76/9,2.
81. 76/10,1.
82. Ibid. The "basic principles" were cited first in a short list of most important measures.
83. 76/10,1.
84. 76/11,1.
85. 66/10,1.
86. 71/9,2. Original quotation italicized.
87. 76/7,1 and 7,2.
88. 76/7,2.
89. Ibid.
90. Ibid.
91. Ibid.
92. Ibid.
93. 71/11,2.
94. 76/7,2 and 8,1.
95. 71/10,1 and 10,2.
96. 71/10,1.
97. 76/14,1.
98. Ibid.
99. 76/4,2. Indicating a possible change of perspective, Brezhnev declared, "There is now probably no spot on earth in which the state of affairs does not have to be taken into consideration, in one way or another, in the formation of our foreign policy."
100. 76/7,2.
101. 66/5,2; 71/11,1; 76/4,1.
102. 66/6,1 and 6,2, and 7,1; 71/4,1 and 8,1; 76/4,2.
103. 76/4,2. As Brezhnev stated, "Probably there has not been one meeting of the Politburo at which we did not consider one question or another related to strengthening the unity of the fraternal countries." This process of unification was encouraged by efforts ranging from cooperation and a "creative" Marxist approach in 1966 (66/6,1), through deeper specialization and closer integration of national

economies in 1971 (71/6,2), to the "gradual drawing together" of socialist countries as a "law-governed pattern" (76/5,11).

104. 76/9,2.

105. 66/10,1.

106. 71/9,2. Italics in original.

107. 76/7,1.

108. 71/9,2.

109. Ibid.

110. 66/10,2.

111. Ibid.; 71/9,2.

112. 76/7,1.

113. Correspondingly, we find the 1966 international report stating that where new states adopting the noncapitalist path were concerned, "the further these countries advance along the road to their chosen goal, the more diversified, deep, and firm our ties with them become" (66/10,2). A decade later, the Central Committee was complimenting itself on the "enrichment" of Soviet political relations with the developing countries in general (76/7,1).

114. 71/9,2.

115. 66/9,2 and 11,1.

116. 71/10,1.

117. 76/8,2.

118. 76/7,2.

119. 66/12,2.

120. Ibid. and 11,1.

121. 71/4,1; 11,1; 13,1.

122. 76/14,2.

123. 76/7,1.

124. 76/6,2 and 7,1.

125. Cf. Franklyn Griffiths, "A Tendency Analysis of Soviet Policymaking," in H. Gordon Skilling and Franklyn Griffiths, eds., *Interest Groups in Soviet Politics* (Princeton, N.J.: Princeton University Press, 1971).

126. For further detail, consult Franklyn Griffiths, "Genoa plus 51: Changing Soviet Objectives in Europe," Wellesley Paper no. 4 (Toronto: Canadian Institute of International Affairs, 1973) and "Images, Politics and Learning in Soviet Behavior toward the United States" (Ph.D. diss., Columbia University, 1972).

127. See Robert C. Tucker, "The Deradicalization of Marxist Movements," in his *The Marxian Revolutionary Idea* (New York: Norton, 1969), pp. 185–186.

3

Consensus Versus Conflict:
The Dimension of Foreign Policy

Hannes Adomeit

One of the surprising realizations after studying a number of international crises is the degree to which Soviet behavior seems to follow engrained patterns of action — as if there existed a broad consensus about operational principles in foreign policy.[1] This realization is even more surprising given important differences at all levels of Soviet domestic politics since World War II, no matter whether such differences concern the personality of the dominant leader, the makeup of the top leadership, or basic elements of the Soviet system. This is true even allowing for major changes in international relations since 1945 and indisputable evidence of domestic political conflict in the Soviet Union.

The possibility exists that Soviet risk taking and crisis behavior merely represent a special case or an exception to the general state of affairs in Soviet foreign policy. More specifically, it could be argued that whereas Soviet foreign policy in general is almost invariably affected by domestic controversy and conflict, Soviet decision making in international crises will typically demonstrate a "rallying around the flag," the concentration of decisions in the hands of a select executive committee, the restoration of important elements of centralization, and a return to traditional reflexes and responses. As will be shown, there is good reason to believe that much of this does in fact occur. Therefore, when examining the relative importance of consensus or conflict in Soviet foreign-policy decision making, it is necessary to make careful distinctions as to the level and type of decisions at issue.

There are obvious limits to the view that Soviet crisis behavior is a special case where consensus is more pronounced than in other areas of Soviet foreign policy. For instance, a crisis of long duration or one flaring up intermittently will tend to bring into play individuals, groups, and forces not represented a priori in the "first circle" of decision making. Similarly, in conditions of protracted international crisis various institutions and organizations will have a greater opportunity to make their interests known. There may also be special circumstances in which a particularly determined domestic faction will refuse to view the crisis as a call for restraint but will see it as a convenient signal to act.[2]

These conditions lead to a basic working assumption: elements of consensus and conflict affect decision making in any political system but conflict in Soviet foreign policy — including international crises — tends to occur within a relatively narrow framework. The analysis proceeds in three stages. The first part examines the aspect of consensus in the form of commonly accepted operational principles in international crises. The second part deals with the aspect of domestic conflict and its actual or potential repercussions, taking some representative examples from the Stalin, Khrushchev, and Brezhnev eras. The third part attempts to create a balance sheet of the respective importance of the two aspects.

I

Unfortunately, much of the theoretical literature has been overshadowed by one single crisis of major importance — the Cuban missile crisis. Most of the works on "crisis management" appeared within a few years after the crisis and were preoccupied with the dramatic aspects of the hectic thirteen days in October 1962. Policymaking, too (at least initially), was overshadowed by the missile crisis, as is evident in Robert McNamara's statement, made shortly after the crisis, that "there is no longer any such thing as strategy, only crisis management."[3] A somewhat Machiavellian idea began to gain ground: If one could understand the dynamics of crisis and could master the art of crisis management, one would be able to outmaneuver a seemingly unsophisticated opponent such as the Soviet Union.

This idea was neither reprehensible nor necessarily a shortcut to political disaster, if only scholars and policymakers had drawn the correct lessons and conclusions from Soviet behavior in the Cuban missile crisis. By and large a twofold error was committed. First, the Cuban missile crisis was elevated to a classic case of how nations go to the brink of war, that is, rung by rung, via a clear and consistent "escalation ladder." This process was later described in detail by Herman Kahn. According to this image, as Karl Deutsch notes, "each power tries to outbid the other by some margin in its verbal or material commitment at each stage," and thus "through threat and counterthreat, retaliation and counterretaliation [matters go] right up to the brink of all-out war — and perhaps across it."[4]

Second, not only was the Cuban missile crisis viewed as a universally valid model of the dynamics of crisis but — more relevant for the present inquiry — Soviet actions in this particular case were taken as the main point of departure for making judgments about Soviet crisis behavior in general. Little did it matter that in reality Soviet behavior in Cuba in 1962 was more the exception than the rule and a deviation from traditional and subsequent patterns of Soviet risk taking rather than a confirmation of such patterns. In order to recognize this more clearly it is necessary to briefly compare Soviet behavior in the Cuban missile crisis with that in other major crises, in particular the Berlin crises of 1948 and 1961.

Certainly, the management of the Berlin crisis of 1948 bears little resemblance to that of the Cuban crisis of 1962. There was little of the postulated outbidding of each power by the other by some margin in its verbal or material commitment, or for that matter any consistent movement of threat and counterthreat, retaliation and counterretaliation. Although there were warning signals at the local level, both of a verbal and material kind, the image of an "escalation ladder" did not fit. At the diplomatic level the Soviet Union adopted a stance of conciliation and compromise. When a major step up the ladder was taken with the imposition of the blockade, it was accompanied by mixed and ambiguous verbal communications—lame excuses, expressions of regret, invocation of the old wartime spirit, and moderately worded statements conveying the idea that compromises on Berlin and Germany were possible and desirable.

On the surface, the consistent escalation of commitments and increases in risks, rung by rung, appear to apply more easily to the Berlin crisis of 1961. On both sides—Soviet and U.S.—a number of moves and counter-moves were made, including maneuvers of forces, speeches emphasizing military preparedness, announcements of increases in defense expenditures, strengthening of conventional forces, and improvements in strategic posture. However, these military measures were spread out over a relatively long period of time (from about May to October 1961) and many of them—paradoxically in the conventional theory of crisis management—were taken *after* the gravest danger point was safely past. Finally, the image of escalation does not fit very well in this case because it was never quite clear what the military measures were all about, whether they were part of the arms race (or arms "competition"), whether they were designed to improve the overall bargaining positions, whether they were meant to be instruments of "compellence" to force the Western powers out of Berlin and to establish a radically different regime on the access routes, or whether—more modestly—they were designed to deter Western counteraction to the measures of 13 August.

By comparison, no such ambiguity applied in the Cuban missile crisis. Verbal and material moves on the U.S. side were unambiguous in their demand that the missiles be removed. Verbal and material moves on the Soviet side were unambiguous in their intention to keep them in, if possible. There was no possibility of compromise, such as keeping medium-range missiles in Cuba and withdrawing intermediate-range missiles or withdrawing only half or a third of them.

Another important deviation from the classic model of crisis management concerns time constraints. In an age of rapid communication and high-speed strategic and conventional delivery systems this is an important problem that did affect the calculations of the major protagonists in Cuba in 1962. However, time constraints did not play an important role in either of the two Berlin crises. In 1948 the "technical difficulties" alleged by the Soviet Military Administration (SMA) in Germany made it appear that the blockade was not final. Patience and watchful waiting were therefore required. It was even agreed by everyone concerned that the important road bridge over the Elbe River and some of the railway bridges were, indeed — as the SMA had officially stated — in need of repair. As the airlift developed, the need to act was postponed even further because the presence of the Western powers and the basic economic activities of the German civilian population could be maintained.

Concerning time constraints and the Berlin crisis of 1961, the parallels with 1948 are again more pronounced than those with 1962. There was pressure for the West to act quickly only if action were to be taken at all. (There is one parallel with the Cuban missile crisis: a fait accompli was being created that could only be removed by acting forcefully.) But as the point of contention in Berlin in 1961 had already been yielded to the Soviet Union by limiting the Allied commitment to uninterrupted access, Allied presence, and the viability of West Berlin (the "three essentials"), and as the population was actively being discouraged by the mayor of West Berlin and the Allies from venting its anger and resentment, time constraints on action were removed almost immediately in the first days after 13 August. The Soviet Union even had to revert to recreating an artificial sense of danger and urgency in its attempt to win more concessions in the next round of pressure.

If, then, it is unwise to take the Cuban missile crisis as the main, or even the only, model for demonstrating universal features of the dynamics of crisis, it is equally inappropriate to use it as the main point of departure for generalizing about Soviet crisis behavior. This can be shown by postulating operational principles of Soviet behavior as derived from observations in international crises other than the Cuban missile crisis and by examining those instances where a crisis might have occurred but did not, due to a failure by the Soviet Union to embark on what Thomas Schelling has called "competition in risk taking." Before presenting some of these principles, definitions and conceptual clarification are in order.[5]

A "risk" is a probability inherent in events and conforming to the subjective notion of *degree of belief*. The assessment of risk in international relations, therefore, is a matter of political judgment of objective conditions and potential costs and benefits. For the sake of convenience only three types of risk will be distinguished here: risks of crisis occurring in normal interaction among states; risks of war in international crises; and risks of annihilation in war. Local conflicts and limited wars directly involving one superpower and the interests of both (Iran in 1946, the succession of Middle East wars, Vietnam, or Soviet intervention in Eastern Europe) initially pose only risks of crisis in the superpower relationship. Two steps and two conditions are required to transform crisis risks into war risks. The first step is a *challenge* posed by one superpower and the second is a *response in kind* by the adversary. The first condition is commitment, resolve, or determination by both powers to engage in a competition in risk taking — by means of treaty obligations or by specific verbal or nonverbal communication. The second condition presupposes the dangers of escalation, imperfect control over local actors, and the "force of events" — that is, the existence of what the Soviet scholarly literature has called the *nekontroliruemyi element* or "uncontrollable element."

What follows from these distinctions are four categories of crisis analysis: cases in which risks of crisis are initiated by local actors or the West to which the USSR (1) does or (2) does not respond in kind and cases in which the USSR takes the initiative and the West (3) does or (4) does not respond. The U.S. blockade of the North Vietnamese harbors in 1972 conforms to the second category, Cuba and the two Berlin crises to the third, and Angola and Ethiopia to the fourth category. No example of the first category can as yet be provided.

The most basic of the postulated operational principles of Soviet behavior[6] in conditions in which risks of crisis or risks of war were present can be stated as follows: *Do not embark on risk taking without careful calculation; move forward only after thorough preparation.* These principles or axioms could clearly be seen in action during the two Berlin crises.

In 1948 the first serious examples of selective interference with access to and egress from Berlin came after Marshal V. D. Sokolovsky's dramatic walkout from the Allied Control Council (20 March). Warning signals of crisis continued in one form or another until the very day of the imposition of the blockade (23–24 June). It was also evident that the blockade was related clearly and unambiguously to the currency reform in the Anglo-American zone. As shown by the severe restrictions imposed by the SMA during the weekend preceding the currency reform (11–12 June), there is no hint of improvisation or spontaneity on the Soviet side. (The restrictions had obviously been put into effect under the erroneous assumption that the reform would be announced during the weekend of 4–5 June.) Similarly, the claim that the currency reform of 18 June came as a surprise to the USSR — a claim advanced by Soviet spokesmen then and repeated in Soviet sources ever since — is completely unwarranted, as the SMA newspaper in Germany had published a report (a correct one) as early as 4 February stating that printed notes for a separate monetary reform were already available in the Western zones.[7] This is not to say that the Soviet calculations were sound or that the result was successful, but only that the measures adopted showed careful preparation and came only after a series of tests of U.S. determination to respond to more severe challenges.

Calculated risk taking and careful preparation were apparent also in the Berlin crisis of 1961. In that case the probing of the extent of Western determination and resolve started as early as November 1958, when the first ultimatum on the Berlin problem was issued; certainly it was well under way at the time of the second ultimatum in June 1961. This probing was designed to reveal the extent to which the Western powers were united on the issues in dispute and to show where action could be taken without risking Western countermeasures. But the most important feature in the present context is the surprisingly long period of delay in taking physical measures. The evidence available points to pressures exerted by Walter Ulbricht on Khrushchev beginning in mid-March 1961. A meeting of the Political Consultative Committee in Moscow on 28–29 March probably discussed the problem, but the course of events justifies the conclusion that the procedure adopted there was only to try all available options of stopping the outflow of East Germans at the local level and avoid the sharpening of conflict at the international level. By June this procedure had proven inadequate. In part as a consequence of this inadequacy and in part as a response to diplomatic opportunities offered by an apparently weak, inexperienced, and irresolute U.S. leadership, the pressure was increased at the international level at the Vienna summit. Even then two more months passed, filled with preparations at the local and international levels, before the Soviet Union decided to risk physical measures. The decision was endorsed at the meeting of the first secretaries of the member countries of the Warsaw Pact on 3–5 August. Another ten days were left to complete the material preparations in East Germany, carefully camouflage the impending action, and prepare for all the contingencies that might arise.

It is instructive to compare this type of Soviet behavior with that shown in other crises and in other situations in which there was only a risk of superpower crisis. During the conflicts in the Middle East in 1956, 1967, and 1973, the principles of "do not embark on risk taking without careful calculation" and "move forward only after thorough preparation" were of limited applicability as the USSR was primarily reacting to local events rather than initiating a risky challenge to the adversary superpower. (See category 2 of the classification of cases introduced above.) Of course, there were some Soviet actions that did threaten to transform the local conflict into an East-West crisis with the risks of war. One example was the so-called nuclear threats issued by Khrushchev (through Nikolai Bulganin as head of government) on 5 November 1956.[8] Another was Kosygin's use of the "hot line" on 10 June 1967, threatening that unless Israel halted its military operations the Soviet Union would take "necessary actions, including military."[9] A final example was the Soviet response to the 1973 Middle East war. The Soviet challenge to the West was demonstrated by the alert of Soviet airborne divisions (approximately 45,000 operational troops) between 8 and 16 October, by other signs of build-up for military intervention, and by a strongly worded letter from Brezhnev to President Nixon on 24 October.[10] But all these examples appear to have had as their primary function (1) to bring pressure to bear on the United States to restrain its presumptive ally, Israel, and (2) to demonstrate to the Soviet Union's presumptive allies, the Arab countries, that the USSR was acting resourcefully on their behalf. To that extent all of these moves were of limited purpose and limited risk. No combat troops of the superpowers participated in the local military operations — Israel did not need such troops and the Arabs did not want them. What both sides in the local conflict wanted was military supplies and political support. This the USSR provided to the Arabs, not in the form of rash moves and blundering but in the form of sober and carefully calibrated threats to achieve maximum effect.

A similar analysis can be made of the Soviet intervention in Czechoslovakia in 1968. Although the events in the CSSR — even more than those in the Middle East — produced only "risks of crisis" in superpower relations, it is useful to consider Soviet behavior in that instance, as the risks and costs involved (though of a different type than in superpower crises) were high, including the possibility of armed resistance by the Czechoslovak armed forces, negative political and economic repercussions in the Soviet bloc, problems in the international Communist movement, and exposure of Soviet forces to the animosity of fraternal workers. Given those risks, the degree to which Soviet behavior in Czechoslovakia in 1968 conformed to the general pattern of behavior manifested in the Berlin crises of 1948 and 1961 is striking. The first harbingers of action to be taken later came at the meeting of the Warsaw Pact member countries (with the exception of Romania) in Dresden, on 23 March 1968, and in a speech by Brezhnev in which he warned that "renegades cannot bank on going unpunished."[11] Yet there were many more bilateral Soviet-Czechoslovak meetings and multilateral conferences; several more months of pressure by diplomatic, economic, and military means; and explicit and implicit threats before actual intervention took place on 21 August 1968. Intervention was delayed for a long time, but when it did take place it caught the Czechoslovak leadership and most Western analysts by surprise. No doubt because of long and careful preparation, the tactical implementation of the measures was skillful, swift, and effective.

But what about Cuba? Was Soviet behavior there an exception to the general pattern, a violation of the axiom under consideration? It is difficult to believe that there was no calculation in advance, but there was certainly a blatant violation of the axiom of careful preparation, particularly technical preparation. Surface-to-air missiles were not operational until after the arrival and construction of strategic offensive missiles; the radar system for detection of U-2 planes and guidance of antiaircraft missiles was built too late; there was no camouflage prior to the detection of the missiles by the United States; and the missile sites were built in a pattern familiar to U.S. intelligence.[12] It is possible to integrate these examples into an "organizational process model," as Allison does, but in regard to the axioms of Soviet crisis behavior they are violations of the principle of "move forward only after thorough preparation."

However, there is more to the axiom of "thorough preparation" than the technical aspect. Even more important is the international *political* aspect, which can be said to include the rules: *Carefully prepare the ground psychologically; make every attempt to demoralize the adversary;* and *soften his potential resistance by an alternation of severe pressure and holding out the prospect of compromise.*

These rules were followed closely in Berlin in 1948 and 1961, and in the CSSR in 1968, but the Cuban missile crisis appears as a significant exception to the rule. The classic procedure would have required gradually reconciling the adversary to the idea of a large Soviet military establishment in the Caribbean, and increasing the level of forces and armaments in the familiar "salami tactics" procedure to demonstrate that, from the Soviet point of view, the presence of Soviet tactical (or any other) nuclear weapons and delivery systems in Cuba was as reasonable as the presence of U.S. nuclear weapons and delivery systems in West Germany. Instead, the Soviets declared officially that "the Soviet Union has such powerful missiles for delivering . . . nuclear warheads that there is no need to seek sites for them beyond the boundaries of the Soviet Union"[13] and even reassured the United States privately on various occasions that no offensive missiles would be placed in Cuba.[14] In the course of gradually increasing the pressure it might have been quite clear that the United States would under no circumstances tolerate the planned scheme, but this is precisely what probing and careful preparation are all about.

When, in the autumn of 1970, the Soviet Union engaged in another challenge to U.S. security interests in the Caribbean it became apparent that the general, or traditional, pattern of Soviet risk taking had been restored. U.S. reconnaissance had found numerous indications that the

USSR was about to provide its navy with a base for nuclear submarines in Cienfuegos, Cuba. U.S. Secretary of State Henry Kissinger presented the full evidence to Soviet Ambassador Anatoly Dobrynin, asserting that such a base would violate the 1962 agreement — that provided for a withdrawal of all Soviet offensive weapons in exchange for a U.S. pledge not to invade Cuba — and outlining the serious consequences that such a move would entail. It did not take long for TASS to declare that the Soviet Union "has not been and is not building its own military base" in Cuba and for Dobrynin to give assurances that the agreement of 1962 existed and would be upheld.[15]

Soviet behavior in Cuba conforms to a second major operational principle. As described by Alexander George, it is *"Push to the limit"* and *"engage in pursuit"* of an opponent who begins to retreat or make concessions, but *"know when to stop"* (in conditions of challenging an adversary); *"resist from the start"* any encroachment by the opponent, no matter how slight it appears to be, but *"don't yield to enemy provocation"* and *"retreat before superior force"* (in conditions of responding to a challenge by an adversary).[16] In the two Berlin crises the axioms of behavior for Soviet leaders taking the initiative were confirmed without qualification. In 1948 the Soviet Union had been pushing against access, the Western Allied presence, and the viability of the Western sectors. However, the pressures were unsuccessful — among other reasons — because the Western Allies were determined to stay in the city and because the German population failed to be demoralized; both depended to a large extent on the unexpected effectiveness of the airlift in supplying the Allies and the city. Under those conditions three alternatives were available to the Soviets: to seriously disrupt the operations of the airlift; to seize the Western sectors directly by the use of military force; or to adopt a more indirect approach by organizing civil disturbances in the Western sectors with the help of local Communists and then intervening to "restore order" and to "safeguard the security of the Soviet zone of occupation."

Soviet interference with the airlift would have resulted in direct military clashes in the air. In the course of probing it had become evident that both the United States and Britain were quite sensitive on the issue of air access — they had reacted strongly to a major air accident caused by a Soviet pilot on 5 April. The SMA was made aware of the fact that fighter protection was being contemplated on the runs to Berlin; any further "accidents" would almost certainly have meant the adoption of such a course of action. At the same time, Soviet extension of the blockade to air communications would have forced the U.S. president to authorize Clay's proposed scheme of reopening ground access by force. (In Clay's and Murphy's opinion Stalin had already overstepped the limits by imposing a blockade on the ground.)[17] Evidently, one of the most important rules of the game on both sides was to avoid the use of force, even at low levels.

This injunction against low-level clashes of military units applied also to the instances of probing ground communications and in Berlin itself. In every instance of pressure on ground access the SMA selected a form of probing that did not require direct backup by military force, and at times strongly discouraged the use of force by the adversary, as this would have been ineffective (e.g. the shunting of locomotives to sidings).

In those instances of pressure in Berlin in which armed units of the Western Allies appeared in response to low-level Soviet challenges, Soviet units were withdrawn as a consequence, without getting embroiled (e.g., the erection of a barrier in the British sector on 2 April and the withdrawal of Soviet units after British forces had isolated the post).

It would also have been a violation of the principle of "know where to stop" if Stalin had decided to adopt either of the two remaining alternatives. Faced with a direct military takeover of the Western sectors, the pressure on the U.S. president to take military counteraction would have been enormous and, with one stroke, all of the Soviet Union's World War II advances would have been endangered. However, everything short of a massive takeover could have been and, almost with certainty, *would* have been resisted by Clay's invoking the legal principle, upheld in low-level counterchallenges, that the Allies were sovereign in their respective sectors.

All these considerations apply with equal validity to the Berlin crisis of 1961. Ground access was beset by problems and challenges, but these challenges were not at all comparable in their importance to the blockade. In fact it is fair to say that the challenges to access were primarily verbal. Where selected stoppages were involved they affected Germans only, they occurred much earlier than in the crisis months of 1961, and they were made through East Germany as a proxy. There was no interference with the reinforcement of the U.S. garrison in Berlin when U.S. troops proceeded to that city on the Autobahn on 20 August. As in 1948 there was some "buzzing" or "frolicking" of aircraft, but even more care was taken in 1961 to avoid incidents and accidents. In the city itself the picture in 1961 was similar to that of 1948. Wherever possible German Democratic Republic (GDR) police, armed units, and border guards were used as buffers to prevent confrontation during East German attempts to check identity papers of Allied military personnel (24 August 1961) and civilians (late October 1961) or during the physical measures of 13 August.

The discussion of the main axiom as it applies to the two Berlin crises shows the operation of the subsidiary rules: *avoid the direct use of military force* and *use proxies wherever possible.* In fact, the use of proxies to avoid the direct use of Soviet military personnel and to scale down the level of risk is a common feature of Soviet foreign policy that applies not only to East Germany in the Berlin crises, but also to North Korea (and China) in the Korean

War, North Vietnam in the Vietnam War, the Arab countries in the Middle East conflicts, Egypt in Yemen in 1967, and Cuba in Angola in 1975–76.[18] In all of these conflicts (which were or seemed favorable to Soviet interests) the Soviet Union attempted — sometimes unsuccessfully — to operate various levers of violence by remote control, thereby leaving open the degree of responsibility it had for the course of events. (Below the threshold of violence the 1955 "Czech"-Egyptian arms deal demonstrated a similar attempt to blur Soviet responsibility.) In all of these instances of trying to further Soviet objectives indirectly — behind the scenes or by remote control — the USSR lowered the risk of direct superpower confrontation. In contrast, U.S. policy often was forced to resort to — and sometimes needlessly volunteered — the physical presence and intervention of its own forces.

From this perspective, the Cuban missile crisis is again a contradiction to preferred patterns of Soviet behavior. The installation of missiles was, and was declared by President Kennedy to be, a direct Soviet challenge involving Soviet military weapons and personnel. U.S. naval forces were moved in position against Russians, and Russian technicians and military personnel on the missile sites were directly exposed to U.S. air strikes. Only one important aspect of the set of axioms was confirmed by Soviet behavior in the Cuban missile crisis: the principle of "know when to stop" and "retreat before superior force." Although it was at a late stage, it was not too late to avoid direct clashes of the military forces of the two superpowers.

There is no example yet where the Soviet Union committed forces directly against the United States or any one of the Allies in the U.S. system of treaties. When the USSR did use force directly it appeared to act in accordance with a principle formulated by the German general, Heinz Guderian, for the use of tank forces in war: If such forces are to be used, do not use them piecemeal and sporadically, but massively, in concentrated fashion, and with determination (*Nicht kleckern sondern klotzen*). This was evident in the large-scale, bloody clashes between Japanese and Soviet armed forces in the summers of 1938 and 1939 and in the Ussuri clashes in March 1969. In both instances the USSR used armed force in the manner described for the limited political purpose of teaching the adversary a severe lesson. But the determined, massive, and swift use of force is also an important feature of Soviet behavior in Eastern Europe in conditions where its supremacy in any particular country appears to be threatened.

Typically in these cases, the Soviet decision to use force has not been dependent on whether or not military success was guaranteed. (Certainly, the Soviet armed forces could, as a favorite Soviet phrase has it, "deal crushing blows" to vulnerable Chinese nuclear and industrial installations, and in 1956 and 1970 they could have been used in Poland without producing a physical confrontation with the other superpower.) The most important criterion for the commitment of forces is not even the degree of resistance to be expected at the local level (e.g., potentially in Yugoslavia or China, or in Poland or Czechoslovakia in the past). The important criteria are, first, whether Soviet security interests are at stake and, second, whether there is no alternative to the use of force to safeguard vital interests.

The third recurring pattern of Soviet behavior is, before engaging in forward operations *carefully construct a fallback position to meet unexpectedly high resistance by the adversary*. It is clear that in 1948 and 1961 the Soviet Union had skillfully constructed a road for tactical retreat, should serious complications have developed. In the Berlin crisis of 1948 the blockade measures were described as being of a technical nature and local significance. Although no one could miss the point that the first multilateral conference of foreign ministers of the USSR and the countries of the Soviet bloc was held at the same time the blockade measures were put into effect (23–24 June 1948), the statement of that conference did *not* establish any direct link between larger political demands on the German problem (which it did mention) and the physical measures at the local level (which it did not mention). In conformity with the axiom, this approach gave the USSR an easy way out: If the United States had reacted immediately by issuing an ultimatum for the reopening of communications, some of the technical difficulties could have been made to disappear as quickly as they had appeared—without loss of face, without making it necessary to shelve the political demands, and without making it necessary to abandon some form of pressure. If, however, the United States had gone beyond that and used force, it could have been accused of acting rashly, without justification, and provocatively, but still would have found itself in the uncomfortable position of having to keep the access routes open on a long-term basis, presumably by establishing a military presence along the access routes—a course of action that was clearly ruled out in Washington and in Berlin, and even by Clay.

Similarly, in 1961, the physical measures initially were easily retractable. At first barbed-wire fencing and wooden barriers were used. Construction of a concrete wall did not begin until 15 August, after the West had demonstrated that it would not take resourceful counteraction. The number of crossing points was only gradually reduced. Also, as noted in the discussion of the foregoing operational principle, Soviet military units were not directly involved in the operation. These combined elements provided the Soviet Union with the tactical flexibility to cope with a vigorous Western response. Various options were still available to achieve the stated purpose of establishing a new border regime and stopping the flow of people from East to West — for instance, the establishment of "border measures" not *at* but *inside* the Soviet sectors. Both crises, therefore, validate a subsidiary axiom of Soviet behavior, the rule *"do not settle for a single probability estimate of unwanted risks" that may develop in the future, but "engage in sequential analysis."*[19]

Again, it is the Cuban missile crisis that is an exception to the general rule of Soviet risk taking and crisis behavior. If Khrushchev had assumed that the United States would react vigorously (as it did), with what sort of tactical flexibility would he have been left in the calculation? It is difficult to find any at all at the local level. Conceivably some flexibility would have been restored to Khrushchev if he had acted elsewhere — for instance, if he had responded to the naval quarantine of Cuba with a land blockade of Berlin. It is possible that the suggestion was made during the crisis, or that it was raised after the fact by Khrushchev's critics. But such action would have compounded the problems for the Soviet Union, rather than alleviating them. Foreign Minister Andrei Gromyko implied as much when he reported to the Supreme Soviet in December 1962 that already the Cuban missile crisis "had brought the world one step, perhaps only half a step, from an abyss." The crisis also made "many people think how the whole matter might have developed if yet another crisis in Central Europe had been added to the critical events around Cuba."[20]

The emphasis in the subsidiary axiom was on *risks*, but — bearing in mind that risks on the one hand and costs, benefits, and objectives on the other are analytically distinct — it may be possible to summarize another operational principle as follows: *do not consider the successful manipulation of risks an end in itself, constantly review costs and gains in the operation, and never lose sight of the important objectives and interests.* These maxims of conduct apply to situations in which Soviet leaders take the initiative and those in which they respond to Western challenges.

To begin with objectives and interests, Western opinion has often attempted to establish with precision "the" Soviet objective in a particular international crisis, thereby neglecting the possiblity that a whole range of objectives — even conflicting objectives — could be pursued at the same time. In fact, if it is correct to say that the maxims do not provide for a single probability estimate but for a sequential analysis of risks, it is a small step to accept the idea that the same could be true for Soviet objectives, i.e., that Soviet leaders continuously make assessments of how the dynamics of crisis affect the potential achievement of important goals.

For the political leaders in the United States and Britain in 1948 it was valid to ask whether Berlin was a lever or a prize in Soviet objectives. But it would have been politically unwise in 1948, as it would be intellectually limiting today, to settle for a single answer. By winning Berlin as a *prize* the

Soviet Union would have improved its own and the German Communists' position in East Germany to a considerable degree. But there was no guarantee that Soviet demands on the "German problem" (reparations, heavy industry, the status of the Ruhr, the social, economic, and political development of the Western zones, plans for the creation of a separate West German state) would suddenly disappear. In fact, those demands might have been put forward even more vigorously. Conversely, the successful use of Berlin as a *lever* for preventing the formation of a separate West Germany would most likely have encouraged Stalin to try harder in Berlin. He probably would have had more success as the morale of the population of Berlin — a crucial factor in the crisis — suffered the shock of Western retreat.

It is equally apparent that the evolution of the crisis in 1961 was constantly being measured against the potential achievement of objectives, and that there was a broad range of objectives to choose from — in Berlin, in Germany, and in Western Europe. Some of the most important objectives can be listed as follows: to induce the Western powers to yield their position in Berlin (the most unlikely to be realized); to enhance the domestic stability and the international status of the GDR; to limit the influence of West Berlin as a "showcase of the West" by increasing its sense of vulnerability and decreasing its ties with West Germany; to win final and irrevocable acceptance of the postwar political and social order in Europe; and to neutralize the threat to this order from West Germany and her declared policy of nonrecognition of the GDR and the postwar borders. The achievement of any one of these major objectives would have opened up a number of additional prospects, including, as Wolfe summarizes, the creation of "an acute sense of insecurity and betrayal in West Germany" and demonstration of "the emergence of a new balance of power, under which the West would have to be prepared to make further concessions on disputed issues."[21]

What follows from this broad range of possible objectives is that it was not necessary to take the Soviet demand for the conclusion of a peace treaty literally. If, from Khrushchev's point of view, progress could be made on any of the major issues without actually signing a peace treaty, so much the better. Nevertheless, in 1958 and 1959 Khrushchev's optimism about significant changes in the correlation of forces in favor of socialism (the acceleration of decolonization, the "missile gap," the Sputnik shock, the prospect of "catching up with and overtaking" the U.S. in per capita production) and the likely political benefits to flow from them, probably extended to hopes that the West would make concessions on the questions of access to the city and the status and viability of West Berlin. By 1961, Soviet expectations had to be scaled down considerably. Developments in the GDR had put the USSR in the position of acting unilaterally and, to make matters worse, acting unilaterally from a position of military-strategic weakness and grow-ing disparity compared to the United States. The measures of 13 August, therefore, took on the character of emergency measures, which explains the significance of Soviet assertions that the measures "were important because they made it possible to solve a series of urgent questions which were then facing the USSR and other socialist countries, chiefly the GDR."[22]

But as soon as the objective of "plugging the loophole" (as it was called in various speeches by Soviet and East German leaders) or the "establishment of a new regime at the borders" (according to official declarations) was suc-cessfully achieved — to Khrushchev's and Ulbricht's great relief and surprise at the lack of any serious complication — new demands (or should one say the old ones?) on the problems of Berlin, Germany, and Western Europe were put forward. This pressure began as early as 23 August, when Western air access came under propagandistic attack, and it continued via revival and abandonment of the peace treaty proposal in various other forms until the Cuban missile crisis.

A subsidiary axiom to the point about not engaging in the manipulation of risk for its own sake and never losing sight of important objectives and interests could be stated as follows: *do not let yourself be diverted by false notions or bourgeois morality* and *resist false considerations of pride and prestige.* Soviet leaders are not insensitive to moral issues, but their morality is different from ours. In 1948, to resort to a medieval siege operation with the purpose (as the West saw and portrayed it) of "starving out a city of more than 2 million inhabitants" was problematic not because it offended Stalin's or the SMA's sense of morality but because it provided the adversary with an ex-cellent propaganda slogan that he could turn into a potent instrument of cohesion. (It is not surprising, therefore, that Marshal Sokolovsky and the Soviet government were quick to express "concern for the well-being of the Berlin population by assuring them normal supplies in all essentials"[23] and to offer the resumption of food deliveries to the three Western sectors — on Soviet terms.) In 1961, too, the sensitivity to moral issues extended less to the human consequences of the border closure than to the negative prop-aganda effect of the wall and the Western charges that the GDR had been transformed into a huge "concentration camp."

Another example of Soviet considerations of pride and prestige was the 1967 defeat of the Russians' Arab protégés. The Soviet General Staff must have felt frustration at the seemingly complete military incompetence of their allies and the large-scale loss of Soviet military material. Nevertheless, the weaponry was quickly replaced, the political commitments became stronger (up to and including the conclusion of a friendship treaty), and the military involvement became deeper, leading to the dispatch of Soviet pilots and antiaircraft personnel to help with the air defense of Egypt in the summer of 1970. A similar sequence of events was replayed between 1972 and 1973: the humiliating expulsion of the Soviet military presence in the summer of 1972 and deteriorating Soviet-Egyptian relations from then on did not prevent the USSR from lending considerable military support to the Arab countries in the October 1973 war (in the form of large amounts of supplies delivered during the emergency) as well as political support (in the form of a "ready-to-intervene" posture). In all of these sequences of events the pursuit of objective interests was more important than the nurturing of hurt pride.

Nothing could demonstrate better the importance of the axiom under discussion than the Soviet failure to respond vigorously to the blockade of the North Vietnamese harbors by the U.S. Navy in May 1972. At that time many respectable observers (Soviet specialists unfortunately among them) feared a competition in risk taking of proportions even more serious than during the Cuban missile crisis. This was based on the assumption that the Soviet Union, having achieved rough military-strategic parity and superpower status, would not tolerate humiliating measures directed against a socialist ally, Soviet ships, and Soviet logistic operations. Yet apart from the difficulty for the USSR of how to successfully challenge U.S. naval supremacy at the local level—a problem of which the USSR must have been aware also in Cuba in 1962—there was the equally important consideration of Soviet goals and interests. By the spring of 1972 it had become obvious that U.S. withdrawal from South Vietnam was only a matter of time; the mining of the North Vietnamese harbors and the bombing of Cambodia could be interpreted as the last convulsions before the final end of the ill-fated U.S. involvement in Southeast Asia. Hence, to engage in confrontation would have risked a great deal and probably achieved nothing. More important, the display of restraint could be made to pay off handsomely at the forthcoming Nixon-Brezhnev summit to be held in June, right after the U.S. blockade measures.[24]

II

The argument that there are a number of interrelated operational principles in Soviet foreign policy raises three questions. First, where do these principles originate? Second, even granting the existence of engrained modes of behavior, aren't these modes constantly changing and, once defined, almost immediately in need of revision? Third, and most important in the present context, if the principles of Soviet behavior are really so straightforward, what are we to do with the extensive and at times reasonably well-documented indications of conflict in the Soviet leadership concerning issues of foreign policy? The problems of origin and change will be touched upon briefly in Section III;

the emphasis in this section is on domestic conflict.

At the outset it is necessary to state that, when looking for evidence of domestic conflict affecting Soviet foreign policy in general and Soviet risk taking and crisis behavior in particular, it may be useful not to subscribe to any particular theory or model to decide whether such conflict is primarily one of institutions, bureaucratic or organizational politics, interest groups or ad hoc groupings, or of individuals and personalities. All potential sources of conflict should be considered if they seem to apply in a particular case.

Next, reality is probably reflected more accurately if one ceases to look at conflict from the perspectives of victors "triumphing," enemies being "crushed," the defeated being "scattered on the battlefield," and policy issues representing mere pretexts in the personal rivalries among ambitious men caught up in the perennial struggle for power.[25] Rather, Soviet leaders — even leaders acting in the Stalinist system — should be credited with opinions of their own and with the will and sometimes the capacity to act on the basis of their own political convictions or in pursuit of functional interests.

As a final introductory comment, it is doubtful whether it is useful to posit a framework of analysis in which the essence of interrelationships (linkages) between Soviet domestic and foreign policy is held to consist of a congruence of elements either of the Left or of the Right, such congruence applying to doctrine and behavior; domestic (including economic), intrabloc, and foreign policy; and policy within the international Communist movement.[26] While this framework of analysis has an indisputable inner logic, looks elegant, and is easily applicable, in practice — as will be shown below in two examples — it poses more problems than it solves. *Kak podtverzhdaet zhizn'*, elegant solutions are not necessarily the right ones. With this in mind, it is time to turn to some actual or probable examples of conflict taken from each of the three postwar eras.

The Stalin Era: Berlin 1948

The Stalinist system (like the German *Führerstaat*) abounds with examples of administrative overlap, internal competition, and bureaucratic confusion. The conditions leading up to the Berlin crisis of 1948 demonstrated the conflict between the Soviet Military Administration (SMA) in Germany and various other organs over policy in the Soviet zone of occupation. Matters of political organization were the primary responsiblity of the SMA, but it had no control over the important issues of reparations, which was a responsibility divided among a number of bureaucracies, including the Office of the Four-Year Plan, the Ministry of Foreign Trade, the Defense Ministry, and the NKVD (MVD after April 1946). Contrary to the prefer-

ences of the SMA these organizations seemed to have taken their job quite
seriously. For instance, Wolfgang Leonhard reports that an officer of the
Main Political Administration of the Red Army, accompanying him in the
Soviet sector of Berlin, referred to the authorities in charge of reparations
as the "reparations gang" and "the enemy."[27] This Russian officer showed
good political sense because the simultaneous pursuit of large-scale reparations and success in winning the loyalty of the German population,
dismantling and reconstruction, was a self-contradictory policy.

However, it would be wrong to think the problems of decision making in
the Stalinist system were caused by organizational autonomy—something
these organizations clearly did not have. If the instructions from the center
to the Milking Organization are to "milk the cow" and to the Slaughtering
Organization to "slaughter it," the result will inevitably be rather messy
or—if this is preferred—one of bureaucratic confusion. But it cannot be
ascribed to mistakes made at the local level (although, of course, this may
be a convenient excuse invoked by those responsible at the top).

In this instance, responsibility of the center in the system of centralization clearly rested at the top because a decision of principle was involved.
As for the course of events during the crisis, all the indications point to
similar responsibility in the form of close, day-to-day supervision of the
local organ entrusted with implementation of the blockade measures (the
SMA). Examples of such day-to-day supervision, with Stalin giving detailed instructions by telephone, are abundant for the wartime and immediate postwar period, but unfortunately for areas other than Berlin.[28]
These examples, particularly of the war period, show that reporting to
Stalin was an almost unbearable strain. A summons to Moscow had a very
ominous ring and instructions had a way of suddenly changing from one
day to the next. Work habits of all the representatives abroad, including
those in the SMA, were synchronized with Stalin's predilection for working
from late evening until early morning. Although the evidence in the Berlin
crisis is only indirect, inferences can be drawn from meetings between the
Western military governors and their Soviet counterpart (Sokolovsky) and
from the numerous sessions in the Berlin *Kommandatura* when the Soviet
negotiators closely adhered to one particular line at each point in time and
showed little room for independent maneuver. These inferences are that
the control from the center most probably applied to minute details of the
operation. This is corroborated by the extremely detailed knowledge that
Stalin showed during the protracted talks in August 1948 in Moscow,
where he enticed the three Western ambassadors to make important concessions—to the embarrassment of Clay, who did "not feel very happy"
about them.[29]

If centralization relegated bureaucratic and organizational politics to a place of secondary importance, there is still the possibility that leadership conflict affected Soviet policy in the Berlin crisis. Although few serious observers at the time were prepared to accept the view expressed by President Truman in a speech in Eugene, Oregon, on 11 June 1948, that Old Joe "is a decent fellow but he's a prisoner of the Politburo,"[30] some of them did subscribe to the view that there were policy differences between Stalin and Vyacheslav Molotov, and also between Georgi Malenkov and Andrei Zhdanov. Regarding the former possibility, it is probably wise to agree with the criticism contained in a dispatch from the U.S. ambassador in Moscow, Walter B. Smith, to Washington in which he pointed out that such views were unfounded and deliberately fostered by Soviet officials as a bargaining device.

> Tough "McCarthy" the dummy, "Bergen" being the name of his ventriloquist, makes exaggerated demands which kind, pipe-smoking "Bergen" Stalin whittles down into so-called concessions which temporarily relieve anxiety of the foreign statesman until he wakes up to the reality of the tough bargain he has been forced to accept.[31]

Assumptions concerning the influence of a power rivalry and dichotomy of view between Malenkov and Zhdanov center on the fact that, in July 1948, Malenkov was crowning his ascendency to the inner circle of Stalin's associates by returning to the Secretariat, while on 31 August Zhdanov died under circumstances that have given rise to suspicions and charges that he was poisoned or died of medical malpractice. Hence the implied or explicit theories that a major reappraisal of Soviet foreign policy — including the Berlin crisis — had taken place in the summer of 1948, away from dogmatism, militancy, and confrontation (the "Zhdanov line") to moderation and conciliation (the "Malenkov line").[32]

The validity of these theories is doubtful, even allowing for some lead time between the taking and implementation of decisions. The Berlin crisis had just begun, and its outcome was uncertain. The policies of pressure vis-à-vis Yugoslavia had also just started after its expulsion from the Cominform in June 1948. The concept of the "imminent crisis of capitalism" was upheld, and the attacks on Eugene Varga and his economic and political theories were resumed in October.

But even granting that the controversies among Stalin's subordinates were real (and they probably were between Malenkov and Zhdanov) and admitting that there might have been a swing from one "line" to another (although it is doubtful that this occured as early as the summer of 1948), the argument developed by Marshall Shulman is still valid: Controversies among subordinates in the Stalinist system were likely to support Stalin's preeminence by allowing him to play one faction and/or line against the other and, if need be, credit one or the other faction with failure if the line didn't work.[33] The main point is that it is not enough to prove that there was power struggle and conflict. What must be shown is how it affected policymaking. The evidence (what little is available) points to the absence of such influence on Soviet decision making in the Berlin crisis of 1948. But perhaps it is valid to say that the real issues of domestic conflict only arise in the Khrushchev and Brezhnev eras.

The Khrushchev Era: Suez, Hungary, and Berlin

The main features of Soviet domestic politics in the period from Stalin's death to Khrushchev's fall were the fluidity of power constellations — rapid changes in the top leadership positions and rivalries of diverse factions. It was also a period of transition from totalitarianism to authoritarianism, with attempts to proceed from coercion to persuasion, from extensive to intensive growth, and from mobilization to modernization. In these conditions of upheaval nothing is more natural to assume than a significant impact of domestic conflict on foreign policy.

One well-documented example of such conflict is the rivalry between Molotov and Khrushchev over policy in the Middle East,[34] the latter arguing that "vast opportunities" were flowing from the disintegration of the British and French colonial system, potentially leading to a breakthrough for socialism in the struggle of the two opposed social systems and justifying stronger support for the national liberation movement — not least because of the seemingly low risks involved. (As Defense Minister Marshal Zhukov erroneously said at the Twentieth CPSU Congress, punitive military expeditions were "a thing of the past.")[35] Molotov thought it was more important to consolidate the Soviet sphere of influence, improve the mechanisms of control and coordination in the Warsaw Pact, and concentrate on building socialism in the USSR itself, rather than squandering resources and enlarging the scope of conflict with imperialism by getting involved in areas secondary to Soviet security interests. The dismissal of Molotov from the post of foreign minister in June 1956 (one month before Nasser's decision to nationalize the Suez Canal Company) was a firm indication that the majority of the Presidium members were by then firmly committed to the new line on the Arab East.

Yet it is important to note that the commitment to a forward-oriented policy in the Middle East did not violate the basic principle of refraining from taking high risks in areas nonvital to Soviet security interests, because Khrushchev limited himself to verbal support, to the threatening letters sent by Bulganin to Anthony Eden and Guy Mollet on 5 November, and to rumormongering about the possible dispatch of volunteers. Both the letters and the rumors were produced after the storm clouds had passed over.

Another point of interest is the fact that Molotov made a comeback shortly after the Suez crisis, as shown by his appointment as minister of state control in late November and his contriving a majority in the December 1956 Central Committee (CC) plenum.[36] But there are no indications that this comeback was in any way related to Suez; there are no signs that a Molotov faction played a role during the crisis or that such a faction was able to exploit it thereafter. In fact, with the upsurge of Arab opinion in favor of the Soviet Union after the crisis, Khrushchev's standing would have been improved had it not been for the serious failure of his *intrabloc policies*, which had led to the Polish October and the violent eruptions in Hungary. The events there were more important from the Soviet point of view and they strengthened the hand of those, like Molotov, who had emphasized concentration of effort and attention on the bloc.

There is a final aspect of the Middle East problem that gives cause for reflection, namely that of possible congruence. Molotov can be regarded almost as the ideal type of an exponent of Left commitments and priorities, by virtue of his consistent support for heavy industry, strengthening of the Soviet military potential, safeguarding of ideological orthodoxy, and opposition to any opening to the West. Yet his type of Leftism lacks the most important attributes ascribed to this state of mind, namely militancy and aggressiveness, or—more specifically in the case at hand—strong support for active involvement in the Middle East. In contrast, his policy prescription was one of caution and conservatism and thus not much different from traditional attitudes of the Soviet military. These observations concerning the lack of evidence that domestic conflict affected Khrushchev's handling of the crisis and my reservation as to the possibility of extrapolating from a Soviet leader's stand on domestic politics to specific attitudes in foreign policy can be made even more strongly in the Berlin crisis of 1961.

On the surface nothing is more tempting to assume than the following: As demonstrated in the promulgation of the Seven-Year Plan (1959–65) Khrushchev had embarked on a comprehensive program of Right priorities and commitments, envisaging cutting defense expenditures, reducing the strength of the armed forces, and channeling resources to agriculture and consumer goods production. Abroad this program was to be one of détente—in particular, improvement of relations with the United States. Khrushchev's grand design, to continue the argument, was opposed by Frol Kozlov, Mikhail Suslov, and the spokesmen for the miltary-industrial complex (both military and managerial). While the fortunes of the respective factions were ever changing, the latter group was able to score substantial victories during the Berlin crisis. Using the crisis as a pretext, their success was evident in the surprise announcement (8 July

1961) of a substantial increase in the defense budget rather than, as
originally planned by Khrushchev, a decrease; in the substantial expansion
of the strength of the armed forces rather than, as originally planned by
Khrushchev, a reduction; and in the unilateral resumption of nuclear
weapons testing in the atmosphere (according to an announcement of 30
August), despite the fact that a moratorium had been in force since 1958
and contrary to assurances by Khrushchev that the Soviet government
would only resume testing if the Western powers did so first. Finally, to
conclude the argument, the hard-line domestic opposition was able to influence the substance of Soviet crisis behavior during the tense months of
the summer and autumn of 1961.[37] There are many problems with this line
of argument.

Foremost, détente — or what went under its name — did not exclude a systematic attempt, beginning (in Khrushchev's view) with the successful
precedent of November 1956, to use nuclear threats for foreign policy
purposes, a device that was used in the Middle East in 1957 and 1958, in
the Taiwan Straits crisis in 1958, and in Berlin in 1961. It did not rule out
challenges to the U.S. in the Congo and in Laos, nor the most dangerous
postwar crisis — in Cuba in 1962. The essence of Khrushchev's détente
policies seemed to lie in the conviction that it was possible to use threats to
force the West to make substantial concessions and at the same time engage
in friendly cooperation and relaxation of tension. This seeming contradiction is not very deep if one bears in mind that détente, or détente rhetoric,
can be an excellent device for the limitation of risks, and the soothing music
of peaceful coexistence a useful instrument for forestalling vigorous
counteraction.

Because it is true that declarations of a Right nature under the heading
of détente coexisted (though not too peacefully) with the diplomacy of the
missile threat, it is not surprising to find a similar lack of congruence in
other fields. This applies to the version in which Khrushchev had been
lowering or keeping defense expenditures constant from the mid-1950s until 1961 and that, suddenly, the hard-line opposition successfully conspired
to reverse the trend. The estimates by various Western specialists on Soviet
defense economics — Franklyn Holzman, William Lee, Phil Hanson, and
Abraham Becker — and by the CIA concur in the view that there was a
dramatic increase in defense expenditures in the USSR in 1959 — the same
year the Seven-Year Plan was introduced, with its verbal emphasis on
agriculture, consumer goods production, and future abundance. The same
high level of expenditures was maintained in 1960.[38] As a consequence, it is
much more realistic to assume that the 8 July announcement of an increase
in the defense budget by almost one-third was merely one of Khrushchev's
signals in the bargaining process over Berlin rather than a reversal of policy

or a sign of a domestic opposition triumph.

Rational explanations appear to be most appropriate also for the increase in the numerical strength of the Soviet armed forces and the resumption of nuclear testing. After an initial cut in 1956, the number of officers and men in the ground forces (compared to those in the other branches) had remained virtually unchanged in the second and third states of reduction (1958–59 and 1960), remaining constant at 2.2 to 2.5 million men. In order to maintain a proper balance among the various branches it was to be expected that in 1961 it would have been the turn of the ground forces to contract in size. But given an international political crisis, deteriorating relations with China and — most important — increasing support in NATO for the strengthening of conventional armaments, nothing could have come at a politically and militarily more inconvenient moment. In the game of military-strategic competition and political confrontation the facts were so compelling that even mediocre political leadership (in the words of Marshal M. V. Zakharov, the reinstated chief of General Staff, even persons who "claim strategic far-sightedness" but lack a "rudimentary knowledge of military strategy") could not have been blind to them.

Nor was it possible to overlook the fact that in 1961 declarations of a growing margin of military-strategic superiority were beginning to replace the fears of a "missile gap." Something had to be done to contain the potentially adverse psychological and political effects of changing Western perceptions of the strategic balance. For this reason Khrushchev skillfully linked space exploits, the quality of Soviet missiles, test series of missiles, and finally the resumption of nuclear weapons testing (including weapons in the megaton range) in one unified campaign to make the West swallow some more "bitter pills."[39]

It is doubtful whether, concerning Berlin, "zigzags in resource allocation can be correlated with clearcut and congruent changes in foreign policy"[40] and unconvincing that domestic opposition forced Khrushchev's hand in the crisis to escalate the contest over Berlin. It is much easier to believe the opposite, namely, that a number of high-ranking Presidium members and military leaders (with due regard to the military-strategic vulnerability of the USSR) were terrified that Khrushchev might be embarking on one of his harebrained schemes and, in a fit of "subjectivism," might carry the Soviet Union to and *over* the brink of Soviet-American confrontation.[41] If domestic conflict relevant to policymaking existed during the crisis, it was probably working for restraint rather than risk taking.

The Brezhnev Era: The Middle East and Czechoslovakia

It is still too early to say whether it is true that there has been just as much domestic conflict in the USSR under Brezhnev as under

Khrushchev; the difference is that the new leadership has managed to conceal the forms and manifestations of such conflict more effectively. Support for the view that there is as much conflict under Brezhnev and that only the forms of conflict have changed could be drawn from the fact that there has been a trend toward functional and specialist representation in the Politburo (e.g., representation of the chiefs of the KGB, the Foreign Ministry, the Defense Ministry and, after Defense Minister Andrei Grechko's death, the chief supervisor — and advocate? — of Soviet military industry), giving rise to what could be called an "institutionalized conflict of institutions." On the other hand this phenomenon could be seen as a trend toward further integration of various interests into a broad consensus and hence a dilution of conflict.

There are other reasons for not overly stressing the element of conflict in the Brezhnev era, including the following: (1) the transition from Khrushchev to Brezhnev was much smoother than that from Stalin to Khrushchev; (2) the leadership seems to be more genuinely "collective," rather than a one-man show as it was — at least at times — under Khrushchev; (3) the severity and scope of changes in the top leadership has been limited (e.g., there has been no discovery and ouster of whole "antiparty groups"); and (4) there has been increasing homogeneity on the basis of long years of common experience and cooperation among an aging leadership. However, conflict has not disappeared and the most serious challenges have come primarily from exponents of a hard line in the political spectrum.

One example of conflict with possible implications for Soviet risk taking and crisis behavior is in the context of the Middle East. Little more than a week after the defeat of the Arabs in the June 1967 war a plenum of the Central Committee (CC) was held in Moscow (20–21 June 1967); the sole item on the offical agenda was Soviet policy in the Middle East. A few days after the plenum it was announced that N. G. Yegorychev, first secretary of the Moscow City Party Committee, was dismissed from his post and demoted to the post of deputy minister for road construction machinery.[42] This relegation is significant for a number of reasons. It involved an official high in the *nomenklatura*, in an office usually considered a stepping-stone to membership in the Politburo — as it was for V. V. Grishin, Yegorychev's successor. Moreover, it involved someone who was but one important member in a faction of "young Turks" who had risen to power and influence in a relatively short time. This faction, centering around Alexandr Shelepin and including — besides Yegorychev — V. Semichastny, D. Goryunov, and V. Tikunov, with their strongholds in the Komsomol, police, and security apparatuses, appeared to have advocated greater commitment and activism abroad in order to cash in on the rise of the USSR to approximate strategic parity with the United States.

There are connections with the Middle East conflict not only because of the June 1967 CC plenum, which dealt with this topic, but also because both Shelepin and Yegorychev had visited the Middle East (in 1964 and spring 1967 respectively) and because *Shelepintsy* of KGB origin reportedly had been sent to various embassies in that area.[43] Finally, the most glaring failure of the Soviet Union immediately prior to the Arab-Israeli war was the failure of intelligence — a major sphere of responsibility of the KGB in conjunction with the GRU. Another glaring failure was that of air defense to protect Egypt and Syria, as well as Soviet military material, from the lightning strike of Israeli aircraft. Hence there may be another link between the Middle East and Yegorychev, who was also a member of the military councils of the Moscow Military District and the Moscow Air Defense District, providing him with the opportunity to voice criticism from a military perspective.[44]

What is unclear about the sudden blow to the young Turks is whether it was Yegorychev who launched an attack against the Brezhnev leadership for having stood by and watched the defeat of the Arabs and/or for having inadequately equipped them before the war, or whether it was Brezhnev who took the initiative and accused the *Shelepintsy* of ineptitude and "adventurist" inclinations, seizing a convenient opportunity to strike a blow at the ambitious younger rivals and selecting Yegorychev as an interim target. (Only a few days after Yegorychev's demotion Shelepin was demoted too, only to stage a comeback in the autumn of the same year.) No matter who started it, the affair seems to reflect *postcrisis* mutual recrimination for failure rather than an example of conflict over measures to be taken *during* the crisis. To that extent the manner in which Yegorychev was demoted is reminiscent of the previously mentioned example of the weakening of Khrushchev's influence after the Hungarian revolt and Molotov's temporary comeback and of Khrushchev's loss of power after the Cuban debacle in 1962.

A final example of conflict with possible implications for risk-taking behavior concerns the Czechoslovak crisis in 1968. Among the elements distinguishing this crisis from others are its long duration and the seriousness of potential repercussions of developments in the CSSR on the Soviet Union. With the time factor providing the opportunity and the direct involvement of various Soviet interests posing the apparent necessity for all top leaders, groups, and forces to assert their influence, it is to be expected that the conflict element will loom large in any analysis of the Soviet decision to intervene.

A summary of the most serious arguments put forward in this context is that economic pressure groups (with Kosygin as their exponent), the trade union organization (with Shelepin as its chief), and "the internationalists" (i.e., Suslov and Boris Ponomarev as the CC secretaries in charge of relations with foreign Communist parties) led their organizations' opposition to the interventionist designs of the security apparatus (with Yuri Andropov as the chief of the KGB, but not yet a Politburo member), the military (with Grechko as defense minister, also not yet a Politburo member), and orthodox sections of the party apparatus, particularly those potentially most affected by the erosive virus of national Communism (e.g., Petr Shelest in the Ukraine and Arvid Pel'she in Latvia).[45] Support for this thesis has been drawn from differences in the statements made by the various bureaucracies, from the fact that the responses in the USSR were characterized by vacillations and frequent shifts between pressure and conciliation vis-à-vis the Czechoslovak reformers, and foremost from the dramatic reversal of the apparent compromise reached at Cierna (29 July– 1 August) and ratified at Bratislava (3 August).[46]

It is a controversial question whether the compromise between the Czechoslovak reformers and the Soviet Union was a genuine one and whether, when the CPSU Politburo met in Moscow some days later and "fully approved the activity of the CPSU delegation at the Bratislava conference,"[47] it had genuinely approved a modus vivendi with Dubček. Four events have been cited in support of Soviet sincerity: an initiative from Ulbricht on 9 August indicating at long last a positive response to Bonn's *Ostpolitik*; Ulbricht's visit to Karlovy Vary on 12–13 August to meet with Czechoslovak leaders; the withdrawal of Soviet troops from Czechoslovakia a few days after the Bratislava conference; and the reports that Brezhnev and other Politburo members were on vacation.[48] Yet, on reflection, one event looks very suspicious: given the considerable evidence that Ulbricht fought USSR pressure to swing in line with Warsaw Pact policy on the *Ostpolitik* after March 1969 — and eventually even had to be replaced — it is highly unlikely that he would have been pressing forward unilaterally in August 1968. It is even more suspect that the only unreconstructed Stalinist leader remaining in East Central Europe would, during his visit in Karlovy Vary, extend a hand of friendship to what he undoubtedly still considered to be a treacherous clique. The sequence of events makes more sense if the Ulbricht initiatives are considered part of the Warsaw Pact's preparations for a surprise attack. The reports that Soviet leaders were on vacation and that troops were being withdrawn would then fit exactly into the pattern, particularly the alleged trooop withdrawal, which had an ominous precedent immediately prior to the full-scale Soviet intervention in Hungary in 1956.

To revert to the central argument of the "bureaucratic politics" explanation, that of interrelationships between functional interests of domestic actors and their attitudes toward intervention, some minor reservations or questions should be noted. If it is true that one of the most outspoken adherents of intervention was the KGB under Andropov, how is it possible that the view tenaciously persists — as expressed recently and affirmatively by someone who has been in a good position to know — that Andropov's "liberal views — in the Soviet context — would surprise many in the West"?[49] If this is correct, why did Andropov's liberal inclinations not find their reflection in Czechoslovakia? Equally incongruously, Suslov has been portrayed as an opponent of intervention, one of the chief reasons (in line with the axiom of "where you stand depends on where you sit") being his alleged concern for the potential impact of intervention on the strength and electoral chances of the nonruling Communist parties. If so, how can this concern be reconciled with the image of Suslov as an orthodox party *apparatchik* and an ideological hard-liner? How does his alleged stance in 1968 fit in with his attitudes toward the severe economic recession in the West in the wake of the 1973 oil crisis and the activities of the Communist party in Portugal in 1975, where Suslov — in both instances — reportedly advocated "exploitation of revolutionary opportunities" and disregard for "mathematical majorities"? All this evidently was advice which, if adopted, would have negatively affected the strength and electoral chances of the most important nonruling Communist parties.

A more important point is implied in Ponomarev's reported statement that, when the decision to intervene was taken, the antiinterventionist coalition found itself "unluckily in the minority."[50] This suggests that the representatives of the various functional interests were opposed to intervention as a matter of *principle* and that the domestic alignments were so finely balanced that intervention, in the final analysis, was a matter of *chance*. A convinced Marxist would probably say that this is an "entirely subjectivist" analysis and he would be right. Notwithstanding differences on tactics, the objective requirements of the situation necessitated drastic curtailment of the Czechoslovak reform experiment. In domestic politics in the Soviet Union in 1965–66 the signs pointed to what observers called "neo-Stalinist" tendencies. In foreign policy from 1967 on — as demonstrated at the Karlovy Vary conference in April of that year — the Soviet Union, in conjunction with the GDR and Poland, made strenuous attempts to contain the negative repercussions of the "dissolution of the blocs" proposals put forward by the Warsaw Pact and also to contain the reverberations of the new *Ostpolitik* after the favorable reception it had received among the Czechoslovak, Romanian, Hungarian, and even Bulgarian leadership. Judging on the basis of the radically diverging trends of Soviet and Czechoslovak domestic and foreign policy it would be difficult to argue that there was anything to govern Soviet responses but a broad consensus on the basic operational principles. Such consensus on principles could have been expressed as follows:

Let us try all available means of pressure on the leadership of the KPČ, unilaterally and jointly with the other members of the Warsaw Pact. Let us exploit all the possible differences within the leadership, but let us never lose sight of the inalienable requirement that the reform experiment must be stopped; if they (the Czechoslovak leaders) won't or can't put a stop to it, we'll help them do it.

III

It is to be hoped that the above two-part analysis has provided sufficient evidence for the following proposition: Decision making in international crises in the Soviet system is shaped much more by consensus on political issues and operational principles than by domestic conflict. Of course, conflict among leaders, groups, and bureaucracies over basic questions of foreign policy—where to take risks, in which way, and up to what threshold—must be expected in any political system, including that of the Soviet Union. However, where such conflict does occur in the USSR it tends to take place within relatively narrow limits.

There may be more room for disagreement over questions such as détente; the Strategic Arms Limitation Treaty (SALT); reduction of armed forces and armaments in Central Europe; East-West economic, scientific, and technological relations, and exchanges of information and ideas. But, as argued in the introduction, there are limits to the notion of separating risk taking from Soviet foreign policy in general. To take some examples: whether or not to reignite the Berlin issue; the amount of support for national liberation movements in the Horn of Africa, Angola, or elsewhere; how deeply to commit the USSR to the Arab "confrontation states" in a possible renewed military conflict in the Middle East; what role to play in the internal affairs of Iran; and how far to go in the support of Vietnam (up to and including military action against Chinese forces)—all of these problems touch both on the narrow aspect of risk taking and the larger one of the overall direction of Soviet foreign policy.

It is important in conclusion not to evade the problem of the likely origins of the postulated narrow framework of disagreement and the roots of the commonly accepted operational principles. As so often is the case in international politics, no single or simple explanation can be offered. But among the complexity of factors at least three should be isolated as being of particular importance: ideology; a common body of experience and similarity of career patterns among the party leaders; and constant reassessment of the validity and effectiveness of the Politburo's own modus operandi in the international arena. All three factors interact and reinforce each other to an extent that makes their separation for analytical purposes a difficult endeavor. None of them can be treated here in as much detail as they deserve, but can only be touched upon.

It has become fashionable to dismiss the role of ideology in shaping Soviet foreign policy — this is quite unfortunate.[51] Of course, revolutionary idealism is very much a thing of the past. Adherence to principle more often than not has given way to exigencies of the moment, pragmatism, and opportunism. Nationalism and — as Lenin deplored — "Great Russian chauvinism" long ago reared their heads and have made a mockery of selfless international socialist solidarity. However, this does not mean that ideology is irrelevant for Soviet foreign policy. It cannot be, as the Soviet state is perhaps the ideal type of an ideology in power. Every major step that is taken, domestically or internationally, is justified in the name of ideology. Although other forms of legitimacy may yet emerge, the Soviet leaders would be destroying the very basis on which they are operating were they to abandon Marxism-Leninism.

Ideological justification applies to the legitimacy and effectiveness of Soviet rule in Eastern Europe, where the Soviet system has been transplanted. Justification of policies in purely nationalist terms would make Soviet control even more unpalatable to the majority of East Europeans than it already is. The same is true for Soviet external policies elsewhere: what might otherwise appear as blatant neoimperialism is less offensive if it is presented as an advance toward the emancipation of all peoples and further progress toward the ultimate victory of socialism over capitalism. (The reverse side of the coin is the concept of "proletarian internationalism," which posits that the first, most powerful, and most mature socialist state has a special claim to the loyalty of every Communist and that — as Stalin so blatantly but aptly put it — it is the duty of every true internationalist "to defend the USSR without reservation, without wavering, unconditionally."[52])

Ideology, therefore, has supplemented nationalism, not supplanted it.[53] Ideology and power aggrandizement, in doctrine and in practice, are pulling in the same direction, and it is impossible to separate them or to say which one of the two is exerting the more powerful pull.

It is also impossible to maintain a strict separation between ideology and pragmatism. That there is no strict dichotomy between the two was argued long ago by Lenin, notably in his *"Left Wing" Communism: An Infantile Disorder*, and there is no reason to consider his arguments on this point invalid. Then as now, rigidity in doctrine does not rule out flexibility in tactics. Experts, including those on international relations, may only serve to make Soviet foreign policy more effective, not to change its character altogether. Most important, it would be erroneous to identify ideology with "irrationality" and "recklessness," and to set it in opposition to pragmatism and caution. Irrespective of whether the top Soviet leaders believe in the utopian aspects of ideology (e.g., full Communism), it is the repeated doctrinal emphasis on the superiority of the socialist over the capitalist system and the ultimate victory of the former over the latter that may explain much of the persisting caution of Soviet foreign policy. If history is assumed to be on one's side it would indeed be foolish to risk nuclear destruction by a succession of adventurist designs.

The Leninist idea of two steps forward, one step backward, and the distaste for dramatic attempts to achieve sudden breakthroughs, unless (as in November 1917) success is virtually assured, are all part of ideological doctrine embodied in party history. They are deeply engrained also — to turn to the second major possible reason for the predominance of consensus over conflict — in the collective consciousness of the party leadership. Other beliefs, prejudices, and images are part of the consciousness shaped by ideology and party history. Foremost is the idea of life (including party and international affairs) as a never-ending struggle, compromise not as an end in itself but merely a means to the achievement of larger objectives, and the notion that to stand still and not to make constant advances would mean to have lost revolutionary dynamism and to have relegated oneself to the proverbial "rubbish heap of history."

To this idea must be added the fact that the current top foreign policymakers have had very similar career backgrounds and have experienced very similar processes of socialization. Most of them came from lower occupational or social status, entered some specialized educational institute, were thrust upward to political leadership after the purges, proved their abilities during the war, and have dominated domestic and foreign policy of the Soviet Union from the late 1940s up to the present.[54] In no other country have top leaders in foreign policy occupied their posts for such a long time.[55]

The final possible reason for the existence of a common outlook and operational principles in Soviet foreign policy lies in the international context. Risk taking and crisis behavior proceed on the basis of precedents. Each new crisis represents a test case for the continued validity of previous operational principles: a successful result of the principles applied (as in the building of the Berlin Wall in 1961) will tend to confirm them; a setback will tend to induce reconsideration (as in 1949 after the Berlin blockade) and possible revision. Departures from proven patterns of behavior, if they are successful, will tend to set new patterns (as in the case of explicit Soviet threats after the Suez crisis) but, if the outcome is unsuccessful, will tend to confirm the old ones (as in the case of the Cuban missile crisis).

Overall, given stringent economic limitations since the Bolshevik Revolution, Soviet policies in foreign policy and military affairs have been remarkably successful. This may not be the case in the future as economic constraints are growing, ideological justifications of Soviet policy are becoming less credible abroad, and suspicions of the Soviet Union as a state bent on power expansion for its own sake are gaining ground. For the time being, however, and until a whole new generation of leaders comes to power, the traditional patterns of Soviet behavior will most likely remain in full force. In the Soviet Union nothing is more successful than success itself.

Notes

1. This observation is based on the following studies by this author: "Soviet Risk Taking and Crisis Behavior: A Theoretical and Empirical Analysis" (Ph.D. diss., Columbia University, 1977); "The Soviet Union and the Middle East Crisis of 1956," manuscript; and "Soviet Risk-taking and Crisis Behaviour: From Confrontation to Coexistence?" Adelphi Paper no. 101 (London: International Institute for Strategic Studies, 1973). The author has also profited from supervision of a Ph.D. dissertation by Fawwaz Yassin, "Patterns of Soviet Intervention in Eastern Europe" (Institute of Soviet and East European Studies, University of Glasgow).

2. For the Berlin crisis of 1961 this is argued, not at all convincingly, by Robert M. Slusser, *The Berlin Crisis of 1961: Soviet-American Relations and the Struggle for Power in the Kremlin, June–November 1961* (Baltimore and London: Johns Hopkins University Press, 1973). Domestic conflict was a major aspect during the Cuban missile crisis, according to the study by Herbert Dinerstein, *The Making of a Missile Crisis: October 1962* (Baltimore and London: Johns Hopkins University Press, 1976).

3. As quoted by Coral Bell, *The Conventions of Crisis: A Study in Diplomatic Management* (New York: Oxford University Press, 1971), p. 2.

4. Karl W. Deutsch, *The Analysis of International Relations* (Englewood Cliffs, N.J.: Prentice-Hall, 1968), p. 113.

5. For more detail concerning theoretical and conceptual problems of risk and crisis see this author's "Soviet Risk-taking and Crisis Behaviour," pp. 2–5.

6. The origin of the term "operational principles" must be attributed to Nathan Leites and his "operational code" of the Politburo. The present discussion has benefited very much from improvements of Leites's approach by Alexander L. George, "The 'Operational Code': A Neglected Approach to the Study of Political Leaders and Decision-Making," in Erik Hoffmann and Frederic Fleron, eds., *The Conduct of Soviet Foreign Policy* (Chicago and New York: Aldine Atherton, 1971), pp. 165–190. Some of George's axioms have been retained and supported here by further empirical evidence, and others have been added.

7. *Tägliche Rundschau*, 4 February 1948.

8. *Pravda*, 6 November 1956.

9. As reported by Lyndon Baines Johnson, *The Vantage Point: Perspectives from the Presidency* (London: Weidenfeld and Nicolson, 1971), p. 302; for details see Adomeit, "Soviet Risk-taking and Crisis Behaviour," pp. 13–14.

10. Galia Golan, "Soviet Aims and the Middle East War," *Survival* 16, no. 3 (May–June 1974): 106–114.

11. *Pravda,* 30 March 1968.

12. These examples are mentioned by Graham T. Allison, *Essence of Decision: Explaining the Cuban Missile Crisis* (Boston: Little, Brown and Co., 1971), pp. 106–108.

13. TASS declaration of 11 September 1962, published in *Izvestiia,* 12 September 1962.

14. Several examples for the time period of 4 September to 13 October 1962 are listed by Allison, *Essence of Decision,* pp. 40–41.

15. The Soviet challenge in Cuba in 1970 has been analyzed by Henry Brandon, "Nixon's Way with the Russians," *The New York Times Magazine,* 21 January 1973, and by George H. Quester, "Missiles in Cuba, 1970," *Foreign Affairs* 49, no. 3 (April 1971).

16. George, "The 'Operational Code,'" pp. 181–182.

17. Robert Murphy was political adviser of the U.S. Department of State to the U.S. military governor in Germany, General Lucius D. Clay.

18. This is not to say that these proxies did not pursue their own interests, or that proxies are to be equated with dependent satellites dancing to the tune of the Soviet leadership's flute. These examples merely show that, wherever possible, the Soviet Union has preferred indirect involvement to direct superpower confrontation.

19. George, "The 'Operational Code,'"pp. 181–182. See note 6.

20. *Pravda,* 14 December 1962.

21. Thomas W. Wolfe, *Soviet Power and Europe: 1945–1970* (Baltimore and London: Johns Hopkins University Press, 1970), pp. 89–90.

22. V. N. Vysotskii, *Zapadnyi Berlin i ego mesto v sisteme sovremennykh mezhdunarodnykh otnoshenii* (Moscow: 1971), p. 237. See also the translated and at times significantly modified English version of the book, Viktor Vysotsky's *West Berlin,* Transl. from the Russian by David Fidlon (Moscow: 1974), p. 160. V. N. Vysotsky is a pseudonym for V. N. Beletsky, a former official at the Soviet embassy in East Berlin.

23. This is the wording used in the note of 14 July 1948 by the Soviet government to the Western powers, published in MID (Ministry of Foreign Affairs) SSSR, MID GDR, *Za antifashistskuiu demokraticheskuiu Germaniiu: Sbornik Dokumentov, 1945–1949 gg.* (Moscow: 1969), pp. 574–578.

24. Nevertheless, there does seem to have been at least one Politburo member, Shelest, who thought that the Soviet Union's self-esteem as a superpower required that Nixon not be received in Moscow prior to the lifting of the blockade or—if the visit were to take place with the blockade still in force—that he be received only after a more "decent" interval. This view did not prevail. Shelest was demoted to the post of deputy chairman of the USSR Council of Ministers (Radio Moscow, 20 May 1972); Nixon arrived in the Soviet Union on 22 May; Shelest's demotion was confirmed on 25 May at the CC plenum of the Ukrainian Communist party (*Pravda,* 26 May 1972). In April 1973 Shelest lost his seat on the Politburo.

25. All these terms are used by Edward Crankshaw, *Khrushchev: A Career* (New York: Viking, 1966), pp. 207, 239 and 245.

26. Alexander Dallin, "Soviet Foreign Policy and Domestic Politics: A

Framework of Analysis," *Journal of International Affairs* 23, no. 2 (1969): 250–265 and repeated, with some modifications, in his "Domestic Factors Influencing Soviet Foreign Policy," in Michael Confino and Shimon Shamir, eds., *The USSR and the Middle East* (Jerusalem: Israel Universities Press, 1973), pp. 31–58.

27. Wolfgang Leonhard, *Child of the Revolution* (London: Collins, 1957), p. 345.

28. The most extensive coverage of such wartime interference can be found in John Erickson, *Stalin's War with Germany*, vol. 1, *The Road to Stalingrad* (London: Weidenfeld and Nicolson, 1975). An interesting example for the postwar period is provided by Malcolm Mackintosh, who reported that Stalin in August 1945 made a telephone call to the Soviet representative at the Allied Control Commission in Bulgaria (characteristically, at the ungòdly hour of 1:40 a.m.) to change the Soviet negotiating line on the elections there. See Mackintosh's article, "Stalin's Policies towards Eastern Europe, 1939–1948," in Thomas T. Hammond, *The Anatomy of Communist Takeovers* (New Haven and London: Yale University Press, 1975), pp. 229–243, esp. pp. 239–240.

29. Clay expressed his disappointment in a teleconference with Washington. See Teleconference TT-1080, Top Secret, 24 August 1948, in Jean Edward Smith, ed., *The Papers of General Lucius D. Clay: Germany 1945–1949*, 2 vols. (Bloomington and London: Indiana University Press, 1974), doc. 502, pp. 781–782.

30. As quoted by Marshall D. Shulman, *Stalin's Foreign Policy Reappraised* (New York: Atheneum, 1965), p. 31.

31. The ambassador in the Soviet Union (Smith) to the secretary of state, 6 March 1948, in U.S., Department of State, *Foreign Relations of the United States, 1948*, vol. 4, *Eastern Europe and the Soviet Union* (Washington, D.C.: U.S. Government Printing Office, 1974), p. 818. To make it more readable, definite articles have been added to the telegram by this author.

32. One important example of this thesis is Shulman, *Stalin's Foreign Policy Reappraised*, p. 47.

33. Ibid., pp. 46–47.

34. Uri Ra'anan, *The USSR Arms the Third World: Case Studies in Soviet Foreign Policy* (Cambridge, Mass.: M.I.T. Press, 1969).

35. *Pravda*, 20 February 1956.

36. Ibid., 22 November 1956. See also Vernon V. Aspaturian, *Process and Power in Soviet Foreign Policy* (Boston: Little, Brown and Co., 1971), p. 346.

37. This theory is expressed most vividly and with intricate detail by Slusser, *The Berlin Crisis of 1961*. Although the various approaches adopted are different, support for various aspects of the theory can be found in the writings of Michel Tatu, Sidney Ploss, Carl Linden, Boris Nicolaevsky, and Alexander Dallin.

38. See, for instance, Abraham S. Becker, *Soviet Military Outlays Since 1955*, The RAND Corporation, RM-3886-PR, Santa Monica, Calif., July 1964, p. 70, and Franklyn D. Holzman, *Financial Checks on Soviet Defense Expenditures* (Toronto and London: D. C. Heath & Co., 1975), p. 11.

39. The metaphor of "swallowing pills" is used by Khrushchev and frequently also by Penkovsky in describing Khrushchev's calculations in the Berlin crisis. See, for instance, *Khrushchev Remembers: The Last Testament*, trans. and ed. Strobe Talbott

(London: Andre Deutsch, 1974), p. 509; and Oleg Penkovsky, *The Penkovsky Papers* (London: Collins, 1965), p. 161.

40. Dallin, "Domestic Factors Influencing Soviet Foreign Policy," p. 43. In line with the framework of congruence, links are said to exist between resource allocations, on the one hand, and relations with Tito, polemics with China, and incidents on the road to Berlin.

41. The most important testimony to this effect is provided by Penkovsky, *The Penkovsky Papers*, esp. pp. 131 and 207. There is no doubt in the mind of this author that the materials provided by Penkovsky are genuine and of some use for scholarly purposes. To that extent it does not matter that the materials were edited by the CIA.

42. *Pravda*, 28 June 1967.

43. *Der Spiegel* (Hamburg), 4 December 1967. Concerning the ramifications of the clique of Shelepin, Semichastny, Yegorychev et al., see also Dallin, "Domestic Factors Influencing Soviet Foreign Policy," p. 50.

44. Malcolm Mackintosh, "The Soviet Military: Influence on Foreign Policy," *Problems of Communism* 22, no. 5 (September-October 1973): 6.

45. Probably the best expression of this view is Jiri Valenta, "Soviet Decision-making in the Czechoslovak Crisis of 1968," *Studies in Comparative Communism* 8, no. 1-2 (Spring-Summer 1975).

46. Cierna was the bilateral meeting between members of the CPSU and the KPČ; at Bratislava representatives of the KPČ and five CPs of the Warsaw Pact countries met to draw up a compromise document. Differences in reporting, as supposedly reflected in *Pravda, Izvestiia, Krasnaia zvezda* and *Trud*, are analyzed by David W. Paul, "Soviet Foreign Policy and the Invasion of Czechoslovakia: A Theory and a Case Study," *International Studies Quarterly* 15, no. 2 (1971): 159-202. The research technique applied in this article is content analysis.

47. *Pravda*, 7 August 1968.

48. All these examples are mentioned by Fritz Ermath, *Internationalism, Security and Legitimacy: The Challenge to Soviet Interests in East Europe, 1964-1968*. The RAND Corporation, Santa Monica, Calif., RM-5909-PR, March 1969, esp. pp. 100-107. In the main, this author very much agrees with Ermath's analysis.

49. By Boris Rabbot, "A Letter to Brezhnev," in *The New York Times Magazine*, 6 November 1977, p. 55. Rabbot was a secretary of the social science section of the Presidium of the Academy of Sciences of the USSR and adviser to the CC.

50. Valenta, "Soviet Decisionmaking in the Czechoslovak Crisis," p. 171.

51. The following is a much condensed summary of this author's "Ideology in the Soviet View of International Affairs" (Paper presented to the Twentieth Annual Conference of the International Institute of Strategic Studies, Oxford, September 1978, to be published under the auspices of the IISS). The role of ideology in Soviet foreign policy is discussed also in Hannes Adomeit and Robert Boardman, eds., *Foreign Policy Making in Communist Countries: A Comparative Approach* (Westmead, England: Saxon House, 1979 and New York: Praeger Publishers, 1979), pp. 17-20 and 155-156.

52. Joseph Stalin, *Sochineniia*, vol. 10 (Moscow: 1951), p. 45.

53. This is a point aptly made by Alexander Yanov, *Detente After Brezhnev: The Domestic Roots of Soviet Foreign Policy,* Policy Papers in International Affairs (Berkeley, Calif.: Institute of International Studies, 1977).

54. Jerry F. Hough, "The Coming Generational Change in the Soviet Foreign Policy-Making Elite " (Paper presented to the National Convention of the AAASS, Washington, D.C., 14 October 1977), p. 3.

55. Ibid.

PART 2

Politics and Society

4

The Pattern of Leadership Politics

Grey Hodnett

The celebration of Leonid Brezhnev's seventieth birthday in December 1976 was accompanied by expressions of esteem and devout fealty from all domestic and foreign constituencies and by new elaborations of Brezhnev's own "cult of personality." Some observers might suggest that this event and other striking manifestations of a Brezhnev cult demonstrate the circular course of history—that the whole spectacle represents the successful culmination of Brezhnev's thrust toward one-man rule. Others, however, would disagree with this judgment. They would argue that there has been a shift to oligarchic rule and greater stability in the Soviet leadership in the post-Khrushchev years. A decade ago, Jerome Gilison identified new factors of stability in Soviet collective leadership,[1] and Vernon Aspaturian observed that "the transition from Stalinist, one-man rule to quasi-pluralistic political behavior is now all but complete. The Khrushchev decade emerges as a sort of transition period between these two types of rule."[2] More recently, T. H. Rigby has urged us to consider the possibility of a "self-stabilizing oligarchy."[3]

A variety of types of evidence can be cited in support of the argument that top decision-making authority is not and can no longer be monopolized by a single individual. One might cite such aspects of the leadership system as control over co-optation and removal of members, physical and career security of members, participation in decision making, the institutional division of labor, the degree of consensual attitudes, and "legitimization" of oligarchic rule. One might also argue that certain features of the broader political elite now tend to promote oligarchic rule. And, one might find reasons why changes in Soviet society could encourage a more stable pattern of oligarchy at the top.

In an earlier study, I argued that the Khrushchev and Brezhnev periods were both marked by a combination of monocratic and oligarchic elements—by the coexistence of "leader" and "leadership" roles.[4] In light of what has (or has not) happened in the interim, I see no reason to revise this appraisal. But such an argument does not imply that changes in the balance between the two roles cannot occur during a single administration nor that the overall balance in one administration is identical to that in another. Seweryn Bialer has commented that

> Khrushchev's Presidium was "collective leadership" as opposed to Stalin's one-man rule. Brezhnev's Politburo shows this kind of leadership in a much more pure and stable version, one much less prone to become only a transitional stage between periods of one-man rule. In the last decade, these competing tendencies, toward oligarchy and a dominant leader . . . were, if not resolved, then settled at least more clearly in favor of the former.[5]

This chapter compares the character of oligarchical tendencies under the two leaders, explores the impact of the current distribution of power upon the satisfaction of various "group" interests, and speculates about the possible effects of a more oligarchic pattern of leadership upon the conduct of foreign policy.

Oligarchic Elements Under Khrushchev

With hindsight it appears that there was truth to both the "dominant leader" and "conflict" models of the Khrushchev years. Khrushchev did exercise power in ways that probably often were not to the liking of his colleagues in the leadership. If we are to believe subsequent testimony, Khrushchev was the one who — against more enlightened opinion in the party Presidium — pushed through such "harebrained schemes" as the disintegration and then piecemeal recentralization of economic administration, dissolution of the Machine Tractor Stations (MTS), universal planting of corn and plowing up of grasslands, bifurcation of the party and state administration into industrial and agricultural branches, and introduction of rotation in office for party and other jobs. It was he who jeopardized the stability of the system with his denunciations of Stalin and re-orientation of party propaganda toward utilitarian concerns. And he was the one who, presumably, decreased the Soviet armed forces and then, in a Cuban gamble that failed, demonstrated the military vulnerability of the USSR. Altogether, these actions reflect the exercise of enormous political influence. Yet it is also apparent — as Robert Conquest, Sidney Ploss, Carl Linden, Michel Tatu, Christian Duevel, and other analysts have persuasively argued — that Khrushchev did not always win policy arguments, that he was forced to attempt to persuade fellow members of the leadership, and that his power was not always sufficient to compel implementation of programs that had his backing. Why was this so? What were the resources that gave weight to "the collective"?

The primary and ineradicable source of weakness of one-man rule under Khrushchev was unquestionably the dissipation of terror as a credible means of dealing with real or perceived opposition within the leadership. Failure to take account of the qualitative change this factor introduced in intraleadership relations is a root cause of the overestimation of Khrushchev's power. The decision to repress Lavrenti Beria and establish party apparatus control of the secret police, coupled with the limited power of *all* members of the leadership before June 1957, created a setting for sharp exchanges of opinion within the Presidium in the 1953–57 period and serious discussion in the Central Committee.[6] Growing certainty that physical violence would not be used against other leaders in the post-1957 period brought about a decisive shift in the stakes involved in top-level political activity.

The high probability that Khrushchev would not or could not resort to police methods in dealing with overt or covert questioning or resistance is likely to have effected still another crucial, if invisible, alteration: namely, an acceleration of *multilateral* communication critical of the leader among other members of the leadership. As Khrushchev's memoirs clearly indicate, this type of communication must have been exceptional—if present at all—under Stalin; one well knew what not to say. One also knew what information not to request, especially in the area of foreign relations.

Communications decapsulation within the leadership was an important condition of a more rapid and accurate flow of information and an essential condition of the transition from narrow, semiclandestine hostility among the lieutenants and courtiers themselves to shared awareness among the leaders or subgroups of leaders of disagreement with the first secretary. In short, the elimination of terror made possible the emergence of "opinion"—and, in time, hostile opinion—within the leadership. The evidence suggests that Khrushchev had to rely heavily upon argumentation in dealing with this opinion and could not close off discussion and debate—and the emergent "groups" that this discussion reflected—simply with threats of violence. This change in the character of interaction within the leadership, despite the overt signs of Khrushchev's power after June 1957, is not given sufficient weight in those interpretations of the period that place predominant emphasis upon Khrushchev's control over personnel appointments and organizational levers. But Khrushchev too did not fully appreciate the power implications of the new communications environment or adequately incorporate anticipation of these implications into his own political behavior.

Directly or indirectly, shifts in information flows and the expansion of political awareness within the leadership and at higher levels in the elite also weakened other sources of possible monocratic rule. Obviously, Khrushchev's inability to prevent the transmission of information about his policy failures in agriculture, industry, foreign affairs, and party building eroded his capacity to evoke respect and even compliance at all levels of the political system. Widespread knowledge of these failures and awareness of general moods within the leadership were probably among the critical factors that qualified and eventually undermined Khrushchev's control over personnel through "patron-client" power. The facts show that in October 1964 the overwhelming majority of Khrushchev's appointees and followers deserted him and not only for careerist reasons. The deserters (almost certainly a large majority of members of the Central Committee) included, inter alia, the leaders of the military and the KGB, who, it has been argued, were handpicked by Khrushchev himself. Is it too much to suppose that their responsiveness to his interests was less than unconditional before 14 October 1964?[7]

Another weakness in the monocratic pattern, and one accentuated by communication flows, was the development of individual prestige on the part of other members of the leadership beside Khrushchev — a prestige that could be translated into personal influence within the Soviet elite. The presence of personas was not unheard of, to be sure; even under mature Stalinism, one might mention Zhdanov, Voznesenskii, Beria, or Marshal Zhukov.[8] But their fate was generally not a happy one. Khrushchev was far less able than Stalin to exclude other leaders from a share of respect within political circles. While the evidence is extremely fragmentary, it seems probable, for example, that Kosygin was not a person Khrushchev himself would have kept on in the leadership had he acted simply on the basis of his own feelings.[9] Similarly, it is very likely that Suslov owed his retention of office under Khrushchev, at least in part, to the support he enjoyed in conservative ideological circles. Brezhnev himself was unquestionably recognized in the functional fields and geographic regions in which he was active as a responsive leader who could get things done.[10] Mikoyan was undoubtedly seen as an experienced and resourceful politician, quite apart from his close relation with Khrushchev; and even Voroshilov seems to have enjoyed some elite standing — attributable, no doubt, to perceptions of his past contribution to the party.

By the same token, Khrushchev had deficiencies in the personality area that no amount of propaganda could overcome. Neither physically nor behaviorally did he command instinctive respect. He lacked even the synthetic charisma of Stalin; there was no authentic Khrushchev cult. The doctrines with which he associated himself did not have the inner psychological compulsion and air of unchallengeable veracity that Stalin's had, although they also did not appear quite as contrived as those of Brezhnev. And

Khrushchev's policy advisers were too lacking in authority, too visible, and often too visibly in error.

Finally, monocratic power under Khrushchev was thwarted by institutional structures, procedures, and political formulas, whose significance was indicated by Khrushchev's attempts to circumvent them. One of the counts in the indictment of Khrushchev was that he used his private staff (and relatives) as a means of bypassing the formal party and governmental institutions of rule.[11] "Back channels" serve various functions, not least of all to compensate for incomplete political power. Thus, one wonders if it would have been necessary for Khrushchev to proceed in this fashion had he simply been able to issue commands to other members of the leadership through normal channels. Judging by the tone of memoranda he dispatched to the Politburo on agricultural questions, Khrushchev felt it necessary to inform the other leaders of his plans and projects, even while he was attempting to preempt their decisions. On the basis of available accounts, it would also appear that approval by his colleagues of the texts of his reports to Central Committee plenums and party congresses, and approval of publication of other documents, was a key constraint that Khrushchev had to deal with—sometimes underhandedly.[12] The propaganda assertion that collectiveness was the highest principle of party leadership, while not taken to heart in all quarters, was a real political obstacle and sufficiently institutionalized that Khrushchev tried to bypass or manipulate it only at his own peril.

But if there were restraints upon monocratic rule during Khrushchev's tenure of office, there were obviously limitations upon the role of "the collective." While the omnipresence of the secret police in leadership relations was no longer a critical factor, the willingness in some quarters of Soviet society to employ violence for political ends had not entirely disappeared. There were, it has been reported, at least two attempts to assassinate Khrushchev.[13] The "antiparty group" did intend to arrest Khrushchev,[14] and—it has often been argued—Khrushchev himself sought to invoke penal sanctions against enemies in the leadership and at lower levels in the elite who could be accused of crimes during the "cult of personality." Khrushchev's treatment of losers in factional battles and leaders who failed his performance tests was not harsh by Stalin's standards, but neither was it especially magnanimous. If, in the long run, the tensions generated by his pressure on leading cadres were an important source of the cohesion that ensured Khrushchev's downfall, in the short run they may have weakened any collective resolve.

As Myron Rush and T. H. Rigby have rightly emphasized, frequent turnover in the Presidium membership after June 1957 was not conducive to the crystallization of a strong sense of collective solidarity. Major changes occurred in May and July 1960, October 1961, and April and November 1962. There was continuity among some members of the Presidium (Brezhnev, Kuusinen, Mikoyan, Shvernik, Suslov, Kozlov, and for a shorter duration, Podgornyi and Polianskii). But one of the key port-folios—the de facto "second secretaryship"—was shifted from one hand to another (Kirichenko to Kozlov in 1960; Kozlov to Brezhnev in 1963, with Kozlov's terminal illness). Moreover, Khrushchev himself simultaneously held the two top positions of first secretary and chairman of the Council of Ministers, plus the post of chairman of the party's RSFSR Bureau, and was consequently in a position to dominate the presentation of proposals and discussion of issues in the Presidium, the Secretariat, and the governmental "cabinet," the Presidium of the Council of Ministers. Judging by his own account, he also dominated the discussion of military issues. (At the Twenty-second CPSU Congress, Marshal Malinovskii referred to Khru-shchev as "our supreme commander-in-chief.")

Frequent changes in the size of the Secretariat, appointments to and removals from the party Presidium, reorganizations of the Central Com-mittee apparatus and government administration, and Khrushchev's tendency to shift the locus of his own base of operations toward the Council of Ministers after 1958 all contributed to an instability of structures at the top and a fluidity of institutional roles. Within the party Presidium there was not a sufficient tradition of functioning "collective" rule, nor a sufficient degree of solidarity to control Khrushchev's procedural deviations, especially his attempts to preempt collective decisions by violating the con-fidentiality of consideration and discussion of policy issues. It was Khrushchev's communications modus operandi—his premature public rev-elation of policy proposals, denigration of counterarguments, solicitation of support from below, talking beyond approved texts, neutralization of debate in the Central Committee through exposure of its deliberations, and use of "back channels " that, above all else, undermined genuine collective leadership.[15] Yet his use of these tactics and insistence on acting as regime spokesman in all areas of policy contributed, over time, to the assertion of collective political will that resulted in his own ouster.

Oligarchic Elements Under Brezhnev

Although Brezhnev's personal influence was significantly greater in 1979 than it was in 1964, the overall structural weaknesses of the leader's role were greater and those of the collective leadership less acute than during Khrushchev's rule. There is probably even less opportunity for Brezhnev than there was for Khrushchev to use the secret police against political op-ponents within the leadership, despite the fact that Brezhnev has taken more pains than Khrushchev to stock the upper echelons of the KGB with personal clients. Whatever the circumstances under Khrushchev, it now seems that there is a clear institutional separation within the party apparatus between the sector responsible for the secret police (the Administrative Organs Department), the sector responsible for personnel affairs (the Organization-Party Work Department), the sector responsible for support of the Politburo and perhaps internal security (the General Department), and Brezhnev's personal secretariat, although there is obviously some overlap in functions.[16]

Probably there is more open discussion of almost all issues by Politburo members than was true in the days of Khrushchev, and on a multilateral basis. In almost all policy areas, including foreign policy, the members of the Politburo, whatever their functional responsibilities, appear to have greater access to relevant official information than they had in previous years. With freer communication, there is greater scope for the formation of broader and more stable opinions within the leadership and greater possibility of linkage between these opinions and "tendencies of articulation" at lower levels in the political elite. The evidence suggests, however, that military information and military policy constitute a special domain and that Brezhnev's chairmanship of the Defense Council may allow him to control or withhold the flow of sensitive military-security information to a majority of Politburo members. (This is treated in more detail below.)

Over the course of his tenure in office as general secretary, Brezhnev has demonstrated less capacity than Khrushchev to use appointments and patronage to reinforce his authority at the highest levels of power. As I have argued elsewhere, one of the particular conditions under which Brezhnev came to office — an agreement to observe the practice of "stability of cadres" — helped to make it impossible for him to achieve the broad placement of his own men in the top leadership attained by Khrushchev.[17] T. H. Rigby has identified four bases of "personal relationship[s] of reciprocal protection and support" in the Soviet system: shared attitudes based on common prior experiences; ties based on prior service together; congruent policy views; and recognition based simply on one man's having appointed another. In Professor Rigby's opinion, prior work together generally produces the strongest linkage and mere appointment, the weakest.[18]

Applying this prior service criterion, it is clear that Brezhnev was able to make the following important appointments between 1964 and 1978: I. V. Kapitonov (a marginal case; secretary for cadres, 1965), A. P. Kirilenko (in effect, "second secretary," 1966), K. U. Chernenko (secretary with administrative and organizational responsibilities, 1976), and K. V. Rusakov (secretary for bloc relations, 1977) in the Secretariat; G. S. Pavlov (administrator of affairs, 1965), K. U. Chernenko (head of General Department, 1965), S. P. Trapeznikov (head of Science and Educational Institutions Department, 1965), and L. M. Zamiatin (head of the International Information Department, 1978) in the Central Committee apparatus; N. A. Tikhonov (first deputy chairman of the Council of Ministers, 1976) in the Presidium of the Council of Ministers; N. A. Shchelokov (minister of Internal Affairs, 1966), S. K. Tsvigun (first deputy chairman of the KGB, 1967), G. R. Tsinev (deputy chairman of the KGB, 1970), and—perhaps —I. A. Grishmanov (minister of the Building Materials Industry, 1965) in the Council of Ministers. To this list of appointee clients may be added two former Brezhnev associates who were already in place in 1964: I. T. Novikov (deputy chairman of the Council of Ministers and chairman of the State Committee for Construction Affairs) and V. E. Dymshits (deputy chairman of the Council of Ministers and chairman of the State Committee for Material and Technical Supply), although Dymshits may owe his longevity in office equally or more to Kosygin's protection. At the Politburo level the clients of Brezhnev (defined in terms of service with him) include the Central Committee secretary, K. U. Chernenko; the Kazakh first secretary, D. A. Kunaev; the Ukrainian first secretary, V. V. Shcherbitskii; and Kirilenko, plus N. A. Tikhonov among the candidate members.

Overall, this is not a very impressive list, although it is relatively strong in the personnel and security areas. It indicates that a substantial element of Brezhnev's patronage support has been based at best upon less binding, more conditional, "exchange-sensitive" sources of allegiance. If we broaden the definition of "clientele" to include individuals who, while not having worked in a subordinate capacity may have been supervised by Brezhnev, we come up with a longer list of people—most of whom are located in the defense industry and moved up through regular carreer channels to their jobs in the 1965 reorganization of Soviet industry.[19] Those who may simply have been appointed by Brezhnev or whose appointments were presumably favorably vetted by Brezhnev make up still another set.[20] In the Politburo these probably include Andropov (1973), Grechko (1973), and Gromyko (1973) among the full members, and G. A. Aliev (1976), V. V. Kuznetsov (1977), and G. A. Shevardnadze (1978) among the candidates. Finally, we may identify a set of leaders whose link with Brezhnev has probably been mediated through service under or appointment at the initiative of Kirilenko.[21] Supportive ties of other leaders with Brezhnev would appear to be cemented by quite conditional sources of loyalty, either common experiences and attitudes or shared policy views.

In sum, among the thirteen voting members of the Politburo in early 1979, there were three full-fledged clients (Chernenko, Shcherbitskii and Kunaev), one semiclient (Kirilenko), and three leaders who probably owed their job appointments more or less directly to Brezhnev (Ustinov, Andropov, and Gromyko). Five members (Kosygin, Suslov, Grishin, Pel'she and Romanov) were not indebted in either way to Brezhnev, and no one in this group should be considered his client even in a looser sense, regardless of any congruency between their past experiences or current policy positions and Brezhnev's. With the expulsion of Podgornyi from the Politburo in 1977 and Mazurov in 1978, the balance of power, however, did shift further toward Brezhnev.

Weakness in Brezhnev's position has been accentuated by the continued presence in the top ranks of the Soviet leadership of persons of independent political standing. It appears that at least Kirilenko, Kosygin, Suslov, and Podgornyi (while he remained in the leadership) have had an all-union reputation and strongholds within the Soviet elite (although Kirilenko's political status and patronage power were brought into question by the removal of his client Iakov Riabov from the defense industry post in the Secretariat in early 1979). Others probably have had strong regional bases (especially Romanov in Leningrad) or renown in particular policy fields (Ustinov in defense production, and Ponomarev and Gromyko in foreign policy). Despite the flood of praise heaped on Brezhnev in recent years for his leadership qualities — his capacity to manage people, his "attentiveness," his commitment to peace (and defense) — there is little evidence that he has developed authentic charisma.[22]

While the monocratic role under Brezhnev has been structurally weaker, the collective role has been comparatively stronger in most important respects. As has often been noted, turnover in the Politburo membership has been much lower than under Khrushchev. If one discounts the retirements of Kozlov (1964), Mikoyan (1966), and Shvernik (1966), there had been only six expulsions from the Politburo up to mid-1977: Shelest (1973), Voronov (1973), Shelepin (1975), Polianskiii (1976), Podgornyi (1977), and Mazurov (1978, perhaps because of illness). The only candidate members removed have been L. N. Efremov (1966) and Mzhavanadze (1972). Of these eight removals, only three might have given pause to other members to reflect upon "collective security" within the leadership: those of Shelest, Mzhavanadze, and Podgornyi.

It is almost certain that Shelest was formally charged with giving aid and comfort to nationalists; he himself may have been described, at least privately, as a "national deviationist" and perhaps even as a "left opportunist."[23] Beyond the very important message for all non-Russian leaders implicit in this affair was the restoration of the weapon of ideological labeling, which as far as we know had not been employed within the leadership since Khrushchev's days. The disgrace of Mzhavanadze, and the Georgian purge with which this was connected, brought to the fore a different type of sin with which other leaders beside Mzhavanadze could conceivably be charged—namely, corruption.

Podgornyi's abrupt removal from the Politburo at the May 1977 Plenum of the Central Committee, and his replacement by Brezhnev as chairman of the Presidium of the Supreme Soviet at the June meeting of the Supreme Soviet had potentially the most profound implications for collective leadership. It is still unclear whether Podgornyi's disgrace was occasioned simply by a refusal to make way for Brezhnev as chairman of the Presidium of the Supreme Soviet; by objections to the draft Constitution (particularly its provisions regarding national relations in the USSR which, had they been in effect in 1962, could have led to criminal charges against Shelest); or, as Boris Rabbot has argued, by Podgornyi's rejection of Brezhnev's détente policy and his advocacy of greater military support for black African guerrilla movements.[24]

Whatever the cause of Podgornyi's removal from the chairmanship of the Presidium of the Supreme Soviet and Brezhnev's succession to this office, these changes did fundamentally alter the existing triangular pattern of power in which one leader (Brezhnev) headed the party, another (Kosygin) supervised the government administration, and still another (Podgornyi) served as head of state. Brezhnev's personal authority was unquestionably enhanced, and the influence of the Secretariat and Central Committee (CC) apparatus vis-à-vis Kosygin and the Council of Ministers was strengthened. Unease in some quarters over Brezhnev's simultaneous occupancy of the general secretaryship and the chairmanship of the Presidium of the Supreme Soviet was signaled by a perceived need to offer elaborate public justifications for Brezhnev's assumption of Podgornyi's role. While Brezhnev's followers were prominent among the speakers at the May 1977 Plenum of the Central Committee and the June session of the Supreme Soviet that endorsed the changes, the most authoritative official rationale was delivered at the Supreme Soviet meeting by Suslov, who has had a vested interest in not jeopardizing collective leadership. It would seem implausible that he was speaking under compulsion.

The fact that Brezhnev wanted personally to take over the Supreme Soviet post rather than simply to install a client in Podgornyi's seat demonstrates conclusively that significant power resources have become associated with the job. This, in turn, indicates at least partial institutionalization of authority at the top leadership level. The job now appears to carry with it the potential for a significant representational role in foreign affairs, initiative with respect to the Defense Council of the USSR, and a certain supervisory authority vis-à-vis the Council of Ministers and its Presidium.

In the short run, Brezhnev's succession to Podgornyi's office strengthens the monocratic leader role. It also sets a precedent for a practice that may have been felt within elite circles to violate the spirit of the 1964 agreement prohibiting dual occupancy of the top party and government jobs. However, the long-term consequences of Brezhnev's accession and the expansion of the constitutional authority of the Presidium of the Supreme Soviet (see below) are ambiguous. Here one should note the ambivalence in public statements about what was in fact decided at the May Plenum of the Central Committee. Where some accounts suggest a structural unification of the *roles* of general secretary and chairman of the Presidium of the Supreme Soviet, others (e.g., Suslov's) suggest a less permanent dual occupancy justified substantially in terms of Brezhnev's *personal* leadership qualities. It would be rash to assume, in any event, that Brezhnev's successor as general secretary will automatically also assume the post of chairman of the Presidium of the Supreme Soviet; the odds are definitely against this. Thus the net long-term effect of what has happened may be a further institutionalization of arrangements that strengthen collective leadership.

Low turnover in the Politburo has effected greater stability in the pattern of hierarchical status among members of the leadership. While the fortunes of some individuals have obviously waxed and waned, there do not appear to have been violent fluctuations in the overall rank order of the leaders. Most important, despite periodic signs of tension there has been exceptional stability in the inner core of the leadership consisting of Brezhnev, Kirilenko, Kosygin, Suslov, and—until recently—Podgornyi. This stability reflects the continued adherence to the pattern of balanced Politburo staffing that T. H. Rigby identifies as a condition of oligarchic self-maintenance. Throughout the period since 1964, CC secretaries have never composed a majority of the members of the Politburo; the Secretariat has never been represented in the Politburo solely by the general secretary, nor solely by members of a single faction; the Presidium of the Council of Ministers has always been represented in the Politburo, and, at least until late 1978, always by more than one individual; and—most significant—the posts of general secretary and chairman of the Council of Ministers have been kept in separate hands.

If we consider the total composition of the Politburo during the Brezhnev years, we can explain the presence of a core of members in terms of "reasonable" positional and institutional representation. Such a concept would cover the general secretary, the senior organizational and ideological secretaries of the Central Committee, the chairman of the Party Control Committee, the chairman and at least one deputy chairman of the Council of Ministers (before Mazurov's release in 1978), the chairman of the Presidium of the Supreme Soviet, and the first secretary of the Communist Party of the Ukraine. Like Khrushchev's Presidium, however, Brezhnev's

Politburo has shown discontinuous membership of the occupants of a number of posts that one might think would have been treated consistently. These include the positions of CC secretary for agriculture, chairman of the Council of Ministers of the RSFSR, first secretary of the Belorussian party, first secretary of the Moscow City Party Committee, chairman of the Trade Unions, and first deputy chairman of the Council of Ministers for agriculture, as well as perhaps first secretary of Leningrad.

Membership has also been assigned during portions of the period to posts that, while meeting the loose test of "reasonableness," have nevertheless not met the test of precedent in the post-1957 years. These include the national security positions of chairman of the KGB, minister of defense, and minister of foreign affairs. Finally, the Politburo has included for part of the time since 1964 the occupants of four posts that definitely do not meet either the "reasonableness" or the precedent criteria—the minister of agriculture, the minister of culture, the chairman of the Ukrainian Council of Ministers, and the first secretary of the Communist Party of Kazakhstan. In other words, the composition of the Politburo full membership during the Brezhnev years can have been no more than half institutionalized: the variation in representation of marginal positions outside the core must be explained largely in terms of factional politics within the leadership, although it is likely that Brezhnev's attempt to build support for his own foreign policy was involved in the promotions of Andropov, Grechko, and Gromyko in April 1973.

If the candidate members are considered together with the full members, a basically "reasonable" and precedent-based pattern of ethnogeographical representation does emerge: We always find some type of representation accorded to the Western (Baltic and Belorussian), Caucasus, and Central Asian republics and nationalities, although the allocation of seats or top seats within regions is certainly not fixed (a Latvian, Pel'she, rather than a Belorussian, Masherov; an Azerbaijani, Aliev, and recently a Georgian, Shevardnadze, but not an Armenian; a Kazakh, Kunaev, rather than an Uzbek, Rashidov).

An important further source of support for the oligarchic role in top-level Soviet politics has been the high degree of organizational stability, regularization of tasks, demarcation of functions and continuity of personnel in the Secretariat and Presidium of the Council of Ministers, and to a lesser degree the corresponding enlivening of the activity of the Presidium of the Supreme Soviet.[25] Since the liquidation in 1965 of Khrushchev's innovations in party organization—the RSFSR Bureau, various Central Committee commissions, bifurcated agricultural and industrial branches, and the Party-State Control Committee—there has been apparently no major change in the structure of the Secretariat and Central Committee apparatus. Following the initial shake-up of the Secretariat after Khrushchev's ouster (Podgornyi's transfer to the Supreme Soviet and the removal of Titov, Il'ichev, and Poliakov), there have been only two noticeable episodes of turbulence: the banishment of Shelepin to the Trade Unions in 1967 and the shift of Demichev to the Ministry of Culture in 1974 (although Demichev remains a candidate member of the Politburo, outranking his belated replacement as propaganda secretary, M. V. Zimianin). To this list may be added the transfer of K. F. Katushev from the bloc relations post in the Secretariat to the position of deputy chairman of the Council of Ministers for CEMA affairs in 1977, and more significantly, the abrupt transfer of Kirilenko's client, Ia. P. Riabov, from the defense industry slot in the Secretariat to the far lower status position of the first deputy chairman of Gosplan in early 1979.

Since 1964 the size of the Secretariat has remained quite constant at between nine and eleven members and continuity of responsibility in almost every area — cadres, propaganda, foreign policy, agriculture, industry, and defense — has been interrupted no more than once. The existing evidence suggests that the Secretariat functions collectively as an institution and that it combines joint deliberation, broad initiative by senior members (e.g., Suslov and Kirilenko), and overall leadership by the general secretary. At the Twenty-fifth Party Congress Brezhnev noted:

> The Secretariat of the Central Commiteee, which has held 205 meetings over the elapsed period [since the Twenty-fourth Congress] has constantly occupied itself with the activity of party organizations, with questions of the selection and distribution of cadres. Much more attention than formerly has been devoted by it to control and verification of fulfillment of decisions which have already been taken.[26]

Occasionally, we find specific references to subjects raised at meetings of the Secretariat. Thus, for example, Brezhnev recently dwelt at length upon a discussion by the Secretariat of the activities of the Ukrainian and Siberian academies of science.[27] The institutional character of Secretariat operations is also suggested, for example, by Brezhnev's greetings to the Trade Union Congress "from the Central Committee of the Communist Party of the Soviet Union, from the Politburo, Secretariat of the CC CPSU and the Soviet government."[28]

In the Presidium of the Council of Ministers, there have been even fewer shifts of responsibility since the reestablishment of the ministerial system in late 1965, the most significant being the demotion of Polianskii from the post of first deputy chairman for agriculture to the job of minister of agriculture in 1973, the appointment of Tikhonov as a first deputy chairman in 1976, and the "retirement" of Mazurov in 1978. This stability of posts and occupants in both the Secretariat and Presidium of the Council of Ministers has provided the basis for a routinization of role relationships between the two bodies in task areas of common concern — namely, planning, foreign economic relations, general industry, defense industry, construction, communications, trade, welfare, agriculture, education, and science.

With its "own" leader (Kosygin), low turnover, sufficient "critical mass," regular assembly,[29] and now a constitutionally legitimized role in the running of government, the Presidium of the Council of Ministers has clearly emerged as a force to be reckoned with in the Soviet leadership. As a group, the members of the Presidium have had — like the ministries they supervise — an impressive amount of experience. If this body did not exist today, it would probably have to be invented, if the Secretariat wished physically to be able to stay on top of policy and personnel questions, rather than be submerged in the increasingly complex details of domestic and foreign economic administration or to undergo a bureaucratic reincarnation.

The Presidium, of course, does not deal with all aspects of Soviet policy; probably its collective mandate does not extend far at all in the ideological, foreign policy, security, and military management areas (although its Military-Industrial Commission, headed by L. V. Smirnov, is thought to play a key role in the coordination of military procurement). There is no evidence that the minister of defense, chairman of the KGB, and minister of foreign affairs are accountable to the Presidium. Since 1973, when they were coopted into the Politburo as participants in top-level decision making, their role in the Presidium has presumably been limited to advising the chairman of the Council of Ministers on secondary matters within their jurisdiction. Also, as noted above, the general secretary's power vis-à-vis the Presidium has been reinforced by his strong patronage ties to at least three of its members — Dymshits (material supply and energy), I. T. Novikov (construction), and Tikhonov (heavy industry and energy).

Finally, it is undoubtedly the case that the Secretariat has enhanced its influence vis-à-vis the Presidium in the years since 1968–1969. The evidence supporting this argument includes the asserted attendance by Brezhnev at some Presidium meetings, public mention of the attendance of Council of Ministers meetings by CC secretaries (Kirilenko, Dolgikh, and Riabov), greater outspokenness about governmental operations on the part of CC secretaries, more CC investigations of and resolutions on governmental agencies, and the extension of the "right of *kontrol*" to ministerial party organizations.[30] Add to this the delivery by Brezhnev of reports on the state of the economy at December plenums of the Central Committee dealing, inter alia, with the next year's budget — reports whose "directions and evaluations" have been declared to be "binding" upon the Council of Ministers since 1975.[31] As long as the general secretary simultaneously occupies the post of chairman of the Presidium of the Supreme Soviet, the provisions of the new Constitution (see below) that emphasize subordination of the Council of Ministers and its Presidium to the Presidium of the Supreme Soviet at the same time tend to strengthen CC Secretariat influence over the government. Meetings of the Presidium of the Supreme Soviet provide a forum in which Kosygin and other government leaders now must (and in fact do) formally account for their actions to the general secretary (in his capacity as chairman of the Presidium), thereby circumventing the Politburo.

At the Politburo level, it is almost certainly the case that procedural rules are followed to assure a higher basic level of information and participation to all members than that which existed under Khrushchev. According to Brezhnev's boast at the Twenty-fifth Party Congress in February 1976:

> The activity of the Politburo of the Central Committee has been robust and operative. During the period after the XXIV Congress it has held 215 meetings. The Politburo has regularly occupied itself with problems of industry, agriculture and capital construction, of the perfection of administration in all branches of the state and economic apparatus. Special attention has been devoted to the measures projected by the XXIV Congress to raise the living standard of the people. Fundamental problems of improving intraparty and ideological work have been discussed. Questions of the foreign policy activity and strengthening of defense of the country have occupied a large place in the work of the Politburo.[32]

The *New York Times* reported an interview in which Brezhnev stated that an attempt is made to reach decisions by consensus, and that if this cannot be achieved issues may be postponed for further deliberation or sent to committee.[33] *Le Monde* correspondent Alain Jacob has written:

> In theory, the Politburo meets every Thursday; and contact between sessions is maintained through memos, passed around for perusal and possible comment by members who are apparently expected to sign them. According to the most trustworthy sources, it is highly improbable that an important decision or a piece of information of major interest is not circulated either for opinion or simply as information to all members of the Politburo within twenty-four hours.[34]

Evidence also suggests that the Politburo is actively consulted, and its consent obtained, in important foreign policy negotiations. Raymond Garthoff has observed that the Politburo "met at least four times" during the five-day

SALT summit of May 1972.[35] And we can see that Brezhnev still takes pains to gain Politburo validation for important foreign policy ventures,[36] just as he has consistently scheduled Central Committee plenums at important international junctures.

Obviously, we should not suppose that the Politburo functions like the proverbial "town meeting." Personal power strivings, gradations of influence among the membership, division of labor, and the inevitable necessity of considering issues jointly with functional specialists all affect the conduct of business. It is undeniable that Brezhnev has sought — and since 1972, attained — a far more important role personally in the conduct of foreign affairs than he played at the outset of the Brezhnev-Kosygin era or even as late as 1971. (One might recall that it was Kosygin who signed the May 1971 SALT communique with Nixon, which set the stage for the subsequent successful conclusion of the SALT I negotiations.) Brezhnev has been supported here by a personal secretariat that, so far at least, has apparently managed to avoid the opprobrium of Khrushchev's "kitchen cabinet" while yet being more in the public eye.[37]

It is generally thought that the Politburo operates with a number of formal and informal specialized subgroups whose membership varies by functional area in keeping with the general Soviet team approach. One analyst has speculated that there may by Politburo-level committees for foreign relations (presumably composed of inner core leaders Brezhnev, Kosygin, Kirilenko, and Suslov, plus Gromyko and — when appropriate — Andropov, Ustinov, and foreign economic relations specialists like Arkhipov, Lesechko, and V. N. Novikov); for agriculture (headed until his death by Kulakov and including the deputy chairman of the Council of Ministers for agriculture, Nuriev, and the minister of agriculture, Mesiats); and perhaps a committee for cultural-ideological problems (whose members would now presumably include at least Suslov, Demichev, and Zimianin).[38] Another analyst refers to "a probable subgroup with the 'portfolio' for national security matters within the Politburo itself."[39] A recent official source observes that throughout Soviet history "commissions have been created by plenums [of the CC], the Politburo, Orgburo and Secretariat and have operated — depending upon the circumstances and complexity of the problem — for a more or less prolonged period, up to several years. Such a method of preparing and deciding questions has permitted various points of view to be more fully taken into account, efforts coordinated, and subjectivism avoided."[40] At the July 1978 Plenum of the Central Committee, Brezhnev mentioned the creation by the Politburo in 1977 of an "authoritative commission" to prepare recommendations on agricultural issues, and at the November 1978 Plenum he referred to the Politburo's formation of a "special commission which is undertaking operative measures to improve transport."

One of the most important Politburo-level committees is undoubtedly the Defense Council of the USSR, which is chaired by Brezhnev. This body is treated at greater length in another chapter of this volume, but several comments are in order here. The Defense Council has been described as "the highest body dealing specifically with military and defense matters."[41] Because of its composition and its access to highly restricted information the Defense Council probably can expect to have its decisions routinely approved by the Politburo. Its core membership is thought to include, in addition to the general secretary, the chairman of the Council of Ministers (Kosygin), the chairman of the Presidium of the Supreme Soviet (Podgornyi, until his ouster), the CC secretary for military affairs (formerly Ustinov and, until recently, Riabov), and the minister of defense (Ustinov).[42] Depending upon the subjects under discussion, its meetings may be attended by the minister of foreign affairs (Gromyko), the chief of the General Staff (Ogarkov), other military leaders, the chairman of the Council of Ministers' Military-Industrial Commission (Smirnov), and the head of the KGB (General of the Army Andropov). In the past the formal status of the council was obscure — whether it was technically a state organ (as its title seemed to suggest), a subcommittee of the Politburo, or really a supercommittee (presidium) of the Politburo.[43] This ambiguity has been resolved by the new Constitution, which stipulates that the Presidium of the Supreme Soviet "forms the Defense Council of the USSR and confirms its membership and appoints and removes the high command of the Armed Forces of the USSR" (Article 119). For our purpose the key point is that an element of collective decision making appears to have been institutionalized in this strategic area of discourse, giving access to the occupants of at least two other senior civilian leadership posts (each with its separate organizational base) and making it extremely difficult for the general secretary to dictate military decisions without coming to terms with the views of other leaders, only a minority of whom have represented the military establishment.

The Future Balance of Monocratic and Oligarchic Elements

With Brezhnev's visibly declining health and the aging of the remaining members of the inner core of the Soviet leadership, it is worth asking whether the forthcoming multiple succession might not be "a succession that could well create a 'succession crisis,' especially if we think of succession as a three-or-four-year process rather than the immediate choice of a new General Secretary."[44] In the context of the present discussion, the practical manifestation of a "succession crisis" would mark the end of the balancing and blending of monocratic and oligarchic elements in the Soviet leadership and a lurch toward either outright autocracy or fragmentation of power. Traditionally, of course, the phrase "succession crisis" does not refer to any sort of conflict or tension that occurs during the succession period, but to a unique kind of turbulence produced by the actual mechanics of the transfer of power. It covers not only the power struggle, but the effects of this conflict as well. It signifies a *general* crisis characterized by a specific syndrome of interrelated features.[45] To restate the matter slightly differently, serious problems in a succession period can, in principle, arise from the dynamics of the transfer of power itself *and* out of the impact on the political system of exogenous factors — Soviet economic dilemmas, nationalist or reformist tendencies in Eastern Europe, the possibilities of war with China, a downturn in relations with the "imperialists." As long as these two sources of tension are analytically distinguished, it is reasonable to draw from the experience of the past two decades in projecting the future. From the standpoint of the classic definition of "succession crisis," the greatest likelihood after the present core leadership goes is the selection of a new general secretary, necessarily of lesser stature, and the strengthening of the collective role in the Soviet leadership. There will be struggle and conflict, but probably not crisis.

As stated above, one of the main sources of erosion of the monocratic role has been the opening of communications within and to the leadership, and the difficulty a leader has in countering this phenomenon without recourse to terror. Under present conditions, the need-to-know explosion is being fueled by the "scientific-technological revolution," the general level of social development, and the impact of foreign involvements. This functional need of the leadership is being met by systematic efforts to develop sources of desired kinds of information in the party apparatus, institutes of the Academy of Sciences, and governmental agencies. While it is not difficult to imagine that a new politics of information channeling has emerged — competing with the old ideological politics of scholastic exegesis — it is difficult to imagine that the overall communications flow can actually be capped or directed solely to the advantage of a new leader.[46] Even more than at present, high-level Soviet politics in the future is likely to be a politics of argumentation rather than a politics of "label-sticking," which is to say a politics probably of accommodation rather than one of winner-take-all.

To be sure, this proposition depends upon the condition that the stakes in power struggles among future leaders be kept within tolerable limits. Is it possible that the military and the KGB can be effectively restricted to the facilitative and temporally restricted role that they have played in the past two successions?[47] One certainly cannot be dogmatic on this score. The unseemly haste with which a civilian, Ustinov, was installed as minister of defense following Grechko's death in 1976 and the evident deliberateness with which Brezhnev has repeatedly demonstrated his patronage base in the KGB (Andropov, Tsvigun, Tsinev, and perhaps Chebrikov) and the MVD (Shchelokov) on various departures from Moscow are cautionary reminders of the potential influence of these organizations. At the same time, however, the refurbishing of the KGB over the past decade may have lessened the temptation, if one really exists, for the military to involve itself in politics outside its areas of professional concern.

Implicit in much of the speculation about the impact of the forthcoming multiple succession would seem to be the notion that sudden rapid turnover at the top will present an opportunity for a new general secretary to establish monocratic rule through the instrument of patronage. As we have seen, patronage proved to be an *unreliable* source of power for Khrushchev and a *limited* source of power for Brezhnev. The chances are that it will be an even more limited one for Brezhnev's successor. Brezhnev built his patronage base partly through "inheritance" from Khrushchev, partly through his postwar service in three different regional party organizations (Dnepropetrovsk, Moldavia, and Kazakhstan), and partly through his lengthy service at high levels in Moscow, where he developed broad contacts in the military-industrial complex and other areas.

If we consider Kirilenko the likeliest short-term successor (but exclude him from the list of long-term successors because of age) and exclude Andropov on the grounds of presumed unacceptability to various elements within the political elite (including the military), then the most likely roster of potential successors at the moment is Chernenko, Romanov, Grishin, and Dolgikh. Of the four, Romanov and Grishin have the most occupationally diverse and professionally competent networks of acquaintances and clients, while Chernenko has had the longest and deepest contact with central officials. Yet in all four cases the clientele pool that can be called upon to fill high-level jobs is far narrower than was Brezhnev's in 1964. This circumstance means that even if the new general secretary were free to staff as he wished, the foundation on which this patronage would be based would tend to be the weakest of the four types noted above—namely, the mere fact of appointment.

But how much reason is there to suppose that a new general secretary will be vouchsafed this degree of appointive discretion? The situation most conducive to such an outcome would probably be an early replacement of Brezhnev, an interval, and then quick replacement of the "old guard" in the leadership. This timing would give the new general secretary an opportunity to get his bearings, line up a team in the wings, and display authority at the moment when the new leaders are being selected. In the absence of such a happy phasing of retirements or deaths, however, it is hard to see how slates of clients of the general secretary could easily be pushed through the Politburo — except, perhaps, under conditions of dire national emergency. The new general secretary, in all probability, will lack even the prestige enjoyed by Brezhnev in 1964. Consequently, the likelihood is that the renewal at the top will tend to follow the bureaucratic pattern, in which the pre-positioning of prospective candidates on appropriate experience-generating stepping-stones will strongly influence probabilities of cooptation. If this turns out to be the pattern, the present absence of a factional majority in the leadership will probably simply be re-created.

But if a sudden coup d'état is unlikely, what about the opposite danger — too much collectiveness, deadlock, and the disintegration of authority? This hinges in large part upon the institutionalization of relationships within the leadership. Disregarding the usual formulation, which implicitly equates institutionalization with constitutionalization,[48] the problem is better approached from a more elementary standpoint. To talk about institutionalization at the most basic level is to talk about social order or social structure. And what is being ordered or structured is, in a literal sense, not simply bodies or behavior, but a certain kind of knowledge in the heads of political leaders (and possibly in the heads of other members of the population). This knowledge amounts to a shared understanding of how leaders who occupy certain specified positions (e.g., general secretary, chairman of the Council of Ministers, minister of defense, etc.) typically will relate — within certain limits, in certain types of situations — to occupants of other leadership and extraleadership positions.[49]

A crucial element of this knowledge is that the pattern of relationships involved in the activity we call leadership will not be dominated by the arbitrary intervention of considerations and resources present in other realms of activity (e.g., personal and factional struggles) in which leaders or other actors are simultaneously engaged. Important factors that differentiate types of institutionalization are the presence or absence of "legitimization,"[50] the stability of the knowledge over time (especially whether or not it is transmitted without fundamental alteration from one generation of leaders to successive generations), and the degree to which awareness of the knowledge extends beyond the leaders themselves.

Looking at institutionalization in this light shows that there are aspects of the knowledge of how the leadership operates. These aspects are publicly expressed and do involve legitimization. The most important of these are Article 38 of the Party Rules (which states that the Central Committee elects the Politburo, the Secretariat, and the general secretary; defines broad spheres of activity of the Politburo and Secretariat; and acknowledges the role of leader within the leadership) and Article 27 ("The highest principle of Party leadership is collective leadership"), although Sections I and III of the rules, which define the rights of party members and principles of party operation, also have a bearing upon intraleadership relations (especially with respect to communications behavior).

The new Constitution also states a number of important principles: the Presidium of the Supreme Soviet exercises ultimate control over the military (Article 119); the Presidium of the Supreme Soviet appoints and releases members of the Council of Ministers "upon submission by the Chairman of the Council of Ministers" (Article 120); the Council of Ministers and Procuracy are accountable to the Presidium of the Supreme Soviet (Articles 129 and 164); and that there should exist a Presidium of the Council of Ministers composed of the chairman, first deputy chairmen, and deputy chairmen (Article 131).

Without dismissing these formal public declarations, which do reflect in some sense an underlying cognitive reality and which can be invoked to maintain balance in the leadership, we must observe that the details of institutionalized knowledge of leadership roles are largely known only to the participants and their close entourage, and may not be well endowed with even the legitimation of formal expression. (An important exception to the latter assertion is a resolution adopted at the October 1964 Plenum of the Central Committee "that the posts of First Secretary of the Central Committee and Chairman of the Council of Ministers be forever separate.")[51]

Thus we are talking about informal understandings: that business will be conducted in official forums, that information will be accessible to members, that participation will be structured in certain ways, that the general secretary will take the initiative in ordering or drawing up reports, and that these reports will be collectively approved. Such understandings are not impervious to extraneous influences and present real problems of intergenerational transmission that should not be disregarded at the present juncture. Nevertheless, one should not ignore the acculturating, congruent experiences that new recruits to the leadership bring with them from having participated in party bureaus at lower levels in the system, nor the weight of routine and ritualization in leadership behavior. Also, one should not divorce business relationships among the leaders from the matrix of social interaction and material privilege in which these relationships are set.[52]

While what exists is more than a "state of nature," we are not likely to see much movement toward a constitutionalization of leadership relations. Apart from its incompatibility with the political culture of Soviet Communism, a constitutionalization of relationships within the party leadership would be inhibited by a calculation of its likely consequences. Because of the universalist mode of legitimization of relationships in the CPSU, it would not be easy publicly to articulate principles regulating leadership behavior at the top that did not apply at lower levels within the party as well. The effect of such a move would inevitably be to undermine democratic centralism in the party. A most important corollary of this effect would be that the party structure would be far more vulnerable to the centripetal influences of non-Russian nationalism and would, through a demonstration effect, jeopardize the pattern of political control in Eastern Europe.

Access to the Leadership and Foreign Policy

The implication of the argument thus far is that, while the role of the general secretary may expand or contract, there has been a tendency in the Brezhnev era — across most policy areas — for the collective to have more access to information, to be consulted, and even to participate more when key policy decisions are being made. Obviously, not all participate equally, nor do all have an equal influence on the agenda. We may assume that Brezhnev has sought and attained a key role in agenda-setting by exercising the legitimate powers of the office of general secretary. His personal secretariat has evidently greatly facilitated his ability to define the issues, especially in foreign affairs. As we have seen, there has been an inner core of the leadership that has almost certainly enjoyed a disproportionate voice in the day-to-day discussion of foreign policy questions, and subgroups have probably acted in other functional areas. Crucial decisions on military policy that have a fundamental impact on the Soviet budget appear to be formulated in the Defense Council by a handful of political and military leaders. But overall, it appears that there are now, and will continue to be, more points of ultimate *access* to the Soviet decision-making process. And this structural condition means, in turn, that more channels are likely to be open, through which more lower-level communicators can dispatch more messages to the decision makers.

While it is sometimes overlooked, it is clear that the impact of communications to the Politburo still ultimately depends not upon the group configuration of the "interest-articulators," but upon how the Politburo members choose to receive messages and respond to them. To oversimplify, the personal political problem facing each Politburo member is how to improve or at least retain his position in the leadership, in a situation in which no fixed tenure is recognized. But in contrast with the classic interest group environment, the direct arbiter of solutions is the group of fellow Politburo members, rather than outside constituencies. In other words, as long as cooptation is the mechanism of recruitment to the Politburo (and there is no sign that this has changed), the linkage between leaders' careers and interests is bound to be looser, more indirect, and more mediated by the whole dynamics of intraleadership politics.

One might suppose, for example, that Dnepropetrovsk oblast would be an especially favored constituency, given its unique points of access to the Politburo, Secretariat, and Presidium of the Council of Ministers. Yet the speeches of Vatchenko, former first secretary of the obkom, over the years, plus much other evidence, indicate that such is far from being the case — especially with respect to the obsolescence of steel mills in the region.[53] It might also be noted that the workers of the oblast (including those of Brezhnev's home town, Dneprodzerzhinsk) were sufficiently dissatisfied with their lot to engage in two major riots in a single year (1972).

Thus we should beware of mechanical or quantitative images of the linkage between "inputs" to and "outputs" from the leadership based merely upon an analysis of patterns of "senders" and "receivers." This caution does not mean that Politburo members do not espouse various causes, sometimes unsuccessfully (witness Shelepin, Shelest, and Voronov). Nor does it mean that Politburo members are not advocates of specific programs and constituencies for which they bear bureaucratic responsiblity. But it does mean that because there is a disjunction between the satisfaction of career ambitions and the satisfaction of interests, there is a tendency for interests to mingle more with other factors in the calculations of leaders. The most important of these factors are immediate considerations of reciprocal power relationships within the leadership, appreciations of policy issues and estimates of likely impacts of different solutions (including impacts on the longer-term configuration of power within the leadership), and mind-sets based on previous experiences that members bring to decision making.

With these caveats in mind, what are likely to be some of the effects of a more oligarchic trend in the leadership? First, broader participation in decision making at the Politburo level almost certainly implies less compartmentalization of foreign and domestic issues. The leaders who gain greater access to the discussion of foreign policy issues than they possessed formerly are leaders whose occupational responsibilities lie more in the domestic area. Despite the role of the inner core of leaders, of individual CC secretaries (Brezhnev, Suslov, Ponomarev, Rusakov, and now Chernenko), and of such institutions as the Defense Council in the conduct of foreign-related activities, greater general participation by other Politburo members means greater awareness of foreign policy issues and, probably, more questioning.

It is worth emphasizing that the exposure of leaders who are not exclusively foreign policy specialists to foreign affairs is not simply a matter of passive observation. We are accustomed, of course, to watching Podgornyi go to the Middle East, or Kosygin deal with Japanese industrialists, or

Kirilenko attend congresses of West European Communist parties. Despite the greetings that they convey on such occasions from "Leonid Il'ich," the authority with which they speak is not simply a reflection of that of the general secretary; there is a significant sharing of responsibilities here that in other systems would tend to fall on the shoulders of a single leader. And this may be considered an element of strength that collective leadership adds to the conduct of Soviet external affairs.

When it comes to the active contact of the other leaders with foreigners and foreign problems, it is not clear that all of this interaction is purely formal. Much of it involves substantive discussions occasioned by integration with Eastern Europe, détente with the West, and the increasingly global scope of Soviet foreign involvements. One might venture to guess that most Moscow-based members of the Politburo, most members of the Secretariat, and virtually all members of the Presidium of the Council of Ministers are engaged in such contacts on at least a weekly basis or even more frequently. This means that foreign affairs are increasingly interwoven in leaders' schedules with domestic tasks, and foreign considerations cannot help but be constantly present in their minds.

Greater collective participation is also likely to affect the style of Soviet foreign policy. More participation is likely to engender a more structured decision-making process, in which compromise is the order of the day. Under these conditions we should expect that the elaboration and implementation of Soviet foreign policy objectives will acquire a still greater bureaucratic coloration, and policies — once established — will have greater inertia, although they may be harder to establish in the first place. With more points of anchorage on the domestic side of the leadership and more immediately visible linkages with domestic concerns, foreign policies are likely to have greater stability. By the same token, the more policy emerges from domestically intertwined compromises, the more difficult it will probably be for Soviet foreign policy managers to agree rapidly to significant compromises abroad.

Finally, is more collectivity likely to affect the direction of Soviet foreign policy? Obviously, this depends in part upon who the members of the collective are. The example of Pel'she's selection should be viewed as advice not to assume without question that technocrats are going to take over the Politburo completely. It is entirely conceivable that Belorussia, for example, will contribute one full member (Masherov) and one candidate member (A. N. Aksenov or I. E. Poliakov) who lack higher technical education and significant specialist experience, but are more than familiar with Komsomol and party organizational work. Nor is it inconceivable, to take another example, that Vatchenko, who has pedagogical training and a career almost exclusively in the party apparatus, will succeed Shcherbitskii as first secretary of the Ukraine and acquire voting membership in the Politburo.

In general, we might expect that with greater participation, there should be a broader range of alternatives under consideration in foreign policymaking. However, the desire to avoid career risk on the part of members could lead to a narrowing of options and an element of conformism within the collective, and most likely a more conservative conformism.[54] We are, perhaps, inclined to assume that because domestic needs are objectively being sacrificed to meet Soviet foreign aims, domestically oriented leaders — or at least those without vested professional interests in international tensions — will tend to adopt more liberal foreign policy positions. This conclusion may be justified in the longer run, if we assume that knowledge and sophistication about the external world make a Soviet leader more accommodating (a highly problematic assumption). But whatever the long-range effects, in the short run participation probably will heighten conservative tendencies, other things being equal.

Michel Tatu has argued that the Soviet leadership is to some extent a captive of the primitive propaganda it beams at lower-level cadres, in the sense that the desire then to carry these officials along inhibits flexibility abroad.[55] The unpublished results of an analysis by Peter Hauslohner of speeches by obkom first secretaries suggest that the younger members of this key middle-elite group are more assertive and uncompromising in their foreign policy positions than the older members. Some members of the top leadership probably share this outlook. They are no doubt exposed to a mass of national security information revealing the hostile designs of the Western imperialists, the unreliability of various elements in Eastern Europe, and the threat from China, and they may have no particular cause to see the world differently. Their speeches indicate that Romanov and Grishin fall into this category as well as Suslov and Pel'she, whom one would anticipate as a matter of course.

Whatever effect collectivity may have on the direction of Soviet foreign policy will also be influenced by the nature of substantive concerns that filter up into the decision-making process. Given the severity of domestic problems today, it is likely that these problems will have a more heightened impact on the resolution of foreign issues than was the case in the 1950s and 1960s. This relationship is most applicable to the sphere of economic affairs, where the Soviet Union is faced with a declining rate of economic growth, declining factor productivity, lack of innovation, a growing labor shortage, inefficient planning, and increasingly tight fuel and raw materials supplies. But there can be no certainty that communication of concern over these difficulties to the leadership will inspire a more accommodating posture toward the West.

The argument will undoubtedly be made that an effective strategy for coping with these dilemmas must include at least a continuation, if not an increase, in trade and scientific exchanges with the West; the involvement of Western financing and technology in the enormously costly development and transportation of Siberian energy and mineral resources; and an easing of the burden of armaments spending. This argument, which prescribes avoiding provocation of the West, is likely to find supporters among officials sensitive to the needs of the emerging "territorial-production complexes," planners, and the foreign trade apparatus.

However, a contrary argument will also be heard. The optimistic assessment of the benefits to be gained from closer economic ties with the West will be questioned, both on economic and political grounds. Greater autarky will be urged, with a corresponding emphasis upon administrative direction of the Soviet economy, social discipline, and "moral incentives." The argument here is likely to be supported by a more threatening depiction of the danger posed by the West and/or China and an evocation of the wartime spirit of sacrifice. Supporters of this position are found everywhere, especially in orthodox ideological circles attuned to the type of views propounded by Suslov, among the military, and among some party officials. Which tendency will dominate cannot be predicted. The outcome will depend partly upon the constellation of forces in the succession setting, but also upon volatile trends in the international environment.

Acknowledgments

I would like to thank Seweryn Bialer, Robert Blackwell, Ben Fischer, T. H. Rigby, Douglas Garthoff, Myron Rush, and Albert Salter for their helpful comments on the first draft of this chapter.

Notes

1. Jerome M. Gilison, "New Factors of Stability in Soviet Leadership," *World Politics* 19, no. 4 (July 1967): 563–581.

2. Vernon V. Aspaturian, *Process and Power in Soviet Foreign Policy* (Boston: Little, Brown and Co., 1971), p. 570.

3. T. H. Rigby, "The Soviet Leadership:Towards a Self-Stabilizing Oligarchy?" *Soviet Studies* 22, no. 2 (October 1970):167–191.

4. Grey Hodnett, "Succession Contingencies in the Soviet Union," *Problems of Communism* 24, no. 2 (March-April 1975):1–21.

5. Seweryn Bialer, "The Soviet Political Elite and Internal Developments in the USSR," in William E. Griffith, ed., *The Soviet Empire: Expansion & Detente* (Lexington, Mass.: D. C. Heath & Co., 1976), pp. 30–31.

6. According to the Medvedevs, plenums of the Central Committee "had an important decision-making function in 1953–57." (See Roy A. Medvedev and Zhores A. Medvedev, *Khrushchev: The Years in Power* [New York: Columbia University Press, 1976], p. 85.)

7. For confirmatory evidence see Michel Tatu, *Power in the Kremlin* (New York: Viking Press, 1969), parts 3 and 4.

8. For a vivid description of Zhukov's popularity and of his bold deportment even in Stalin's presence see A. Iakovlev, *O zhizni i o sebe* (Moscow, 1974), pp. 311–312.

9. See Strobe Talbott, ed., *Khrushchev Remembers: The Last Testament* (Boston: Little, Brown and Co., 1974), p. 419.

10. For an admittedly partisan account of Brezhnev's behavior in Kazakhstan and Moscow during the Khrushchev years see Fedor T. Morgun, *Khleb i liudi* (Moscow, 1975), pp. 80–84, 123–125.

11. According to the Medvedevs, Suslov's condemnation of Khrushchev at the October 1964 Plenum of the Central Committee included the charge that he had "a small unofficial 'cabinet' of friends and relatives as advisors instead of consulting the Presidium, and of bringing his entire family into politics — his son-in-law, A. Adzhubei, the editor of *Izvestiia*, was a sort of unofficial 'minister of foreign affairs' and many foreign policy decisions had been made without consulting Gromyko, a rather confusing state of affairs for Soviet ambassadors abroad." (*Khrushchev*, p. 175.)

12. Mikoyan is reported to have declared to a local party meeting in December 1964: "You have heard many good speeches by him, but the CC had to correct all these speeches, since during the course of a speech he would depart from the theme and talk about a lot extra that was not written in the text." And Mikoyan also observed: "The transition to the Seven-Year Plan also took place abnormally. When the planning organs had prepared the draft of the Seven-Year Plan, Khrushchev told Satiukov to publish this draft in *Pravda* without its preliminary discussion in the Presidium of the CC and at a plenum. Thus, the CC was confronted by the fait accompli of publication of the draft, and there was nothing left for the CC to do but approve it." (*Politicheskii dnevnik* [Amsterdam: The Alexander Herzen Foundation, 1972], pp. 6–8.) According to the Medvedevs, at the time of the Twenty-second Party Congress "the preliminary version of Khrushchev's speech that had been approved by the Party Presidium did not include any mention of these new and even more shocking disclosures of Stalin's crimes." (*Khrushchev*, p. 146.)

13. Medvedev and Medvedev, *Khrushchev*, p. 21, and *Politicheskii dnevnik*, p. 15.

14. Medvedev and Medvedev, *Khrushchev*, p. 76.

15. The emphasis placed here on Khrushchev's communications behavior is justified by the fact that — as far as I am aware — he was never accused of actually countermanding substantive decisions of the Presidium or of acting dictatorially in the literal sense of the word. The truth seems to be that after June 1957 the other members of the Presidium may have grumbled, or even vigorously resisted various Khrushchev initiatives, but in the end did not persist in their objections and collectively consented to what Khrushchev wanted to do. Individually, they "went along to get along." The majority of them had risen to Presidium membership under Khrushchev's aegis and none of them apparently had been willing to put his own job on the line by unequivocally breaking with Khrushchev on policy or procedural

grounds. Thus, a basic reason why the new leadership had even less desire than the post-Stalin leadership to face up to the question, "Where were you when all this happened?" was that it really had no answer. This is why, in justifying nondisclosure of the charges against Khrushchev, Brezhnev allegedly stated: "We should not pour muck on ourselves." (Medvedev and Medvedev, *Khrushchev*, p. 176.)

16. See Leonard Schapiro, "The General Department of the CC of the CPSU," *Survey* 21, no. 3 (Summer 1975): 58 ff.

17. Hodnett, "Succession Contingencies," p. 5.

18. T. H. Rigby, "The Soviet Regional Leadership: The Brezhnev Generation," mimeo (December 1976), p. 20.

19. Included here are D. F. Ustinov (secretary for defense industry, 1965, and minister of defense, 1976); V. A. Kirillin (deputy chairman of the Council of Ministers and chairman of the State Committee for Science and Technology, 1965); L. V. Smirnov (deputy chairman of the Council of Ministers and chairman of the Military-Industrial Commission, 1965); N. V. Goldin (minister of construction of heavy industry enterprises, 1967); S. A. Zverev (minister of the defense industry, 1965); A. I. Shokin (minister of the electronics industry, 1965); S. A. Afans'ev (minister of general machine building, 1965); K. N. Rudnev (minister of instrument making, automation equipment, and control systems, 1965); V. V. Bakhirev (minister of machine building, 1968); A. I. Kostousov (minister of the machine tool and tool building industry, 1965); E. P. Slavskii (minister of medium machine building, 1965.)

20. These include F. D. Kulakov (secretary for agriculture, 1965) and M. S. Solomentsev (secretary for heavy industry, 1966 — but probably not in fact an unconditional supporter of Brezhnev) in the Secretariat; N. I. Savinkin (head of the Administrative Organs Department, 1968), K. V. Rusakov (head of the Department for Relations with Communist and Workers Parties of Socialist Countries, 1968), P. K. Sizov (head of the Light Industry Department, 1965), and V. I. Stepakov (head of the Propaganda Department, 1965) in the Central Committee apparatus; and G. S. Zolotukhin (minister of procurement, 1973), A. M. Shkol'nikov (chairman of the People's Control Committee, 1974), and Iu. V. Andropov (chairman of the KGB, 1967) in the Council of Ministers.

21. Those who served under Kirilenko include Ia. P. Riabov (secretary for defense industry and administrative organs, appointed in 1976 and released in 1979) in the Secretariat and G. A. Karavaev (minister of construction, 1967) and F. T. Ermash (chairman of the State Committee for Cinematography, 1972) in the Council of Ministers. Kirilenko nominees probably include V. I. Dolgikh (secretary for heavy industry, 1972) and K. F. Katushev (secretary for bloc relations, 1968) in the Secretariat; I. N. Dmitriev (head of the Construction Department, 1969) in the Central Committee apparatus; perhaps M. T. Efremov (deputy chairman of the Council of Ministers, 1965) in the Presidium of the Council of Ministers; and B. E. Shcherbina (minister of construction of petroleum and gas industry enterprises, 1973), A. M. Tokarev (minister of industrial construction, 1967), K. N. Beliak (minister of machine building for animal husbandry and fodder production, 1973), and S. D. Khitrov (minister of rural construction, 1967). Another nominee is possibly V. M. Chebrikov (deputy chairman of the KGB, 1968).

22. Jerry F. Hough, "The Brezhnev Era: The Man and the System," *Problems of Communism* 25, no. 2 (March-April 1976):6.

23. See Grey Hodnett, "Ukrainian Politics and the Purge of Shelest" (Paper for the annual meeting of the Midwest Slavic Conference, Ann Arbor, Michigan, 5-7 May 1977).

24. See Boris Rabbot, "Ouster of rival shows Brezhnev is serious about detente," *The Globe and Mail* (Toronto), 30 June 1977, reprinted from *The Christian Science Monitor*. Rabbot's description of Podgornyi's foreign policy preferences tallies well with my reconstruction of the views of Podgornyi's client, Petr Shelest (see "Ukrainian Politics and the Purge of Shelest," pp. 33 ff.).

25. On the Presidium of the Supreme Soviet see Shugo Minagawa, *Presidia and Standing Commissions of the Federal and Republican Supreme Soviets in the USSR 1958*-1972 (Ph.D. diss., The Australian National University, 1973); and "The Functions of the Supreme Soviet Organs, and Problems of Their Institutional Development," *Soviet Studies* 27, no. 1 (January 1975):46-70.

26. *XXV s'ezd Kommunisticheskoi Partii Sovetskogo Soiuza, stenograficheskii otchet*, vol. 1 (Moscow, 1976), pp. 91-92.

27. *Pravda*, 18 February 1977. It is interesting to note that the decisions that emerged from the discussion were presented as decisions of the Central Committee.

28. *Pravda*, 22 March 1977.

29. The Presidium of the Council of Ministers is said to meet each week. See Alain Jacob, "The Soviet System," *The Guardian*, 2 March 1974, p. 15.

30. See T. H. Rigby, "The Soviet Communist Party and the Scientific and Technical Revolution," in T. H. Rigby and R. F. Miller, *Political and Administrative Aspects of the Scientific and Technical Revolution in the USSR* (Occasional Paper no. 11, Department of Political Science, Research School of Social Sciences, Australian National University, Canberra, 1976), pp. 39-42. It might be noted that Kirilenko has attended and, on occasion, addressed meetings of the entire Council of Ministers. See *Pravda*, 18 January 1977 and 26 January 1978.

31. See T. H. Rigby, "The Soviet Government under Kosygin," mimeo (June 1976), pp. 20-21.

32. *XXV s'ezd*, p. 91.

33. *New York Times*, 15 June 1973.

34. *Le Monde*, 12 February 1974, p. 1. The translation of this passage in *The Guardian* of 2 March 1974 is incorrect.

35. Raymond L. Garthoff, "SALT and the Soviet Military," *Problems of Communism* 24, no. 1 (January-February 1975):29.

36. For example, see the statements in *Pravda* on 2 and 3 December 1976 approving Brezhnev's trips to Yugoslavia and Rumania in November.

37. It also appears that Brezhnev likes to work informally with formal members of the leadership. Jacob reports that the members of this "Kremlin coterie" include the deputy head of the International Department of the CC, Vadim Zagladin, Katushev (now demoted to the Presidium of the Council of Ministers), Gromyko, Kirilenko, Patolichev, and Dolgikh — "they are all men personally trusted by the 'boss.' Meetings of this circle," Jacob continues, "can occasionally be very relaxed with people showing up in shirt-sleeves or sweaters; and they do not necessarily

meet in the Kremlin nor in the austere Central Committee building on Moscow's Staraya Square." (*The Guardian*, 2 March 1974).

38. Rigby, "The Soviet Government under Kosygin," pp. 22–23.

39. Thomas W. Wolfe, "Military Power and Soviet Policy," in Griffith, ed., *The Soviet Empire*, p. 157.

40. N. A. Petrovichev, ed., *Partiinoe stroitel'stvo*, 4th rev. ed. (Moscow, 1976), p. 154. Specifically, this handbook notes: "In the 1948–1953 period there existed a permanent commission of the Politburo for foreign policy questions; in 1953 and in 1962–1966 a permanent ideological commission of the CC; in the period 1956–1959 a permanent commission on problems of ideology, culture and international party ties, which held regular meetings and kept its own minutes. At different times permanent commissions on military (defense) and organizational-party questions have operated.

If the creation of permanent commissions has been a comparatively rare phenomenon, the organization of temporary commissions for reviewing and solving individual questions or preparing proposals has been and is widely applied in the activity of all organs of the Central Committee. Commissions have been created on military questions, work in the countryside, questions relating to the cooperatives, various problems of the development of industry, transport, construction, trade, etc." (p. 154).

41. Garthoff, "SALT and the Soviet Military," p. 29.

42. Ibid. Another author lists as probable members Brezhnev, Podgornyi, Kosygin, Kirilenko, Suslov, and Ustinov. (Harriet Fast Scott, "The Soviet High Command," *Air Force Magazine*, March 1977, p. 53.)

43. See William E. Odom, "Who Controls Whom in Moscow," *Foreign Policy*, no. 19 (Summer 1975), pp. 120–121. Douglas Garthoff has also observed: "The historical precedent of a Soviet state defense committee and the likely presence of [those leaders holding the top party, government, and state posts] suggest that it may be a super-coordinating body." But he goes on to argue that a more plausible interpretation would be to view the Defense Council as an instrument used by Brezhnev to constrain the discussion of military issues in the full Politburo: "[Although] political considerations introduced in the Politburo would broaden the scope of discussion, the actual policy options would be narrower than if no Defense Council stage had occurred. By leaving the final approval to the Poltiburo, the Defense Council would not actually challenge the authority of the Politburo, including its non-defense expert members (e.g., Suslov), as the top policy-making body." (Douglas Garthoff, "The Soviet Military and Arms Control," Center for Arms Control and International Security, UCLA, ACIS Working Paper no. 10 November 1977, pp. 14–15.)

44. Jerry F. Hough, "Soviet Succession—Challenge for Kremlin and the U.S.," *The Guardian*, 1 May 1977, p. 15.

45. These include: (1) competition for supreme power; (2) a qualitative acceleration of power-oriented factional conflict in the leadership; (3) re-orientation of leaders toward their elite power bases; (4) intensification of high-level "party/state" conflict; (5) inability of the leadership to take decisive necessary policy actions; (6) change in the dominance relationship between the leadership and lower ad-

ministrative agencies; (7) weakening of influence by the party apparatus over other institutions in the society; (8) general loosening of social controls; (9) possible transformation of the political system. Only (1) and (2) *must* occur in "succession crises"; the remaining features *may* occur, depending on the way in which the crisis is resolved. "Crisis," it should be noted, thus refers to *potential* as well as actual instability, to a "state of affairs in which a decisive change *could* occur." (Myron Rush, *Political Succession in the USSR,* 2d ed. [New York: Columbia University Press, 1968], p. 72.) (My emphasis)

46. As "A. Pravdin's" account of the rise and fall of the Information Sector of the CC apparatus demonstrates, one must not assume that there is anything automatic about the solicitation or reception of information at the top. (See A. Pravdin and Mervyn Matthews, "An Interview with a CPSU Functionary," *Survey* 20, no. 4 [Autumn 1974]:97–98.)

47. More information on June 1957 and October 1964 would be highly desirable, but the latest account available (Medvedev and Medvedev, *Khrushchev,* ch. 15) does, I believe, strongly support my reconstruction of the role of force in the ouster of Khrushchev (see: "Notes and Views," *Problems of Communism* 24, no. 4 [July-August 1975]: 87–88).

48. The key elements in the implicit conventional definition are (a) the presence of some sort of juridically binding rules, usually thought of as statutory in form; (b) the "regulation" by these rules of relationships among organizations and occupants of leadership roles; (c) fixity of the "regulated" relationships over time; (d) overt articulation and public awareness of these rules; and (e) availability to the public of information indicating observance or violation of these rules. Where the stipulated elements obtain, leadership relationships are said to be endowed with "legitimacy." Where they do not obtain, leadership relationships are considered both illegitimate and arbitrary—in the sense of being based upon the purely discretionary use by all concerned of any and all efficacious power resources, including physical and "ideological" violence.

There are conceptual objections to this definition. It is not "constitutionally" articulated rules that in fact "regulate" leadership behavior, but understanding on the part of leaders either that they ought to observe the rules or that failure to do so is likely to be visited with painful consequences. Not printed words, but the certainty that sufficient legislators were prepared to use the relevant constitutional provision and vote for his impeachment led Nixon to resign.

Second, the "legitimacy" of leadership arrangements does not inhere in formal statements about these arrangements, but in the eyes of observers of them. Perceptions of "legitimacy" can vary, and the extent to which legitimization is a function of formalization is a problem. But if we disregard these objections and employ the package of five criteria listed above, we would have to declare straightaway that institutionalization has never existed within the Soviet leadership, does not exist at the present, and is most unlikely to exist in the foreseeable future.

The notion of juridically binding rules that "legally" constrain the political behavior of leaders has little basis in Russian historical experience and stands in complete opposition to Leninist doctrine and the practice of "Communist construction" from 1917 to the present. The discrepancy between various articles of the

Party Rules and established practice is a matter of commonplace observation, and the concept of "regulation" implies the existence of some type of juridical mechanism superordinate to the political decision makers, the existence of which would be fundamentally and immediately incompatible with the entire Soviet system of rule. And publicity of actual leadership relations is completely antithetical to the in camera practice characteristic of decision making at all levels in the Communist party.

49. "Institutionalization occurs wherever there is a reciprocal typification of habitualized actions by types of actors. Restated, any such typification is an institution. What must be stressed is the reciprocity of institutional typifications and the typicality of not only the actions but also the actors in institutions." (Peter L. Berger and Thomas Luckmann, *The Social Construction of Reality: A Treatise in the Sociology of Knowledge* [New York: Doubleday & Co., 1967], p. 54.)

50. "Legitimization" can be thought of as an attempt to "explain" a particular pattern of role performance knowledge by setting it within some broader framework of meaning (see ibid., pp. 92 ff.). Looking at "legitimization" in this way emphasizes — in contrast to Parsonian-influenced social science — the fusion of cognitive, judgmental, and emotive elements in practical human knowledge. As Berger and Luckmann observe: "It is important to understand that legitimation has a cognitive as well as a normative element. In other words, legitimation is not just a matter of 'values.' It always implies 'knowledge' as well. . . . Legitimation not only tells the individual why he *should* perform one action and not another; it also tells him why things *are* not what they are. In other words, 'knowledge' precedes 'values' in the legitimation of institutions." (Ibid., pp. 93–94.)

51. Medvedev and Medvedev, *Khrushchev*, p. 175.

52. See Alexander Yanov, *Detente After Brezhnev: The Domestic Roots of Soviet Foreign Policy* (Berkeley: Institute of International Studies, University of California, 1977). Also see Albert L. Salter, "Portrait of an Emerging Soviet Elite Generation," in Dimitri K. Simes et al., *Soviet Succession: Leadership in Transition* (Beverly Hills, Calif.: Sage Publications, 1978), pp. 26–31.

53. See Hodnett, "Ukrainian Politics and the Purge of Shelest," p. 41.

54. For an elaborate argument emphasizing the possibility of an evolution toward "Russian Nazism" see Yanov, *Detente After Brezhnev.*

55. See Michel Tatu, "Decision Making in the USSR," in Richard Pipes, ed., *Soviet Strategy in Europe* (New York: Crane, Russak & Co., 1976), p. 62.

5
The Impact of the Military
on Soviet Society

Timothy J. Colton

"The Army is a part of Soviet society and is nurtured by it not only materially but spiritually. In the Army are reflected all those socioeconomic and ideological-political processes taking place in society."[1] In these words a major Soviet text clearly states the first lesson a Western observer grasps about the military — that it must be understood as a part of the whole Soviet social and political system. While it has many of the universal characteristics of military organizations (and of all bureaucracies), its molding by unique and often paradoxical circumstances must never be forgotten. It is the largest peacetime army in history yet the leader who presided over its founding had opposed standing military forces until weeks before coming to power, and six decades later his writings are cited to support indefinite accumulation of military "might." The army is subject to strict civilian control (as official pronouncements never tire in declaring) yet the country's foremost civilian recently arranged to acquire, in his seventieth year, the military rank of marshal. The army uses the latest in nuclear and electronic technology yet the press routinely describes shortages of fresh fruit, footwear, and shower facilities in military garrisons.

The purpose of this chapter is to explore the military's effect on the overall social and political order by which it so obviously has been shaped, and in particular its effects on those aspects of society that influence foreign policy. This is a question of clear and present significance, both for our overall understanding of Soviet reality and for the formulation of Western foreign policies. The last decade has seen not only a general increase in Western interest in Soviet military affairs but also an introduction into journalistic, academic, and government discussion of themes reminiscent of the notion of "Red militarism" that flourished between the wars.

The Military and Society: Western Views

In the past Western scholars have tended to be more interested in the substance of Soviet military policy than in political and social processes in which the army is involved. Inasmuch as such processes have been analyzed, the dominant concern has been with relations between the military and the ruling Communist party and the overwhelming consensus has been that these relations are basically adversarial. The military's quest for autonomy is said to clash with party desires for complete hegemony over all potential rivals, thereby resulting in deep-seated and irresolvable conflict. In the words of Roman Kolkowicz, "The relationship between the Communist Party and the Soviet military is essentially conflict-prone and thus presents a perennial threat to the political stability of the Soviet state."[2] This antagonism is thought to be resolved in the party's favor principally through bureaucratic control mechanisms (the most important of which is the party's apparatus within the military, the main political administration), but even these controls do not prevent aspects of the conflict from surfacing.

This interpretation has recently been seriously questioned by some scholars. In an ambitious and widely read essay published in 1973, William Odom argued that "value congruence rather than conflict" characterizes army-party relations, and he drew attention to linkages between the two institutions and to symbiotic aspects of their relationship.[3] The present author has found the original model to be particularly misleading when applied to the behavior of the military party apparatus, whose officials have tended, contrary to earlier predictions, to function on most political issues as allies rather than adversaries of military commanders. Rarely does one see sharp lines drawn between an army seeking autonomy and a party wishing to maximize control, or between the military command and the political organs tied to the civilian leadership. Rather, consensus and cleavage normally cut across institutional boundaries and involve coalitions primarily based on location and including *both* military commanders and party officials.[4]

Such a pattern of horizontal linkages between party officials and specialized elites, far from being unique, probably applies to many other particularized groups and issue-areas. For example, in the field of industrial management managers and party workers are in basic agreement on overall goals, and on individual questions most conflicts "arise between one group of industrial and party officials who support one project and another group of industrial and party officials who support another project."[5]

The question that Odom has raised in his more recent work is whether the specific tendency toward civil-military "congruence" and interpenetration is found with regard to issues *other* than specialized military ones. In a 1976 article Odom points to what he calls "the militarization of Soviet society." Concentrating on civil defense, basic military training, and paramilitary programs since 1967, he draws a picture of a society in which military values and institutions increasingly permeate all aspects of life. Odom's views about exactly *who* is managing the militarization process are somewhat unclear. At times he speaks in general terms of the regime as a whole "organizing the civil society to support the military," and implies that it is soldiers themselves—the professional military establishment, as organized in the Ministry of Defense—who are appropriating an ever greater role.[6]

We have then an approach that—particularly in versions lacking the subtlety of Odom's—conceives of the military's social impact in terms almost diametrically opposed to traditional ones. Kolkowicz's army exerts a sharply limited impact on Soviet society as a whole, its influence being circumscribed by the party's controls and tendency to "Regard any increment in the military's prerogatives and authority as its own loss and therefore as a challenge."[7] In Odom's conception, on the other hand, soldiers and their values, with party encouragement, are acquiring more influence.

This chapter will present somewhat of a middle course. It will concur with Odom that military and civilian elites share certain fundamental objectives and interests as well as commitments to major defense programs. However, it will also strive toward greater specificity in identifying issues on which the military affects policy outcomes and the means by which this influence is exerted. The army's impact on society will be examined in terms of three major roles—agent, educator, and claimant—and tentative conclusions will be drawn regarding trends in its overall influence and implications for foreign policy.

The Military as Agent

The most important role Soviet military officers play is that of administrative agents of civilian politicians. This is the dominant image of the military in the rudimentary Soviet theory on civil-military relations. "The Soviet commander," according to the leading text on military strategy, "is the representative of the party and people. He carries out their will and implements party policy in the forces."[8] The line of vertical subordination (extending from party leadership through the successive command and staff layers of the Ministry of Defense) is an obvious and straightforward one.

Perhaps less obvious is what the agent role implies for the military's effect on Soviet society. First, it means that officers exercise a great deal of delegated authority over the lives of a large number of subordinates, including the several million young men (most of them aged eighteen to twenty) serving as conscript soldiers and sailors. One half of all Soviet youths undergo compulsory military service, a proportion that has been considerably higher in the past and will probably increase in the future. For several years their work, social, and even sleep habits are regulated by officers whose orders are, as military regulations state crisply, law (*zakon*) for their subordinates. Under officers' direction they operate a vast and intricate system of activity that includes an enormous store of fighting equipment and most of the facilities needed to train, police, clothe, house, feed, transport, heal, clean, counsel, and entertain the men who make the equipment work.[9]

The vast majority of the officers who exercise this authority are members of the party or Komsomol (this is especially true in troop command posts and almost universally at ranks of major and above), and the military hierarchy is saturated with a network of appointed and voluntary party agencies. Yet this has never made the army anything other than an organization whose prime purpose is to prepare for, wage, and win armed conflict. Even the military party organs' activity has for most of their history been tailored to military purposes. Soviet officers are soldiers of the party, but they are soldiers nonetheless. They leave their imprint upon their temporary charges as surely as do their counterparts in other armies.

Not only has the party delegated to the military a mission and the authority to perform it, it has also assigned consummate importance to that function. In the belief that defense is, as Stalin said, "the primary task for us,"[10] the regime has created an innovative and productive infrastructure for the military effort — a military-industrial complex, to use the phrase the Soviets often apply to other countries. This system, undoubtedly "the most privileged segment" of the economy,[11] is best seen as registering the impact of military *goals* — as defined by a basically civilian leadership — rather than of the military *establishment*. But the requirements of their administrative mission do bring Soviet officers into contact with numerous other segments of society and of the governmental system.

For instance, military officials, usually in quite specialized agencies, participate as administrators in several areas of mainly civilian jurisdiction into which they have been allowed to extend their efforts to augment military capabilities. Several issue-areas stand out. In the field of construction, the military has long participated in extramilitary projects on a major scale, partly to enhance its own capacity and partly to compensate for civilian deficiencies. Soldiers (usually specially drafted construction troops) build telephone lines, housing, office and other public buildings, and irrigation facilities.[12] In the area of transport, too, construction has been a major activity. Since 1945 specialized railroad troops have laid about a thousand kilometers of track a year and have built hundreds of bridges and other structures; they are currently responsible for the eastern sector of the massive Baikal-Amur Railroad project.[13] All facets of military and civilian transport were tightly integrated during World War II, and even in peacetime complex arrangements exist to coordinate use of rail lines, airports, canals, harbors, and other facilities.

Officers also seek to secure specific contributions to their delegated mission from a number of civilian organizations, a fact that implies some military participation in realms of decision entrusted primarily to civilians. The ties with the other parts of the military-industrial complex (scientific institutes, defense production ministries, planning bodies) are often mentioned in Western research. There has been rather less heed paid to collaboration concerning civil defense, civil aviation, maritime navigation, and diplomatic representation abroad. Almost nothing has been written about how the army deals at several levels with civilians providing it with routine goods and services. Its headquarters negotiate agreements with the Ministry of Agriculture (for use of farmland), the Ministry of Oil Refining and Petrochemical Industry (for fuel and lubricants), food-processing ministries, and the Ministry of Trade, Ministry of Light Industry, and other consumer goods producers (for supply of clothing, consumer durables, and other items). At the local level, housing is sometimes leased from civilian authorities, contacts are made with party and government authorities during disaster relief operations and harvest campaigns, conscription call-ups entail close communication with local health and school officials, and annual contracts are made with republican and local agencies for supply of perishable foods, leisure and sporting equipment, household appliances and chemicals, and a range of other commodities.

The Military as Educator

Implicit in its role as the regime's principal agent in military policy is the army's role as educator. Any peacetime army is essentially an educational organization, teaching citizens how to apply violence in the interests of the state. Yet the role of educator is so important in Soviet military theory and practice and so central to any discussion of the military's impact on society that it merits separate consideration.

Much of the education that occurs within the Soviet military would be familiar to conscripts in other armies: the drill, technical instruction, field exercises, and the like. What is striking about Soviet military training is its deliberate interweaving with a system of ideological and moral upbringing (*vospitanie*). Since the Civil War, Soviet theorists have argued that the train-

ing of the good soldier is inseparable from the forming of the good citizen
and that wars are won by the side that can field the soldier "who is able in
the most difficult of conditions to maintain his high moral spirit and will to
victory."[14] To this end all servicemen are constantly bombarded with
political information and exhortation, most of it administered by the
political organs. Each man attends four hours a week of obligatory political
classes and an additional hour of "political information." About 80 percent
of all troops are members of the Komsomol (70 percent are already
members when conscripted), and a much smaller proportion are party
members.[15] Cultural and recreational activity (supervised by the political
organs) is also laden with ideological content.

It is thus readily understandable that the army is referred to as a "school
of Communism," an arena for political socialization as well as specialized
military training. Indeed, in the first several decades of Soviet rule the
military was frequently heralded as the country's single most important
vehicle for this purpose. Stalin described it as "the sole . . . point of
assembly where people from various provinces and regions come together,
study, and are schooled in political life."[16] Thousands of servicemen,
especially from rural areas, received their first exposure to party ideas (not
to mention mass organization and machine technology) in the interwar
Red Army. The subsequent growth of the regime's systems of public education and communication has outdated any claim to preeminence, but
political training in the military remains an important thread in the overall
weave, "continuing the process of Communist education . . . begun in the
family, school, and productive process."[17] Because soldiers have already
been familiarized with the regime's basic values, the emphasis is now on
reinforcing and maintaining the desired attitudes against "nihilism and skepticism."[18]

During the last decade there has been an upsurge of official interest in
military service — in all its aspects — as an inculcator of civic virtue. One
now finds statements that the army provides "particularly favorable circumstances for organizing the entire business of upbringing."[19] At the
Twenty-fifth Party Congress in 1976, Leonid Brezhnev's only reference to
the military was in precisely this connection: "In speaking about educational work, comrades, it is impossible not to dwell on the enormous role
which the Soviet Army plays in this matter. Young men arrive in the
soldierly family with no experience in the school of life. But they return
from the Army already people who have gone through the school of tenacity
and discipline, who have acquired technical and professional knowledge
and political training."[20]

Two educational goals are now receiving emphasis. One is the development of such individual lines of character as "tenacity and discipline," which

military and party leaders alike often see as lacking in the generation born after 1945. The other reflects what may be an even deeper source of anxiety — the goal of solidarity among the Soviet Union's many nationalities. The army is clearly designed as an integrating and Russianizing institution. Russian is the sole language of instruction and command and facility in it is a prerequisite for admission to officers' schools. There is an "attempt to reinforce in every soldier the awareness of belonging to a single socialist Motherland, to a great international army."[21] Political officers operate "circles for the study of the Russian language" in some units, and they are urged to combat "elements of national conceit and harmful habits of seeing a national basis for every disagreement or personal insult."[22] This struggle will no doubt become more important as it becomes necessary to conscript larger numbers of non-Russians (particularly Central Asians) in future years.

The development of the last decade that has most caught the eye of foreign observers has been the perceptible increase in military and military-related education *outside* the army. This growth has occurred in three areas.

First, the revised military service law of 1967, while reducing active duty for most conscripts by one year, required all predraft-age youths to undergo basic military training (*nachal'naia voennaia podgotovka*) at their places of study or work. Introduced in stages from 1968 to the mid-1970s, the system placed military instructors (*voennye rukovoditeli*) — most of them reserve or retired officers — in secondary and vocational schools and major production enterprises. The two-year, 140-hour program covers military regulations, use of light weapons, drill, and a technical military specialty (usually operation of a vehicle). Since the early 1970s many postsecondary students (who normally receive draft deferments) have been required to attend courses in new military faculties. They ultimately are given reserve commissions and are thus liable to later call-up. In addition, the preinduction and other programs of DOSAAF (the Voluntary Society for Assistance of the Army, Air Force, and Navy) have continued to expand, particularly in the area of technical specialties. DOSAAF's capital expenditures increased by almost 60 percent from 1972 through 1976, and by 1977 it was claiming a membership of 80 million — two-thirds of the entire adult population.[23]

A second area of growth has been the civil defense program, which has acquired greater visibility and perhaps a higher degree of coordination. Civil defense themes have been more prominent in the mass media and in specialized publications, and since 1971 they have been included in curricula for all second- and fifth-grade pupils. The program of instruction in factories and other workplaces was standardized in 1972 (at twenty hours of nonworking time a year for each employee), and both large-scale exercises and specialized courses for officials have become more common.[24]

Third, the regime has placed greater emphasis on the general "military-patriotic education" of the population, particularly the young. The commemoration of past martial exploits, especially the "Great Patriotic War" of 1941–1945, reached a crescendo with the celebration of the thirtieth anniversary of victory in 1975. In the five years 1972–1976, 80 major war monuments were unveiled; from 1974 to 1976, more than 500 books and 300 serialized novels and short stories on the war were published in Russian alone.[25] Perhaps the major innovation has been in terms of participatory and organized forms of inculcation for young people. These various activities include "red pathfinders" clubs, which mount excursions to monuments and battlefields; groups of "young friends" of the army and navy; and military-patriotic "schools" and "universities" (most of them attached to elementary or secondary schools or to DOSAAF clubs). Most ambitious have been the two "military-sports games" organized by the major youth federations — *Zarnitsa* (Summer Lightning) for Young Pioneers (aged 10 to 15), claiming 16 million participants by 1972;and the Komsomol's *Orlenok* (Eaglet), established only in 1972 and, as of 1976, claiming 8 million participants in their later teens.[26]

In terms of sheer ambition and energy, all of these programs warrant further attention from Western scholars. But would such attention establish that Soviet society is being "militarized" and in particular that the power of the military itself is growing? Here a number of cautions are in order.

To begin, one should be careful not to overstate the innovativeness of some of this activity. Preinduction training in the schools does mark a major change (although one accompanied by another change — shorter terms for conscripts — which markedly reduces the exposure of most young men to active military service). Civil defense, on the other hand, dates in its current form from 1961 and, indeed, grew out of a local air defense network established in 1932; the 1972 directive on workplace instruction did not necessarily imply an increased effort, merely a set of minimum standards.[27] DOSAAF, too, has a long history (its predecessors were founded in the 1920s). And military-patriotic propaganda and education are by no means a recent creation. If 80 monuments were built between 1972 and 1976, in 1966 there were already 675 military monuments and memorials in the Ural Military District alone (an area in which no land battles were fought during World War II).[28] The entire military-patriotic program is fundamentally backward-looking, an attempt to foster by deliberate government effort feelings that for earlier generations emerged more spontaneously from experience. Even tributes to the plethora of war novels protest that authors are now more likely to slight martial themes than in the past.

In the second place, it should be realized that many of the measures reviewed here have complex objectives, and that at least some are essentially used to shape civilian society in accordance with the preferences of civilian leaders and in ways that go beyond merely heightening military capability. This is especially true of military-patriotic education, in which several kinds of values that have long been important to the civilian elite — discipline, nationalism, and respect for past achievements — are at the very heart of the process. It is certainly significant that the regime has chosen the army and the military idiom as the focus for the effort, but it is true nonetheless that broader civilian purposes prevail. Nationalism is heavily stressed in the program, particularly in non-Russian republics (where it is often referred to as "internationalist" as well as military-patriotic). The appeal to the accomplishments and heroes of the past is an omnipresent theme (to the point that a story can refer to long-dead revolutionaries and soldiers as "standing invisibly" in a Komsomol honor guard at a monument).[29] Here, too, the ideals being promoted far transcend the military realm.

A third pitfall to avoid is confusion of the objectives and exertions of the programs with their actual impact on society. Militarizing government programs do not necessarily mean a militarized society, any more than a "war on poverty" in the United States automatically implies greater equality.

Quantitative descriptions of the programs should be treated with great care. It is useful to know that 85,000 young people a year took part in the red pathfinders movement in Turkmenistan in 1971–1972; that 2,000 children and teenagers attended summer military-sports camps in Latvia in 1972 and 16,000 were enrolled in military-patriotic schools in Belorussia in 1973; or that in the summer of 1975, 30,000 students from Dnepropetrovsk oblast visited local monuments and another 8,000 went on excursions to four "hero cities."[30] What none of these figures indicates (and what Western analysts rarely seek out) is the ratio of participants to eligible populations. The 1970 census makes clear that in these cases the participants amounted, respectively, to 17.6, 0.6, 0.9, 7.5, and 2.0 percent of the relevant populations (aged ten to nineteen) — proportions that imply far less substantial impact than the absolute numbers might intimate at first glance.

Even where quantitative saturation is indisputably high (as with DOSAAF and the Zarnitsa and Orlenok games, which between them involve half of the ten-to-nineteen-year-olds), no analysis can refrain from raising questions about program quality and effect. While this is not the place for detailed examination, it should be noted that no serious Soviet discussion of the programs fails to pose such questions.

Basic military training is a partial exception here, at least in the secondary schools; despite construction and other problems, it seems to have produced the desired effect. Nonetheless, even a favorable Soviet overview must conclude that the program "suffices only to acquaint students with the general structure of [a military] machine, with its most important features and basic operating principles. To put it briefly . . . students acquire elementary knowledge and habits concerning only a single military-technical specialty."[31] Soviet evaluations of nonschool programs are often much less positive. Reviews of civil defense preparations refer to "formalism and vulgarization" and remark on officials "who 'forget' about civil defense, justifying this by their preoccupation with production affairs"; reports about both basic training and civil defense mention "indifference" in building and maintaining basic facilities; a speech on war novels scores their "primitiveness" and facile moralizing; and stories tell of participants in military-patriotic projects being assembled from predetermined lists (*po spisku*).[32] The bloated DOSAAF network has been excoriated for similar sins for decades, and this evidence is reinforced by the private testimony of present and former Soviet citizens and the obvious absurdity of some of DOSAAF's self-appraisals.[33] If Zarnitsa and Orlenok seem to be more efficacious, it is probably because they are firmly rooted in the schools; most competitions take place on school grounds (under Pioneer and Komsomol auspices), and only a small proportion of competitors seem to participate in the regional and national games in midsummer.

The fourth and final qualification regarding these programs has to do with their relation to the power of the military itself. Militarizing programs — even a militarizing society — may go hand in hand with greater political power for the professional military, but in the Soviet Union under Brezhnev there is little evidence that they have.

Basic military training, to take the first area, is formally a responsibility of civilian ministries of education, all of which have departments for that purpose. Military instructors are appointed and dismissed by local education departments on recommendation of the school director and with the consent of the local military commissariat. They are paid by the schools and responsible to their directors. In 1972, after receiving letters from several military instructors recommending that they be subordinated to military commissariats rather than to civilian school authorities, the deputy minister of education in charge of the national program dismissed the suggestions as being "so obviously [mistaken] as hardly to warrant comment." The deputy minister went on to observe: "The school must not be transformed into the likeness of a troop subunit. The Soviet school has its own regulations and educational traditions, which the military instructor is obliged to observe."[34]

DOSAAF, which plays a substantial role in several military-related areas, is not under immediate control of the army. It finances its own operations—with considerable difficulty, as many accounts clearly show—from membership dues, lotteries, charges for sports events, and a variety of recreation services. Military officials do not seem to be involved in DOSAAF's perennial campaigns to persuade local authorities to implement the vague guidelines on assistance to the organization's construction efforts.[35]

The fact that civil defense has a uniformed national chief (*nachal'nik*)—currently General of the Army Aleksandr T. Altunin, who has since 1972 also been a deputy defense minister—seems to imply more concerted penetration of civilian society by the military. Yet one should be careful about inferring the "dominant administrative role of the Ministry of Defense"[36] from Altunin's dual appointment (his predecessor had similar status from 1961 to 1964) or on any other grounds. At republican and local levels, the civil defense chief is invariably the civilian chairman of the relevant council of ministers or municipal council. While most administrative responsibility probably lies with their full-time chiefs of staff, who are professional officers, the fact that civilians remain formally in charge is noteworthy and underlines the regime's intention to keep implementation of the program at least partly in nonmilitary hands. Official pronouncements refer to civil defense as being "under the leadership of the [local] Party and Soviet organs" and describe "constant attention" to it on the part of local party executives.[37] No such statement would ever be made about operations within army jurisdiction, which are essentially outside the purview of local politicians.[38] At the plant level, the chief of civil defense is the enterprise director and the part-time chief of staff is one of the director's line subordinates, often an engineer and sometimes a man with minor military experience. All formations within the enterprise are created by order of the director, and they are explicitly characterized as nonmilitarized (*nevoenizirovannye*) groups. A number of other civilian organizations participate in civil defense planning and exercises—including the Komsomol, Red Cross, railroads, medical and sanitation services, electrical and gas utilities, sports organizations, and territorial planning agencies—and the evidence suggests that whatever coordination is imposed comes from civilian authorities rather than from the military.[39]

A similar situation applies to military-patriotic education. Active and retired military officers, political organs, and occasionally military units are involved in program implementation, but planning is subject to local party control.[40] The Komsomol is actively involved (all its committees have departments for sport and mass defense work), as are the Pioneers, sports organizations, trade unions, ministries and departments of culture, *Znanie* (the mass information organization), school administrators, and the

Academy of Pedagogical Sciences. At best, the military is a partner in a program dominated by civilians and using military values to achieve largely civilian ends.

The Military as Claimant

Besides participating in (and often monopolizing) political decisions within the military establishment, Soviet officers also take part in a variety of decisions together with civilian politicians and administrators. In doing so, they often put forward claims for recognition and resources in much the same manner as bureaucratic officials elsewhere in the Soviet system.

Clearly their main resource with national leaders is their status as specialists and experts worthy of consultation. Even Stalin, when confronted by specialized military decisions, "repeatedly asked, 'What does the General Staff think?' or, 'Has the General Staff examined this question?' And the General Staff always gave its opinion."[41] Since the early 1960s official statements have been much more explicit than before in referring to consultation as routine: "Before deciding one way or the other on questions of military development, the Party Central Committee and Politburo carefully study the state of affairs in the Army and Navy and consult with the high command and the most important specialists of the Armed Forces."[42]

Consultation is formalized to some extent through military membership in bodies such as the Council of Ministers, the Defense Council (a collegium for discussing military policy, currently chaired by General Secretary Brezhnev), and the Military-Industrial Commission, which deals with defense production. The military is also represented on the formal decision-making organs of the party. The thirty military members and candidates on the 1976 Central Committee (7 percent of the total) made up by far the largest contingent from any bureaucratic constituency. At the peak level, most Politburos prior to 1955 contained one nonprofessional defense administrator (Trotsky, Frunze, Voroshilov, Bulganin). Since then there have been two experiments to seat a defense minister who was also a professional soldier (Georgii Zhukov in 1956–1957 and Andrei Grechko in the three years before his death in April 1976). Grechko's successor, Dmitrii F. Ustinov (a civilian Politburo member who has spent almost his entire career dealing with defense production, most recently as party secretary), marks at least a temporary reversion to the pre-1955 pattern and shows that the professional military can in no way view a Politburo seat as an institutional entitlement. Military officers sit on lower-level party organs as well. As of the early 1970s individual officers belonged to seven of fourteen republican bureaus, an average of eight sat on republican central committees, and there was substantial representation at the local level.

Less formalized channels are probably of equal importance (as is true for all bureaucratic claimants in Soviet politics). Marshal Grechko, for example, is said to have attended Politburo discussions on military matters even before his elevation to that body,[43] and war memoirs depict similar informal interaction. Some officers seem to have benefitted from personal connections with civilian politicians based on friendship and common experience (Grechko is said to have had such a relationship with Brezhnev). One can also assume the existence of less personalized linkages with civilians involved in defense research and production. As in most consultative relationships, there has been no sharp line drawn between advice solicited by civilians and prodding at the military's own initiative. Khrushchev may have grumbled in his memoirs about military "pressure" or even "intimidation" of the party leadership, but there is no evidence he sought to prevent soldiers from speaking their minds on military issues. "I don't reproach the military for that—they're only doing their job."[44]

The Soviet military is denied some of the bargaining resources available to its counterpart in the United States. In particular, the structural primacy of the party executive has precluded the direct appeals to an independent legislature encountered in the United States. Nonetheless, some structural factors clearly work in the Soviet officers' favor. Special weight is lent to their counsel by the fact that their expertise is not widely shared outside the military establishment. Notwithstanding party, KGB, and defense industry involvement in some aspects of military affairs (and the evident growth of military competence in several civilian research institutes over the last decade), the Soviet officer corps does seem to control far more of the information relevant to its mission than do armies in Western societies. The Soviet system does not contain the major nonmilitary sources of military information found in U.S. politics—there is no equivalent to the Central Intelligence Agency or to private consulting firms such as the RAND Corporation.

Officers' status as claimants on the leadership is also reinforced by the high degree of instability and danger that civilians have perceived as inhering in the international milieu, the environment in which military decisions take effect. The tendency of Soviet leaders to resolve uncertainty in foreign policy on the side of safety has clearly made them more receptive to military advice than to that of most other expert groups. Khrushchev's remarks to President Eisenhower in 1959 display this receptivity as well:

> Some people from our military department come and say, "Comrade Khrushchev, look at this! The Americans are developing such and such a system. We could develop the same system, but it would cost such and such."

I tell them there's no money; it's all been allotted already. So they say, "If we don't get the money we need and if there's a war, then the enemy will have superiority over us." So we discuss it some more, and I end up giving them the money they ask for.[45]

Such high-level consultations on foreign policy issues are, of course, closed to foreign social scientists (for the period since 1945, at least). So are most of the bureaucratic channels at all levels through which influence on civilians is exerted. Much more readily observable are the public discussions in which army officials participate. Officers are subject to the same constraints as other citizens (for instance in relation to criticism of Stalin) and to special restrictions in the cause of secrecy. Still, one finds a remarkably wide range of military-related concerns and anxieties aired in public: the status of the army and its mission, specific questions on military policy (such as the relative weight given to different branches of the military), the quality of civilian goods and services, and others. In approaching these public articulations, and less open ones as well, several general points should be kept in mind.

The first is that the military does not claim to be a monolithic or isolated organization. Military participation is specialized according to issue and actor (logistics officers are most concerned with relations with the railroads, political officers with military-patriotic education, and so on). Officers are not necessarily coordinated or unanimous in their preferences and may in fact differ among themselves in major ways. And whatever the range of military opinion, the likelihood is that important aspects of military positions will find support from at least some civilians and not offer a frontal challenge to civilian party leaders or to the interests of the regime as a whole. It is clear, for example, that Khrushchev's force reduction proposals in 1960 were opposed by a wide range of civilian party and state officials as well as by the military high command (and the military party organs).

Precisely such a pattern of ongoing discussion has been visible in this decade of relations with the West regarding the desirability and preferred modes of détente. Most military spokesmen share the ambivalence that infuses almost all official pronouncements about the "relaxation of tensions." While valuing its contribution to Soviet security (they have had virtually nothing to say about the presumed benefits of increased trade and technological exchange), they are anxious about possible Western second thoughts and wary of the long-term effects of relaxation of vigilance on the Soviet population — particularly on the youth.

Undoubtedly it is the latter train of thought that has been emphasized in public military statements. Soviet soldiers have had to make no apologies for the fact that, as Marshal Grechko said, "For us military men it is impossible to forget" the experience and dangers of war.[46] Military officers have been most forthright in arguing the hazards of failing to extract reciprocal concessions from the West, especially on arms control issues: "A unilateral slackening in the USSR's defense power might call forth sharp changes in the policy of the ruling circles of the imperialist states. . . . Life dictates the necessity of unflagging concern for strengthening . . . the military power of the Soviet Union."[47] It is interesting that some of the most outspoken declarations about the possible pitfalls of détente have come from the Main Political Administration (MPA), a component of the military establishment whose central task is to interpret and enforce party policy in the military realm. MPA chief Aleksei A. Epishev has repeatedly warned against imperialism's "aggressive nature": "In a situation where imperialism, in its efforts to regain its lost initiative, has become even more aggressive and adventuristic, Lenin's words about the need to keep our Army 'fully ready for battle and increase its military potential' are particularly appropriate."[48] Such sentiments have recently been echoed by Ustinov, his civilian background notwithstanding.[49] They are, moreover, sentiments that resonate in many civilian quarters (as is surely the case for corresponding viewpoints in the United States).

In considering the military as a claimant in politics it is also important to understand that in the majority of cases the target of military advice and pressure is not the national party leadership at all, but other organizations or groups whose cooperation is necessary for some specific purpose. For instance, the Ministry of Defense and the MPA have repeatedly urged artists and their professional unions to do more work on martial themes. The latest illustration of concerted pressure occurred in April 1977, when General Epishev addressed a hall full of cultural dignitaries (including officials of the Ministry of Culture, the editor of *Literaturnaia gazeta*, and leaders of the writers', composers', filmmakers', and sculptors' unions), demanding more attention to "soldierly labor, which is just as necessary to society as that of the worker or peasant."[50] Quite frequently, at least on routine service issues, it is local officials who are the targets of military efforts. A bottleneck or disagreement may mean that officers will "turn for a decision to the corresponding Party and soviet organs."[51] Public criticisms are many and varied, with officers pressing, for instance, for improved housing and nursery facilities for military families, better treatment of reserve officers and veterans (particularly now that many World War II veterans are reaching pension age), more attention to civil defense and paramilitary programs, or more investment priority for local factories producing materials for military construction units.[52]

The final point to be made here is that military claims, for all their complexity, essentially relate to areas of policy in which the army's institutional

interests are directly engaged. Soviet leaders have been assiduous in restricting soldiers' participation in administration and politics to questions
relating in some way to their professional function and immediate interests.
Stalin's conviction that "the military should occupy themselves with their
own business and not discuss things that do not concern them"[53] has been
retained by his successors. In a way the list of issues on which the military
does not play a major role as agent or claimant — including questions of internal order and rural development, to mention two areas where the
Chinese military is much more active — is as impressive as the set of issues
in which the army's role is significant. Soviet officers have displayed no
tendency to expand their participation into new problem areas and some
have even declined minor opportunities to do so. For instance, the construction of military retail outlets is often not coordinated with that of
civilian stores because "military clients and construction agencies do not
maintain close working contacts with local executive committees."[54] Some
military trade executives "do not meet their local suppliers for years on end"
and fail to obtain delivery of goods already contracted for due to the fact
that they "do not insist on having their orders filled."[55]

Trends and Implications

The crucial prerequisite for careful examination of the military's impact
on Soviet society and politics is the acceptance of the fact that this impact is
complex — complex in its determinants, modes, and consequences. It is
surely incorrect to reduce the military's role to that of anxious adversary of
the party leadership. Yet it would also be dangerous to accept some of the
more simplistic notions (particularly those broadcast by Western journalists
and Western generals) about pervasive military influence or about a
militarizing or militarized Soviet society.

The army's impact has not changed qualitatively during the Brezhnev
era. The prospects for qualitative change are not to be dismissed out of
hand yet they will depend essentially on developments outside the military
establishment, developments that are extremely difficult to forecast. Any
outright disintegration of the political system will inevitably bring the
military to center stage, as has happened in other societies. The Brezhnev
succession will offer the potential for military involvement in the selection
of civilian leaders, but that potential will be realized only if civilians fail to
observe the restraint in appealing to military assistance that they have exercised in the past. Short of such dramatic developments, the most likely
stimulator of a change in the military impact in the next decade is the
emerging labor shortage. This dilemma may force the regime in the 1980s
to contemplate ways of fusing military training, civilian education, and

economic production that have not been seriously entertained since the 1920s.[56] If past experience is any guide, changes in this or any other area will be incremental and considered. Inroads on civilian authority are likely to come, as Bruce Russett has written of the U.S. military, "not [from] a sudden take-over by . . . soldiers but [from] slow accretions in the scope of military influence in the 'normal' political system."[57]

What do the military's impact and possible changes in it imply for foreign policy? Clearly the weight of military goals and the availability of military instruments in Soviet policy are major data for consideration in the West. Yet in both cases these basically reflect the same factor that has been the main determinant of the impact of the military itself on Soviet society — the values and objectives of Soviet *civilians*. The army is an important focus for political socialization, but this is principally due to civilian acceptance of many of the ideals it embodies. The military-industrial complex is a major constituency in Soviet politics, but largely because nonsoldiers have made it one. And if the counsel of generals is heard with respect in Moscow, it is primarily because civilian leaders take seriously the goals that officers pursue. In the 1970s, as in the 1920s when Mikhail Frunze summarized this symmetry in perceptions, Soviet soldiers and civilians seem to agree: "The stronger and more powerful [the army] is, and the more it is a threat to our enemies, then the more our interests will be served."[58]

Notes

1. V. V. Sheliag et al., *Voennaia psikhologiia* (Moscow, 1972), p. 3.

2. Roman Kolkowicz, *The Soviet Military and the Communist Party* (Princeton, N.J.: Princeton University Press, 1967), p. 11.

3. William E. Odom, "The Soviet Military: The Party Connection," *Problems of Communism* 22, no. 5 (September–October 1973):12–26.

4. Some of my findings are reported in "Military Councils and Military Politics in the Russian Civil War," *Canadian Slavonic Papers*, no. 18 (March 1976), pp. 36–57; and "The Zhukov Affair Reconsidered," *Soviet Studies* 29, no. 2 (April 1977): 185–213.

5. Jerry F. Hough, *The Soviet Prefects: The Local Party Organs in Industrial Decision-Making* (Cambridge, Mass.: Harvard University Press, 1969), p. 265.

6. William E. Odom, "The 'Militarization' of Soviet Society," *Problems of Communism* 25, no. 5 (September–October 1976): 34–51; quotations on pp. 35, 50. I do not mean to slight the complexity of Odom's argument by making selective reference to it, or to equate it with the less sophisticated discussions about Soviet "militarization" that one encounters elsewhere.

7. Kolkowicz, *The Soviet Military*, p. 105.

8. V. D. Sokolovskii et al., *Voennaia strategiia* (Moscow, 1968), p. 445.

9. Most aspects of Soviet military management have been neglected by Western scholars, even though the Soviet military system encompasses huge and costly operations. No serious work has been done, for example, on the expanding system of military state farms (*voennye sovkhozy*), enterprises operated by civilian laborers that "occupy many thousands of hectares of land, contain tens of thousands of cattle and sheep and hundreds of thousands of hogs and fowl, [and produce] tens of thousands of tons of grain, potatoes, and vegetables." *Tyl i snabzhenie Sovetskikh vooruzhennykh sil*, 1973, no. 4, pp. 52–53.

10. I. V. Stalin, *Sochineniia*, vol. 10 (Moscow, 1949), p. 85.

11. Karl F. Spielmann, "Defense Industrialists in the USSR," *Problems of Communism* 25, no. 5 (September–October 1976):52.

12. Aggregate statistics are not available, but descriptions of major projects evince substantial effort. See, for example, the report that in Sergeli, a new suburb of Tashkent, troops built 150,000 square meters of housing in only seven months of 1976, complete with amenities and services (*Krasnaia zvezda*, 23 November 1976, p. 2).

13. Statistics in *Tyl i snabzhenie Sovetskikh vooruzhennykh sil,* 1968, no. 9, p. 75.

14. *Izvestiia*, 9 August 1964, p. 3.

15. The 70 percent figure for conscript Komsomol membership is in *Krasnaia zvezda*, 25 April 1974, p. 3. The 80 percent overall figure is inferred from partial data from several sources. Party organizations in the military are dominated, as they have been at almost all other times, by officers.

16. Stalin, *Sochineniia*, vol. 5, p. 205.

17. *Krasnaia zvezda*, 9 May 1973, p. 2.

18. *Morskoi sbornik*, 1969, no. 8, p. 6.

19. *Krasnaia zvezda*, 9 December 1976, p. 2.

20. *XXV s'ezd Kommunisticheskoi Partii Sovetskogo Soiuza: stenograficheskii otchet*, vol. 1 (Moscow, 1976), p. 101.

21. *Tyl i snabzhenie Sovetskikh vooruzhennykh sil*, 1972, no. 10, p. 13.

22. Quotation from *Kommunist vooruzhennykh sil*, no. 3 (February 1970), p. 24. For the language circles, see ibid., no. 21 (November 1972), p. 32, and *Bloknot agitatora*, no. 7 (1972), p. 5.

23. DOSAAF statistics in *Krasnaia zvezda*, 23 January 1977, p. 2, and 26 January 1977, p. 1. Capital expenditures for 1972–1976 totalled 28.2 million rubles. For useful overviews of the three programs being discussed here, see Odom, "The 'Militarization' of Soviet Society," and Herbert Goldhamer, *The Soviet Soldier* (New York: Crane, Russak, 1975), ch. 2–3.

24. Many civilian officials chafed at having to attend these courses. See, for instance, *Sovetskaia Belorussiia*, 18 October 1972, p. 3, and *Kommunist Tadzhikistana*, 24 August 1973, p. 4.

25. *Krasnaia zvezda*, 7 April 1977, p. 2.

26. Statistics in *Sovetskii patriot*, 29 November 1972, p. 2; *Krasnaia zvezda*, 17 August 1976, p. 4.

27. In Belorussia, for example, the 1971 program required twenty-one hours, that is one hour *more* than after standardization (*Sovetskaia Belorussiia*, 2 April 1972, p. 3).

28. *Izvestiia,* 5 May 1966, p. 3.

29. *Krasnaia zvezda,* 21 August 1976, p. 4.

30. These numbers are given in *Turkmenskaia iskra,* 26 May 1973, p. 3; *Sovetskaia Latviia,* 17 May 1973, p. 2; *Sovetskaia Belorussiia,* 18 November 1973, p. 2; and *Krasnaia zvezda,* 8 February 1976, p. 2.

31. *Sovetskii patriot,* 31 March 1974, p. 4.

32. The quotations here are from *Sovetskaia Moldaviia,* 15 August 1972, p. 3; *Krasnaia zvezda,* 28 March 1976, p. 2; *Turkmenskaia iskra,* 7 September 1973, p. 3; *Krasnaia zvezda,* 7 April 1977, p. 2, and 7 May 1976, p. 2.

33. In 1977, for example, DOSAAF claimed to have "prepared" 2.8 million machine operators for work in agriculture in the previous five years (*Krasnaia zvezda,* 26 January 1977, p. 1). Yet the total number of machine operators registered by the 1970 census was only 3.4 million.

34. *Sovetskii patriot,* 16 August 1972, p. 3.

35. For a particularly frank discussion of DOSAAF's financial difficulties, see ibid., 3 December 1972, p. 2.

36. Odom, "The 'Militarization' of Soviet Society," p. 47.

37. These references are common in both civilian and military statements on civil defense. In the first ten months of 1975 the executive of the Zhdanov raion soviet is said to have discussed civil defense questions on fourteen occasions, and the party bureau considered "important questions" a number of times (*Krasnaia zvezda,* 16 November 1975, p. 1). Other stories report regular discussions in both soviet and party executive organs. The administrative organs departments of local party organs are often reported as being involved in civil defense planning; science and education departments also play some role.

38. Several dozen local party secretaries sit on the military councils of military districts and fleets, but their participation in decision making seems to be minimal. Soviet sources are quite categorical in denying any legitimate role for local party organs as such in intramilitary affairs.

39. The Gosplan of the Udmurt autonomous republic has established a commission for overcoming "interdepartmental barriers" on civil defense matters (*Krasnaia zvezda,* 28 March 1976, p. 2). In some areas civil defense formations are being increasingly used by civilian executives for rescue and recovery work following natural disasters and even "major production accidents" (*Kazakhstanskaia pravda,* 4 July 1973, p. 2). The availability of trained and equipped civil defense groups may actually lessen the likelihood of civilian use of military assistance in such cases.

40. Local first secretaries are said to confirm (*utverzhdat'*) annual plans for military-patriotic work (*Krasnaia zvezda,* 6 May 1976, p. 1).

41. S. M. Shtemenko, *General'nyi shtab v gody voiny,* vol. 1 (Moscow, 1968) p. 116.

42. *Partiino-politicheskaia rabota v Sovetskikh Vooruzhennykh Silakh* (Moscow, 1974), p. 103.

43. Raymond L. Garthoff, "SALT and the Soviet Military," *Problems of Communism* 24, no. 1 (January–February 1975):29.

44. Strobe Talbott, ed., *Khrushchev Remembers: The Last Testament* (New York: Bantam, 1976), p. 540.

45. Ibid., p. 572.

46. *Krasnaia zvezda*, 9 January 1976, p. 2.

47. *Kommunist vooruzhennykh sil*, no. 16 (August 1972), p. 16.

48. *Pravda*, 25 March 1971, p. 2.

49. See, for example, Ustinov's article in *Pravda*, 23 February 1977, p. 2, which refers to dangers to Soviet security posed by the governing circles (*praviashchie krugi*) of the Western states. Compare this to Brezhnev's speech in Tula in January (ibid., 19 January 1977, p. 2), which discusses not only "aggressive forces" within the Western countries but "other forces, ones which . . . are capable of taking into account the realities of the contemporary world."

50. *Krasnaia zvezda*, 7 April 1977, p. 2. Since the late 1960s the Main Political Administration and the Ministry of Defense have awarded a number of prizes and diplomas designed to induce creative artists to work on military-related themes. They currently award annual prizes for novels, essays, songs, and films.

51. *Tyl i snabzhenie Sovetskikh vooruzhennykh sil*, 1973, no. 7, p. 63.

52. Such criticisms are found in a number of sources: individual letters to newspapers, investigative articles in military newspapers and journals, articles by officers in civilian publications, and speeches by commanders and political officers to republican and local party congresses, conferences, and plenums (many of which are printed in republican newspapers).

53. Quoted in P. I. Iakir and Iu. A. Geller, eds., *Komandarm Iakir* (Moscow, 1963), pp. 111–112.

54. *Tyl i snabzhenie Sovetskikh vooruzhennykh sil*, 1973, no. 7, p. 62.

55. Ibid.

56. At current rates of conscription, the military would have to draft almost 85 percent of all eighteen-year-olds in 1987 to maintain manpower levels (*New York Times*, 17 April 1977, p. 8).

57. Bruce M. Russett, *What Price Vigilance? The Burdens of National Defense* (New Haven, Conn.: Yale University Press, 1970), p. 181.

58. M. V. Frunze, *Sobranie sochinenii*, vol. 1 (Moscow and Leningrad, 1925), p. 365.

6

The "Nationality Problem" in the USSR: Domestic Pressures and Foreign Policy Constraints

Jeremy Azrael

For the past quarter century, the Soviet "nationality front" has been relatively tranquil. Certainly, there have been no armed uprisings or mass insurgencies of the sort that occurred in both the 1920s and the 1940s. Nor have there been any counterparts among the contemporary ruling elite of such ideologically and politically formidable "national Communists" as Sultan Galiev, Mikola Skrypnik, and Faisal Khodzhaev. Moreover, far from reflecting a worldwide trend this seeming deescalation of international and center-periphery tensions has coincided with an upsurge of nationalism and ethnocentrism in nearly every other multinational polity. Despite these comforting comparisons there is no warrant for Brezhnev's claim made on the occasion of the fiftieth anniversary of the formation of the USSR that his country's "historical nationality problem" has been definitively solved.[1] Although his claim ultimately might be vindicated, it is certainly premature and may turn out to have been rashly overconfident.

I

Although Beria is the last member of the ruling elite to have been denounced as an outright nationalist,[2] numerous high officials have been charged with overstepping prescribed limits in defending local claims or interests against the claims and interests of the center or of other localities. Despite the almost exclusively prosecutory character of the available evidence, there is no reason to doubt the validity of such typical allegations as the following: that the first secretary of the Kazakh party organization, R.O. Shayakhmetov, resisted Khrushchev's Virgin Lands program because it implied massive "European" in-migration; that a large group of Latvian party and state leaders attempted to restrict investment in their republic in order to retard its further Russianization; that Politburo members D. S. Polianski and A. N. Shelepin headed a Russia-first faction within the leadership; and that Ukrainian first secretary and Politburo member Petr Shelest opposed any buildup of Siberia and the Far North at the Ukraine's expense and sought to shield Ukrainian intellectuals against central pressures.[3] Furthermore, what is true of these paladins of the Soviet establishment is undoubtedly true of lower-ranking officials, who have frequently been "guilty" not merely of excessive localism but of ethnocentrism in such matters as the utilization of local resources, the selection and deployment of cadres, the designation of budget priorities, the awarding of honors and emoluments, and the enforcement of nominally "universalistic" norms and regulations.

None of the evidence suggests that we are witnessing or are about to witness a resurgence of full-blown "national Communism." Within limits the evidence in question may be misleading. In some cases, charges of ethnic particularism are undoubtedly trumped-up rationalizations for purges that are initiated for other reasons. Further, many of the accused officials are probably unwitting victims of shifts of emphasis in the prevailing party line. In this connection, it is important to remember that local officials are expected and even encouraged to mobilize their constituencies for interregional competitions, to develop local personnel "reserves," to promote "indigenization," to respect native sensibilities, etc. Even if one allows for such eventualities the evidence clearly indicates the persistence of strong impulses toward "national deviationism" at all levels of party-state machinery.

Along with the problems posed by its own cadres, the regime has also had to contend with an apparent upsurge of national self-consciousness among mainstream students and intellectuals. A great many literary and artistic creations testify to this and further corroboration is provided by the mushroom growth of republic- and local-level ethnographic societies and societies for the conservation of historical and cultural monuments that have proliferated in recent years.[4] In many instances these societies are direct outgrowths of what were originally completely unofficial clubs or circles that attracted more and more volunteers for their self-generated projects. As a result, the regime quickly established parallel official organizations whose growth it has sponsored and financed. This support is often grudgingly given, however, and its purpose is clearly to accommodate sentiments that the regime does not wish to foster but sees no way to eradicate and hopes at least partially to coopt.

Although the regime has taken steps to ensure that these societies do not become incipient nationalist movements on the model of the not-so-remotely analogous Matica Hrvatska and Matica Srpska societies in

Yugoslavia, it has apparently been unable to prevent some of them from falling under the sway of outspoken nationalists, at least partially and temporarily. In any event, the KGB is reported to have acted on this premise on several occasions, and a reliable emigré source contends that the Moscow headquarters of the Society for the Preservation of Historical and Cultural Monuments is colloquially known as the Russian Club and provides a forum for blatantly Russocentric propaganda and agitation.[5] Pending further developments, there is no reason to conclude that most or even many of the millions of members of these societies are potential national dissidents. By the same token, however, there is no reason to doubt the contemporary relevance of the comments of a late nineteenth century Baltic German observer of imperial Russia, who wrote, "when politics are quiet, antiquarianism, entomology, and other harmless sciences flourish. Quiet concern for the history of the fatherland may, in particular, serve as a surrogate for other passionate kinds of patriotic activity."[6] Today, as under the ancient regime, there are intrepid citizens who engage in highly "passionate kinds of patriotic activity" and refuse to accept any surrogate for the direct expression of their national grievances and aspirations.

In four cases, this refusal has culminated in the emergence of what can be described as communal movements involving a combination of structured leadership and grass-roots activism. With one or another stress, this description fits not only the highly publicized Jewish exodus movement but also the repatriation movements that have arisen within the Volga German, Meskhetian Turkish, and Crimean Tatar communities and that have attracted mass support and preserved their momentum and coherence despite the frequent arrest and/or dispersal of key leaders.[7] Like their Jewish counterparts the participants in the Volga German and Meskhetian Turkish movements are so poorly integrated into the allegedly indivisible Soviet people or *narod* that they are eager to renounce their Soviet citizenship in favor of repatriation to what are in fact the quite foreign "homelands" of West Germany and Turkey. Ironically, however, the regime probably feels less threatened by these would-be defectors than by the Crimean Tatars who appear to be even better organized and more solidaristic and whose demand for repatriation can only be satisfied by dispossessing many of the current Russian and Ukrainian inhabitants of the Crimea and reinforcing an already palpable Slavic backlash against the regime's "overindulgence" of the country's "yellow" minorities.

Although the repatriation movements that have arisen among the Soviet Union's diaspora nationalities provide the only current examples of sustained national protest on a communal scale, they are by no means the only examples of organized national dissidence or of grass-roots national self-assertiveness. Thus, there has been a steady outpouring of nationality-oriented *samizdat* publications from virtually all of the country's Slavic and Baltic nationalities, including Russian, Lithuanian, and Ukrainian publications that clearly depend on a fairly extensive network of active collaborators. In addition, national dissidents have circulated and submitted hundreds, if not thousands, of protest letters and petitions, including one to UN Secretary General Waldheim with seventeen thousand Lithuanian signatories.[8] Finally, mass protest meetings and large street demonstrations on behalf of national rights have taken place in Abkhazia, Armenia, Uzbekistan, Georgia, and Lithuania, including at least three (two in Lithuania and one in Georgia) that became riots warranting military intervention.[9]

II

Despite his insouciant rhetoric, there is little question that Brezhnev is seriously concerned about the escalatory potential of such nationalist challenges. Indeed, shortly after he proclaimed that the nationality problem had been solved, the regime established a special Council on Nationality Problems directly under the Presidium of the USSR Academy of Sciences. Although too little is known about this council to draw any firm conclusions about its precise mandate or modus operandi, its very creation is a sign of official disquiet, and published accounts of its activities suggest that it is heavily engaged in policy research for the Central Committee and the Council of Ministers.[10] Most of this research appears to be directed toward the economic, social, and demographic aspects of "the nationality problem" rather than to its explicitly political manifestations. However, this impression may well be an artifact of Soviet classification procedures, since there are unofficial reports that council members have also been involved in surveys of *samizdat* publications and analyses of police interrogations of national dissidents. In any event, the council was clearly not convened to perform a collective autopsy on a patient who is believed to be terminally ill, if not yet clinically deceased.

Further evidence of Brezhnev's real attitudes can be found in the new Soviet constitution, which was finally promulgated in October 1977, almost fifteen years behind schedule. An easily overlooked but particularly instructive feature of the new constitution is its omission of any reference to the right of the country's constituent republics to maintain their own armed forces.[11] Since all of the other trappings of republican sovereignty — including the right of secession — are explicitly reaffirmed, this omission is clearly not the result of a general purge of "obsolescent" clauses. On the contrary, a more likely explanation is the existence of operational and/or contingency plans to permit a partial revival of "military federalism" in actual practice. In this connection, it is worth noting not only that the

Brezhnev-Kosygin regime is about to face the same kind of demographic constraints on military recruitment that prompted Khrushchev to propose the replacement of certain active-duty units by territorial militias, but also that the changing ethnic composition of the Soviet population has strengthened purely military arguments for more ethnically homogenous patterns of organization and deployment.[12] These arguments have almost certainly surfaced in the inner councils of the Ministry of Defense, and credible rumor indicates that they have already contributed to a favorable response by the Kremlin to a request that Kazakh recruits be allowed to perform their military service within the Kazakh republic. However, this same rumor alleges that a similar request by the Estonian party leadership was summarily rejected, and there is little doubt that the regime is anxious to minimize such requests and to ensure that it can reject them without patently violating a constitutional right. Far from reflecting a mere desire to retain the utmost flexibility, this anxiety almost certainly reflects the same instinctive mistrust that governed Khrushchev's 1956 decision to cancel the routinely issued marching orders of the army regiment that was closest to riot-torn Tbilisi but that happened to contain an "overrepresentation" of Georgians, even though this decision meant leaving the city in the hands of the rioters for twelve additional hours.[13]

The elimination of the provisions for republic-level armed forces once noted, the most immediately interesting and relevant feature of the new constitution is the retention of the ethno-federal system. As soon as the "need" for a new constitution was announced in 1961 it became evident that many Soviet officials were eager to dismantle or drastically alter this system. Almost immediately thereafter, a spate of articles appeared in which critical attention was directed to the rising costs of institutional parallelism and jurisdictional immobilism that continued ethno-federalism would allegedly entail, as well as to the fact that a number of nationalities no longer constituted majorities within their own republics and hence had no better claim to a sovereign status than the Karelians whose union-republic had been unceremoniously liquidated on precisely this ground in 1956.[14] Although these articles did not go unanswered, Khrushchev's heavy stress on the imminent "merger" (*sliianie*) of nationalities and his active promotion of an array of inter-republic policymaking and management bodies strongly suggested that their authors enjoyed the highest backing and that ethno-federalism was about to become a thing of the past. Once the dust had settled after Khrushchev's ouster, this impression was reconfirmed by a series of measures that abolished all surviving republic-level councils of the national economy, liquidated the RSFSR Bureau of the CPSU, and emphasized the importance of so-called large economic regions as foci of long-term planning.

It is possible, of course, that these measures were misleading and that the

Brezhnev-Kosygin leadership always intended to retain the ethno-federal system intact. There is a stronger possibility, however, that Khrushchev's successors backed away from their original intention as the result of a growing appreciation of the depth of their subjects' national feelings and a growing apprehension that the abolition or modification of the ethno-federal system would mobilize these feelings against the regime and raise the temperature on the "nationality front" to a very uncomfortable level. That these fears were not unfounded was shown in April 1978, when a reported 20,000 demonstrators took to the streets of Tbilisi to demand that the draft of their new republic constitution be revised to restore Georgian to its formerly authorized status as an official state language.[15] The fact that this demand was promptly honored and that corresponding revisions were made in the draft constitutions of Azerbaidzhan and Armenia provides further evidence that the regime feels far more vulnerable on its "nationality front" than it likes to pretend.[16]

Another — and, for present purposes, final — sign of the intensity of the regime's concern is the trebling between the Twenty-second and the Twenty-fifth Party Congresses of the number of Turkic representatives on the Politburo, with the addition of D. A. Kunaev and G. A. Aliev to the incumbent Sh. R. Rashidov.[17] Although these promotions undoubtedly were prompted by considerations other than ethnic origins, the latter were almost certainly not fortuitous. On the contrary, there is every reason to surmise that they figured prominently as part of a highly premeditated effort to mitigate the spectre of a destabilization of the "nationality front" in the country's Turkic republics. It is true that in comparison to the country's other nationalities the native inhabitants of these republics have been notably quiescent since the early 1930s. Even now, there is no evidence of the sort of organized national dissidence that has appeared nearly everywhere else. However, a sizable contingent of Uzbeks does appear to have participated in the Tatar-led street demonstration that shook Tashkent in 1969 and to have made its presence felt by demanding not only that the Tatars be allowed to leave Uzbekistan but that the Russians be forced to do so.[18] If Igor Shaferevich is to be believed, Russians in a number of Central Asian cities "often hear the cry, 'Just wait til the Chinese come, they'll show you what's what.'"[19]

In addition to such anti-Russian sentiments, Pan-Turkic sentiments have also resurfaced lately and been widely disseminated in published as well as unpublished form. In a recently published interview no less a personage than the renowned Kirgiz novelist and playwright Chingiz Aitmatov invoked the inculcation of "Turkic national pride" as a legitimate and important objective for his fellow Turkic writers.[20] Far from speaking academically, Aitmatov was wittingly or unwittingly allying himself with the Kazakh poet Olzhas Suleimenov, the author of a highly polemical book, self-consciously entitled *Az i Ya* (*Aziya* or Asia). Suleimenov claimed that the Russian epic, *The Igor Tale*, was written half in Turkic and was a testament among other things to the extremely important role of the Turks and the Semites (!) in world civilization in general and the civilization of Russia (with its "miserable past" and legacy of "ignorance, credulity and timidity") in particular.[21] Although the regime allowed Suleimenov to defend himself against his outraged Russian critics, it was undoubtedly deeply disturbed by what probably was in fact and certainly was widely construed as a deliberately provocative and intensely nationalistic declaration of faith.[22]

Apart from its general fear of escalating inter-national and center-periphery tensions, there are a number of contextual factors that make the regime particularly sensitive to signs of emergent or reemergent Turkic nationalism, especially in its Pan-Turkic variant. For one thing, much of the Turkic population lives in close proximity to the Sino-Soviet frontier and is hence a particularly high-priority target of anti-Muscovite Chinese propaganda.[23] In addition, and perhaps more important in view of the deep-rooted Sinophobia of the Turkic nationalities and the well-known mistreatment of the Turkic minorities in the Peoples Republic of China (PRC),[24] the Turkic nationalities are in the midst of an extraordinary population explosion. To be precise, they have been growing at an average rate of well over 3 percent per annum during the past fifteen years, as compared to an average of only slightly over 1 percent per annum for the country's other major nationalities.[25] In consequence, the Turkic share in the total population has increased from 11 to 17 percent and will almost certainly reach 25 percent by the end of the century.[26]

As these figures imply, the Turkic share of the country's young and youthful population is even greater than its share of the whole and will remain so for the foreseeable future. Although there is no compelling reason to believe that the Turkic nationalities will automatically become more self-assertive as their demographic weight increases, their increasing demographic weight undoubtedly makes the prospect of heightened militancy more threatening from the point of view of the regime. Furthermore, as the regime is well aware, the Turkic nationalities may be on the verge of precisely the sort of intensive "modernization" that could make them much more accessible and susceptible to nationalist appeals.

To date, although far from unaffected by its impact, most of the country's Turkic population has remained outside the mainstream of Soviet socio-economic development. The vast majority of the Turkic population still lives in relatively remote rural areas and has managed to preserve a great deal of its traditional social and cultural heritage. As a result of the prolonged stagnation of non-Turkic population growth rates, however, a situation has emerged in which the Turkic nationalities constitute the only potential source of substantial future increments to the country's industrial work force.[27] Barring an improbably sharp increase in labor productivity, the only way the regime can hope to maintain anything close to current economic growth rates is either to shift the country's industrial center of gravity sharply eastward or to mobilize large numbers of Turkic nationals to work in the country's already industrialized "European" republics.[28]

The first of these intentionally, but not grossly, overstated alternatives would greatly antagonize the already restive "European" nationalities. It is not surprising that Brezhnev's initial response to what he recently described as "a number of population problems which have lately become exacerbated" has been to call for the design of a new "population policy" and to establish a new All-Union State Committee on Labor and Social Problems under the chairmanship of the erstwhile (Russian) second secretary of the Uzbekh Communist party rather than to accelerate investment rates in what some Soviet publications have once again begun to refer to as "Turkestan."[29] Nevertheless, the record clearly indicates that the country's Turkic nationalities have been extremely loath to migrate to non-Turkic regions, and the present circumstances are such that they are unlikely to change their behavior in the absence of indirect and direct sanctions of a sort that would severely antagonize the victims and could well be economically counterproductive. Furthermore, native officials and intellectuals have lost much of their former ambivalence about the industrialization of their homelands and tend to resent "Eurocentric" investment decisions instead of viewing them as safeguards against massive European inmigration. In consequence, Brezhnev's successors may take a different approach from the one that he seems to favor and initiate an all-out effort to bring the industrial mountain to Muhammed.

For a variety of reasons, this latter alternative is also unlikely to be a completely satisfactory economic panacea. At a minimum, it portends a much slower pace of development for underdeveloped regions such as Siberia and the Far North, which are far richer than Turkestan in essential natural resources, including many that are of great importance in maintaining a viable balance of East-West trade. What matters most for present purposes, however, are not the problematic economic consequences of a "Turkocentric" investment program, but the even more problematic consequences for the center-periphery and inter-national relations. From this perspective, to repeat, one can foresee not only an exacerbation of national discontent among the already disgruntled "European" nationalities but a hostile Turkic reaction to unwelcome central encroachment on local political and administrative autonomy and to the inevitable social and cultural stresses inherent in rapid industrialization.

III

The Turkic nationalities merit special attention in a discussion of the Soviet "nationality problem," because of the distinctive contribution they make in the field of foreign policy. For one thing, they are a magnet for the persecuted Turkic minorities in the PRC, who (in a reversal of the situation that obtained in the 1920s and 1930s) have fled across the border into the USSR in large numbers in recent years and whose express conviction that their Soviet kinsmen enjoy a relatively satisfactory life makes them not only receptive subjects and useful objects of Soviet propaganda (including domestic propaganda and counterpropaganda) but also makes them promising intelligence targets and potential fifth column allies whose presence on the Sino-Soviet border is a deterrent to Chinese "adventurism."[30] In addition, Soviet efforts to penetrate the Middle East rely heavily upon Turkic personnel, a disproportionate number of whom can be found in nearly every Soviet embassy, aid office, and military mission.[31] Similarly, Soviet information and exchange programs in the area have been highly "Turkocentric," with a strong emphasis on the vitality and richness of Soviet Muslim political, economic, and cultural life and on the "lessons" that other Muslims can draw from the Soviet Turkic experience.

Continuation and expansion of these programs indicate that the regime evaluates these programs positively, and that there is no reason to doubt that they yield positive results. At a minimum, they probably generate a certain amount of diffuse goodwill for the Soviet Union and make it easier for the regime to preserve its credibility in the face of the bitter attacks on Soviet colonialism in general and anti-Muslim colonialism in particular that have been mounted not only by Chinese and Western spokesmen but by a number of prominent foreign mullahs and by such Muslim political leaders as Libya's Colonel Qadaffi and Morocco's King Hassan.[32] In addition, the programs almost certainly serve useful intelligence functions and facilitate the recruitment of cadres and members for overtly or covertly pro-Soviet front organizations, pressure groups, and political parties. The same general points probably apply to the regime's assiduous promotion (by similar means) of the Turkic republics as generic models of socialist development for the entire Third World. Although few countries in the Third World seem prepared to emulate such models exactly, many of their leaders and citizens are undoubtedly favorably impressed by what is, after all, plausible evidence of formerly backward territories that have not only made rapid socioeconomic progress under the Kremlin's tutelage but also seem to be politically contented.

Should the seeming tranquility of the Turkic segment of the "nationality front" be disrupted by the emergence of outspoken national dissidence and public protest, the Turkic nationalities would undoubtedly lose much of their value as foreign policy assets and could easily become net liabilities. In doing so, they would be following in the footsteps of the Jews, the Volga Germans, the Armenians, the Ukrainians, and other nationalities that once performed useful exemplary, diversionary, or liaison functions in Soviet foreign policy but have largely ceased to do so.[33] As was true in the past, the regime still tries to cultivate the foreign kinsmen of nearly all of its major nationalities through a wide array of special, nationality-oriented newspapers, magazines, radio broadcasts, culture exchanges, scholarship programs, etc. However, the regime is well aware that most members of the intended audience have long since shed any illusions about the possibilities for national self-fulfillment under Soviet rule. Although it undoubtedly hopes for and receives occasional unexpected windfalls of active sympathy and support, the regime's basic purpose is to reduce the intensity of anti-Soviet sentiments in politically influential diaspora and emigré communities and to curb the militancy with which these communities lobby their host governments to appeal to the Kremlin on behalf of their kinsmen in the USSR. Unwelcome under almost any circumstances, such representations are particularly undesirable at present, when the regime is eager to secure foreign credits and better terms of foreign trade.

It is no revelation that the Kremlin has not, in fact, managed to keep its nationality problem off the diplomatic agenda. Despite the reservations of many concerned officials, a number of governments have found it virtually impossible to resist the pressure of emigré and diaspora communities that, after years of more or less halfhearted lobbying, have been re-energized by the eloquence of national dissidents and the courage of national protesters within the USSR. Moreover, various governments have made more or less formal commitments to monitor violations of human and communal rights on a regional and/or global basis and to take such violations into account in their conduct of foreign affairs.[34] One ironic consequence of this internationalization of the nationality problem is that the Kremlin has been able to transform its liabilities into bargaining chips to be traded for economic and political concessions by other governments. This tactic clearly has been used in the case of the Volga Germans and the Jews, and was at least arguably a key ingredient of Soviet strategy in the CSCE negotiations in Helsinki. In order to employ this tactic, however, the Kremlin takes substantial risks.

First, the very fact of bargaining over what are widely regarded as basic rights exposes the Soviet regime to a certain amount of international opprobrium. Moreover, the regime's willingness to bargain is tantamount to a public admission of its serious need for outside economic assistance, if not to a public affirmation of the legitimacy of foreign intervention in Soviet internal affairs. Third, every bargain it strikes weakens the argument that intervention cannot yield positive results and thereby strengthens the hand of would-be interventionists, including those who, like the Arab states in the case of Jewish emigration to Israel, may feel that a bargain has been made at their expense. Finally, any sign of vulnerability or susceptibility to foreign pressure is likely to further destabilize the "nationality front" by convincing Soviet citizens that more impressive feats of national self-assertiveness could result in stronger foreign interventions on their behalf.

The history of the Jackson-Vanik Amendment suggests that the regime is so sensitive to these risks that it will repudiate bargains that involve public commitments and formalized agreements. At the same time, as already indicated, circumstances are now such that the regime can only take an adamant stance and refuse to negotiate if it is willing to jeopardize other important goals. These goals are not so compelling that the regime would negotiate away any of the essential attributes of monolithic central control over political and economic life on the peripheries. So long as foreign governments insist on keeping the nationality problem on the diplomatic agenda, however, the domestic pressures for a rectification of national grievances will be considerably harder to resist.

Even if the nationality problem were to disappear from the diplomatic agenda, Soviet foreign policy would remain susceptible to its actual and potential influence. Rising national self-consciousness and self-assertiveness could make the regime more hesitant about international undertakings that restive Soviet nationalities might perceive as inimical to either their own interest or the interests of their foreign conationals. Conversely, the regime could find it more difficult to refrain from international actions that were deemed imprudent from an all-union perspective but were intensely desired by particular Soviet nationalities. Although it is hard to imagine national lobbies as powerful as the Jewish or Greek lobbies in the contemporary United States, it is not completely farfetched to posit circumstances in which the regime's response to an Israeli occupation of Syria, or a Kazakh-Kirgiz-Uighur uprising in China, or a Turkic-Pushtun civil war in Afghanistan, or a Ukrainian separatist movement in Canada would be importantly conditioned by its concern for the national sensibilities of its own citizens. Apart from such highly speculative possibilities, there is every reason to believe that concern about the spillover effects on its own national constituencies is and will remain a significant factor in the regime's behavior toward Eastern Europe, where any move toward independence could seriously exacerbate centrifugal pressures within the USSR. Finally, it seems probable that the existence of the nationality problem is and will remain one of the many constraints against the initiation or continuation of foreign policy "adventures" that might expose the Soviet Union to the danger of military retaliation against its own territory and thereby (either by design or by accident) create the appearance of separatist options for national communities and/or nationalist elites.

IV

Short of a highly improbable (though not impossible) military intervention by outside powers, there is little prospect that the centrifugal pressures on the regime will lead to an early breakdown of the Soviet system or even to a full-fledged political crisis. Although a prolonged and intransigent succession struggle could lead to a mobilization of national constituencies and to a sharp escalation of center-periphery (and periphery-periphery) conflict, the power of inertial forces and of centripetal sanctions and incentives seems adequate to keep the nationality problem within manageable bounds for the foreseeable future. At the same time, there are forces at work on both the domestic and international scenes that could make its management considerably more difficult and retard whatever tendencies exist toward its long-term solution. With sufficient imagination, commitment, consensus, and good luck, the regime might be able to design and implement internal-system reforms that would weaken these forces and keep them in abeyance. Otherwise, the regime is not only likely to become much more deeply embattled on the "nationality front" per se but also likely to find that the nationality problem exacerbates many other problems from which it can no longer be successfully disentangled.

Notes

1. L. I. Brezhnev, *O piatidesiatiletii SSSR* (Moscow, 1973), p. 19.

2. On Beria, see Charles H. Fairbanks, Jr., "National Cadres as a Force in the Soviet System: The Evidence of Beria's Career, 1949-53," in Jeremy R. Azrael, ed., *Soviet Nationality Policies and Practices* (New York: Praeger Publishers, 1978).

3. On Shayakhmetov, see Strobe Talbott, ed., *Khrushchev Remembers: The Last Testament* (Boston: Little, Brown and Co., 1974), pp. 120-121. On Latvia, see Robert Conquest, *Russia After Khrushchev* (New York: Praeger Publishers, 1965), pp. 209-210. On Yegorichev, Semichastny and Shelepin, and Shelest, see S. Enders Wimbush, "The Great Russians and the Soviet State: The Dilemmas of Ethnic Dominance," and Yaroslav Bilinsky, "Mykola Skrypnyk and Petro Shelest: An Essay on the Persistence and Limits of Ukrainian National Communism," in Azrael, ed., *Soviet Nationality Policies and Practices.* On Poliansky and Shelepin, see Grey Hodnett, "Succession Contingencies in the Soviet Union," *Problems of Communism* 24, no. 2 (March–April 1975):18; Michael Agursky, "Selling Anti-Semitism in Moscow," *New York Review of Books*, 16 November 1972, pp. 19–23, and "Polit-

buro Axe Falls on Polyansky," *Jerusalem Post*, 14 March 1976, p. 8; and Alexander Yanov, *The Russian New Right* (Berkeley: Institute of International Studies, University of California, 1978), pp. 51, 61, 141.

4. See "Preservation of Historical and Cultural Monuments," *Soviet Union* 10 (1972):4, and S. T. Palmer, "The Restoration of Ancient Monuments in the USSR," *Survey*, no. 74/75 (Spring 1970).

5. For KGB suspicions, see *Soviet Analyst* 3, no. 19 (19 September 1974):1-2. For the "Russian Club," see Yanov, *The Russian New Right*, pp. 13, 113, 141.

6. As quoted by John A. Armstrong, "Mobilized Diaspora in Tsarist Russia: The Case of the Baltic Germans," in Azrael, ed., *Soviet Nationality Policies and Practices*, pp. 94 ff.

7. See Ann Sheehy, *The Crimean Tatars, Volga Germans, and Meskhetians* (London: Minority Rights Group, no. 6, 1973). The Jewish case is too well known to require specific documentation.

8. See V. Stanley Vardys, "Modernization and Baltic Nationalism," *Problems of Communism* 24, no. 5 (September-October 1975):47.

9. For a good survey of militant Soviet national protest activities, see *Conflict Studies*, 30 December 1972, pp. 1-27; also, *Soviet Analyst* 2, no. 12 (7 June 1973):3. For more recent, especially Caucasian, examples, see the articles by Craig Whitney in the *New York Times*, 25 June 1978, p. 1, and 26 June 1978, p. 3.

10. See, for example, M. H. Guboglo, "V sektsii obshchestvennykh nauk Prezidiuma AN SSSR — V nauchnom sovete po natsional'nym problemam," *Voprosy istorii*, no. 4 (1976), pp. 148-150.

11. Compare Article 73(8) of the new constitution with Articles 14-g and 18-b of the previous constitution, where the right of each union republic to have its own military formations, organized according to centrally established "guiding principles," is explicitly affirmed.

12. See Jeremy R. Azrael, *Emergent Nationality Problems in the USSR* (Santa Monica, California: The RAND Corporation, 1977), section 4, for a fuller treatment of these and subsequent points concerning "military federalism," as well as for detailed references and citations.

13. See Paul K. Cook, "The Soviet Union in the Year 2000" (Seminar notes, Russian Research Center, Harvard University, 19 December 1974), p. 15.

14. See Jerome M. Gilison, "Khrushchev, Brezhnev, and Constitutional Reform," *Problems of Communism* 24, no. 5 (September-October 1972):69-78.

15. See Craig Whitney, "Soviet Georgians Take to Streets," the *New York Times*, 15 April 1978, p. 3. Later reports lowered the number of demonstrators to 5,000.

16. See the *New York Times*, 25 April 1978, p. 11.

17. Rashidov, who was elevated to candidate membership on the Politburo in 1962, is an Uzbekh; Kunaev, elevated to candidate membership in 1966 and full membership in 1971, is a Kazakh or Uighur; and Aliev, elevated to candidate membership in 1976, is an Azeri.

18. On the Tashkent demonstration, see *Chronicle of Current Events*, 8 (30 June 1969). Another nationality-related disturbance is reported to have occurred in 1970 in the Narab region of Tadzhikistan, which is inhabited by many Turkic Uzbeks as well as Iranian Tadzhiks. (See Barbara Wolfe Jancar, "Religious Dissent in the

Soviet Union," in Rudolf L. Tökés, ed., *Dissent in the USSR* (Baltimore, Md.: Johns Hopkins University Press, 1976), p. 219. Also, a large Tadzhik riot is rumored to have occurred in the spring of 1978.

19. See Igor Shafarevich, "Separation or Reconciliation," in Alexander Solzhenitsyn et al., *From Under the Rubble* (New York: Bantam Books, 1976), p. 87.

20. See N. Khudaiberganov, "An Inspired Confession," *Pravda vostoka*, 10 December 1976, p. 3.

21. See "Discussion of a Book by Olzhas Suleimenov," *Voprosy istorii*, no. 9, 1976, pp. 147–154, abstracted in *Current Digest of the Soviet Press* 28, no. 51 (19 January 1977):15–16.

22. Ibid. for Suleimenov's response to his critics. Lest this point be overinterpreted, however, it is also worth noting that no apology or recantation has been demanded from the Russian scholar L. N. Gumilev, whose critics allege that his writings lead to the conclusion that virtually all of the non-Slavic peoples of the USSR are "illegitimate" and could not survive without the aid of the genetically better-endowed Slavs, who are only able to preserve this superior endowment by avoiding intermarriage with non-Slavs. (See V. I. Kozlov, "On the Biological-Geographical Conception of Ethnic History," *Voprosy istorii*, no. 12, 1974, pp. 72–85, abstracted in *Current Digest of the Soviet Press* 27, no. 20 [11 June 1975]: 1–5.)

23. For representative Chinese attacks on Soviet nationality policy, see Hung Chuan-yu, "The New Tsars—Common Enemy of the People of All Nationalities in the Soviet Union," *Peking Review* 27 (4 July 1969):25–27, and the unsigned "Soviet Social-Imperialism Pursues a Policy of National Oppression," ibid., 22 (28 May 1976):19–23. Attacks of this kind are regular features of Chinese propaganda broadcasts to the USSR.

24. For one of many Soviet efforts to publicize the plight of the Chinese Turks, see V. A. Buguslavskii, A. M. Kuzmina et al., *Velikoderzhavnaia politika maoistov v natsionalnykh raionakh KNR* (Moscow, 1975).

25. A full breakdown of national growth rates, based on data from the 1959 and 1970 Soviet census and later Soviet demographic studies, can be found in Azrael, *Soviet Nationality Policies and Practices*, p. 366.

26. See G. A. Bondarskaia, *Rozhdaemost v SSSR: Ethnodemograficheskii aspekt* (Moscow, 1975).

27. There are foreign *gastarbeiter*, but their large-scale importation would require drastic changes in long-established policies and is at best a very remote possibility.

28. See Azrael, *Emergent Nationality Problems in the USSR*, section 2, for a fuller discussion of these two alternatives and the underlying situation from which they emerge. The immediately following paragraphs draw heavily on this discussion.

29. See Brezhnev's report to the Twenty-fifth Party Congress, translated in *Current Digest of the Soviet Press* 28, no. 8 (24 March 1976):7. On the new State Committee, see *Radio Liberty Dispatch*, 20 August 1976. The head of this committee, V. G. Lomonosov, reportedly worked in the Central Asian section of the CPSU Secretariat before he became Uzbekh's second secretary.

30. The precise number of Chinese Turkic refugees in the USSR is uncertain but has been estimated in the tens of thousands. See, for example, Christopher S.

Wren, "Kazakhstan Beckons Refugees from China," the *New York Times,* 24 April 1976, p. 8. Well-informed Soviet authorities have allegedly told U.S. interlocutors that these refugees are purposely segregated from their Soviet kinsmen, lest they lose interest in the reclamation of "their own" territory on the Chinese side of the border.

31. See Yaacov Ro'i, *The Role of Islam and the Soviet Muslims in Soviet Arab Policy* (Jerusalem: Jerusalem Academic Press, 1975).

32. Cf. Mu'ammar al-Qadhaffi, *Fi-al-Naziriyyal al-Thalithah* [On the third theory] (Benghazi, 1974), p. 28, and "The Islamic and Chinese Peoples in the Soviet Union Should Determine Their Own Destiny," *Al-Alam* (Rabat), 9 November 1975, pp. 2–3 (trans. in *JPRS* 66295, 5 December 1975, pp. 13–14) as well as the sources cited in note 29, above.

33. See Rasma Silden Karklins, "*The Role of 'Foreign Minorities' in Soviet Foreign Policy*" (Ph.D. diss., University of Chicago, 1975).

34. The Helsinki Final Act is, of course, the prime example.

7

Mass Expectations
and Regime Performance

Walter D. Connor

It is not clear that a nation's internal dynamics have a great deal to do with the foreign policy options it perceives or the policies it eventually follows — at least it cannot be taken as universal that foreign policies can always be traced back to domestic determinants. Yet the lack of clarity reflects changes wrought in the modern age. When wars, conflict, and accommodation were a matter of monarch-to-monarch deals, requiring or dispensing with the use of forces that extended little beyond mercenaries and feudal vassals, foreign policy had little to do with domestic conditions.

Characteristic of the developed world since the industrial revolution is the reliance of rulers on both large national armed forces and the production of a large range of goods within their borders, with the consequent involvement of the whole population in laying the human and material base for policies of any sort. Over the shorter term populations can be coerced into involvement — but it becomes harder. The USSR, a latecomer to development, has not escaped this pattern. This chapter explores some aspects of the regime's reliance on the Soviet population — specifically, the pressures on and ability of the regime and the economy it manages to provide: (1) material goods in the here and now; (2) the prospect, in career terms, of a good or at least tolerable life at work for the majority of its citizens, beyond everyday bread-and-butter concerns; and (3) the yet more intangible spiritual goods in the broad sense, which go beyond material and career concerns. Presumably, satisfied populations will more readily acquiesce to government foreign policy directions, having more confidence that the correct lines are being pursued. Short- or long-term economic grievances or strong reservations about the moral atmosphere a regime creates will detract from such support. We shall attempt to specify in what ways, stressing at various points that this is an exploratory and very speculative enterprise.

Background

Today the Soviet Union, for all the tremendous human cost recorded in its almost sixty-year history, is by any measure a politically stable entity. Its stability is rooted in history and based on elements of political legitimacy and practical effectiveness. Its legitimacy is based on the fact that, making use of its coercive resources and its control over education, the media, etc., the regime has managed to convince the vast majority of the population (barring the dissidents) that the political institutions and their mode of operation are appropriate — perhaps that they are in fact the only conceivable institutions.[1] Convincing the population was easier because a democratic alternative — liberal political institutions operating within rule-of-law limits on the basis of real elections — was not something that the masses, either at the birth of the Soviet state or in more recent years, demanded or even understood.

Soviet legitimacy is based on the positive grounds of effectiveness as well. The basic functions of government have been performed in a fitting manner. A continual emphasis on growth has satisfied big business — in its Soviet variant the ministerial hierarchy and managers who cope better with demands for quantity than for quality and variety. Allocations of resources and status to national defense have been sufficient to keep the armed forces happy. Presumably, other powerful groups (the regional party bosses and the KGB — still a power, if not what it once was) are also satisfied enough with the effectiveness of governmental functioning.

What of the mass of the population? How does it see the basic functions of government and how does it rate the effectiveness with which they are performed? As far as directly political functioning is concerned, I doubt that most Soviet citizens have serious complaints. National defense and the role the USSR plays as a superpower are positive values for the population. With respect to internal order, most are used to and respect a government that gives orders — and most probably believe that things are, after all, not much different in the West despite democratic propaganda (while those who do recognize the differences often view the polity-society interaction in the West, the crime problem, and the proliferation of alternative lifestyles as some species of anarchy). While these observations do not all apply to the programmatic political dissidents with alternative designs for the Soviet polity nor to religious and nationalist activists who challenge the state's code of operation in these areas, they do apply to the majority. The latter understands the rules, written and unwritten; knows what sorts of deviant behavior are tolerated; and knows that, in this post-Stalin era, one will not be arrested for doing nothing. It is a livable, if repressive, set of rules and surely more tolerable than the Stalinism that older Soviet citizens remember.

Effectiveness has another side, however—economic performance. As the trustee of national productive capacity for the population-as-owner, the state is committed to delivering the goods. This is the secular side of the claim to legitimacy, a side that has grown in importance in the USSR as the use of coercion on a mass scale has abated and as, despite all the recent détente-related vigilance rhetoric, the state comes to a tacit agreement with the population that apoliticality is sufficient, carrying on its agitprop more from habit and organizational inertia than from any confidence that the population will emerge politicized and conscious.

What are the current expectations of the Soviet population with respect to both the political conditions of their life and the material basis of that life? What can the regime deliver in the light of those expectations? And, on the assumption that official perceptions of public demand and the adequacy of regime response to that demand color official views of what is possible in foreign policy, how are these linked to the formulation of that policy in the USSR now and in the years to come? These are questions to be explored— hardly answered in any definitive sense—and the exploration can appropriately begin with the peculiar consciousness that, it seems to me, is now characteristic of the Soviet masses.

Soviet Man, Trade-Union Consciousness, and Goulash Communism

To those who would make revolutions, transform systems, and reshape the context of human social experience, the tension between the utopias and the common person's preference for a quiet life among familiar things, for improvements within understandable bounds, is vexing. Lenin, in a well-known passage, labeled the phenomenon "trade-union consciousness."[2]

The status of trade-union consciousness becomes more ambiguous when it exists within the context of a successful revolutionary regime, presumably able to provide the appropriate and correct ideological guidance. Stalin made some obeisance to it when, in naming the targets for the First Five-Year Plan, he specified (through his mouthpiece, V. V. Kuibyshev) a 70 percent increase in real wages and a major increase in the supply of consumer goods for the Soviet masses: a promise to tickle the consciousness of any trade-unionist, but rapidly broken by the logic of the plan era.

Yet with the decompression after Stalin's death, trade-union consciousness reemerged, almost by invitation. Far from being the object of derision it was to Lenin, it is now a critical element in Soviet political stability and one the regime wishes to promote, albeit within limits. As Lenin correctly understood, trade-union consciousness is an impediment to developing demands for systemic change, and his contemporary heirs have no revolution to make, but a large political stake to protect.

In a more general sense, secularization has come to the Soviet polity, however poorly official rhetoric may reflect this reality; it is manifest in the regime's relations with the masses, and vice versa. Secularization refers to the apparent forbearance of the regime from asking any heroic efforts of the population, from attempting to mobilize it in the pursuit of the gigantic goals of the 1930s. It also means that the population does not look to the regime for grand collective purposes to which to bend their efforts — the joys and concerns of today's Soviet citizens are private, and this is understood by the regime.

In the positive sense, secularization entails the increasing reliance of the regime on material effectiveness as a basis for legitimacy. As long as it can deliver the goods people expect, at the rates they expect, the regime correctly anticipates that it will receive support. For the mass, secularization means what I have earlier called "expectancy":[3] that a "good" government can and will provide jobs, housing, decent wages, and a supply of goods on which to spend them. Years ago, research on Stalin-era Soviet emigrés showed a marked orientation toward welfare-state paternalism under socialist auspices, most pronounced among the younger emigrés (contemporaries of today's Soviet middle-aged population).[4] While the expectations were not met in Stalin's time, they have been met in more recent years.

Ideological appeals still are made to the population, but in the years of Brezhnev and Kosygin more has been staked on the secular exchange of the regime's material delivery for the population's support. The population is apolitical, but this is no problem. Soviet leaders have not yet gone so far as Kadar to say that "he who is not against us is with us," but their implicit message to the mass has been close to this and the target has been the preservation of internal stability with minimized reliance on the expense and dysfunctional instrumentalities of coercion and terror. Thus delivery of everyday goods is important — and a complex process.

Regime as Producer, Citizen as Consumer

Satisfactory performance in this aspect of material life depends on at least three factors: (1) the ability of the regime to manipulate and control demand — not in the economist's sense as much as in the sense of consciousness; (2) the ability of the regime to manipulate perceptions of how the economy works; and (3) the actual rate of success in delivering goods and services for which the demand is legitimate, i.e., recognized by regime and mass alike.

On the first factor, it seems that the ability is considerable and has been effectively used. In many dimensions the living standard of the Soviet population is still deplorably low compared to other industrialized countries, yet those countries have not become elements in the frame of reference of most Soviet citizens. Barred from travel abroad and limited in access to nonofficial sources of information about the outside world, they compare their own past and that of their parents with the present and find the present better. The frame of reference is comparative chronologically, but still largely limited to the USSR. This frame of reference imposes limits on what is considered possible and conceivable. Against such a backdrop, the modest but real and cumulative improvements of recent years in food, housing, and consumer durables are quite important.

The Soviet regime — since Stalin as before 1953 — has also been effective in manipulating perceptions of the operations of the economy as far as the common man is concerned. Quite reasonably, a Soviet propagandist can cite the large income tax endured by the public in Western capitalist and social-democratic states and compare it to the much more moderate Soviet rate, all without clarifying for his listeners the large percentage of the retail prices they pay that is a (quite regressive) tax itself. Citing the real pains of inflation in the West, the propagandist need not specify the role shortages play as an alternative in the Soviet economy nor the inflation hidden in the retirement of a given item at a certain price from the market and its replacement by an improved equivalent item at a higher price. There are no radical economists to demystify economics for the Soviet citizen nor does his secondary-school instruction in *obshchestvovedenie* (social science) reveal how the economy functions. On a more general level, the unique quality of Soviet economic accomplishments is stressed in a manner that conveniently and effectively ignores qualifying facts. It has been in the interest of Soviet leaders since 1953 to contrast the rising living standards of the post-Stalin period with the grim years preceding — but it would scarcely be in their interest to remind the man in the street that the pre–1928 standards of living were much higher than those of 1928–1953. Similarly, citing impressive time-series of economic indicators, one can demonstrate tremendous progress in per capita provision of education, medical care, and a whole variety of goods and services that make the USSR seem a uniquely successful experiment in the promotion of human welfare. Given the political dividends such facts produce, one undestands why so little attention is paid to the fact Cyril Black demonstrated a decade ago: that on most major per capita indicators of progress the USSR, despite its achievements, has not passed the nations that were ahead of the Russian Empire in 1914.[5] Those nations, too, have progressed mightily since then, generally at a lower cost in human life and social upheaval than that imposed on the Soviet people.

On the third point, from the perspective of the Tenth Five-Year Plan, facts are not so clear. There is evidence of a disjunction between the recent past and the near- and middle-term future that might, under certain circumstances, pose problems for the maintenance of domestic morale and thus for the foreign policy options the USSR can entertain.

As a whole, the past ten to fifteen years have been ones of adequate and more than adequate Soviet economic performance. Consumption grew in the 1966–1970 period at an annual average of 4.8 percent — a healthy figure — with the soft goods and consumer durables components leading at rates of 6.5 and 8.9 percent, respectively.[6] Food supply and diet quality similarly saw marked improvement, all within the context of an Eighth Five-Year Plan that had not announced any precedent-breaking inversion of the time-honored priority of heavy industry over the consumer sectors.

Such an announcement was made for the Ninth Five-Year Plan (1971–1975), but growth in consumption failed to respond to this rhetorical prod. Total consumption increased at a more modest annual average of 3.1 percent, while foods fell to 2.7 percent per annum from the 4.0 percent of 1966–1970.[7] Group A growth rates exceeded those of group B even in this consumer-oriented plan period. In any case, a real consumption growth rate in the 3 percent range is not bad performance, and we can allocate some of the shortfall it represents to the harvest disasters of 1972 and 1975. However, given its climatic and geographic characteristics, the USSR will remain hostage to its agricultural economy and the slowdown of 1971–1975 depends on other factors for a more complete explanation, including the trends for the future of consumer satisfaction it indicates.

Improving the lot of Soviet consumers has, in the past, been mainly a matter of adding more producers to the labor force. But, as Gregory Grossman notes, around 1970 the Soviet economy "began to run out of plentiful reserves of labor for industrialization and modernization."[8] Rates of increase in nonagricultural employment tailed off markedly in 1971–1975 and the Tenth Five-Year Plan targets a less than 1 percent per year average increase in industrial employment. Had the USSR a history of rapidly increasing labor productivity, had it evidenced effective substitution of capital for labor over the years, and had it shown prospects of steadily increasing capital formation, the deficit of producers would not loom so seriously. But none of these is the case and the goals of the Tenth Five-Year Plan demonstrate appropriate moderation: It is a leaner plan, with consumption increases targeted at less than the 1971–1975 plan level, but higher than the actual growth achieved in that period. Lack of new manpower, expected difficulties in achieving greater productivity per unit of capital invested, and the ever-present threat of bad harvests all must be sobering to the Soviet leaders and planners, since they have staked much on the ability of the economy to meet consumers' demands. If popular expectations are mounting at a rapid rate the question of how much support the regime can command from the population will be sharply posed. If expectations as to nature and rate of material improvement remain roughly constant, there may still be room for concern, since the goals of the plan clearly indicate, along some fronts, a deceleration of growth rates. Should its negative results become evident across a broad enough spectrum of consumption, this deceleration may raise some questions in the minds of workers: Why send foreign aid to unreliable and exotic Third World regimes when Soviet citizens are tightening their belts? Why give subsidies to Czechoslovakia and Poland to keep such uncertain socialist allies quiescent when Soviet citizens have been loyal and docile?

Still, such questioning seems fairly distant. The impact of more than a decade of improvement is still palpable. People today are better fed, shod, and provisioned as consumers than in the past and they know it. The general stability of the ruling Politburo, despite the Podgorny affair, must reassure those who think about the potential connections between instability at the top and changes in the consumer economy. If the new plan is lean, it means only that the pace of improvement will decelerate, not that things will become worse in general. In the past ten years many citizens in urban USSR have attained their basic needs — a private apartment, a decent wardrobe, an assortment of foods, and a television set. They will not lose these and more citizens will acquire them. As far as the relatively affluent citizens are concerned (affluent generally because of their valued skills and thus people whose satisfaction is important to the regime) the situation is hardly bleak. Considerable resources, for instance, went into the automobile complex at Togliatti for a product that comparatively few citizens will be able to afford for some time to come. Many more who can already pay for automobiles will have Zhigulis just as they will be able to acquire Finnish-Estonian furniture suites, color TVs, and the like. The increasingly cooperative housing strategy not only allows the state to absorb more of the excess rubles of the affluent, but allows people to satisfy discretionary cravings for better residences.

Something of a balance has been struck between supply and demand, the ability of the state to offer and provide goods, services, and growth and the public's expectations that life will get better and certainly not fall below certain material minima all too well remembered by some. Different sectors of the public, with different levels of demand, have been taken care of, each commensurate with its anticipated ability to affect the stability of the system. From the elites, who enjoy special distribution networks and special rubles, down to the masses, who have much less but enough to keep them from anomic collective outbursts, the reward structure is adequately if roughly calibrated. Given its continued monopoly over coercive resources, the regime has a certain amount of maneuvering room in this regard: Things could worsen somewhat for the masses without a compromise of stability serious enough to affect Soviet external postures. Rioters were shot in Novocherkassk in 1962; they will be shot again in similar situations. But this is scarcely a desirable situation and one may assume that the leadership wishes to alienate neither mass nor elite.

In sum, to look at the future is to see the prospect of reductions in the regime's room for maneuver. The slowing of the economy as it reaches, in Grossman's words, "middle age " is apparently a given. Beyond this other problems arise, independent of any quantum jumps in consumer expectations. Real per capita incomes have risen faster than consumption — funds accumulated in savings deposits have reached an awesome total. The 1976–1980 plan aims at bringing income and consumption into better balance, but no such outcome is guaranteed. From planners' viewpoints, the shortages so familiar to Soviet citizens are in large measure a product of subsidized low prices — meat and bread are too cheap. Yet the price increases that might reconcile demand to supply would not be popular with the consumers. The lessons of Poland in 1970 and 1976 are not readily transferable to the more docile Soviet population, but Soviet leaders cannot ignore them completely.

Imports of consumer goods and Western technology are no panacea for the problems. Inflation has increased the prices since the early 1970s and the USSR is unlikely to repeat some of the bargains of the recent past. Not yet viewed as a real credit risk, it still faces the prospect of closer examination when dealing in the hard-currency markets. Its reliance on technology import may increase but the results, at their best, will not completely suffice to counteract the trends already identified.

Economics, Careers, and Social Mobility

A longer-term aspect of economic performance and popular satisfaction reaches — in scope — well beyond the supply and demand of foods, services, and durables and — in time — beyond the beginning of the post-Stalin era: the impact of economic growth on occupational or social mobility. What can be more impressive to those whose early life (or that of their parents) reflected the twilight of a semifeudal estate society, what better fodder for the success stories parents and grandparents tell the young than the changes that made urban workers out of the hitherto-despised peasants and briefcase-carrying white-collared intelligentsia of workers and their children? As prices fall or stabilize and supplies stabilize or rise, one can live better — but this is a matter of everyday life, its ups and downs. It is very different from change that involves a whole new way of life, a new career that makes one a new person.

The massive process of industrialization in the USSR since 1928 has reshaped the occupational structure, creating the demand that children abandon the occupations of their fathers for expanding sectors of the economy. And it is the way of the modern world, of the process of industrialization, that these structural changes diminish the lowly and disreputable occupations while increasing those generally held in higher regard—an upward shift in the occupational prestige profile of a society's employed persons.

The changes over time in the USSR reflect two basic trends: an increase in the relative and absolute numbers of clean (nonmanual or white-collar) jobs and a shift in the manual sector, with agriculture contracting and industrial blue-collar work expanding. In great measure, nonmanual jobs are viewed as better than manual ones even in those cases where pay is similar. For all the revolutionary rhetoric the USSR has been, and remains, a rather European country in the degree to which headwork is valued over handwork. Similarly, it is better to be a worker, with an urbanized life, a bounded work day, and regular wages, than to be a peasant.

Judged in the perspective of many individual experiences, such structural changes signify millions of cases in which children can compare their jobs with those of their parents and conclude that they have, indeed, advanced. This is an important asset for a government that, on the whole, imposed severe privations on its population through much of its existence, reflected so graphically in the decline of the average standard of living after 1928.

The historical impact has been of major importance and can be summarized thus:

1. During the Soviet period, despite the large number of peasants still on the land, the pronounced trend has been toward increasing the supply of higher prestige and generally higher paid nonmanual jobs at the expense of manual ones and the supply of nonfarm manual jobs at the expense of farm occupations. The relatively modern Soviet occupational structure of today is weighted more heavily than in the past toward better jobs.

2. The holders of the better jobs throughout much of Soviet history have, of necessity, been recruited to these expanding sectors from lower origins. Nonmanuals were heavily of worker, somewhat less of peasant, background; the working class derived largely from former peasants and their offspring. Thus, all were upward-mobiles.

3. The linked processes of structural changes in occupational distribution and social mobility have increased the supply of people with some stake in the system (nonmanuals and workers, especially skilled) while diminishing the percentage of peasants who have had little reason to like the

system. In essence, development and the mobility it created have increased the number of people with some positive attitudes toward the system and the regime.[9]

4. This social mobility was a possibly critical element in the preservation of political stability at relatively low cost (i.e., limiting the coercion necessary) when other economic changes threatened to undermine it. Mobility was probably greatest during the heroic period of industrialization and reconstruction (1928–1953) during which the standard of living of all major social strata declined. Workers, peasants, and nonmanuals in their majority lived less well after 1928 than before—but the old (prerevolutionary and NEP) nonmanual and industrial working classes were not the same as the new ones. Peasant recruits flooded the old working class and the expansion of state activity meant that the mass of workers and peasants recruited to nonmanual positions inundated the old nonmanuals. The new men lacked the comparative frame of reference of the old and for them this mobility generally meant real advancement in material and prestige terms, even if the objective situations of nonmanuals and industrial workers were worse after 1928 than before. Mobility absorbed the shock of a declining standard of living.[10]

What of future prospects for economic performance in this respect? Will the USSR be able to produce intergenerational mobility rates commensurate with popular expectations? Have popular expectations increased such that the demands placed on the system are now more pressing?

We do not have the data necessary to assess current against past performance. We can, however, point to some potential stress points, where mass desires and governmental policy (and capacity) are not and probably cannot be synchronized. First, while the number of secondary school graduates and the number desiring a place in a university expands, the space in higher educational institutions has not kept pace. Nor, since the late 1950s, has the regime thought that it should. Hopes and desires have not yet responded to realities and, as the Soviet press and journals continually document, the failure to be admitted to the university is a crisis in many young lives. Specialized secondary education and a technician's career are small compensation for such a failure, although it is exactly this sort of education into which planners have tried to direct the young.[11]

Second, the phenomenon of shrinking space exacerbates an already inegalitarian pattern of access to higher education by class origin. As V. N. Shubkin and other Soviet researchers have demonstrated,[12] children of the intelligentsia are greatly overrepresented and children of routine white-collar employees somewhat overrepresented in universities, while worker and peasant children occupy a smaller share of lecture hall seats than their proportion of the population would dictate. As the number of spaces available constricts in relation to the demand, the cultural and motivational (to say nothing of financial) advantages of the more fortunately born amplify in value.

Given that education is the sine qua non of upward mobility, this would suggest, third, that fewer persons born outside the intelligentsia enjoy real chances of being upwardly mobile into it and that it will tend to become an increasingly hereditary stratum. To the degree that worker and peasant children accept the desirability of intelligentsia occupations (and Soviet research indicates that they share essentially the same perceptions of occupational prestige, attractiveness, and desirability as the children of the urban intelligentsia)[13] this raises the level of career frustration we may anticipate.

Fourth, the mobility from peasant to worker and from rural farming to urban industrial employment, which made the fundamental social transformation of the USSR, has entered a new and ambiguous phase. For all the alarm about youth (especially better educated males) leaving the village, a large percentage of the population remains in agriculture, though there is no indication that it wants to. Given the low skill levels of so much of this labor force and the rather low efficiency of the large capital investments made in agriculture under Brezhnev, the question arises whether the economy can tolerate any substantial downturn in the number of hands in agriculture without exacerbating the food supply situation.

There is an element of paradox in this last point. While agricultural investment, greatly increased under Brezhnev, has been low in its productivity yields, the real incomes of collective farmers have been increasing at a faster rate than those of the nonagricultural labor force. Thus there has been real improvement here, too—yet not enough to moderate desires to leave the villages.

This brings us to a consideration of the longer-run consequences of the social mobility that is now part of Soviet history. Economic development policies and the mobility they created have led in the USSR, as in Eastern Europe, to an expansion of the intelligentsia and routine nonmanual ranks and of the working class and a contraction of the relative size of the peasantry. The nonpeasant strata's growth through upward mobility from the peasantry meant that the new members of these strata had received benefits from the regime, while the process itself creamed off the young and talented from a peasantry that was severely exploited, thus releasing pressures among what was then the largest occupational stratum.

Today, however, intelligentsia and working class are more typically hereditary in composition—the upward-mobiles of the Stalin years have seen their children find places in the same strata. These children lack the reference points of their parents and thus have less reason to feel that, despite scarcities and long lines, they are doing well. Collectively, these strata dispose of considerable resources—education, skill, the complex of characteristics that distinguish urbanites from villagers—and make for more readily mobilizable strata. Economic development has increased the size of the very strata on which the regime must depend, but their current composition suggests that these strata are not necessarily as dependable as they were in the past. Similarly, for all its privations the peasantry remained outside politics, immobile and dispersed—a source of stability, if not active support, for the system. But now it represents a smaller proportion of the population than ever before and even if increased incomes render it more supportive of the regime, the value of its support is moderated by its size. Poland has become a victim of this process, exhibiting since 1970—and especially since 1976—marked social instability. Though the process has not gone so far in the USSR (nor is it likely to), a future in which Soviet intelligentsia and the industrial working class no longer are content with the economy's, and hence the regime's, performance cannot be discounted. To go beyond what is presently evident to what is at least conceivable if not probable in the future is to see the prospect of resentments welling up from working-class parents and their children as those children see their early ambitions for success turned into the same working-class reality as that of their parents. Will they readily support a system that increasingly locks them into their original stratum or will resentment grow as they come to view themselves as passive objects of economic manipulation?

Underlying all this is a changing demographic picture within which the future processes of mobility will take place.[14] Declining birth rates have taken their toll—the prospect for the 1980s and beyond is reduced numbers of able-bodied persons entering the labor force. Nothing can be done to reduce this deficit, which impinges on prospects for the supply of both industrial and military manpower. Both need to be conserved. For industry this implies even less favorable regime attitudes toward outflow from the working class, especially by the children of the skilled-worker cadres in the large cities. For the military it raises the prospect of lengthened enlistment periods, squeezing industry. Neither of these possibilities accords with the cumulative individual aspirations of many Soviet youths. (The ethnic dimension of the manpower dilemma, which reveals low urban-Slavic fertility, higher fertility among Central Asians, and thus a change in the ethnic composition of the new cohorts entering the labor force, is also important and will be dealt with later.)

Hearts and Minds

The economic aspects of career satisfaction or lack thereof shade off into the noneconomic sphere. How well does the Soviet regime satisfy the non-material aspirations of citizens in terms of feelings of security, satisfaction, a measure of autonomy, and an acceptable quality of life? The evidence seems to indicate that it has done rather well for the majority of the population. On the whole, workers, peasants, and much of the intelligentsia are adjusted to the system — to government regulation of so many areas of private life, to the recurring collective ritual of elections, to the regime's refusal to countenance the notion of a loyal opposition. The mass political culture, if not parochial, is subject to nature.[15] Soviet citizens, in the mass, expect to be governed, not to be left free to pursue any path they might choose. Freedom of communication, expression, travel, etc., means little. Indeed, some Soviet citizens find the growing complexities of an increasingly urban life and its toll on family stability and intergenerational relations hard to encompass. The harsher but simpler and surer years of Stalin seem attractive at times, a feeling that is expressed in what Hedrick Smith has called a "nostalgia for a strong boss."[16] But by and large the Soviet citizenry is politically undemanding — mature enough to see mobilizational rhetoric as pro forma, mature enough to understand that the days of grand alternatives for which collective energies must be mobilized are past, but not mature enough to resent the restrictions under which it lives. Order prevails, terror does not; it is only terror, the sadistic and unpaternal behavior of a regime, to which they really object.

The dissidents, at least those of the "democratic movement," are more demanding. The freedoms of the West are reference points and salient considerations to them. But they are few and they lack public support. They are alone in their self-claimed participant orientation to politics.

Today a Soviet patriotism linked mainly to Russian-Slavic symbols and identity and promoted rather effectively by the regime provides a common rallying point for citizens, a basis for ready identification. Widespread fear of China — certainly the greatest external-enemy obsession of citizens — links regime, mass, and even many dissidents, providing the corresponding negative reference point. All in all, it seems fair to say that at least for the Slavic near-majority, expectations about an appropriate political life have been met and have contributed to popular support for and acquiescence to the regime's foreign policy orientations, whatever they might be. The risks of shortfalls in meeting expectations lie more in the material sphere.

Mass Demands, Delivery, and Foreign Policy

The previous pages indicate the difficulty in tying the discussed issues in any direct way to issues of present or future Soviet foreign policy and its direction. To go beyond suggestion — when one is faced with a largely apolitical population that is not much concerned with foreign affairs and is content to see politics remain the preserve of an elite — and to consider the effect of that population's level of satisfaction on foreign policy is to enter a realm of fairly broad speculation.

Matters are further complicated by the fact that public moods affect foreign policy only as they are perceived by the political leadership as refracted through the leadership's vision of what mass aspirations and convictions mean. This, in turn, raises the question of which leadership? The time is ripe for the beginnings of a succession, but we have yet to see them. Even allowing for the possibility of several more years of Brezhnev, some contingencies of the succession must be taken into account.

Given the complexities, the aim here is to elaborate some potential future lines of development in the Soviet external stance that in various ways reflect the regime's taking account of different possibilities and constraints imposed by perceived public moods.

First, perceptions may turn the leadership inward toward a de-emphasis on foreign engagements, a tactical and strategic retreat from some forward positions. Such perceptions would focus on the constraints posed by the economy's probable future performance, constraints that give cause for concern if not yet for alarm. A slowing growth rate, increasing ratios of capital inputs to outputs when nonhuman as well as human capital is no longer so plentiful, and the general industrial-military implications of the manpower shortage raise the prospect of imposing greater burdens on the population than the Brezhnev regime likes to contemplate. To some in the leadership or close to it the prospect of assuring internal stability through a program that will not impose such burdens must have its attractions.

Such a program would involve the promotion or acceptance of a more substantial détente than is yet evident, up to and including some moderate quid pro quo in Soviet internal policy to attract further Western (primarily U.S.) technological inputs on a stable basis and reallocation of investment from the military budget to civilian producer and consumer sectors to service the new technology and meet consumer expectations. This, in turn, would entail a somewhat less activist posture in some areas of Soviet foreign policy concern.

The idea of such a program is optimistic from the U.S. viewpoint, but there are also reasons why it might appear attractive to Soviet policymakers. First, the economic problems may well be insoluble (barring severe cuts in the growth of consumption) without external inputs and, in their readiness to continue grain purchases at less advantageous terms, Soviet leaders have shown themselves quite sensitive to the implications of declines in welfare. Second, involvements in Africa (in the Horn, in Angola) have not paid large dividends and could be cut without any outcry from a populace lacking in Third World sympathies. (The use of Cuban soldiers in Angola shows the USSR no more ready than it has been in the past to involve Soviet troops in operations far from Soviet borders and in some measure must be attributable to anticipated morale and discipline problems.) Third, the time may seem ripe — and running against the USSR — for broad-ranging arms agreements with the U.S. and the West. The Carter administration thus far has combined signals of desire for progress on SALT with signals indicating a readiness to contemplate stepped-up military programs if the USSR continues in what seems to many a rather inflexible posture. Soviet defense expenditures and military manpower needs are expensive to a troubled economy; matching a U.S. buildup will increase the expenses. To some, the present period may appear as a window in time, when certain accommodations may be possible at minimal cost but expensive and perhaps unattainable when the window closes.

There are reasons for an optimistic projection of Soviet concerns about mass material satisfactions onto foreign policy, but the current leadership probably does not read things this way. The problems delineated here have been clear to the leaders for some time and, in more favorable circumstances, they have not acted. A substantial change in the leadership would seem to be a sine qua non for such movement; but not just any change and not a change of the kind that is most probable.

A second set of possibilities is quite different; perceptions of a slowing economy and an extended manpower shortage may point to a window in time of another kind altogether. These perceptions can promote adventurism as well as retrenchment. Western technology may be perceived as carrying too high a price tag not only in the immediate concessions that might be demanded in tougher negotiations, but over the long term in its effects on the structure of Soviet administration and the CPSU's leading role. Without such external inputs, a further slowing of the economy can be predicted, precipitating the need to cope with prospects of mass material demands beyond the economy's power to deliver. Viewing the manpower situation, one could conclude that the increasing proportion of new hands who will be rural, nonindustrial, and Turkic in background signals problems in industry and in the military.

An adventurist reading of the portents might suggest that if the USSR wishes to push ahead, to garner new advantages through pressure, threats, or actual use of military force (in China, the Middle East, Europe, or Africa), the time to act is soon, before adverse trends have increasing effect. Warsaw Pact forces are as reliable as they are likely to be a decade from now; the Soviet population is still disciplined and reasonably content, still reflexively patriotic and — if properly appealed to on the basis of foreign threats to the Soviet position — ready to endure some belt-tightening to meet those threats. Thus far, the Western powers have not shown a tougher stance toward the USSR in the areas that seem to count most. But from Moscow the trend may be interpreted as moving in that direction, encouraging some to urge quick action.

The details must remain vague here — we are after all dealing in speculation — but again, such a line of development seems to require a substantially new leadership. Many will dismiss the probability of a leadership with this orientation emerging from the succession, but it is far from impossible. It is comforting to predict, as one respected analyst and student of Soviet politics recently has, that "Once the generation of leaders who benefited from the purge has retired, there will be a strong natural tendency for Soviet internal policy to evolve in a more liberal direction — toward the more relaxed type of authoritarian state found in Poland."[17] But this is also misleading. Parenthetically, Poland's relaxed authoritarianism is to a large degree a function of an incomparably more demanding and politicized population, the counterbalance of the Church, and the still-flawed legitimacy of the regime — conditions that do not exist in the USSR and are not likely to exist. A younger leadership, unmarked by the purges and by World War II, hardly need be more liberal or less aggressive in foreign policy. Those men in their early to middle fifties, of whom we know so little but from whom we presume a new leadership must come — why should they be so accommodative to (questionable) strong natural tendencies? One could argue more reasonably that the scar tissue of collectivization, the plan era, the purge, and the war provided both Khrushchev and Brezhnev with a sense of the "possible" — within limits, a moderation of impulses to dominate, internally and abroad. The experience of a terrorized society followed by that of a nation almost destroyed by war reminds one that anything is possible, including the paralysis and collapse of one's own system or the rapid advancement of one's goals. Post-Stalin liberalization and a more moderate (though still expansionist) foreign policy than the USSR might have undertaken can be attributed as well to these experiences of the Khrushchevs and Brezhnevs as to any others. Younger people who lack such experiences may well have a lesser sense of "possibility"[18] and, faced with a situation where Brezhnev's foreign policy gains appear small compared to their view of current Soviet potential, may be all the more tempted to move sooner rather than later, whatever the risks. If the prospects for growing prosperity at home seem dim, the temptation may be a strong one. As Robert Conquest says, "Governments incompetent at home but capable of demagogic expansionism abroad have traditionally — one might almost say automatically — turned to foreign adventure."[19]

But neither is this, it seems to me, the likeliest reading of the internal situation and its implications by even a new leadership. The optimistic projection first given and this pessimistic one both imply more substantial shifts in the Politburo, Secretariat, and even perhaps the CPSU Central Committee than will come over a short period. The fortunes of younger men at the top have not been good. No chosen successor to Brezhnev is identifiable from this new generation and none probably exists. Despite the calendar, which reminds us that Brezhnev Kirilenko, Kosygin, Suslov et al. cannot live forever, the succession is probably more a matter of years than months.

If this is the case, there will be enough elements of gradualism to make most probable a balance much like that which seems to underlie the current policy of the Politburo. Both of the previous projections assume a certain alarmism in leadership views of Soviet prospects, a quality the current leaders do not manifest. Their concern seems to be with "satisficing" rather than "maximizing" — a preference to limit risks. Although the leaders desire technology, they refuse to countenance economic reforms that might make better use of that which they import. Although they want stability at home and in Eastern Europe above all, they cannot refrain from foreign involvements with risky and dubious payoffs. Concerned with meeting mass expectations, they continue to take measures to control the growth of those expectations and remain ready to use coercion, to some unspecified point, to respond to any disorderly overflow.

The recipe is inelegant, but it has worked thus far. It bears the marks of compromise among the interests and persuasions represented in the Politburo. This Politburo will probably recruit one much like itself — a body that will include men who could accommodate to our first projection as well as the more aggressive who would lean toward the second. The next Politburo, with a substantially different group of full members, should resemble the current one in this respect as well. It will probably be as attentive to mass satisfactions as the current one, as likely to take half-measures to increase technological imports for the consumer sector to maintain some increase in living standards and to hold coercion in ready reserve should belt-tightening be necessary on a large scale. It may attempt various economic measures to sweeten the pill of less extraordinary career prospects for ambitious offspring of the manual strata or it may decide to attempt to ride the dissatisfactions out, assuming that aspirations will eventually be moderated. In all this it will rely on a population that has shown it can endure a great deal without revolting, but whose composition includes more and more younger persons who, by Soviet standards, have not had to endure a great deal.

Anything is possible, but the internal and foreign operating context of the Soviet leadership now and a few years hence, as it is perceived by that leadership, should not be one of grand or horrific alternatives. For such a group does not seem likely to perceive the world in terms quite so extreme.

Notes

1. See, for instance, Valery Chalidze's comments in *To Defend These Rights: Human Rights in the Soviet Union* (New York: Random House, 1974), p. 149.

2. V. I. Lenin, *What is to be Done?* (New York: International Publishers, n.d.), pp. 32–33.

3. Walter D. Connor, "Generations and Politics in the USSR," *Problems of Communism* 24, no. 5 (September-October 1975):26–27.

4. See Alex Inkeles and Raymond A. Bauer, *The Soviet Citizen: Daily Life in a Totalitarian Society* (Cambridge: Harvard University Press, 1961), esp., pp. 242, 254.

5. See Cyril E. Black, "Soviet Society: A Comparative View," in Allen Kassof, ed., *Prospects for Soviet Society* (New York: Praeger Publishers, 1968), esp., pp. 40–43.

6. Estimates from Rush Greenslade, "Economic Development and Popular Expectations" (Paper for Workshop on Political Stability and Socio-Economic Change in the Soviet Union, Research Institute on International Change, Columbia University, 4–5 May 1976), p. 2.

7. Ibid.

8. Gregory Grossman, "An Economy at Middle Age," *Problems of Communism* 25, no. 2 (March-April 1976):18.

9. Inkeles and Bauer, *Soviet Citizen*; see, for various tabular data related to this, pp. 239–265.

10. For a more detailed consideration of the impact of mobility in this respect, see Walter D. Connor, *Socialism, Politics and Equality: Hierarchy and Change in Eastern Europe and the USSR* (New York: Columbia University Press, 1978).

11. See Mervyn Matthews, *Class and Society in Soviet Russia* (London: Penguin Press, 1972), p. 282.

12. See V. N. Shubkin, *Sotsiologicheskie opyty* (Moscow, 1970); M. N. Rutkevish and F. R. Filippov, *Sotsial'nye peremeshcheniia* (Moscow, 1970); see also the articles in Murray Yanowitch and Wesley A. Fisher, eds., *Social Stratification and Mobility in the USSR* (White Plains, N.Y.: International Arts and Sciences Press, 1974).

13. That is, workers' children aspire in almost as large numbers as intelligentsia's children to intelligentsia occupations. Peasant children express lower aspirations in some instances, focus more on the industrial worker stratum than on the distant intelligentsia, but this seems to indicate a tempering of aspirations by reality rather than a different type of aspiration. See, e.g., Shubkin, *Sotsiologicheskie opyty*, p. 180.

14. For the most recent treatment of this whole complex of issues, see Murray Feshbach and Stephen Rapawy, "Soviet Population and Manpower Trends and Policies," in U.S. Congress, Joint Economic Committee, *Soviet Economy in a New Perspective* (Washington, D.C.: U.S. Government Printing Office, 1976) pp. 113–154.

15. Connor, "Generations and Politics," pp. 25–26.

16. Hedrick Smith, *The Russians* (New York: Quadrangle Books/NYT, 1976), pp. 248–254.

17. See Jerry F. Hough, "The Soviet Succession: A Challenge for the Kremlin — and the U.S.," *Washington Post*, 17 April 1977, pp. C1–C2.

18. This, it sems to me, is a point Hough (ibid.) misses. Much has been said of

the self-confidence, the better education, etc., of the younger range of Soviet officials as compared with their elders of the Brezhnev generation. In some sense this makes them "easier to talk to" in various governmental or academic contacts—but these characteristics can cut two ways, and the generally positive impression one receives on the surface is of course not necessarily the most revealing one.

19. See Robert Conquest, "A New Russia? A New World?" *Foreign Affairs* 53, no. 3 (April 1975):492.

PART 3

Economics

8
Soviet Economic Development, Technological Transfer, and Foreign Policy

Herbert S. Levine

Introduction

Erosion in the growth of total labor and capital productivity in the Soviet economy during the 1960s and 1970s is the key aspect of Soviet economic performance that dominates all others in its effect on Soviet foreign policy. In an effort to counteract lagging productivity, Soviet leaders embarked on a program of massive imports of advanced technology and machinery from the advanced capitalist nations. The conduct of such a program, requiring as it does a significantly increased level of interaction with the capitalist world, has had a profound effect on Soviet foreign policy.

This chapter analyzes the economic elements in the developments just described, opening with a brief discussion of the productivity problem and some of its future implications, then examining past Russian involvement in the world economy. A historical pattern of this involvement and its relation to the process of technical change are described, followed by an analysis of current and projected Soviet economic relations with the advanced nations and the possibility of the Soviets pursuing a more intensive and long-term involvement in international economic interrelationships. The chapter concludes by stating some of the implications for the United States of the issues raised.

The Productivity Problem

An examination of the postwar record of Soviet economic growth provides the framework for understanding recent shifts in Soviet policy toward economic relations with the capitalist West. Such an examination forms the basis for an assessment of the Soviet economy's need for and potential gains from increased interrelatedness with advanced capitalist countries, and in particular Soviet imports of modern technology and machinery from the West.

If the postwar period is divided into three subperiods—the 1950s, the 1960s, and the first half of the 1970s—a significant relationship can be observed. First, the rate of growth of the Soviet national product has been steadily decreasing (though still remaining at a respectable level). Western calculations of Soviet growth and official Soviet data uphold this statement. According to certain Western calculations, the rate of growth of Soviet GNP in the 1950s was 6.7 percent per year; in the 1960s, 5.4 percent; and in the first half of the 1970s, 4.2 percent.[1] Official Soviet data show higher rates, but also a downward trend: 10.2 percent, 7.1 percent, and 5.7 percent.[2]

Second, while the rates of growth of output were declining, the rates of growth of labor plus capital inputs into the economy remained relatively stable over the entire 1950–1975 period (capital stock grew 8–9 percent and labor employment about 2 percent). What has been occurring is a decrease in the rate of growth of factor productivity. When a statistical comparison is made between the Western calculations of the rates of growth of output and the rates of growth of combined labor and capital inputs, it is evident that the rate of growth of total factor productivity in the Soviet Union has persistently decreased: from 1.7 percent per year in the period 1950–1960, to 0.7 percent in 1960–1970, and 0.1 percent in 1970–1975.[3] Thus during the most recent period output has grown slightly more rapidly than inputs.[4]

In developed industrial economies, increasing factor productivity is an important source of economic growth. Its decline in the Soviet economy has, therefore, become a matter of grave concern to Soviet leaders.[5] It may be seen as an erosion of the effectiveness of the Soviet growth model, which—in somewhat oversimplified form—has required Soviet authorities to concentrate on the maintenance of a steady growth in the supply of inputs into the economy with the expectation that this will lead to a more than proportional increase in output.

Moreover, the decline in factor productivity casts its shadow and leads to forecasts of serious tensions in the economy during the 1980s. In some long-term projections produced with the Stanford Research Institute/Wharton Econometric Forecasting Associates Soviet Econometric Model (SOV-MOD), future productivity problems and their consequences are indicated. While rates of growth of national product may remain in the 4–4.5 percent per year range in the 1975–1985 period, declining capital productivity combined with low labor force growth (the result of demographic factors) leads to an increasing share of investment in GNP and a decline in the share of consumption. In addition, agricultural output and productivity is projected to remain a difficulty.

Demographic and resource problems are serious and certain of their locational aspects not adequately taken into account by the model may constrain the growth of output below the relatively optimistic levels projected by the model. For example, while demographic data used in model calculations project the rate of growth of the working-age population declining from the current 1.5 percent per year to an extremely low 0.4 percent per year in the first half of the 1980s,[6] the model is not sensitive to the fact that the higher rates of growth of the non-Russian populations of the Soviet Union will tend to make the available labor force increasingly non-Russian in origin and located in outlying parts of the USSR, particularly Central Asia. This, coupled with the location of the bulk of Soviet industry far from Central Asia and the evident immobility of the Central Asian nationalities, may well reduce labor productivity and output growth below projected levels. Similarly, the looming energy shortage and the location of energy reserves in remote, difficult to exploit areas will add further downward pressure on Soviet growth prospects.

Another aspect of this prognosis is that although the data indicate that Soviet gross output could perhaps continue to grow in the 4 percent per year range to the mid-1980s without dramatic systemic changes, it is not likely that the Soviet Union would be able to keep up with the West in terms of modernity. This issue is of crucial importance to the Soviet leadership.

These clear and perceived needs have contributed to the Soviet interest in Western advanced technology, which increased in intensity at the end of the 1960s. As implied in the Tenth Five-Year Plan, these needs will contribute to the continued interest of Soviet leaders in Western technology, machinery, and equipment to the end of the 1970s and most likely beyond. Soviet trade with the nations of the developed West was (in nominal terms) five times as high in 1975 as it was in 1968, and machinery and high technology industrial materials imports were six times as high. And although the Soviet econometric model projections beyond 1980 do not show the same surge, they do indicate continued substantial growth. Total Soviet trade with the developed West is projected to be almost two and one-half times as high in 1985 as in 1975, and Soviet imports of machinery and industrial materials from the developed West are projected to increase by about the same ratio.

One aspect of this rapid growth of trade with the West is the increase in the share of Soviet trade, especially Soviet imports, accounted for by the

West. In 1968 the nations of the developed West accounted for 23 percent of Soviet imports; in 1975, this figure had risen to 36 percent; however, by 1985 it is projected to decline slightly to 32 percent.[7]

Past Pattern of Russian Involvement in the World Economy

This is not the first time in history that Russia has turned to the advanced West to acquire modern technology. In fact, it is possible to perceive a historical pattern of periodic forays into the international economy, primarily to procure inputs required for growth and modernization, associated with Russia's generally fitful pattern of economic development. Intense periods of rapid economic growth, in which Russian leaders attempt to catch up with the advanced nations of the West, are followed by periods of withdrawal and relative stagnation.[8]

Since the mid-fifteenth century, the history of Russia has been dominated by the theme of territorial expansion — originating in the small principality of Muscovy just emerging from Mongol rule, Russia has grown to its present size. During this process of expansion, the Russian state frequently came into contact and conflict with more advanced and more powerful Western nations. In such confrontations the expansionary ambitions of the Russian leaders were thwarted, primarily because of the relative backwardness of the Russian economy. The tension between ambition and ability led to the state's assuming the role of initiator of economic development, applying pressure on the international economy to grow rapidly to be able to support Russia's foreign policy aims. Thus the fitful nature of economic development observed in Russian history: When the military needs of the state were intense, the economy was pressured into rapid growth; and when a degree of power parity was reached with the West, the need for rapid growth subsided and the state removed its pressure for growth. As a consequence, a period of rapid growth was followed by a period of little or no growth. In past periods of importation of advanced technology the Russians were able, within a compressed period of time, to approach contemporary levels of economic development in the West and to some extent even the levels of contemporary technology in the West. Yet in the longer run, as the advanced nations of the West continued to develop new technology, the Russians were not able to maintain their relative position and fell back.

This pattern is seen in the period of Peter the Great at the beginning of the 1700s, the period of rapid growth of the 1890s, and the period of massive industrialization launched by Soviet leaders in the 1930s. At the beginning of the eighteenth century, under Peter the Great, the Russian economy experienced a tremendous surge of growth that brought it toward the existing levels of industrial development in advanced Western nations. Peter emphasized the importation of foreign technology and massive numbers of foreign technologists and built an economic base for the support of his military ambitions.

Within the past century there have been two major periods of concentrated Russian involvement in the world economy, again with major emphasis on the acquisition of advanced foreign technology. The first of these was connected with the industrialization spurt in the 1890s. It was led by the Russian minister of finance, Count Sergei Witte, whose policy was to encourage foreign investment in Russia. Foreign capital, especially French and Belgian, accounted for almost 50 percent of all new capital invested in Russia during the industrialization drive of the 1890s. In 1900, foreign companies owned more than 70 percent of the capital in mining, metallurgy, and machine building in Russia.

With this high level of foreign investment, not only was the capital stock of Russia greatly expanded but foreign technology was brought into Russia in the form of advanced capital equipment and human capital. Foreign technologists, experienced businessmen, managers, and engineers came to Russia as foreign companies were established. Direct foreign investment was thus responsible for the implantation of advanced techniques in several key industries. New technology was often incorporated with little or no adaptation. For example, the steel mills built in southern Russia after the mid-1880s were of the same technological level and size as those being built in Western Europe. In this period, with the continuing participation of foreigners in management, these steel mills kept up with West European progress and remained in the mainstream of world progress in steelmaking. Moreover, because foreign firms competed with Russian firms inside Russia, the latter were forced to be more efficient in order to survive.

During this period, Russian trade manifested characteristics typical of an underdeveloped economy: Russia exported raw materials and imported machinery and other industrial commodities. Its exports consisted chiefly of grain, lumber, and oil. Before the turn of the century, Russia was the second largest producer and the largest exporter of oil in the world. Its imports, in addition to machinery and equipment, consisted of certain commodities that it did not produce (rubber and nonferrous metals) and certain commodities that it did produce but for which the domestic demand exceeded the domestic capacity to produce (rolled ferrous metals, copper, coal, and cotton).[9]

A second period of major involvement in the world economy within the past century was the interwar period, especially the early 1930s. During the relatively free market-oriented period of the New Economic Policy of the

1920s, the Soviets attempted to import primarily foreign machinery and technology through the program of foreign concessions. The quantitative importance of this program is a matter of debate. Nevertheless, the actual number of business arrangements with foreign concerns was larger than commonly has been believed.[10] However, it was during the period of the First Five-Year Plan, 1928–1932, that major efforts were made to import foreign machinery and technology in connection with the industrialization program that was then being initiated.[11] With the emphasis on industrial capital formation, imports of machinery and equipment began to assume greater importance. By 1932, imports of machinery and equipment rose to a level of more than half of the total imports of the Soviet Union and imports of certain types of machines—turbines, generators, boilers, machine tools, metal-cutting machines—accounted for between 50 and 90 percent of the growth in the supply of these machines during the period of the First Five-Year Plan. On the whole, imports of capital goods from abroad totaled almost 15 percent of gross investment in the Soviet Union during this period. Furthermore, imports of certain basic industrial materials— lead, tin, nickel, zinc, aluminum, rubber—accounted for perhaps 90 to 100 percent of these materials consumed in the Soviet industrialization program. Clearly, imports of machinery and industrial commodities played an important role in Soviet economic growth during the First Five-Year Plan.

After the completion of the First Five-Year Plan, Soviet involvement in this type of trade declined. The decline can be attributed to several factors. First, trade policy was aimed at building import substitution capacity and was severely reduced after the delivery of necessary machinery. Second, in the recession of the 1930s, terms of trade worsened for the Soviet Union, i.e., the export prices of raw materials dropped significantly compared to machinery import prices. Third, the attitude in the United States toward trade with the USSR, after the granting of Most Favored Nation (MFN) status to the Soviet Union, shifted away from giving credit on favorable terms and toward conditioning trade terms on political concessions.[12]

In the next five-year plan—the period 1933–1937—imports of foreign capital goods fell drastically to about 2 percent of gross investment. Dependence upon the West for major products decreased dramatically. Sometimes imports of equipment fell rather suddenly. For example, imports of tractors in 1931 accounted for about 60 percent of the growth of the tractor stock in that year; in the next year they fell to zero.

From this brief survey of past Russian involvement in the international economy it can be seen that underlying the spasmodic historical pattern of Russian economic development has been the desire to catch up economically with advanced Western nations, to achieve military parity with them, and to protect and increase the national security and power of Russia.

The objective of assuring national independence and avoiding dependence on other nations has been of fundamental importance. In the 1890s there were many, especially among Russian nobility, who were opposed to Witte's policies. They charged that his program of bringing in foreign capital was endangering the national independence and was leading Russia into a position of colonial dependency on foreign capitalists. Witte, in defending his program, appealed to Russian nationalism. His program, he argued, was designed to free the country from dependence on foreign supplies of manufactured goods.[13] Only by building its productive forces could Russia remain independent and attain the position of a world power. He assured critics that Russia had the means and the power to control foreign investors who were being used to help develop the economy: "Only a disintegrating nation has to fear foreign enslavement. Russia, however, is not China."[14]

Soviet industrialization in the 1930s was imbued with the goal of gaining economic independence and strengthening the defense capabilities of the nation. In a famous speech in 1931, Stalin stated:

> One feature of the history of old Russia was the continual beatings she suffered for falling behind, for her backwardness. . . . Do you want our socialist fatherland to be beaten and to lose its independence? If you do not want this you must put an end to its backwardness in the shortest possible time. We are fifty or a hundred years behind the advanced countries. We must make good this distance in ten years. Either we do it, or they crush us.[15]

The pursuit of nondependence was written into the 1936 USSR Constitution and, according to Soviet foreign trade authorities, became the guiding objective in the formulation of Soviet foreign trade policy and planning. Although there were other factors, as indicated above, the political policy of nondependence made an important contribution to the drastic drop in Soviet trade in the middle and late 1930s.

Under this traditional pattern of Russian involvement in the world economy, the Russians in the past were able to approach (but rarely reach) contemporary world levels of technology with the technology they imported. In the longer run, however, as Western nations continued to develop new technology the Russians were not able to keep pace with the changes. Why have they had trouble in fully assimilating advanced technology and why have they been particularly weak in maintaining technology at world levels? Certain aspects of the situation under the Soviets have been amply discussed in the literature on the Soviet economy.[16] We will mention these briefly and add some observations that will help to explain Russian difficulties before the Revolution.

Among the Soviet economic institutions that affect the ability of the economy to absorb, to master, and to create new technology, the one that has received primary emphasis in both Western and Russian literature on the Soviet economy is the managerial incentive mechanism, which has more or less dominated the Soviet scene since the 1930s. In the past decade the Soviet economy has been undergoing certain administrative changes; while the current picture is not totally clear, the incentive mechanism is still basically related to the fulfillment of performance targets. In any situation such as this there are two ways of assuring success or increasing the possibility of success: (1) performance and (2) keeping the target within reasonable distance. The second aspect of target-type rewarding is detrimental to the innovation process. Innovation always involves risk. The compensation for risk contained in the reward for possible over-plan fulfillment is reduced by the fact that success today will mean a higher target tomorrow and managerial success in the system requires the rather regular meeting of targets. Thus managers resist innovation and try to keep targets low. There is much discussion in the Soviet Union about how to get around this problem, but nothing very effective has been introduced so far. Indeed, it can be argued that no significant results should be expected from attempts to improve Soviet technology assimilation such as the modification of specific forms of success indicators, cost sharing and pricing devices, and the length of the plan time period against which enterprise results are evaluated. What is perhaps necessary is a change in the basic managerial philosophy itself: a shift from making managerial income and promotion rewards direct and immediate functions of measurable objective performance indicators to a system where, as in the West (and in East Germany), these rewards are decided upon by superiors using less precise subjective evaluation criteria.[17]

A second factor inhibiting the absorption and diffusion of advanced technology in the Soviet Union involves the organization of research and development (R&D). Substantial effort is put forth on research and development in the Soviet Union, but to a great extent it is separated from production and insufficient attention is paid to development in comparison with research. As a result a fair amount of new technology is generated or foreign technology identified, but the implementation and diffusion of it are limited. For the reasons discussed above, the managers of industrial enterprises try to avoid incorporating new technology because it will cause problems and will not lead to sustained rewards. Thus giving the control of R&D to production managers is not an acceptable solution, since the expectation is that they will not encourage the development of new products and processes. Furthermore, the constant pressure to meet current output targets militates against using resources for experimentation and for the introduction of new methods that might, for a while, result in lower output.[18] One of the reforms currently underway — the creation of large "scientific production associations" — promises to bring the Soviet organizational relationship between research, development, and production more into line with the pattern dominant in the West, of having a scientific institute as the managerial unit in the association to give primacy to technical change as an objective. Whether this reform will have significant results — operating within the present incentive, planning, and control environment — is difficult to say, though it might be considered one of the more promising current reforms.

Third, the technology transfer process is primarily a people-process. That is, technology is best transferred from firm to firm and from country to country by people (managers, engineers, sales engineers, etc.) rather than by publications (including blueprints) or products themselves. The Soviets have in the postwar period, until recently, concentrated on the latter approaches while making limited use of the former. However, they currently appear to be paying more attention to the people part of the process.

Current Soviet discussion of new forms of industrial cooperation with Western businesses also has been directed toward increasing Western interest and participation in effective technology transfer to the Soviet Union. As Kosygin has stated, "We are convinced that for the realization of such cooperation there can be found various organizational forms which would be to the interest of all participants."[19]

Finally, the absence of a threat of bankruptcy in the noncompetitive Soviet economy has a profound effect. In competitive economies, while the innovational process responds in a positive way to high rewards for successful innovation it also responds to the fear of being driven out of business by dynamic competitors. Indeed, the spur to innovation from the drive for survival may be more important to the system than the drive for high rewards. The absence of defensive innovation in the Soviet economy removes a fundamental incentive element in the diffusion of new technology. Though Soviet authorities might be able to improve their institutional arrangements to foster innovation (as with the scientific production associations) they cannot change the basic nature of the system. They cannot introduce competitive arrangements, which involve the unplanned destruction of economic units, without changing the basic nature of the system. Thus it can be argued that a noncompetitive, nonmarket system will by its nature be less innovationally dynamic than a competitive economy. This is not the place to engage in a long discussion of the matter, but it should be noted that the foreign policy implications are more intense and of a more permanent nature to the extent that the innovational lag is considered to be an intrinsic part of the Soviet system, rather than one correctable by organizational reform.

The elements discussed have related to Soviet institutions and practices, but the Russians under the tsars also had trouble mastering modern technology and maintaining its dynamic change. What common elements in the pre- and postrevolutionary Russian scene may explain these common difficulties?

One element concerns the creative destruction aspect of technical change — that is, when something new is introduced and it is successful, the old is destroyed. In a politicized, bureaucratized economy such as that found under both the tsars and Communists, those who operate the existing activities are better able to protect themselves against the threat of new kinds of activities and technologies than they would be in a private enterprise, competitive economy. In this respect, one of the advantages of a private enterprise system is that it does not internalize within the state decision-making sector the destruction of the old. The price paid for new technology is absorbed by individual elements in the society rather than by the society as a whole. In the Soviet Union and in tsarist Russia creative destruction has been limited by the bureaucracy; this has been an important and difficult aspect of the whole process of technical change in the Russian economy.

In general, bureaucracies tend to possess a high degree of risk aversion and ability to protect themselves against the pains of change. Bureaucracies tend to penalize failure more than they reward innovational success. Bureaucracies tend to favor large-scale output — this has always beeen true in Russia — and large-scale output itself increases the cost of change. Bureaucratic rules and lines of authority hamper change and experimentation with new ways of doing things. Firmly established lines of administration prevent "invasion" of a stagnant branch by groups from a more dynamic branch. Such "innovation by invasion" has been a significant source of innovation and technology diffusion in the West. Frequently, dynamic persons who press for change appear in leadership positions in a bureaucracy. While they may enjoy some success through the exercise of their power, these leaders are not at the production level and thus their influence over day-to-day operations is limited.

A final, key factor in the picture is that the Soviets have primarily imported foreign technology for domestic growth purposes rather than for exports that would have to be internationally competitive. Thus once the new technology is in place, there has been no pressure on those using it to keep it up to changing foreign levels, and the technology has languished. This was also important in the tsarist period. The success experienced by the

Japanese from the mid-1800s on in developing a self-sustaining technological advancement through the import of technology for international competitive purposes highlights the importance of the *purpose* of imported technology, i.e., whether it is to be used only internally or also for international competitive purposes. This argument contributes to an explanation of why the Soviets have been much better in military technology than in civilian technology. Military equipment is by nature competitive; its performance and utility can be judged only in relation to the equipment possessed by the (potential) enemy, where as this is not true of nonmilitary equipment.

Possible Alternative Pattern of Russian Involvement in the World Economy

The foregoing discussion describes the difficulties experienced by the Russians in absorbing advanced technology and in mastering the process of technical change. But this does not necessarily mean that the Soviets derive little or no benefit from the importation of advanced technology. First, what was presented above is qualitative analysis. The literature on Soviet importation of foreign technology is based primarily on case studies, which do not provide macro, quantitative information. Second, the thrust of most of these cases is misdirected. Even though the Soviets do not handle foreign technology nearly as well as other nations do, the foreign technology imported into the Soviet Union may still be significantly more productive than the existing domestic technology and therefore may be of substantial benefit to the Soviet economy.

With the aim of deriving a quantitative estimate of the relative productivity of imported and domestic machinery in the Soviet Union and the gains from imported technology, a series of calculations were conducted using the SRI-WEFA Soviet Econometric Model.[20] In the model, industrial capital is disaggregated into domestic and imported capital. Using a form of a production function that treats technical change as embodied in factors of production, we calculated the separate effects on output of domestic and imported capital. When we applied a rough estimate of the additional domestic investment required for putting imported machinery into use (three rubles of domestic investment for every ruble of imported machinery),[21] the model indicated that imported industrial machinery is approximately three times as productive as domestic industrial machinery. In addition, a counterfactual scenario, which removed an estimate of the détente-associated increase in machinery imports from the West during the period 1968–1973, showed that the total increment to industrial output would have been almost 10 percent lower than it actually was. Projections into the future, however, indicate decreasing returns to imported technology.

These quantitative results indicate a fairly substantial payoff to imported machinery and technology, more than might have been assumed from the anecdotal literature and the qualitative analysis presented above. Because of this and because of still unresolved questions of methodology, the calculations are controversial; it is quite possible that future econometric work will yield substantially lower results. On the other hand, some recent microeconomic analyses of Soviet imports of advanced fertilizer technology also indicate substantial gains to the Soviet economy.[22] If the order of magnitude of these calculations is generally accurate and, more important, if they reflect Soviet leaders' perceptions of the gains from technology transfer, then the current Soviet desire for expanded economic relations with the West may be strong indeed.

A crucial question in assessing the impact of economic factors on Soviet foreign policy is whether the Soviet leaders will follow the traditional pattern described above and, after acquiring a substantial injection of foreign technology, will return to reduced levels of economic interaction with the West. This possibility cannot be denied and must be given significant consideration in the formulation of U.S. policy. However, there is an alternative pattern that the Soviets may begin to follow.

The second pattern for assessing future Soviet trade policy differs from the first in that it focuses on a more general pattern of trade and development among industrial nations rather than on a unique Russian one. It argues that as Russia progresses along the path of industrialization it will come increasingly under the influence of this general pattern of industrial development.

According to the long-term data compiled by Simon Kuznets, the international flow of goods and resources grew at rapidly accelerating rates in the period from the 1820s to World War I, declined in the interwar period, and then accelerated again in the post–World War II period.[23] In the pre–World War I and post–World War II periods, international trade flows for developed industrial nations appear to grow more rapidly than does domestic product, and while the share of total trade accounted for by the advanced nations remains at a fairly constant high level in the pre–World War I period, it shows marked growth in the post–World War II period.[24] Thus the general pattern for industrialized nations appears to be one of increasing international involvement as economic development proceeds (the interwar period can be viewed as a recession-ridden anomaly in regard to the role of international trade).

The Marxist-Leninist literature has always asserted that this is the pattern for capitalist nations. What was not clear was whether the pattern also applied to socialist nations. Soviet foreign trade literature, following the political positions taken in the 1930s, did not stress the economic efficiency advantages of foreign trade and thus did not argue that the international economic relations of a socialist economy would increase with economic growth. Although after World War II the advantages of the international division of labor within the socialist bloc and the expansion of intra-CMEA trade were stressed, the emphasis on the advantages of trade was muted. But after the death of Stalin arguments in support of the advantages of trade began to be made with more force, both by economists and by Soviet officials. From the beginning of the 1970s, major emphasis also has been placed on the expansion of Soviet economic relations with developed capitalist nations.[25]

An important theme running through current Soviet discussions of the advantages of trade is the role played in contemporary developed economies by the "scientific-technical revolution."[26] The development of modern science and its application through modern technology to economic activity, it is argued, has profoundly increased the role of international economic relations in advanced economies, primarily due to the effects of the international nature of science and the manner in which it develops. This argument is similar to Kuznets's fundamental point about the crucial importance of the internationalization of knowledge.[27]

Do these recent pronouncements on the advantages of international economic relations mean that the Soviets have abandoned their policy of nondependence on foreign countries and have adopted a policy of interdependence? For the present, this is clearly not the case. First, much of the Soviet discussion on the advantages of foreign trade has been directed toward trade within the socialist bloc and thus has not involved the issue of interdependence with capitalist countries. Furthermore, the literature on intra-CMEA trade and planning consistently stresses the maintenance of the sovereignty of the individual nations within the bloc rather than stressing the growth of their interdependence.[28] This is, however, only a partial answer for increasingly in the current period Soviet discussions have emphasized the need for extending Soviet economic relations beyond the socialist camp into the capitalist camp. A key early pronouncement here was Kosygin's speech at the November 1971 Supreme Soviet in which he openly invited Western participation in the development of the Soviet economy:

> With the transition to the practice of long-term agreements, which guarantee stable orders for industry, new possibilities are opened up in our relations with Western nations. Consideration can be given to the mutually beneficial

cooperation with foreign firms and banks in the working out of a number of important economic problems, connected with the use of the natural resources of the Soviet Union, the construction of industrial enterprises, and the search for new technologies.[29]

The advantages of trade with Western nations were described in the following terms in the 1973 annual report of Minister of Foreign Trade Nikolai S. Patolichev:

> Mutual advantage is one of the leading principles of Soviet foreign trade associations, and they adhere to this principle in trade with their Western partners. In developing economic ties with Western Europe, our country receives an opportunity to make fuller and more rational use of its own resources and possibilities, and at the same time to acquire, by way of commercial exchange, goods of other countries that are not produced in our country or whose production would cost more than it does to import them. Thus, foreign economic ties offer a more efficient solution to a number of problems arising in the course of economic construction.[30]

And in 1976, at the Twenty-fifth Party Congress, Kosygin reemphasized the continuing and growing importance of international economic relations with capitalist nations, but also added a reference to the need for political support and cooperation in capitalist countries for the development of such economic relations.

> The role of international economic cooperation in accomplishing the five year plan's task will grow. . . .
> In conditions of the easing of international tension, our economic relations *with the developed capitalist countries*, which can expand successfully on the basis of the principles set forth in the Final Act of the Conference on Security and Cooperation in Europe, are taking on new qualitative aspects. We shall continue the practice of concluding large-scale agreements on cooperation in the erection of industrial projects in our country and on the participation of Soviet organizations in the construction of industrial enterprises in Western countries. Agreements on a compensatory basis, especially with short reimbursement periods for new enterprises, various forms of industrial cooperation and joint scientific research and design work, are promising forms of cooperation.
> Needless to say, our trade and economic ties will develop faster with countries that show a sincere willingness for cooperation and concern for ensuring normal and equitable conditions for its development. Only in this event is it possible to have truly broad and lasting economic relations, which will be reflected in our national-economic plans.[31]

Second, the Soviet policy of nondependence is related to the level of economic development that has been attained by the Soviet Union. Clearly, Stalin's original objective of acquiring sufficient economic development to guarantee the national independence of the Soviet Union has been achieved. The development of economic relations with capitalist nations at this stage extends beyond this core of economic power but does not endanger it. In other words, under present conditions expanded economic relations with the West do not involve capitalist countries in the basic core of the Soviet economy (which is now sufficiently developed to guarantee the independence and national security of the Soviet Union), but operate at the margin to improve the performance of the Soviet economy. Thus the expansion of economic relations with the West represents for the Soviet Union an increase in interrelatedness with Western economies, but does not involve in any significant sense an increase in Soviet-Western interdependence or in Soviet dependence on the West.[32]

Third, this distinction between interrelatedness and interdependence is further illustrated when account is taken of the kind of international specialization or division of labor that has been developing among industrialized nations and that is envisioned by the Soviets. In an important 1966 article, Bela Balassa argued that postwar trade among advanced European economies, especially after the founding of the Common Market, has not followed the precepts of traditional comparative cost specialization; it has been marked by intraindustrial rather than interindustrial specialization:

> Only a few manufactured goods (e.g., steel ingots, nonferrous metals, paper) traded among the industrial countries are standardized commodities, while the large majority are differentiated products. . . . In the presence of national product differentiation, multilateral tariff reductions may lead to an increased exchange of clothing articles, automobiles, and other consumer goods, for example, without substantial changes in the structure of production. Further, the expansion of trade in machinery and in intermediate products at a higher level of fabrication . . . may entail specialization in narrower ranges of products rather than in the demise of national industries. These changes, then, would involve intraindustry rather than interindustry specialization.[33]

This leads to different conclusions about the advantages of trade. The economies of scale resulting from long production runs associated with narrow specialization within industrial branches replace the more general productive efficiency advantages that, in the traditional explanation, result from intersectoral specialization.

Soviet trade authorities have long stressed the principle of intraindustrial specialization. It is reflected in the 1962 CMEA "Basic Principles of International Socialist Division of Labor"[34] and emphasized in discussions of contemporary capitalist trade and development and in discussions of the expansion of Soviet trade with the West.[35] This is a very important principle for it means, as Balassa indicated, that trade between countries can expand without necessitating substantial changes in the internal structure of production of the trading partners. To the extent that intraindustrial trade with Western nations involves final rather than intermediate goods the Soviets can increase their international interrelatedness with little immediate danger of becoming dependent upon capitalist nations.

The implications of the second pattern are then quite different from those of the first. Instead of another periodic Russian expedition into the international economy, the expectation would be for a greater and more lasting Russian involvement in the international economy. It would also be expected that the Soviets would press for intraindustrial trade and would thus try to develop the production of exportable manufactured goods of a relatively high level of fabrication rather than continue to rely on their traditional raw material exports.

Though the second pattern may appear to be radically different from past Russian involvement, this is only part of the picture. During the period 1905–1913, the traditional Russian, state-dominated, inwardly focused pattern of development did show signs of giving way to the more general, international involvement pattern of the Western industrialized nations. After 1903, with the removal of Witte, the Russian state withdrew from its role as initiator of economic development. It was replaced by Russian banks, which began to perform managerial and entrepreneurial functions and which also began to take over these functions from foreign managers, leading to a process of Russianization of industrial management. With the encouragement of the banks, cartels and syndicates were formed, giving the banks and a growing group of Russian industrialists significant control over the Russian economy. These bankers and industrialists, while supporting the need for the Russian economy to become independent in crucial areas of manufacturing, opposed as medieval the "desire to shut oneself off from the world by a Chinese wall."[36] They advocated that Russia follow the path of the advanced nations of the West and they called for the development of foreign markets for the products of Russian industry. During the 1905–1913 period, Russian trade increased significantly and Russian banks and corporations began to participate in West European capital markets.[37]

This process was cut off by the Bolshevik Revolution and the return to inwardly focused economic development under the Soviets. But now that the Soviet economy has attained a level of development that assures national independence, the underlying forces that gave rise to the short, prerevolutionary period of growing Russian international interrelatedness may again move the Russian economy in that direction.

Conclusion

In drawing some brief conclusions from the material presented above, three issues predominate:

First, the possibility that the Soviet Union will pursue the more stable, second pattern of involvement in the world economy in place of the traditional Russian pattern;

Second, Soviet hard-currency problems in managing its expanded trade with the West; and

Third, "leverage" — the potential political utility to the United States of expanded economic relations with the USSR.

The Two Patterns

Although the resolution of the differences between the two patterns will be visible only in the long run, Soviet behavior in the medium run (ten years) will be affected by which pattern is dominant. For example, to the extent that the traditional first pattern is currently felt by Soviet leaders to be the dominant strategy, major decisions in regard to export expansion and long-term hard-currency earnings will be put off and reliance will be placed on the current composition of exports with its emphasis on raw materials exports to the West. However, it is wrong to view Soviet policymaking as a monolithic, totally centralized process. Even within a dominant environment of pattern one, some appearances of pattern two are possible, especially in regard to intraindustrial specialization.

It is sometimes said that central planning itself inhibits trade and thus would reduce the possibility of pattern two. Although there is some merit to this argument, it is also true that under planning the entire national interest can be internalized in a centrally formulated policy. Thus trade can have great advantages and will be increased. There is even discussion of possible Soviet participation in international trading institutions and agreements such as the International Monetary Fund (IMF) and the General Agreement on Trade and Tariffs (GATT). The issue is not settled, but clearly central planning in Eastern Europe and the USSR has not led to the destruction of trade. Furthermore, trade is not as inhibited by the establishment of specific plans as some think. As Soviet leaders have made clear, plans can be adjusted to meet the changing demands and opportunities in the international market. There is, however, great concern that increased involvement in the world economy might excessively expose the Soviet

Union to the instabilities of Western capitalist economies. An example of this was the sharp increase in the Soviet hard-currency deficit caused by decreased Soviet exports associated with the Western recession in 1974 and 1975.

An additional observation on the two patterns concerns the process of change in Soviet policymaking. When Khrushchev visited the United States in 1959 and observed heavy automobile traffic on U.S. highways, he indicated that it was Soviet policy to avoid the wastes of the automobile age, i.e., that the Soviets would limit the production of private automobiles. Yet a decade later this policy was changed. The imperatives of industrialization—in this case the obvious fact that Soviet industry could have the capacity to mass produce automobiles plus the workings of the "demonstration effect" on Soviet demand (especially elite demand)—led to the alteration of Soviet policy. Likewise, it can be argued that although most Soviet leaders today support expanded economic relations with the West with the traditional first pattern in mind, there are forces that promote the second pattern. Over time, more members of the Soviet decision-making strata will become involved in economic relations with the West. To the extent that they are successful relations, these decision makers will benefit directly from their own work. Given a sufficiently long period without a major world crisis disrupting East-West relations, the size of this group may approach a critical mass.

Soviet Hard-Currency Problems

In the rapid growth of Soviet trade with the West since the end of the 1960s, Soviet imports from the West have increased more rapidly than exports. As the two were about equal in 1968, this has meant a growing hard-currency trade deficit for the Soviet Union, which in 1975 reached the extraordinary level (in Soviet experience) of $6.3 billion.[38]

One of the ways in which the Soviet Union has attempted to finance these deficits has been through the sale of gold. These sales have reached fairly substantial levels in recent years (approximately $1 billion per year in the period 1973-1976). The value of gold sales reflects both the amount of gold sold and the price of gold in world markets. While in 1973 the Soviets sold more gold than they produced, thus decreasing their gold stocks in that year, the great increases in the price of gold in 1974 and 1975 allowed them to halve the physical amount of gold sold in 1974 with only a 20 percent reduction in the value of gold sales and to sell slightly more than half the 1973 amount in 1975 with an equal value of sales. On the other hand, the subsequent drop in gold prices in 1976 required a 65 percent increase in the amount of gold sold in that year to achieve a 25 percent increase in the value of gold sales. The amount of gold sold in 1976, however, was still somewhat less than the amount of estimated production, so that the gold stock most likely did not decline. (The Soviet gold stock is currently estimated to be about 1,925 metric tons, which at the present price — August 1977 — of $145 per ounce has a value of approximately $10 billion.)

Until the latter part of the 1960s the Soviets did not borrow heavily from the West, but when the campaign to import advanced technology was launched all of this changed. Annual Soviet credit drawings from the West doubled between 1968 and 1972 and then quadrupled between 1972 and 1976. Over the entire period Soviet medium- and long-term hard-currency indebtedness rose from about $1 billion to $10 billion. At the same time Soviet hard-currency holdings changed from a small positive amount — $0.6 billion — to a negative amount, or short-term debt, of $2.3 billion. Thus the total Soviet hard-currency debt at the end of 1976 can be said to have been over $12 billion. A further aspect of the Soviet hard-currency debt position, reflecting its ability to carry the debt, is seen in its hard-currency debt service ratio — the ratio of annual debt service payments (interest plus principal repayments) to Soviet exports to the developed West. This ratio rose from a low 12 percent in 1968 to a not insignificant 23 percent in 1976.

This recent record of high Soviet hard-currency deficits and growing indebtedness, especially when viewed against the background of a marked increase in total CMEA hard-currency debt (estimated to be approximately $40 billion at the end of 1976), has raised questions about the future of Soviet hard-currency dealings. The issue essentially boils down to the questions: Will the Soviets be able to continue in the future as they have in the recent past? If not, *what* might change?

Discussions of this issue usually explore the willingness of Western lenders to continue increasing credit to the Soviet Union and the possibilities of altering the composition of Soviet import-export balances with the developed West. The general consensus in regard to credit seems to be that although Western lenders have confidence in Soviet credit worthiness, there is now less willingness to lend to the Soviets. Some U.S. banks are reaching their legal limits for single borrowers and other banks are reaching their own informal country limits. Banks are being more careful with loans to the Soviet Union and are asking higher rates of interest. Furthermore, the Soviets themselves may well be worried about their increasing indebtedness and may not want to increase it. As a recent *Euromoney* article stated: "It may, in the end, be Soviet concern about its own indebtedness with the West, and the damage this does to its international status, that will limit the long-term level of borrowing, rather than any more cautious approach to the risk on the part of the international banking community."[39]

The main elements in Soviet import demand are machinery, other high technology industrial inputs, and grain. Given the crucial role of productivity increases in the Tenth Five-Year Plan targets and in the Soviet growth strategy, it is unlikely that the Soviets will easily or for long cut machinery imports from the West, although they may, under pressure, try to shift some of these machinery purchases to CMEA suppliers. Grain imports in the long run could be reduced by increased agricultural productivity, which might result from increased investment in agriculture and better managerial and organizational methods. In the near future, grain imports will vary with variation in the weather (given the 6-million-ton minimum annual import in the U.S.-USSR Grain Agreement, in effect through 1981).

There is much talk in the Soviet Union about increasing the exports of manufactured goods to the West, but most Western analysts discount this as a potential source of significant increases in hard-currency earnings in the near future. The usual view is that raw materials will remain the major export to the West. Increases in these are strongly affected by economic conditions in the West; that is, slow growth in the West will have a deleterious effect on Soviet exports. Moreover, of increasing importance in Western analyses is the recent CIA projection of decreasing Soviet oil production in the first half of the 1980s. Since fuel exports (oil, gas, and coal) accounted for over 50 percent of total Soviet exports to the developed West in 1976, a decrease in oil production could have drastic effects on the Soviet hard-currency position.

In the study referred to in note 38, a projection to 1985 of the SRI-WEFA Soviet Model was calculated with special reference to Soviet hard-currency transactions. Though the baseline reference projection used in the analysis was rather optimistic in regard to the performance of the Soviet economy, Soviet hard-currency problems were projected to continue into the 1980s. By 1985 the Soviet hard-currency deficit was estimated at 3.4 billion dollars, its debt at over 22 billion dollars, and its debt service ratio at 31 percent.

Leverage

The possible political utility to the United States of economic relations with the USSR has become a subject of controversy among government policymakers and in public arenas. Interest in this aspect of economic relations has been stimulated by the expansion of U.S.-Soviet trade and a recognition in the West of the problems the Soviets are having in increasing labor and capital productvity, thereby sustaining the growth and development of their economy. This interest has been further stimulated by a concern in the United States that economic benefits from expanded economic relations are asymmetric in favor of the Soviet Union, given the U.S. lead in technology and the negotiating advantages held by the Soviet state trader when dealing with individual U.S. firms. Thus it is argued that benefits from our economic relations with the USSR are necessary to balance the putative net economic gains accruing to the Soviets.

Essentially, the issue is how much economic leverage the United States possesses in its relations with the USSR and to what extent it can exercise that leverage. While this controversy encompasses an extremely broad set of issues that are not discussed comprehensively in this chapter, it is the view of this writer that the United States does possess the potential for meaningful economic leverage, which could be realized if certain conditions were met and principles followed. The list is long and complex, but four elements will be mentioned.

First, a multiplicity of possible objectives may be attained through a program of economic leverage. These objectives range from those of great importance to the United States to those of lesser importance. Much of the confusion in the debates on leverage arises from the failure to delineate objectives and from the oft-made implicit assumption that if U.S. political policy objectives of greatest importance cannot be achieved, then the development of an economic leverage program is not worth pursuing. On the contrary, a well-formulated, balanced foreign policy involves instruments to achieve a range of different objectives. Decisions on instruments and programs are in their nature cost-benefit decisions. For example, where the cost is low the benefit need not be very great to make the program worth introducing and developing.

Second, the objectives and policies of different agencies within the U.S. government and of the public and private sectors in the United States must be coordinated in order to operate an effective leverage program. Multilateral coordination between the United States and its allies regarding policy toward economic relations with the USSR is of major importance; since in many areas the USSR can substitute relations with other developed industrial nations for those with the United States, it is vital that the United States pursue coordinated policies with other Western countries in order to make leverage effective.

Third, if leverage is to be an effective instrument it should be possible to vary its application, to increase or decrease its scale quickly and easily. For example, this is true of credit, especially if the credit is being provided by a U.S. government agency (such as the Eximbank). On the other hand, it is not true of MFN status. In addition, leverage instruments should be capable of responding to the interests of different groups in the United States. For example, if grain exports are to be used in a leverage program the government must have the means of maintaining U.S. farm income if it intends to reduce such exports.

Fourth, the fact that major policy decisions in the Soviet Union are made by a small group of party leaders in the Politburo offers some advantages to the exercise of leverage by the United States. Since the Politburo is responsible for all major policy decisions, it has the power to deliver on agreements, including unpublicized agreements, with the United States. Moreover, since the Soviet economic bureaucracy resists change and innovation, the Soviet political leaders — if they are to maintain national power parity with the United States — must exert pressure from above to introduce and spread new methods and new technology. Thus their commitment to the import of advanced foreign technology is great. Operating as they do in the political sector, these pressures take the form of high priorities and campaigns usually focused on a few major projects that receive substantial public attention and become identified with senior party officials. As a consequence, Soviet leaders would be somewhat more vulnerable to a U.S. leverage effort directed toward such major projects. (U.S. government support and encouragement of American involvement in such major projects would help to create the base for the exercise of leverage.)

If the application of leverage is to be effective, it must consider certain salient Soviet sensitivities. Soviet leaders are concerned with issues of political legitimacy; therefore, they are particularly sensitive to any threats to the sovereignty of the Communist government. Thus the tactic of a quiet, diplomatic application of leverage is preferable to a declaratory, overt application of leverage.

Finally, the role of middle- and lower-level Soviet party and state officials regarding a Soviet policy response to a U.S. leverage initiative is heightened by certain administrative practices in the Soviet Union. Specific agent responsibility, continuous monitoring of agent performance, and the awarding of material and status rewards and penalties in relation to performance encourage responsible agents to pursue the means of achieving their assigned tasks. To the extent that imports of U.S. machinery and technology help in this regard, Soviet administrators, especially at the ministerial level, may support the maintenance of expanded economic relations with the United States. This is a significant aspect of the Soviet system that contributes to the potential for the exercise of economic leverage by the United States.

Acknowledgments

I am indebted to Donald W. Green, Daniel L. Bond, Charles Movit, Mark Earle, W. Francis Rushing, and James Cole for their contributions in the preparation of this chapter, and to SRI International for its research support.

Notes

1. Data on Soviet growth of GNP are given in 1970 established (market) prices but cover Western concepts of GNP. Unless otherwise indicated the data in this paper are from the SRI-WEFA Soviet Econometric Model (SOVMOD) databank, basically derived from U.S. government data, much of which have been published in recent Joint Economic Committee studies of the Soviet economy. See, for example, U.S. Congress, Joint Economic Committee, *Soviet Economy in a New Perspective* (Washington, D.C.: U.S. Government Printing Office, 1976), hereafter JEC, *Soviet Economy in a New Perspective*, and the previous volumes in the series cited in the Foreword to that volume.

2. See the Soviet annual statistical abstract: Tsentral'noe Statisticheskoe Upravlenie, *Narodnoe Khoziaistvo SSSR* (Moscow, various years).

3. For these calculations a Cobb-Douglas production function was used, with a labor exponent of 0.6 and a capital exponent of 0.4.

4. In fact, certain interesting calculations of the late Rush Greenslade, measuring GNP at factor cost, indicate that total factor productivity growth in 1970–1975 was actually negative (–0.2 percent). See JEC, *Soviet Economy in a New Perspective*, p. 279.

5. What is important here of course is the Soviet leaders' perception of the productivity issue. Although it is sometimes argued that Soviet leaders pay substantial attention to Western calculations of Soviet economic performance, it is safer to assume that they primarily look at Soviet data. If a calculation similar to the above is made using official Soviet data (with a total employment series based on Soviet data), growth of total factor productivity drops from 5.5 percent per year in the 1950s to 2.1 percent in the 1960s and 1.2 percent in the early 1970s.

6. Murray Feshbach and Stephen Rapawy, "Soviet Population and Manpower Trends and Policies," in JEC, *Soviet Economy in a New Perspective*, p. 133.

7. Measured in current U.S. dollars; SOVMOD databank, and SOVMOD III Reference Solution, 1975–1985, July 1977.

8. Alexander Gerschenkron, *Economic Backwardness in Historical Perspective* (Cambridge, Mass.: Harvard University Press, 1972), pp. 17–18.

9. See Franklyn Holzman, "Foreign Trade," in Abram Bergson and Simon Kuznets, eds., *Economic Trends in the Soviet Union* (Cambridge, Mass.: Harvard University Press, 1963), pp. 287–320.

10. See Anthony C. Sutton, *Western Technology and Soviet Economic Development, 1917 to 1930*, vol. 1 (Stanford, Calif.: Hoover Institution Press, 1968).

11. Holzman, "Foreign Trade."

12. See, for example, Michael R. Dohan, "The Economic Origins of Soviet Autarky, 1927/28–1934," *Slavic Review* 35, no. 4 (December 1976): 603–635.

13. Margaret Miller, *The Economic Development of Russia, 1905–1914*, 2d ed. (New York: A. M. Kelley, 1967), p. 219.

14. Theodore Von Laue, *Sergei Witte and the Industrialization of Russia* (New York: Columbia University Press, 1963), p. 182. Soviet historians today generally agree with Witte's critics and argue that Russia at the turn of the century was a colonial dependent of Western capitalist nations.

15. Joseph Stalin, *Selected Writings* (Moscow, 1942), p. 200.

16. See, for example, Joseph S. Berliner, *The Innovation Decision in Soviet Industry* (Cambridge, Mass.: M.I.T. Press, 1976).

17. David Granick has made such an argument in an unpublished SRI study, "Soviet Introduction of New Technology: A Depiction of the Process" (SSC-TN-2625-7, SRI/Strategic Studies Center, 1975). He argues that the Soviet managerial system is essentially Taylorism, which was originally designed to increase the direct productivity of semiskilled workers, not the administrative and innovational activity of managers.

18. The impending problems of the Soviet oil industry, as projected by U.S. government economists, are a classic illustration of how the Soviet economic bureaucracy operates: the overcommitment of resources to meet current output targets, rather than the use of resources to develop future capabilities.

19. Aleksei Kosygin in Gosplan SSSR, *Gosudarstvennyi piatiletnyi plan razvitiia narodnogo khoziaistva SSSR na 1971–1975 gody* (Moscow), p. 56.

20. Donald W. Green and Herbert S. Levine, "Macroeconometric Evidence of the Value of Machinery Imports to the Soviet Union," in John R. Thomas and Ursula M. Kruse-Vaucienne, eds., *Soviet Science and Technology*, George Washington University (Washington, D.C.: National Science Foundation, 1977), pp. 394–424 (reprinted in *Survey* 23, no. 2 [Spring 1977/78]:112–126). See also the earlier paper: Green and Levine, "Implications of Technology Transfers for the U.S.S.R.," *East-West Technological Co-operation* (Brussels, 1976).

21. This ratio has been suggested by Soviet economists in private conversations with the author.

22. Philip Hanson, "The Impact of Western Technology: A Case Study of the Soviet Mineral Fertilizer Industry" (Paper presented at the Conference on Integration in Eastern Europe and East-West Trade, Bloomington, Indiana, October 1976). See also Philip Hanson, "Western Technology in Soviet Economy," *Problems of Communism* 27, no. 6 (November–December 1978):20–30; and John Hardt and George Holliday, "Implications of Commercial Technology Transfer Between the Soviet Union and the United States," in Congressional Research Service, *Technology Transfer and Scientific Cooperation Between the United States and the Soviet Union: A Review* (Washington, D.C.: U.S. Government Printing Office, 1977), pp. 55–103.

23. Simon Kuznets, *Modern Economic Growth: Rate, Structure and Spread* (New Haven, Conn.: Yale University Press, 1966), ch. 6.

24. Ibid., and M. Maksimova, *Osnovnye problemy kaptialisticheskoi integratsii* (Moscow, 1972).

25. See, for example, Kosygin's speech at the November 1971 session of the Supreme Soviet, Gosplan SSSR, *Gosudarstvennyi piatiletnyi plan*. See also his speech at the Twenty-fifth CPSU Congress (February–March 1976), in *Pravda*, 2 March 1976, pp. 2–6. (Trans. in *Current Digest of the Soviet Press* [*CDSP*] 38, no. 10 and no. 11 [7 and 14 April 1976, respectively.])

26. This phrase is likely to appear in almost every current Soviet discussion or pronouncement on foreign trade. For an extensive treatment, see M. Maksimova *Osnovnye problemy*, ch. 2.

27. Simon Kuznets, *Modern Economic Growth*, pp. 286–294.

28. "International economic relations between socialist countries take the form of relations between sovereign owners of the means of production, and not as relations built on the base of unified international property . . . this is one of the basic differences between CMEA and imperialist economic organizations like the 'common market' which aspire to take for themselves functions of supra-national institutions." V. Ladygin and Iu. Shiryaev, *Voprosy ekonomiki,* no. 5 (May 1966), p. 82.

29. Gosplan SSSR, *Gosudarstvennyi piatiletnyi plan,* p. 56.

30. *Pravda,* 27 December 1973, p. 4. (Trans. in *CDSP* 25, no. 52, 23 January 1974, p. 3.)

31. *Pravda,* 2 March 1976. (Trans. in *CDSP* 28, no. 10 [7 April 1976]:5, 10.)

32. The degree of involvement of a nation in the world economy may be said to lie along a continuous scale. The scale measures the amount of economic disruption that would be caused to a nation's internal economy if its external economic relations were broken. That is, increasing degrees on the scale of involvement in the world economy reflect the dependence of an economy on external relationships as measured by the extent of economic disruption that would be entailed in the breaking of these relationships. The zero point or lowest range of the international involvment scale is "autarky" and the highest range is "interdependence." The range above autarky may be called "nondependence" and the range above that "interrelatedness."

33. Bela Balassa, "Tariff Reductions and Trade in Manufactures Among the Industrial Countries," *American Economic Review* 56, no. 3 (June 1966):469. On the role of product differentiation in the commodity composition of trade, see I. Kravis, "'Availability' and Other Influences on the Commodity Composition of Trade," *Journal of Political Economy* (April 1956):143-155.

34. Michael Kaser, *Comecon* (London: Oxford Press, 1965), p. 194. See also C. H. McMillan, "Soviet Specialization and Trade in Manufactures," *Soviet Studies* 34, no. 4 (April 1973):529.

35. M. Maksimova, *Osnovnye problemy,* ch. 2; M. Maksimova, "Vsemirnoe khoziaistvo i mezhdunarodnoe ekonomicheskoe sotrudnichestvo," *Mirovaia ekonomika i mezhdunarodnye otnosheniia,* no. 4 (April 1974):13-14; and Patolichev in *Pravda,* 27 December 1973.

36. Ruth A. Roosa, "Russian Industrialists Look to the Future: Thoughts on Economic Development 1906-17," in J. S. Curtiss, ed., *Essays in Russian and Soviet History* (New York: Columbia University Press, 1963), p. 201.

37. Margaret Miller, *The Economic Development of Russia*; Olga Crisp, "Russia 1860-1914," in Rondo Cameron et al., *Banking in the Early Stages of Industrialization* (New York: Oxford University Press, 1967), pp. 183-238; and John P. McKay, *Pioneers for Profit: Foreign Entrepreneurship and Russian Industrialization 1885-1913* (Chicago: University of Chicago Press, 1970).

38. See H. S. Levine and D. L. Bond, *Soviet Responses to Hard Currency Problems,* SRI International, TN-CEPR-5814-1 (prepared for the Council on International Economic Policy, The White House), Washington, D.C., August 1977. All data in this section are from the SOVMOD III Reference Solution 1975-1985, July, 1977. See also H. S. Levine and D. L. Bond, "Oil, Wheat and the Soviet Union," *Wharton Magazine* (Summer 1978):36-43.

39. *Euromoney,* March 1977, p. 62.

9
Demographic Trends and Soviet Foreign Policy: The Underlying Imperatives of Labor Supply

Warren W. Eason

Introduction

Although it is difficult to link foreign policy directly to demographic trends, we can regard population patterns as creating a context that helps to shape the alternatives available to policymakers in foreign affairs. This can be particularly well studied in the Soviet case, where population variables have been sharply drawn and the future contrasts sharply with the past in demographic terms.

The point of departure is the fact that recent trends in the major Soviet population indices have evoked considerable concern about their economic and social consequences and implications for policy formulation in a number of fields. Concern is expressed most generally in terms of the growth of the *total population* and arises from the fact that declining fertility over much of the country in recent decades, despite low levels of mortality, implies minimal growth or even an absolute decrease in the total population in the future, rather than the long-run moderate increases that Soviet demographers and planners prefer.

Concern is also expressed about marked *differences* in population growth in different parts of the country and especially about regional differentials in the fertility rates. While extraordinarily high fertility persists in Soviet Central Asia and parts of the Caucasus, in much of the rest of the country in the recent past fertility has reached levels below those necessary for population reproduction.

The focus, however, is on what these trends imply for other variables, particularly *labor supply*. Declining fertility has already led to a slowdown in the rate of growth of the working-age population and therefore of the labor force, and the trend is expected to worsen markedly in the next decade.

There are also serious and persistent imbalances in the *distribution* of labor, reflected in the dearth of labor available for transfer to nonagricultural occupations and in the existence of labor surplus and deficit areas in different parts of the country. The latter arise in part from the reluctance of certain national groups — in many instances those of relatively high fertility and high proportions in agriculture — to respond to economic and other incentives to move. These regional imbalances in labor supply will also worsen if the regional differentials in fertility persist.

But the real problem is not in the demographic and labor supply variables; rather it is in the *pressures* that they generate for planners, administrators, and policymakers. With respect to the domestic economy, for example, if the decline in the rate of growth of the labor force and the growing misallocation of labor are not to be translated into a continuing decline in the rate of growth of production, major accommodations and reforms must be introduced to increase the effectiveness with which human resources are developed and utilized in the production process. It is therefore not surprising that in order to meet production targets, Soviet economic plans are already relying on significantly greater increases in *labor productivity*, through the introduction of new technology and practices designed to bring about more effective utilization of labor resources (*trudovye resursy*) at all levels.

To a certain extent the need to raise productivity is simply the universal imperative of successively higher stages of economic development. There is a note of urgency in the Soviet case — given their ambitious economic objectives — because the changes in the population variables are of sufficient magnitude and their appearance is so timed that they render the pattern of labor supply in the immediate future fundamentally different from anything the Soviets have had to live with since the beginning of rapid industrialization in 1928.

What has happened is that in a very short span of time the Soviet Union is making the transition from a country in which labor was a relatively abundant resource — and labor policies and practices reflected this abundance — to one where labor is scarce and must be treated as such if economic performance is not to suffer. The fact that the major economic growth rates (GNP, industry) have been declining on the average since the peak growth years of the late 1950s and early 1960s — reaching some of the lowest levels ever in the 1978 annual plan — evinces the failure of the system thus far to compensate by higher productivity for the slowdown in the rate of growth of the working-age population and other manifestations of growing labor scarcity that first appeared in the 1960s.

The objective of this chapter is to outline the nature of the emergence of the primary and secondary demographic forces that have given rise to pressures for change in policies affecting human resources and in particular to shed as much light as possible on the situation in the immediate future. The assumption is that it is through the various dimensions of labor supply that the demographic variables will influence policy formation in various fields, in some instances directly, in others indirectly.

The curious if not surprising aspect of Soviet demographic history is that the pressure for change in response to a developing scarcity of human resources took so long to become evident—considering the awesome population losses suffered during World War I, the Civil War, and World War II, as well as the pattern of declining fertility in both rural and urban areas over much of the country that has been a feature of Soviet experience since the earlier years. By all logic, the relative scarcity of labor as a factor of production should have begun to be apparent well before the 1960s and 1970s. The reason that it has not been apparent until recently seems to lie with the timing or periodization of the basic sources of labor supply, in both quantitative and qualitative terms, namely:

1. With the timing of births and deaths and the respective contribution to future labor supply of *secular*, peacetime trends in fertility and mortality on the one hand and *episodic* or one-time demographic events involving primarily major wars on the other;

2. With the length of time it has taken for the pool of human resources supplied by the agricultural sector to be depleted and for certain related imbalances in the regional distribution of labor to become critical; and

3. With the response of policymakers at various stages of development to the question of raising the qualitative dimension of labor supply through formal education and on-the-job training.

These three dimensions of Soviet labor supply will be examined in this chapter in a historical framework, first, because the present and future demographic picture is recognized as being the result of past as well as present demographic events; second, because attitudes and patterns of behavior affecting population variables at a given moment grow out of what they were in the past; and third, because it may be possible to form hypotheses about the possible existence (or absence) of links between population variables and policy formation in the future on the basis of such links in the past.

Primary Demographic Determinants of Labor Supply

Figure 9.1 portrays the effect of the timing of births and deaths on the rate of growth of the working-age population during the Soviet period. The working-age population, known in Soviet literature as the "able-bodied

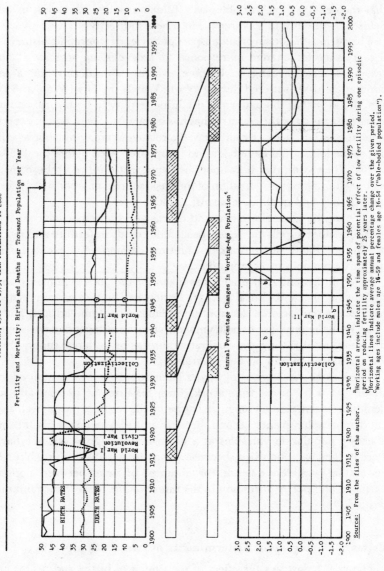

Figure 9.1

PERIODIZATION OF SECULAR TRENDS AND MAJOR EPISODES IN FERTILITY AND MORTALITY
COMPARED TO THE RATE OF CHANGE IN THE WORKING-AGE POPULATION:
U.S.S.R., 1900 TO 1975, WITH PROJECTIONS TO 2000

Fertility and Mortality: Births and Deaths per Thousand Population per Year[a]

Annual Percentage Changes in Working-Age Population[c]

Source: From the files of the author.

[a] Horizontal arrows indicate the time span of potential effect of low fertility during one episodic
period on reducing fertility approximately 25 years later.
[b] Horizontal lines indicate average annual percentage change over the given period.
[c] Working ages include males age 16-59 and females age 16-54 ("able-bodied population").

population" (*trudosposobnoe naselenie*), is composed of males aged 16–59 and females aged 16–54, and therefore stands as the principal determinant of the size and rate of growth of the labor force. Focusing here on the rate of growth, the working-age population is represented in Figure 9.1 in terms of its annual percentage rate of change.

Certain *episodic events* that had a severe effect in reduced fertility and increased mortality are identified in Figure 9.1 by vertical bars bracketing the periods involved. These events include World War I and the Civil War and its immediate aftermath (1916–1921); the period of forced collectivization (1931–1936); and World War II and its immediate aftermath (1941–1946). The respective periods of declining or lowered fertility are similarly identified by vertical bars.

The several episodic periods of low fertility and the most recent period of declining fertility can be expected to have a depressing effect on the rate of growth of the working-age population sixteen years later. The direction and timing of these effects are indicated in Figure 9.1 by means of diagonally linked bar graphs. The episodic periods of low fertility can also be expected to depress fertility rates in the next generation, as the reduced number of potential parents pass through the reproductive ages. For purposes of illustration, the potential *generational* effect is indicated in Figure 9.1 by horizontal arrows each covering a span of twenty-five years. That span was selected because it represents approximately the peak of the prime reproductive years (20–29).

The information in Figure 9.1 indicates how the immediate future differs from the historic past in terms of the primary determinants of labor supply, and in particular why it has taken so long for past trends and variations in fertility and mortality to have a substantial effect on the rate of growth of the working-age population and therefore on the rate at which human resources are being made available to the economy and society. The information thus portrays the periodization of the basic demographic forces that are only now transforming the country from one long accustomed to labor abundance to one that must adjust quickly, almost precipitously, to conditions of overall shortage.

The first point of interest from Figure 9.1 is why the secular decline in fertility (indicated by the crude birth rate) did not lead directly to a decline in the rate of growth of the working-age population long before this. The reason is the parallel decline in mortality, shown in the generally declining crude death rate, especially after World War II. A large proportion of the decline in total mortality is infant mortality, which means that the number of infants born and surviving to adulthood from the 1920s to the 1950s declined by less than the birth rate or even increased. Thus it was not until the late 1950s — when the crude death rate was stabilized at less than ten per thousand—that a projected rate of growth of the working-age population (after 1977) fell significantly below the long-run average of about 1.5 percent per year to less than 0.5 percent.

The generational effects of the several episodic events beginning with World War I that temporarily but severely reduced fertility and increased mortality tend to be obscured in the Soviet case by the coincidence of the events themselves. Thus the generational effects of the 1915–1921 episode on slowing down the rate of growth of the working-age population sixteen years later, in 1931–1937, were obscured by the turmoil attending collectivization (the large-scale rural-urban migration and the transformation of 25 million individual peasant households into almost 20 million collectivized households) as well as by higher mortality rates.

We do not have direct information on the working-age population during these years but indirect evidence of the generational effect of the 1915–1921 episode appears in the relatively low rate of growth of the estimated total labor force during the 1930s (see Figure 9.2 below). The nonagricultural labor force, however, grew very rapidly (if erratically) during the 1930s by drawing to a certain extent on the large surplus of human resources in agriculture. For this reason the impact of the earlier episodic event on the labor component of development and industrialization during these years was minimal.

Similarly, the depressing effect of 1915–1921 on the level of fertility some twenty-five years later—through reduction in the number of potential parents passing through the prime reproductive ages—fell squarely in the years affected by World War II (1940–1946). The result was to aggravate the decline in fertility that took place during the war for other reasons, leading to perhaps 20 million fewer individuals born and surviving the decade of the 1940s than would have been the case without the war.[1]

Losses among the adult population during World War II were staggering: An estimated 25 million of the population in 1940 died by 1950 who would not have died if there had not been a war.[2] However, the effect on reserves of human resources during the war as well as in the years following was cushioned by the timing of the flow into the working ages (beginning at age 16) of individuals born during years of high fertility.

As shown in Figure 9.1, those born from about 1923 to 1931, when birth rates were very high, entered working and military ages from 1939 to 1947, encompassing all years of the war. It is estimated that between 1940 and 1945 the working-age population actually declined by about 1.6 percent per year; this decline would certainly have been greater except for the support of the cohorts born during the 1920s.

Similarly, from about 1952 to 1957 the working-age population increased from 1.5 to 2.6 percent per year, a higher rate of increase than in the 1930s (1.4 percent average between the 1926 and 1939 censuses) or probably than in any earlier period. This unusual increase was caused by the entry into the working ages of the cohorts born from about 1936 through 1941, when birth rates had recovered temporarily to relatively high levels, and by the relatively small number of individuals leaving at the other end (males aged 60 and females aged 55).[3] Those entering were young enough to have suffered less than any other age group; those leaving, especially males, had borne the full brunt of all three earlier episodic events.

Nor was the rate of growth of the working-age population in the intervening period — 1947 to 1952 — particularly deficient, as far as can be ascertained by reconstructing cohort growth from the 1959 census results (see Figure 9.1). The rate of growth during the immediate postwar years may have been as high as 1.5 percent per year. Although the decline in fertility during 1931–1936 did affect the number entering working ages beginning in 1947, the decline had been only to intermediate levels (probably not below 25 per thousand) and, as with the cohorts immediately preceding and following them, they probably suffered less during World War II than those in older age brackets.

The first real curtailment in the rate of growth of the working-age population during peacetime began in 1958, but it was an episodic event caused by the coming of age of the depleted cohorts born during the war. The effect was great enough, however, to bring almost no increase in the working-age population for a period of several years (1959–1961), which sent the shock waves of labor scarcity through the system for the first time.

But the shock was short-lived and the recovery was strong. From 1963 to the present, the working-age population has been increasing by 1 to 2 percent per year, a relatively high rate caused by moderate and stable birth rates (about 25 per thousand) during the 1950s, at the same time that infant mortality declined to very low levels, and the continued retirement of relatively small numbers of older people.

It is therefore only from the present forward, as shown in Figure 9.1, that a serious and long-term slowdown in the peacetime rate of growth of the working-age population is projected. The reason is the decline in fertility that accelerated beginning in 1961, stabilizing at relatively low levels (about 17 births per thousand population) in the late 1960s. Allowing for the number leaving the working ages at the upper end, the rate of growth of the working-age population is projected to decline from almost 2 percent per year in the 1970s to less than one-half of one percent per year from 1981 until the mid–1990s.

Figure 9.1 predicts an increased rate of growth to 1.0 percent or perhaps a bit more when individuals born in the 1980s begin to enter working ages. This small recovery results from assuming a continuation of very recent trends in fertility, which have shown a slight reversal from their long-term downward movement.[4] Whether this represents a serious reversal remains to be seen, but the effect of these recent developments in fertility is at least to stabilize—at positive but modest levels—the overall growth of Soviet labor supply entering the twenty-first century.

Secondary Demographic Determinants of Labor Supply

Supply of Labor from Agriculture

Another major reason why the Soviet Union is facing a fundamentally different set of circumstances in labor supply compared to the first half-century (1928–1978) of economic growth is that the pool of labor resources from agriculture is finally being depleted, compounding the pressure of scarcity relationships caused by the pattern of fertility discussed above.

As shown in Figure 9.2, the industrialization drive began in 1928 with about 85 percent of the labor force in agricultural occupations. Although the total labor force was growing at only 1.5 to 2.0 percent per year (also shown in Figure 9.2) it was relatively easy in the first decade to draw from the agricultural labor pool and provide for an average annual increase of the nonagricultural labor force of almost 10 percent, without seriously depleting agricultural labor resources.[5]

In fact, had it not been for the demographic effects of the collectivization drive, in which millions of adults died prematurely and millions fled to the urban areas, the planned rapid growth of the nonagricultural labor force during the early five-year plans could have taken place while the agricultural labor force remained unchanged or even increased. As it was, the agricultural labor force declined from about 70 million in the 1920s to less than 60 million in 1939; however, it was still almost 70 percent of the total civilian labor force.

Because the Soviet Union entered World War II with such a high percentage of its labor force in agriculture, it was able to withstand frightful losses in population and still emerge with more than half of the labor force in agriculture. The proportion of females in the surviving population was of course very high, but reliance on female labor in agriculture has always been a feature of the Soviet (and pre-Soviet) economy.

During the 1950s the nonagricultural labor force increased by 3–4 percent per year, at the same time that the total labor force was increasing at historically high rates averaging in the vicinity of 2 percent because of the entry of the relatively large cohorts that had survived the war as young children (Figure 9.2). The net effect on the agricultural labor force in the 1950s was an average annual decline of only one-half of one percent per

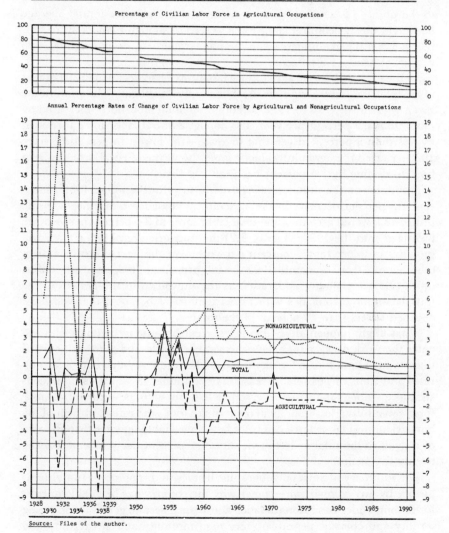

Figure 9.2

PERCENTAGE DISTRIBUTION AND ANNUAL RATES OF CHANGE OF THE CIVILIAN
LABOR FORCE BY AGRICULTURAL AND NONAGRICULTURAL OCCUPATIONS:
U.S.S.R., 1928-39 AND 1950-74, WITH PROJECTIONS TO 1990

Percentage of Civilian Labor Force in Agricultural Occupations

Annual Percentage Rates of Change of Civilian Labor Force by Agricultural and Nonagricultural Occupations

Source: Files of the author.

year. By the end of the decade the percentage of the labor force in agriculture had declined from 54 to 43, thereby passing through an important phase in the direction of the tightening of the labor supply available from agriculture.

The brief but sharp drop in the rate of growth of the working-age population in the late 1950s and early 1960s (Figure 9.1) caused an accelerated drain from the agricultural labor force into the nonagricultural sector. By the mid-1960s the proportion of the labor force in agriculture had declined to the point (38 percent) where it required a 2.5 percent annual average decline in the agricultural labor force to release enough individuals to support a 3.5–4.0 percent increase in the nonagricultural, despite annual total growth of nearly 1.5 percent.

By the early 1970s, the agricultural labor force had declined to 30 percent of the total and the real squeeze in labor supply had begun to be seen. In the seven years from 1970 to 1977, although the total labor force increased by more than 1.5 percent per year, the nonagricultural labor force increased by less than 3 percent. Even that increase — the lowest in peacetime since 1928 — caused the agricultural labor force, by virtue of rural-urban migration, to decline by 1.5 percent per year.

From now on the situation takes a major turn for the worse, for if the recent 1.5 percent decrease in the agricultural labor force together with the projected lowered growth of the total labor force to 0.5 percent per year are projected into the 1990s (Figure 9.2) the nonagricultural labor force will grow by no more than 1 percent per year over the next fifteen years. In other words, from now until 1995 the full pressure of labor scarcity will be on the Soviet planning apparatus, as the slowdown in the growth of the total labor force coincides with an agricultural labor pool that will have declined to less than 20 percent of the total.

What might happen after 1995 is less clear because individuals who will enter the working ages then have not yet been born and there is the usual uncertainty about future fertility trends. The recent stabilization of fertility rates and signs of possible increase may continue, in which case the constraints on labor supply may ease somewhat. But with the agricultural labor force constituting less than 20 percent of the total, the rate of growth of the nonagricultural labor force can be at best only slightly greater than the rate of growth of the total or in the vicinity of 1 percent per year entering the twenty-first century.

The summary of Soviet demographic history to this point — a tumultuous history by any comparison — shows why the country has been able to exist for so long under conditions of labor abundance despite generally declining fertility and episodic periods of very high mortality and low fertility and why, on the other hand, it will suddenly be thrust into an era of labor scarcity that will probably be the state of affairs Soviet planners and policymakers must deal with for some time to come. The problem is whether they can adjust and adapt to these basic changes in the supply of labor resources to minimize their potentially depressing effect on economic performance and therefore on the options open to them in domestic and foreign activities that are dependent on economic performance.

Supply of Labor by Regions and Nationalities

For the purpose of discussing trends in population growth and labor supply by regions and nationalities, the Soviet Union may be divided into the three distinct regions pictured in Figure 9.3.

Region I is commonly referred to as European Russia — the Russian and other Slavic nationality groups living in the Ukraine and Belorussia and in the oblasts of the RSFSR adjacent to Europe, together with the three Baltic republics and the Georgian Republic in Transcaucasia. What the parts of this region have in common for our purposes is the adoption — beginning in the late nineteenth century and continuing through the Soviet period — of the pattern of declining fertility found in earlier European experience. Since the major share of the total population of the country lives in Region I, it is from this region that the declining fertility and now the labor scarcity of the country as a whole is derived.

Region II includes the Urals, Siberia, and the Far East and although sparsely populated, resembles Region I in its demographic history, except that (a) the decline in fertility took place later; (b) the region has always been characterized as a relatively unattractive place to work and by labor scarcity; and (c) certain so-called autonomous republics within Regions I and II, such as the Tatar Republic, tend to follow the corresponding native populations of Region III in their demographic history.

Region III includes the five republics of Central Asia plus Armenia and Azerbaidzhan of Transcaucasia, and in demographic terms it stands in starkest contrast to Region I. Defying all of the "normal" responses to economic development and modernization that are found in the notion of the "demographic transition," fertility rates in Region III have remained very high throughout the Soviet period — except for a temporary but sharp decline during the early 1930s and of course during World War II. In fact in the rural parts of the Uzbek, Tadzhik, Kirgiz, and Turkmen republics, fertility rates in the recent past have increased to levels approaching those associated with natural fertility devoid of any effort at birth control.

Even in the urban areas of these four republics fertility has been comparatively high over the years, in direct relation to the proportion of native, non-Slavic peoples in the respective populations. Kazakhstan, on the other hand — the fifth and largest republic in Central Asia — has always had the smallest proportion of native peoples (and the highest proportion of Slavic

214

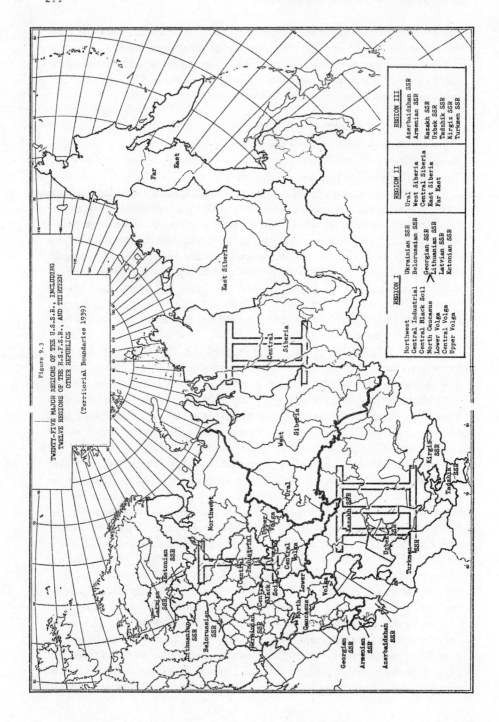

Figure 9.3

TWENTY-FIVE MAJOR REGIONS OF THE U.S.S.R., INCLUDING TWELVE REGIONS OF THE R.S.F.S.R., AND THIRTEEN OTHER REPUBLICS

(Territorial Boundaries 1939)

REGION I	
Northwest	Ukrainian SSR
Central Industrial	Belorussian SSR
Central Black Soil	Georgian SSR
North Caucasus	Lithuanian SSR
Lower Volga	Latvian SSR
Central Volga	Estonian SSR
Upper Volga	

REGION II
Ural
West Siberia
Central Siberia
East Siberia
Far East

REGION III
Azerbaidzhan SSR
Armenian SSR
Kazakh SSR
Uzbek SSR
Tadzhik SSR
Kirgiz SSR
Turkmen SSR

in-migrants), and has therefore always had somewhat lower fertility rates than the other republics. Moreover, fertility in Kazakhstan and in Armenia and Azerbaidzhan has recently been declining. Whether fertility will continue to decline in these three republics, and whether and for how long fertility elsewhere in Region III will remain at a maximum are interesting and important questions. But for the next several decades such hypothetical possibilities for fertility can have no effect on the rate of growth of the working-age population, the immediate prospects for which will be dominated by the high birth rates of the recent past.

Table 9.1 illlustrates the projected growth of the working-age population in Region III compared to that of Regions I and II together, not counting possible interregional migration. The comparison is startling. Even in the five-year interval through which we are now passing (1976–1980) the

TABLE 9.1

RECENT AND PROJECTED CHANGES IN THE WORKING-AGE POPULATION: USSR, TOTAL AND REGIONS I AND II COMPARED TO REGION III

(In thousands)

Periods	Total	Region III*	Regions I and II*
1971–75	12,726	4,782	7,944
1976–80	10,408	4,643	5,765
1981–85	2,687	3,524	− 837
1986–90	2,830	3,469	− 639
1991–95	4,020	4,193	− 173
1996–2000	9,012	6,081	2,931
1981–95	9,537	11,186	−1,649

*Regions are listed in Figure 9.3. Table 9.1 groups Georgian SSR with Region III.

Source: Murray Feshbach and Stephen Rapawy, "Soviet Population and Manpower Trends and Policies," in U.S. Congress, Joint Economic Committee, Soviet Economy in a New Perspective (Washington, D.C.: U.S. Government Printing Office, 1976), p. 129

working-age population in Region III will have increased by 4,643,000 (44.6 percent of the total increase) although only 25 percent of the Soviet population lives there. However, during the next 15 years (1981–1995), while the working-age population of Region III continues to increase by 11,186,000 overall, that of Regions I and II will *decline* by 1,649,000.

These sharply differing growth rates will exacerbate the regional imbalance in labor supply between the surplus of Region III and the deficit of Regions I and II, an imbalance caused by historically low levels of interregional migration of population and the fact that Region III has remained relatively underdeveloped up to this point. Resistance of the native populations to migration from Region III has perpetuated the regional imbalance in labor supply; if this resistance continues, it cannot but bring even more depressing pressures in the future in terms of implications for productivity. Options to relieve the pressures are examined in the last section of this chapter.

Supply of Labor by Age and Sex

The evidence to this point shows that there will be a serious tightening of planners' options in labor supply in the very near future because of the slowdown in the overall rate of growth of number of individuals available for work and because of changes in their distribution by agricultural/nonagricultural occupations and major regions of the country. There will also be related problems in terms of particular age groups and the changing age distribution of the population.

The first of these problems—and one that frequently receives attention—concerns the male population of prime military age, 18–34. To the extent that the demand for Soviet military manpower may be assumed to be relatively inelastic, the brunt of the slowdown in the rate of growth of this age group will be borne by the civilian economy. The effect may be seen in terms of changes in the prospective size of the cohort of males age 18, the age of initial liability for military service. According to recent estimates and projections[6] the number of males age 18 in the population will reach a historical peak (2,646,000) in 1978 and decline to about three-quarters of that level (2,012,000) in 1987, increasing thereafter only slightly as a result of the small increase in the crude birthrate that began in 1969, 18 years earlier (Figure 9.1).

Assuming that the number of conscriptees at age 18 remains unchanged at the 1975 level (1,866,000), after allowance for possible exemptions from military service, it may be shown that the number of 18-year-olds available for the national economy would decline absolutely after 1982. The net downward shift over this period would be about 600,000 at an annual rate, from a plus 398,000 in 1978 to a minus 199,000 in 1987.

Some time ago the Soviets suffered an even greater change in the number of 18-year-old males — it declined to a low of 974,000 in 1962 (the "war babies" effect) or about one-third of the 1978 level — but this was only a temporary decline and its effect on the civilian economy was tempered by the fact that it took place when the agricultural source of labor had not yet reached the limit. The "trough" of the early 1960s, moreover, was followed by unusual increases in the number of 18-year-olds, climaxing in 1978 in the all-time high of 2,646,000, compared to an average of about 1,900,000 in the 1950s. The effect on the civilian economy of the forthcoming decline of this critical age group — although to levels that are not too low by recent experience — will be cushioned neither by alternative sources of supply nor by a strong recovery in the 1990s and thereafter.

In what may be seen as a positive side to these prospective trends by age groups, the declining numbers of young people should reduce the demand for specialized education and training, as it has already done at the level of general education. Releasing resources for other uses, it opens the possibility of paying greater attention to the quality of specialized education than has been possible during the very rapid expansion of the system that took place during the 1960s and 1970s. A section of this chapter is devoted to the question of "quality" in labor supply.

A perceptible "aging" of the Soviet population will also take place over the next few decades as the reduced number entering the young ages is balanced by the rising number of those reaching the older age groups — those who were young enough to be spared some of the hazards of World War II. Feshbach and Rapawy project the "aging" process to the year 2000 in the percentages given in Table 9.2.[7] While the proportion of the population in the working ages remains essentially unchanged from 1950 to 2000, the proportion of ages 0–15 shows a decline and that beyond the working ages an increase.

One implication from these figures is that the "dependency ratio" will not

Table 9.2
Aging Process of the Soviet Population to the Year 2000

Age Group	1950	1960	1970	1980	1990	2000
0–15	32.2	31.8	30.7	26.1	27.0	25.2
16–59/54 (working ages)	57.4	55.7	54.2	58.3	55.4	55.5
60/55 and over	10.4	12.4	15.1	15.5	17.6	19.2
	100.0	100.0	100.0	100.0	100.0	100.0

change significantly, even as the rate of growth of the working-age population declines (Figure 9.1). The increased burden of dependents in the older age groups will be balanced by the reduced burden of those under 16.

It can be expected that the process of "aging" will also take place *within* the working-age population, as the reduced number of young entrants combines with the expanded number now moving into the older years (50 and over) who entered the labor force just after the war. This aging of the work force would tend to reduce upward mobility in jobs and in other ways perpetuate a conservative style in management at the very time when the demands for genuine reforms in planning and management—to compensate for the depressing changes in labor supply—will undoubtedly increase.

In one respect, at least, the Soviet Union in the coming decades will be returning to a more "normal," long-run state of affairs in labor supply. The sex ratio among the adult population throughout the Soviet period has reflected episodic population losses that fell much more than proportionately on males—during World War II, but also during World War I, the Civil War, and the period of collectivization of the early 1930s. At the end of 1944, when the situation was at its worst, there were estimated to be 32 million fewer males than females in the adult population.[8]

Now, 35 years after the most recent episodic catastrophe, this extraordinary deficit of males appears only in the population over 50 years of age. What impact this "recovery" will have on effective labor supply is difficult to say, since the proportion of the female population in the labor force has always been high and jobs are open to women without discrimination. Still, the absence of women continues to be noticeable in the most senior positions of the economy, government, and party; therefore, we can probably assume that the return to a more normal ratio between the sexes in the adult population will lessen one constraint under which Soviet administration has been operating.

Qualitative Dimensions of Labor Supply

The Soviets have always recognized the need to raise the quality of their labor force—through general education, specialized training, and the acquisition of knowledge and experience on the job—in the interests of effective industrialization and the achievement of social goals. The mix of methods chosen to achieve this objective, however, has varied at different stages of development.

During the first three decades (1928–1958) labor was regarded as a relatively abundant resource and the economy was geared to labor-intensive methods of production and to the extensive and wasteful use of secondary labor in many capital-intensive sectors. The demand for formal, full-time, specialized training under these conditions was minimal and the number of individuals admitted to such training programs grew very slowly (Figure 9.4). As a result, in these first thirty years of industrialization the vast majority of the labor force in industry as well as agriculture was required to learn on the job, even among specialists in positions of responsibility. This approach, in which the factory and the office were the school, was justified in terms of the most effective use of educational and other resources.

It was not until the late 1950s—coincident with the first sign of ap-

Figure 9.4

THE NUMBER OF ENTRANTS EACH YEAR INTO PROFESSIONAL (HIGHER), SEMI-PROFESSIONAL (SPECIALIZED SECONDARY) AND VOCATIONAL (PROFESSIONAL-TECHNICAL) EDUCATIONAL INSTITUTIONS: U.S.S.R., 1930-40 AND 1945-75

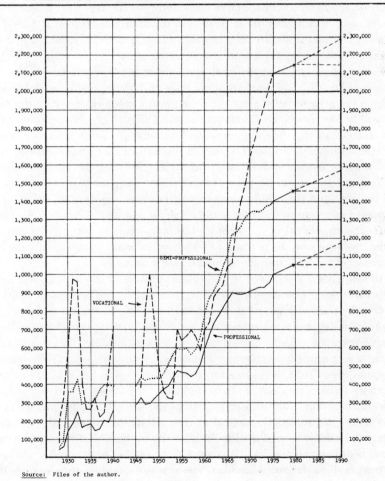

Source: Files of the author.

proaching labor scarcity—that the Khrushchev educational reform was launched which, among other things, set the three-track system of specialized education on a steep growth path. It is only recently that this growth has approached the point where a high percentage of young people can expect to receive formal, specialized training in one track or another early in their productive lives.

It is important to keep in mind that this more or less universal availability of specialized training programs is a very recent development. In the late 1950s, when Sputnik called our attention to the possible contribution of the educational system to Soviet successes, only about one-third of Soviet young people could expect to receive formal, specialized training outside the work place. Insofar as the specialized educational system contributed to Sputnik, it was on a very selective basis. Now and in the future the demand for specialized education must be seen in much broader terms, affecting all levels of training if quality is to any significant degree to be substituted for quantity in the drive for economic performance.

This is not to say that the total numbers in these programs will not increase, although it is unlikely that the scale of the system will develop much beyond the present level, since the number in a given cohort of young people will be decreasing by 20 percent in the 1980s. Nor is it to say that the distribution among the three tracks will not change. Since 1965, for example, the number of students admitted annually into *professional* programs (universities, institutes) has been held to near 900,000; the number admitted into *semiprofessional* programs (technicums) has risen slowly from 1.2 to 1.4 million; and the number completing *vocational* training off the job has increased at a continuous rate to over 2 million in 1975 (Figure 9.4). Currently the equivalent of 20 percent of an age cohort is admitted to professional training and 30 percent to semiprofessional training, with the remaining 50 percent completing vocational training.[9]

Allowing for a slowdown in the rate of growth of the system and for a redistribution of entrants by program, a range of possible growth paths to 1990 is sketched in Figure 9.4. From 1975 to 1980, the number of entrants to professional and semiprofessional programs is extrapolated on the basis of recent trends, which themselves represent a slowdown in growth after 1965; the number completing vocational training, which has grown unabated since 1958, is assumed to grow more slowly. From 1980 to 1990, alternative paths for each are indicated that range from no further growth to a continuation of the slower growth of the preceding quinquennium.

Whether the Soviet educational system will make a significant contribution to the substitution of quality for quantity in the labor force in the years ahead is difficult to predict. The fact that the quality of the product has not been as high as desired when the system was expanding rapidly does not mean that it cannot be improved in the future, when the system is growing at a moderate rate, if at all.

Conclusions

The demographic changes that have been taking place constitute for the most part not a temporary phase or minor aberration in trend lines, but a fundamental and rather precipitous departure from the historical past, and are essentially irreversible, given the likely demographic prospects and the state that Soviet economic development has reached. In and of themselves, the changes will tend to depress Soviet economic performance and, if effective countermeasures are not taken, will bring about a further deterioration in growth rates. The latter have been gradually declining since the 1950s and the forthcoming trends in labor supply can only make matters worse.

Although the ultimate implications of the changes in labor supply are beyond the scope of this chapter, it may be useful to conclude with a brief outline of four major options that are open to Soviet planners for dealing directly with the problem. Three of the options would attempt to modify the trends themselves, tempering if not reversing their effect on economic performance. The fourth option, taking supply as given, would be directed toward improving the structure and quality of economic activity and the utilization of labor on the job, in the interest of raising per-worker productivity. Raising per-worker productivity is an objective that must be achieved in any event if long-run economic goals are to be attained and the downward drift in growth rates is to be reversed. It has acquired a sense of urgency because the prolonged era of labor abundance and the wasteful labor and management practices that it has perpetuated — so characteristic of the first fifty years of Soviet industrialization — has finally come to an end.

One option would be to try to influence the primary demographic variables by creating conditions that would be conducive to higher fertility rates in Region I and II and lower rates in Region III. The aim would be to increase the overall rate of growth of the working-age population (the future labor force) and at the same time to reduce the differentials in fertility and population growth among regions. Although the effect of changes in the birth rate of the working-age population and its distribution would not be felt for fifteen or twenty years, the idea of trying to influence fertility — for this and other reasons — has been receiving considerable attention in Soviet literature.[10] From this discussion has come some understanding of past fertility trends, but less than agreement on what to do about these trends. For example, Soviet demographers think they know at least some of the reasons why the number of children per family in Region I has decreased (e.g., insufficient housing space), but they really do not know what it would take to reverse the trend. They think they know why fertility in Central Asia is so high (e.g., the retention of certain traditional attitudes despite the modernization of many social institutions), but they do not know what would be required to change the attitudes enough to influence decisions on family size. Not only do they not agree on whether a given approach would really change fertility patterns, but they are also uncertain as to whether the potential benefits would justify the costs. In other words, whether the considerable resources that might be required to alter the growth of the *future* labor force should better be channeled into efforts to raise the productivity of the *present* labor force.

It is unlikely that Soviet planners in the near future will undertake a major program directed specifically at influencing fertility. Although improvements in housing and other social services may have as one consideration their potential effect on fertility, it is unlikely that the modification of fertility rates would become a priority objective involving a substantial reallocation of resources for its implementation. In the absence of such a program, there is reason to believe that the stabilization and slight increase of birth rates that has taken place in Region I in the past decade may continue. The downward trend in fertility of the 1950s and 1960s may have bottomed out.

Less certain, perhaps, is the future of the very high rates in the rural areas of certain republics in Central Asia. For a population that has clung stubbornly to traditional practices in family formation during the first sixty years of living under the Soviet system, it is not immediately clear why things might change now. On the other hand, the decline in fertility already evident in Azerbaidzhan, Armenia, and Kazakhstan may be suggestive of a turn of events that will become general for the whole region in the not too distant future.

A second option for influencing labor supply focuses on untapped labor reserves in the form of able-bodied women who are not yet in the labor force, as well as prospective retirees of both sexes. Although the option has a certain appeal, at least in principle, the fact is that such reserves have never been large in Soviet experience and are now smaller than ever.[11] A high percentage (by international standards) of the Soviet (and pre-Soviet) female population has always been in the labor force and in the last decade or two successful efforts have drawn even more into the labor force. The number working beyond normal retirement (males age 59, females age 54) also has been relatively high and has shown an increase in the recent past. And the import of foreign labor, although carried out on a small scale in recent years and feasible in the future for selected projects, presents logistical and political problems that argue against its extended use in the future. In short, the possibility of increasing labor supply out of the existing and projected population that is not in the labor force is quite small.

As far as the distribution of the labor force by surplus and deficit areas is concerned, the most direct way of alleviating the growing imbalance is to facilitate interregional migration on a fairly large scale. For such migration to have a salutary effect on productivity, however, it must be accompanied by the effective integration of the migrants into the population of the receiving regions and particularly their introduction into positions at all levels of the work force, which heretofore they have not held in very large numbers. Past experience suggests that these accommodations will not readily be made and that resistance to migration on the part of the native populations of Region III will not easily recede. The primary method employed—relocation through bonuses or pay incentives—has not worked well in the past. And administrative mobilization of one type or another—beyond that already practiced on graduates of specialized training institutions but so far with little lasting effect on interregional mobility—if carried out on a large scale, may incur political and social costs that could outweigh benefits.[12]

Another view, although held by the minority of Western analysts, is that the responsiveness of the native populations of Central Asia to the economic pressures of overpopulation at home and opportunities elsewhere may have reached the point (in the 1980s) of a significant increase in out-migration.[13] Finally, it must be recognized that there remains a latent demand for labor in the *urban* parts of Central Asia that could decrease some of the surplus from the immediate area and that the Soviets are inclined to take the Central Asian population as given and to think in terms of moving new (labor-intensive) industries into the area in order to take advantage of supply factors.

Nevertheless, even if during the 1980s there is a greater responsiveness to pressures and inducements to migrate and a greater flow of investment resources into the region, the effect on productivity will probably not be felt until later. The crunch of the numbers in the next few years, as shown above, will be such that any feasible accommodation in terms of migration and/or investment will have a relatively small countereffect. The benefits of such accommodation, although they may ultimately be great, will probably not be felt until close to the next century.

The foregoing options for dealing directly with numbers of people—by modifying fertility rates, finding hidden reserves, encouraging migration—may possibly appear as priority programs under the mounting pressure of labor supply in the years immediately ahead, but their countereffects to the quantitative pressures will probably not be great even under the most optimistic assumptions.

The remaining option, therefore, concerns what might be called the "qualitative" factors affecting production. These include: (1) the elements of quality inherent in education, training, experience on the job, and attitudes toward work and a career, and (2) the technological and managerial factors that determine the effectiveness with which the given labor supplied at different levels of skill and responsibility are utilized in their respective jobs.

It has been shown that major strides have been made since the Khrushchev educational reform (1958–1965) in providing Soviet young people with something approaching universal specialized training at one level or in one form or another. Also taken into account are the acknowledged shortcomings in the quality of the product produced by the system and the opportunities for improving this quality in the years immediately ahead. Now that the major institutional growth phase has been completed and the number of young people graduating from the secondary school system will decline, the greater attention that can be paid to the quality of the various specialized education programs could make a slow but steadily improved contribution to the national economy in the future.

Of all the areas affecting the contribution of labor to production, however, the most sensitive, if not critical, for countering the contractions in the overall labor supply are those concerned with the effectiveness with which labor is utilized on the job. It is partly a function of the institutions and technology of the workplace and partly a function of the structure of the work force on the job and the effectiveness of management and the relations between the managers and the managed. It is probably in these related areas — at all levels of activity involving technology and management — that the weaknesses of the Soviet system are most apparent to the Western observer. Despite a keen awareness by Soviet leadership of the contribution of technology and management to economic growth and performance, and the rather substantial attempts that have been made, in and through the economic reforms of 1965, to bring them into play, it is in this area more than any other that the reason for the gradual but continued slowdown in the growth of the Soviet economy since the early 1960s can be found.

It is also through technological progress and the improved use of human resources on the job that the long-run growth in *productivity* must be found. Even without the impending problems in labor supply that lie ahead the Soviets are faced with the need to solve the related problems of technology and management of the work force, if the gradual depression of economic activity is to be turned around and long-term economic goals achieved within an acceptable period.

The forthcoming shortage of human resources simply makes the solution of the problem of technology and management all the more imperative. In fact, the existence of a shortage of labor already being felt in many parts of the country is the result of the failure to use labor more effectively. Underemployment or "hidden unemployment" of labor in Soviet enterprises has been a characteristic of the Soviet system for a long time, and the decline in the rate of growth of labor supply turns this underemployment into a shortage before it would have if labor had been utilized more efficiently to begin with.

To the extent that improvements in the institutional-technological-managerial setting do not keep pace with the requirements implied by each successive level of economic development, the pace of growth itself, for a given supply of human resources, will suffer. As a chronic complaint about the Soviet system, this is what has been hampering the growth rates for the past twenty years or more. The changes in the overall quantitative dimensions of labor supply that will unfold in the 1980s have brought the problem into an acute phase, and the question is whether the Soviets will be able to rise to the terms in which the crisis of productivity appears and do something about it at last. The fact that they have not really solved the technological-managerial problem of the higher stages of development in recent decades may easily lead one to conclude that the solution is beyond their grasp, at least to the degree required to stem the fall in growth rates if not to turn them around. The fact that the economic reforms launched in 1965 with some promise of dealing with the question have been substantially abandoned supports the pessimistic views of genuine improvement in the Soviet economic system in these terms.

On the other hand, the pressures of shortages that lie just over the horizon because of the impending changes in labor supply are of an order of magnitude and severity never before experienced by Soviet planners. Despite warnings in the literature of what is coming, the inertia of fifty years probably does not prepare the planners to face what is really in store, nor can we predict their reaction to the further downturn in growth rates that is almost certain to occur within a few years.

The big unknown is what kind of effect these new pressures must exert to force Soviet leadership to undertake a really agonizing review of their approach and to consider some serious changes that could have far-reaching effects on the performance of the economy and on its very nature. We must keep an open mind on what the considered reaction to this very new set of circumstances will be. The fact that the top leadership of the party and government is soon due for a major turnover, coincident with the first phase of the new pressures from labor supply, further encourages us to keep our own options open before judging how the Soviets will handle the impending crisis of productivity.

Notes

1. See Warren W. Eason, "The Soviet Population Today: An Analysis of the

First Results of the 1959 Census," *Foreign Affairs* 37, no. 4 (July 1959).

2. Ibid. Taken together, Soviet population losses during World War II came to 45 million people — who would have been alive in 1950 if there had not been a war — a figure equivalent to almost one quarter of the total population (including annexed territories) in 1940.

3. The number of males who became 60 years of age, and thereby left the working-age population, during the 1950s included those born from 1890 to 1900. Having experienced the special hazards of both wars, their numbers had been severely depleted by the 1950s. Females who became age 55 during the 1950s were born in 1895–1905 and, to a lesser but not insignificant degree, their numbers were also affected by the two wartime periods.

4. Warren W. Eason, "Demographic Problems: Fertility," U.S. Congress, Joint Economic Committee, *Soviet Economy in a New Perspective* (Washington, D.C.: U.S. Government Printing Office, 1976), pp. 155–161.

5. Cf. Warren W. Eason, "Population Changes," in Allen Kassof, ed., *Prospects for Soviet Society* (New York: Praeger Publishers, 1968), pp. 230–240, for a discussion of the relationship between the proportion of the labor force in agricultural occupations and possibilities for the growth of the nonagricultural sector.

6. Murray Feshbach and Stephen Rapawy, "Soviet Population and Manpower Trends and Policies," in JEC, *Soviet Economy in a New Perspective*, p. 150.

7. Ibid., p. 115.

8. Derived from the population by sex and five-year age-groups on 1 January 1950, estimated in Frederick A. Leedy, "Demographic Trends in the U.S.S.R.," U.S., Congress, Joint Economic Committee, *Soviet Economic Prospects for the Seventies* (Washington, D.C.: U.S. Government Printing Office, 1973), pp. 474–477, by "reverse projection" techniques, to 1 January 1945, assuming mortality on the basis of fragmentary published figures.

9. These are "equivalent" percentages of a given age cohort, because some members of the latter will go directly to the labor force from general education and a similar number will enter specialized training from the labor force.

10. A recent review of this literature may be found in David M. Heer, "Three Issues in Soviet Population Policy," *Population and Economic Review* 3, no. 3 (September 1977):229–252.

11. Murray Feshbach and Stephen Rapawy, "Labor Constraints in the Five-Year Plan," in JEC, *Soviet Economic Prospects for the Seventies*, pp. 491–507.

12. Cf. Jeremy Azrael, "Emergent Nationality Problems in the USSR," RAND Report R-2172-AF, pp. 9–16; and a paper by Murray Feshbach, "Prospects for Massive Out-Migration from Central Asia During the Next Decade" (February, 1977).

13. For example, Robert A. Lewis, Richard H. Rowland, and Ralph Clem, *Nationality and Population Change in Russia and the U.S.S.R.* (New York: Praeger Publishers, 1976), pp. 354–381.

10
Soviet Economic Growth and Foreign Policy

Morris Bornstein

An important factor in the conduct of Soviet foreign policy in the coming years clearly will be the extent to which serious problems of resource allocation are confronted. Such problems derive from both the physical constraints on supplies of major factors of production and the measures designed to utilize these supplies. After examining allocation patterns in the context of overall economic performance since 1960, I shall analyze resource constraints, and conclude with implications for Soviet foreign policy toward Eastern Europe, the industrialized capitalist nations, and the less developed countries.

Resource Allocation Patterns and Economic Performance

The allocation of resources in a country is commonly analyzed in terms of where gross national product (GNP) is created and how it is used. Table 10.1 shows the shares of major sectors of origin in total Soviet national product at factor cost[1] in 1970, the latest year for which a comprehensive calculation has been published. Although industry is the largest sector, agriculture remains very important, contributing about one-fifth of national product. Thus agricultural fluctuations strongly affect total national product, and economic performance is best judged over a period such as five years, long enough to span good and bad harvests.

Table 10.2 presents estimates of the distribution of Soviet national product by major end uses in recent years. A little less than half of total output is

This chapter draws on a research project at the University of Michigan Center for Russian and East European Studies, funded by a grant from the Rockefeller Foundation. I wish to thank the foundation for its support; Dennis A. O'Hearn for his assistance in research; and Gerhard Fink, John P. Hardt, Marie Lavigne, and Jan Rylander for helpful comments.

227

available to households for individual consumption from family income. Another 8 percent of national resources goes to communal consumption in the form of government health and education programs. One-fourth of total product is devoted to investment in machinery, equipment, buildings—and capital repair (major reconstruction) of them—plus expansion of livestock herds. Research and development, general administration, military programs, net exports, and net inventory change account for the remaining one-sixth of total resources. It is noteworthy that these estimates show no significant changes in the respective shares from 1965 to 1976.

TABLE 10.1

USSR: Shares of Gross National Product at Factor Cost[a] by Sector of Origin, 1970

Sector	Percent
Industry[a]	28.7
Construction	8.8
Agriculture	20.4
Transportation	7.8
Communications	0.7
Trade	6.1
Services	23.9
Other	3.6
Total[a]	100.0

Source: Computed from ruble values in U.S. Central Intelligence Agency, USSR: Gross National Product Accounts, 1970 (Washington, D.C., 1975), p. 10.

[a]Including weapons production.

Also striking is the inclusion of military programs — sometimes called the "defense" end use — in the "Other" category in Table 10.2. This reflects, on the one hand, the great and apparently successful effort of the Soviet authorities to conceal the total size and detailed composition of military expenditures and on the other hand, the resulting controversy among Western specialists and their organizations. Western experts agree that the official Soviet budget appropriation for "Defense," announced in the annual budget speech of the minister of finance, includes only a part, perhaps less than half, of total military outlays. But these specialists disagree in their subsequent efforts to estimate total military expenditures and composition or to ascertain which ones are covered by the budget item for "Defense" and which are financed elsewhere, and where.

For example the U.S. Central Intelligence Agency (CIA) has recently estimated that military programs absorbed 11-13 percent of Soviet GNP during 1970-1975. This share was relatively stable over the period because military spending increased at about the same rate as total GNP.[2] The same order of magnitude for the defense share of national product appears in some other studies, which take the defense share of GNP as 10 percent in 1970[3] and 11 percent in 1973.[4] However, other specialists question these estimates — both the figures and the underlying methodology.[5]

The performance of the Soviet economy may be evaluated from various standpoints: growth, productivity, and welfare.

Table 10.3 presents estimates of average annual rates of growth since 1960 of the major sectors of the economy and of GNP as a whole. Because of the methodology used (explained in the source cited), weapons production is excluded from the figures for industry and for total GNP. The table shows the steady but gradual decline in industrial growth and also the sensitivity of GNP to variations in agricultural output. Good agricultural results boosted the average annual growth rate for GNP in 1966-1970 above the rate achieved in 1961-1965, whereas bad harvests in 1972 and 1975 depressed the GNP growth rate for 1971-1975.[6]

Average annual rates of growth by end use, for the same periods, are given in Table 10.4. Because these estimates include weapons production, the figures for total GNP are slightly higher than those in Table 10.3, but the time trend is the same.[7] Poor agricultural results in 1971-1975 are reflected in the smaller rate of growth of household consumption and the sharp drop in livestock herds. The pattern of investment also changed as machinery, equipment, and capital repairs grew more rapidly but construction more slowly in 1971-1975 compared with 1966-1970. However, the continuing decline in the "Other" category is not very informative, because it is a residual covering the net results of such disparate items as defense, net exports, inventory changes, and statistical discrepancies.

TABLE 10.2

USSR: Shares of Gross National Product,[a] by End Use, 1965, 1970, and 1974-76

(Percent)

End Use	1965	1970	1974	1975	1976[b]
Consumption	58	57	56	58	57
Household consumption	49	48	48	n.a.[c]	n.a.
Communal consumption[d]	9	9	8	n.a.	n.a.
Fixed Investment	26	27	28	27	28
New fixed investment[e]	22	23	23	23	23
Capital repair	4	4	5	4	5
Research and Development	3	3	4	15	15
Administration	3	3	3		
Other[f]	10	10	9		
	100	100	100	100	100

Sources: 1965, 1970, 1974: Rush V. Greenslade, "The Real Gross National Product of the U.S.S.R., 1950-1975," in U.S. Congress, Joint Economic Committee, Soviet Economy in a New Perspective (Washington, D.C.: U.S. Government Printing Office, 1976), p. 277. 1975-1976: U.S. Central Intelligence Agency, Handbook of Economic Statistics 1977 (Washington, D.C., 1977), p. 49. These sources use the same concepts and methodology.

[a]At factor cost in 1970 prices.

[b]Preliminary.

[c]N.a. = not available.

[d]Government expenditures on education and health.

[e]Including machinery and equipment, construction, and net additions to livestock herds.

[f]Including military outlays, net exports, net inventory change, and statistical discrepancy.

TABLE 10.3

USSR: Average Annual Rates of Growth of Gross National Product[a]

by Sector of Origin, 1961-65, 1966-70, and 1971-75

(Percent)

	1961-65	1966-70	1971-75
Industry	6.6	6.2	5.9
Construction	4.5	5.8	5.6
Agriculture	2.4	4.2	-2.0
Transportation	8.7	6.7	6.3
Communications	7.1	8.9	7.2
Trade	4.9	6.5	5.0
Services	4.7	4.2	3.6
Gross National Product	4.9	5.3	3.7

Source: Greenslade, "The Real Gross National Product
of the U.S.S.R....," p.272.

[a]At factor cost in 1970 prices, excluding weapons production.

Trends in productivity are shown for GNP in Table 10.5, and for industry alone in Table 10.6. In both tables, it is clear that growth has been primarily a result of rapid expansion of capital inputs (as a result of the high rate of investment shown in Table 10.2), while labor input (in man-hours) has been increasing much more slowly. In turn, although (in Table 10.6) labor productivity in industry has been growing at a modest rate, capital productivy changes are negative, as diminishing returns to capital occur when the capital-labor ratio increases.[8] Thus more investment is required to achieve a given increase in output. However, investment competes with both defense and consumption for resources. Hence, efforts to raise labor and capital productivity play a crucial role in Soviet economic growth.

One factor in labor productivity is the population's perception of the real income attainable by spending wages or salaries to buy consumer goods and services. Table 10.7 shows that the improvement in consumer welfare in the USSR has been steady but modest. Per capita consumption grew

TABLE 10.4

USSR: Average Annual Rates of Growth of Gross National Product[a]
by End Use, 1961-65, 1966-70, and 1971-75

(Percent)

End Use	1961-65	1966-70	1971-75
Consumption	4.0	5.1	3.8
Household consumption	3.8	5.3	3.9
Communal consumption[b]	5.1	4.0	3.6
Fixed Investment	7.1	6.3	5.4
New fixed investment	6.8	6.4	4.5
Machinery and equipment	10.8	7.6	8.4
Construction	4.3	6.5	5.0
New addition to livestock herds	23.1	-0.2	-14.7
Capital repair	8.9	6.0	9.4
Research and Development	8.8	6.7	6.1
Administration	3.4	4.7	3.9
Other[c]	6.3	3.2	-3.7
Gross National Product	5.0	5.5	3.8

Source: Greenslade, "The Real Gross National Product of the U.S.S.R....," p. 276.

[a]At factor cost in 1970 prices, including weapons production.

[b]Government expenditures on education and health.

[c]Including military outlays, net exports, net inventory change, and statistical discrepancy.

more slowly in 1971-1975 than in 1966-1970 in all categories except durables (no change) and education (a small increase). Food supplies remain a problem, with diet quality poor although caloric intake is adequate. And the housing shortage is still serious, although improved now that the majority of urban families live in their own apartments.[9]

The basic trends in Soviet resource allocation and economic performance depicted in Tables 10.4-10.7 are likely to continue in the near future. A careful analysis of the Tenth Five-Year Plan for 1976-1980 reveals the Soviet leadership's recognition and grudging acceptance of the retardation of growth of inputs, productivity, and output. Thus, compared with actual

TABLE 10.5

U.S.S.R: Average Annual Rates of Growth of Gross National Product,

Factor Inputs, and Factor Productivity,

1961-65, 1966-70, and 1971-75

(Percent)

	1961-65	1966-70	1971-75
Gross National Product[a]	5.0	5.5	3.8
Factor inputs			
Labor, capital, and land combined[b]	4.1	3.9	4.1
Labor[c]	1.6	2.0	1.9
Capital	8.7	7.5	7.9
Land	0.6	-0.3	0.9
Factor Productivity			
Labor, capital, and land combined	0.9	1.5	-0.2
Labor	3.4	3.4	1.8
Capital	-3.3	-1.9	-3.8
Land	4.4	5.8	2.9

Source: Greenslade, "The Real Gross National Product of the
U.S.S.R....," p. 279.

[a]Including weapons production.

[b]Inputs combined using a Cobb-Douglas (linear homogeneous)
production function with weights of 60.2, 36.7, and 3.1 percent
for labor, capital, and land, respectively.

[c]Man-hours.

performance in the Ninth Five-Year Plan period (1971-1975) the Tenth
Plan projects slower growth for national product, fixed investment, industrial employment and labor productivity, industrial production, and per
capita consumption.[10] Furthermore, this deterioration in economic performance appears likely to intensify in the early 1980s, when severe resource

TABLE 10.6

USSR: Average Annual Rates of Growth of Industrial Production, Factor
Inputs, and Factor Productivity, 1961-65, 1966-70, and 1971-75

(Percent)

	1961-65	1966-70	1971-75
Industrial Production[a]	7.0	6.8	6.0
Factor Inputs			
Labor and capital combined[b]	6.4	5.5	4.5
Labor[c]	2.9	3.1	1.5
Capital	11.2	8.7	8.7
Factor Productivity			
Labor and capital combined	0.6	1.3	1.5
Labor	4.0	3.6	4.5
Capital	-3.8	-1.8	-2.4

Source: Greenslade, "The Real Gross National Product of the
U.S.S.R...," p. 279.

[a] Including weapons production.

[b] Inputs combined using a Cobb-Douglas (linear homogeneous)
production function with weights of 57 and 43 percent for labor and
capital, respectively.

[c] Man-hours.

constraints will further curtail growth. Competition among consumption,
investment, and defense in the allocation of available resources will increase, with important implications for domestic and foreign policies.

Constraints on Growth

One can approach constraints on Soviet growth by studying the three
basic factors of production — land (including both agricultural land and
energy resources), labor, and capital — and related problems in technological progress and the balance of payments. Because of these constraints,
Soviet economic growth in the 1980s will be slower than in the 1970s.

TABLE 10.7

USSR: Average Annual Rates of Growth of Per Capita Consumption,

1961-65, 1966-70, and 1971-75

(Percent)

	1961-65	1966-70	1971-75
Total Consumption	2.5	4.7	3.2
Household consumption	2.4	4.9	3.2
Food	2.0	3.5	2.1
Soft goods[a]	1.8	6.6	2.7
Durables	4.4	9.7	9.7
Services	4.9	5.4	4.3
Communal consumption	3.6	3.1	2.9
Education	5.1	3.2	3.4
Health	1.3	3.0	2.2

Source: Gertrude E. Schroeder and Barbara S. Severin, "Soviet Consumption and Income Policies in Perspective," in U.S. Congress, Joint Economic Committee, Soviet Economy in a New Perspective, p. 622.

[a]Clothing, footwear, publications, etc.

Land

Agriculture. The poor performance of Soviet agriculture is explained in part by natural handicaps and in part by unfavorable policy decisions. The environmental constraints on agriculture in the USSR are formidable.[11] Three-fourths of the area is climatically comparable to the Prairie Provinces of Canada and the northern Great Plains of the United States. In all three the land suffers from insufficient heat, moisture, and nutrients. Almost one-third of the USSR is too cold for farming and an additional two-fifths is so cold that only hardy, early-maturing crops can be grown. Only the southern areas are warm enough to permit a variety of crops, but moisture is often deficient. Drought-resistant plant varieties and dry-farming techniques are helpful, but irrigation is the most effective solution. However, it is costly in terms of both capital and labor and in some areas soil deterioration makes the benefits of irrigation short-lived. Also, large quantities of organic and mineral fertilizers are required. Furthermore, a recent study[12] suggests that climatic conditions were unusually good from 1960 to 1974, with greater precipitation, warmer winters, and cooler summers. Perhaps half of the increase in Soviet grain production from 1963 to 1974 may be explained by these favorable circumstances. A return to the harsher climatic conditions of the early 1960s may have begun with the severe drought of 1975.

Overcoming such serious natural obstacles requires a considerable commitment of resources and skillful, imaginative management of them. The Soviet authorities have been more successful at meeting the first than the second requirement. In 1971-1975, for example, ambitious plans for agricultural investment and the delivery of machinery and materials to farms were generally completed, with only minor exceptions. New fixed investment in agriculture grew at an average annual rate of over 9.5 percent, almost two-thirds faster than investment in the rest of the economy. As a result, productive (e.g., machinery) and nonproductive (e.g., housing) investment in the agricultural sector accounted for 26 percent of total investment. If investment in branches supporting agriculture (e.g., chemical fertilizers and agricultural machine building) is added, the figure rises to 34 percent of total investment.[13]

The picture for 1976-1980 in the Tenth Five-Year Plan is not so encouraging. The agricultural sector (proper) is again to receive one-fourth of total fixed investment, but this total will be rising much more slowly in 1976-1980 than in 1971-1975. Thus investment in agriculture is to increase at an average annual rate of only 3.5 percent in 1976-1980, a sharp cut from the 9.5 percent achieved in 1971-1975.[14] At the same time, the Soviet authorities wish to continue shifting labor from agriculture to industry and service activities.

In these circumstances, improvement in the productivity of labor and capital is critical for increased output, but the record of productivity in Soviet agriculture is dismal. According to a recent estimate[15] the combined productivity of land, labor, and capital increased at an average annual rate of only 1.0 percent in 1961-1970 and actually decreased at an average annual rate of 1.1 percent in 1971-1975. There are a number of causes of low productivity.[16] The composition of the agricultural labor force in terms of age, sex, and education is highly disadvantageous. Price and wage policies inadequately motivate the labor force. Traditionally, the private sector has been grudgingly tolerated, rather than encouraged by lifting restrictions on the size of plots and herds and increasing supplies of fodder and industrial inputs. Decision making is overcentralized and as a result often rigid and unrealistic.

Thus rapid growth of Soviet agricultural output appears unlikely. The land area under cultivation will not increase and may even fall as withdrawals because of neglect and heavy use exceed additions from reclamation and restoration. The agricultural labor force is declining, while the rate of capital formation in agriculture and related industries is decreasing. At the same time, in view of the high income elasticity of demand for meat, dairy products, and fruits and vegetables, shortages of these products will increase as household incomes rise. Hence, the USSR will continue to import substantial quantities of grain, especially animal fodders.[17]

Energy resources. In the coming decade the USSR may face a serious energy crunch. Even with continued steady growth of the output of oil — the most important element in the Soviet fuel balance — the USSR would find it hard to meet domestic fuel demand and maintain net exports of oil at the present level.[18] But Soviet oil production faces a number of difficult problems in the next decade. First, the Soviet oil industry uses production techniques, such as rapid water injection methods, that boost output in the short run but ultimately recover less of the oil in a field. Second, drilling has emphasized exploitation of known fields rather than exploration for new sources. As a result, proven oil reserves have been falling in recent years and the reserves-to-production ratio will probably deteriorate further in the next five to ten years.

Since 1970, nearly all output growth has come from West Siberian fields, as production fell in the Ukraine, North Caucasus, and Azerbaidzhan and leveled off in the Urals-Volga area. It is questionable whether in the next decade Siberian production can increase enough to offset the decline in output west of the Urals. Geological conditions are favorable to future discoveries in East Siberia, offshore regions in the Arctic and Caspian, and off Kamchatka and Sakhalin in the Sea of Okhotsk. However, exploration and development of these areas will require many years, very large outlays, and foreign equipment. In East Siberia, production and transportation are hampered by vast distances, forbidding terrain, and severe climate.[19] The technology to cope with pack ice in the offshore Arctic has not yet been developed even in the West. Weather and ice conditions in the Sakhalin area are harsher than in the North Sea, where development of commercial-scale production took ten years. Climatic conditions are more favorable in the Caspian region, but difficult deep drilling is required.

Third, exploration for and exploitation of new oil reserves have been hampered by shortages, outdated design, and inferior quality of equipment available to the Soviet oil industry. For example, most Soviet seismic recording uses a technology employed in the United States twenty years ago. There is a shortage of drilling rigs, the service life of components is short, and the quality of bits is inferior to those produced in the West. Soviet pumps are inferior to U.S. units in efficiency, capacity, and service life.

Domestic production of large-diameter pipe meets about two-thirds of Soviet requirements, with the remainder imported. Finally, the most serious deficiency for the future is lack of modern offshore technology using mobile (including submersible) drilling platforms. Some indication of Soviet needs for foreign equipment and technology is given by Soviet orders for Western oil and gas equipment and technology (excluding large-diameter line pipe) in 1972–1976 totalling about $3.1 billion.[20]

Western specialists' assessments of the negative impact of these problems on Soviet oil production and exports differ, depending upon their assumptions about various key factors, including the following: Will the Soviet authorities expand oil production through a crash program of exploration and development? What will be the effectiveness of Soviet efforts to restrain domestic oil consumption through conservation programs and the substitution of coal and gas for oil? To what extent will OPEC-led price increases on the world market offset possible decreases in the quantity of Soviet oil exports, thereby sustaining Soviet hard-currency earnings from them?

A widespread—but not universal—view among specialists is that Soviet oil production may peak in the early 1980s in the neighborhood of 600 million metric tons per year (about 10 percent above the 1977 output) and then level off or perhaps even decline. It would then be very difficult for the USSR to continue to meet its own requirements and those of Eastern Europe and to send non-Communist countries the quantity of oil exports that has recently been the USSR's largest single source (about 40 percent) of hard currency. Unless domestic consumption and oil exports to Eastern Europe could be curtailed sufficiently, hard-currency exports of oil would fall. At the same time, sustaining and raising Soviet oil production over the longer run will require large imports of Western equipment and know-how.[21]

Expansion of natural gas production will also introduce problems. Most new gasfield development and pipeline construction will be in the permafrost areas of West Siberia. In addition, there are serious shortages of large-diameter pipe and ancillary equipment such as compressors, valves, and turbines. Yet gas production may still grow at an average annual rate of about 6 percent to 1990, with rising exports to the West adding substantially to Soviet hard-currency earnings.[22]

In the Soviet energy balance, coal is important primarily for use in boilers to produce electricity, steam, and hot water—which together account for two-fifths of total Soviet energy consumption. In these uses the technical and economic advantages of oil and natural gas over solid fuel are smallest. Plans to substitute coal for oil and gas in existing power stations have been announced, but it is questionable how far they can be implemented because the massive amounts of new specialized equipment required to convert the stations are not available. In turn, the expansion of coal production for use in new facilities faces formidable obstacles. Coal production west of the Urals is constrained by the exhaustion of old seams, unfavorable and even dangerous geological conditions, labor force problems, and lack of mechanization of many operations. Thus more than three-fourths of additional coal output must come from strip mines in Siberia. Although surface operations are cheaper than underground mining, the Siberian deposits are far from consumers in the western USSR and the poor physical properties (such as high ash content) of some of the coal preclude its shipment over long distances.[23]

In summary, the USSR faces serious energy problems in the next five to ten years. Over the longer term, these problems can be overcome only by massive investment and foreign help.

Labor

The growth of the Soviet labor force will slow down markedly in the 1980s because of a decline in the growth of the working-age population that cannot be offset by an increase in the already high "participation rate"—the share of employed in the eligible population.[24] There are two reasons for the decline in the growth of the working-age population. First, beginning in 1978 the number of new entrants will fall because of low birth rates in the 1960s. Second, the number of people retiring each year will increase, reflecting the rising birth rates of the postrevolutionary but precollectivization period of the 1920s. (For a fuller discussion, see Chapter 9.)

Thus, as Table 10.8 shows, in 1981-1990 the average annual rates of growth of the adult population (16 and over) will be only half those of 1971-1975. But the drop will be even sharper for the working-age group (16-59 for men and 16-54 for women). Its average annual rate of growth will fall in the 1980s to only 0.3-0.4 percent—less than one-fourth the rate in the 1970s. In contrast, the pension-age group (60 and over for men and 55 and over for women) will grow much faster in the 1980s than in the 1970s.

However, within the USSR there will be important regional differences in the growth of the working-age population in the 1980s. It will be concentrated in Central Asia, Kazakhstan, and the Caucasus, where birth rates remained relatively high in the 1960s. In the Ukraine and the Baltic region the working-age population will remain essentially the same, while in the RSFSR it will actually decline absolutely in the 1980s. Furthermore, these regional differences in population growth due to differences in fertility are likely to be reinforced by internal migration. On balance over the last decade there has been a net inflow of people from other regions of the USSR into Central Asia, Kazakhstan, and the Caucasus. One reason was the availability of urban industrial jobs not filled by the local population.

TABLE 10.8

USSR: Average Annual Rates of Growth of Population and Labor Force, Actual 1966-70 and 1971-75, and Estimated 1976-80, 1981-85, and 1986-90

(Percent)

	1966-70	1971-75	1976-80	1981-85	1986-90
Population (Ages)					
16 and over	1.6	1.7	1.5	0.8	0.7
16-59(men) or 16-54(women)	1.2	1.9	1.5	0.4	0.3
60(men) or 55(women) and over	3.3	1.3	1.2	2.3	2.1
Labor Force					
Total civilian	1.5	1.6	1.5[a]	0.9[a]	0.5[a]
Agricultural	-1.3	-1.4	-1.6	-1.7	-1.8
Nonagricultural	3.0	2.8	2.5	1.6	1.1

Source: U.S. Central Intelligence Agency, USSR: Some Implications of Demographic Trends for Economic Policies (Washington, D.C., 1977), p. 13, based on Stephen Rapawy, Estimates and Projections of the Labor Force and Civilian Employment in the USSR, 1950 to 1990 (Washington, D.C.: U.S. Department of Commerce, Bureau of Economic Analysis, Foreign Demographic Analysis Division, 1976).

[a] Assumes (1) continuation of 1970 rate of participation of population in labor force and (2) no change in the size of the armed forces after 1975 (Rapawy, pp. 18-25).

Another was the attractiveness of the southern climate to workers from other areas, especially the far east and north.

In turn, if (as in the estimates in Table 10.8) it is assumed that there will be no change in the participation rate and no reduction in the armed forces, the average annual rates of growth of the total civilian labor force will drop from 1.5 percent in 1976–1980 to 0.9 percent in 1981–1985 and 0.5 percent in 1986–1990. Within this total, the growth of the nonagricultural labor force will be slowed sharply, from 2.5 percent in 1976–1980 to 1.6 percent in 1981–1985 and 1.1 percent in 1986–1990. This will occur despite a slightly faster contraction in the agricultural labor force, estimated at an average annual rate of 1.8 percent in 1986–1990 compared to 1.6 percent in 1976–1980.

The possibilities for government action to offset the unfavorable trends in labor supply appear limited. Raising participation rates could be successful only to a limited extent. Regional differences in culture, language, and education make migration policies difficult to achieve and it is unlikely that output per man-hour can be raised enough to offset the drop in labor input. (Eason provides a fuller discussion of the options open to policy-makers in Chapter 9.)

Capital

A major source of Soviet economic growth has been expansion of the capital stock. In the last fifteen years capital inputs have increased much faster than labor inputs (Table 10.5). This investment effort has absorbed more than one-fourth of GNP (Table 10.2). It is unlikely that this already high investment share can be boosted significantly because of the implications for consumption and military programs. Hence, Soviet policymakers' attention must focus on ways of increasing the efficiency of investment and reducing the marginal capital-output ratio (the amount of additional capital needed to secure a given increase in output).

The low productivity of Soviet investment is caused partly by some basic features of the Soviet economy.[25] For example, the evaluation of investment projects is hampered by the failure of the price system to reflect the relative scarcities of different types of labor, machinery, and materials and by the use of unduly low normative rates of return in comparing more and less capital-intensive techniques. Also, new machinery and equipment are often unsuitable because the specifications have been worked out by research institutes and design bureaus administratively and physically remote from the actual producers. Once produced, the machinery is inefficiently allocated among users by the cumbersome material-technical supply apparatus.

Other causes of low capital productivity are more specific to the investment process.[26] In total Soviet investment the share of construction is high and that of machinery is low in comparison with the industrialized market economies. For example, construction has accounted for about 60 percent and machinery and equipment about 40 percent of total Soviet investment in industry. In the United States, the respective shares are about 25 and 75 percent. However, technological progress is embodied in machinery and equipment rather than structures. One reason for the high share of construction in Soviet investment outlays is that the Soviet construction industry is much less efficient than the machine-building branches. Both large cost overruns and long delays in the completion of projects are common. Plan fulfillment reports and press accounts often complain about the backlog of "unfinished construction"—in the form of projects started but not yet completed to the point where production can begin.

Another reason for the importance of construction in total investment is the emphasis of Soviet planners on expanding the scale of output by building new installations rather than by modernizing and re-equipping existing plants with new machinery incorporating the latest technology. Thus replacement investment has accounted for only about one-fourth of total investment in the USSR, compared with about half in the United States. Soviet investment planners are reluctant to retire capital stock because of physical deterioration or obsolescence. Instead, they strive to extend service life by "capital repairs" involving major renovation, but these outlays merely purport to restore the assets to original working potential rather than increasing productive capacity or cutting costs through the introduction of new technology. Such capital repairs were the fastest growing element in investment in 1971–1975 (Table 10.4) and accounted for almost one-fifth of total investment in 1976 (Table 10.2).

The Tenth Five-Year Plan for 1976–1980 seeks to alter past practice by emphasizing modernization investment at existing sites. In the European part of the country the bulk of investment is to involve re-equipment and modernization of present facilities. Investment in new installations is to be concentrated in Siberia, where large new productive and also infrastructure facilities are required to develop fuel and raw material resources. In addition, the perennial campaign to cut construction delays has been reaffirmed. However, the various investment problems are so deep-rooted and persistent that it is questionable to what extent Soviet planners can overcome them in the next decade and improve capital productivity, arresting the unfavorable trends shown in Tables 10.5 and 10.6.

Technological Progress

Economic growth depends not only on increasing the quantities of inputs of land, labor, and capital but also on raising output per unit of input by better coordination of factor use and by improving the quality of materials, equipment, and production processes through technological progress. Better coordination of the use of available factors involves the system of economic planning and management. The USSR's highly centralized system has been more successful in mobilizing resources — raising the rates of investment and labor force participation and transferring workers from agriculture to industry — than in increasing the productivity of these resources. Proposals for economic reform in the 1960s sought to improve economic performance by devolving to lower levels in the administrative hierarchy some decisions over the composition of output and production methods. However, a careful evaluation of the changes actually made in such important dimensions as administrative organization, output plans, distribution of material inputs, labor and wages, investment, prices, performance indicators, and incentives shows that the economic system was altered very little in the USSR and Eastern Europe (with the exception of Hungary to some extent). The reasons included continued powerful opposition to reform, internal inconsistencies in reform programs, excessive tautness of ambitious plans, and developments in the world economy.[27]

There are serious obstacles to technological progress in the present organizational, price, and incentive structures of the Soviet economy.[28] The organizational structure is unfavorable to innovation in several ways. First, Soviet firms' lack of autonomy over their products and processes discourages innovation. Second, firms' supplies and sales usually are not negotiated directly with other producers but instead are determined by central allocation agencies not anxious to change existing arrangements. Third, as already noted, research and development organizations are dissociated from producing enterprises. As a result, design work for new equipment is often done by institutes unacquainted with the production and technological conditions in the plants in which the equipment will be used. The price structure discourages innovation because prices on new products are often set with great delay and frequently do not provide producers with a profit adequate to justify the risks inherent in making new and different rather than old and familiar products. Finally, incentive systems reward regular increases in sales and profits, without sufficient recognition that innovation competes with production because a changeover to a new production process can result in a slowdown in the growth of output. Special bonuses for innovation are too small to induce managers to take the risks involved.

For these reasons, domestically generated technological progress has been slow in the USSR, leading to great interest in the importation of technology from industrially advanced capitalist countries. The principal fields in which foreign technology is sought include energy extraction and processing equipment, facilities for building transportation equipment, chemical plants, computers and related systems, and agricultural production and processing. Foreign technology has been obtained through a variety of mechanisms, including ordinary imports of goods, licensing, purchase of complete plants (turnkey arrangements), coproduction, and subcontracting, but excluding joint ventures.[29]

The contribution of imported technology to Soviet economic growth is difficult to assess, because of conceptual, methodological, and data problems. The importance of the direct stimulative effect on Soviet output from the foreign technology embodied in imported machinery and equipment is limited by the small share of these imports in total Soviet investment in machinery and equipment. However, in addition one would ideally like to consider indirect effects, such as (1) productivity increases in the equipment produced by imported machinery, (2) the incorporation of the new technology in machinery subsequently designed in the USSR, and (3) the "ripple" or "feedback" influence on Soviet suppliers of materials and components that must be improved for use with the imported machinery. Because these direct and indirect effects are difficult to measure, there are few estimates and no consensus of Western specialists about the magnitude of the contribution of foreign technology to Soviet economic growth in an aggregate sense.[30] Nonetheless, foreign technology and equipment are clearly important in particular branches of Soviet industry, such as petroleum and gas, chemicals, and various categories of machine building.

Thus the USSR is energetically seeking foreign technology in many fields from many countries — subject to availability of financing. Despite efforts to expand Soviet exports to the West,[31] the USSR had hard-currency merchandise trade deficits of $6.3 billion in 1975 and $5.1 billion in 1976 as a result of heavy imports of machinery and equipment, steel products, and grain. These deficits were financed partly by sales of gold and arms but chiefly by Western supplier credits and general-purpose loans on the Euromarket. Thus the USSR's gross hard-currency indebtedness to the West grew from over $11 billion at the end of 1975 to about $14 billion at the end of 1976. (The corresponding figures for net indebtedness — allowing for Soviet deposits in Western banks — were about $3 billion less.) As a result, a rising share of annual Soviet merchandise exports is now going to repay principal and interest on earlier borrowing. This share increased from 15 percent at the end of 1973 to 26 percent at the end of 1976.[32]

These financing problems explain Soviet interest in obtaining foreign technology — embodied in machinery and equipment and also in the form of licenses and processes — through "industrial cooperation agreements" involving repayment in kind in the output of an installation after it begins operation.

Future Prospects

Published projections of possible rates of Soviet economic growth to 1980, 1985, or 1990 vary according to the methods employed and the assumptions made about base-year conditions and choices among policy options thereafter. Most authors insist on presenting a complex set of estimates to show the range of possibilities, but these projections[33] reach two common conclusions:

1. Under what these authors deem the most plausible of various alternative assumptions considered, Soviet economic growth rates will decline in the next decade because of the trends in growth of factor inputs and factor productivity (including technological progress) analyzed in the preceding sections. For instance, recent CIA projections for the average annual percentage rates of growth of Soviet GNP run from a "best case" of 3.75-4.25 in 1977-1980 and 3.25-3.75 in 1981-1985 to a "worst case" of 3.5-4 in 1977-1980 and 2-2.5 in 1981-1985.[34] A variety of calculations to 1990 by Hunter, Earle, and Foster—using the Stanford Research Institute–Wharton Econometric Forecasting Associates econometric model of the Soviet economy—show even greater ranges but also conclude that Soviet growth will slow down unless implausibly favorable domestic and external conditions prevail.

2. In principle it might appear that the slowdown in growth could be moderated by transferring resources from defense and/or consumption to growth-promoting investment. But the room for maneuver in these respects is quite limited. Military programs occupy an estimated 4 million people in the armed forces and absorb large shares of the production of major investment goods industries, such as machine building (about a third), metallurgy (about a fifth), chemicals (about a sixth), and energy (also about a sixth), according to recent U.S. government estimates.[35] Moreover, military outlays will be rising as the USSR completes the development, production, and deployment of new weapons systems, which typically are more complex and thus more expensive both to produce and to maintain than earlier systems. It would require a major reappraisal of Soviet military requirements to arrest these trends and release military manpower and industrial capacity on a scale sufficient to boost investment significantly.

In turn, any slowdown in the already modest recent improvement in per capita consumption could retard the growth of labor productivity by dampening incentives and might even cause public unrest. In particular, the low level and variability of the grain crop and the resulting persistent serious meat shortages make it inadvisable to reduce agricultural programs in favor of industrial investment. Also, because the share of consumer durables in total machinery output is small, a large cut in production of automobiles, refrigerators, and electrical appliances would be necessary to secure a significant increase in production of machinery for investment. Thus it will be very difficult for the Soviet leadership to reduce the growth rates of defense and consumption, cutting their shares in a total GNP that will be rising more slowly in the 1980s than in the 1970s.

Foreign Policy Implications

Eastern Europe

The retardation in Soviet economic growth—and particularly the energy problems contributing to it—will exacerbate existing tensions in the USSR's economic relations with Eastern Europe. Although it is impossible to determine the exact magnitudes involved,[36] during 1970–1976 the East European nations as a group benefited from a net resource transfer from the USSR due to intra-CMEA price relationships and Soviet credits.[37] During this period the USSR supplied fuels and raw materials to Eastern Europe in bilateral barter transactions at prices below those the USSR could have obtained in hard currency on the world market.[38] It also extended credits of $2.4 billion to Poland.[39] Before 1975 intra-CMEA prices for a prescribed interval, like a five-year period, were based on world market prices of an earlier period. For example, intra-CMEA prices in 1971–1975 were supposed to be related to world market prices of 1965–1969. By this arrangement East European purchases of oil from the USSR were insulated from the sharp rise in world energy prices in 1973–1974. Beginning in 1975 a new pricing scheme was adopted, with annual price adjustments based on a rolling average of earlier world prices.[40] As a result Soviet oil prices to Eastern Europe doubled in 1975 and rose 8.0 and 22.5 percent, respectively, in 1976 and 1977. Even so, in 1977 they were still about one-fourth below current world oil prices.[41]

In addition to charging Eastern Europe more for fuels and raw materials, the USSR has obtained that area's participation in large-scale projects to develop Soviet natural resources. These include the $5 billion (initial cost estimate) Orenburg natural gas pipeline from Soviet fields to Eastern Europe, and smaller cellulose, asbestos, copper and nickel, and electric power projects. Typically, East European participants provide equipment (sometimes purchased by them in the West for hard currency) and are to be repaid in output from the project over a ten- to twenty-year period.[42]

In forthcoming CMEA discussions over the coordination of plans and trade in 1981–1985, the USSR will press the East European countries to invest further in joint projects on Soviet territory, at the cost of investment within their own borders. There will also be hard negotiations over how to share with Eastern Europe the burden of slower growth or perhaps even a decline in Soviet oil production. How much will the USSR enforce Soviet domestic energy conservation or sacrifice badly needed hard-currency earnings in order to supply oil to Eastern Europe at prices below the world market level? If the USSR stabilizes or reduces oil deliveries to Eastern Europe, the latter would have to use more scarce hard currency to buy petroleum – instead of industrial materials, machinery, and equipment – on the world market. The result would be a decline in rates of growth of industrial production, national product, and per capita consumption in Eastern Europe, with unfavorable consequences for regime-society relations in the area.

On the one hand, the USSR may gain increased leverage over East European internal and foreign policies as a result of the latter's dependence on Soviet petroleum and gas. On the other, in the search for ways to ease such pressure on Eastern Europe – and thus itself – the USSR might, for example, decide to pursue more vigorously an accommodation between CMEA and the European Economic Community (EEC) that would lead to greater East European exports to Western Europe and an expansion of industrial cooperation agreements with Western firms to secure capital and advanced technology.[43]

The Industrialized West

The USSR needs machinery and equipment, steel products, and grain from the industrialized capitalist market economies – the United States and Canada, Western Europe, and Japan. As noted above, hard-currency exports of petroleum, the USSR's principal earner of convertible currency, are likely to decline. It is unlikely that the loss of hard-currency earnings from petroleum can be offset by increases in merchandise exports (such as timber, diamonds, and manufactured products) and in sales of gold and arms. Thus the USSR will seek additional credit from Western private and government banks.

It is estimated that at the end of 1976 the gross hard-currency debt of the USSR amounted to about $14 billion, with the East European countries together owing $28 billion and the CMEA banks about $4 billion – for a total CMEA gross indebtedness to the West of $46 billion.[44] (Net indebtedness, allowing for Eastern deposits in Western banks, was about $40 billion.) Service (payments of principal and interest) on this debt absorbed 25–30 percent of the hard-currency earnings of most of the CMEA countries in 1976 and it will rise as payments on more recent loans start. By 1980 service on past Soviet debt may exceed new drawing on credits, so that the latter will have little effect on import capacity.

Will this need for Western credit make the USSR more vulnerable to Western pressure for changes in Soviet internal and external policies? This appears doubtful for two reasons. First, Western banks now have a stake in keeping Eastern borrowers "afloat" and avoiding default by continuing to lend to them in order to protect loans previously made. Second, there are strong political and economic forces against Western coordination of lending policies toward the East. Competition among Western countries for markets for capital goods, for raw material supplies, and perhaps for associated political influence has impeded the development of common trade or credit policies toward the East or even the simple exchange of information about them.[45]

In turn, the inability of the United States to secure such joint action by its allies limits the possibilities to use "economic cards" in bilateral negotiations with the USSR over arms control and other issues. The USSR has been able to obtain from Western Europe and Japan most of the equipment and credit denied it by restrictions on U.S. Export-Import Bank financing linked to Soviet emigration policies. Nonetheless, the USSR is concerned about these restrictions, as well as the denial of Most Favored Nation tariff treatment, which hampers Soviet exports to the United States. The USSR may search for a new accommodation on these and other matters in order to obtain U.S. participation in large-scale projects to develop Siberian oil and gas. Although Western Europe and Japan can provide much of the equipment, technology, and credit, some U.S. participation in such large projects may be necessary to secure unique U.S. technology and to spread the risk.

In principle, arms control could help Soviet economic growth by potentially releasing resources from defense to investment or consumption uses. But modest arms limitation agreements — for example, on where forces may be stationed or on the quantity or deployment of missiles already in production — would not significantly reduce defense spending and ease the pressure on the Soviet economy. Furthermore, the Soviet authorities consider that one type of arms control — limitation on arms sales — could hurt Soviet economic growth. These sales are important not only for political purposes but also because they earn hard currency that makes an important contribution (an estimated $1.5 billion in 1976) to covering Soviet import needs from the industrialized capitalist market economies.

Less Developed Countries

Soviet trade and economic and military assistance programs are concentrated in selected target countries in the Middle East, South Asia, and Africa. These activities support various objectives of Soviet foreign policy in these areas, including the following:[46]

1. Strengthening Soviet influence, in competition with the West and China;

2. Supporting revolutionary "national liberation" (especially Marxist) regimes;

3. Promoting the "Soviet model" of economic development through expansion of heavy industry under public ownership and comprehensive planning; and

4. Securing naval and air bases for Soviet forces.

The less developed countries (LDCs) are a significant source of Soviet imports of food, raw materials, and fuels and an important market for Soviet exports of machinery and equipment and, in particular, arms. Soviet military agreements with the LDCs have been growing rapidly since 1969, reaching new commitments of $2.5 billion and actual deliveries of $2.2 billion in 1976.[47] The USSR has been successful in boosting arms sales because it furnishes sophisticated weapons to many LDCs, quotes lower prices than Western suppliers, and offers fast delivery from current stocks.[48] Before 1974, about two-thirds of Soviet military transactions with LDCs were financed by credits. Since then, cash sales for hard currency — chiefly to petroleum-rich Middle Eastern countries — have increased sharply, accounting for about 60 percent of total arms sales to LDCs in 1976. As a result, by 1977 40 percent of Soviet-LDC trade was paid for in hard currency — rather than through bilateral barter agreements or settlements in nonconvertible currencies — compared with 20 percent in 1970.[49]

Almost all of Soviet economic "aid" is in the form of repayable credits, rather than outright grants, which account for only 5 percent of the total. Most of the aid involves highly visible heavy industry projects, like steel mills. In addition, technical assistance is provided by sending Soviet technicians to LDCs and training their nationals in the USSR. New economic aid commitments from the USSR to LDCs averaged $890 million annually in 1971–1976. However, deliveries lag behind commitments by an average of seven years because of the long lead times for heavy industry projects and the difficulties in assembling complementary resources in the LDCs. Thus actual LDC drawings on Soviet credits averaged only $492 million annually in 1971–1976.[50] Furthermore, when allowing for repayments of principal and interest on earlier credits, the amount of *net* aid per year is still less — estimated at about $100 million in 1975, or less than 0.05 percent of Soviet GNP.[51] Hence, a slowdown in Soviet economic growth in the 1980s is not likely to curb significantly the USSR's ability to pursue those economic aid programs it considers politically advantageous.

On the other hand, the USSR will continue to give only "moral" support to LDCs' demands for a "New International Economic Order." The LDCs seek (1) agreements to stabilize commodity prices or index them to changes in prices of industrial products; (2) rescheduling or cancellation of some of their outstanding debts to more developed countries (MDCs); (3) reductions in MDC trade restrictions hampering LDC exports; and (4) more aid from MDCs.[52] The USSR rejects a division of the world along MDC-LDC or North-South lines, insisting instead that the proper groupings are industrialized capitalist nations, LDCs, and socialist states. The USSR holds that the LDCs should seek redress for their grievances only from the industrialized capitalist nations because the latter have exploited the LDCs and are responsible for recession and inflation in the world economy. In contrast, the LDCs have no legitimate claims on the socialist countries, which did not cause the problems of the LDCs.[53]

Conclusion

Soviet economic growth will slow down for various reasons beyond the control of the Soviet leadership. As a result, some changes in foreign policy may occur, while other Soviet positions remain largely unaltered. The USSR's influence over internal and external policies of the East European countries will be strengthened. However, common Soviet–East European interests may lead to an effort to increase trade and investment relations with the EEC. Although the USSR will seek credit from the West — especially to develop Siberian petroleum and gas — possible political leverage for the West will depend on how extensively coordination of trade, technology, and credit policies replaces the present competition among West European countries, Japan, and the United States. To pursue its objectives in the Third World, the USSR will continue to use trade — especially arms sales for hard currency — and economic aid, but it will seek a bystander role in North-South disputes.

Notes

1. In order to show resource use more accurately, calculations of national product at factor cost adjust data in established prices by deducting indirect taxes and by adding subsidies and allowances for factor charges not included in established prices. In the case of the USSR, such charges include interest on capital and rent on land. The tables in this chapter present Western estimates rather than Soviet official statistics. Although derived from Soviet official data, the Western estimates use statistical concepts and methods more appropriate for the analysis of the questions considered here.

2. U.S. Central Intelligence Agency, *Estimated Soviet Defense Spending in Rubles, 1970–1975* (Washington, D.C., 1976), p. 16.

3. Lars Calmfors and Jan Rylander, "Economic Restrictions on Soviet Defense Expenditure," in U.S. Congress, Joint Economic Committee, *Soviet Economy in a New Perspective* (Washington, D.C.: U.S. Government Printing Office, 1976), p. 379.

4. Hans Bergendorff and Per Strangert, "Projections of Soviet Economic Growth and Defense Spending," in JEC, *Soviet Economy in a New Perspective*, p. 411.

5. See for example, Herbert Block, "Soviet Economic Power Growth—Achievements Under Handicaps," in JEC, *Soviet Economy in a New Perspective*, pp. 255–261, and William T. Lee, *The Estimation of Soviet Defense Expenditures, 1955–75: An Unconventional Approach* (New York: Praeger Publishers, 1977).

6. Soviet official statistics show essentially the same time trend, although their corresponding numerical values differ for conceptual and methodological reasons. Thus, for example, the Soviet official percentage figures for the average annual growth rate of "national income produced" (i.e., net material product) are 6.5 for 1961–1965, 7.8 for 1966–1970, and 5.7 for 1971–1975. (USSR, Tsentral'noe statisticheskoe upravlenie, *Narodnoe khoziaistvo SSSR v 1975 g.,* Moscow, 1976, p. 49.)

7. Rush V. Greenslade, "The Real Gross National Product of the U.S.S.R., 1950–1975," in JEC, *Soviet Economy in a New Perspective*, pp. 272–276.

8. Martin L. Weitzman, "Soviet Postwar Economic Growth and Capital-Labor Substitution," *American Economic Review* 60, no. 4 (September 1970); and Padma Desai, "The Production Function and Technical Change in Postwar Soviet Industry: A Reexamination," in ibid. 66, no. 3 (June 1976).

9. Gertrude E. Schroeder and Barbara S. Severin, "Soviet Consumption and Income Policies in Perspective," in JEC, *Soviet Economy in a New Perspective.*

10. Gregory Grosssman, "An Economy at Middle Age," *Problems of Communism* 25, no. 2 (March–April 1976); and U.S. Central Intelligence Agency, *Soviet Economic Plans for 1976–80: A First Look* (Washington, D.C., 1976).

11. David W. Carey, "Soviet Agriculture: Recent Performance and Future Plans," in JEC, *Soviet Economy in a New Perspective*, p. 577.

12. U.S. Central Intelligence Agency, *USSR: The Impact of Recent Climate Change on Grain Production* (Washington, D.C., 1976).

13. Carey, "Soviet Agriculture: Recent Performance," pp. 585–586.

14. Ibid., pp. 590–592.

15. Estimated by Douglas B. Diamond; cited in James R. Millar, "The Prospects for Soviet Agriculture," *Problems of Communism* 26, no. 3 (May–June 1977):8.

16. Ibid., pp. 11–15.

17. Ibid., p. 15, and D. Gale Johnson, *The Soviet Impact on World Grain Trade* (Washington, D.C.: National Planning Association, 1977), pp. 32–34.

18. Leslie Dienes, "The Soviet Union: An Energy Crunch Ahead?" *Problems of Communism* 26, no. 5 (September–October 1977).

19. Alan B. Smith, "Soviet Dependence on Siberian Resource Development," in JEC, *Soviet Economy in a New Perspective.*

20. U.S. Central Intelligence Agency, *Prospects for Soviet Oil Production: A Supplemental Analysis* (Washington, D.C., 1977), pp. 24–27.

21. Space limitations do not permit a more detailed explanation of the various factors involved or a description of possible alternative scenarios. The issues, the available data, and alternative assumptions and projections are examined at length in U.S. Central Intelligence Agency, *Prospects for Soviet Oil Production* (Washington, D.C., 1977), and U.S. Central Intelligence Agency, *Prospects for Soviet Oil Production: A Supplemental Analysis*; Robert Campbell, "Implications for the Soviet Economy of Soviet Energy Prospects," *The ACES Bulletin* 20, no. 1 (Spring 1978); Leslie Dienes, *Soviet Energy Policy and the Hydrocarbons* (Washington, D.C.: Association of American Geographers, 1978,); and John P. Hardt, Ronda A. Bresnick, and David Levine, "Soviet Oil and Gas in the Global Perspective," in U.S. Congress, House of Representatives Committee on Interstate and Foreign Commerce, Senate Committee on Energy and Natural Resources, and Senate Committee on Commerce, Science and Transportation, *Project Interdependence: U.S. and World Energy Outlook Through 1990* (Washington D.C.: U.S. Government Printing Office, 1977).

22. Dienes, *Soviet Energy Policy and the Hydrocarbons,* p. 42; and U.S. Central Intelligence Agency, *USSR: Development of the Gas Industry* (Washington, D.C., 1978), pp. 25–29.

23. Dienes, "The Soviet Union: An Energy Crunch Ahead?" pp. 51–56.

24. Murray Feshbach and Stephen Rapawy, "Soviet Population and Manpower Trends and Policies," in JEC, *Soviet Economy in a New Perspective;* and U.S. Central Intelligence Agency, *USSR: Some Implications of Demographic Trends for Economic Policies* (Washington, D.C., 1977).

25. Alec Nove, "Investissement et progrès technique," *Revue d'Études Comparatives Est-Ouest* 7, no. 4 (December 1976).

26. Stanley H. Cohn, "Deficiencies in Soviet Investment Policies and the Technological Imperative," in JEC, *Soviet Economy in a New Perspective.*

27. Karl W. Ryavec, *Implementation of Soviet Economic Reforms* (New York: Praeger Publishers, 1975); and Morris Bornstein, "Economic Reform in Eastern Europe," in U.S. Congress, Joint Economic Committee, *East European Economies Post-Helsinki* (Washington, D.C.: U.S. Government Printing Office, 1977).

28. Joseph S. Berliner, *The Innovation Decision in Soviet Industry* (Cambridge, Mass.: M.I.T. Press, 1976).

29. Maureen R. Smith, "Industrial Cooperation Agreements: Soviet Experience and Practice," in JEC, *Soviet Economy in a New Perspective.*

30. Philip Hanson, "International Technology Transfer from the West to the U.S.S.R.," in JEC, *Soviet Economy in a New Perspective,* pp. 796–800.

31. Paul Ericson, "Soviet Trade and Payments with the West," in JEC, *Soviet Economy in a New Perspective*; and U.S. Central Intelligence Agency, *Soviet Commercial Operations in the West* (Washington, D.C., 1977).

32. U.S. Central Intelligence Agency, *USSR: Hard Currency Trade and Payments, 1977–78* (Washington, D.C., 1977), p. 17.

33. For example, U.S. Central Intelligence Agency, *Soviet Economic Problems and Prospects* (Washington, D.C., 1977); Calmfors and Rylander, "Economic Restrictions on Soviet Defense Expenditures"; and Bergendorff and Strangert, "Projections of Soviet Economic Growth."

34. U.S. Central Intelligence Agency, *Soviet Economic Problems and Prospects.*

35. Ibid., p. 2.

36. The reasons include uncertainty about (a) the coverage of trade figures, particularly in regard to arms; (b) actual deliveries, as distinct from commitments, for joint investment projects; (c) individual countries' transactions with the CMEA Investment Bank; (d) how net balances for arms and invisibles (such as tourism) are settled; and (e) switch trade, under which balances with a CMEA partner are offset by balances with third countries outside the CMEA area (Paul Marer, "Economic Performance, Strategy, and Prospects in Eastern Europe," in JEC, *East European Economies Post-Helsinki*, p. 544).

37. Ibid., p. 546.

38. Paul Marer, "Has Eastern Europe Become a Liability to the Soviet Union? The Economic Aspect," in Charles Gati, ed., *The International Politics of Eastern Europe* (New York: Praeger Publishers, 1976), pp. 60–72.

39. U.S. Central Intelligence Agency, *Handbook of Economic Statistics 1977* (Washington, D.C., 1977), p. 71.

40. For intra-CMEA prices in 1975, average world prices for the three-year period 1972–1974 were used. Beginning in 1976, a five-year period was adopted, with 1976 CMEA prices based on 1971–1975 world prices, 1977 CMEA prices on 1972–1976 world prices, and so on.

41. John R. Haberstroh, "Eastern Europe: Growing Energy Problems," in JEC, *East European Economies Post-Helsinki*, pp. 383–384.

42. Arthur J. Smith, "The Council of Mutual Economic Assistance in 1977: New Economic Power, New Political Perspectives and Some Old and New Problems," in JEC, *East European Economies Post-Helsinki,* pp. 155–157.

43. Edward A. Hewett, "Recent Developments in East-West European Economic Relations and Their Implications for U.S.-East European Economic Relations," in JEC, *East European Economies Post-Helsinki.*

44. Richard Portes, "East Europe's Debt to the West: Interdependence Is a Two-Way Street," *Foreign Affairs* 55, no. 4 (July 1977):757.

45. Ibid., pp. 777–779.

46. U.S. Congress, House of Representatives, Committee on International Relations, *The Soviet Union and the Third World* (Washington, D.C.: U.S. Government Printing Office, 1977).

47. The respective amounts for East European countries were $75 million and $200 million, as deliveries on earlier commitments exceeded new agreements.

48. U.S. Central Intelligence Agency, *Communist Aid to the Less Developed Countries of the Free World, 1976* (Washington, D.C., 1977), pp. 1–3.

49. U.S. Central Intelligence Agency, *Changing Patterns in Soviet-LDC Trade* (Washington, D.C., 1978).

50. In addition, in 1971–1976, credits and drawings from East European countries averaged $584 million and $194 million, respectively, per year. U.S. Central Intelligence Agency, *Communist Aid to Less Developed Countries of the Free World, 1976*, p. 7.

51. Orah Cooper, "Soviet Economic Aid to the Third World," in JEC, *Soviet Economy in a New Perspective,* p. 193.

52. C. H. Kirkpatrick and F. I. Nixson, "UNCTAD IV and the New International Economic Order," *The Three Banks Review,* no. 112 (December 1976).

53. *Pravda,* 5 October 1976, p. 4; trans. as "In the Interests of Cooperation," *Current Digest of the Soviet Press* 28, no. 40 (3 November 1976).

11
Soviet Agriculture: Domestic and Foreign Policy Aspects

Arcadius Kahan

The general thrust of post-Stalinist agricultural policies in the Soviet Union can be described by two developmental strategies: land-expansionist and land-intensive. Each strategy was based upon a distinct technology, the first emphasizing the mechanization of basic farm operations (plowing, harvesting, etc.) and the second stressing the use of chemical fertilizers, irrigation, and drainage of the agricultural land.

Both policies were designed to increase agricultural production, primarily of grains and feed, and also to lessen the impact of the yearly fluctuations in crop output, which had a spillover effect upon the level of livestock production. However, each relied upon a different strategy and technology to achieve these objectives. The first strategy, followed by Khrushchev, involved a radical expansion of the planted areas under grains into the dry areas of the eastern grain belt (primarily for spring wheat). The rationale was not only to expand grain production but to have the eastern regions compensate for shortfalls of grain yields in the European regions, thereby effectively diminishing the annual deviations from the average of grain production, on the assumption that droughts do not occur simultaneously in both areas. An additional benefit of this strategy was the expected expansion of corn output for feed in areas previously occupied by food grains.

This policy required a substantial increase in capital inputs, particularly in means to mechanize grain production. The rate of increase of capital in the agricultural machinery industry and other complementary current inputs from the industrial sector into agricultural production was rapid indeed. The required increase in labor inputs related to the expansion of the planted area and to the higher labor requirements of corn production was short-lived, until the growth of mechanization of grain production began to reduce the labor inputs. The shifts of labor eastward into scarcely populated regions was in part achieved by the use of the institutions of state farms, a solution that increased the mobility of labor and saved on initial expenditures for the capital overhead in the "new lands" regions.

Relying upon mechanization in grain production and the scope and speed of land expansion, with a belief in achievable economies of scale, made this strategy appear biased with respect to the size of farms. The result was a growth of the average farm size, not only because of the establishment of large farms in the "new lands" areas, but also because of the amalgamation of the existing farm units. Such a strategy and the technology that it embodied had not only a scale effect but also an income effect upon the Soviet agricultural labor force. Actually, one can speak about a number of related income effects.

A part of the increase of agricultural production was used to raise the labor incomes of the grain producers, thus reducing the income differential between the grain producing regions and the regions supplying the industrial crops (cotton, etc.), a differential that marked the later years of the Stalin era. Increased incomes for the labor force operating agricultural machinery were a stimulus for the acquisition of skills in the state farms, and also in the Machine Tractor Stations (MTS) that were subsequently turned over to the collective farms. Discriminatory taxation of the auxiliary household plots of collective farmers and state farm workers was curtailed; more importantly, the monetization of the collective farmers' incomes was increased, thereby broadening their consumption choices.

The land-expansionist policy was accompanied by certain institutional reforms that facilitated change. One of the institutional consequences was the rise in farm prices, so that the increments in agricultural incomes could be transferred by the farms to the population in income and wage payments. Another institutional consequence was the abolition of the MTS, in order to integrate the use of the farm machinery in the operations of the collective farms and subordinate the farm operations to unified management. The political consequence of the latter institutional change was to strengthen party controls from within the farms instead of the previous system of control from without.

Until 1964 the above strategy was hardly reexamined by Soviet policymakers, nor were any alternative strategies considered. Most of the criticism was voiced abroad and summarily dismissed by the Soviet policymakers. The criticism of the strategy from abroad pointed to the availability of other variants of planted area expansion, namely to the heavy use of summer fallow which was widely practiced in the Canadian Prairie Provinces, areas analogous to the Soviet "new lands." The use of summer fallow permitted not only the achievement of yields substantially higher than in the analogous areas of the USSR, but also maintenance of the level of yields without major year-to-year fluctuations because of unfavorable weather

◆

conditions. The maintenance of a regime of summer fallow enabled Canada to save on costs of labor and to produce large quantities of grain at reasonable costs.

The Soviet policymakers, however, exhibited a very short time-horizon and decided in favor of cropping the land continuously with a monoculture, depriving it of the opportunity to collect moisture, exposing it to weed infestation, and taking chances with the frequent droughts, expending seed and labor in the process. The results were predictable: increased fluctuations of yields and very high costs of production in view of the increased inputs. In the early 1960s, when the growth rate of agricultural production began to decline and the fluctuations in grain output became more pronounced and affected the size of the livestock herd as well as the level of livestock production, Soviet policymakers became disenchanted with the existing strategy. The downfall of Khrushchev signalled a new set of policies. The scope of the corn program was reduced, the expansion of the cropland area halted, and a technology that combined grain and feed production with the aid of massive fertilizer utilization and irrigation was introduced to remedy the ills of Soviet agriculture.

Thus the objective of raising the level of output of food and feed grains had to be achieved by massive investment in land reclamation and irrigation and supported by a high level of industrial production by the chemical fertilizer industry. The investment package producing the technology is much more varied and complex than the one that was devised by the earlier strategy. It involves not only the chemical industry and the machine-building industry, but also the construction of large-scale storage facilities and the use of heavy equipment for the building of irrigation systems, pipes for drainage, etc. Obviously the days are gone when half a million or more Uzbeks could be forced to dig the giant ditch that was called the Fergana Canal. Labor is too scarce and too expensive to engage in such undertakings. Using modern machines requires not only diversion of resources from other tasks, but the taxing of the system of industrial organization at its most vulnerable points: cooperation, coordination, and synchronization of efforts among different branches and components.

The present technology is expected to raise the level of agricultural production and has demonstrated both abroad and within the Soviet Union that it can raise the level of yields, particularly under favorable weather conditions. This technology exhibits a tendency to increase the labor inputs per unit of land, unless checked by labor-saving devices such as the increased use of mechanization in both crop and livestock production. Thus the reduction of the agricultural labor force has slowed down despite its economically unfavorable skill composition. Labor shortages in a number of areas during the harvest season become apparent. The present technology appears also to be neutral with respect to the scale of farms. Neither the application of fertilizer nor the feeding of livestock provides a greater advantage outside a particular range, in spite of the various cost data provided by the authors in Soviet journals (the data are never complete enough to permit an independent check). As far as irrigation projects are concerned, the volume of water supplied to a given area determines the scale of farming operations. The neutrality of land drainage with respect to farm size is an established rule.

The incessant drive of Soviet planners for larger size operations recently shifted from the area of crop production to the area of livestock production, presumably because of the desire to economize on capital expenditures (such as construction materials, equipment, etc.). The constant refusal by planners to consider the costs of intrafarm transportation, dangers of diseases, etc., keeps the drive toward concentration of production facilities very much alive.

It it still difficult to evaluate the impact of the new strategy and the advantages of the new technology. Costs are soaring, but production is increasing and, as in the earlier phase of the previous strategy, the additional output generated provides an opportunity to increase the supply of agricultural products to the total population as well as to raise the incomes of agricultural producers. In this climate it is possible for the Soviet government to act more cautiously at the institutional level.

Will the present set of policies or the presently applied technology bring the desired results for the Soviet Union? Will the Soviet Union be capable, if it chooses, of becoming agriculturally self-sufficient and able to support its population at a reasonable consumption level? I have grave doubts whether these goals will be achieved during the next decade. According to an elementary calculation, based upon the Soviet population figures and the official Soviet index of agricultural production (no doubt an inflated one), the average yearly per capita growth rate of agricultural output for the last 25 years was about 1.7 percent.[1] This represented an upper limit for the growth of per capita consumption in the past and will probably, at best, remain the upper limit for the future.

As long as capital investment continues to encompass a relatively large portion of overhead capital expenditures, the short-run rate of return will be low. Spectacular increases in agricultural production are therefore hard to envisage. The past destruction and neglect are taking their toll; this is the price paid by those who built trucks before roads, who discarded the wheelbarrow while still learning to operate cranes, and who, while designing tractors of hundreds of horsepower, were oblivious to the minimum comfort of the driver's seat, assuming a limitless endurance of the "heroes of socialist labor."

The Soviet Union will be able, by maintaining a high rate of investment and pursuing the present strategy, to achieve increases of crop yields that the United States and other countries have achieved at lower cost. Soviet agricultural output carries a high price tag, even during the present period of relatively high world prices in agriculture. The suppressed and hidden cost inflation in the industrial and agricultural sectors appears to reinforce itself.

There is an additional caveat—the bureaucratic structure of decision making. It is not the mere existence of a bureaucracy that is at issue; it is the problem of the locus of effective decision making and its remoteness from the farm level that becomes critical. The peculiar bureaucratic habit of inserting oneself between two parties who can otherwise resolve their problems through contractual relationships (presumably to their mutual advantage), of imposing oneself as the judge and decision maker, issuing commands and instituting controls in nonadversary situations, flourishes in the Soviet system. The mastery of the Soviet regime in devising intermediaries (monopolistic institutions in the dealings between industry and agriculture, between agriculture and trade, etc.,) is unsurpassed; the impact upon efficiency of operations and coordination is quite predictable.

The wisdom of the policies of the top decision makers is not impressive. Their time-horizon in agriculture, contrary to the prevailing doctrine, is very short and the mood varies with the quality of the harvest, a situation reminiscent of subsistence farming in tsarist Russia. Such vacillation between a state of despair and a state of euphoria was not unique to Khrushchev's era, but is typical of the Brezhnev and Kosygin era as well. It results in interruptions of plans, changes in targets, shifts in resource use, and confused or wrong signals to the farms.

To what extent can the term "crisis" be used with regard to Soviet agriculture? Qualitatively, the "crisis" of the 1970s is different from that of the 1950s. During the 1950s Khrushchev publicly reported both the exhaustion of on-the-farm and commercial grain reserves and the concomitant pressure to use the state's strategic reserves for current food consumption. During the 1970s no one doubted or questioned the availability of a food-grain supply for human consumption even under the most adverse weather conditions. The "crisis" of the 1970s is one of feed grains to meet the population's demand for livestock production. Our temptation to view Soviet agriculture as being in a state of crisis is the result of our bewilderment at observing a system that works sluggishly, sloppily, with enormous waste, bureaucratic inertia, and resistance to change. How can we be impressed by statistical data that do not even abide by the law of "equal cheating" and by figures that often simply do not make sense? How can we comprehend the prevailing arrangements when combines are idle during the harvest because trucks are transporting grain from the fields to a distant state elevator or when precious fertilizer is being washed by the rains and bleached by the sun due to the scarcity of appropriate storage? Our inability to comprehend such inefficiency prevents many of us from acknowledging and viewing the progress of Soviet agriculture as a process made more difficult and less pliable in its function or performance by existing rigidities. But this is more our problem as observers than the Soviets'. We cannot, or perhaps should not, judge Soviet progress by our criteria of economic efficiency; we should respect the reality of differing priorities. The difficulties in producing butter are in part a function of the success in producing guns over a long period of time.

Soviet agriculture is beset by a number of serious problems that tend, at this stage of Soviet economic performance, to limit rather than stimulate Soviet economic growth. The problems listed above can be classified in a few categories:

1. Decreases in the growth rate of production;
2. Lowering of returns to investment;
3. Inability to raise labor productivity combined with a low response to incentives;
4. An unyielding institutional setup within agriculture (relative immobility of interfarm resources, excessive centralization of decision making) and between agriculture and other sectors of the economy.

The Soviet Union is paying a heavy price for the growth of its agricultural output in view of the existing problems and imperfections. In the process, Soviet agriculture has become a drain on available resources and will remain one for many years to come—a drain, but not one of crisis proportions.

If one extends the effects of Soviet agricultural policies to the political universe, one would probably encounter some constraints upon political flexibility at home and abroad. There is no doubt that such constraints exist and are exacerbated by the slowness of agricultural development. But we would assume that the direct repercussions create choices primarily between consumer goods and services and not between consumption and armaments. The latter choice would constitute a crisis for the Soviet regime, while the former is just Soviet reality.

Agricultural policies in the Soviet Union, even under ordinary circumstances, address themselves to technological or economic issues, but often intrude into the area of politics. An interesting example of such intrusion, which in turn leads to important economic consequences, is provided by measures that resulted in a change in the prevailing pattern of interregional income differentials. In the Soviet Union interregional income differentials have a special meaning—when such regions coincide with particular republics, with nationality groups, etc., income differentials cease to be confined to the area of economics; they intrude into the area of politics.

In the search for new sources of raw materials for the mineral fertilizer industry, important deposits were unearthed in Belorussia (at this point Belorussia is producing about 12 to 13 percent of the total output and almost as much as all Central Asia). Belorussia has been able to retain about half of its mineral fertilizer output within its boundaries and has reached the highest level of mineral fertilizer application, exceeding all other republics by a wide margin. Given such information, the performance of crop yields in Belorussia during the last decade ceases to be a mystery. A similar situation has developed in Lithuania. There is little doubt that the apportionment of mineral fertilizers to Belorussia and Lithuania required not a decision by the bureaucrats in the state planning committee but a decision by the Politburo.

The use of fertilizer in Belorussia and Lithuania is linked with the problems of the Russian Nonblackearth zone. As long as mineral fertilizers were sent to the cotton plantations of Central Asia or to the sugar fields of the Ukraine and Moldavia, the sensitivity of the Russians could be contained. But when the younger brothers (Belorussians) next door began to apply fertilizer to their potato fields, their grains, and even the pastures on the drained Polesia marshes, a program to restore the productive capacity of the Nonblackearth region had to be hastily designed. This seems to reflect the dialectics of the relationship between economics and politics within the present setting of the Soviet Union.

While the case of the Nonblackearth zone illustrates the politicization of some economic decisions and measures in the agricultural sector, it is necessary to consider some of the political consequences that resulted from the changes in Soviet agriculture.

Since the most visible result of the government's policies was the decline of the agricultural and rural population,[2] one could safely assume that the Soviet regime is less dependent upon the goodwill of the agricultural population than in the past. Since the numerical decline of the agricultural population coincided with an increase of the real incomes of the agricultural labor force and population, it would follow that the regime feels relatively secure with respect to the loyalty of this social group. Although in the past the majority of army recruits were of rural and agricultural background, the present composition of the armed forces follows more closely the overall distribution between urban and rural elements. But there is a complicating aspect involved in this issue. To an increasing degree, the proportion of non-Russian nationalities in the agricultural population has grown. The proportion of the Central Asian nationalities, the Moldavians, and others is increasing at the expense of the ethnic Russians, since urbanization in some of the areas of the periphery is lagging behind the central regions inhabited by Russians. In other words, nationality problems might complicate what at first glance appears in the political sphere to be a decrease in government dependency upon the agricultural population.

Another complicating factor in the dependency relationship of the regime and the agricultural population is the indirect result of a foreign policy constraint. The Soviet Union has not given up its drive toward self-sufficiency in agricultural production primarily because of foreign policy considerations. The goal of self-sufficiency is apparent from all recent major policy documents, including the resolution of the Central Committee Plenum of 4 July 1978. The expansion of agricultural production, it is stipulated, should proceed in all directions and apparently without much regard for comparative advantages. In order to move toward self-sufficiency, the agricultural labor force is provided with an increasing range of incentives, and price increases for goods produced by the farms will swell the already high subsidies for agriculture in the state budget. But if the present regime has tried to placate the farm population to some extent by raising the level of payments for agricultural labor and preserving the auxiliary plots of collective farmers and state farm workers, this policy has not met with acclaim from the industrial workers. In fact, the workers appear to resent the fact that Soviet agriculture does not provide the supply of foods and fibers that the regime continually promises the population. There is reason to believe that the urban population's resentment of the agricultural producers is increasing, whereas in the past they were considered merely victims of the institutions of socialized agriculture. If this impression of intensified resentment is correct, then we are dealing with a lowering of social cohesion that might have a number of political repercussions.

There is not much that the regime can do politically to improve the performance of the agricultural sector, as long as it is committed to avoiding the use of wholesale terror and to preserving the basic institutional structure in agriculture. The preceding discussion suggested that the pattern chosen by the present policymakers in the Soviet Union is one of small institutional changes and of incremental measures in the existing basic policies. A pattern of increasing use of mineral fertilizers, more and larger tractors, and differentiation between specialized meat producing and diary producing livestock was followed during the last three years of the current plan period and is also being envisaged for the next plan period (1981–1985). Such incremental changes will not make a significant difference in the situation of Soviet agriculture. They will not drastically reduce the rising production costs, nor will they cause spectacular increases in agricultural output.

There is hardly any mention in Soviet economic or political literature of major institutional or policy changes in agriculture. "Caution" appears to be the watchword in Soviet agriculture as much as in Soviet industry. The caution exercised in the realm of agricultural policies, the reluctance to experiment with other institutional arrangements, the unwillingness to grant more freedom to the collective farms or more leniency to the private initiative of those producing on their auxiliary plots appears to be more politically than economically motivated.[3] It certainly suggests a sense of insecurity on the part of the political leadership, a fear of relinquishing direct controls.

One observes, instead, the repetition by the leadership of time-proven methods — such as the continuous conversion of collective farms into state farms, the increase or promise of increase of collective farmers' pensions, and continuing investment in the infrastructure of the farm areas, in order to keep the dwindling farm population in agriculture. Western political scientists often discuss the hypothesis that the Soviet leadership hesitates to introduce changes in the management or institutional structure of agriculture because it does not have sufficient "elbow room" to sustain losses in reserves or consumption that might result during the transition period. It is difficult to accept this line of reasoning in view of the absence of evidence of experimentation on the part of Soviet policymakers. No one would expect them to be so bold as to change the system overnight, to take a leap into the unknown. But there are many ways in which limited experiments could be undertaken that might indicate whether a change would in fact result in any curtailment of production.[4] Although the regime appears not to be concerned about domestic political attitudes and is satisfied to follow previous patterns, foreign policy considerations justify its concern with agriculture's performance.

The foreign policy considerations that originate from the performance of Soviet agriculture have a number of dimensions. One is striving toward self-sufficiency in agricultural production by the Soviet Union discussed earlier. The other aspect pertains to the relations between the Soviet Union and the Communist countries of Eastern Europe. Leaving aside the specific problems of the relationship to Yugoslavia and Rumania, the Soviet Union during the previous decades has carried the responsibility of supplying agricultural products to the Eastern European countries as a part of the mutual trade agreements of the COMECON. During the 1970s, especially during years of decreased agricultural production, this obligation became a real burden resulting in increased food and feed imports outside the Soviet bloc. It appears that for both political and economic reasons[5] the Soviet Union can only temporarily shirk its long-term responsibility as a supplier of food, feed, and agricultural raw materials, and may be compelled at best to act as a supplier of last resort. During the heyday of détente, the Soviet Union encouraged its Eastern European allies to enter independently into bilateral trade relations with the chief food-producing countries in order to obtain credits for agricultural imports. However, the Soviet Union is becoming painfully aware that because the most easily obtainable sources have been exhausted and a ceiling in the availability of credits has been reached (under conditions of complications with the spirit and conditions of détente), the continuation of direct dealings between the Eastern European countries and the West harbors political risks. Soviet inability to supply Eastern Europe in the long run would undermine its political stature in the eyes of the East Europeans vis-à-vis the West and China.

The option of obtaining agricultural products from the developing—or Third World—countries, which would be preferable politically and economically for both the Eastern European countries and for the Soviet Union, is not available. There would be no foreign exchange problem, since the agricultural imports would be paid for through bilateral agreements either in manufactured goods or in armaments, but the developing countries are often importers of those agricultural products that are in demand by the COMECON countries. Thus the world market in agricultural products, largely supported by the exporting countries of the West, is the only place where the needed imports can be obtained when a deficit appears in the domestic supply of Eastern Europe and the Soviet Union. This is a situation in which the Soviet Union is affected both by its own deficiency and by the foreign policy constraints that increase its dependency upon Eastern Europe. But to the extent that the leverage that the Soviet Union possesses vis-à-vis Eastern Europe (which it has proven able to use when it feels threatened) is a part of the foreign policy reality, no such leverage exists vis-à-vis the major industrially developed countries of the West.

By its own admission, the Soviet government considers that its most urgent economic task is to take advantage of the present "scientific-technical revolution." The "scientific-technical revolution" is a euphemism for the totality of technological advances of the last twenty to twenty-five years—the utilization in industry and services of electronic, atomic, and biophysical technology. The Soviet Union needs technology in order to benefit from labor-saving features and to keep pace with technological progress in the West. The easiest way to acquire this technology, together with the practical applications in industrial processes, is to purchase it from other advanced countries. Thus the importance of machinery, equipment, etc., from the West became the barometer of recent Soviet activity to close the technical gap.

The ability of the Soviet Union to earn a sufficient amount of foreign exchange in order to finance technology imports is limited by its export volume and gold reserves. The difficulties of increasing exports to hard-currency countries has been demonstrated by the record of Soviet foreign trade. For the Soviet Union to have food imports competing with the imports of capital goods, under conditions of limited export possibilities, is painful and frustrating. The Soviet Union succeeded in importing grains during 1972–1973 at very favorable prices. But during 1975–1976, with smaller grain stocks in world trade and the absence of a U.S. wheat subsidy, the USSR had to pay $153 per metric ton of wheat instead of the $59 that it paid in 1972–1973. In addition, in October 1975 the Soviet Union signed a grain agreement with the United States that institutionalized the grain trade for five years, beginning October 1976. The terms of the agreement amounted to a commitment to purchase an annual minimum of 6 million tons of wheat and corn. By accepting the terms of the agreement, the Soviet Union agreed to cost increases to assure itself an adequate feed-grain supply and to lessen its impact as a monopoly buyer. It could be assumed that the motives of the Soviet Union in signing the agreement were not only to ensure against even the remote possibility of encountering an export embargo, but also to create a climate in which its purchases of capital goods could be financed through foreign loans. Thus access to Western credit markets was probably the chief motive in signing the agreement, since the Soviet policymakers probably discounted the recurrence of U.S. embargoes on grain exports. The Soviet policymakers also are aware of the fact that the position of the United States in the grain market is much stronger than its position in the capital goods market, where the Soviet Union can try to gain from the competition between the United States and other industrialized countries.

The Soviet dilemma and experience of importing both capital goods and grain can be illustrated by the relative figures for both types of imports during the years 1973 through 1978. Capital goods imports amounted to $14.5 billion, compared with $9.6 billion for grain imports. By the Soviets' own definition grain imports tend to be a poor substitute, even when they are necessary, for capital goods, given the short time-horizon for the retooling of industrial capacity. The volume of credits awarded to the Soviet Union by the end of 1977 was estimated at $17 billion and the problems of refinancing some of the earlier loans arose.

The hope that the competition among the industrialized countries would help the Soviet Union to acquire the necessary capital goods was also dampened; economic recovery, increases in domestic demand, differences in quality and technical sophistication of the capital goods, rising exports to the OPEC countries, and political factors (in part stemming from the ceaseless growth of the Soviet military arsenal) all contributed to a diminished enthusiasm for exports to the Soviet Union that had to be financed through or by the exporters. It is also possible that recent overtures by China, offering to some of the potential exporters of capital goods shares in the development of its oil resources and promising orders for capital goods, had at least a marginal effect. Competition from China meant the Soviet Union was no longer the actual and potential major importer of capital goods and therefore capable of taking advantage of such a position, at least with respect to Japan. With respect to the United States and the European countries, a Soviet shift from purely military production to capital goods (obviously consumer goods production would be even better) would probably help to improve the climate for massive sales of modern technology embodied in Western capital goods. One might wonder whether this is acceptable to the Soviet leadership and whether it is realistic to expect their acquiescence. Under the terms of SALT II it is likely that the rearmament of both the NATO alliance and the Warsaw Pact countries will continue at an agreed upon pace. Thus for the Soviet Union, retooling of its industrial plant and the need for continued grain imports will remain competing objectives.

On balance, the performance of Soviet agriculture, which is not capable of meeting the demand of rising domestic consumption levels, appears to have more serious foreign policy implications than purely domestic consequences.

Notes

1. In addition to the official Soviet data, a minor adjustment was made for the effect of urbanization upon the consumption pattern of agricultural products.

2. The share of the rural population in the total declined from 60 to 38 percent during the third quarter of this century and the agricultural population now constitutes about 26 percent of the total.

3. Obviously no one can take seriously the claim that it makes any difference to the leadership whether the grain produced is of collective farm or state farm origin, except for political considerations.

4. A palatable area of experimentation could be one of the industrial crops, in which case there would be no possibility of competition between government demand and private demand because there are no private cotton factories in the Soviet Union.

5. The main economic reason is the inability of the East European countries to pay for agricultural imports by exporting to the West. Needless to say, a long-run adjustment process of developing exportable goods for Western markets would lessen their dependency upon the Soviet Union.

PART 4

Eastern Europe

12

The Economies of Eastern Europe
and Soviet Foreign Policy

Paul Marer

The purpose of this chapter is twofold: to summarize the economic situation in Eastern Europe and to discuss its foreign policy implications for the USSR.[1]

The East European region is defined as including the six East European members of the Council for Mutual Economic Assistance (CMEA)— Bulgaria, Czechoslovakia, the German Democratic Republic (GDR), Hungary, Poland, and Rumania—plus the two Balkan countries of Yugoslavia and Albania. The inclusion of the latter two countries makes sense when looking through the prism of Soviet foreign policy: The ups and downs of the Soviet Union's past relations with these two maverick countries is certainly one of the "inputs" into formulating Soviet policies vis-à-vis the rest of Eastern Europe.

These eight countries differ in most respects: size, resource endowment, historical and cultural experience, nationality, language, level of economic development, direction and speed of changes in their economic systems, development strategy, economic performance, and political orientation. They would differ from one another even if Albania and Yugoslavia were not included; their inclusion increases the diversity. The roots of the diversity in the region can be traced to the enormous differences in the initial postwar "environments" under which the centrally planned economic system was introduced. These differences were, in some cases, further accentuated or diminished by certain postwar events and the special economic links that some countries were able to forge with countries within or outside the region, such as Bulgaria with the USSR, Albania with China, and the GDR with the Federal Republic of Germany (FRG).

The first section discusses the economic situation in the region, covering the period to the end of 1977 in most cases and the plans and prospects of the 1976–1980 five-year plan. After comparing the economic performance of the eight East European countries and their plans to 1980, we consider the sources of growth, stressing both the important growth contribution of Western credits and the economic problems created by the inevitable repayment burdens. We then compare the various economic strategies, systems, and policies of the countries.

The second section discusses the political economy of Eastern Europe's relations with the USSR, first offering an overview of the evolution of postwar economic relations and then discussing recent developments regarding the terms of trade and the so-called "joint" CMEA projects in the USSR.

The implications of the foregoing for Soviet foreign policy is the topic of the third section. Listed and discussed briefly are the issues and developments that, from the Soviet perspective, "aggravate" and those that help "smooth" Soviet–East European relations. Implications for Soviet foreign policy are then considered, first with regard to Eastern Europe and then for other areas.

THE ECONOMIC SITUATION IN EASTERN EUROPE

Indicators of Economic Performance

Economic performance is multidimensional. The five indicators most often relied upon by economists to measure performance are: economic growth rates; production efficiency (i.e., how much input is needed to produce a unit of output that, over time, can be measured by the growth of productivity); improvements in the standard of living and the distribution of income among individuals, groups, and regions (a very important aspect of which is the rate and nature of inflation); the rate of unemployment; and the status of the balance of payments.

Even if one had accurate data on each of the five performance indicators, how one should interpret them is not always clear. This problem is especially important in the case of Eastern Europe. Sometimes the data may not mean exactly the same under an East European economic and social system as they would mean in our Western society and sometimes a comparatively good or improved performance can be achieved only by a concurrent or postponed weaker performance in some other area of the economy.

Economic Growth Performance

Aggregate Growth

A comparison of the officially published (Net Material Product = NMP) and recalculated Western aggregate output (Gross National Product = GNP) is presented in Table 12.1 for each of the eight East European

TABLE 12.1

Ranking of the East European Countries by
Growth Performance, 1965-76 Actual
and 1976-80 Plan

(Average Annual Rate of Growth in Percent)

Country and Measure	1965-70	1970-75	1976	1977 p.	1976-80 p.
1. Romania					
NMP	7.7	11.3	10.5	11.3	10.5
GNP	4.5	6.1	7.1		
2. Poland					
NMP	6.0	9.8	6.6	5.7	7.1
GNP	3.8	6.7	5.7		
3. Bulgaria					
NMP	8.7	7.9	6.6	8.2	7.7
GNP	4.8	4.5	4.6		
4. Yugoslavia					
Social Product	6.1	6.6	4.0	n.a.	7.0
5. Albania					
NMP	9.0	6.3	n.a.	n.a.	6.3-7.0
6. Hungary					
NMP	6.8	6.2	3.5	6.2	5.5
GNP	3.1	3.6	1.2		
7. Czechoslovakia					
NMP	6.8	5.7	2.6	5.2	5.0
GNP	3.5	3.4	1.9		
8. GDR					
NMP	5.2	5.4	3.7	5.5	5.0
GNP	3.2	3.5	2.4		

Source: Paul Marer, "Economic Performance, Strategy,
and Prospects in Eastern Europe," in U.S., Congress,
Joint Economic Committee, East European Economies Post-
Helsinki (Washington, D.C.: U.S. Governemnt Printing
Office, 1977).

countries as available, for subperiods between 1965 and 1975 and annually
for 1976. Available plan figures are also shown for 1977 and 1976-1980.[2]
The official NMP series, while upward biased, is believed to be one of the
most important indicators used by the leadership in the East European
countries to judge their own economic performance. The recalculated GNP
series is our best estimate of how rapidly the East European economies are
growing.

In Table 12.1 the eight countries are ranked on the basis of their overall
growth performance during 1970-1975 according to official (NMP) data.
The ranking remains pretty much the same on the basis of GNP data (not

available for Yugoslavia and Albania), but would change slightly if 1965–1975 growth rates were the criterion. The eight countries can be divided into two groups: the three relatively fast-growing countries of Rumania, Poland, and Bulgaria and the less rapidly growing other countries. Taking the 1965–1976 actual and 1976–1980 plan figures into account, Rumania can probably claim first place and Bulgaria second. It is interesting to note the position of Yugoslavia and Albania. Yugoslavia places right in the middle, performing about the same as Hungary during 1965–1976. In the period 1965–1970 Albania claims to have grown roughly on a par with Rumania and Bulgaria, but its growth slowed during 1970–1975 and its performance was roughly on par with that of Hungary. To be sure, Albania's exceptionally poor and incomplete statistics and the absence of a Western recalculation undermine our confidence in the data and makes it particularly difficult to compare its performance with those of other countries.

Per Capita Growth

Population growth figures are presented in Table 12.2. At one end of the spectrum stands Albania, where the annual population increment is about 2.5 percent—an extremely high rate even by world standards—reducing Albania's growth rates on a per capita basis by at least 1.5 percent vis-à-vis every other East European country. At the other end is East Germany, whose population has recently been declining by about one-quarter of one percent per annum, raising its per capita performance slightly. Registering small population increases—in the one-third to two-thirds of one percent per annum range—are Bulgaria, Czechoslovakia, and Hungary. In the one percent per annum growth range are Rumania, Poland, and Yugoslavia. Comparing growth performance in the 1970s on a per capita basis and taking into account plan projections to 1980 would change the relative position of Albania, moving it down among the relatively slow-growing countries; of the GDR, moving it slightly ahead of Czechoslovakia on the NMP; and also of Hungary, on GNP basis.

Perhaps the most important—certainly the most frequently cited— statistic is economic growth performance, i.e., how rapidly the aggregate output of goods and services produced by the economy is growing. A rapid growth in real production (versus the money value of production that may rise due to inflation) tends to make other economic targets easier to attain. These targets include improving the standard of living, bettering the distribution of income by giving a larger slice of a growing pie to the poorest groups or regions, providing jobs to those willing and able to work, and increasing exports to pay for needed imports, thus keeping the country's external accounts (balance of payments) in balance.

TABLE 12.2

Index of Population Growth in the East European Countries, 1960-1976

(Average Annual Percent Change)

Period	Bulgaria	Czechosl.	GDR	Hungary	Poland	Romania	Yugosl.	Albania
1965-70	0.70	0.28	0.04	0.36	0.80	1.28	1.04	2.80
1970-75	0.56	0.65	-0.24	0.39	0.91	1.00	0.95	2.50[1]
1975-76	0.38	0.86	-0.30	0.48	0.92	1.00	0.95[3]	2.50[2]

[1] 1970-73.

[2] Assumed to be the same as 1970-73.

[3] Assumed to be the same as 1970-73.

Source: Paul Marer, "Economic Performance..." op. cit. Table 3.

Sources of Growth

Conceptual Issues

The three fundamental sources of growth (positive or negative) involve inputs, productivity, and changes in the terms of trade. A positive foreign contribution to capital inputs is made by an inflow of foreign credits; to labor inputs, a net inflow of migrant or temporary workers.[3] An economy growing rapidly that derives much of its growth from growth of inputs and at the same time undergoes rapid change in the economic structure (e.g., the importance of industry is rising rapidly at the expense of the agricultural sector) is said to follow an "extensive" growth path. Conversely, an economy that achieves the greater part of its growth from improved productivity without rapid change in the structure of the economy is said to follow an "intensive" growth path. Extensive growth requires economic mobilization — putting all able-bodied people to work or to school, undertaking a high level of investment (which means holding down consumption), and directing investment into sectors yielding high output per unit of investment, at least in the short run. Such a mobilization was carried out by all East European countries after the war and continues in a few countries, notably Rumania and Albania. But the gain in output that can be obtained from resource mobilization will diminish gradually in all countries and sooner in the more advanced ones like the GDR and Czechoslovakia. To maintain rapid growth, countries must rely increasingly on productivity, i.e., improved production efficiency, whose growth is hindered by the well-known inefficiencies of central planning. Attempts to reduce these obstacles have led to experiments with partial or comprehensive reforms of the economic system as well as increased reliance on trade and industrial cooperation with Western countries.

Changes in terms of trade usually have a significant impact on a country's growth rates only when relative prices on the world market shift substantially (as was the case after the 1973 explosion in the price of energy) and affect principally countries that have a relatively large foreign sector, i.e., high foreign trade to national income ratios. The decisive issue is whether a country is a net exporter or importer of the goods and services whose relative prices increased on the world market: if a net exporter, it benefits; if a net importer, it loses from such shifts in relative prices.

Capital and Labor Inputs and Productivity

Thorny statistical problems make it extremely difficult to estimate with any degree of confidence how much of a given country's rate of growth — and differences in rates of growth across countries — might be explained by differences in growth of factor inputs or productivity.[4] These difficulties notwithstanding, the following broad generalizations seem to emerge from the available statistics:

1. The increase in total employment since 1960 has been under 2 percent per annum in every East European country in each five-year period, except as noted below; hence, employment growth has not been a dominant growth factor in most countries.[5]
2. In all countries achieving a high rate of growth of output, industrial employment increased rapidly, in many cases between 3 percent and 6 percent per annum. Much of the increase was provided by declining agricultural employment.
3. In all countries achieving a high growth of output, accumulation (investment and depreciation funds) as percent of distributed national income used was high, rising to 30 percent or more by the early 1970s or sooner. In the relatively slow growing countries, accumulation as percent of national income remained below 30 percent. The lowest share is by the GDR, which needs to maintain consumption growth because of the politically sensitive competitive pressure it faces from West Germany in this regard. It must be stressed, however, that comparisons of national income shares devoted to accumulation versus consumption are notoriously problematic.
4. To sum up, both labor and capital productivity indexes have been growing much more slowly in all countries and in most periods than the corresponding output measures.[6] This indicates, as do the facts enumerated above, that a continued rapid growth of inputs explains a significant part of the rapid growth of the fast-growing East European countries. But neither our statistical data nor our theoretical and measurement techniques are adequate as yet to be able to determine accurately what proportion of growth is due to increased inputs versus increased productivity.

Foreign Borrowing

All East European countries except Albania have recently become net borrowers from the West.[7] From 1961, for more than a decade and a half, Albania has been a large borrower — or grantee — from the People's Republic of China. The six East European members of the CMEA combined are net lenders to the East, principally to the USSR, through their participation in so-called CMEA joint investment projects, although periodically the USSR makes large loans to individual East European countries. These countries also run trade surpluses with the less developed socialist states, principally Mongolia and Cuba, participating in what might be called intrasocialist foreign aid programs. The East European countries occasionally also invest in projects located on the territory of a regional partner, but intra-East European credit flows are small and hence can be disregarded. Finally, several East European governments extend credits to finance the sale of their machinery to less developed countries.

Although all countries in the region are involved in both borrowing and (with the possible exception of Albania) lending, the hard-currency credits the seven East European countries have recently obtained from the West and the credits in kind Albania obtained from China have been of overriding importance. Although Albania's borrowing has not been predominantly in hard currency, its inclusion in the comparison is appropriate because the resources it obtained came from outside the region. The distinction that much of the credit it has received may have been (or will be) forgiven, whereas the rest of Eastern Europe will have to repay what it has borrowed, is important when considering the burden of indebtedness but not its contribution to growth, in the short run.

Table 12.3 shows the increase in hard currency indebtedness of the East European countries between 1970 and 1977. It presents also the indebtedness of the two CMEA banks—because this debt is the shared responsibility of all CMEA members—in proportion to each country's equity in these institutions, and, for comparative purposes, the debt of the USSR and the soft-currency debt of Albania, mainly to China. The tabulation reveals that the indebtedness of the six East European members of the CMEA increased almost sevenfold in seven years, from $4.6 billion in 1970 to $31.7 billion by 1977. Almost one-half of this $27 billion increase in debt has been incurred by Poland (more than $12 billion) since 1973.

It is very difficult to establish precisely the relationship between foreign borrowing and the debtor country's growth rates. Still, to go beyond simply giving the dollar amounts, since the countries are of different size and level of development, in Table 12.4 we juxtapose the increase in indebtedness with the increment of the same country's GNP since 1967. Both debt and GNP are expressed in current U.S. dollars. To be sure, a borrowed dollar spent on investment tends to contribute more to current and future growth than if the loans were used to import consumer goods. But still, the comparison does provide a useful point of departure for establishing a common denominator. The year 1967 was chosen as the base year because previous borrowing from the West was not on a significant scale. The years 1972 and 1975 were selected to divide the subperiods because the indebtedness position of some countries changed considerably and current dollar GNP estimates were available.

Ranking countries by the highest to the lowest ratio of increase in in-

TABLE 12.3

Eastern Europe and the USSR:
Net Hard Currency Debt 1970-1977
($ billions)

	1970	1974	1975	1976	1977
Bulgaria	.7	1.2	1.8	2.3	2.7
Czechoslovakia	.3	1.1	1.5	2.1	2.7
GDR	1.0	2.8	3.8	6.0	5.9
Hungary	.6	1.5	2.1	2.8	3.4
Poland	.8	3.9	6.9	10.2	13.0
Romania	1.2	2.6	3.0	3.3	4.0
Total Eastern Europe six	4.6	13.1	19.1	25.7	31.7
USSR	1.9	5.0	10.0	14.0	16.0
CMEA Banks*	0	.1	.5	1.1	1.7
Total European CMEA	6.5	18.2	29.6	40.8	49.4
Albania**	.3	n.a.	.8	n.a.	n.a.
Yugoslavia	1.9	n.a	5.6	n.a.	n.a.

*
The International Investment Bank, which at the end of 1977 had outstanding Eurocurrency loans of approximately $1.5 billion and the International Bank for Economic Cooperation, whose outstanding hard-currency obligation at the end of 1977 was under $.2 billion.

**
Cumulative import surplus, as calculated by Michael Kaser in "Trade and Aid in the Albanian Economy," in East European Economies Post Helsinki .

Source: Compiled from the reports of various Western banking and government institutions.

debtedness to incremental GNP during 1967–1976, we find that Albania is in a class by itself. The resources it was able to obtain abroad were of the same order of magnitude as the increments to its GNP. Albania's unique position in Eastern Europe is further emphasized if we consider that since World War II it has relied continuously on large infusions of foreign resources (whereas East Europe was not borrowing on a significant scale before the mid-1960s) and that a substantial portion of those resources were obtained, or became, grants rather than loans.

Focusing on the entire 1967–1976 period, the remaining seven countries

TABLE 12.4

The Contribution of Hard-Currency Debt to Economic Growth, 1967-76

(Billions of Current Dollars and Percent)

Country	1967-72 (5 years)[3]			1972-75 (3 years)			1975-76 (1 year)			1967-76 (9 years)		
	ΔDebt (A)	ΔGNP (B)	A/B (%)	ΔDebt (A)	ΔGNP (B)	A/B (%)	ΔDebt (A)	ΔGNP (B)	A/B (%)	ΔDebt (A)	ΔGNP (B)	A/B (%)
Bulgaria	0.3	4.6	7%	1.0	6.0	17%	0.5	1.9	26%	1.7	12.6	13%
Czechoslovakia	0.1	12.5	1%	0.9	15.4	6%	0.6	3.8	16%	1.6	31.7	5%
GDR	0.8	13.9	6%	2.3	18.2	13%	1.0	4.7	21%	4.1	36.7	11%
Hungary	0.4	5.2	8%	1.2	7.3	16%	0.6	1.6	37%	2.2	14.2	15%
Poland	0.0	20.4	--	5.8	28.7	20%	3.3	9.2	36%	9.1	58.2	15%
Romania	0.9	13.0	7%	1.4	14.4	10%	0.2	5.8	3%	2.5	33.3	8%
Eastern Europe Six[4]	2.4	69.6	3%	12.6	90.0	14%	6.2	27.0	23%	21.2	186.7	11%
Yugoslavia[5]	1.9	7.1	27%	2.3	18.4	13%	.9	5.2	17%	5.1	30.8	17%
Albania	0.331[1]	0.374	88%	0.322	0.374[1]	86%	n.a.	n.a.	n.a.	0.653[2]	0.748[2]	87%[2]

[1] Cumulative import surplus, principally with the People's Republic of China. [3] From 12/31/67 til 12/31/72.

[2] 1967-75. [4] Weighted average.

[5] Social product

Source: Paul Marer, "Economic Performance," Table 4.

fall into two groups. The increase in debt was 10 percent or more of the increase in GNP in Yugoslavia (17 percent), Poland (16 percent), Hungary (15 percent), Bulgaria (13 percent), and the GDR (11 percent), and less than 10 percent in Rumania (8 percent) and Czechoslovakia (5 percent). On a per capita basis, the countries rank from most to least resources borrowed (1976 data) as follows:

Albania	$365
Yugoslavia	$300
Poland	$297
GDR	$286
Bulgaria	$263
Hungary	$255
Rumania	$149
Czechoslovakia	$141

What factors can explain the rapid rise of debt of these countries? That the debt of the East European countries is large, in fact extraordinarily large, cannot be disputed. If anyone had predicted ten years ago that by the end of 1977 the Communist countries would owe about $50 billion to the industrial West, that forecast would have been considered wildly unrealistic, with a probability of occurrence near zero. Several events in combination helped to bring about the present situation. First, détente made improved East-West economic relations possible. Second, the Communist countries changed their cautious credit policy and were willing to borrow large sums. Third, much of the huge trade surplus generated by the OPEC countries was deposited in Western banks that were seeking opportunities to lend these funds profitably. And since borrowing by Western businesses was sluggish (due to the oil-price-rise-induced recession), East European borrowers were (and still are) courteously accommodated. Fourth, the recession in the West created excess capacity and high unemployment, which made Western governments eager to promote exports to willing buyers with guaranteed and sometimes subsidized credits. Fifth, strong competition among Western exporters and government credit agencies for Eastern orders practically eliminated earlier restraints on loans to Communist countries (although gradually stronger voices, once again favoring credit restraint, are now being raised in many Western countries).

Terms of Trade

Implicit in our discussion of foreign borrowing and lending were the assumptions that an increase in Eastern Europe's indebtedness provides additional resources for growth, and credits granted by Eastern Europe reduce the amount of resources that can be harnessed for development, at least in the short run. This assumption needs to be modified: only by considering changes in the country's terms of trade can we determine, for example, whether foreign borrowing has provided additional resources or whether it was needed simply to cover the higher price of imports that remain un- compensated by the higher price of exports.

Export and import price indices and terms of trade for 1970–1975 have been published or can be derived for five East European countries (see Table 12.5). The overall terms of trade did not change significantly until 1973, but then deteriorated by 17 percent for Hungary, 14 percent for the GDR, 5 percent for Yugoslavia, 4 percent for Bulgaria, and improved by 3 percent for Poland. Czechoslovakia's terms of trade were probably similar to those of the GDR, while Rumania's were probably closer to Poland's. No price data are available on Albania's trade, but one may speculate that since Albania is self-sufficient in energy and a large share of its exports is made up of raw materials, its terms of trade have probably improved since 1970. But since Albania trades predominantly with China and the pricing mechanism they use is not known, any conjecture about Albania's terms of trade is highly speculative.

Price trends and terms of trade are known to differ in trade with socialist and nonsocialist countries not only because the commodity compositions differ in the two directions, but also because prices in intrasocialist trade follow world market price changes with several years' lag. Separate price and terms of trade indices with these two groups of countries are available only for Hungary and Poland, and these are shown in Table 12.6.[8] Two slightly different price and terms of trade indices are shown for Hungary under each of the two main headings: one calculated on the basis of country of export and import (called socialist versus nonsocialist trade), the other on the basis of the settlement price used (called ruble versus dollar settlement trade). The difference is that a certain portion of trade with CMEA part- ners—usually made up of above-plan "hard good" exports and imports—is priced according to current world market prices. This commerce is in- cluded under "socialist" but excluded from "ruble-settlement" trade.[9]

Table 12.6 reveals that between 1972 and 1975, in trade with socialist countries Hungary's export prices rose by 17 percent to 19 percent while its import prices increased by 32 percent to 39 percent, resulting in a deterioration in its terms of trade by 12 percent to 15 percent (depending on whether or not dollar-priced trade is excluded). Since the commodity com- position of GDR and Czechoslovak trade with the socialist countries is not too different from that of Hungary, one may reasonably speculate that their terms of trade would also be comparable. Poland, on the other hand, is in a much better situation: As it is both an exporter and importer of energy and

TABLE 12.5

Export and Import Price Indices and Terms of Trade of Five East European Countries, 1970-75

(1970=100)

Year	Bulgaria			GDR			Hungary			Poland			Yugoslavia		
	X	M	TT	X	M	TT	X	M	TT	X	M	TT	X	M	TT
1970	100.0	100.0	100.0	100.0	100.0	100.0	100.0	100.0	100.0	100.0	100.0	100.0	100.0	100.0	100.0
1971	100.8	102.3	98.6	100.5	100.7	99.8	100.3	101.7	98.6	102.4	98.2	104.3	105.3	103.8	101.4
1972	100.4	100.8	99.6	100.9	101.9	99.7	101.9	104.1	97.9	103.8	97.8	106.2	110.6	111.5	99.2
1973	103.4	104.3	99.2	102.6	108.2	94.8	107.0	110.7	96.6	109.8	106.4	103.1	133.3	130.7	102.0
1974	110.9	113.1	98.1	110.1	122.2	90.1	115.3	128.9	89.4	127.8	124.4	102.6	175.5	192.2	91.3
1975	120.5	125.3	96.2	117.8	136.3	86.4	122.3	147.2	83.1	146.0	141.8	102.8	191.3	201.8	94.8

Source: Paul Marer, "Economic Performance," Table 6.

TABLE 12.6

Export and Import Price Indices of Hungary and Poland

with Socialist and Nonsocialist Groups of Countries, 1970-75

(1970=100)

Year	Hungary[1]						Poland		
	Exp.		Imp.		T of T		Exp.	Imp.	T of T
	Soc.	R.S.	Soc.	R.S.	Soc.	R.S.			
						With Socialist Countries			
1970	100.0	100.0	100.0	100.0	100.0	100.0	100.0	100.0	100.0
1971	99.8	99.6	101.5	101.8	98.4	97.8	100.7	99.6	101.0
1972	100.1	100.2	103.7	104.0	96.5	96.3	102.5	99.8	102.5
1973	101.8	100.7	104.7	104.2	97.3	96.6	103.1	99.4	103.5
1974	106.2	102.0	112.5	105.2	94.4	97.0	105.6	102.9	102.5
1975	119.2	117.0	139.4	132.2	85.5	88.5	128.2	129.7	98.7
						With Nonsocialist Countries[2]			
	N.S.	D+O	N.S.	D+O	N.S.	D+O			
1970	100.0	100.0	100.0	100.0	100.0	100.0	100.0	100.0	100.0
1971	101.4	101.4	104.8	102.2	99.2	99.2	106.4	94.2	113.0
1972	106.2	105.0	97.6	104.4	100.8	100.6	107.7	92.2	115.8
1973	120.0	119.3	118.7	121.6	97.0	98.1	125.7	118.0	105.5
1974	142.5	141.8	169.0	169.6	85.3	83.6	182.6	156.8	116.5
1975	133.7	132.5	179.2	170.2	81.1	77.8	198.3	161.9	122.5

[1]
Soc. = Socialist countries
R.S. = Ruble-settlement countries
N.S. = Nonsocialist countries
D+O = Dollar-and Other devisa-settlement countries

[2]
Advanced industrial countries for Poland only.

Sources: See source cited for Table 12.5.

Table 12.7

Exports from Eastern Europe to Western Europe (1975)

	Fuels (SITC 3)	Primary Products (SITC 0 + 1 + 2 + 4)	Manufactures (SITC 5–8)	1975 Terms of Trade (1970 = 100)
Poland	37.0%	25.0	38.0	122.5
Romania	20.8%	28.3	50.8	(100.0)
Czechoslovakia	14.3%	20.3	65.4	(90.0)
GDR	6.8%	23.2	70.0	(80.0)
Hungary	2.1%	43.1	54.8	80.0
Bulgaria	1.9%	48.2	49.9	(80.0)

raw materials, its terms of trade with all socialist countries as a group did not significantly change. The terms of trade of Rumania, which neither imports nor exports energy in trade with its socialist partners, probably did not change very much either. Bulgaria's terms of trade vis-à-vis socialist countries probably falls between that of Hungary and Poland.

In trade with nonsocialist countries, during 1972–1975, Hungary's terms of trade deteriorated by about 20 percent while Poland's improved (with the industrial West only) by more than 20 percent, thanks to coal, which made up 30 percent of Poland's hard-currency exports in 1975. The terms of trade of the other East European countries would be influenced greatly by the commodity composition of their exports to the West: the larger the proportion of fuels and other primary products, the more they were helped, or the less hurt, by developments during 1972–1975 on the world market. Based on data compiled by Wolf, the 1975 compositions of East European countries' exports to the twelve main West European countries that accounted for most of the East-West trade, were as given in Table 12.7.[10]

Shown in parentheses in the last column are my rough estimates of the terms of trade of the five East European countries for which data are available. The estimates are based on the commodity composition of these countries' exports to Western Europe and the terms of trade indices of Poland and Hungary.

With respect to nonsocialist trade, the tentative conclusion is that Poland was the only East European country that obtained resources from the West, not only through borrowing large amounts but through an improvement in its terms of trade. Rumania was probably neither hurt nor helped much in its Western trade from price developments on the world market, but the other four countries had to devote a significant part of the resources borrowed from the West to maintain the real volume of their imports in the face of deteriorating price relations. Moreover, it seems that the same countries that were most hurt by price developments in their trade with the West were also most adversely affected in their trade with socialist countries, although the brunt of the impact has been delayed by a few years.

Economic Strategies, Systems, and Policies

To provide an overview for the eight East European countries, the countries are divided into two groups: the Southern Tier, made up of the Balkan countries of Bulgaria, Rumania, Yugoslavia, and Albania, which—on the basis of official statistics—have been growing more rapidly than the rest of Eastern Europe (except Poland); and the Northern Tier, made up of the more highly developed but still very diverse countries to the north of the Balkans—the GDR, Czechoslovakia, Hungary, and Poland. Three issues are discussed briefly: broad economic strategy, major changes in the economic system, and policy on Western credits.

Southern Tier (Balkan) Countries

Bulgaria, Rumania, Yugoslavia, and Albania share the Balkan historical region (along with Greece), and have in common the fact of economic backwardness and foreign domination before World War II. Although the economic system and political orientation of Yugoslavia are quite different from the rest of Eastern Europe, Yugoslavia and Albania are similar in one respect: both have had continuous leadership since the war. Tito in Yugoslavia and Hoxha in Albania came to power as leaders of a liberating army and initially without Soviet backing. Of the four countries, only Bulgaria has not quarreled with Moscow. The common denominator of the economic systems, strategies, and policies of the other three has been the quest for and preservation of independence.

In a comprehensive essay on the economy of Rumania, Jackson argues that perhaps the single key to Rumanian policy since the 1950s has been the pursuit of independence under constraints.[11] Since the leadership believes that a backward, unindustrialized country has no hope for independence, the first priority has been and remains rapid industrialization. The Rumanians recognize, however, that industrialization breeds new threats to independence if countries supplying raw materials, capital, and technology and providing markets impose conditions that may hinder further development. The Rumanians chose to reduce this threat by (1) limiting the level of imports via import substitution; (2) distributing imports among many domestic branches to avoid excessive specialization; and (3) diversifying imports and exports as much as possible among other countries. This last strategy explains in part Rumania's increased orientation toward the less developed countries (LDCs): nearly one-third of Rumania's commerce is scheduled to be with Third World countries by 1980.

In its drive to achieve economic independence, Rumania had a significant edge over its Balkan (as well as other East European) neighbors: energy independence. In 1974 it could supply 86 percent of its needs from domestic sources. This is claimed to be the highest rate of energy self-sufficiency in Europe. Rumania received no significant aid from East or West (unless one classifies large commercial credits as aid). Yugoslavia had been a recipient of Western aid as well as substantial remittances from its nationals working in Western Europe, while Albania had obtained large amounts of aid from the CMEA countries up to 1961 and from China since then. Based on this comparison, Rumania has been the most self-reliant.

In Yugoslavia, the early 1970s witnessed a growing disenchantment with excessive dependence on market forces, stemming from "worries about the apparent increase in economic inequality both among republics and among individuals within each republic and from concern over the perceived concentration of economic power in the hands of financial institutions, the managerial elite, and wholesale, retail and foreign trade enterprises."[12] The response has been to assign a somewhat greater role to planning (a new planning infrastructure was laid out by law); to give new emphasis to social arrangements, as opposed to market considerations, on the basis of which fundamental economic decisions are to be formulated; and to enhance the influence of the party over economic policy.

Despite these modifications, the Yugoslav economic system remains fundamentally unchanged: an imperfect market system based on the principles of social ownership of the means of production and workers' self-management in enterprise decision making.

In Albania,[13] 1965–1966 marked the transition from a Soviet-type planning and management system to a specifically Albanian one in which ideological and moral incentives and outcomes ranked higher than economic results. In 1966, on the one hand, there was a significant reduction in the number of plan indicators, a conventional step in the East European setting; on the other hand, decision-making power was devolved not to enterprise management but to the workers, which is quite unconventional. The mobilization of workers was intended to come up with "counterplans" to prevent managers from hiding capacity and drawing up inflated requests — an attempt to supplement hierarchical pressures on enterprise directors with party-led pressure from below.

Bulgaria's economic strategy contrasts sharply with that of the other countries in the Balkan region. It has received favorable economic treatment from the Soviet Union and the resulting economic dependence on Moscow has reinforced the political ties between the two.[14] The Bulgarian economy has been subject to considerable and, in the view of many observers, excessive organizational change during the past ten years. At the same time, the record indicates that the leaders are more concerned with establishing practical rather than ideologically motivated solutions. Reform proceeds by testing rather than a priori reasoning. The most fruitful organizational experiments were carried out in agriculture.[15]

To what extent does an increased reliance on Western credits stem from an *ex ante* policy decision to make use of borrowed resources to accelerate growth or consumption or both, and to what extent is increased indebtedness the unplanned *ex post* outcome of unforeseen domestic developments (e.g., investment or consumption growing faster than planned) and international events (e.g., deteriorating terms of trade and Western recession hurting exports)? It is probably correct to state that every East European country's increase in hard-currency indebtedness was partly planned and partly unplanned. Nevertheless, there appear to be significant differences among them.

Rumania made planned use of large Western credits to accelerate its growth via large-scale Western machinery and other technology imports earlier than other East European CMEA countries. A rapid growth in trade with the West for the early 1960s was projected in 1958; even before the shift was made, the Rumanians began looking for credits to buy Western plants and equipment. Once the biggest borrower in Eastern Europe, Rumania followed a cautious credit policy during the early 1970s. During 1974–1975 its debts increased by $1 billion, largely due to unforeseen and uncontrollable external developments, i.e., rising import prices and reduced demand for its exports in recession-plagued Western Europe. In 1976 Rumania restored its trade balance by cutting imports and expanding exports. Its estimated $4 billion outstanding debt at the end of 1977 required that about 40 percent of its hard-currency exports be devoted to service the debt rather than pay for current imports.[16]

In the case of Bulgaria, one has the impression that the rise in its indebtedness is largely the outcome of unforeseen domestic developments, such as the establishment of overly ambitious goals that are attainable only by extraordinary efforts. These efforts required bottleneck-breaking industrial imports from the West in the 1960s and machinery and consumer goods imports in the 1970s. Efforts to balance the economy between 1973 and the first half of 1976 were inadequate and of course were made more difficult by external developments; the economy seemed to be drifting while huge external debts piled up and consumer purchasing power ran ahead of supplies. A serious effort was made in 1976–1977 to reduce the trade deficit, but the indebtedness continued to rise.[17]

In Yugoslavia, the recent increase in indebtedness seems to have been largely unplanned, resulting from external developments. Periodically, the country's balance-of-payments problem has posed a major constraint on growth. Yugoslavia finds it difficult to restore the foreign balance, given the country's priority for growth and commitment to a decentralized economic system.[18]

Albania is a special case: although it ran deficits during 1970–1973 amounting to something like half the value of its small imports from the industrial West and obtained commercial credits from Italy (its major supplier among market economies), more recently it pledged not to rely on Western credits. Albania is believed to be the only country whose new constitution contains a legal prohibition against (presumably long-term only) external loan, although credits from China were for a time the exception.[19]

Northern Tier Countries

For the GDR, its ambiguous relations with the Federal Republic of Germany (FRG) are one of the chief determinants of its economic policy. The GDR feels that it is taking part in an economic race whose outcome affects the very stability of the regime. It cannot permit itself to fall far behind the FRG in consumption standards, a consideration underscored by the Polish riots in 1970 and 1976 which led to a reassessment of the consumer's place in East Germany's development policy. This dilemma also conditions the GDR's relations with the Soviet Union and the rest of the CMEA, where its potential weakness vis-à-vis the FRG gives it strength and leverage.[20] Internally, its return to the fold of traditional Soviet-type economies marked the dismantling of its unique New Economic System.

For Czechoslovakia, the restoration of economic normalcy and control became the chief determinant of economic policy after 1968. The economic reforms were terminated by Husak, and central planning has been resurrected more thoroughly than was thought possible.

Poland is the site of one of the most notable developments since 1970: adoption of a rather extreme version of import-induced growth as a development strategy, with a large part of imports financed by credits. Two environmental considerations, external and internal, played a large role in inducing this new strategy. The external consideration was the signing of a "normalization treaty" with the FRG in December 1970, followed by the Soviet-American détente of the early 1970s, which created a climate conducive to reorientation toward the West. The internal consideration was the confrontation in December 1970 between the workers and the government following the rise in food prices. The government acquiesced in the workers' combined demand for a price freeze and substantial wage increases. This in turn ruled out an acceleration of investment growth based on internal resources — the strategy followed by Gomulka — and ushered in the import-induced growth strategy of Gierek, initially planned on a moderate level but realized in a rather extreme version. The resulting large indebtedness, reinforced by repeated poor harvests requiring large grain imports and Western recession adversely affecting Polish exports, is one of the many serious problems Poland faces today.

Changes in the Economic System

Internally, Poland experimented with limited economic reforms during the early 1970s, but elements of reform were introduced and often modified in a haphazard, inconsistent manner. As soon as there was an unfavorable change in the environment, there was an increase in the use of direct commands and intervention by central authorities. Looking to the near future, Fallenbuchl concludes:

> No serious economic reforms are envisaged for . . . 1976–80. For the time being there seems to be no return even to the limited reforms which had been started in the first years of the decade. At least in 1977, the "new economic and financial system" will remain inoperative, the autonomy of the large economic organizations (WOG) will continue to be seriously limited, and the use of command directives rather than parametric steering will still be retained.[21]

In Hungary during 1972–1974 there was a widely noted "retrenchment" with regard to its New Economic Mechanism (NEM) introduced in 1968. But the essence of the NEM remains intact, which is "remarkable in view of the extremely unfavorable impact from the foreign sector in 1974–75. . . . The fundamental success of the reforms is demonstrated by their resistance to a powerful set of forces, any of which alone might have brought back central physical allocation, obligatory plan targets and incentives based on them, and all else associated with the 'standard system' of command planning."[22] We might add that if recent statements by Hungarian economists can be taken at face value, Hungary has made a tentative commitment to enlarge gradually the scope of the NEM by 1980, notably in the foreign trade and foreign exchange area.[23] One may speculate that the Hungarian NEM might possibly then serve as a model for a new reform movement in at least some East European countries.

The countries of the Northern Tier have followed a pattern of increased indebtedness to the West in recent years. This may have implications for Soviet foreign policy if Moscow is regarded as the ultimate guarantor of these countries' repayment obligations, as will be considered in the concluding section.

The GDR increased its debts sharply during the last few years, due to a combination of internal developments (the increased appetite for Western machinery, grain, and other investment and consumption goods) and external problems (skyrocketing import prices in 1974, lower Western demand for exports in 1975, and slowed Soviet deliveries of industrial materials and grains). More than 20 percent of its nearly $5 billion debt at the end of 1976 consisted of net liabilities to the FRG, a portion of which remains under the special, interest-free "swing credit" arrangement.[24]

Czechoslovakia has traditionally followed a conservative borrowing policy since 1968, meaning not that it shunned Western credits entirely but that it borrowed relatively small amounts until 1974. During 1974–1975 it faced the same adverse external developments as the other East European countries and its debts rose sharply, a trend that continued during 1976 when it was the only East European country whose exports to the West declined and whose imports continued to rise. Its debts rose further in 1977. Thus this once conservative country no longer lags behind the rest of Eastern Europe in terms of orders of magnitude of indebtedness to the West, the result apparently of unforeseen developments rather than deliberate policy.

Poland, with a debt at the end of 1977 estimated to have reached $13 billion, ran large deficits since 1972 partly as a result of a deliberate new policy by Gierek and partly as a consequence of unforeseen domestic as well as external developments. The unforeseen domestic development was that the investment boom got out of hand, an issue on which Fallenbuchl offers a most interesting insight:

> The excessively high rate of investment happened not because of an increased degree of autonomy of economic organizations [the reason Portes gives for the large fluctuations of investment in Hungary], but because there was a general expansionary attitude at all levels of the administrative structure. . . . There also seemed to appear a tendency for . . . a "multi-center direction of the economy," with the Central Planning Commission, the Central Committee and the Presidium of the Council of Ministers each making its own decision in response to different pressures from local party and state authorities, the industrial branch ministries, and lobbying by various managers of economic organizations. [Everyone attempted] to "hook on to the plan," . . . on the basis of unrealistically low estimates [of investment costs], knowing well that once the project is included in the plan, it will subsequently receive all that is needed for its completion.[25]

In 1975, huge deficits were incurred due in part to a record 7 million tons of grain and fodder imports required by shortfalls in domestic production and the suspension of Soviet deliveries due to Moscow's own grain problems. An even larger deficit was incurred in 1976 due to continued large imports of Western grain and machinery and reduction of coal and meat exports to alleviate potentially explosive shortages after the ill-advised large increases in consumer prices were cancelled. Today Poland reportedly has some difficulty in servicing and arranging credits and has to pay a higher interest than most other East European countries.[26] A fundamental question that remains for Poland is whether its leadership is unified enough and whether it has enough credibility with the population to find a new course to lead the country out of its current serious economic difficulties.

Hungary has been reasonably conservative in its policy on Western credits. Still, lack of effective control over investments and large deterioration in its terms of trade during 1974–1975 created large deficits, financed largely through commercial bank loans. A further factor has been a deliberate policy of continuing the improvement in the standard of living — for political as well as for economic reasons — which meant greater imports and smaller exports than if a policy of "growth at any price" had been followed. Stringent and apparently successful measures were introduced in 1976–1977 to reduce the deficit, although the indebtedness continued to grow.

Prospects

Two of the common, and in several countries the most serious, problems that remain to be solved are: (1) how to correct the economic imbalance created by the rapid rise in hard-currency indebtedness and other obligations; and (2) how to improve the efficiency of production, since productivity must generate a larger share of growth to compensate for slowdowns in the rate of growth of factor inputs — capital and labor. The two problems are interrelated.

Meeting foreign obligations and commitments — whether to the West for servicing the debt or to the USSR for investment participation or debt service — involves a faster rate of growth of national income produced than national income domestically used. But additions to domestically available national income are an important source of new investment as well as increased consumption. The latter is also, indirectly, a factor of production because increased consumer goods serve as incentives to elicit improved performance by labor.

A first approximation of the repayment burdens of East European countries on their hard-currency debts is their debt-service ratio (share of hard-currency exports that must be devoted to interest and repayment of principal and thus is unavailable to pay for current imports). At the end of 1976, the ratios of the East European countries were estimated as:[27]

Bulgaria	.85
Poland	.60
Hungary	.44
Rumania	.42
GDR	.40
Czechoslovakia	.31

Thus the figure for Bulgaria means that 85 percent of its hard-currency exports at the end of 1976 were used to service its hard-currency debt. (Bulgaria also has, to be sure, revenues from such "invisible" exports as tourism and shipping.)

The debt service burden is reflected in the plans and recent policy changes of these countries. For example, in Bulgaria in July 1976 the Central Committee Plenum adopted a new stabilization policy, mobilizing the entire party apparatus to solve problems of waste and overinvestment. The plans of 1977 projected a rise in produced national income of 8.2 percent versus domestically utilized national income of 4.5 percent.[28]

Poland also plans to start repaying loans during the current five-year plan. During 1971–1975 utilized national income grew by 12 percent per annum while produced national income grew by less than 10 percent; the plans for 1976–1980 project a 4.8 percent utilized versus 7 percent produced national income growth per annum ratio.[29] The situation is similar in Rumania, where utilized national income is scheduled to increase by 8 percent per year versus produced national income at more than 10 percent.

One country that is affected particularly adversely by a combination of worsening price developments, the investment participation required in the USSR, and the hard-currency debt service burden is the GDR. The reasoning and quantification by an expert on East Germany of what these developments signal for the GDR is of particular interest, for the methodology—which is applicable to the other East European countries—as well as for the specific figures he derives:

In 1970 . . . the share of exports and imports was about 31 percent each of NMP. [But by 1975 the deterioration in terms of trade meant] that to balance imports quantity-wise, exports would have to rise by another 15 percent . . . nearly 5 percent of NMP, nearly 4 percent of GNP.

Without any other changes in the price level on Western markets, we know that prices on CMEA markets are going to adjust to the present Western prices by the end of the decade. Assuming that the total deterioration in the terms of trade will amount to 20 percent, the damage by 1980 will be [somewhat more than] 6 percent of NMP if the ratio of imports in NMP does not change. [But if] foreign trade continues to increase at a rate 60 percent faster than NMP, and NMP rises by 26 percent [as planned] by 1980, imports should rise by over 40 percent to some 35 percent of NMP, and the damage in terms of growth of exports will amount to 7 percent of the 1980 NMP.

[But] balancing accounts in 1980 is not sufficient. Assuming that (1) the GDR leadership wants debts [to the West] to remain at their present [1975] level in 1980, and that only additional deficits amassed during the first two years of the present FYP are to be repaid during the final two years; and (2) participation [by the GDR in projects in the USSR] of 8 billion marks over the 1976–80 FYP at annual rates, [we can] sum up all the increases [required] in exports: 7 percent to balance trade at the [worsened] terms of trade, 2 percent to keep the deficit at the present level, and 1 percent for investment in CMEA, altogether 10 percent of 1980 NMP will be used up by increased exports. Any smaller room for increasing the export surplus means an increase in indebtedness; any larger share, a reduction of indebtedness.[30]

The East European countries plan to meet the hard-currency payment pressures and deteriorating terms of trade by increasing exports rather than by restricting imports. The question is whether exports can in fact be increased as rapidly as planned. This depends in part on economic conditions and commercial policies in the main Western countries, on the exporting countries' ability to produce high-quality goods readily marketable for hard currency, and on Soviet willingness to supply energy and other inputs.

Whether an export surplus can be generated with or without a cutback in imports, a sizable export surplus means, ceteris paribus, a slowdown in the growth rate of utilized national income. This in turn suggests that the growth rate of consumption will fall, unless investments are drastically curtailed. Crucial for these countries' future prospects is an assesssment of how the population will react. Soviet actions can amplify or cushion the expected slowing (or possible reduction) in the growth of consumption. Preliminary evidence suggests that the Soviets would lean, for political reasons, toward cushioning a decline by letting East European countries run up debts to be repaid in the 1980s or by reducing the amount of resources required to invest in projects in the USSR. Both of these actions would free exports to the West.

Regarding the second problem of improving the efficiency of the economy, all countries face difficulties. The systematic and organizational obstacles to improved efficiency are well-known problems. To improve productivity, a renewed emphasis has been placed in all countries on reducing the share of labor-, material-, and fuel-intensive products in output, on technological innovation, and on expanding industrial cooperation with Western countries.

The Political Economy of East Europe–Soviet Relations

Overview

The most significant general factor in the relations between the Soviet Union and the countries of Eastern Europe is the large disparity between the population, territory, resource endowment, and military power of the USSR and those of the countries of East Europe, individually and collectively. Given these differences, and given Soviet policy, intrabloc relations involving the USSR are inevitably asymmetrical. They are, in the most general terms, marked by the dominance of a superpower and the dependence of six relatively small client states. Yugoslavia's relationship with the Soviet Union has differed in substance from that of the other six since the Stalin-Tito break in the early 1950s, when Yugoslavia first became politically and economically independent from the USSR and subsequently reestablished relations, carefully guarding its independence. The USSR and Albania severed practically all relationships in the early 1960s.

Any relationship of asymmetrical interdependence offers opportunities for the strong to take advantage of the weak. In the political-military sphere the six East European nations have certainly been subordinated to the Soviet Union. An interesting question is, therefore: Has the Soviet Union also asserted its power to dominate the East European countries economically? Has the Soviet Union exploited its political-military position for its own economic advantage? The logic of the situation would seem to support an affirmative answer, as do the well-documented cases of economic coercion by the Soviets under Stalin and of Soviet military intervention in East Germany in 1953, in Hungary in 1956, and in Czechoslovakia in 1968.

Until after Stalin's death in 1953, the Soviet Union's political domination of East Europe was accompanied by conventional types of economic extraction, taking the form of reparations transfers (mainly from East Germany and also from Bulgaria, Hungary, Rumania, and, indirectly, from Poland), so-called joint-stock companies in East Europe through which the Soviets took some of these countries' resources, and by the Soviets' paying unfairly low prices for East European exports (particularly well-documented in the case of Poland). The size ($14 billion) of the unrequited flow of resources from East Europe to the Soviet Union was approximately equivalent to the flow of resources from the United States to West Europe under the Marshall Plan, with East Germany shouldering the brunt of the burden.[31]

The economic relationship between the Soviet Union and East Europe, after Stalin, changed substantially. Since the mid-1950s, the Soviet Union apparently has not been obtaining large unrequited resource transfers from East Europe. In fact, some specialists argue that until 1975 the USSR had been paying an increasingly steep price for the continued dependence of the East European countries on the Soviet Union. This net cost to the Soviets is said to be reflected in adverse and deteriorating terms of trade until 1975 and in an unfavorable commodity composition of that trade. That is, a large share of Soviet exports to East Europe consists of energy and raw materials that the Soviets could readily sell to the West for hard currency with which to buy urgently needed machinery and other commodities from Western countries, goods the East European countries are unable to supply to the USSR.

Terms of Trade

During 1971–1974, Soviet–East European terms of trade did not change very much. Soviet crude oil exports to Eastern Europe in 1974, for example, were priced at less than $20/ton, or about one-quarter of the world price. Because of the special pricing system in effect on the CMEA market, under which historical rather than current world market prices are used, the Soviet Union's hypothetical terms of trade with Eastern Europe gradually deteriorated during 1971–1974 by an estimated 30 percent to 40 percent below the levels which would have prevailed if Soviet–East European prices had moved with changes in world prices.[32] Almost all of this "grant" was accounted for by their not following the dramatic rise of oil prices on the world market. This benefited the five oil-importing countries (all but Rumania).

In January 1975, one year before the expiration of the fixed CMEA price agreement, the Soviet Union nearly doubled oil prices to CMEA, providing substantial additional income to the USSR: 1.4 billion transferable rubles (almost $2 billion), equal to total Soviet imports from Hungary in 1975. In that year, energy accounted for 25 percent of Soviet export proceeds from Eastern Europe. The 1975 doubling of oil prices still permitted the five East European countries to buy energy cheaper from the Soviet Union than from the world market.

Using detailed but not fully specified quantity and value data published by the USSR, two experts independently calculated changes in Soviet–East European terms of trade from 1974 to 1975 (see Table 12.8). Depending upon the choice of weights and the small differences in methodologies used, in 1975 Eastern Europe's terms of trade deteriorated vis-à-vis the USSR by 11 percent to 14 percent, with the largest loss suffered by the GDR, Czechoslovakia, and Hungary; a somewhat smaller loss by Bulgaria; and only a 3–4 percent deterioration for Poland and Rumania.

TABLE 12.8

Soviet Export and Import Price Indices and Terms of Trade with
Six East European Countries, 1975

(1974=100)

Partner Country	Soviet Export Prices			Soviet Import Prices			Terms of Trade		
	1974 Weights	1975 Weights A	B	1974 Weights	1975 Weights A	B	1974 Weights	1975 Weights A	B
Bulgaria	139	156	137	130	137	126	107	112	109
Czechoslovakia	142	144	139	123	121	119	115	119	117
GDR	147	154	143	121	125	122	121	125	117
Hungary	140	150	140	126	129	124	110	116	113
Poland	141	151	141	139	144	136	102	104	104
Romania	134	143	131	132	138	127	102	105	103
Six Countries Combined	142	151	140	128	132	126	111	114	111

Sources: 1974 weights and 1974 column A: M.J. Kohn and N.R. Lang, "The Intra-CMEA" Table 1; column B:Raimund
Dietz, "Terms of Trade im sowjetischen Aussenhandel gegenüber den RGW-Landern in Osteuropa" (tentative
title) (Vienna, Austria: Wiener Institut für Internationale Wirtschaftsvergleiche, 1977).

Kohn and Lang calculated that the negative impact of deteriorating terms of trade with the USSR in 1975 in effect forced the four most seriously affected countries to give up resources by amounts equivalent to roughly one percent of GNP for the GDR, Hungary, and Bulgaria, and over .5 percent of GNP for Czechoslovakia.[33]

Further increases in oil prices occurred after 1975, because of the new system of setting intra-CMEA prices on the basis of moving-average world market prices. According to the new price rules reportedly agreed upon, 1975 prices were based on a three-year (1972–1974) world average, changed to a five-year world average in 1976 (1971–1975). Thus 1977 prices were based on 1972–1976 world prices, 1978 prices on 1973–1977 world prices, and so on.

One of the most critical economic questions for Eastern Europe is the Soviet Union's future ability and willingness to supply oil to Eastern Europe. The CIA predicted that unless the Soviet leadership takes some drastic policy action soon, Soviet oil output will peak by 1980 and decline thereafter, so that by the mid-1980s the Soviets may well be forced to import rather than export oil.[34] One of the world's leading experts on Soviet energy, Campbell, believes that the CIA forecast is likely to be proved correct and that

> there is not much that the Soviet oil industry can do to avoid this outcome in the short run. The irony is that the more heroically [they] struggle to get the . . . annual increments the plan calls for, the more desperate they make the situation for the following years [because] their current actions heavily mortgage the prospects for future increments. The industry is getting these outputs by drilling for more wells than called for by the plans, injecting very large volumes of water, and probably diverting drilling meterage from exploration to development.[35]

Campbell sees the Soviets as having three options: (1) continue to drift with respect to energy policy, in which case exports to the East Europeans will have to decline drastically during the early 1980s and the Soviets themselves will have to spend billions of dollars to buy oil (probably an unacceptable option); (2) substantially reduce oil exports to the West (which account for almost 50 percent of Soviet hard-currency earnings), which would force them to modify their current development strategy's reliance on Western technology imports (probably also an unacceptable option); or (3) try to break the energy bottleneck by a massive importation of Western technology for oil exploration, production, refining, transport, and utilization, paying partly with other exports (the most probable option).

The point of going into all of these details is that each of the alternatives described is highly unfavorable for Eastern Europe, the effects varying according to each East European country's energy and hard-currency situation.

> The general implication of the situation described is that these countries can probably expect to receive Soviet oil at the levels fixed for the [current] five year plan, but that this will not grow, and might well decline in the eighties. Thus, they will have to obtain incremental needs, and perhaps seek replacement supplies, on the world market. . . . It seems impossible to escape the conclusion that the countries of Eastern Europe will find their growth prospects depressed by these changes.[36]

Joint CMEA Projects in the USSR

One of the most important items determining resource transfers between the USSR and the six East European countries is East European participation in CMEA investment projects. Since the signing of the Comprehensive Program in 1971 there has been a dramatic increase in the size and number of these projects, with multilateral participation but not joint ownership. The largest projects are located in the USSR. The largest and by far the most important project is the $5 billion (initial cost estimate) Orenburg natural gas pipeline, channeling gas from Soviet fields to Eastern Europe. According to the arrangement, each East European country except Rumania is to build a section of the pipeline (Rumania is to provide only pipe and equipment) and supply labor and above-plan deliveries of equipment, technical services, and the hard currency with which to pay for the pipe and machinery that must be purchased in the West.

The valuation of the individual countries' contribution to the project and the financing arrangements were not published. But it is known that early in 1976, and again in 1977, the International Investment Bank (IIB) of the CMEA borrowed $600 million and $500 million, respectively, on the Eurodollar market for the Orenburg project and provided these funds to the USSR, which has made purchases, largely of pipe, for the entire project. The East Europeans owe the IIB for their share of the Soviet hard-currency purchases and, according to IIB rules, must repay in hard currency at world market rates of interest.

Direct participation by Eastern Europe in construction in distant Soviet territory has proved to be a difficult and very expensive proposition. To compensate for the hardship — and to provide incentives and special support facilities — the wages of a typical worker sent from East Europe to these inhospitable regions of the USSR can be up to five times as much as the worker would be paid at home, making direct labor participation increasingly difficult to justify economically. There are further problems in providing the needed technical services plus labor skilled in pipeline construction. As a consequence, each East European country has reduced its commitment and, except in the case of Poland, much of the actual pipeline construction will be done by the Soviets themselves. Hungarian economists, however, stress that not a reduction but a transformation in the individual country's commitment has been taking place lately. Hungary and some other East European countries are finding that rising national currency costs and lack of specialization in certain tasks — such as the laying of pipelines which each country was supposed to perform in the USSR — makes it more attractive to commission other countries to perform some of the installation (in the case of Hungary, Poland will help out), since the initial contract provides that the signatory countries can redistribute the scope of the tasks among themselves, and to increase the share of the country's direct hard-currency contribution to the USSR in fulfillment of its obligation to the project.

THE ECONOMIC SITUATION IN EASTERN EUROPE AND SOVIET FOREIGN POLICY

As a point of departure for attempting to link economic trends in Eastern Europe with Soviet foreign policy, let us speculate on how the Soviet Union might view economic trends from the point of view of its own economic interests. Some of the trends in Eastern Europe must adversely affect Soviet interests, while others are probably complementary.

Economic Developments Aggravating and Smoothing Soviet–East European Economic Relations, Viewed from the Soviet Perspective

Developments Aggravating Soviet–East European Economic Relations

1. Worsening of the USSR's actual and prospective hard-currency balance of payments because this increases the pressure on the USSR to reorient energy and other "hard good" exports from Eastern Europe to the West. During 1975 the USSR incurred a more than $6 billion hard-currency deficit; in 1976, another $5 billion. Its debt service ratio continues to rise, so evidence suggests that the burden of remaining a large net supplier of hard goods to Eastern Europe is increasing. How large this burden is for the

Soviet Union depends upon the rate of growth of its net hard good exports to Eastern Europe, the current assessment by the Soviet leadership of the contribution of Western imports to its economy, the availability of Western credits (short- and long-term goverment-sponsored and private), and the prospects for increasing Soviet exports to the West.

2. Worsening of the Soviet Union's current and prospective energy balance. More than 25 percent of Soviet exports to Eastern Europe consists of energy, predominantly oil. The rapid worsening of the Soviet energy balance aggravates Soviet–East European economic relations directly, and through its adverse impact on Soviet hard-currency balance of payments.

3. Too high a share of trade with the West. Although it is believed the Soviets do not lay down guidelines or ceilings for the level or share of total trade with the West that is "acceptable," rapid reorientation of trade toward the West probably meets with Soviet disapproval because it increases Western influence. To be sure, the economic benefits to the East European country — and possibly to the USSR itself (see below) — must be welcome. Soviet criticism of Eastern Europe's turning to the West is also probably constrained by the Soviets' own rapid trade expansion with the West.

4. Rapidly growing hard-currency indebtedness of the East European countries. This is almost certainly not to the Soviets' liking for several reasons: (a) it increases Western influence, one form of which is creditors seeking and obtaining more financial information and Western analysts scrutinizing the East European economies more thoroughly; (b) creditors insist more and more on granting further credits only for projects tied to developing exports to the West, which preempts some of Eastern Europe's valuable resources for the West; (c) heavy indebtedness may increase the leverage of Western governments in East European countries, leverage that may be used to gain political concessions from them; (d) servicing the debt may require Soviet assistance in the form of hard-currency grants or loans (allegedly granted to Bulgaria in the late 1960s as emergency aid) or by permitting the debtor country to redirect to the West hard good exports earmarked for the Soviet Union; (e) default or forced rescheduling (which is more likely) of the debt would impair the Soviet Union's own credit rating (economic cost) and would demonstrate a lack of economic and political cohesion in the Soviet bloc (political cost).

There is little doubt that, for the reasons stated, large and rapidly growing hard-currency indebtedness by Eastern Europe increases

Soviet–East European tensions, although the extent to which the Soviets can (publicly or even privately) "blame" an East European country probably is constrained by the Soviets' own borrowings from the West, and also depends on the perception as to whether the increase in debt was caused by circumstances beyond the control of the decision makers in the East European country (such as, for example, a sharp deterioration of the terms of trade, Western recession, or the Soviets' own inability or unwillingness to supply needed commodities, forcing the East European country to turn to the West) or due more to irresponsible policies of the country. (We analyzed this issue briefly in Section 1.)

5. Irresponsible experimentation with "dangerous" economic reforms. It would be overly simplistic to argue that the Soviets uncompromisingly oppose economic reforms in Eastern Europe. Their attitude is probably influenced by their leadership's own cost-benefit assessment of reforms in general; by whether any given reform measure is viewed as a pilot experiment whose outcome might be relevant to their own economy or those of other East European countries; and by whether the reforms are assessed as having undesirable political consequences, such as dangerously weakening the control of the party.

6. Permitting equity joint ventures with Western firms. Since up to now the Soviets have rejected equity joint ventures (but accept the principle of contractual joint ventures) with Western firms in their own country (most likely for ideological reasons), they probably look unfavorably upon such ventures entered into by Yugoslavia since 1967 and Rumania and Hungary since 1972. This may be one reason why the latter two countries have been proceeding cautiously in this regard.

7. Uncooperative attitude toward participation in joint CMEA projects the Soviet Union considers important, namely those located in the USSR.

8. Poor quality East European exports to the USSR. Soviet complaints are often heard about problems with the quality and modernity of East European machinery as well as consumer manufactures exports.

9. Subsidies requested by East European countries with a notably higher standard of living than the median standard in the USSR (or even European Russia). Resentment is surely felt, if not by the top leadership at least by the thin layer of informed public opinion. Yet the Soviets appear to be ready to support, grudgingly, a policy of rising consumption even in the GDR because of the politically im-

portant competition the GDR is engaged in with the FRG and because rising consumption is viewed as contributing to political stability in Eastern Europe.

10. Soviet terms of trade with Eastern Europe that are less advantageous to the USSR than the hypothetical terms of trade would be if current world market prices were used.

Developments Smoothing Soviet–East European Economic Relations

1. The opposite, or the reversal, of developments aggravating these relations, in 1–10 above.
2. East European countries serving as channels transmitting to the Soviet Union Western know-how, technology, and products. As a rule, this takes the form of incorporating Western imports and technology into products sold by these countries to the USSR. (This is an issue on which little factual work has been done in the West up to now.)
3. East European countries contributing resources to carry out Soviet objectives outside the region, such as economic and military aid to the less developed, centrally planned Third World economies.
4. Agreements to settle so-called "above quota" hard good exports in hard currency because the USSR tends to be a net supplier of such goods to Eastern Europe.
5. Low-interest credits by the East European countries to the Soviet Union to participate, on a bilateral or multilateral basis, in investment projects located in the USSR.

Developments Whose Impact on
Soviet–East European Relations Is Not Clear

1. Subregional integration among the East European countries. To the extent that such effort makes good economic sense, it strengthens the participating countries and may reduce need for Soviet subsidy, so the Soviets should support it. But we know that Stalin viewed with great suspicion all such efforts, afraid of sowing the seeds of potential anti-Soviet policies. How the current leadership views subregional integration is not clear.
2. East European countries joining international organizations, such as the IMF, the World Bank, and GATT. The economic benefit that membership provides is probably viewed positively, the strengthening of Western influence, negatively.
3. Substantial increase in West-East and East-West tourism. An inflow

of Western tourists provides needed foreign exchange, but it, as well as East European tourists going to the West in large numbers, makes those economies more "open" and their people more skeptical about Soviet propaganda claims.

Implications for Soviet Foreign Policy with Regard to Eastern Europe[37]

The primary Soviet *motive* (interest) with regard to Eastern Europe is to control the individual countries and the region for the military, political, and ideological gains this yields to the USSR. The principal Soviet objectives here are *strategic*: control of the East European buffer region denies it to any other great power and can serve as a springboard in case of Soviet military engagement in Western Europe; *political*: control of Eastern Europe serves to validate Moscow's credentials as leader of one of the two principal alliance systems in the world; and *ideological*: control of Eastern Europe under a one-party "socialist" rule represents an extension of the Soviet social system, important in view of the fact that the Soviet Union does not consider itself merely a state but a representative of a particular form of social and economic organization that has universal validity and application.[38]

From the Soviet perspective, economic considerations in relations with Eastern Europe are probably secondary — or derivative — whereas from Eastern Europe's perspective, they are of overriding importance. Although immediately after World War II the Soviet Union had — along with military, political, and ideological objectives — economic designs on the region (namely, to obtain a net flow of advanced technology and other goods), more recently economics has become an important instrument — *a means of control* — by which to enforce Soviet military, political, and ideological objectives there. At a minimum, Eastern Europe's economic dependence on the USSR serves as leverage designed to influence — or possibly veto — certain policies or actions in those countries without having to intervene militarily, which the Soviets clearly consider an undesirable action of last resort.

Soviet *power* to maintain control of East European governments and to press its demands for their help in implementing Soviet foreign policy objectives outside the region is based, in the last resort, on the presence of the Soviet armed forces and the demonstrated willingness to use them. But because the cost to the Soviet Union of using its army to repress movements in the region is high, a high priority is almost certainly assigned to preventing a situation in Eastern Europe from "deteriorating" to a point where the Red Army would have to be actively used again to maintain control. Hence, the Soviet leaders must welcome the economic leverage that dependence creates and use it as an instrument of control. If the preservation of Eastern Europe's economic dependence on the Soviet Union involves costs — and at the moment it apparently does — these are probably viewed as the costs of empire maintenance. The nature of the costs, and how one might go about quantifying it, were outlined above.[39]

That the Soviet Union worries about the *risks* of following certain policies vis-à-vis Eastern Europe is certain. One risk the Soviet leadership tries to avoid is the harm that could result from exercising power too exploitatively, or simply in a clumsy way. As they look back on what happened in Yugoslavia in the early 1950s and in Albania and Rumania in the 1960s, they probably conclude that increased sophistication in exercising control is essential if Soviet actions are not to help create — or cement — a united national front against Soviet domination and control.

Another risk the leadership seems to be concerned about is inaction — standing idly by — while seemingly innocuous trends in Eastern Europe develop into crises threatening Soviet control of the region. Trends the Soviet leadership must be concerned about include: consumer dissatisfaction that could snowball into antigovernment riots; dissident intellectual movements that could develop into anti-Communist political movements; growing economic dependence on and interaction with the West that could lead to a dangerously high level of ideological contamination; and excessive dependence on Western creditors that in case of actual or potential default could lead to a serious embarrassment of or financial drain on the Soviet Union.

Soviet conduct in Eastern Europe in the 1970s suggests that the leadership is trying the minimize the risks of harm that could result either from exercising power in a too heavy-handed manner or from lack of response to potentially explosive trends.

That the Soviet Union calculates the cost-benefit tradeoffs of its policy in East Europe is suggested by the fact that it does not push the region's economic dependence on the USSR to its limit, which could be very costly. In fact, it is trying to minimize these costs without unduly weakening the leverage it maintains through dependence. (Paradoxically, an East European country's economic dependence on the USSR increases as the country approaches the [self-imposed or Western-imposed] limits of its indebtedness to the West.)

More direct evidence of cost-benefit calculation by the Soviets is their recent urging that the East European countries reduce their ambitious growth rates in 1976–1980. The Soviets must reason that a somewhat less impressive economic performance by these countries would be "traded" for the more tangible benefit of lower demand for Soviet energy and raw materials, for all types of imports from the West, and for an increased supply of exports, which would moderate Eastern Europe's balance of payments problems vis-à-vis the USSR as well as the West.

With respect to *opportunities* to formulate new policies vis-à-vis Eastern Europe or to implement existing policies more effectively, the current and near-term future environment does not seem particularly auspicious for the USSR. Current Soviet policies appear to be "drifting" and may be characterized as defensive rather than imaginative and forceful. That is, the Soviet Union seems to be responding, defensively and uncertainly, to events and trends in the region. To be sure, it has one clear objective — prevent the loss of control — but it appears that it is not able to forestall a gradual erosion of control in some countries. What we are observing reflects the age — tiredness — of the Soviet leadership, the increased complexity of the situation in Eastern Europe, and perhaps also a disagreement among Soviet leaders over policy.

Implications for Soviet Foreign Policy
Outside Eastern Europe

These implications are more difficult to discern and are speculative. The following implications for Soviet foreign policy outside Eastern Europe may be drawn.

1. The Soviet leaders' perception of policy success, failure, or simply the cost and difficulty of implementation in any region, including Eastern Europe, is likely to be an important determinant of current and prospective future policies, just as Vietnam taught the United States that a policy of direct intervention must be avoided. What might the Soviets have learned in Eastern Europe that could shape their foreign policy outside that region?

As they look back on what happened in Yugoslavia in the early 1950s, Hungary in the mid-1950s, Albania and Rumania in the early 1960s (and Egypt in the early 1970s), the Soviets probably conclude that their interests will be harmed if Soviet power is imposed and exercised vis-à-vis any country too brutally, exploitatively, or simply in a clumsy way. Their experience in Eastern Europe should tend to make them seek an arsenal of more sophisticated instruments for exercising power vis-à-vis potential or actual client countries. This arsenal may consist of improving knowledge about the modus operandi of client states and their elites, and creating and effectively using economic, military, or political leverage. If so, this new sophistication probably creates the appearance of a moderation in Soviet foreign policy, which would also be consistent with the USSR's objectives regarding détente policy.

2. The more the Soviet Union wants détente — principally for the economic benefits this policy yields by creating an environment under

which East-West trade, technology transfer, and credits can flow more readily—the more inclined it will be to avoid actions that could fundamentally damage détente. While the Soviet leadership has an option on whether or not, and to what degree, it wishes to harness Western trade, technology, and credits, its most likely option is continued and possibly increased economic involvement with the West, as indicated above in the discussion of why Soviet oil supply problems worry Eastern Europe.

Increased economic instability in Eastern Europe poses a danger for Soviet détente policy for the following reasons: if economic problems in an East European country worsen (for example, consumer goods shortages increase or retail prices are raised substantially in Poland), such developments might trigger demonstrations or uprisings that may take an antigovernment, possibly antiregime, turn. Such developments would probably prompt the Soviet Union to intervene militarily. Such intervention, especially if it resulted in bloodshed, would probably fundamentally damage if not destroy for a certain period the environment of détente.

3. Soviet attitude toward the Eurocommunist movement, which is probably shaped in part by Soviet concern over Eurocommunism's impact on Eastern Europe. Eurocommunism differs from Soviet Communism in that the former rejects the dictatorship of the proletariat, formulates a national road to socialism, and criticizes Soviet policies in Eastern Europe. The more the Soviet leadership is concerned with centrifugal political tendencies in the region—to which independent economic policies tend to contribute—the more it is forced to take a hard-line attitude toward Eurocommunist movements. How can it appear to sanction "revisionist" views of the Communist party of one country and condemn similar views of the Communist party of another—East European—country?

4. Perhaps the most direct link between East European economies and Soviet foreign policy outside the region is that Eastern Europe can help to promote Soviet *global* foreign policy ends in two ways. One of these is psychological:

> Soviet control of Eastern Europe serves to validate Moscow's credentials as a regional power, as a leader of a group of states, and as a leader of one of the two principal alliance and political systems in the world. . . . The United States and the Soviet Union are the only two alliance leaders in the world today, and a certain amount of prestige is derived from that particular role. Furthermore, much of the Soviet Union's prestige in international affairs derives from the fact that it is the leader of a group of states.[40]

The other aspect is economic. East European governments provide valued support—individually and through the CMEA—in behalf of Soviet diplomatic, economic, and military objectives throughout the world. This includes supporting the less developed Communist movements or countries, like Mongolia, where the CMEA governments were to assist by helping to construct more than 240 projects during 1976–1980;[41] aiding Cuba, possibly on a stepped-up scale since Cuban soldiers have been sent on military missions to Africa; helping North Vietnam during the war and now during its reconstruction; and absorbing and aiding a significant number of refugee families from Chile, to mention just a few examples. The point is simply that these efforts tend to serve Soviet rather than East European foreign policy interests. Such assistance is valued by the USSR not only for the resource contribution it makes to Soviet efforts but also because in certain situations the Soviet Union may prefer to act through a proxy rather than directly, either because this is more efficient (if the East European country has a special skill or its presence is more acceptable to the target country) or because the Soviet Union derives propaganda benefits from an "international" effort. Such internationalization also makes the Soviet effort less visible and creates less chances of conflict with the United States. For example, in deviation from its past practice, the Soviet Union agreed to grant aid to Mexico and Iraq under the auspices of CMEA, and CMEA conducted negotiations for a similar aid treaty with Angola.[42] The East European countries are increasingly active also in the Third World, especially in Soviet foreign policy targets such as Iraq and Angola. (To be sure, one cannot deny that economic and even aid relations might be motivated also by Eastern Europe's own long-term economic interest.)

In 1973 the IIB established a "Special Fund" of one billion transferable rubles for financing projects in the Third World. Although little if any of these funds have been disbursed up to now, if and when they are activated, the allocation of funds is likely to be consistent with Soviet political interests. Special aid and cooperation agreements in recent years between the CMEA and other countries indicate an emerging global strategy on the part of the CMEA. Some examples are the agreements with Finland and Mexico; negotiations with Colombia, Guyana, and Angola about signing such agreements; and expressions of interest about entering into formal economic relations with Afghanistan, Argentina, India, Iran, and Jamaica.

While one may argue that such a strategy makes sense from the point of view of each country's economic interest, others contend that these agreements represent one manifestation of

a quest by the Soviet Union for strategic, political, economic and last but not least, "ecumenical" influence as the leader of the world "progressive forces." In other words [Soviet] strategy has shifted, from securing the [East European] region for its own value, to transforming it into a staging area for further expansion, with East Europeans playing a role of junior partners in the endeavor.[43]

Notes

1. Much of the discussion is based on information contained in U.S. Congress, Joint Economic Committee, *East European Economies Post-Helsinki* (Washington, D.C.: U.S. Government Printing Office, 1977). Parts of this essay follow closely the wording of the author's contribution to that volume, "Economic Performance, Strategy, and Prospects in Eastern Europe." Parts are also based on the author's "East European Economies: Achievements, Problems, Prospects," in Teresa Rakowska-Harmstone and Andrew Gyorgy, eds., *Communism in Eastern Europe* (Bloomington: Indiana University Press, 1979).

2. The official NMP figures measure, in constant prices, gross output by sector less material costs, excluding the so-called nonmaterial service sectors. The recalculated GNP figures measure aggregate economic activity, including the service sectors, by summing indices of sectoral output in constant prices using factor cost weights. Because NMP and GNP differ in coverage, methodology, and bases of valuation, the two series are not expected to present the same picture on performance.

3. Growth of inputs is difficult to separate from growth of productivity. One reason is that a dollar's worth of new machinery or a worker newly entering the labor force may be more productive than machinery already in place or workers already in the work force. Another problem is that the growth of productivity is measured as a "residual," i.e., the difference between growth of output and growth of inputs. Hence statistics on productivity will be especially vulnerable to the formidable measurement problems of both output and input as well as the weighting used to determine the rate of growth of combined capital and labor inputs.

4. Little systematic information on inputs is available for Albania. Most other countries have gaps in coverage and poor quality data. But the biggest problem by far is that the definitions and methodologies of calculation are not standardized among the countries, so that in most cases meaningful statistical comparisons cannot be made. This is why, even for a given country, alternative estimates of capital stock and growth of inputs and productivity often differ widely, depending on the (often unstated) definitions, the relative prices used as weights, and so on.

5. The exceptions are: Poland, where total employment has increased by 2 percent or more since 1960 because of a combination of demographic factors, increased participation rates in agriculture, and the movement of younger people from agriculture to industry and construction; Albania, for which no information is available, but rapid employment growth can be deduced from the exceptionally rapid increase in population (Table 12.2) and the rapid rise in the labor participation rates of women; and Yugoslavia, where during 1971–1975 a combination of the rapid increase in the labor supply and government policy had created substantial new domestic employment. This recent situation contrasts with the 1965–1970

period when the labor supply also increased rapidly (by about 5 percent per annum) but employment in the socialist sector grew by less than 1 percent per year. This caused a large number of Yugoslavs to seek employment outside the country (emigration, primarily to Western Europe, provided twice as many new jobs as domestic employment) or to become unemployed.

6. Thad P. Alton, "Comparative Structure and Growth of Economic Activity in Eastern Europe," in JEC, *East European Economies Post-Helsinki*, pp. 247–248.

7. For a comprehensive survey of the Western perspective on lending to centrally planned economies, see Paul Marer, ed., *U.S. Financing of East-West Trade: The Political Economy of Government Credits and the National Interest* (Bloomington, Ind.: International Development Institute and Indiana University Press, 1975).

8. Price indices for earlier periods are shown in Paul Marer, *Postwar Pricing and Price Patterns in Socialist Foreign Trade (1946–1971)* (Bloomington, Ind.: International Development Research Center (IDRC) Report 1, 1972).

9. There is some question whether socialist "dollar" trade is only priced at current world prices or is also settled through hard-currency payments. For Hungary, dollar trade evidently means current prices, not settlement in hard currency, at least in its trade with the USSR.

10. Thomas A. Wolf, "East-West European Trade Relations," in JEC, *East European Economies Post-Helsinki*, Table 3.

11. See Marvin Jackson, "Industrialization, Trade, and Mobilization in Romania's Drive for Economic Independence," in ibid.

12. Laura D'Andrea Tyson, "The Yugoslav Economy in the 1970's: A Survey of Recent Developments and Future Prospects," in ibid., p. 946.

13. See Michael Kaser and Adi Schnytzer, "Albania—A Uniquely Socialist Economy," in ibid.

14. The Soviets have given Bulgaria substantial aid in various forms. For example, it gave several large, long-term, subsidized credits at an average interest charge of 2 percent—some in hard currency—totaling 2.3 billion rubles in 1970. See K. Pecsi et al., *As europai szocialista orszagok gazdasaga* (Budapest: Kossuth, 1975), p. 388. The figure cited is probably in "old" rubles, in which case it converts into $575 million. Pecsi also mentions that Soviet deliveries to Bulgaria have always fitted exactly the requirements of the rapidly developing Bulgarian economy. No similar statement is made in discussing Soviet economic relations with the other East European countries.

15. See Mark Allen, "The Bulgarian Economy in the 1970's," in JEC, *East European Economies Post-Helsinki*, pp. 676–682.

16. William F. Kolarik, "Statistical Abstract of East-West Trade Finance," in U.S. Congress, Joint Economic Committee, *Issues in East-West Commercial Relations* (Washington, D.C.: U.S. Government Printing Office, 1979), Table 10, p. 201.

17. See Allen, "The Bulgarian Economy in the 1970's," in JEC, *East-European Economies Post-Helsinki*.

18. See Tyson, "The Yugoslav Economy in the 1970's," in ibid.

19. See Kaser and Schnytzer, "Albania—A Uniquely Socialist Economy," in ibid.

20. See Michael Keren, "The Return of the Ancien Regime: The GDR in the 1970's," in ibid.

21. Zbigniew M. Fallenbuchl, "The Polish Economy in the 1970's," in ibid., p. 858.

22. Richard Portes, "Hungary: Economic Performance, Policy and Prospects," in ibid., p. 788.

23. Personal interviews with Hungarian and Polish economists, April 1977 and March 1978.

24. Joan C. Zoeter, "Eastern Europe: The Growing Hard-Currency Debt," in JEC, *East European Economies Post-Helsinki*, p. 1358.

25. Fallenbuchl, "The Polish Economy in the 1970's," in ibid., pp. 850–851.

26. Lawrence Theriot, "Communist Country Hard Currency Debt in Perspective," in JEC, *Issues in East-West Commercial Relations*, Table 3, p. 184.

27. See Zoeter, "Eastern Europe: The Growing Hard-Currency Debt," in JEC, *East European Economies Post-Helsinki*, Table 10.

28. See Allen, "The Bulgarian Economy in the 1970's," in ibid., p. 661.

29. See Fallenbuchl, "The Polish Economy in the 1970's," in ibid., p. 857.

30. Keren, "The Return of the Ancien Regime: The GDR in the 1970s's," in ibid., pp. 744–745.

31. For details, see Paul Marer, "Soviet Economic Policy in Eastern Europe," in U.S. Congress, Joint Economic Committee, *Reorientation and Commercial Relations of the Countries of Eastern Europe* (Washington, D.C.: U.S. Government Printing Office, 1974).

32. Martin J. Kohn and Nicholas R. Lang, "The Intra-CMEA Foreign Trade System: Major Price Changes, Little Reform," in JEC, *East European Economies Post-Helsinki*, p. 139.

33. Ibid.

34. U.S. Central Intelligence Agency, *The International Energy Situation: Outlook to 1985* (Washington, D.C., 1977).

35. Robert W. Campbell, "Implications for the Soviet Economy of Soviet Energy Prospects," *The ACES Bulletin* 20, no. 1 (Spring 1978):37–52.

36. Ibid., p. 38.

37. Vernon Aspaturian suggested a useful framework for analyzing the variables shaping Soviet foreign policy. The key concepts in his framework are: purposes and intentions (i.e., goals and readiness to act); capabilities and power (the means whereby demand is pressed or policies carried out); risk (subjective assessment of results from following a certain course of action or inaction); cost/benefit calculation; and opportunities (when intentions, capabilities, risks, and cost intersect fortuitously to maximize the possibility of realizing goals at a minimum cost). See Vernon V. Aspaturian, *Process and Power in Soviet Foreign Policy* (Boston: Little, Brown and Co., 1971), pp. 56–81.

38. Vernon Aspaturian, "Has Eastern Europe Become a Liability to the Soviet Union? — The Political-Ideological Aspects," in Charles Gati, ed., *The International Politics of Eastern Europe* (New York: Praeger Publishers, 1976), pp. 23–25.

39. For a more detailed discussion of the issues, facts, and reasoning, see Paul

Paul Marer

Marer, "Has Eastern Europe Become a Liability to the Soviet Union? — The Economic Aspects," in ibid.

40. Vernon Aspaturian, "Eastern Europe in World Perspective," in T. Rakowska-Harmstone and A. Gyorgy, eds., *Communism in Eastern Europe.*

41. S. A. Skachkov, "Soviet Aid to Mongolia Activated," *Ekonomicheskaya gazeta,* July 1977, JPRS trans. 69878, p. 12. This reference was pointed out by Stephen J. Millar, a student at Carleton University.

42. *The Soviet Union and the Third World: A Watershed in Great Power Policy?* Report to the Committee on International Relations, House of Representatives (Washington, D.C.: U.S. Government Printing Office, 1977), p. 131.

43. Teresa Rakowska-Harmstone, "Nationalism and Integration in Eastern Europe: The Dynamics of Change," in Rakowska-Harmstone and Gyorgy, eds., *Communism in Eastern Europe.*

13
Eastern Europe as an Internal Determinant of Soviet Foreign Policy

Andrzej Korbonski

It is now commonplace to assert that the relationship between the Soviet Union and the smaller East European countries has undergone several metamorphoses in the past twenty-five years. The Stalinist monolithic bloc or, if one prefers, the Moscow-ruled satellite empire, gave way in the late 1950s to a "socialist commonwealth of nations" that in turn has been replaced in recent years by a more conventional political-military-economic alliance. The change has been accompanied by a transformation of the power relationship between the core and the periphery, or between the Soviet Union and its six junior partners in Eastern Europe.[1] The power configuration in which all policies originated in Moscow, which maintained an absolute monopoly on decision making, has now become a more complex relationship with lines of authority somewhat blurred.

It would be tempting to view the nature of current relations between the Soviet Union and Eastern Europe as interdependent rather than as primarily dependent. However, any alliance — even one as asymmetrical as the Warsaw Pact — involves some degree of interdependence and therefore this concept is not very helpful in explaining the relationship in the late 1970s contrasted to that of thirty years earlier. A much more useful description is that of a dependency that has been called "a highly asymmetric form of interdependence" and that assumes some reciprocity on the part of the actors.[2]

Regardless of whether the Warsaw Pact is institutionalized dependency or interdependence between the USSR and Eastern Europe, whether the Soviet Union considers itself the undisputed leader of a political-military alliance willing to some extent to bear the cost of managing it, or whether the relationship between the Soviet Union and Eastern Europe may be called "organic" or "inorganic,"[3] it may be taken for granted that Soviet policies — both external and internal — have been, at least since the death of Stalin, influenced to some degree by domestic developments in the various East European countries.

The purpose of this chapter is to identify and analyze the various noneconomic linkages between the smaller East European countries and the Soviet Union. This is not easy as the borderline between politics and economics in all societies, but especially in Communist societies, tends to be fuzzy. Furthermore, economics rather than politics appears to be one of the strongest glues currently holding the alliance together.[4] Still there is no doubt that noneconomic factors influence the Soviet–East European relationship and their impact should not be underestimated, as illustrated, for example, by the case of Czechoslovakia in 1968 or Poland in 1970.

No attempt will be made here to develop a theoretical framework of influence transmission or innovation diffusion from Eastern Europe to the Soviet Union. This has been thoroughly analyzed by Zvi Gitelman and his pioneering work can hardly be improved.[5] It will be taken as an axiom that such transmission does indeed take place and the major objective of this chapter will be to discuss the two types of linkages and influences (political and strategic-military), to trace the manner in which they act as determinants of Soviet behavior on the international scene, and to speculate on how they are likely to evolve in the future.

Although it may be presumed that the influence of the smaller Warsaw Pact allies has been most visible with regard to Moscow's policy toward Eastern Europe, it may also be assumed that Soviet policy toward the West, the Third World, and the rest of the Communist camp outside Europe has not been unaffected by the presence of a formal, Moscow-led alliance in Europe. Therefore an effort will be made to trace the impact of that alliance and the changes therein on the conduct of Soviet foreign policy. The various linkages, channels, and processes will be mentioned briefly here — an in-depth analysis of the Soviet–East European dependence would require a separate treatment.

The past two decades have witnessed a major transformation of East European societies. They have been subjected to strains and stresses of modernization reflecting different stages in the process of socioeconomic development or decay and to changes in the international arena characterized by the transition from the cold war to East-West détente. There is no doubt that many, if not all, of the East European countries have faced a series of developmental challenges and crises, the solving of which has occupied the attention of their regimes for many years and continues to do so today. I shall discuss the political developments in Eastern Europe in a more or less systematic fashion by focusing on the five well-known systemic components suggested by Samuel Huntington[6] (culture, structure, groups, leadership, and policies) and on the five generally accepted developmental challenges or crises (identity, legitimacy, penetration, participation, and distribution).[7] The systemic components and the crises are closely inter-related and they will be discussed together.

If one defines culture broadly as "values, attitudes, orientations, myths and beliefs relevant to politics and dominant in the society,"[8] it may be argued that following the excitement generated by the emergence of ideological revisionism in some East European countries in the late 1950s there was a long hiatus, interrupted by another wave of revisionist think-ing—a byproduct of the Prague Spring of 1968. Another long pause fol-lowed, only to be interrupted again in 1976 by the birth of the human rights campaign in Poland, Czechoslovakia, East Germany, and even Rumania. Without going into the causes of this rather striking phenomenon—be it Basket Three of the Conference on Security and Cooperation in Europe (CSCE), President Carter's open advocacy of and support for the cam-paign, or internal developments in the individual countries—the fact re-mains that the dissident movement was perceived by most Communist regimes in the region as representing a serious challenge to the legitimacy of the established political systems, perhaps more serious than the revi-sionism of the early post-Stalinist era or even the doctrine of "socialism with a human face."

The revisionism of the late 1950s represented a major challenge to the ex-isting ideology, yet it did not seriously threaten the basic assumptions and foundations of the regimes in power. The Hungarian Revolt of 1956 was not the result of a lengthy process of revisionist thinking—in the final analysis it was triggered by a series of erroneous political decisions, many of which could have been avoided or postponed, made by the ruling elite. One may argue that ideological revisionism played a role in the Polish "bloodless revolution" of October 1956, but even in this case the existing system did not appear in serious danger. Moreover, however exciting and ex-hilarating, revisionism as a movement was confined to a narrow and rather elite group of academics and intellectuals with relatively little impact on the rest of society, with the possible exception of youth. The major conse-quence of the 1956 changes in Poland—the return of agriculture to private ownership—was not an outcome of a serious analysis of the economic situa-tion but the result of a spontaneous and highly pragmatic ad hoc decision made by Wladyslaw Gomulka shortly after he assumed power in Warsaw.

Nevertheless, 1956 was obviously the watershed in Soviet–East Euro-pean relations. The upheavals in Hungary and Poland gave Moscow con-siderable food for thought and the Soviet leaders—most likely on the advice of their Chinese counterparts—were forced to adopt a new policy toward

Eastern Europe that differed markedly from Stalin's.[9]

The spirit of the Prague Spring reflected in the Action-Program of the Czechoslovak Commmunist party and the "Manifesto of Two Thousand Words" was a more complex phenomenon. Although the authors strenuously denied it, both documents were seen by Moscow (and the West) as representing a serious threat to the established Communist rule in Czechoslovakia and to the regimes in the neighboring countries of Poland and East Germany. In the final analysis this perceived threat provided the major reason for the invasion of Czechoslovakia in August 1968.[10] The invasion was eventually justified by the Soviet leadership in the proclamation of the "Doctrine of Limited Sovereignty" which, in a sense, changed once again the rules of the game between the USSR, its East European allies and even other Communist-ruled countries.[11]

The most recent human rights campaign is especially dangerous because it not only openly challenges the legitimacy of the Communist regimes but—at least in some countries—it is conducted by an alliance of workers and intellectuals, in itself a very rare phenomenon in East European societies. Testifying not only to the broad support for the campaign among all social classes, including the working class, but also to the emerging regional character of the movement were the following: the open resistance to constitutional amendments in Poland in the winter of 1975–1976; the emergence of a worker-intellectual coalition in the same country following the June 1976 food riots; the overt criticism of the regime by East German intellectuals in the fall of 1976 accompanied by a widespread expression of dissatisfaction illustrated by the mass application for exit visas to West Germany; the birth of the "Charter 77" movement in Czechoslovakia; and the protest statements issued by top Rumanian literary and artistic figures.

Until now, broad support and identifiable regional character in reform movements have been either rare or absent. Each time the intellectuals, students, and workers formed an alliance (Czechoslovakia in 1968, Hungary in 1956, and Poland in 1956 and 1976) the local regimes were forced to amend their policies or face serious threat to their survival. The striking new factor on the East European domestic scene was the growing politicization of the blue collar working class which, in Poland at least, succeeded in getting rid of an increasingly unpopular leader (Gomulka in December 1970) and forcing his successor to call off a major increase in food prices (Gierek in June 1976).

The area-wide character of the protest movement also represented a novelty on the East European scene. In the past, expressions of dissent and discontent were largely confined to individual countries and the more orthodox and conservative regimes were usually quite successful in closing off potential channels of influence transmission and isolating their countries from outside pressures. The policy of isolation broke down partially in 1968 when the East German, Polish, and Soviet regimes were powerless to stop or neutralize the "demonstration effect" of the Prague Spring as it began to have an impact on their respective societies. It appears that by 1976 the local regimes were even less able to control the situation and prevent the spread of discontent. One possible reason for this was that the human rights movement took the East European governments as well as the world at large by surprise. As a result the respective ruling elites tended to over-react, which in turn stimulated Western criticism and focused the world's attention on conditions in the region, contributing further to the escalation of tension in the area. The only regime that thus far has tried to deal with the situation in a relatively moderate fashion has been that of Poland. Elsewhere in the area, even in Yugoslavia, the protest movement has been strongly attacked in terms occasionally reminiscent of the Stalinist past.

The widespread dissent made it clear that behind the supposedly stable facade laboriously constructed by the various East European regimes, the gap between the rulers and the ruled not only continued to exist but in fact seemed to widen. Much of the discontent was due to economic hardships and unfulfilled expectations for a better life. Still, there is little doubt that it was the Helsinki Final Act of the CSCE and especially its Basket Three, followed by the Belgrade Conference to review the implementation of Helsinki agreements, that played a major role in providing some legitimacy to the protest movement, making it more difficult for the respective governments to use crude force to suppress it.

There were some signs that the Soviet Union as the leader of the East European alliance was not only caught off guard but also embarrassed by the area-wide protests. It appears that initially, at least, it tried to warn its junior allies against overreacting and, as illustrated by its promise of aid to the relatively moderate Polish regime, might have preferred to deal with the dissenters in a noncoercive fashion. It was only after the proclamation by the Carter administration of official U.S. support for the movement in the Soviet Union and Czechoslovakia that the official Soviet stance hardened perceptibly.

As suggested earlier, the human rights campaign represented a major challenge to the legitimacy of the established East European regimes. It is a well-known fact that acquisition of some degree of legitimacy has been one of the major objectives of the East European regimes ever since the Communist takeover of the area in the early postwar period.[12] It is also clear that the combination of coercive measures and massive indoctrination and resocialization campaigns that characterized the first decade or so of Communist rule did not result in legitimacy for the established political systems. Consequently, in the mid-1960s a decision was made to reduce the role played by coercion in favor of a significant improvement in the level of welfare enjoyed by the respective populations. "Consumerism" was seen as the most promising path leading to at least a modicum of legitimacy and popular acceptance for the regime. The decision to focus on the consumer was also seen as an attempt to deal with another major crisis facing the various Eastern European regimes: the crisis of distribution. A significant rise in the living standards was intended to perform the double function of neutralizing the impact of the two crises of legitimacy and distribution.

It can be argued that in Eastern Europe, at least until recently, the frustration, alienation, or anomie produced by social mobilization and economic development were related more to problems of distribution and welfare than to political issues such as greater participation. One could of course point to Czechoslovakia in 1968 as a contrary example, but a good case can be made that throughout Eastern Europe economic demands tended to take precedence over political desiderata and it is only recently that the two have begun to converge, putting additional pressure on the ruling regimes. While it is easy to overstate the significance of economic discontent as a causal factor of popular dissatisfaction with the performance of the existing political and economic systems, the fact remains that the history of Eastern Europe over the last twenty-five years is replete with examples of governments giving way to popular pressures resulting from economic hardships, either by modifying their harsh economic policies or by instituting economic reforms (East Germany, 1963; Czechoslovakia, 1966–1969; Hungary, 1953–1955 and 1968; Poland, 1956–1958, 1971, and 1976). And economic liberalization more often than not has been accompanied by some political relaxation.

So far, at least, the policy aimed at achieving greater legitimacy through the satisfaction of economic demands has met with mixed success. The policy itself was represented by a multipronged effort to raise the level of consumption by increasing the domestic output of foodstuffs and consumer goods and by expanding their import from the West. Other measures aiming in the same direction included efforts to raise labor productivity, to modernize industrial plants, and to keep down the price level of consumer goods.

Has the new emphasis on raising the level of welfare in Eastern Europe affected the conduct of Soviet foreign policy? There is evidence that the Soviet leadership has been aware of the growing ferment in the region. It is concerned with the maintenance of economic and political stability in the various countries and thus appears willing to tolerate dissident activity. In fact there have been indications that the Kremlin would be willing to allow a greater degree of liberalization for the sake of preserving the status quo. While a repetition of the invasion of Czechoslovakia could not be entirely excluded, the probability of its happening in the post-Helsinki period is not very high.

The concern for economic well-being as an instrument of legitimacy undoubtedly influenced the Soviet attitude toward Basket Two at Helsinki and Belgrade as well as toward East-West trade in general. It was that trade that was seen as being of crucial importance for the improvement of economic performance in different countries. So far, at least, there are no signs that the Soviet Union has been putting pressure on its junior allies to curtail the volume of trade with the West, although Moscow is reducing its own imports from the United States because of the growing unfavorable balance of payments.

The emphasis on economics necessitated greater involvement of two systemic components — structures and groups — both of which had to undergo changes in order to deal with the new situation. In the East European context the two most important structures — "formal organizations through which the society makes authoritative decisions"[13] — were the Communist parties and the bureaucracies. The major task facing both was how to cope with the imperatives of modern industrial society and with the multiple challenges to their supremacy and monopoly of political and economic power. This was a far cry from their earlier tasks — the takeover and consolidation of power. The current stage, which can be described as that of system maintenance, clearly required some major changes in their attributes. Moreover, the thirty years or so since the establishment of Communist regimes in the area have produced a new generation of entrants into the political arena who for a variety of reasons differ greatly from their predecessors.

It is not surprising that the ruling parties in the region have been undergoing a crisis of their own. The gradual emergence of modern industrial societies in several countries in the region required some adjustments in the authority structures in order to change the character of the regulatory and extractive capacity of the political and economic systems. The process of adjustment, which is in its early stages, emphasizes the rationality and secularization as well as the efficiency of decision-making considerations at the expense of teleological ones. Insofar as the ruling parties were concerned it meant growing emphasis on achievement rather than ascription as the criterion of political recruitment. To be sure, "oligarchic petrification"[14] — defined as the retention of strict social controls by the ruling party with the help of dogmatic ideology and conservative bureaucracy, without major systemic innovations — is likely to be maintained, at least for some years to come, in Bulgaria, Czechoslovakia, and Rumania, but even in those countries the demands of modernization are bound to introduce some changes.

The transformation of the ruling parties in such countries as East Germany, Hungary, and Poland has emphasized the growing role of "experts" at the expense of "reds," manifested in the ascendance of technocrats and the gradual demise of ideologues and some categories of party and government bureaucrats. As demonstrated by Fleron, the process takes place through the "cooptation" of experts into the party ranks and greater stress on professionalization of the rank and file of party membership.[15] An alternative to be discussed below is the greater participation in decision making by interest groups.

The growing realization by the top party leadership in some countries that the strains and stresses of modernization required different kinds of political and economic elites than the earlier processes of takeover, penetration, and mobilization coincided with the arrival on the scene of a younger, better educated, and more pragmatic group of recruits into the political and bureaucratic establishment. The result appears to be a growing conflict between the old and the new guards that may have far-reaching implications for the future of Eastern Europe.[16] Although until now the struggle for political power has been largely confined to the lower and middle ranks of the party and the bureaucracy, it is only a matter of time before it reaches the top echelons of the ruling elite.

The process of "circulation of elites" in the area is likely to be one of the most important political developments in Eastern Europe in the near future. As suggested earlier, the leaders in several East European countries have gradually become aware that the problems of the postmobilization stage, with its emphasis on reforms to improve the efficiency and effectiveness of systemic performance, could not be successfully solved by the same elites who had created the "command" system in the first place. This was especially true of the bureaucracy, which in some cases may have tacitly accepted the various economic and political reforms only to sabotage their subsequent implementation.[17]

The above changes, however, may lead to another crisis, that of party identity. Judging by the frequency and level of discussions emanating from Eastern Europe, two problems seem to concern the ruling elites in various countries: the concept or idea of "developed socialism" and the impact of the "scientific-technical revolution" on Communist societies. Both concern the future role of the ruling party.

Denying the validity of supposedly Western assertions that the importance of the party was likely to decline in the context of the postindustrial state, considerable attention was devoted in the discussions to stressing the fact that, on the contrary, the ruling party's role would be strengthened to allow it to provide leadership and guidance to an increasingly complex society. The party was no longer seen as the traditional Leninist narrow elite of revolutionaries but as the "party of the whole people," yet its leading role in the system was to be upgraded. The same was true for the state, which was not expected to wither away in the foreseeable future but was to remain as strong as ever. Discussion was accompanied by frequent appeals for tighter controls and discipline, which mirrored concern about dilution of party authority and cohesiveness under the impact of growing economic prosperity resulting from technological progress and substantial injections of Western know-how, which by now has become common in most East European countries.

There is little doubt that the elite turnover thus far has not resulted in a significant democratization of East European politics. The new elites are younger, better educated, and more pragmatic and efficiency-minded than their predecessors. They are also more nationalistic and more deeply steeped in the traditional culture of their societies. None of this provides a guarantee that they will also be more democratic. On the contrary, the traditional East European political culture always contained an anti-democratic bias which, one may suspect, has not significantly diminished over the years. On the other hand, although not necessarily inclined toward democracy, the new elites appear to be more liberal in the sense of favoring some pluralist evolution and a somewhat greater participation by selected functionally specific groups, in the name of higher efficiency of the system.

Groups—"the social and economic formations, formal and informal, which participate in politics and make demands on political struc-tures"[18]—have now become an integral part of most Communist systems in Eastern Europe. It can be shown that specialized or professional groups have been generally recognized by the ruling parties as performing the necessary and legitimate function of providing expert advice to political leaders. Other groups, such as those representing various intellectual and artistic activities as well as the interests of particular social classes were previously treated as simple "transmission belts"; they have been acquiring some autonomy and making demands on political leadership.

The reasons for the emergence and growing institutionalization of interest groups in Eastern Europe have been analyzed extensively in the literature and need not be elaborated here.[19] The fact remains that earlier expectations to the contrary, their impact on East European politics has been minimal, at least until now. There is no doubt that various specialized groups played a significant role in the formulation and implementation of several important reforms—especially in the economic realm—and that their participation in decision making reduced to some extent the importance of dogmatic, rigid, and conservative elements in the party and bureaucracy. However, it can be shown that few if any of the groups showed interest in going beyond their own specific and parochial areas of concern and that by and large they appeared satisfied with the status quo, especially when the latter guaranteed their privileged status and protected their interests. Although there were some exceptions, professional groups such as managers, planners, academics, and members of the "creative intelligentsia" were rather easily bought off by the ruling party and appeared reconciled with the existing state of affairs.

The two major exceptions to the rule were the workers and some segments of the intellectual community. Although their importance and their willingness to become politically engaged varied from country to country, there is little doubt that they represented a potentially serious threat to the political stability of individual East European countries and contributed to at least three systemic crises facing the Communist regimes — those of legitimacy, distribution, and participation.

The blue collar workers as a group remained relatively quiescent throughout the early years of Communist rule. However, in the last twenty years or so they were responsible for the most serious upheavals encountered by the various regimes in Czechoslovakia (1968), Hungary (1956), and Poland (1956, 1970, and 1976). The causes of this apparent militancy are complex. Possibly the most crucial element in the chain of causation lies in the attitudes and behavior of the "new working class," consisting mostly of men and women who entered industrial and other non-agricultural employment in the course of the massive migration from villages into the cities that accompanied industrial revolution in the region. Over time this particular group has shed its previous values, traditions, and attitudes and has acquired the characteristics usually associated with a modern, industrial working class. The synthesis of socialization, education, and urbanization has left its mark and, although the links between the factory and the village have not entirely disappeared, the peasant heritage has slowly given way to modern industrial and urban culture. Another segment of the new working class was in fact quite new, having been recruited in the late 1960s and early 1970s from among urban young people, who did not have to go through the painful process of acculturation.

It can be argued that the East European regimes succeeded beyond expectation in creating the new proletariat that was presumed to provide strong support for the system that, after all, was responsible for the workers' privileged status, at least as compared to other segments of society like peasants. That support has proven to be at best problematical. However, it would be a mistake to assume that the potential growing activism of the working class in some countries is likely to augur an era of greater liberalization and democratization. In the end, the attitudes of the East European working class may not be all that different from the attitudes of the French workers in May 1968 or of American "hard hats" in the latter stages of the Vietnam War, when the workers sided with their governments against the intelligentsia and students demanding political and other reforms. The evidence from Eastern Europe is mixed. On one hand there is the example of the Warsaw workers who remained at best indifferent during the events of March 1968, providing living proof of continued deep social cleavages and conflicts in Poland that ultimately stymied the formation of a united front against the regime. The lack of collaboration between students and workers was reaffirmed in December 1970 during the Baltic Coast riots, when the students remained clearly on the sidelines. On the other hand, the collaboration between Czechoslovak workers and students before and after the Soviet invasion in 1968, and between Polish workers and intellectuals following the events of June 1976, is testimony that the conflicts and cleavages can be bridged in a moment of crisis.

The East European regimes have dealt with the potential and actual discontent of the workers in a variety of ways. The most obvious, which until now has not been very successful, was to raise the standard of living of the workers. Another option was to move in the direction of more genuine worker self-government á la Yugoslavia. Some regimes tried to distract the workers from their own concerns by resorting to and encouraging traditional nationalist and even chauvinist tendencies (as in the case of Rumania) and ultimately by invoking the threat of a possible foreign (i.e., Soviet) intervention. Thus far, however, none of the options has shown much success and it may be assumed that the problem of dealing with the new proletariat will occupy the attention of East European policymakers in the near future. The regimes' lack of success in dealing with citizen discontent also explains the continuing great concern with the improvement of the economic performance of the system.

As indicated earlier, the East European intellectual community appears to be deeply divided at present between those who decided not to challenge the legitimacy of the various regimes in return for many (mostly material) privileges and those willing to become politically engaged. It is clear that the policy of individual governments aimed at improving the economic and social status of the intellectuals, reemphasizing traditional national cultures and values, partially relaxing censorship, and lowering barriers to foreign travel and contacts met with only partial success. It also appears that at least in some countries the politically active intellectuals realized that the only way to force the regimes to change their policy in a more liberal direction was to ally themselves with the workers, thus creating a new and powerful pressure group able and willing to articulate political and economic discontent.

The above process provides an excellent illustration of the crisis of participation. As Huntington suggests, there is a chain reaction linking social frustration (resulting from social mobilization) with political participation. The latter must be enlarged in order to accommodate the demands of the mobilized and frustrated populace. Unless and until legitimate channels for participation are established and institutionalized, systemic instability will follow.[20] It is therefore not surprising that one of the standard responses to popular discontent has been the promise to expand participation at various levels and to make the different "representative" institutions more important.

One of the key systemic elements in Eastern Europe that has been changing in a significant fashion is the leadership — "the individuals in political institutions and groups who exercise more influence than others on the allocation of values."[21] Even though the importance of individual East European leaders as initiators of the process of change may have declined in recent years, there is little doubt that the top Communist party leaders in individual countries still exercise considerable influence over their respective societies.[22] Moreover, the leaders themselves have been changing. In addition to changes over time in their personal characteristics, two other types of leadership changes have been present in Eastern Europe: the transition from individual to collective leadership and the transition from strict control to "benign neglect" of the leadership succession process on the part of the Soviet Union.

It can be shown that the sixteen individuals who led the six Communist parties — and hence the six countries of Eastern Europe since 1953 — can be divided into those who could be termed undisputed rulers and those who were forced to share their power. In four countries — Czechoslovakia, East Germany, Hungary, and Poland — there was a sharp break with the traditional one-man leadership following the death or removal of the top ruler. Although the collective leadership often included members of the ruling elite closely identified with the previous one-man leadership, there is little doubt that the decision-making process at the top changed significantly as a byproduct of the transfer of power, giving rise to further changes throughout the system. Moreover, the degree of change was often magnified by striking differences in the style of rule between the old and the new rulers.

In some cases (Czechoslovakia 1969, Poland 1970) the transition from one collective leadership to another did represent a drastic turnover in personnel and had a much greater impact on the political system than a changeover from individual to collective leadership. Similarly, at times the replacement of one undisputed ruler by another gave rise to major systemic changes, even though both rulers were recruited from the same or similar milieus. This was particularly true in Rumania, where Nicolae Ceausescu's succession following Gheorghiu-Dej's death in 1964 was soon reflected in an acceleration of the process of change in that country.

The transition from individual to collective leadership during 1953-1977 appears to have been irreversible; once the latter was established, the probability was high that sooner or later it would become institutionalized. However, institutionalization of collective leadership did not automatically guarantee a more liberal leadership, as illustrated by the replacement of Dubček by Husak in Czechoslovakia in 1969. Nevertheless, as a rule, collective leadership tended to be more liberal and open than individual rule.

The other factor that had a major impact on the process of leadership succession was, of course, the Soviet Union. At least until 1956 Moscow's influence was powerful and nearly overwhelming: the Kremlin's support of one leader against another was for all practical purposes the sine qua non of success. After 1956 the situation was much less clear-cut.[23] Whatever the explanation of the irregular pattern of Soviet intervention in the East European succession process, it may be speculated that Moscow's official attitude toward the new leaders played a major role in their acquiring some popular legitimacy, which affected their ability to govern and to initiate change.

It may be argued that in most cases leadership succession exerted its strongest effect on political structures — the ruling party and the bureaucracy — and that the effect on other systemic components was much more difficult to determine and evaluate. It also seems that the replacement of one leader by another did not exert as strong an influence on East European politics as might have been expected. This means that succession no longer represents a drastic and radical transition from one political formula to another, but that it has been regularized and institutionalized, with a high premium being put on continuity or on gradual, incremental change.

A second corollary is that leadership as a systemic component may not be so important in the East European context as we have been led to believe on the basis of the early post-Stalinist experience of the middle and late 1950s. To put it differently, while the absolute weight of the leadership variable may have remained unchanged, its relative importance may have declined in favor of other systemic components such as party or interest groups. Although based on impressions and intuition rather than on hard data, this hypothesis is not entirely implausible, especially when postulated in the context of an "advanced socialist" or a "postindustrial" society.

Have the individual East European leaders had much influence on the formulation and direction of Soviet foreign policy? The answer to this question must be highly speculative. It can be argued that the influence of individual leaders was largely dependent on the type and character of the personal relationship between them and the ruling Soviet oligarchy. This relationship could and did range from close rapport through indifference to actual dislike and ultimately it affected the strength of personal influence.

Judging from highly impressionistic reports, the Polish leader Gomulka succeeded in developing good personal relations with both Khrushchev and Brezhnev and it is not inconceivable that he was able to play a part, however small, in influencing Soviet policy. The so-called Rapacki and Gomulka Plans of nuclear-free zones in Central Europe represented essentially Polish initiatives that were eventually adopted by the Soviet Union.[24] Gomulka's attitude toward the crisis in Czechoslovakia in 1968 and his response to Chancellor Willy Brandt's overtures in the following year appeared to have had some impact on the Soviet decision to intervene in Czechoslovakia in August 1968 and to pursue the dialogue with Bonn that culminated in the Soviet-German Treaty of July 1970.[25]

There is also some impressionistic evidence of other East European leaders' influencing Soviet foreign policy. For years Walter Ulbricht had considerable success in torpedoing Soviet attempts to improve relations with the Federal Republic and he was also the strongest single advocate of armed intervention in Czechoslovakia.[26] In the final analysis his removal and replacement by Erich Honecker — with Soviet blessing — paved the way toward the normalization of relations between the two German states. Similarly, Soviet policy toward Rumania was undoubtedly influenced by Moscow's perception of Ceausescu as a party leader firmly in control of the country's internal situation — in sharp contrast to the Kremlin's view of Alexander Dubček, who was seen as losing his grip over the developments in Czechoslovakia.

The final systemic component to be discussed involves the policies or "patterns of governmental activity which are consciously designed to affect the distribution of benefits and penalties within the society."[27] It is here that the remaining systemic components converge and it is these policies that ultimately give rise to the various crises confronting the rapidly changing societies.

It is axiomatic that ever since the Communist takeover in the middle and late 1940s, the policies of the East European regimes represented by and large an imitation, emulation, or adaptation of policies that originated in the Soviet Union. It is only in the past decade or so that the individual countries began to deviate from this pattern and to embark on policies of their own. This was due primarily to the changes in systemic components such as parties, bureaucracies, groups, and leadership and — last but not least — to the change in the attitude of the Soviet Union, which for various reasons decided to adopt a more benign stance vis-à-vis its junior allies.

It is not surprising that the changes in policies took place above all in the economic realm. The decision to undertake major reforms of the economic systems was intended to accomplish several tasks at once. The major objective has been alluded to earlier: it was an attempt by the regimes to acquire some degree of legitimacy and popular acceptance through a significant improvement in the living standards of the respective populations. This goal could be achieved only through an increase in the rate of growth of the economy, which showed signs of lagging in the early and mid-1960s when the shortages of labor and other inputs forced the decision makers to switch from the extensive to the intensive model of economic growth. This, in turn, necessitated introduction of greater rationality and efficiency into the economic system, the former through the reduction of the central planning mechanism and the latter through the modernization of the industrial plant and management methods, supplemented by increasing imports of technology from the West.

The initiation and execution of economic reforms was the result of changes in all systemic components. In the realm of political culture, the ideological revisionism of the late 1950s had as its corollary economic revisionism, which provided the theoretical underpinnings of the reforms. The changes in the character and composition of the ruling parties and bureaucracies resulted in the emergence of a political climate that was receptive to innovation and experimentation. The growing importance of interest groups of all hues tended to favor the reforms and, finally, the new generation of better educated and more pragmatic party and government leaders was also interested in a more efficient and rational allocation of resources and better performance of the economic systems. Economic reforms could also have been seen as preventing or neutralizing the various crises that accompanied the process of modernization and change, particularly those of legitimacy, distribution, and participation.

While the reforms represented the most important example of autonomous or semiautonomous policies on the part of the smaller East European countries, other examples can also be cited, both in the domestic and foreign arenas. The process of political liberalization in countries such as Czechoslovakia, Hungary, and Poland is a case in point.[28] It consisted of a series of political, economic, and social reforms that taken together constituted a major change in the system, affecting both the institutions and processes in individual countries. With regard to foreign policy issues, the decisions to expand economic contacts with the West, to establish diplomatic relations with some Western countries previously considered mortal enemies, to settle territorial issues, or to offer major new ideas in the area of arms control and disarmament testified to the ability of some East European countries to undertake important initiatives of their own. Here again, the motives behind these decisions reflected changes in the various endogenous systemic components in addition to changes in the exogenous variables, such as the change in the attitude of the Soviet Union and changes in the international environment as a whole.

The question to be asked now is whether all these changes affected, influenced, or determined the conduct of Soviet foreign policy and, if so, how? It was hypothesized at the outset that in view of the change in the character of the Warsaw Treaty alliance the Soviet–Eastern Europe relationship has begun to approximate interdependence rather than one-sided domination or dependency, which means that changes in Eastern Europe are likely to have some impact on Soviet decision making, both foreign and domestic.

If this assumption has any validity, the first problem to be analyzed concerns the manner in which the influence is being transmitted from Eastern Europe to the Soviet Union. In other words, what were the agents, channels, and targets of influence penetration?[29] Without going into the details of Soviet foreign policymaking, one can identify several "linkage groups" or agents that, intentionally or not, directly or indirectly, serve as "transmission belts" for influences, views, and ideas from the smaller East European countries into the Soviet Union. Some of them are obvious. They include top party leaders who meet with their Soviet counterparts in the bilateral and multilateral conferences that have become a standard feature of Communist international relations since the death of Stalin. Regular meetings of the executive committee and of standing commissions and committees of the Council of Mutual Economic Assistance (CMEA) provide a forum for the exchange of information and, ipso facto, for influence transmission. The same is true for the sporadic gatherings of the Warsaw Treaty Consultative Committee and meetings of the top military leaders of the alliance. At the less exalted level there are frequent contacts between the representatives of the Communist party bureaucracies when the Soviet and East European *apparatchiki* representing the different departments of their party Secretariat get together to coordinate ideological or political propaganda and education campaigns. In general it may be said that, with some significant exceptions, the personal contacts between Soviet and East European elites have been and are quite extensive.

An important channel of information is obviously represented by Soviet embassies in the East European countries. As a rule, the individuals chosen for those posts belong to the party hierarchy and this alone guarantees that their views receive considerable attention in Moscow. There are indications that in some instances the information provided by Soviet ambassadors played a crucial role in influencing the conduct of Soviet foreign policy.[30] Other channels of communication and influence transmission include personal contacts between various professional and cultural groups, exchange of books and publications, showing of films and plays, and other conventional instruments of influence penetration.

Have all these linkage groups and agents affected the conduct of Soviet foreign policy? The answer is both yes and no. As a working hypothesis it may be assumed that the existence of the Warsaw Treaty Organization and of the CMEA does play a role in Soviet foreign policy that would be different were both organizations nonexistent. In other words, the Soviet Union for some time has been a leader of two important political-military and economic alliances and hence no longer a free agent or actor able to disregard the wishes and interests of its junior partners. Several examples can be cited to show that this indeed has been the case — whether in the various East-West negotiations or with respect to the Sino-Soviet conflict.

The existence of the Soviet-controlled Warsaw Pact and the need to legitimize the post–World War II boundary arrangements in Eastern Europe were directly responsible for the Soviet push in favor of the Conference on Security and Cooperation in Europe as the instrument for the ratification of the territorial status quo in that part of the world. In the same vein — eager to achieve Western and particularly U.S. approval of its sphere of influence in Eastern Europe — the Soviet Union was willing to make some concessions in SALT I and Mutual Balanced Force Reduction (MBFR) negotiations, thus accelerating the process of East-West détente in the early and mid-1970s.

What about the impact of systemic changes in Eastern Europe on the conduct of Soviet foreign policy? Beginning with the changes in the ideological component, there is no doubt that the revisionism of the 1950s and 1960s, the rebirth of nationalism, and the recent human rights campaign influenced Soviet policy not only toward Eastern Europe but also vis-à-vis the West. Soviet policy toward Czechoslovakia, Rumania, and Yugoslavia are cases in point. More interesting are the changes in Moscow's attitude and policy toward the United States and Western Europe. For example, there is little doubt that Soviet policy toward Eurocommunism has been closely related to the Kremlin's policy vis-à-vis East European Communist parties. Several of the latter have had traditionally close relations with the Italian and French parties and it may be assumed that the criticism of the USSR voiced by these parties in recent years did not go unnoticed in Eastern Europe and was also likely to affect and possibly strengthen the dissident movement in some of these countries. Thus Eurocommunism was seen by the Kremlin not only as a direct challenge to its leadership of the international Communist camp but, more directly, as a threat to Soviet control of the East European periphery. The area-wide campaign in support of human rights clearly contributed to the recent hardening of Moscow's stance vis-à-vis Washington, which was perceived as the chief instigator of the drive.

Changes in East European parties, bureaucracies, and interest groups do not appear to have much impact on Soviet foreign policy unless they lead to the initiation of major systemic changes that are perceived by the Soviet

Union as being inimical to Communist rule in the given country and the area as a whole. The same seems to be true of changes in leadership.

Insofar as changes in policies are concerned, the Soviet attitude may be described as one of benign neglect. Thus Moscow did not object, by and large, to economic reforms as long as they tended to be confined to the economic sphere and did not spill over into politics. The successful expansion of economic relations with the West, which clearly benefited Eastern Europe, may have persuaded the Soviet leaders to imitate their junior partners and increase Soviet trade with the West. One may also speculate that Rumania's and Poland's interest in establishing diplomatic relations and settling territorial and other issues wth West Germany forced the Soviet Union to follow suit in seeking accommodation with Bonn. Thus it can be seen that various systemic changes and crises in Eastern Europe did play a role in Soviet foreign policy. It is clear that Moscow has been particularly sensitive to the crisis of legitimacy and in at least two cases intervened to prevent an actual or potential collapse of the Communist regime. Similarly, when the crisis of distribution threatened the foundations of the Polish regime in 1976, Moscow stepped in with economic aid to prop up the Gierek government.

There is, of course, a whole range of influences emanating from Eastern Europe that clearly affects the conduct of Soviet foreign policy and that requires a separate treatment. I refer to the security considerations stemming from the military and strategic position of Eastern Europe. A good case can be made to show that in the final analysis it is these considerations that govern and determine the shape of the relationship between the Soviet Union and Eastern Europe and that the internal socioeconomic changes in the region have only a marginal impact on the conduct of Soviet foreign policy. Nevertheless, since the borderline between political, economic, and military problems and policies tends to be fuzzy, the changes discussed above cannot be entirely ignored.

Notes

1. Bulgaria, Czechoslovakia, East Germany, Hungary, Poland, and Rumania.

2. For an interesting recent discussion of the various conceptual issues, see James A. Caporaso, "Dependence, Dependency, and Power in the Global System: A Structural and Behavioral Analysis," *International Organization* 32, no. 1 (Winter 1978):18–21.

3. For a discussion of the latter concept, see "United States National Security Policy vis-à-vis Eastern Europe," Hearings before the Subcommittee on International Security and Scientific Affairs of the Committee on International Relations, House of Representatives, 94th Congress, 2nd Session, 12 April 1976 (Washington,

D.C.: U.S. Government Printing Office, 1976).

4. Paul Marer, "Prospects for Integration in the Council for Mutual Economic Assistance," *International Organization* 30, no. 4 (Autumn 1976):631–648.

5. Zvi Gitelman, *The Diffusion of Political Innovation: From Eastern Europe to the Soviet Union*, Comparative Politics Series 3, no. 27 (Beverly Hills, Calif.: Sage Publications, 1972) and "The Impact on the Soviet Union of the East European Experience in Modernization," in Charles Gati, ed., *The Politics of Modernization in Eastern Europe* (New York: Praeger Publishers, 1974).

6. Samuel P. Huntington, "The Change to Change: Modernization, Development and Politics," *Comparative Politics* 3, no. 3 (April 1971):316.

7. Lucian W. Pye, *Aspects of Political Development* (Boston: Little, Brown and Co., 1966), pp. 63–66.

8. Huntington, "The Change to Change," p. 316.

9. For an interesting discussion, see Morton Schwartz, *The Foreign Policy of the USSR: Domestic Factors* (Encino, Calif.: Dickenson Publishing Company, 1975), ch. 5 and 6.

10. During a visit to Prague in December 1968, I heard from reliable sources that beginning in 1966 the Soviet embassy in Prague had systematically distorted the situation in Czechoslovakia, suggesting among other things that the Communist rule was on the verge of collapse.

11. See "Czechoslovakia and the Brezhnev Doctrine," Paper prepared by the Subcommittee on National Security and International Operations of the Committee on Government Operations, United States Senate, 91st Congress, 1st Session (Washington, D.C.: U.S. Government Printing Office, 1969).

12. For an interesting discussion of this problem, see Paul Hollander, "Comparing Socialist Systems: Ends and Results," in Carmela Mesa-Lago and Carl Beck, eds., *Comparative Socialist Systems* (Pittsburgh, Pa.: University of Pittsburgh Center for International Studies, 1975), pp. 429–431.

13. Huntington, "The Change to Change," p. 316.

14. Zbigniew Brzezinski, *Between Two Ages* (New York: Viking Press, 1970), p. 165.

15. Frederic J. Fleron, Jr., "Toward a Reconceptualization of Political Change in the Soviet Union: The Political Leadership System," *Comparative Politics* 1, no. 2 (January 1969):228–244.

16. See Zygmunt Bauman, "Twenty Years After: The Crisis of Soviet-Type Systems," *Problems of Communism* 20, no. 6 (November-December 1971): 45–53.

17. Andrzej Korbonski, "Political Aspects of Economic Reforms in Eastern Europe, " in Zbigniew Fallenbuchl, ed., *Economic Development in the Soviet Union and Eastern Europe*, vol. 1 (New York: Praeger Publishers, 1975), pp. 8–25.

18. Huntington, "The Change to Change," p. 316.

19. See, for example, H. Gordon Skilling and Franklyn Griffiths, eds., *Interest Groups in Soviet Politics* (Princeton, N.J.: Princeton University Press, 1971).

20. Samuel P. Huntington, *Political Order in Changing Societies* (New Haven, Conn.: Yale University Press, 1968), pp. 53–56.

21. Huntington, "The Change to Change," p. 316.

22. Andrzej Korbonski, "Leadership Succession and Political Change in Eastern

Europe," *Studies in Comparative Communism* 9, nos. 1-2 (Spring/Summer 1976):3-22.
    23. Ibid., pp. 10-11.
    24. See Lincoln P. Bloomfield, Walter C. Clemens, Jr., and Franklyn Griffiths, *Khrushchev and the Arms Race* (Cambridge, Mass.: M.I.T. Press, 1966), pp. 148-151.
    25. Erwin Weit, *Eyewitness: The Autobiography of Gomulka's Interpreter* (London: Andre Deutsch, 1973), pp. 197 ff.
    26. Ibid., pp. 201-203.
    27. Huntington, "The Change to Change," p. 316.
    28. Andrzej Korbonski, "The Pattern and Method of Liberalization," in Mesa-Lago and Beck, *Comparative Socialist Systems*, pp. 192-214.
    29. For a discussion of the general issue of influence penetration in the Soviet and East European environment, see Andrzej Korbonski, "External Influences on Eastern Europe," in Charles Gati, ed., *The International Politics of Eastern Europe* (New York: Praeger Publishers, 1975); Sarah M. Terry, "External Influences on Political Change in Eastern Europe: A Framework for Analysis," in Jan F. Triska and Paul M. Cocks, eds., *Political Development in Eastern Europe* (New York: Praeger Publishers, 1977); and Erik P. Hoffman, "External Influences on Soviet Domestic Politics: An Introduction,"*Soviet Union* 4, part 1 (1977), pp. 3-16.
    30. It is common knowledge that the Soviet ambassador to Warsaw, Stanislav Pilotovich, frequently criticized the relatively moderate policy of the Polish regime. The Soviet ambassador to Czechoslovakia at the time of the Prague Spring, Stephan Chervonenko, was well known for his conservative attitude with regard to developments in Czechoslovakia.

PART 5

Domestic Context: An Overview

14

The Domestic Sources
of Soviet Foreign Policy

Alexander Dallin

The Character of Soviet Foreign Policy:
An Introduction

Of all the major political concerns of the Soviet authorities, the conduct of foreign policy was the one the Bolsheviks had least expected and were least prepared for when they took power more than sixty years ago. By the same token, the course of world affairs has often challenged and belied the beliefs and expectations of Soviet analysts and decision makers. The record of Soviet foreign policy is replete with remarkable successes and stupendous failures—both successes and failures having been due in part to Soviet perception and behavior and in part to factors beyond Soviet control.

Soviet foreign policy behavior can be seen as the product of an encounter between the expectations and values of Soviet decision makers and the reality as they found and perceived it. In practice, it has required (and in turn reflected) a series of adaptations—an imperfect learning process, which they have at times resisted and at other times sanctioned, though often only belatedly.

The survival of the Soviet state, between the two world wars, in a capitalist encirclement (as well as the failure of revolutions abroad sponsored or supported by Moscow) heightened the tension between conventional (state) and transformational (revolutionary) perspectives and impulses, a tension that has remained alive down to our days.[1] Similarly, conflicting pressures have stemmed from the simultaneous attractions of "expansion and coexistence" (to cite the title of a standard history of Soviet foreign policy).[2] Whether the Soviet Union has more to gain from a (political or military) stabilization of the international environment or from the fallout from destabilization has been a matter of further uncertainty. These are but a few of the many areas of ambiguity and tension in the Soviet approach to public policy—foreign policy included—that Soviet secrecy and ritual reiteration of orthodox formulae have at times made to appear more single-minded, more unambiguous, and more relentless than seems warranted by closer inspection of the record.[3]

The past sixty years have seen a remarkable growth, not of Soviet Communism but of the Soviet state. From an impoverished, inexperienced, and underdeveloped pariah in the family of nations, it has grown into a formidable superpower, possessing the ability to project its power globally, to exercise effective control over a number of other polities, and to wield considerable but uneven influence in many other areas. Victorious in World War II, the USSR emerged onto the postwar scene both exhausted and exhilarated. Its expanded control over territories and resources — as well as Stalin's behavior — were essential elements in the etiology of the cold war, which both mirrored and validated the axiomatic belief in the inevitability of conflict ("contradictions") between the Soviet camp and its adversaries and the "two-camp" images underlying the Soviet leadership's perception of world affairs.

The quarter-century since Stalin's death has seen a substantial increase in Soviet power — economic, military, and political — along with evidence of serious strains and failures; considerably heightened professionalization and competence in the conduct of public policy, but also pockets of serious and dysfunctional rigidities and bureaucratic irrationality; international assertiveness and involvement, but also a measure of restraint in Soviet conduct abroad.

Considerable attention has been paid to the emergence of the Soviet Union as a global power, insistent on its right to a global presence and voice. No doubt new Soviet capabilities have generated new options and new expectations, in pursuit of what has been described as an expanding Soviet concept of security. Far less light has been shed on the notion of Soviet restraint, clashing as it does with American stereotypes; yet the record (with some glaring exceptions) confirms a fairly pervasive Soviet proclivity to avoid high risks in foreign affairs and, even when apparently committed to "adventurous" behavior, to back down or shy away in crisis situations, such as the Cuban missile crisis of 1962, the Middle Eastern crisis of 1973, and the Ethiopian affair of 1978.[4]

Yet precisely in this period, when it has involved itself far more massively in international interaction across a broad front, the Soviet Union in the post-Stalin era has not been guilty of direct aggression or forcible territorial expansion outside the bloc: the only instances in which Soviet armed forces have seen action have been in East Germany (1953), Hungary (1956), Czechoslovakia (1968), and the border incidents with China (1969) — with the Cuban (1962) and Egyptian (1970) crises the limiting cases that essentially confirm the point.

In exploring the characteristics of foreign policy performance in the Brezhnev era, with its mix of successes and failures, it is useful to take as a point of departure the general outlook of the Khrushchev era that preceded it. That outlook, in its original and optimistic version, may retrospectively be boiled down to three sets of expectations:

- The Soviet-controlled socialist camp would grow in strength, cohesion, and influence, as would the international Communist movement abroad;
- The capitalist world, in the West and Japan, would be plagued by general economic and political crises that, coming on the heels of decolonization, were bound to weaken its relative weight in the "correlation of forces" with the Communist bloc;
- The Third World, finally freed from imperialist fetters, would inevitably gravitate toward the Soviet camp, with which it shared common interests and common adversaries.

None of these expectations has come true. The Sino-Soviet split has been but the most dramatic and divisive cleavage in the Communist world. Time and again, Eastern Europe has caused Moscow alarm—with the Czech events of 1968 the most obvious and best known but by no means the only recent example. For all intents and purposes, international Communism has ceased to function as a unitary, let alone Moscow-controlled, movement.

In the Third World, Moscow has sustained a long series of setbacks in its extensive and expensive efforts to profit from its support of nationalist movements: at least until the mid-1970s none of its favorite clients (and recipients of considerable assistance)—from Sukarno's Indonesia to Sadat's Egypt, from the Congo to Algeria to Iraq, from India to Cambodia to Mali—had "come through." The only substantial successes Moscow could point to in the Third World resulted from unanticipated circumstances over which it had no control, such as Cuba, and perhaps (but by no means permanently as yet) Angola and Ethiopia. In these instances, and in some others, it has acquired a fair measure of influence where, except for Afghanistan, it previously had little or none. But this precisely has been a source of considerable Soviet frustration: both Leninist axioms and the experience of earlier Soviet generations reinforce the lingering assumption that influence, being transient and evanescent, is not good enough, whereas airtight control is apparently not to be achieved. Similarly, whereas the increasing resort to proxies (notably, the role of Cubans in Africa) has been successful (and has confirmed the Soviet disposition to avoid taking high risks), it has also reinforced the traditional Soviet fear of being used for its clients' purposes—of making the proxies into tails wagging Soviet dogs.

And while the West in recent years has had its own share of serious difficulties—inflation, unemployment, energy crisis, problems of morale, lack of solidarity and leadership—these have not been such as to change the overall "correlation of forces" fundamentally (in spite of Vietnam—which again was a crisis Moscow could scarcely take credit for) and, in the view of most Soviet observers and decision makers, not such as to invite a fundamental change in Soviet strategy vis-à-vis the West. If anything, Soviet elite perceptions of continuing Soviet needs and of Soviet backwardness relative to the West in regard to technological innovation, industrial and agricultural productivity, and economic efficiency have become markedly stronger in the recent past; they have provided a far-reaching rationale for stepped up interaction between the USSR and the "developed" West.

This indeed has been one of the major stimuli for the overall policy orientation to which the Brezhnev leadership has been committed in the 1970s. From Moscow's perspective, it presupposes approximate parity in strategic weapons, which enables the Soviet Union to act as a coequal superpower, to demand to be treated as one, and to pursue what one astute observer has labeled its "global vocation." But if in Moscow's view the 1970s have witnessed the "objective" shift in the balance of power away from previous Soviet inferiority, Moscow apparently neither holds to, nor acts on, the belief that the USSR has gained a substantial edge in military power, let alone in other indicators of what it calls the "correlation of forces" over its potential adversaries.

Soviet foreign policy may be seen as the pursuit of a number of interrelated objectives in the face of complex constraints and pressures, both internal and external to the USSR. These objectives range from self-preservation and security to a number of others whose relative priority may depend on the expected price to be paid for their attainment. Those to which the commitment is presumably high include: the recognized need to avoid military conflicts with the United States; the commitment to promote control and integration of Eastern Europe under Soviet auspices; the desire to derive benefits from the stepped-up interrelationship with the West in science, technology, and economy; the calculation that an improved climate in East-West relations can both offset the deterioration in Sino-Soviet relations and help stem a further rapprochement between China, Japan, and the developed West that might revive Soviet fears of encirclement; the belief in the possibility of maintaining a relatively diffused relationship with the NATO powers (including the relaxation of Soviet–West German tensions, Western recognition of the GDR, the summit meetings of the early 1970s, and the Helsinki accord); the serious pursuit of arms-control negotiations with the United States and other powers, but also a continued commitment to the buildup of Soviet military forces, with a rather steady and substantial share of the GNP going to defense-related activities, development, and procurement; and a habitual inclination to exploit political crises and power vacuums in third areas insofar as these can be exploited without incurring undue costs or risks.[5]

It is not surprising that at times the simultaneous pursuit of these and other policy objectives has given rise to tensions and incongruencies among the component policies. These have been heightened still further by the perceived inconsistencies and ambiguities in the behavior of other powers, in particular, the United States.[6]

The pressure in Moscow to move forward unilaterally in the international arena, at times in a manner apt to jeopardize the "limited adversary" relationship with the West, appears to stem from several mutually reinforcing sources, notably, the perceived opportunities abroad, on the one hand, and the pressure from within the Soviet elite for a more vigorous, more militant, or more dynamic Soviet foreign policy, on the other. While it is difficult to assess its relative importance, the awareness by Soviet analysts and decision makers that the available military forces at the disposal of the USSR have grown substantially (and that correspondingly, the presumed balance has shifted) is likely to have heightened the disposition to pursue such opportunities, though not to the point of jeopardizing other parameters of conduct abroad, such as the avoidance of confrontation with the United States.

Given this new capability, it is perhaps surprising that Moscow has as yet relatively little to show for it in terms of tangible gains and benefits. But, while there clearly has been hesitation, confusion, and reassessment in Moscow, there is no evidence of a fundamental abandonment of the assumptions and approaches referred to above.[7]

The balance sheet of Soviet foreign policy is then a rather mixed one, and so are the considerations that go into it. It is well to warn against oversimplified formulae. Russia is neither a conventional imperialist state nor an old-fashioned, satiated, status quo power. The USSR is not simply "traditional Russia" in new garb, nor another variant of the Nazi system. Its foreign policy, as one U.S. analyst has remarked, is "based on rational, calculated motives to an indeterminate degree and on nonrational, often spontaneous, motives to a similarly indeterminate degree; it is neither totally predictable nor hopelessly whimsical, neither perfectly constant nor endlessly fluctuating."[8] While its role abroad has often been troublesome and quarrelsome, even foolish and provocative, it will be argued below that—even if it cannot be conclusively demonstrated—whenever it comes to fundamental choices in preferences, orientations, and values, the dominant decision makers in the Soviet Union remain fundamentally wedded to the primacy of domestic over foreign affairs.[9]

Domestic Determinants:
The Concept and the Soviet Case

"The importance of the domestic political roots of foreign policy is increasingly evident," begins a recent editorial in *Foreign Policy* dealing with the United States.[10] And an academic specialist begins a paper on foreign policy as adaptive behavior by declaring, "Never before has consciousness of the interdependence of national and international life been so pervasive."[11] The domestic sources of foreign policy behavior have indeed come to attract the attention of various analysts, observers, and actors in international affairs. Before addressing the question of to what extent such considerations are relevant or useful for an understanding of Soviet conduct, we should review the various views of the concept in general.

The focus on the domestic context of foreign policymaking may be seen, in part, as a reaction against the earlier "realist" stress on the international system and also against the conventional view that foreign policy is conducted essentially in insulation from the vagaries of domestic pressures and politics, whose role is—and ought to be—ultimately trivial in the pursuit of national interests and for the outcome of international interaction. It has also been reinforced by the sense that the boundary between comparative politics and international relations, as academic subdisciplines, is artificial at best (and similarly the boundary between national and international systems). In the United States, the experience of Vietnam dramatized the impact of domestic sources on foreign policy and apparently has had a lasting effect on the process of foreign policy formation, for example, in the role of the legislative branch. In any event, some of the most interesting and innovative academic work of the past decade has been concerned with various aspects of domestic inputs into foreign policymaking.[12]

But although different models and paradigms can be valuable under different circumstances, it is important to keep an open mind concerning the applicability of various approaches and techniques. Given a comparative, transnational, and multivariate perspective, none of these various approaches appears to commend itself as universally adequate. Such an eclectic attitude does, of course, raise questions of how to integrate, conceptually and operationally, not only the bureaucratic with the interest-group approaches, but especially the various political paradigms with the cognitive-process approach. In lieu of a more rigorous weighing of variables, it may be necessary for the time being to limit oneself to inquiring about rival tendencies over time, since unfortunately a proper integration has apparently not yet been achieved for political science in general, and *a fortiori* not for Soviet studies.

While some scholars have rejected or resisted applying these concepts and approaches to Soviet studies,[13] there is a good reason to consider them: this is after all (as Charles Gati has remarked) but another look at what George Kennan, a generation ago, labeled the "sources of Soviet conduct."

In brief, it will be my conclusion that there is a substantial and often significant interrelationship between the external and internal aspects of Soviet foreign policy — including both inputs and outputs — involving structural as well as cognitive elements. While the nature of this relationship and its manifestations have undergone considerable changes over time, the linkage is real and important though often imperfectly perceived or understood.[14]

And yet it would be entirely unwarranted to assume that theories and hypotheses generated in the context of U.S. politics and often informed by assumptions about a particular cultural, institutional, and historical setting can readily be applied to a particular (and peculiar) "case" such as the USSR. Indeed, there has been some academic malaise in this field because of the seeming impropriety of applying to the Soviet experience the elaborate typologies and matrixes invented or proposed by ingenious American methodologists and model-builders. Academic unhappiness has also — quite plausibly — been fed by the realization that there is yet to be produced any sort of body of propositions or paradigms that satisfactorily explains (rather than merely suggests or describes) perceived Soviet "linkages." And yet, this differs only in degree from the problems of research and analysis in the field at large. As one of the principal advocates of the "linkage" approach has written:

> Notwithstanding the varied and impressive accomplishments [of recent scholarship], the dynamics of the processes which culminate in the external behavior of societies remain obscure. To identify factors is not to trace their influence. To uncover processes that affect external behavior is not to explain how and why they are operative under certain circumstances and not under others. To recognize that foreign policy is shaped by internal as well as external factors is not to comprehend how the two intermix or to indicate the conditions under which one predominates over the other. And in these respects progress has been very slow indeed.[15]

Still, the numerous company of the frustrated must not obscure the genuine distinctiveness of the Soviet process and system, nor of the special problems of information regarding them. There is the self-evident lack of empirical data (and the near-impossibility of securing them) regarding many aspects of decision making, and the even greater lack of information concerning cognitive processes, in the Soviet elite. There is the related difficulty of doing any kind of significant quantification in this area.[16] On the other hand, this may not be a grievous loss, since the field as a whole has had an abundance of relatively limited quantitative studies that have not "cumulated" or significantly helped answer the "big" questions.

Even in full awareness of these limitations, it is still possible to discuss, for instance, the growth of a diffuse climate of opinion in Moscow indicative of an acquisitive society without being able to specify how such a mood is communicated to the ultimate decision makers. It is important to know the range of opinions in the Soviet elite on arms control questions even if we remain uncertain what options are placed before the Politburo (or even who places them there).

Much of the American political science literature on "linkages" has focused on crisis behavior. Whatever the arguments for such a concentration of effort (and some foreign analysts have found them peculiarly "American"), the centrality of crisis studies is unsatisfactory and inadequate in the Soviet case.[17] For one thing, the distinction between routine and crisis may not be as sharp or self-evident as in other polities. For example, in a severe crisis (the Cuban missile crisis has become the classic example) Soviet decision making reverts to the smallest and most closed body (as was true in the United States as well)—a phenomenon that serves to conceal or distort the interplay of bureaucratic and societal forces in Soviet politics, and in any event obscures some of the diversity of images and perceptions that at other times can be detected on the Soviet scene.[18] In more general terms, research attention to conflict and crisis in the Soviet system would tend to slight the study of continuing (or changing) mind-sets and perceptions—be it of the international system, of the self, or of others. This argues in favor of the "relative importance of unarticulated, as distinct from articulated, images in decision makers' foreign policy choices."[19]

There are, furthermore, certain structural or systemic peculiarities to be taken account of. Compared with American institutions, for instance, the Politburo naturally plays a unique role, positioned as it is to minimize the impact of bureaucratic politics on the top decision makers (as well as to minimize access outside of narrowly defined channels). This suggests that a bureaucratic-politics approach to the Soviet scene requires some redefinition or adaptation.[20] Unlike the virtual free-for-all of U.S. politics, its Soviet analog—while real—is bound to reserve greater authority to the ultimate decision-making body, to limit the scope of political discourse, and to deny almost all institutionalization of subsystem groups. Yet tacitly tolerated and de facto political contests and articulations have been realities of Soviet life at virtually all times; indeed, they have varied not only over time but also by issue-areas that suggest patterns deserving of further study.[21]

Finally, there is bound to be particular difficulty in identifying individual mind-sets because of the necessity for any Soviet public figure to adhere to official jargon, and because public pronouncements cannot normally be taken to be the "true" indications of an actor's mind-set or beliefs.[22] But this too must not be taken as an argument against efforts to identify differences in outlook or beliefs among particular Soviet leaders: there are examples of outstandingly successful work doing just that.[23]

In the perennial debate whether secular or systemic forces or individual actors are the proper focus for an understanding of foreign policies, there is still another consideration that militates for greater attention to the mind-sets of Soviet decision makers: of all political systems, the Soviet seems most likely and most able to override, ignore, or distort what might otherwise or elsewhere be identified as natural or secular trends. This argument, to be sure, must not be absolutized either: the Soviet system is not immune to the general manifestations — and unintended consequences — of modernization, for instance. But the difference in degree is here sufficiently great as to make for a difference in research priority as well. This sense is reinforced by an empirical look at the Soviet experience, in which the role of three individuals in succession — Lenin, Stalin, and Khrushchev — must be given substantial explanatory weight in any realistic effort to account for what happened over a half-century of Soviet history.[24]

We are thus led to conclude that, despite all caveats and reservations, certain universals and concepts must apply to the Soviet experience as much as they do anywhere else. This would be true, for example, of the role of belief systems, cognitive processes, and mind-sets, and of processes like learning or small-group dynamics. At the same time, it is important especially in the Soviet case to distinguish between the formal, ritual, explicit, and overt public images of states and systems, friends and foes — and the actual, often unstated, and at times unwitting or unacknowledged operational asumptions and beliefs of particular actors. What follows from this, as a minimum, is the proposition that Soviet institutional and ideological imperatives cannot be so directive, compelling, or unambiguous as to permit an analyst to be certain regarding cause-and-effect relationships in decision making. On the contrary, the fact that a variety of contradictory and mutually exclusive policies (and corresponding images) have all been legitimized by reference to common ideological authority suggests that (while it may impose some constraints on policy options and perhaps also on cognition) Marxism-Leninism does not validate resort to a rational-actor model and in fact remains a component of uncertain weight in the making of Soviet foreign policy.[25]

It is then important to recognize the elements of ambiguity that we detect in the Soviet leaders' outlook. Ignoring for the moment the differences among them, we can hypothesize that this ambiguity is a characteristic of the present decision makers' mind-sets. Is the political future predictable? How much control can one have over historical developments? Does the Soviet Union have an interest in stabilization? On all these questions (among those suggested by Alexander George) there are hints of significant ambiguities. The same is true of the Soviet leaders' and experts' images of the United States, China, and the Third World, as a number of recent studies have shown.[26]

Linkage Patterns: From Brest to Brezhnev

The course of Soviet history rather overwhelmingly supports the general proposition that time and again basic policy orientations in Moscow have had inescapable foreign policy components and implications. This suggests an inner logic in the pattern of linkages between internal and external policy choices in Moscow, and while no single formula will serve to explain all the instances of such linkages that can be adduced, the single most pervasive and persistent pattern of political cleavages and linkages—at least down to the post-Stalin years—has been the dichotomy between what has customarily been labeled as "left" and "right" (within the Communist sector of the political spectrum). While these categories provide diagnostic and descriptive tools that are at times utterly inadequate, they do reflect serious divergencies in attitudes and approaches: in their more extreme manifestations the differences between "left" and "right" are a function of conflicting values, political tempers, preferences, strategies, and policy orientations.[27]

In essence, the left describes a syndrome centered on "transformation" whereas the right opts for "stabilization"; mobilization is found on the left, normalcy on the right; tension-management on the left, consensus-building on the right; a willingness to resort to militancy and if need be to violence would be characteristic of the left, a characteristic preference for incrementalism of the right. Partisanship and the priority of politics belong on the left; rationality and the priority of economics (or, more generally, science) on the right: this is also the substance of the "Red versus expert" cleavage so often encountered in Communist systems. The priority of the development of heavy industry, on the left, as against the more vigorous development of agricultural priorities and/or consumer goods, on the right, is congruent with this cleavage. Voluntarism tends to be identified with the left, determinism with the right. Going it alone, autarky, and self-isolation are correlates of the left, alliances and interdependece of the right. These are some of the major rational components of the two Communist tempers and outlooks, at least in their extreme, polarized manifestations.

In practice, of course, expressed opinions (as well as presumed opinions, where we can derive them indirectly) range all over the political spectrum. Nor are individual political actors typically consistent in occupying the same "space" on a range of different issue-areas; this is true even in societies where political issues are openly debated and it is bound to apply even more to Soviet conditions, where information and sophistication are very unevenly distributed throughout the elite, where the range of alternatives is scarcely ever publicly ventilated, and where "ideological" coherence and consistency across a number of issue-areas are even less likely obtainable.

Despite these (and possible other) reservations about the adequacy of the left/right dichotomy, it is still the single most meaningful and useful set of explanatory labels as a first gross approximation of reality. This perspective, for instance, helps us to understand the underlying traits of an outlook that combines a distinctly "radical" perception of revolutionary opportunities abroad (be it by a Zinoviev in the early 1920s, or a Zhdanov after World War II, or a Mao Tse-tung after 1957) with a predilection for drastic, direct action and a disposition to tighten controls and discipline at home. The same perspective helps us understand the logic of the linkage, in the Khrushchev era and after, of divergent Soviet views of U.S. intentions with bitter arguments over resource allocation, military posture, and arms control.[28] In the same years one could also speak of a linkage of détente and welfare priorities, as against "vigilance," repression, preparedness, and a forward foreign policy.

At the risk of oversimplification, we can reduce the patterns in which linkage variables have occurred to two, which for the sake of brevity I will label, respectively, congruence and reciprocity.[29] Historically the most frequent has been a congruence between domestic and foreign strategies and orientations. By this, however, we may mean either of two things.

Congruence: Rational Linkage

This pattern describes a congruence between the political and ideological content of the decision makers' domestic priorities and preferences and their foreign policy priorities and preferences; at times, these may be operationalized in budgetary terms. Both domestic and foreign policies are informed by a single, dominant "general line" (or, in more conventional terms, are merely different components of a single policy).

The congruence of political orientations can be illustrated by selecting representative spokesmen for them — persons with fairly coherent political views — at different periods of the Soviet era; for instance, Leon Trotsky or Nikolai Bukharin in the early years; later, Andrei Zhadanov or Viacheslav Molotov; after Stalin, Frol Kozlov and Mikhail Suslov. The division of opinion over the inevitability of a new "two-camp" polarization between the Communist and capitalist systems in 1945–1946 (as reported by Maxim Litvinov) provides another example.[30] The period 1946–1947 saw a tightening up inside the Soviet Union across the board, leading to the policies generally identified as *Zhdanovshchina,* as well as the congruent rise of the cold war abroad.

Similarly, allowing for hesitations, inconsistencies, and infighting during the first several years, the general ethos of the post-Stalin era meant a significant shift from confrontation to relaxation both at home and abroad. In each instance (and in others that could be cited) there was a single dominant political mood and/or strategy that created predispositions to pursue policies congruent with it in each of the two environments, domestic and foreign.[31]

At the same time, it would appear that the identification of a single overarching political orientation for each given period—and of clear "turning points" that dramatically mark the shift from one period to the next—is more appropriate and more correctly reflects the policymakers' approach for the period approximately from 1917 to 1956. As we will see, apparently the complexity of the system, the stress on incremental change, the sophistication involved in the simultaneous pursuit of seemingly incongruent policies, and the abandonment of the earlier simplicities of a "general line," make it harder to apply this pattern to the post-Stalin era.[32]

Congruence: Political Linkage

A different pattern of congruence is suggested by the Soviet equivalent of bureaucratic and other forms of elite politics. There is good reason to claim that different Soviet institutions have at times tended to promote or accept different policies—say, with regard to such telltale issues as resource allocation and arms-control policy, which cut across a wide variety of jurisdictions—in a manner suggestive of bureaucratic politics *a l'americaine.* Indeed, as for instance with the Soviet ABM system in the 1960s, one may relate policy outcomes (and policy differences within the elite) to bargains and the relationships of rival factions and cliques, rather than to the rationality of substantive linkages. No doubt the inclination of informal factions and cliques not to contest a divergent policy of a rival group as part of a tacit trade-off or deal is even more frequent. Of course, in the Soviet case, given the virtual absence of secondary associations and of organized public lobbies as well as the inclusion of virtually all formal and informal groups within the official hierarchy, the distinction between bureaucratic politics and interest groups is not nearly so sharp as in the United States.

The two patterns of congruent linkages just outlined need not be mutually exclusive. Indeed, one may speculate that the commitment to a détente policy in 1971 and its maintenance since then have involved both substantive calculus and bureaucratic postures.

Curiously, some of the leading quasi-public (albeit esoteric) attacks on Soviet détente policy from within the establishment (coupled with calls for a greater exploitation of the ostensible crisis of capitalism and of "revolutionary opportunities" abroad in 1975-1976) have tended to come from individuals (like Ponomarev, Zagladin, Zarodov, and Sobolev) identified with "Communist internationalist" sectors, careers, or bureaucracies, such as survivors of the old Comintern apparatus and the editorial board of *World Marxist Review*. On the other hand, the most articulate and persuasive advocates of more substantial and improved U.S.-Soviet relations have included senior staff members of the Institute for the Study of the United States and Canada (which, it has been argued, has begun to acquire something akin to a vested interest in détente).[33]

One may assume that—holding the external environment constant—the stability of a given Soviet policy orientation tends to be greatest when there is a reinforcement or cumulation of (a) perceived national interest at the top; (b) self-serving interest on the part of multiple subnational groups and actors; and (c) a network of bureaucratic politics that creates vested interest in the status quo.

Reciprocity

A very different pattern, which I will call reciprocal linkage, is suggested by the periodic recurrence of contrasting rather than congruent relations between domestic and foreign policies. There are two major examples of this phenomenon—each logical in its own paradoxical way.

During the first Five-Year Plan, Soviet foreign policy was remarkably conciliatory—clearly as part of a calculated effort to minimize the chances of international crisis and Soviet involvement in foreign wars at a time of exceptionally severe strain and disarray within. These, of course, were the years of the "second" (and for many Soviet citizens, including the bulk of its peasantry, the "real") revolution, with extreme mobilization and change.

Most significantly, the 1970s exhibit such a pattern of reciprocity—in contrast with the simpler and more direct linkage that in the Khrushchev years tended to mirror (whatever the exceptions) a coherent approach to domestic and international relaxation or reorganization. Current Soviet conduct obviously involves a calculated reciprocal linkage between the search for increased interaction with the outside world *and* increased Soviet efforts to minimize the domestic political costs of such a foreign policy (for instance, by stifling political deviance).[34]

Foreign Policy Comes Home

The Post-Stalin Era

Stalin's death marked a profound watershed in Soviet history. It is true, of course, that whatever the novel trends and conflicting pressures, power to make final decisions in the Soviet state remained and remains normally concentrated in the hands of a very few; especially at moments of severe crisis the leadership can in effect ignore "outsiders" and "public opinion" and function with only minimal concern for its subsequent accountability. The Cuban missile crisis provides an example of such a concentration of decision-making authority in a circle even smaller than the party's Politburo.[35]

And yet it would be a serious distortion of Soviet reality to write off the nature and scope of changes that have occurred since 1953; at times the elements of seeming continuity have so impressed foreign observers as to preclude an adequate recognition of the transformations.[36] Some of these changes may be seen as natural, secular trends predictable in terms of developmental regularities. Others must be considered volitional, political, often unpredictable, and contingent.

Insofar as the regular, systemic changes are concerned, it will be useful to refer to the general literature on modernization. Thus, one can readily formulate several applicable propositions:

1. All developing systems tend to bring an increasing part of the population into passive or active political participation.
2. Such systems eventually tend to produce integration at the level of the nation-state, at the expense of both parochial and internationalist preoccupations.
3. Over time, developing systems tend to focus priority of attention, resources, and operationally relevant objectives on the domestic, rather than the foreign, arena.[37]

These three tendencies are identifiable in the Soviet system. Yet their influence is countermanded in part by the fact that foreign affairs are least susceptible to direct involvement by broader strata of the population. As in other polities, foreign affairs are bound to require greater reliance on authoritative institutions or individuals.

Furthermore, the Soviet system may be best able to override, ignore, or distort the typical tendencies of modernization to bring about certain changes in political development. It tends to reduce licit discussion of political choices to relatively insignificant issues, to the local level, and to means rather than ends; and it tends to limit the delegation of decision making to functional-instrumental rather than political, issue-areas. It has also successfully resisted, thus far, institutionalization of the elements of unintended pluralism.

Several political and volitional tendencies have been studied in recent years. A few deserve to be identified in this discussion:

1. Once the mobilization mentality and political terror associated with Stalin had abated, it was only natural that diverse priorities and demands should be voiced. The leadership thus faced a range of opinions reflecting different preferences and values, but lacked any mechanism to adjudicate such divergences.

2. Soviet society experienced the gradual but inescapable process of functional differentiation. At the same time, political articulation increased as the pressures of forcible mobilization were relaxed somewhat. In over-simplified terms one might suggest that members of the Soviet elite became informal spokesmen for various interests or, more rarely, issues or "tendencies."

3. The more highly modernized society must rely more heavily on "experts," who tend to press for better and more information and for an element of greater rationality. At least some experts, by securing access to policymakers, gain the ability to introduce new notes into the policy dialogue that often clash with the refrains of ideologues and timid bureaucrats. On the other hand, policy differences between experts exist and are articulated.

4. Although there are obvious and substantial differences in influence and power among the small group of members of the "collective leadership," joint decision making by its very nature creates conditions in which idiosyncratic attributes of individual leaders play a lesser role and outside influences may be more readily brought to bear on the policy-makers. Likewise, the vastly enhanced possibility, in the post-Stalin years, of losing on policy issues without losing one's job (let alone one's head) is likely to promote greater candor in expressing divergent views within the Soviet establishment. Thus candor, competence, and communications seem to have combined to substantially improve the type and quality of information available to a large number of high Soviet officials and specialists.

5. The termination of the mandatory priorities in economic allocation and development characteristic of the Stalin era and the significant growth of the Soviet GNP in the first post-Stalin generation has meant that available assets have permitted decision makers a wider range of choices, have imposed fewer constraints on them, and have more readily permitted

satisfying all perceived constituencies to some significant extent.

6. A wider range of choices also becomes permissible due to the greater uncertainty within the Soviet elite about the validity of developments with manifestly disorienting implications for the faithful believers in the existence of a single Communist truth.

While the specific weight of these and other elements has changed over time, the dynamics of change in the Soviet Union have nonetheless tended to follow a plausible and intelligible pattern. It may be said, in brief, that Leonid Brezhnev has brought foreign policy home to the USSR. On the one hand, there are the trends that are "objectively" given, as economic development proceeds and as the Soviet Union undergoes what is called the "scientific-technological revolution." In this respect the situation in the USSR is not qualitatively different from trends elsewhere in the world, including the United States, which Graham Allison, Edward L. Morse, and others have described as marked by the growing erosion of the boundaries between foreign and domestic policy areas. Developments in fields such as energy, weapons, and communications illustrate this trend.[38]

On the other hand, the same tendency has been reinforced and promoted by "subjective" political choices made by the Politburo. As a number of studies have described, these decisions have included a departure from the time-honored commitment to economic self-sufficiency in favor of greater interaction with the outside world, including foreign trade, advanced technology transfers to the Soviet Union, and other ways to benefit the Soviet economy. In essence, these are efforts to remedy continuing, and in some instances chronic, deficiencies of Soviet economic and technological development (especially in such areas as innovation, incentives, management, efficiency) and to do so without embarking on economic or administrative reforms at home that would be apt to provoke more serious political fallout as well as perhaps tacit resistance and potentially more serious disruption.[39]

Soviet policy thus seeks to call on the external to help the internal environment, on condition that the political costs at home are held to a manageable minimum. Regardless of whether or not in retrospect Brezhnev and his colleagues will be seen to have correctly gauged their ability to keep this price at a minimum — in terms of access to "alien" ideas, values, and attitudes — the policy commitment itself once more underscores the indissolubility of the domestic and foreign policy spheres.

The overall effects of these trends may be summarized as:

1. A spillover effect greater than in the past of discrete decisions in other sectors (e.g., dissent, weapons, R&D, energy) on foreign affairs;

2. A growing complexity — technical, administrative, and intellectual — of Soviet foreign policymaking;

3. A growing awareness by Soviet foreign policymakers of the domestic arena in which they function.

This point deserves additional comment. Without any dramatic or sudden changes in process or institutions, the relationship between Soviet state and society (and in particular between decision makers and attentive elites) has begun to be transformed in perhaps fundamental ways. Stalin could effectively ignore "public opinion" in making foreign policy decisions; in turn, the dominant mood—whether out of necessity, resignation, or dedication—was to leave foreign affairs to the Kremlin. As John Scott recalls in his *Behind the Urals*, when the Nazi-Soviet pact was concluded "Semichkin shrugged his shoulders: 'Stalin did it,' he said. 'Yemu vidnyei—He knows what he is doing.'"[40] And speaking of the war years, Frederick C. Barghoorn later recalled, "It was always my impression that the vast majority of Soviet people were politically indifferent and apathetic. I often heard ordinary Soviet people say, 'We are little people,' or 'That is not our affair.'"[41] No longer so.

As Adam Ulam has cogently argued, Soviet leaders today cannot afford great political defeats abroad of the sort Stalin could: presumably severe setbacks would reflect on the perceived legitimacy of the regime. By the same token, Ulam suggests, foreign policy successes are for the Soviet elite a "principal means of legitimizing their policy system."[42]

By implication then Soviet decision makers no longer have quite the same free hand in foreign affairs as their predecessors had. There is emerging a sense of quasi-accountability—to a circumscribed elite rather than a mass public, to be sure—even while formal and institutional requirements for it are lacking (other than the ritual fictions of Central Committee and Supreme Soviet reports). This in turn implies a quest for what has aptly been called foreign policy legitimation.

The concept of policy rather than regime legitimacy has lately been gaining acceptance; the process by which such legitimacy is acquired and maintained is legitimation.[43] If it tends to create no problems for governments in periods of general policy successes, at times of questionable performance doubts regarding the assumptions underlying the policy calculus are likely to grow. The rather uneven record of the Brezhnev leadership—especially vis-à-vis the United States—has in all likelihood put the senior decision makers in Moscow on the defensive to a greater extent than has been true of foreign policy issues within the political lifetime of the present incumbents. To be sure, toward the outside world (and this includes the bulk of the Soviet Union itself) the elite continues to present, whenever possible, a united front; and the constituency toward which this informal accountability is directed remains narrowly circumscribed.

Within these limits, one may posit that the necessity to seek continual policy legitimation will remain in force for any Soviet leadership. This imposes a new parameter of constraints on policymaking and at least in this regard moves it closer to the public-relations management (rather than the traditional agitprop) familiar to U.S. politicians who know that there is commonly more support to be gained from flag-waving and grandstanding than from measured sophistication. If true, this is another ironic, albeit unintended, consequence of the "development" of Soviet politics and society.

All this describes an imperfect learning process. Sooner or later some of the new images and insights were bound to clash with time-honored stereotypes. Under Stalin, none dared exclaim that the emperor had no clothes. After him there were neither clothes nor emperor, and then the questions were bound to come. "What happens when the Soviet Union reaches a point in history, as it did in 1956, when the inadmissible gap between Marxist-Leninist theory and Soviet practice becomes blatant? Sooner or later this gap must be closed—not by changing the practice, which will continue to be dictated, in Marxist terms, by Life itself, but by changing the theory"[44]—or else, one might add, by minimizing references to theory altogether.

There has clearly been, in Soviet outlook and articulation, a marked increase in ambiguity and in unreconciled diversity of approaches and cognitions. It has been suggested that it is particularly important to inquire whether the image of the opponent has changed.[45] To put things simply, the answer is yes. While Soviet ideological treatments, textbooks, and some other media continue to convey the image of a crisis-ridden, declining enemy camp, the operational presuppositions of greater interdependence between socialist and capitalist systems and economies include implicit elements of mutual benefit, symbiosis, and recognition that the Soviet Union stands to gain from closer ties with the presumably degenerate and contagious opponent (if the latter will permit them). Similarly, the anticipated benefits from growing interdependence presuppose that the United States and other capitalist systems will *not* collapse. Nor are these entirely novel insights: the evidence of pragmatic emancipation from ideological stereotypes goes back many years and was clearly an element in the Sino-Soviet dispute as far back as the early 1960s.[46]

The competing images of the United States that can be found in Soviet statements, scholarship, and media have been the subject of several thorough studies and cannot be reexamined here. In substance, all serious inquiries have found evidence of the existence of rival images (with rival behavioral implications)—or evidence of significant changes over time in the dominant imagery and its underlying assumptions.[47]

While the process is at times slow and reluctant, there is solid evidence of

Soviets learning from experience. The inclusion of a "mutual hostage" posture in the SALT I treaty marked, for the Soviet Union, a recognition of interdependence that had previously been resisted in an atmosphere of Leninist *kto kovo*. Negotiators who have been involved with Soviet opposite numbers in arms control talks over ten or more years give various and numerous examples—along with instances of infuriating stubborness—of the gradual adoption and absorption of "American" concepts and assumptions in the fields of military doctrine and arms control theory on the part of the USSR.[48]

There is also considerable anecdotal evidence of the vastly improved familiarity of the Soviet public, or at least of that part that evinces interest, with conditions abroad. This would seem to be due to a coincidence of several developments, such as improved access to communications media (including radio as well as television reception and long-distance telephone dialing), and some modest improvement in opportunities to travel abroad and to meet foreigners within the USSR. While the explicitly political payoff of all these transactions and opportunities remains in dispute, one can point to a slow but real, cumulative impact of seemingly apolitical transactions between the Soviet population and the outside world. It is easy for an outsider to underestimate the scope and importance of the striking contrast between the virtual isolation of the Soviet citizen from the world abroad a generation ago and the current state of affairs in which channels and arenas of interaction have multiplied by the hundreds, if not thousands, and now cover a gamut from athletics to professional meetings, from blue jeans and Pepsi to the Grateful Dead.[49]

Linkage Patterns: Why and Whither?

It remains to ask why there are such connections and patterns linking seemingly distinct areas of public policy. There are apparently three distinct roots of linkage in the Soviet case.

The Structural Base. One set of connections among seemingly discrete dimensions of policy stems from the nature of the Soviet polity and economy. This structural or institutional aspect is a function of the central command system and in particular of the centrality of decisions regarding resource allocation.

Given a pool of limited resources, options—say, regarding the procurement of weapons—are bound to affect the availability of assets for agriculture, light industry, and capital construction—and vice versa. Priority given to the acquisition of foreign grain or chemical fertilizer or technology implies appropriate measures calculated to promote these priority objectives and restraint from others that might imperil them. This is not to argue that foreign policy decisions are made strictly in terms of financial cost-benefit analyses; but the alternative uses of scarce resources clearly militate for a rational coordination of domestic and foreign options consistent with a rank-ordering of priorities. Moreover, as suggested earlier, certain trends in technology and science policy serve to intensify the linkages in this field and at least require a clearer perception of anticipated costs and benefits.[50]

Elite Politics. One may suggest, tentatively, the existence of another source of linkages in recent years in the emergence of tacit, informal, or incipient coalitions, where the pursuit of a given foreign policy may be in the nature of side payments in return for a consensus or "deal" on domestic policies or vice versa. Here the linkage is not so much substantive as political.[51]

The Mind-set. The obvious place to focus, in addition, is on the minds of the actors. As a universal proposition, individuals filter information, respond to impulses, and choose among alternative behaviors in a fashion consistent with personal norms, perceptions, prior experiences, and beliefs. Some psychologists have formulated theories of "cognitive consistency" based on the assumption (some would say, evidence) that there exists in any person a natural search for congruence among one's attitudes, beliefs, and behavior—an assumption other specialists would vigorously deny.[52] But even if such a hypothesis is problematic, in the Soviet case we encounter a special and important trait that might be called a psychoideological compulsion, rooted in the Leninist tradition, to provide a totalist, holistic, homogeneous analytical framework for the entire domain of public policy. More specifically, one may speak of a special Soviet predisposition to perceive or provide "linkages" in the environment, due to a combination of (1) the notion of a "general line"; (2) the operational assumption of the relatively high penetrability of foreign polities; (3) the claims to be engaged in "scientific" analysis and the definition of strategy and tactics; (4) the predisposition to make entire societies the target of Soviet foreign policy behavior; and (5) the axiom that there are no accidents.

While the mind-set is always a relevant dimension, the specific weight of Leninist assumptions such as those sketched above—their saliency and impact and the corresponding attitudes—is bound to vary.

Both conceptually and empirically, at any given instance several or all of the above sources of linkage may be present. It is not clear whether the different sources just outlined make for different operational consequences. It would appear that they may occur and persist differentially. Thus the "reciprocal" posture of the 1970s implies both a weakening of the traditional compulsion to find and act on consistent totalist beliefs and images and a greater instrumental skill and sophistication in the simultaneous pursuit of seemingly conflicting courses — as it were, the capacity to play a different tune with each hand at once.[53]

Of course, it must be remembered that adaptation need not mean moderation. But the evidence suggests that while the specifically Leninist elements among the "subjective" variables sketched above are declining in practical importance, the other two complexes — the structural and the political dimensions — appear to have gained in weight in explaining Soviet policy in the 1970s.[54]

The Wider Context

Having surveyed some of the concepts and trends, it remains for us to look briefly and selectively, at some of the variables in Soviet life that seem to be particularly significant or controversial in relation to our topic.

Traditional Political Culture

What is the relevance of earlier experience, traditions, and myths for the conduct of Soviet foreign policy? Clearly, discrete policy decisions cannot be related to any such diffuse, long-range phenomena in a cause and effect relationship. Just as clearly, these may be important sources of memories, attitudes, and beliefs that, as part of contemporary mind-sets, constitute at the very least a wider context that may set conditioning or constraining parameters.

In substance, we are dealing with political culture — not in the sense of official (and often fictitious and ritualized) beliefs, but as "the subjective perception of history and politics, the fundamental beliefs and values, the foci of identification and loyalty, and the political knowledge and expectations which are the product of the specific historical experience of nations and groups."[55]

Methodologically, unfortunately, this proves to be an exceptionally amorphous subject matter whose operational relevance and weight are difficult to assess or demonstrate under the best of circumstances.[56] It is hard enough to identify the distinctive elements of any society's political culture(s); it is harder yet to do better than to give an intuitive response to the question whether such elements remain "alive" and, if so, what bearing they have on current attitudes and behavior. Dealing with such questions in regard to foreign affairs, finally, is bound to be most hazardous of all.

This section, therefore, is likely to reflect the author's biases more openly and substantially than do other parts of this chapter. It amounts to an inclination *not* to give undue weight to historiopolitical predispositions that, of late, have served far too generously as an ostensible master key to an understanding of Soviet conduct. "Political culture" has repeatedly become the residual category that has served as the catchbasin for everything that could not otherwise be explained. In the Soviet case it has all too often been invoked by "essentialist" ideologues arguing—at times with massive erudition—a historical predeterminism: the Soviet Union, as it were, trapped by and unable to escape its own past.[57]

Although this is not entirely a yes or no proposition, I find far more merit in the contrary view, and I am delighted not to be alone.[58] A senior historian recently warned, in regard to Germany, that "too great a desire to prove continuity leads to a tendency to ignore nuances and to confuse chance likenesses and similarities of formulations with identity in essence."[59] Other scholars have shown, with massive evidence and considerable sophistication, the common features that modernization tends to produce, regardless of the cultural peculiarities of particular societies—not only in socioeconomic institutions but also in individual values and attitudes.[60] The whole notion of political socialization hinges, after all, on the possibility of altering prior norms; and the justified skepticism regarding the concept of "national character" underscores the need to relativize the importance of cultural, political, and historical continuity and distinctiveness as an input into present and future decisions.[61]

It is a sound proposition that the relative weight of traditional political culture is bound to be diminishing.[62] Still, it is useful to refer to a few elements which are at times put forth as still influential. Some features, of course—no matter for our purposes whether their existence is proven, problematic, or fictitious—are at best of marginal relevance to our topic. These encompass the so-called oriental mode of production, the ostensible Byzantine influences, and the impact of the Mongols on Russia. My underlying assumption is a preference for parsimonious explanations of causality, and it is sound to posit that no significant insights are to be gained by factoring in variables such as the "Tatar yoke."[63] Essentially the same may be said of other studies, however informed, astute, and imaginative the analyses.[64]

One problem is that for every "tradition" thus identified (for which one can claim some evidence of continuity) one can also find not only exceptions but countertrends and countertraditions. As a shorthand formulation to characterize currents in Russian intellectual thought, for instance, it might be said that if there was a tradition linking Dostoyevsky, Berdiaev, and Solzhenitsyn, there is also another spanning events and actors from the *veche* to Miliukov, on to the elections to the Constituent Assembly, and to Andrei Sakharov. If Russian culture was marked by a lack of institutionalized give-and-take in political life (at least prior to 1905) this did not prevent the emergence of political pluralism including organized parties and partisan media; nor did it doom or frustrate the growth of politics within the Bolshevik party or the Soviet elite after the Revolution of 1917. Other scholars, too, have recently challenged the assumption of the significant inheritance of a highly centralized government, a command economy, a large economy, and an official ideology. As S. Frederick Starr remarks,

> It need hardly be said that this is a highly selective characterization of Russia's political heritage. One might suggest, for example, that Russia has suffered as much from undergovernment as from overgovernment; that its undermanned elites have ruled as much by default as by design; or that centralization has existed more as an ideal than as a functioning reality.[65]

The question then comes back to the marginal utility of introducing hypothetical assumptions.

Soviet "Ideology" as Political Culture

What about political culture as it has emerged and developed since the Bolshevik Revolution? Here it is well to distinguish clearly between *official* Communist political culture—both the formal ideology and the ritual orthodoxy of Soviet officialdom—and the dominant culture as actually internalized and assimilated by major segments of the population. We are not dealing here with either the operational code of particular actors or with formalized doctrine. The latter has been the object of intense and sustained socialization, and in the virtual absence of countervailing experiences and exposure for the bulk of the Soviet population, its effects must of course not be dismissed out of hand. Yet for our purposes what matters is the practical relevance of the belief system, as it is widely and commonly accepted, to the extent that it serves to order or filter experience.

The role of Marxism-Leninism as a motive force or as a determinant of policy choices by the Soviet leadership has been discussed so extensively and debated so fiercely that new perspectives cannot be expected here.[66] I can do no more than indicate my own location on the spectrum of viewpoints articulated in this debate and illustrate what appears to me the most plausible position with a few examples.

In essence, the argument has centered on the question of whether the Soviet state is "an ideology in power" (whether ideology was, to use the standard formula, a "guide to action") or whether (the phrase is, I believe, R. V. Daniels's) action is a guide to ideology; whether, in other words, the formal and explicit belief system impels, informs, shapes, and directs decisions and set goals or, on the contrary, amounts to a bundle of means in the pursuit of national (or special) interests as defined by the elite or the leader.

To put it briefly, over the course of Soviet history the same formal ideology has permitted—and has been used to justify and sanction, by reference to the "classics" of Marxism-Leninism—such a wide range of different, conflicting, and at times mutually incompatible courses of action that it cannot be properly seen as a "guide to action." War and peace, coexistence and confrontation, going it alone and broad alliances have all been legitimized by reference to ideological authority.

It does not follow from this that the Soviet leaders use Marxism-Leninism merely as a veneer for traditional (Russian) objectives or for the pursuit of policies rooted in their own power hunger, nor that they hypocritically decide, after making a given decision, how to cloak their conduct in proper Communist phraseology to rally the faithful and confound the foe. Surely in the early years the Bolshevik leadership took its theory quite seriously, even if from the outset the top theoreticians—such as Lenin, Bukharin, and Trotsky—disagreed over fundamental questions of doctrine, such as the primacy of state or revolution. It can also be shown that over time the long-term aspects of the creed, including its vision of the future, have become increasingly fuzzy and irrelevant to day-to-day decision making in Moscow.

In a world in which the first enemy is China, another Communist state, the two-camp doctrine makes no sense. In a world in which (to quote Khrushchev) "the atomic bomb does not follow the class principle," it is hard to speak of the ineluctable course of human history. In a world in which Moscow relies on the West for more grain, better computers, and an occasional Cadillac or crate of Pepsi-Cola; where proletarian revolutions have been the exception rather than the rule; where war is no longer deemed inevitable; where Soviet successes abroad have been due to conventional means—state power, political and military; where it is acknowledged that at times ideological preconceptions have blocked a correct reading of reality (a reality that turned out to be far more complex than the "classics" had given their disciples reason to expect); and where reference to Communism as a belief system has served to legitimize every turn and twist of policy, hard and soft, left and right, rigid and flexible, a good case can be made that today the actual decisions—be they on automation, Afghanistan, or antisubmarine warfare—are not uniquely or even primarily informed by Leninist dogma.

It seems sensible, then, to accept the notion of a gradual, uneven, and unacknowledged erosion, decline, or "relativization" of the unique elements of the faith insofar as they were taken to provide, in earlier years, perceptual blinders and to set goals to which all else had to be subordinated. The process of erosion may be manifested in two ways: first, in the adaptation of ideological formulations to reality and second, in the decreasing intensity, scope, and operational impact of ideological statements as handed down "from above." It is probably fair to assume that such an approach is more easily assimilated into the dominant political culture.

This is another example of a learning process that has led to growing sophistication and "emancipation" from doctrinal stereotypes on the part of a relatively small number of members of the intellectual and political elites, but that has not been explicitly acknowledged nor affected the reiteration of orthodox clichés in and by the mass media and routine propagandists.[67]

The official style requires, within limits, continued adherence to the conventional formulae and jargon (though experienced Soviet officials and scholars know how to ignore, manipulate, or circumvent these when necessary or when possible). On the one hand, this makes for a greater gap between public pronouncements and private beliefs; on the other hand, given the elaborate reiteration of doctrinal formulations (and the fact that they are "taken seriously" by authoritative figures), something rubs off and becomes part of the diffuse body of assumptions accepted in the dominant culture.[68] It is scarcely surprising that in a system in which the entire society has been systematically and frequently subjected to the same stream of political stereotypes, many people are bound to accept their terms uncritically and unthinkingly; after all, the same is essentially true of societies in which the verbal and "educational" bombardment is far less intense and less uniform.

The most that can be said about the continuing role of "ideology" in this era, for the dominant Soviet culture, is to describe it as a partial guide to perception — shaping categories and expectations and often limiting the range of the permissible. But to what extent, specifically, it functions must be assumed to vary not only from time to time but also from individual to individual, and cannot be deduced from a generalized, aggregated, abstracted discussion of "ideology" and "political culture."

We must also note here the existence of contradictory elements, side by side, in the body of what we have been calling political culture. There is, for instance, a deeply engrained animus against the capitalist world. In all likelihood, this is a widespread, genuine, and deep-seated feeling among many Soviet citizens. This does not, however, prevent them from engaging in semi-licit activities that smack of private enterprise; of knowing, admiring, or envying the high standard of living and the consumerist "luxuries" of American-style capitalist life; and of accepting, endorsing, even fervently wishing for increased contacts with the outside world, not only as an alternative to war but also as a way of sharing in a world they do not trust but want to be a part of.

Similarly, there is an engrained assumption that "time is on their side." Yet there is confusion here, too. When pressed, Soviet citizens will acknowledge that "their side" no longer automatically comprises all Com-

munist powers and parties and that China, as an adversary of the Soviet
Union, could not also have time on its side. Similar confusion applies to the
world Communist movement, to Russian nationalism, to the roll of personalities, and to numerous other contradictions in the domestic "political
culture."

What we find then is that the culture, insofar as it can be identified,
today represents a somewhat amorphous amalgam of traditional Russian,
orthodox Communist, and more recent eclectic elements. While there
seems to be widespread agreement over the recession of Communist
"ideological" elements — most obviously in their role of operationally shaping policy decisions — there is uncertainty or disagreement among observers
over the question whether traditional elements are reemerging or are also
bound to wither as Soviet society becomes increasingly modernized. There
is a manifest increase in beliefs, perceptions, and assumptions that do not
readily fit either the "Russian" or the "Communist" stereotypes, if only
because the present world is marked by what Moscow likes to refer to as the
scientific-technological revolution, and some of its products — be it digital
computers or intercontinental ballistic missiles or frozen food — were not
provided for by, and are not readily accommodated within, the categories
provided by the Leninist heritage.

This then adds to the aura of ambiguity, which is heightened by the fact
that, at least in a limited form, the mass audience is exposed to conflicting
signals from elites, experts, and decision makers who tend to see the world
in different and at times conflicting terms. Different images serve to support and justify different foreign policy preferences.[69]

It remains doubtful then whether the study of political culture as a diffuse
collective phenomenon is of marked value in any attempt to identify and
explain Soviet foreign policymaking and motivations. This would seem to
apply to "traditional" as well as to "Communist" features of the culture.

Soviet Politics: Trends and Actors

Various studies have examined, in considerable detail and with expert
knowledge, some of the "objective" dimensions of Soviet power. Not only
geography and climate but natural and human resources and economic,
technological, and scientific capabilities are among the factors that make up
the environment in which the Soviet Union functions and in which policy
decisions are made. These variables may be assumed to impose constraints
or to apply pressure on the decision makers insofar as they communicate
needs or opportunities, comparative advantages, or disadvantages vis-à-vis
other states. While for many purposes it may be important to have a precise
picture of Soviet assets and liabilities in all these fields, for our subject what
counts is their role as inputs into policy decisions — that is, how these prob-

lems are perceived and operationalized. And here there is much that we do not know.

We do know that the Soviet Union has been firmly and lastingly committed to maximizing its power. Under Stalin this was the overriding objective of state policy, pursued at considerable cost to other sectors of public (let alone private) life and economy. While the methods and the mix of objectives have changed since his death, the impetus toward the acquisition of power has remained and become virtually an end in itself.

If we ignore the price—which has at times been staggering—the USSR has clearly been successful in this quest, as measured by a number of conventional indicators. Its emergence as one of the two superpowers, its GNP, its military might, its space program, and its global reach are all examples of achievements and capabilities that enhance its international position. They create political opportunities as well as responsibilities, temptations as well as dangers for the USSR.

Just as obviously, the Soviet Union is very far from having solved the many problems of economic development, use of resources, management, distributive justice, or the challenges of bureaucracy, inadequate incentives, and resistance to scientific and technological innovation. If we can believe recent assessments, the Soviet Union faces serious problems in the years ahead, not only in its growth rates (which have already slowed) but also in a number of other sectors, from manpower to fossil fuel. As is the case in other societies, developmental "progress" has a way of generating unintended and often highly unwelcome consequences even before older problems are substantially resolved.

No effort will be made here to summarize basic economic, geographic, or demographic data.[70] Instead, to explore how Soviet authoritative observers perceive these problems, it may be useful to differentiate among several questions.

How has Soviet weakness or strength, as perceived by them, affected the outlook and behavior of Soviet decision makers? It would be an error to equate perceived weakness with Soviet willingness to compromise or yield, and perceived strength with inflexibility or intransigence in Soviet foreign policy. And yet historically much of Soviet policy in the early years of the regime can be shown to have been the product of keenly perceived inferiority compared to the "capitalist" environment. Whether or not the sense of danger was exaggerated or contrived, there is little doubt that from 1927 on Moscow saw the "correlation of forces" between the Soviet and non-Soviet worlds menacingly to Moscow's disadvantage. This perception, after all, was the rationale for the breakneck buildup. As Stalin declared in 1931, the USSR had to do in ten years what it took others fifty or one hundred years to achieve!

Militarily, the sense of Soviet weakness was explicitly acknowledged in

Lenin's regret that he was unable to come to the aid of Béla Kun's embattled Hungarian Soviet Republic in 1919; in Stalin's policy of appeasing Japan in 1931 and again in 1939. It was a prime motivation for the Nazi-Soviet Pact: repeatedly in 1939–1941 remarks were made in Moscow that time was needed to stockpile weapons and supplies, to prepare and train Soviet forces. After World War II, Stalin told Tito that regrettably the Soviet armed forces were in no condition to provide the support the French and Italian Communists would have needed to take power in their homelands. Such examples are but the tip of the iceberg; one may well posit a pervasive undercurrent of comparative weakness, relative disadvantage, and perceived inferiority that have informed so much of Soviet behavior—both when it meekly folded and when it hoarded whatever it could (as with reparations from Germany after World War II, and to some extent in Soviet economic relations with its "fraternal" allies in Eastern Europe and the Far East). And although in sizing up the West the Soviet sense of strategic inferiority has in recent years begun to vanish (though even here a distinct time lag may be observed), no similar erosion has affected the perceived asymmetry in relative economic and technological development nor of living standards—and with good reason.

Independently of specific events or decisions, a large part of responsible Soviet officialdom appears to be intensely aware of at least some of the systemic problems connected with the economy, resources, manpower, and energy. It is true that some of the chronic handicaps and vulnerabilities have become less salient in the post-Stalin years. Technology has begun to overcome such problems as distances and permafrost. Territory—and the absence of natural borders—has been of decreasing importance for national security in the nuclear age. But, ironically, no sooner do some problems recede than others, of equal or greater gravity and complexity, move to the fore.

How then do they see the present and future short falls and inadequacies on the Soviet homefront? It is not too much to assert that—after the obvious priorities of security, legitimacy, and control—issues of economy and resources, and the "scientific-technological revolution," are among the uppermost concerns of the Soviet elite, objects of intense attention, sustained study, and often bitter debate.

An analysis of the Soviet political scene must deal with a number of trends basic to an understanding of it. Once we transcend Soviet constitutional and ideological myths, we find informal political behavior that comes closer to a "conflict model" than to the stereotype of consensual authoritarianism. Rather plausibly, members of the Soviet elite, "acting as individuals or as members of factions and interest groups, seek to convert inputs or . . . demands, based on often divergent interests and values, into outputs of public policy."[71] This has been particularly true in the post-Stalin years, when "elite politics has evolved from arbitrary, personalistic rule to a competitive oligarchy. Group access to the principal policymaking arenas has become more regularized and less dangerous."[72]

To be sure, these changes must be seen against the continuities of the "bureaucratic and mobilizational bias" of the Soviet political system. The Soviet Union remains a one-party dictatorship, with a political life marked by the tradition and mystique of party unity, hierarchy, discipline, and centralization, a pronounced institutionalization of party supremacy, and a habit of (at least formal) consensus and compliance. And yet it would be a grievous error to accept Soviet claims and pretense as reality and to neglect the multitude of tensions, functional and jurisdictional disputes, role conflicts, groups, lobbies, informal groupings, individual idiosyncracies, bureaucratic politics, vested interests, intellectual and perceptual differences, regional and ethnic rivalries, power struggles, technical disputes, and various other antagonisms. Indeed, it is precisely the variable relationship among these elements that makes it so difficult to provide simple analytical formulae for the inputs into Soviet policymaking.

We admittedly have a woefully inadequate knowledge of these magnetic fields that undergird the surface of Soviet public life. This does not make them any less real or important.[73] The difficulties of analyzing political conflict in the Soviet system have been amply commented on. They are rooted, on the one hand, in Soviet inability to deal candidly with the subject and Soviet unwillingness to reveal what might be considered compromising information (a preference elites elsewhere might share but are not usually able to implement with equal effectiveness); and, on the other hand, in the methodological challenges of reconstructing factional alliances and alignments, coalitions and cleavages from highly inadequate and often unreliable fragments of information. But while the handicaps have been immense, a review of the record shows a formidable accumulation of instances supporting and illustrating the hypothesis of Soviet political conflict and, in spite of a frequent sense of frustration (and a number of false starts) on the part of many observers, a remarkable increase over time in insight and sophistication in analysis and interpretation.[74] Indeed, one might well agree with Frederick Barghoorn's observation that

> we should not make the mistake of assuming that uniform socialization, centralized recruiting of executives, and the hierarchical structure of the political bureaucracy ensure unity of perspective or purpose among Soviet decisionmakers. On the contrary, much evidence indicates that discord, conflict, and political infighting may play a larger, though concealed, role in one-party systems than in democracies.[75]

What does remain in dispute are the bases of political alignments. While the original "Kremlinological" preoccupation with personalities has been largely superseded in the work of many specialists, there are no doubt many instances in which personal (or personality) conflicts are a major part of the story. There has been an inclination to pursue the hypothesis that different institutions and bureaucracies tend to breed vested interests that promote the identification and support of policy preferences functionally congruent with the professional concerns of a given agency or with its collective political posture.[76]

This approach has helped to correct the "totalitarian" misconceptions of earlier studies. But it turns out that empirically the available evidence does not fully support this hypothesis either (any more than its equivalent does regarding bureaucratic politics in the United States). The political behavior of individual leaders, to the extent that we can reconstruct it, does not always bear out the pattern of quasi-representation of institutional interests at the apex of the Soviet power pyramid. Institutional policy preferences (say, of the military) turn out not to be homogeneous and, where we can identify them, the options endorsed by subgroups or individuals do not always correspond to what we would "rationally" expect to be the functional preferences of the institutions with which they are associated. In light of our earlier discussion of mind-sets, this should scarcely be surprising, with innumerable variations — from mental laziness to a lack of adequate information to the spillover effect of other issue-areas that preoccupy a particular actor — accounting for some of the remaining variance.

The role of groups and groupings, though still contested by some commentators, is increasingly hard to deny. In brief, since 1953 there have been

> expanded opportunities for interest articulation and political access for the myriad occupational, associational, and opinion groupings in Soviet society. Economists have had increasing influence on decisions affecting the organization of the economy; teachers have had an impact upon educational reforms; scientists have influenced the priorities of scientific research; and lawyers have helped in the determination of legal policy. . . . And throughout the hierarchy, commissions of experts are attached to Party and state executive organs, to provide input related to their fields of specialization.[77]

In turn, the dissatisfaction with the bureaucratic politics model and the stress on interest groups have strengthened the case for analysis by issue-areas or, in Franklyn Griffiths's terminology, the study of "tendencies of articulation." These amount to orientations toward issue-areas — attitudes and opinions rather than institutional groups — and have served as a framework for various studies.[78]

I posited earlier that the single most significant, or useful, axis on which to locate different substantive policy positions in the Soviet Union — and indeed political tempers — is the conventional left/right spectrum. It is proper to identify various other dichotomies current in the typology of groups with this cleavage — for example, the division into orthodox/traditionalists and modernizers/reformers; the hiatus between maintenance and innovation; the split between "expert" and "Red."[79] Curiously, such an approach is reinforced by recent U.S. research. Snyder and Diesing conclude from a series of case studies that, rather than seeing attitudes of decision makers as largely role-conditioned, "individuals' views seemed at least as often to be the function of personal predilection toward 'hard' or 'soft' strategies." Indeed, applying this to foreign policy preferences, they find that

> the stances taken by individual participants tend to mirror the spectrum of external bargaining options available to the state. The salient options are coercion . . . , accommodation, or some mixture of these two. . . . While the softliner underrates the danger of looking weak, the hard-liner discounts the risk of provocation and escalation.[80]

In general terms, these propositions are equally plausible as hypotheses in regard to Soviet elite politics.

Nonetheless, a left/right yardstick by itself is an inadequate tool. For one thing, we find significant differences *within* each end of the spectrum — for instance, among moderates on the Communist "right," tension over resource allocation between consumer goods and agriculture; or differences among "hard-liners" in the military-industrial complex. Moreover, the alternatives between left and right no longer pose so stark a dilemma, as options have become attenuated with the growing GNP. Soviet policy manages to produce a mix of "left" and "right" elements; it is not "guns *or* butter" but rather "how many guns (of what kind, at what price, and for whom) *and* how much butter (of what quality, for whom)."

Furthermore, other sources of cleavage do not fit the left/right dichotomy at all: staff/line differences; tensions between center and periphery; regional rivalries — say, between Siberia and the Ukraine over resources and investments — with foreign policy overtones vis-à-vis China and Czechoslovakia; generational, occupational, or experiential alignments; and last but not least, patronage networks and cliques.[81]

All this underscores the need to recognize the existence of multiple sources of cleavage and alignments in Soviet politics and society. It is also well to remember that political differences may be healthy rather than dysfunctional. As Hodnett has remarked, what we see now is often the politics of accommodation rather than a winner-take-all style or attitude.[82]

It is equally important to avoid being boxed into inflexible definitions. One of the hallmarks of current Soviet politics is its ambiguities and inconsistencies, and many observers would agree that recent practice often comes closer to "muddling through" than to the pursuit of any grand design.

Two related points should be added here. One is to refer to the dynamics of collective decision making. It may be suggested that there is a built-in tendency — given divided opinion or unwillingness by any individual or faction to expend political credit for "victory" on a given issue — in case of doubt, to do nothing.

The other is to refer to the interesting proposition by K. J. Holsti regarding the variability of national role conceptions. As he shows in a comparative ranking, the USSR stands near the top in the multiplicity of roles conceived for it by its key actors — decision makers and advisers — vis-à-vis the outside world. For instance, they see the Soviet Union at various times as liberator, as model, as regional leader, as developer, as defender of the faith.[83] These multiple roles are bound to invite different strategies and give rise to divergent priorities, thus further compounding the problems of inconsistency and ambiguity.

Actors in the Decision Process

Decision making in Soviet foreign policy — what little is known of it — has been discussed in other studies. While a broader circle of persons and a greater number of institutions are now involved than were a generation ago (especially if we include all the phases, such as consulting, research, and policy planning), it remains true that the party's Politburo has the decisive say in determining foreign policy lines.[84] However, the Politburo may now be considered more inclusive insofar as "all major specialized hierarchies of the Soviet Party-state have their chief executives represented in the Politburo"[85] (highlighted by the cooptation into the Politburo of the main spokesmen for the three security bureaucracies — the Ministry of Foreign Affairs, the Ministry of Defense, and the Committee of State Security).

The experience of the post-Stalin leadership offers a number of signal instances of top-level disputes centered on foreign policy issues or distinctly linked to them, and in a number of instances resulting in the ouster of losers. One outstanding case, on which the evidence from Soviet and non-Soviet sources is particularly ample, is the duel between Nikita Khrushchev and Viacheslav Molotov, which saw its climax at the Central Committee meeting of July 1955 and amounted to a confrontation of two fundamentally different political orientations.[86] Their clash may be seen as epitomizing the conflict of Stalinist and anti-Stalinist outlooks in Moscow; as a test of strength between left and right Communist tempers; as a confrontation of optimism and pessimism; as reflecting a fundamental difference in approaching a number of specific foreign (as well as domestic) policy issues, ranging from the Austrian peace treaty to diplomatic relations with Japan and the German Federal Republic, from joint-stock companies with "fraternal" states to the settlement of Soviet-Yugoslav and Soviet-Finnish differences.

In the post-Khrushchev era, the primary cases of top-level confrontations that led to the ouster of at least one Politburo member in each instance and that in varying degrees involved foreign policy issues are those of Aleksandr Shelepin, along with his associates and followers; of Piotr Shelest; and of Nikolai Podgorny. In none of these is the polarization of contending tendencies as clear-cut or consistent as it was in the 1955 duel. But the Shelepin case clearly involved far more than the removal from power of an ambitious and somewhat younger rival of Leonid Brezhnev. While Shelepin's public pronouncements were on occasion self-contradictory (whether out of genuine changes in outlook, confusion, or obedience, or out of attempts to anticipate political criticism on the part of some of his colleagues is not clear), his general outlook and the support he sought and to some extent enjoyed (e.g., in the secret police, trade unions, youth and sports organizations) ranged him (along with associates like Pavlov and Semichastnyi) on the side of the action-oriented, know-nothing, anti-Western, anti-intellectual elements. Perhaps most indicative of the foreign policy implications of those identified with the *shelepintsy* is the purge of Nikolai Egorychev, first secretary of the Moscow party organization, in the aftermath of the 1967 Middle Eastern crisis.[87]

As for Shelest, he had been amply identified as one of the prime advocates of Soviet intervention in Czechoslovakia, at a time in 1968 when most Politburo members still resisted such a move. Shelest's orientation—on other occasions zenophobic and anti-"revisionist"—apparently was linked to his sensitivity to the possible (or real) effect of developments in Czechoslovakia on the neighboring Ukraine, over whose destiny he was in effect presiding. His dramatic ouster from the leadership on the eve of the Nixon visit to Moscow in May 1972, on the heels of the stepped-up U.S. bombing of Hanoi and mining of Haiphong, ties Shelest circumstantially to a position in which he found the symbolic Soviet-American embrace intolerable. Though it is apparent that the Shelest ouster had other important strands as well, the distinct position regarding détente that it suggests links it to the broader issue of Soviet-American relations and the major latent cleavage in the Soviet elite over that issue.[88]

Even if they have not led to a showdown, other differences in priorities and outlook among the remaining members of the Politburo can from time to time be documented (and will be illustrated at various points below).[89] Between Brezhnev and Kosygin, for instance, these may be seen as expressions of the perennial tension between party and state apparatuses, as reflections of personal rivalries and competing patronage networks, as an example of the transformation/maintenance dichotomy, or as the product of issue-specific technical considerations. Constance Friesen has shown an interesting connection between the Brezhnev-Kosygin relationship and the prospects of Soviet-American trade. A comparison of their speeches on the subject shows clear differences between them, with Kosygin the more skeptical and restrained (in the 1970s) about the prospect of foreign trade— perhaps out of greater awareness of the rigidities in management, organization, and other aspects of the Soviet economy and administration.[90]

Another sophisticated content analysis of speeches and writings of Soviet leaders is based on the hypothesis that technology acquisition from abroad is a political issue in the Soviet elite. The findings suggest that Brezhnev has been the most important advocate of expanded U.S.-Soviet economic ties, while Suslov, Grechko, Andropov, and Ustinov have shown the least interest in them; but that in general the subject appears to have become less controversial, at least among Politburo members, in the course of the 1970s. As the author of the study puts it, content analysis "also provides a corrective to arguments that explain policy conflicts within a given group of leaders as due merely to differences in their official roles."[91]

There have been a number of efforts to study the nature of bureaucratic politics and bargaining at levels *below* the Politburo and Central Committee Secretariat. Thus the study of foreign trade problems confirms what others too have observed— the growing role of the State Committee on Science and Technology, compared to the USSR Ministry of Foreign Trade; the great variety of institutions, from Gosplan to banking agencies, involved in various aspects of trade and technology acquisition, often with rival outlooks and ill-defined boundaries of jurisdiction; and the "problems resulting from overlapping jurisdictions of foreign trade organizations, from competing claims of industrial ministries, and from high-level debates over the degree of centralization in the economy."[92]

A curious example of jurisdictional rivalry was provided by the handling of Senator Edward Kennedy's trip to the Soviet Union in September 1978. His visit with Brezhnev was arranged without the asssistance of the Soviet Foreign Ministry, much to its apparent annoyance. Press reports upon Kennedy's departure implied that he had received private assurances that questions he had raised would be sympathetically reviewed, including those regarding the issuance of exit visas to a list of individuals he submitted; subsequent events seemed to indicate Soviet implementation of these promises. Rather surprisingly, an article in *Pravda* was distinctly critical of Kennedy (without identifying him by name) and belittled the importance of his intervention.[93] According to members of his staff, it became known that the article had been placed in *Pravda* at the initiative of the Foreign Ministry, jealous as it was to maintain its sweeping responsibility for the field of foreign affairs.

Another careful and informed study of Soviet behavior, in the negotiations with the United States and United Kingdom that led to the conclusion of the 1963 partial nuclear test ban treaty, relates changes in Soviet behavior in these negotiations to "internal bargaining" between protreaty and antitreaty groupings within the Soviet establishment.[94] As others have shown, arms control is likely to be (in any society) a particularly controversial issue, as it tends to provide a focus for rival policy definitions both by diverse "tendencies of articulation" and by conflicting institutional, budgetary, and political interests. This particular case study tends to reinforce the general approach offered here, including the dichotomy between orthodox and reformist outlooks and coalitions. In this instance the "orthodox" elements were apt to oppose the treaty, whereas the "reformers" were likely to favor it. Interestingly, "both the scientists and the foreign affairs intelligentsia seem to have been divided, including 'orthodox' as well as 'reformist' elements. The military, on the other hand, seemed rather unified in its 'orthodox' outlook and displayed no significant internal divergences. Data on the views of industrial managers are inconclusive but suggest 'orthodox' leanings on the part of heavy industry."[95]

Informal coalitions among individuals or bureaucratic subunits have repeatedly been pointed to as indicative of considerable and probably growing importance in Soviet politics. As one recent study confirms, "Coalitions in Soviet politics are loose, temporary, issue-oriented, heterogeneous alliances of convenience among different subgroups powerful enough to carry out their policies."[96] And another study, based on an analysis of the Soviet press, concludes that "the Soviet political system is probably characterized by many criss-crossing, inter-institutional alliances. The various groups are presumably in a state of constant flux, coalescing on the basis of a similarity of views on one issue and changing sides when another issue is concerned."[97] While such volatility may have been more characteristic of the 1960s than of the 1970s, the existence of informal coalitions and at least some fluidity in their composition are beyond doubt.

Less well understood are the dynamics by which rival positions are staked out, explored, or reconciled. Given the paucity of information about the influence process and access to decision makers, the following comments are tentative and perhaps excessively taxonomic.

Policy studies elsewhere have distinguished between "systemic" and "marginalist" critics and critiques.[98] While the former relates to fundamental differences over policy objectives, the latter describes conflicts over alternative ways and means of achieving shared goals. Normally, of course, systemic dissent is not tolerated in the Soviet Union (though ambiguities may awkwardly persist, as with Roy Medvedev). In foreign policy, systemic differences have characteristically been "resolved" by silencing the losers in one manner or another (for instance, in regard to Maxim Litvinov after 1945 and Viacheslav Molotov after 1955–1957).[99] One problem for the foreign analyst is the fact that (precisely because of the impermissibility of fundamental disagreements) such "systemic" differences must be camouflaged in "marginalist" jargon. Cases of "marginalist" dissent may then (but need not) conceal more basic policy conflicts.[100]

It is plausible to distinguish among those who frontally and directly clash over foreign policy; those who seek to make opportunist or instrumental use of foreign policy issues in the course of a contest for power; and those who are engaged in what might be called derivative arguments, in which the logic of "linkages" extends the identification of individuals or groups with political "tendencies" (as well as patron/client alignments) to foreign policy preferences, as if by inevitable indirection.[101] What may be a more helpful categorization emerges from an excellent discussion of the economic and political aspects of East-West trade: a distinction between *direct* participants (e.g., the Ministry of Foreign Affairs or the Politburo), *"collateral"* participants (e.g., the State Committee on Science and Technology or the Academy of Sciences' Institute for the Study of the USA and Canada), and *indirect* ones (e.g., economic reformers or *apparatchiks*). In the framework of a Soviet-American comparison, the authors establish important structural differences. Not only is decision making more centralized in the Soviet Union, but "the number of collateral participants in the Soviet Union is far smaller than in the United States, and the importance of indirect participants is much less striking."

> The first results, in general, from the monopolistic position of the Party, and the second, from its authoritarianism. Third, in contrast with the direct participants, the contribution of collateral participants in the Soviet Union appears to be far more compartmentalized than in the United States. International relations specialists in the Soviet Union interpret United States behavior. They do not offer approaches to arms control. That is the sphere of the military. The Committee on Science and Technology explains how much it means for improved planning to enlist the services of Control Data, but it does not worry about the political implications of getting involved with the major capitalist power.[102]

Interestingly, as Holzman and Legvold show, despite the essential asymmetry of institutions, there are remarkable similarities in the configuration of Soviet and American attitudes toward economic interdependence — a fact that reinforces the utility of a tendency-oriented approach rather than strictly institutional analysis.

We know of very few instances in which individuals or groups not bureaucratically concerned with a given policy issue have taken the initiative to make their views known to those who have the power to decide. No doubt there are numerous instances and numerous variations of informal communication of personal preferences to, say, Central Committee staff members at suburban dachas over a game of chess or a bottle of vodka. By their nature, these instances are hard to document and to assess. One senior Soviet scholar who is also a government consultant (on the Third World) states privately that when he disagrees with official policy, he has the choice of (1) trying to argue with the decision makers—in effect, his superiors; (2) contacting his former students, who are now department heads, ambassadors, and other officials, seeking to influence their views; or (3) writing a personal letter, officially, to the appropriate party or state agency. While he does the latter reluctantly, he says that he has done so more than once. He remarks that he expects to be consulted on major policy problems and he recognizes that, as an established authority, he may be in a better position to voice his opinion than are many others in the Soviet elite.

It is clear that there are such elements of initiative and individual choice in the Soviet system. They appear to be growing. On the other hand, it seems that such practices are not yet widespread and there is no information about their effect, if any.

Soviet Politics: Cases and Issues

Even a cursory survey of the available materials suggests the wide range of issues over which there have been significant differences, overt or otherwise, within the Soviet elite. There are no doubt many more that could be discovered with a variety of analytical techniques, and then all those that an outsider cannot detect from the available record.[103]

Some of the issues in dispute have only indirectly addressed Soviet foreign policy; the perennial tug-of-war over priorities in resource allocation inevitably has implications for Soviet posture and policy abroad and, conversely (in Vernon Aspaturian's words), "the foreign policy and defense posture of the Soviet state establishes a certain configuration of priorities in the allocation of budgetary expenses and scarce resources. Various individuals and groups develop a vested interest in a particular foreign policy or defense posture because of the role and status it confers upon them. Correspondingly, other individuals and groups in Soviet society perceive themselves as deprived in status and rewards because of existing allocations of expenditure and resources."[104]

At one time the linkages between domestic and foreign policies also tended to align those favoring reform, de-Stalinization, and welfare-consumer priorities with advocates of better relations with the capitalist West; and the traditionalists with the isolationists. This, as we have seen, is no longer so simply, so logically (or so ideologically) the case.

What have unmistakably remained major sources of divergencies of outlook are perceptions of the international scene: the prospects of war and peace;[105] the size, structure, and deployment of Soviet armed forces; the "correlation of forces" and the assessment of "revolutionary opportunities" abroad (or their absence); and along with all this, the images of self, of the United States, of China, and of other parts of the globe.[106] From this complex flows the very central set of problems often described as "strategy and tactics" vis-à-vis the adversary camp, in its various mutations over time. The current differences over détente, as will be seen below, are but the latest manifestation of this continual cleavage reflecting, at least in part, different Communist tempers and temperaments, perceptions, outlooks, and mind-sets.

Subsidiary to these broad questions, but often congruent with the individual actors' orientations toward them, are divergent attitudes toward particular means of promoting or implementing policy directives. This would include such issues as emigration as a quid pro quo for a more forthcoming American attitude; the benefits and risks of intellectual and cultural contacts abroad; and the more general quandary whether Soviet purposes are better served by international tension or stabilization.

Where we are able to glimpse insights into recent elite politics in Moscow, we find hints of divergences over Soviet policy toward international Communism — toward Eurocommunism in particular — and toward China.[107] The same is true of a variety of regional issues, including in recent years Portugal and Angola. But there is little point in such an enumeration; it should be clear that the gamut of issues over which there have been differences in the Soviet elite and bureaucracy covers virtually all the major (and a good many minor) policy decisions in foreign affairs, though of course these have not always been confronted or fought out. Nor should this be at all surprising, given the wide range of differences in outlook and value which are represented within the spectrum of what was once considered monolithic Communism.

To what extent have Soviet policymakers themselves been aware of the "linkage" patterns that have been suggested in this chapter? The answer is somewhat tentative, but we can find several examples suggesting at least an intuitive awareness of the linkage. Thus Khrushchev's comment at the time of the nuclear test ban treaty in 1963 that "We shall reduce expenditures on defense, and this money shall be directed to the production of chemical fertilizer"[108] turned out to be as naively overoptimistic as the equivalent American hopes for arms control as an economy measure. But the linkage is there. More diffuse but also more fundamental was the point made in 1969, when the SALT negotiations were about to begin, and reiterated in various ways thereafter, that "experience has shown that only under conditions of a relaxation of tensions is it possible to concentrate a maximum of resources on accomplishing the plans for the building of communism."[109] Soviet sources would of course not explicitly acknowledge the existence of bureaucratic politics or differences within the elite. Only exceptionally does one find a comment made to a foreign correspondent to this effect (but not printed inside the USSR). Valentin Falin, first deputy chief of the Central Committee's International Information Department, was quoted by Craig Whitney as telling him in regard to the SALT II treaty:

> Your Administration has different views about the treaty in the State Department, the Pentagon and the National Security Council. On our side, the Defense Ministry may think one way, the Foreign Ministry may have another view, the Defense Council a third. Both of us have to resolve these differences and take political decisions to complete a treaty.[110]

There is no doubt that close scrutiny and imaginative use of Soviet sources would permit the development of a number of valuable case studies in this field, as indeed has been done with such topics as the Soviet intervention in Czechoslovakia in 1968[111] and Soviet policy toward the Middle East.[112]

Perhaps the most important cluster that currently brings together divergent assessments and preferences, linking a number of domestic and foreign policy issues, might best be identified for our purposes under the headings of

- Soviet assessment of the United States
- SALT
- Détente
- Autarky *vs.* foreign trade and technology transfer.

Each of these deserves a thorough study, far more extensive and systematic than any comments that can be made here.[113]

The various Soviet perceptions and images of the United States have been the subject of several sophisticated studies and detailed examinations. In a thorough analysis of Soviet writings since World War II, Franklyn Griffiths has shown the striking continuity of images (and their underlying assumptions) over time and the consistent correlation of particular clusters of images and approaches with distinctive policy inferences and tendencies. While a dichotomy into a relatively benign and a relatively hostile perception of the American scene (or even its extension into a more complex typology) is bound to be an oversimplification, it does convey an important cleavage reflected in the available literature.

In another dissertation, Robert W. Hanson has analyzed Soviet images of U.S. foreign policy for the 1960–1972 period and very sensibly identifies both the major divisive issues and the impact of events and politics on the balance in Moscow. Morton Schwartz, in a recent book-length study, has analyzed the views of Soviet "experts" on the United States clustered around the Institute for the Study of the USA and Canada. These and other studies would permit further hypotheses as to the extent to which perceptions and misperceptions were (and are) essentially projections of domestic experience within the USSR; and also as to the differential learning process among various Soviet constituencies.[114]

The most important cleavage, in the present political setting, of course deals with Soviet-American détente. Those who tend to perceive the United States in relatively more moderate, unideological (and, Americans will be quick to add, realistic) terms are also more likely to be optimistic about the prospects of détente — both its expected benefits, as seen from Moscow, and the likelihood of its enduring in spite of American attempts to "sabotage" it. The division of opinion on this cluster of issues — reflecting a basic difference concerning both the Soviet outlook on the outside and the choice of political strategies — likewise tends to follow a persistent cleavage, aligning on the one side those who have stressed the unchanging nature of imperialism and the inevitable crisis that world capitalism will face in the years ahead; and on the other side, those who have been willing and able to recognize the qualitatively novel aspects of international relations in the nuclear age, the possibility of state regulation modifying the "iron laws" of capitalist economic crises, the continuing need for Soviet economy and technology to borrow extensively from the capitalist West (or else face the need for drastic reforms), and the implied failure of "history" to fulfill its preordained task.[115]

Though hints of it abound, the cleavage has rarely been made explicit. On occasion documentary evidence has become available, such as a highly plausible summary of a speech by Vladimir Iagodkin, secretary of the Moscow City Committee of the CPSU, at a symposium at the Institute of the History of the USSR of the Academy of Sciences, in June 1973. According to this account (by a witness), Iagodkin assailed both "dogmatic negativism" regarding Soviet policy toward the United States and "opportunist illusions." The "dogmatic negativists," he declared, did not wish to sit down at the conference table with the imperialists (this was on the eve of

Brezhnev's visit to Washington); the victims of "opportunist illusions" were engendering the notion of ideological coexistence—itself, according to Iagodkin, a specimen of ideological subversion.[116] Presumably it was the same "dogmatists" that Gromyko had in mind when he referred to unnamed comrades in his speech at the Twenty-fourth CPSU Congress.

> Sometimes the question is posed: How dependable is this? How realistic is the meaning of agreements with some states if those agreements are not always honored by them? This question is sometimes posed in a different—bluntly speaking, directly provocative—way, and any agreement with the capitalist states is said to be almost a plot.[117]

But in most cases the latent differences are less directly alluded to or are left to the reader or listener to infer from significantly different uses of esoteric telltale symbols and signals that the Soviet insider has learned to "decode."

There is a fair amount of evidence that the basic decisions in favor of Soviet détente policy were made in 1969–1971, as part of a number of "linked" options—regarding SALT, military priorities, Sino-Soviet relations, a reversal of growth rates for sectors "A" and "B" in Soviet economic development in the Ninth Five-Year Plan, and so forth.[118] The divergent comments of the Soviet military on the U.S. likewise fit this pattern.

It is easier to ask than to answer the question, "Who in the USSR speaks for détente?"—whether, in other words, there are particular attributes (be they demographic, generational, occupational, ethnic, or bureaucratic) that would permit us to identify individuals and groups who have tended to support or oppose what may be called the Brezhnev line in the 1970s. That there are considerable differences, even in the top leadership, is clear from an examination of their public utterances. Grey Hodnett, on the basis of leader speeches for the years 1970–1974 identified as opponents of détente, among those who were then Politburo members: Grechko, Grishin, Mazurov, Pel'she, Shelest, Suslov, Masherov, and Ustinov.[119] Since then, several of the above have been relieved or have died; others have moved up, and new issues and circumstances have shifted the precise balance but have hardly affected the underlying cleavage.

If this is so, who is behind these leaders? Here a word of caution from Michel Tatu may be in order. He reminds us that the top leadership of relatively better informed and more realistic men "finds itself opposed to a mass of lower grades (cadres) who are prisoners of the dogmas and the primitive views of the world imposed upon them by the same governing body. . . . How can they avoid being more 'hawkish' than their leaders?"[120] If this is the result of primitive mass propaganda, its counterproductive effects must be taken to include not only the doubts it instills abroad regarding Soviet intentions, but also the ballast they constitute for a leadership seeking greater flexibility for unorthodox departures in foreign affairs.

Marshall Shulman has proposed an even broader scheme:

> Foreign policy in the Soviet Union, as elsewhere, is not purely an exercise in rational choices but also involves the interplay of domestic politics. As Brezhnev has indicated, his movement toward the fuller implementation of a policy of "peaceful coexistence" has not been without opposition. . . . As might be expected, some of the skepticism is to be found among the professional military services, which, like their opposite numbers in the United States, identify their claims upon the national budget with national security, with mistrust of the SALT process and assumed deviousness of their adversary. The main source of opposition, however, comes from the orthodox wing of the Party and its large ideological apparatus, and from the even larger apparatus of the political police. For them, "peaceful coexistence" means trouble—a weakening of the ideological elan that is their stock in trade, an opening of the country to influences that they can only regard as "subversive," increased trouble with intellectuals and nationality groups, and an erosion of the image of the "imperialist threat" that legitimizes their power and on which their careers depend.

As for the other side of the argument,

> The debate is joined by spokesmen of the "peaceful coexistence" policy from different lines of defense. Some, like Georgii Arbatov, the head of the Institute on the USA, . . . seek to persuade the hardliners that under present circumstances "peaceful coexistence" represents the most effective form of struggle against U.S. imperialism. Others, like Dimitrii Tomashevsky [of IMEMO] . . . argue forcefully and openly the need for Western capital and technology as the paramount considerations of the moment. An unusually broad perspective was represented in an article in *Izvestiia* . . . by Vladimir Osipov [who] concluded that "the global nature of the interdependence of states makes anachronistic foreign policy concepts of former centuries based on the opposition of some countries to others and the knocking together of military alliances."[121]

This analysis accords with the evidence as I see it.

Perhaps the most extensive effort to identify groups in Soviet society who may be seen (or who may see themselves) as either beneficiaries of international tension or else as beneficiaries of détente has been provided by Vernon V. Aspaturian.[122] Many of his interpretations are not only informed but coincide with the observations of other analysts. Still, given the variations we have earlier observed within each large bureaucracy and each social group, there is something excessively mechanical and wholesale in identifying, say, the party apparatus as protension and the state bureaucracy as prodétente, or the industrial managers as protension and the cultural and scientific intelligentsia as well as the consumer as prodétente (the latter being probably the closest to a correct label among the above). Nonetheless, with all due reservations, it is not only a pioneering effort but also an exceptionally skillful and original survey.

A German Sovietologist, Astrid von Borcke, finds ample evidence — e.g., in a comparison of speeches by leading members of the Soviet elite — that there was a serious debate underway that amounted to "nothing less than a confrontation between the innovative forces and those committed to persistence in the Soviet system."[123] Among the proponents of détente she identifies the foreign service bureaucracy, captains of industry seeking know-how and additional resources from abroad, and (somewhat more ambiguously, but in line with several other analysts) parts of the secret police apparatus. Among the enemies of détente she places leading military men, party *apparatchiki*, and ideologists.

The fact that in some particulars her analysis may well be open to challenge is neither surprising nor crucial; more important is the far-reaching coincidence and congruence of a number of separate efforts, by different scholars in different countries, to sort out "linkage groups" — pro and con — in Soviet politics, society, and economy, in regard to the broad outlines of Soviet-American détente.

Special attention should be paid to the reports and analyses of several scholars and observers who were themselves active in or close to the Soviet elite until a few years ago. Dimitri K. Simes, who until 1973 was a research associate with the Institute of World Economy and International Relations in Moscow, has dealt with the politics of détente in several papers. In an early summary, he too found that "the policy of détente, its domestic political prerequisites, and its reactions on the Soviet system, stand at the center of the continuing debate within the Soviet leadership." He too analyzed the speeches of Soviet leaders to discover telltale differences; and he too listed among proponents of détente the foreign policy establishment but also technocrats and managers; among its opponents, some parts of the armed forces (such as the traditionalist ground force commanders and the Main Political Administration), and the apparatus.[124]

More recently he has provided another summation, which makes further distinctions that seem realistic even if they complicate the picture: defense industrialists in large measure also welcome Western technology; the new Soviet military command, competent and realistic, has no reason to oppose the SALT treaties; the foreign ministry does not hold a unanimous view of détente; the research institutes that often serve as consultants to Central Committee departments are "usually more sophisticated and broadminded than their bureaucratic counterparts," and so forth.[125]

What becomes clear from these as well as other studies is the complex of domestic constraints on the Soviet pursuit of détente. That there are serious differences over it is taken for granted by Alexander Yanov, a former Soviet sociologist and journalist who in a well-informed and thoughtful essay also identifies the military, the "little Stalins," economic centralizers, and other party officials among those who oppose a détente strategy for the USSR.[126]

Finally, Boris Rabbot, formerly with the Academy of Sciences, once a consultant to party officials and active in the Moscow elite, also considers axiomatic the existence of pervasive arguments over questions of foreign policy within the Soviet leadership and among those they consult. Although a number of assertions made in his writings on the basis of hearsay are open to challenge, some of his general observations based on firsthand knowledge would seem to confirm the thrust of the argument made in this chapter. It should scarcely come as a surprise that

> the internal debates over detente in Moscow reflected uncertain perceptions of American intentions among the Soviet leaders. . . .
>
> The idea that the United States wanted to exacerbate the Sino-Soviet dispute and liberalize Soviet society prevailed among the mass of old apparatchiki of the Stalin school, the Party and its Central Committee, among employees of the KGB's domestic service, the Defense Ministry, the armaments industries, and the leaders of military units along the border with China, Mongolia and Afghanistan. . . . Supporters of the theory that the West sought to liberalize the Soviet system through detente included the foreign, or external, branches of the KGB, the Ministry of Foreign Affairs, the General Staff, and a number of specialists on the Central Committee staff. The minority view that the United States was seeking only to reduce the danger of nuclear war was supported by just two groups — . . . a large group from the so-called 'creative intelligentsia' . . . [and] Brezhnev and a small group of his Politburo supporters and consultants. . . . [They] believed that detente could produce Western economic and technological aid.

After stressing the impact that increased interaction with the outside world has already had on the Soviet population, Rabbot remarks that "the simultaneous necessity for cooperation with the West and measures to counteract the effects of that cooperation created numerous fissures in the Soviet monolith. . . . Detente and the Soviet leadership's response to it evoked struggles both between institutions and within them."[127]

It might be more correct to say that the challenge of détente did not introduce the cleavages into what had long since ceased to be a monolith; but it may have made them more manifest for those whose political consciousness peaked in the 1970s.

Finally, it would be an error to see the alignment over détente exclusively in terms of logic, tendencies, or institutions. A number of observers have properly stressed the growing role of "experts" — consultants, advisors, and quasi-academics — in Soviet policymaking in general and in regard to Soviet-American relations in particular. It is probably the consensus of those who have examined the specialists' output that the quality of insights and information of these specialists exceeds by far the level of realism and knowledge of others in the Soviet system (with some obvious exceptions). But beyond the substantive and advisory aspects of their role, these experts — exemplified by the Institute for the Study of the USA and Canada, under Georgii Arbatov, and the Institute of World Economy and International Relations, under Nikolai Inozemtsev — have acquired something of a vested interest in détente. As Morton Schwartz has sought to show, "the relaxation of international tension between the Soviet Union and the United States has resulted in the creation of forces in the USSR with a long-term interest in a temperate and restrained foreign policy" — forces that, he argues cogently, could not have come to the fore except under conditions of détente, such as it is.[128]

Indeed, it will be well not to minimize the material, acquisitive, and philistine aspects of Soviet interest in détente and in the opportunities it provides for the cultivation and satisfaction of creature comforts — and the craving for status — by members of the Soviet elite. This is another way of feeding fads and fashions, of indulging the peculiar *veshchizm* (as some Soviet observers have begun to refer to materialism) that extends across the whole spectrum of Soviet society and especially its urban part.[129] In this light the collectivity of those Soviet citizens who have an opportunity to travel abroad, at least from time to time, becomes committed to a multiplication of contacts (and of opportunities for contacts) with the outside world — for a variety of reasons among which many are not at all political or intellectual.[130] The number of abstemious ascetics who oppose this orientation can hardly begin to rival the legions hungry for the West.

The problems of détente continue to be debated in the Soviet elite. Has it paid off? What price is the Soviet Union paying, explicitly or unwittingly? Can the United States be trusted? What is the effect of détente on the United States, as people in Moscow perceive it? These are but a few of the questions on which Soviet expert opinion, visceral preferences, institutional loyalties, vested interests, idiosyncratic mind-sets, political traditions, and sheer ignorance, prejudice, and naiveté combine and divide in untidy and changing shapes and forms.

Weights and Trends: Conclusions

The preceding pages have referred to a bewildering spectrum of variables. Even if we assume that they have been correctly identified as relevant to our concerns, their relative importance is not self-evident. What is the formula for mixing personalities and politics, groups and individuals, logic and effect, heredity and environment, "objective" and "subjective" constraints, institutional loyalties and ad hoc alignments?

The simple answer is that there is none. I know of no technique or methodology that would permit us to assign weights to the ingredients in the mix. Hence any hypotheses are likely to be largely intuitive, neither demonstrable nor falsifiable. Some years ago, Vernon Aspaturian concluded his pioneering essay on this subject by saying that "the relationship of internal politics to foreign policy in the Soviet system remains in a state of flux and has yet to find its characteristic equilibrium."[131] This remains true. Moreover, it has become clear that we look in vain for a single pattern that would provide useful and reliable explanations. As Donald R. Kelley remarked in a paper on Soviet decision making, "We are pursuing a chimerical analysis goal in thinking that there is a single model both broad enough to encompass the wide range of bureaucratic and political modes of behavior characteristic of Soviet politics and specific enough to suggest anything more than self-evident truisms about the system."[132] Indeed, part of the analytical difficulty arises from the fact that in every identifiable "case" we find a number of variables operating in combination, not susceptible to isolation one by one.

Perhaps the best that can be done is to attempt, rather impressionistically, some comparative judgments concerning

- the relative "weight" or saliency of a given variable or cluster as compared to others;
- the relative "weight" or saliency of a given variable or cluster over time;
- the relative "weight" or saliency of a given variable or cluster compared to its equivalent elsewhere, for instance, in the United States.

The following may be suggestive of such assessments.

What we have seen above indicates that culture patterns have diminished in weight as explanatory variables as modernization has progressed over time. Similarly, formal, official Soviet ideology has been of decreasing operational weight. What remains, it appears, is part ritual and part composite mind-sets, which must be plumbed individually to determine what role ideology plays.

The political dimensions have all gained in weight over time. In the post-Stalin era this has been true of elite politics, bureaucratic politics, groups politics, and coalition politics. The role of "experts" as advisers and consultants has likewise been on the increase, as has the role of the military.

In the societal sphere, public opinion, mood, and values have typically been a passive constraint on policymakers. Even if it is increasing (as it appears to be), their role remains secondary at best.

The weight of the geographic, territorial environment has tended to decline in the age of television, jet flights, and space exploration. As for economy and resources, their relative "weight" may have described a curvilinear transformation. The original perception of economic weakness as a constraint on foreign policy has eroded over time. Resource allocation has become less painful and contested, at least for the past ten to fifteen years. On the other hand, there is a growing awareness of slowing growth rates, looming manpower shortages, energy problems, and lags in innovation, efficiency, and management, which are bound to have troublesome overtones for foreign policymaking.

As for the role of personalities, the relative weight of the individual and his or her idiosyncracies (as against group or institutional variables, for instance) tends to be less in an era of "collective leadership" than was true under Stalin or even Khrushchev.

If these are the correct directions of the trends in the Soviet Union today, we may be surprised to discover that many of them are not too dissimilar from those we identify in other, non-Communist societies including the United States; in substance, they are variants of secularization, bureaucratization, the growing role of specialists, and an increasing awareness of resource problems. However, the relative weight of individuals at the apex of the political structure remains far greater in the Soviet Union than in the United States and the total range of licit alternatives that may be articulated in Soviet esoteric communication (which takes the place of open political discourse) is markedly narrower than that in the United States. Likewise, for obvious structural reasons, the universe of domestic pressures from outside the establishment is far greater in the United States than in the USSR.

The principal problem with translating these rather general and perhaps unhelpful observations into more operational conclusions is the utter inadequacy of the one set of variables we would need most at this point: the mind-sets of the individual decision makers. Thus it is not at all clear what the implications for foreign policy are of the forecasts of Soviet economic difficulties in the years ahead. Will they make future Soviet leaders more willing to coexist abroad out of a sense of internal constraints? Or, on the contrary, are they more likely to be tempted to opt for greater adventurism abroad? To attempt a responsible answer to this, we would need to know far more about the individuals who will be there to make decisions. Had we the requisite information and insight, this would be the place to apply some of the lessons from the study of cognitive processes and personalities that were discussed at the beginning of this chapter.

The world at home and abroad looms as an important but missing piece of our puzzle. We would need to know more of the Soviet leaders' self-image; their awareness of multiple constituencies and audiences at home; the time lag in their learning; the impact of their previous successes and failures in other issue-areas; the relative political and personal sensitivity of particular issues; their attitudes toward risk-taking; their personal insecurities; their quest for status and recognition; their need for approval and support; their instinct for role-playing and small-group dynamics; and of course their perception of the Soviet domestic scene, its strains and weaknesses and strengths as they bear on foreign affairs.

It would be important to study the potent role of the various actors' earlier images and experiences — the "lessons of the past," including false lessons and false analogies (whose awesome weight, albeit in a different setting, various post mortems on U.S. policy in Vietnam have helped make clear). If Anthony Eden expected Gamal Nasser to behave much as Hitler had, and if Dean Rusk and Paul Nitze continued to operate with mental images carried over from Munich and Pearl Harbor to Yalta and Vietnam, then there is no reason to think that Soviet analysts and policymakers have an easier time shaking off old stereotypes and misconceptions, or fail to carry around mutually incompatible "scratches on their minds" (to use Harold Isaacs's phrase). Indeed, the learning curve of Soviet officialdom remains to be studied, too.

These are among the many tasks that remain to be undertaken. If this chapter has failed to provide simple, operational answers, it has shown that the approach outlined above can be as fruitful and realistic when applied to the Soviet scene as it has proven elsewhere. Thus one message is for further research.[133] Another is the utility of a comparative perspective, especially in regard to the interplay between external and internal bargaining and postures. And while once again it is impossible to prove (or disprove) the hypothesis, there seems to be merit in applying to the Soviet case the conclusion of an American study: "The process and outcome of international bargaining is more the adventitious result of configurations of attitude and influence *within* states than of the 'balance of bargaining power' *between* them."[134] Others, such as Franklyn Griffiths, have made a persuasive case for reconceptualizing supposedly "bilateral" Soviet-American problems as multilateral with various domestic voices as parts of the process. This is a perspective that invites a look at tacit, or latent, coalitions between adversaries.

The Tacit Alliance

The hypothesis that there is a significant connection between Soviet domestic developments and Soviet foreign policy is supported by common sense, empirical evidence, and political science theory. Of course, foreign policy is not merely a dependent variable of bureaucratic intrigues and power struggles. Nor does the foregoing imply that discrete decisions concerning foreign and security affairs must be taken in full awareness of all these complexities. In fact (as William Zimmerman and others have suggested) the decision process may well vary from issue-area to issue-area.

Herbert Dinerstein has observed that many distortions in Soviet-American relations have been due to "each side's failure to comprehend the complexity of the other's decision-making."[135] In this sense, Soviet foreign policy is but a particular case of a larger class of phenomena. The same is true of the lingering assumptions of monolithic consensus and compliance in the Soviet polity — assumptions more often rooted in stereotypes, distance, and ignorance than in solid research. It is interesting that at present Japanese historians are similarly challenging the orthodox assumptions of "consensus" theory as applied to the Japanese past. On closer examination, life — including political life — invariably proves to be varied, rich, and complex.

All this, of course, is not meant to deny the particular handicaps — institutional, ideological, and intellectual — under which Soviet foreign policymakers have labored. These are highlighted by Roy Medvedev's critique of the Soviet system. "A country's domestic situation influences its foreign policy," he writes, perhaps tongue in cheek. "There can be no doubt that surviving elements of totalitarianism or authoritarianism in the USSR, the United States, and other great powers, the existence of ideological intolerance and artificial restrictions on scientific, economic, and cultural cooperation all act as an obstacle to relaxation of the cold war." In the Soviet Union, he continues, "democratization would make government policy subject to public scrutiny." More pointedly,

> the whole process of decision making in foreign affairs should become more democratic. Although the very nature of these problems often means that final decisions can be taken only within a narrow circle or sometimes by one person alone, there should be preliminary debate about options, the possibility of a clash of views, and full discussion even if only within the relevant department. . . . One cannot avoid the impression that actions are often committed without adequate advance scrutiny.[136]

It may be the wrong question to ask, as is often done, whether the United States can influence Soviet outlook and policy. One implication of this chapter is that, whether it wants to or not, whether it knows it or not, the United States by what it says and what it does—and what it fails to say and fails to do—inevitably contributes to the dialogue being carried on among members of the Soviet elite. While it is naive to expect the United States to manipulate Soviet behavior and perspectives, it is clearly true that at least at the margins the mutual perceptions of the two superpowers are being shaped by each other's behavior. The fact that this is true "only" at the margins need not be of great concern: marginal differences often turn out to be decisive. (Similarly, it may well be true that there is a basic consensus on the general values shared by the Soviet elite, but once again the marginal differences—which do exist—may be crucially important.) The United States is then properly perceived as an unwitting participant in the internal debates and assessments going on in the Soviet Union, much as Soviet behavior in turn provides contending schools of American analysts with ammunition.

One implication of this interpretation is the error of "black-boxing" Soviet foreign policy outputs. Admittedly, there is also a danger in overstressing conflicts and cleavages in Soviet policymaking circles. But, on balance, it seems to be a danger that conceals fewer booby traps for the policy analyst abroad and one that far fewer foreign observers have succumbed to.

Such a perspective has implications for many areas of Soviet-American interaction. One American specialist on the Soviet Union who has had considerable experience in observing and negotiating with Soviet officials in recent years writes (in reference to academic exchanges, but with equal applicability to other subjects):

> The vision of an essentially adversarial relationship with a monolithic opponent was never entirely accurate and is less so now. Strategies based on such an assumption fail to take into account the existence in the Soviet Union of conflicting (although seldom publicly expressed) views in rather high places about how to cope with the considerable impact of the American academic presence in the USSR and of the experiences of returning Soviets who have spent some time here. These conflicts and differences create a constantly shifting set of openings through which to promote and encourage a freer exchange of people and ideas—which is what the exchanges are about.[137]

A careful analysis of the crisis over Czechoslovakia in 1968 concludes that "the failure of Dubček's advisers and most Western observers to understand the significance of the internal dynamics of Soviet decision-making accounts in part for their being unable to anticipate the invasion of Czechoslovakia on August 20, 1968.[138]

In a strange inversion Robert W. Hansen has documented the "tendency of [Soviet] hard-line writers to continue to rely on an undifferentiated model of American conduct. They were much less sensitive to the debate within U.S. society on foreign policy."[139] The same phenomenon, it will be seen, works in the opposite direction: so-called "hard-liners" in the United States have tended to ignore or deny the existence or significance of political debate within Soviet society.

That such external postures can be important is documented in the findings of Snyder and Diesing, based on a number of closely examined cases.

> Even if certain agencies or individuals can be expected regularly to take hard or soft positions, their influence will be greater or less depending on whether the external situation seems to favor an accommodative or coercive strategy, in the eyes of the central decision maker and in terms of the core of consensus in the group.

Their inference—easier to draw logically than it is to begin implementing—is, "If you want to influence another government, find out what group(s) in that government are already inclined to do what you want, and shape your moves so as to strengthen those groups in their own government's internal debate."[140]

What we have in fact is not merely a pattern of mirror images, which have been pointed out repeatedly in the literature on Soviet-American relations,[141] but what may properly be called (though neither side likes to hear it said) tacit alliance between adversaries.

Not only do the "moderates" on each side share an interest and in fact cooperate to promote agreements they deem to be mutually beneficial, but others as well help each other—in deed if not in intent. It can be shown how the military-industrial establishment on each side cites the research and procurement of the other in justification of its demands for larger budgets and allocations. It has been suggested that in a number of branches—for instance, the navy and foreign trade—Soviet and U.S. counterparts are in effect "functional bureaucratic allies" and "external pacers" for each other.[142]

Even more than these functional congruencies, the "hawks" on both sides help validate each other's expectations. Their commitment to worst-case analysis requires the assistance of the adversary to provide support, at least in their own minds, for their prophecies of doom and gloom.[143] Much like the familiar action-reaction phenomenon in the arms race, the vociferous affirmation of the "present danger" to the United States cannot but strengthen the hand of, and provide evidence cited by, Soviet diehards who deny the possibility of meaningful accords with the United States; who see no evidence of American good will but firmly expect an eventual military showdown; and who represent the Neanderthal end of the Soviet political spectrum.

Fortunately, this is not the only possible perspective. Experience suggests that those whom we would consider our friends inside the Soviet Union are far more likely to have an opportunity to make themselves heard and to influence the course of events under conditions of greater relaxation and transnational interaction than under circumstances reminiscent of the cold war.

But, regardless of the merits of this argument, there is one general point that needs to be made in conclusion. If there is one lesson that suggests itself, it is above all the need for sensitivity to the Soviet domestic scene on the part of foreign observers and policymakers, and for greater awareness of the likely effects of American pronouncements and behavior on internal Soviet dialogues and debates. This calls for a massive effort at consciousness-raising in foreign affairs.

Acknowledgments

I have worked on the subject of this manuscript at various times over a number of years and am indebted to a number of institutions for their support. The Albert Shaw Lectures, at Johns Hopkins University in 1964, provided the initial stimulus to explore the topic. A conference organized at Tel Aviv University in 1971, on Soviet policy in the Middle East, offered an opportunity to develop some of the themes more thoroughly, as did a conference on Soviet foreign policy at the University of Michigan in 1975, sponsored by the Research and Development Committee of the American Association for the Advancement of Slavic Studies. I am most grateful for the support of facilities provided for research, at various times, by the Center for Advanced Study in the Behavioral Sciences at Stanford, California (1970–1971); the Hoover Institution on War, Revolution, and Peace (1972–1974); the Research Institute on International Change at Columbia University (1977–1978); and the Kennan Institute for Advanced Russian Studies at the Woodrow Wilson International Center for Scholars, Washington, D.C. (1978–1979). None of these institutions bears any responsibility for the statements and views expressed herein, which are entirely my own. Finally, I should add that this chapter is part of a larger study in progress.

Notes

1. For a recent restatement, see, for example, Jon D. Glassman, *Arms for the Arabs* (Baltimore, Md.: Johns Hopkins University Press, 1975), ch. 6.

2. Adam Ulam, *Expansion and Coexistence*, 2d ed. (New York: Praeger Publishers, 1974).

3. See, among recent publications, U.S. Congress, House of Representatives, Committee on International Relations, Subcommittee on Europe and Middle East, *The Soviet Union: Internal Dynamics of Foreign Policy, Present and Future* (Washington, D.C.: U.S. Government Printing Office, 1978); and Alexander Dallin, "Retreat from Optimism: On Marxian Models of Revolution," in Seweryn Bialer et al., eds., *Radicalism in the Contemporary Age*, vol. 3, *Strategies and Impact of Contemporary Radicalism* (Boulder, Colo.: Westview Press, 1977), pp. 117-157.

4. The evidence supports the findings of Jan F. Triska and David D. Finley in "The Soviet Union: Reckless or Cautious?," ch. 9 of their *Soviet Foreign Policy* (New York: Macmillan, 1968), even if there is room to question them on methodological grounds. Nor does there appear to have been any perceptible change in Soviet risk taking since the ostensible attainment of gross strategic parity with the United States. This is not meant to question the plausible hypothesis that the Soviet view of what constitutes a risk may itself change as Soviet capabilities grow. For a view challenging these hypotheses, see Hannes Adomeit, "Soviet Risk-Taking and Crisis Behavior: A Theoretical and Empirical Analysis" (Ph.D. diss., Columbia University, 1977).

5. On various aspects of this Soviet posture and outlook in the 1970s, see (in addition to other titles cited in this chapter) Robert Legvold, "The Nature of Soviet Power," *Foreign Affairs* 56, no. 1 (October 1977):49-71; Lawrence T. Caldwell, *Soviet-American Relations: One-Half Decade of Detente Problems and Issues* (Paris: The Atlantic Institute for International Affairs, 1976); Dimitri K. Simes, *Detente and Conflict: Soviet Foreign Policy 1972-1977*, The Washington Papers 5, no. 44 (Beverly Hills, Calif. and London: Sage Publications, 1977); Marshall D. Shulman, "Trends in Soviet Foreign Policy," in Michael MccGwire et al., eds., *Soviet Naval Policy* (New York: Praeger Publishers, 1975), pp. 3-22; Robert Legvold, "The Soviet Union and Western Europe: Expansion and Detente," in William E. Griffith, ed., *The Soviet Empire* (Lexington, Mass.: Lexington Books, 1976), pp. 217-258.

6. On the latter, see also Lawrence Caldwell and Alexander Dallin, "United States Policy Toward the Soviet Union," in Kenneth Oye, Donald Rothchild, and Robert J. Lieber, eds., *The Eagle Entangled* (New York: Longman, 1979), pp. 199-227.

7. See the analysis in Vernon V. Aspaturian, "Internal Politics and Foreign Policy in the Soviet System," in R. Barry Farrell, ed., *Approaches to Comparative and International Politics* (Evanston, Ill.: Northwestern University Press, 1966), pp. 212-287. See also George F. Kennan, *The Cloud of Danger* (Boston: Little, Brown and Co., 1977), ch. 12. But consider also the following comment: "I do not *know* what Soviet objectives are. It is surely pointless to deduce them from published statements, whether by Lenin or Brezhnev, and this for two reasons: there are certain ideologically 'compulsory' declarations which they feel compelled to make, which may or may not mean that they set much real store by them, and, more important, the term 'objective' or 'aim' is operationally meaningless. One has to know the weight attached to this objective or aim as compared to others, the price they are prepared to pay, the risks they are prepared to take." Alec Nove, "On Soviet Policy and Intentions," *Survey* 22, no. 3/4 (Summer/Autumn 1976):112.

8. David W. Paul, "Soviet Foreign Policy and the Invasion of Czechoslovakia,"

International Studies Quarterly 15, no. 2 (June 1971):159.

9. On this subject, see further discussion below. See also Aspaturian, "Internal Politics and Foreign Policy in the Soviet System," pp. 229–230; and Sidney Ploss, "Studying the Domestic Determinants of Soviet Foreign Policy," in Erik P. Hoffmann and Frederic J. Fleron, Jr., eds., *The Conduct of Soviet Foreign Policy* (Chicago: Aldine/Atherton, 1971), pp. 76–90.

10. *Foreign Policy*, no. 27 (Summer 1977):108.

11. James Rosenau, *The Adaptation of National Societies: A Theory of Political System Transformation* (New York: McCaleb-Seiler, 1970), p. 1. While I find the sophistication of Rosenau's concepts stimulating and creative, I do not think they help significantly in understanding the particular problem to which this chapter is addressed.

12. For convenient and competent summaries of the various schools, see, for example, Michael Brecher, Blema Steinberg, and Janice Stein, "A Framework for Research on Foreign Policy Behavior," *Journal of Conflict Resolution* 13, no. 1 (March 1969):75–79; and Christopher Hill, "A Theoretical Introduction," in William Wallace and W. E. Paterson, eds., *Foreign Policy Making in Western Europe* (Farnborough, England: Saxon House, 1978), pp. 7–30.

I will not be concerned in this chapter with such macrotheoretical approaches as imperialism or geopolitical imperatives.

Historically, the relative priority of foreign domestic policy goals acquired special saliency in nineteenth-century Germany. Leopold von Ranke was the most prominent among historians and politicians arguing for the *Primat der Aussenpolitik* (see his "Dialogue on Politics"), asserting, in essence, that foreign policy was a test of a state's greatness in the pursuit of its natural interests and its *raison d'état*. The implication was that internal concerns could not be permitted to interfere with these pursuits.

Foreign policy, conceived as a dependent variable, is shaped by a combination of external (international) and internal (domestic) inputs. Such an approach is inherently multivariate and includes such diverse variables as economic capabilities, manpower, perceptions and attitudes of the actors and of the attentive public, bargaining, special interests, and so on. For systematic examination and ordering of such variables see: Patrick J. McGowan and Howard B. Shapiro, *The Comparative Study of Foreign Policy: A Survey of Scientific Findings* (Beverly Hills, Calif.: Sage Publications, 1973); Howard Lentner, *Foreign Policy Analysis: A Comparative and Conceptual Approach* (Columbus, Ohio: Charles E. Merrill Co., 1974), p. 136; Richard W. Cottam, *Foreign Policy Motivation, A General Theory and A Case Study* (Pittsburgh, Pa.: University of Pittsburgh Press, 1978), p. 34 ff; Glenn H. Synder and Paul Diesing, *Conflict Among Nations: Bargaining, Decision Making and System Structure in International Crises* (Princeton, N.J.: Princeton University Press, 1978); and Michael Brecher, "Images, Process and Feedback in Foreign Policy: Israel's Decisions on German Reparations," *American Political Science Review* 67, no. 1 (March 1973):75.

For a helpful survey of the decision-making literature, the principal organizing concept in this field, see Dan Caldwell, "Bureaucratic Foreign Policy-Making," *American Behavioral Scientist* 21, no. 1 (September–October 1977):87–110. For a competent restatement that offers background for Soviet foreign policy studies, see

"Models of Decision in the Social Sciences," ch. 2 of Arnold L. Horelick, A. Ross Johnson, and John D. Steinbruner, *The Study of Soviet Foreign Policy: A Review of Decision-Theory Related Approaches* (Santa Monica, Calif: RAND R-1334, 1973; also Sage Publications, 1975).

There is no need to review Graham Allison's *Essence of Decision*, which very persuasively argues that "where you stand depends on where you sit." However, the organization and bureaucratic-politics approach to decision making, as well as the stress on system characteristics, has been challenged by those who emphasize perceptions, attitudes, values, information-processing, mind-sets, and styles of particular decision makers. For our purposes, these diverse perspectives may be grouped around the "cognitive process" paradigm. See: Ole R. Holsti, "Cognitive Process Approaches to Decision-Making: Foreign Policy Actors Viewed Psychologically," *American Behavioral Scientist* 20, no. 1 (September–October 1976):11–32, and his "Foreign Policy Decision Makers Viewed Psychologically: 'Cognitive Process' Approaches," in James N. Rosenau, ed., *In Search of Global Patterns* (New York: Free Press, 1976), pp. 120–144 (including an excellent bibliography) .

Alexander George, another proponent of this perspective, argues that "A political leader's beliefs about the nature of politics and political conflict, his views regarding the extent to which historical developments can be shaped, and his notions of correct strategy and tactics — whether these beliefs be referred to as 'operational code,' Weltanschauung, 'cognitive maps,' or an elite's political culture — are among the factors influencing that actor's decisions." See Alexander George, "The 'Operational Code': A Neglected Approach to the Study of Political Leaders and Decision-Making," *International Studies Quarterly* 13, no. 2 (June 1969):197.

An important variant of the cognitive approach is the "cybernetic" paradigm, stressing the shortcuts to decision making that typically take place in conditions of imperfect information and imperfect alternatives to choose among. See John D. Steinbruner, *The Cybernetic Theory of Decision* (Princeton, N.J.: Princeton University Press, 1974). All these formulas tend to focus on feedback and learning theory.

For a recent discussion, with valuable bibliographic and methodological references, see also Lloyd S. Etheredge, "Personality Effects on American Foreign Policy, 1898-1968," *American Political Science Review* 72, no. 2 (June 1978):434–451.

Reference should also be made to the insights generated by Robert Jervis's brilliant study of perceptions in international relations. It supports the argument that the value biases and idiosyncratic elements of a decision maker's perception tend to be more important than institutional rules in shaping policy. Such a finding, among other things, would militate in favor of complementing the bureaucratic politics approach with a perspective paying attention to the decision makers' mind-sets. See Robert Jervis, *Perception and Misperception in International Politics* (Princeton, N.J.: Princeton University Press, 1976).

13. For an argument denying the importance of domestic constraints and pressures, see Richard Pipes, "Domestic Politics and Foreign Affairs," in Ivo J. Lederer, ed., *Russian Foreign Policy* (New Haven, Conn.: Yale University Press, 1962), pp. 145–170. This perspective is consistent with its author's more recent policy advocacy. For a more sophisticated critique of the approach represented in this chapter, see Adomeit, "Soviet Risk-Taking and Crisis Behavior." A stimulating

critique of prior efforts to apply (or fail to apply) decision-making and related approaches to the study of Soviet foreign policy is Horelick, Johnson, and Steinbruner, *The Study of Soviet Foreign Policy*, pp. 35–48.

A different argument (which I consider erroneous) is presented in John A. Armstrong, "The Domestic Roots of Soviet Foreign Policy," *International Affairs* (London) 61, no. 1 (1965):37–47. It argues that "in the short run contestants for leadership in the Soviet Union will manipulate policy issues to strengthen their domestic power position. . . . In the longer run, any victorious contestant tends to take a position which is consonant with a rational calculation of Soviet interests." Graham Allison rather summarily places Sovietologists among advocates of his Model I. See Graham Allison, *The Essence of Decision: Exploring the Cuban Missile Crisis* (Boston: Little, Brown and Co., 1971), ch. 1.

A question that remains to be studied is the "linkages" in comparative Communist perspective. Some interesting attempts in this direction are to be found in James E. Kuhlman ed., *The Foreign Policies of Eastern Europe: Domestic and International Determinants* (London: Sijthoff, 1978). Of the several efforts to deal with similar problems in regard to China, I found the most valuable to be Harry Harding, "Linkages Between Chinese Domestic Politics and Foreign Policy" (manuscript, 1976), and Thomas W. Robinson, "Political and Strategic Aspects of Chinese Foreign Policy," (manuscript, 1976), pt. 1.

As for the relative importance of domestic versus external factors in shaping Soviet policy—an issue that has stirred some controversy in the field—it is assumed, by definition, that domestic and foreign inputs are always present and that their respective weights vary from case to case. The comparative neglect of external variables in the subsequent discussion is not meant to imply their insignificance.

14. Reference should be made here to some of the studies dealing, in varying degrees, with this subject. In addition to those cited above, see in particular Vernon V. Aspaturian, "Internal Policies and Foreign Policy in the Soviet System" and his "The Soviet Military-Industrial Complex—Does It Exist?" *Journal of International Affairs* 26. no. 1 (1972):1–28; Sidney Ploss, "Studying the Determinants of Soviet Foreign Policy," *Canadian Slavic Studies* 1, no. 1 (Spring 1967):44–59; Morton Schwartz, *The Foreign Policy of the USSR: Domestic Factors* (Encino, Calif.: Dickenson Publishing Co., 1975), p. 27. See also the editor's introduction to Part 2 of Erik P. Hoffmann and Frederic J. Fleron, eds., *The Conduct of Soviet Foreign Policy*. In addition to myself and others cited in subsequent notes, those who have addressed these problems in their writings include Lawrence T. Caldwell, Herbert S. Dinerstein, Oded Eran, David Finley, Douglas Garthoff, Raymond Garthoff, Harry Gelman, Franklyn Griffiths, Roy Grow, Grey Hodnett, Richard Horn, Christer Jonsson, Roman Kolkowicz, Wolfgang Leonhard, Ronald Letteney, Carl Linden, Richard Lowenthal, Paul Marantz, G. Grant Pendill, Morton Schwartz, Marshall D. Shulman, Michel Tatu, Ben T. Trout, Thomas W. Wolfe, Donald Zagoria, and William Zimmerman. There is also a useful literature on decision making in Soviet arms control policy, space exploration, and foreign economic policies, some of which is cited below.

Reference is made, at various points in this chapter, to doctoral dissertations by Hannes Adomeit (Columbia, 1977); Robert W. Hansen (Princeton, 1975); Samuel

B. Payne (Johns Hopkins, 1976); C. Grant Pendill, Jr. (Pennsylvania, 1969); Ronald Pope (Pennsylvania, 1975).

The collection of essays edited by Egbert Jahn (Jahn, ed., *Soziookonomische Bedingungen der sowjetischen Aussen-politik* [Campus-Verlag, 1975]; English ed., *Soviet Foreign Policy: Its Social and Economic Foundations* [New York: St. Martin's Press, 1978]), seem to focus on the subject of this study. However, they deal primarily (though not entirely) with variants of far-left critiques of Soviet polity and society. These contributions, legitimate as critiques, vary substantially in sophistication and level of political information but for the most part adhere to presuppositions and analytical categories that are not helpful in the pursuit of questions the present study seeks to address.

15. Rosenau, "Pre-Theories and Theories of Foreign Policy," in Farrell, *Approaches to Comparative and International Politics*, p. 31.

16. This too should not be asserted too sweepingly. Whatever the methodological strictures, there is value in such studies as David W. Paul, "Soviet Foreign Policy and the Invasion of Czechoslovakia"; Kuhlman, ed., *The Foreign Policies of Eastern Europe*; and Milton Lodge, *Soviet Elite Attitudes Since Stalin* (Columbus, Ohio: Charles E. Merrill, 1969). Additional references to quantitative studies will be made later in this chapter.

17. See, for example, C. J. Hill, "A Theoretical Introduction," pp. 11–12. Douglas F. Garthoff, "The Domestic Dimension of Soviet Foreign Policy: The Kremlin Debate on the Test Ban (1962–1963)" (Ph.D. diss., Johns Hopkins University, 1972), p. 9, aptly points out that on the nuclear test ban issue different opinions in the Soviet elite could be articulated precisely because it was not a crisis situation.

18. See also Allen S. Whiting, "The Scholar and the Policy-Maker" in Raymond Tanter and Richard H. Ullman, eds., *Theory and Policy in International Relations* (Princeton, N. J.: Princeton University Press, 1972), p. 242.

19. Brecher et al., "A Framework for Research on Foreign Policy Behavior," p. 85, n. 14.

20. A similar subject of considerable academic discussion has of course been the applicability of "interest group" concepts to the Soviet scene. Some of the contributions to the debate are listed in Horelick et al., *The Study of Soviet Foreign Policy*; to the list of fiercest critics should be added William Odom and Andrew Janos; to that of scholars using variants of an interest-group approach, Theodore Friedgut and Philip Stewart.

21. On this, in addition to the writings of Jerry F. Hough, see in particular William Zimmerman, "Issue Area and Foreign-Policy Process: A Research Note in Search of a General Theory," *American Political Science Review* 67, no. 4 (December 1973):1204–1212.

22. It is important to identify individual mind-sets rather than to limit oneself to spotting "collective," long-term predispositions. It is sound, if elementary, that one cannot deduce an individual's attributes or idiosyncracies from the aggregate characteristics of any group he or she belongs to. See Suzanne Keller, *Beyond the Ruling Class: Strategic Elites in Modern Society* (New York: Random House, 1963).

23. See, for instance, the work of Stephen F. Cohen, Grey Hodnett, Carl Linden, Michel Tatu, and some of the earlier writings of Robert Conquest.

24. Indeed, this is a serious objection to the "systemic" arguments of cold-war revisionists (a la Gabriel Kolko) who—whatever the merits of their analysis of the American side—tend to dismiss the idiosyncratic characteristics of Joseph Stalin or other individual actors. On the Stalin issue, see also Robert C. Tucker, ed., *Stalinism* (New York: W. W. Norton and Co., 1977), and Tucker, "The Emergence of Stalin's Foreign Policy," *Slavic Review* 36, no. 4 (December 1977):563–589, and comments on it, ibid.

25. For further discussion, see William Zimmerman, "Elite Perspectives and the Explanation of Soviet Foreign Policy" in Hoffmann and Fleron, eds., *The Conduct of Soviet Foreign Policy*, pp. 18–30; and Zimmerman, *Soviet Perspectives on International Relations* (Princeton, N.J.: Princeton University Press, 1969).

26. "Ambiguity may result from a scarcity of information, from information of low quality or questionable authenticity, or from information that is contradictory or is consistent with two or more significantly different interpretations, coupled with the absence of reliable means of choosing between them." (Holsti, "Foreign Policy Decision Makers Viewed Psychologically," p. 127.)

27. There is room for a closer look at the defining characteristics of "left" and "right," "softness" and "hardness," militancy and moderation in Soviet political behavior. At times these terms are too vague and vast to permit useful operationalizing; at other times they are too sweeping or ambiguous to permit differentiating adequately among distinct phenomena. One reason for continuing to use the terms "left" and "right," in spite of their inadequacy, is the absence of an alternative set; another reason is the fact that they continue to be used in Communist discourse, in and out of the Soviet Union. Thus "revisionism" has typically been a pejorative term in referring to "rightist" political strategies dealing with domestic, foreign, and ideological matters. Similarly, "sectarianism" or "dogmatism" have been labels used to condemn "leftist" political postures dealing with internal, external, and doctrinal matters.

28. On the latter linkage, see Michel Tatu, *Power in the Kremlin: From Khrushchev to Kosygin* (New York: Viking Press, 1969). The works of Franklyn Griffiths, Carl Linden, and Thomas Wolfe are also relevant to this subject.

29. A word might be added here in response to those who see no patterned or organic interrelation between Soviet domestic and foreign policies. First, my argument is not that there must be a direct causal connection among all aspects of foreign and domestic policy. Second, the assumed disjunction has repeatedly been a result of the observer's ignorance of Soviet politics. To cite but one example: in 1959–1960 hardly any Western observer linked Khrushchev's behavior during his visits to the United States (including the famous shoe-pounding at the UN General Assembly) with the Sino-Soviet dispute, with his arguments with Soviet military commanders over the reduction of ground forces, with the dispute over reliance on a nuclear deterrent, with the upgrading of consumer goods targets, and with the transfer of manpower to the "virgin lands" of Central Asia. In retrospect the view that all these issues were linked in Soviet political analysis and decision making is rather convincing.

And third, even where no explicit policy linkage is detected from the outside, it is always true, by definition, that foreign policy decisions are shaped by perceptions of opportunities and threats, risks, costs, and anticipated benefits, as well as a (frequently imperfect) awareness of alternative options and their implications. As Henry Kissinger wrote, before his years of public glory, "The domestic structure is not irrelevant in any historical period. At a minimum it determines the amount of total social effort which can be devoted to foreign policy. . . . Aside from the allocation of resources, the domestic structure crucially affects the way the actions of other states are interpreted." (Henry A. Kissinger, "Domestic Structure and Foreign Policy," in *Daedalus, Journal of the American Academy of Arts and Sciences* 95, no. 2 [Spring 1966]:503–529; reprinted in Harold K. Jacobson and William Zimmerman, eds., *The Shaping of Foreign Policy* [New York: Atherton Press, 1969], pp. 141–142.)

In any case, empirical inspection of Soviet policy over time argues strongly that the hypothesis of a random or disjointed relationship between internal and external policies must be abandoned.

30. On Litvinov, see Alexander Dallin, "Allied Leadership in the Second World War: Stalin," *Survey* 21, no. 1/2 (Winter/Spring 1975):15–18; and Vojtech Mastny, "The Cassandra in the Foreign Commissariat," *Foreign Affairs* 54, no. 2 (January 1976):366–376.

31. Such a pattern does not assume the existence of a unitary rational actor. Given the reality of politics, such linkages may be taken to reflect the dominant political orientation of an individual, a group, or a coalition. This does presuppose that the jockeying for power is indeed closely tied to, and marked by, distinct differences in political choices (if these are not always "ideologically" consistent). Thus the Stalin-Trotsky duel in the 1920s, the Malenkov-Zhdanov struggle in 1944–1948, and the Khrushchev-Molotov fight in 1955 each involved conflicts over domestic, foreign, and ideological positions as well as a struggle for power.

32. It is possible that some continuity could be shown and the answer to the linkage problem found if one were to disaggregate "foreign" and "domestic" policies further into a number of specific and simultaneous issue-areas. On this question, see Thomas L. Brewer, "Issue and Context Variation in Foreign Policy: Effects on American Elite Behavior," *Journal of Conflict Resolution* 17, no. 1 (March 1973):89–114.

33. For a discussion of their role, see the work of Morton Schwartz, Oded Eran, William Taubman, Boris Rabbot, and William Zimmerman,

34. It should not be assumed that a single or identical calculus need underlie all instances of the same pattern's occurrence. Moreover, there need be no linear correlation between perceived weakness and a conciliatory mood in foreign (or domestic) affairs; nor does a willingness to pursue compromises, deals, or détente abroad need necessarily to stem from weakness.

35. U.S. Senate, Committee on Government Operations, Subcommittee on National Policy Machinery, *National Policy Machinery in the Soviet Union* (Washington, D.C.: U.S. Government Printing Office, 1960).

36. For a succinct and effective statement of the political changes, see Seweryn Bialer, "Stalinism and Soviet Political Systems" (manuscript, 1978), pp. 55–57.

37. See Karl W. Deutsch, "Social Mobilization and Political Development," *American Political Science Review* 55, no. 3 (September 1961):497–500.

38. On the general theory of modernization, see Edward L. Morse, *Modernization and the Transformation of International Relations* (New York: Free Press, 1976), p. 84. "As the government's role in the economic and social life of a society increases, concern for foreign policy must decrease relative to the concern for domestic affairs. . . . And unintentional policy consequences must also increase, since the interconnectedness of different policy realms increases. Thus undesirable policy consequences also increase." For the counterargument, see Peter Gourevitch, "The Second Image Reversed: The International Sources of Domestic Politics," *International Organization* 32, no. 4 (Autumn 1978): especially 907–911.

39. This is not meant to suggest that there are not also other and genuine motivational components in the Soviet search for détente, such as its anti-Chinese aspect, the search for arms-control agreements, the attempt to influence political attitudes in the West, and so forth.

For general discussions of the foreign policy calculus in the Brezhnev era, see Morton Schwartz, *The Foreign Policy of the USSR*; Kennan, *The Cloud of Danger*, ch. 12; Robin Edmonds, *Soviet Foreign Policy 1962–1973* (London: Oxford University Press, 1975); Michael MccGwire et al., eds., *Soviet Naval Policy;* and MccGwire, ed., *Soviet Naval Influence* (New York: Praeger Publishers, 1977); Legvold, "The Nature of Soviet Power"; Stephen Cohen, "Soviet Domestic Politics and Foreign Policy," in Carl Marcy, ed., *Common Sense in U.S.-Soviet Relations* (Washington, D.C.: American Committee on East-West Accord, 1978); Peter H. Juviler and Hannah J. Zawadzka, "Detente and Soviet Domestic Politics" in Grayson Kirk and Nils Wessell, eds., *The Soviet Threat*, Proceedings of The American Academy of Political Science, vol. 33, no. 1 (1978), pp. 158–167; Dimitri K. Simes, "Detente, Russian-Style," *Foreign Policy*, no. 32 (Fall 1978):47–62; U.S. House of Representatives, Subcommitte on Europe and the Middle East, *The Soviet Union: Internal Dynamics of Foreign Policy, Present and Future* (Washington, D.C.: U.S. Government Printing Office, 1978).

40. John Scott, *Behind the Urals* (Bloomington: Indiana University Press, 1973), p. 264.

41. Frederick C. Barghoorn, *The Soviet Image of the United States* (New York: Harcourt Brace Jovanovich, 1950), pp. 245–246.

42. Adam Ulam, "Russian Nationalism," ch. 1 in this volume.

43. See the discussion in B. Thomas Trout, "Rhetoric Revisited," *International Studies Quarterly* 19, no. 3 (September 1975):251–257; and the paper by Alexander George, "American Foreign Policy: The Problem of Legitimacy" (paper for the symposium on U.S. Foreign Policy in the Next Decade, St. Louis, University of Missouri, 15 April 1977). I am grateful to Alexander George for drawing my attention to this problem.

44. Edmonds, *Soviet Foreign Policy 1962–1973*, p. 155. See also Triska and Finley, *Soviet Foreign Policy*, ch. 4, "Doctrinal Stereotype Quotient."

45. See Alexander George, "The 'Operational Code,'" p. 216 ff.

46. Alexander Dallin, "Russia and China View the United States," *Annals of the American Academy of Political and Social Science*, vol. 349 (September 1963):153–162.

47. See Franklyn Griffiths, "Image, Politics and Learning in Soviet Behavior

Toward the United States" (Ph.D. diss., Columbia University, 1972); William Zimmerman, *Soviet Perspectives in International Relations, 1956–67*, and his "Soviet Perceptions of the United States" in Alexander Dallin and Thomas B. Larson, eds., *Soviet Politics Since Khrushchev* (Englewood Cliffs, N.J.: Prentice-Hall, 1969), pp. 163–179; Morton Schwartz, *Soviet Perceptions of the United States* (Berkeley: University of California Press, 1978); and Alexander Dallin, "The United States in the Soviet Perspective," in *Prospects of Soviet Power in the 1980's, Part I, Adelphi Paper*, no. 151 (London: International Institute for Strategic Studies, 1979).

48. A good example is the U.S. effort to persuade Soviet officials and scholars (including Kosygin at Glassboro in 1967 and scientists at Pugwash meetings) that improvements in offensive weapons can easily cancel defensive systems, and that, therefore, even operational ABM systems would be ineffectual; and that instead, limitations on offensive (strategic) systems need to be negotiated. See Wolfgang K. H. Panofsky, "The Mutual-Hostage Relationship Between America and Russia," *Foreign Affairs* 52, no. 1 (October 1978):109–118; and Raymond L. Garthoff, "SALT I: An Evaluation," *World Politics* 31, no. 1 (October 1978):1–25.

49. On this subject, see Alexander Dallin, "The Fruits of Interaction," *Survey* 22, no. 3/4 (Summer/Autumn 1976): 42–46.

50. I do not believe that the framework proposed here is invalidated by the fact that the Soviet ship of state, like those elsewhere, may at times succumb to a process of "muddling through."

51. The same may be true of trade-offs among different aspects of foreign policy.

52. See, for example, Robert Abelson et al., eds., *Theories of Cognitive Consistency: A Source Book* (Skokie, Ill.: Rand McNally & Co., 1968).

53. An illustration of this change is provided by the Sino-Soviet conflict. While in the Khrushchev years there was a clear linkage in Soviet domestic policy of what Maoists and Stalinists would call "revisionism" with anti-Maoism, the Brezhnev leadership has in effect decoupled the two environments: It is now possible to pursue the anti-Chinese line without political or ideological overtones and without implications for Soviet domestic policy. If anything, Soviet domestic policy has in at least some areas swung back to a somewhat "tougher" course.

54. One might then ask whether (a) reciprocal linkage policies are not inherently more unstable than congruent linkage policies, and (b) policies based on coalition bargaining are not inherently more unstable than structurally or even ideologically anchored policies. As for the stability of the reciprocity pattern, one may hypothesize that there is indeed a built-in tension in the pursuit of conflicting policy orientations in the domestic and foreign environments. No doubt an instinctive preference for coherent approaches across the board remains alive, and there is reason to think that at least some Soviet observers see the current course as inherently inconsistent.

On the other hand, the pursuit of such different courses has not been unknown elsewhere either. Differential attitudes toward in- and out-groups are normal in any system. To date the Soviet authorities do not appear to be troubled by the tension just described. Ultimately, it can be safely predicted, Moscow must resolve the matter by opting for a more coherent approach across the board, sacrificing the "reciprocal" approach. But this is an almost meaningless assertion, as (1) it is not falsifiable; (2) there is no time limit attached to it; and (3) in any event, it is impossible to predict in what direction such a "resolution" would go.

55. Archie Brown and Jack Gray, eds., *Political Culture and Political Change in Communist States* (New York: Holmes and Meier, 1977), p. 1.

56. See, for example, Frederick C. Barghoorn, *Politics in the USSR*, 2d ed. (Boston: Little, Brown and Co., 1972), especially ch. 1 and 2; and Robert C. Tucker, "Culture, Political Culture and Communist Society," *Political Science Quarterly* 88, no. 2 (June 1973):173–190.

57. See, for example, Richard Pipes, *Russia Under the Old Regime* (New York: Charles Scribner's Sons, 1974); Tibor Szamuely, *The Russian Tradition* (New York: McGraw-Hill Book Co., 1974). For two opposite approaches to the question of self-serving and distorting foreign images of Russia in the past, see George F. Kennan, *The Marquis de Custine and His Russia in 1839* (Princeton, N.J.:Princeton University Press, 1971), and Sergei G. Pushkarev, "Russia and the West," *The Russian Review* 24, no. 2 (April 1965):138–164.

58. The most systematic rebuttal by a historian, especially in regard to foreign policy, is Dietrich Geyer, "Der Geschichtliche Hintergrund und das Problem der Tradition," in Geyer, ed., *Sowjetunion: Aussenpolitik 1917–1955*, vol. 1 (Koln: Bohlau, 1972), pp. 1–19. See also note 65 below.

59. Gordon A. Craig, Review of Imanuel Geiss and Bernd Jurgen Wendt, eds., *Deutschland in der Weltpolitik des 19. und 20. Jahrhunderts*, in *American Historical Review* 81, no. 2 (April 1976):403.

60. See especially Alex Inkeles and David Smith, *Becoming Modern: Individual Change in Six Developing Countries* (Cambridge, Mass.: Harvard University Press, 1974); and Alex Inkeles, "The Modernization of Man in Socialist and Nonsocialist Countries" in Mark G. Field, ed., *Social Consequences of Modernization in Communist Societies* (Baltimore, Md.: Johns Hopkins University Press, 1976), pp. 50–59.

61. See Richard Fagen, *The Transformation of Political Culture in Cuba* (Stanford, Calif.: Stanford University Press, 1969); and Alex Inkeles and Daniel J. Levinson, "National Character: The Study of Modal Personality and Sociocultural Systems" in Gardner Lindzey, ed., *Handbook of Social Psychology*, vol. 2 (Cambridge, Mass.: Addison-Wesley Publishing Company, 1954), pp. 977–1020.

62. For a thorough examination of the historical dimension in the context of Soviet foreign policy formation, see Morton Schwartz, *The Foreign Policy of the USSR*, ch. 3, especially p. 92.

63. On the theory of "oriental despotism," see Karl A. Wittfogel, "Russia and the East" in Donald W. Treadgold, ed., *Development of the USSR* (Seattle: University of Washington Press, 1964), pp. 323–339. See also James H. Billihgton, *The Icon and the Axe* (New York: Alfred A. Knopf, 1966).

It would go beyond the framework of this chapter to examine the characteristics of Russian imperialism in a comparative perspective. On parallels with Western expansionism, see in addition to Dietrich Geyer (cited above), Michael M. Karpovich, "Russian Imperialism or Communist Aggression?" in Alexander Dallin, ed., *Soviet Conduct in World Affairs*, pp. 186–195.

64. A prime example would be Edward L. Keenan, "Muscovite Political Folkways: Some Prolegomena to the Study of Great Russian Political Culture"

(manuscript, Harvard University, 1976). See also the contributions of Theodore H. Von Laue, Robert F. Byrnes, and Cyril E. Black in Ivo Lederer, ed., *Russian Foreign Policy*, part 1. Cyril Black identifies four objectives that, he seeks to show, all Russian governments have pursued over the centuries: stabilization of frontiers; creation of conditions for economic growth; promotion of the unification of national territories; and assurance of international security through arrangements with other states. Without disputing these categories, one may wonder to what extent these are distinctive, let alone unique, concerns.

65. U.S. Senate, Committee on Foreign Relations, *Perceptions: Relations Between the United States and the Soviet Union* (Washington, D.C.: U.S. Government Printing Office, 1979), p. 65.

66. For seminal earlier discussions, see, for example, Barrington Moore, *Soviet Politics — The Dilemma of Power* (Cambridge, Mass.: Harvard University Press, 1950); the symposium on "Ideology and Power Politics," with Richard Lowenthal, Samuel Sharp, and R. N. Carew Hunt in *Problems of Communism* 7, no. 2 (March-April 1958):10-29 (reprinted in Dallin, ed., *Soviet Conduct in World Affairs*, ch. 2, and in Hoffmann and Fleron, eds., *The Conduct of Soviet Foreign Policy*, ch. 7); Alfred G. Meyer, "The Functions of Ideology in the Soviet Political System," *Soviet Studies* 17, no. 3 (January 1966):273-285 (and comments in ibid., April and July 1966). See also Zbigniew Brzezinski, *Ideology and Power in Soviet Politics* (New York: Praeger Publishers, 1962); and Vernon V. Aspaturian, *Process and Power in Soviet Foreign Policy* (Boston: Little, Brown and Co., 1971).

67. In terms of the typology, discussed elsewhere, of Soviet foreign policy as viewed in "essentialist," "mechanistic," or "cybernetic" terms, the learning aspects support the latter model.

The above comments are not meant to suggest the absence of interaction between elite and mass opinion. Thus in the Brezhnev era the tendency to play down ideological formulae has been translated into policy passed down from the top to the mass media and local officialdom.

68. For more specific discussion of the role and content of "ideology" in this context, see Morton Schwartz, *The Foreign Policy of the USSR*, ch. 4.

69. For a sophisticated and informed discussion of the effect of events on explicit doctrine, see Paul Marantz, "The Soviet Union and the Western World: A Study in Doctrinal Change 1917-1964" (Ph.D. diss., Harvard University, 1971).

70. Among the many convenient summaries, one might cite Morton Schwartz, *The Foreign Policy of the USSR*, ch. 1; U.S. Congress, Joint Economic Committee, *Soviet Economy in a New Perspective* (Washington, D.C.: U.S. Government Printing Office, 1976). For a summary of economic performance, see Gregory Grossman, "The Soviet Economy Before and After the Twenty-fifth Congress" in Dallin, ed., *The Twenty-fifth Congress of the CPSU: Assessment and Context* (Stanford, Calif.: Hoover Institution Press, 1977), pp. 53-78.

71. Frederick C. Barghoorn, *Politics in the USSR*, p. 200.

72. George W. Breslauer and Stanley Rothman, *Soviet Politics and Society* (St. Paul, Minn.: West Publishing Co., 1978), p. 209. See also Morton Schwartz, *The Foreign Policy of the USSR*, pp. 176-189.

73. As one close student of the problem stated, "Policy conflicts, personal

rivalries, and personnel shifts at the top levels bear on [the Soviet leader's] continuing effort to sustain or expand his dominance. . . . He inevitably offends some political forces and pleases others in pressing his policies, thereby generating conflict within the regime. . . . In fact, it is the way [an] issue is defined by the leader or faction in power that gives shape and tone to all the tensions and contentions within the present regime." (Carl Linden, *Khrushchev and the Soviet Leadership* [Baltimore, Md.: Johns Hopkins University Press, 1966], pp. 5, 15.)

74. For a fine summary, as this applies to foreign policy in particular, see Horelick, Johnson, and Steinbruner, *The Study of Soviet Foreign Policy*, esp. pp. 32–38. See also, in addition to Linden (*Khrushchev and the Soviet Leadership*), among the many earlier titles, Robert Conquest, *Power and Policy in the U.S.S.R.* (New York: St. Martin's Press, 1961); Michel Tatu, *Power in the Kremlin*; Sidney I. Ploss, ed., *The Soviet Political Process* (Waltham, Mass.: Ginn, 1971); T. Harry Rigby, "Crypto-Politics," *Survey*, no. 50 (January 1964), pp. 183–194, reprinted in Frederic J. Fleron, ed., *Communist Studies and the Social Sciences* (Chicago: Rand McNally & Co., 1969), pp. 116–128; as well as the newer studies, Archie H. Brown, *Soviet Politics and Political Science* (New York: Macmillan, 1974); Seweryn Bialer, "The Soviet Political Elite and Internal Developments in the USSR," in Griffith, ed., *The Soviet Empire*, pp. 25–55.

A number of monographs and dissertations deal with particular time periods or subjects of Soviet politics. Some good examples are Philip S. Gillette, "The Political Origins of American-Soviet Trade, 1917–1924" (Ph.D. diss., Harvard University, 1969); David E. Langsam, "Pressure Group Politics in NEP Russia: The Case of the Trade Unions" (Ph.D. diss., Princeton University, 1971); Werner G. Hahn, *The Politics of Soviet Agriculture, 1960–1970* (Baltimore, Md.: Johns Hopkins University Press, 1972); Sidney Ploss, *Conflict and Decision-Making in Soviet Russia: A Case Study of Agricultural Policy, 1953–1963* (Princeton, N.J.: Princeton University Press, 1965); James B. Bruce, *The Politics of Soviet Policy Formation: Khrushchev's Innovative Policies in Education and Agriculture*, Monograph Series in World Affairs 13, no. 4 (Denver, Colo.: University of Denver, 1976); C. Grant Pendill, "Foreign Policy and Political Factions in the USSR, 1952–1956" (Ph.D. diss., University of Pennsylvania, 1969); and others cited below.

The use of a conflict model does not preclude the recognition that an individual leader, such as Khrushchev, can try to push through his own policy preferences at some risk and cost. Nor is it contradicted by the observation that, with some striking exceptions, the post-Khrushchev era has been marked by considerable stability and security in bureaucratic roles.

75. Barghoorn, *Politics in the USSR*, p. 202.

76. See, for example, Aspaturian, "Internal Politics and Foreign Policy in the Soviet System"; Wolfgang Leonhard, "The Domestic Politics of the New Soviet Foreign Policy," *Foreign Affairs* 52, no. 1 (October 1973):59–74; Michael J. Brenner, "Bureaucratic Politics in Foreign Policy," *Armed Forces and Society* 2, no. 2 (Winter 1976):326–332.

77. Breslauer and Rothman, *Soviet Politics and Society*, pp. 212–213.

78. Perhaps a word should be added on the tension between the bureaucratic politics and the group approaches to policy analysis. While the distinction between

the two is fundamental in the United States, it is not nearly so basic in the U.S.S.R. This is true primarily because "everybody" (except for a handful of extreme dissidents) is, as it were, part of the "system" and therefore an insider. Nonetheless, it probably remains true that the bureaucrat is concerned with the preservation of the status quo, whereas the spokesman for a group is engaged in special pleading, more often than not pleading for a change.

On both group and tendency analysis, see H. Gordon Skilling and Franklyn Griffiths, eds., *Interest Groups in Soviet Politics* (Princeton, N.J.: Princeton University Press, 1971). See also Theodore M. Friedgut, "Interests and Groups in Soviet Policy-Making: The MTS Reforms," in *Soviet Studies* 28, no. 4 (October 1976):524–547; Philip Stewart, "Soviet Interest Groups and the Policy Process: The Repeal of Production Education" *World Politics* 22, no. 1 (October 1969):29–50; Barghoorn, *Politics in the USSR*, pp. 206–227.

79. While the categories have remained similar, the Brezhnev years have seen a curious reversal of argumentation, compared to the Khrushchev era. Carl Linden, the author of an excellent analysis of politics under Khrushchev, writes, "The antagonism in the post-Stalin period between those leaning toward orthodoxy and conservatism on the one hand, and those disposed to reform and innovation, on the other, can be roughly defined in terms of an internal vs. an external orientation in policy. The more orthodox emphasize the necessities of the world struggle and the dangers from the outside enemy. Those inclined toward reform stress internal problems, the prospect for a relatively safe international environment, and the possibilities of developing less dangerous forms of struggle with the adversary abroad." (Linden, *Khrushchev and the Soviet Leadership*, pp. 18–19.) In the 1970s, by contrast, the moderate/reformist elements have been more likely to look abroad for positive ties, at best holding the domestic scene constant.

80. Glenn H. Snyder and Paul Diesing, *Conflict Among Nations: Bargaining, Decision Making, and System Structure in International Crises*, pp. 512–513.

81. Grey Hodnett appropriately reminds us that T. H. Rigby has stressed four bases of protection and support in the Soviet system: shared attitudes based on common prior experience; ties based on prior service together; congruent policy views; and patron-client relations (see Chapter 4). See also his excellent article, "Succession Contingencies in the Soviet Union," *Problems of Communism* 24, no. 2 (March–April 1975):1–21, especially p. 11. Vernon Aspaturian attributes differences and conflicts over foreign policy to personality differences; group differences; differences over doctrinal interpretation, stemming largely from differential perceptions of self-interest; and differences over strategy and tactics to achieve common goals. (See Aspaturian, "Internal Politics and Foreign Policy," p. 250.)

82. Hodnett, ch. 4. See also Ilana Kass, *Soviet Involvement in the Midde East: Policy Formulation, 1966–73* (Boulder, Colo.: Westview Press, 1978), p. 233. Breslauer cogently criticizes traditional Kremlinology for failing to differentiate between the "routine political conflict" and "destabilizing" political infighting. (George W. Dallin, ed., *The Twenty-fifth Congress of the CPSU*, pp. 19–20).

83. K. J. Holsti, "National Role Conceptions in the Study of Foreign Policy" *International Studies Quarterly* 14, no. 3 (1970):233–309.

84. See Benjamin Fischer, "The Soviet Political System and Foreign Policy-

Making in the Brezhnev Era," (manuscript, 1978); Morton Schwartz, *The Foreign Policy of the USSR;* Triska and Finley, *Soviet Foreign Policy;* Aspaturian, "Internal Politics and Foreign Policy in the Soviet System"; Grey Hodnett, "The Pattern of Leadership Politics"; Jon D. Glassman, "Soviet Foreign Policy Decision-Making," in Andrew W. Cordier, ed., *Columbia Essays in International Affairs*, vol. 3 (New York: Columbia University Press, 1968), pp. 373–402; Vladimir Petrov, "Formation of Soviet Foreign Policy," *Orbis* 17, no. 3 (Fall 1973):819–850; Peter H. Juviler and Henry W. Morton, eds., *Soviet Policy-Making* (New York: Praeger Publishers, 1967); Boris Meissner, "The Foreign Ministry and Foreign Service of the USSR," *Aussenpolitik*, English ed., 28, no. 1 (1977):49–64; Dimitri K. Simes, *Detente and Conflict: Soviet Foreign policy 1972–1977*, The Washington Papers, vol. 5, no. 44 (Beverly Hills, Calif. and London: Sage Publications, 1977); Kenneth Myers and Dimitri Simes, "Soviet Decision Making, Strategic Policy, and SALT," (ACDA/PAB-243, Washington, D.C., 1974); Michel Tatu, "Decision Making in the USSR" in Richard Pipes, ed., *Soviet Strategy in Europe* (New York: Crane, Russak Co. Inc., 1976), pp. 45–64.

For a systematic presentation of Soviet decision making, as the United States knows it, and a brief acount of the various institutions involved (using a variety of sources), see the statement submitted by Thomas W. Wolfe, "The Military Dimension in the Making of Soviet Foreign and Defense Policy," U.S. House of Representatives, Subcommittee on Europe and the Middle East, *The Soviet Union: Internal Dynamics of Foreign Policy, Present and Future* (Washington, D.C.: U.S. Government Printing Office, 1978), pp. 85–114.

85. Bialer, "Soviet Political Elite and Internal Developments in the USSR," p. 31. If it is true even in the United States that "hardly any work has been done on the relationships between characteristics of foreign policy elites . . . and foreign policy behavior" (Patrick J. McGowan and Howard B. Shapiro, *The Comparative Study of Foreign Policy* [Beverly Hills, Calif.: Sage Publications, 1973], p. 14), the same is surely true of the study of Soviet foreign policy.

86. See, for example, Seweryn Bialer, testimony before the U.S. Senate, Comittee on the Judiciary, *Scope of Soviet Activity in the United States,* 8–29 June 1956; David J. Dallin, *Soviet Foreign Policy After Stalin* (Philadelphia: J. B. Lippincott Co., 1961), pp. 227–233; Paul Marantz, "Internal Politics and Soviet Foreign Policy: A Case Study," *Western Political Quarterly* 28, no. 1 (March 1975):130–146; and V. A. Zorin, ed., *Vneshniaia politika SSSR na novom etape* (Moscow, 1964), pp. 8, 34.

87. See Malcolm Mackintosh, "The Soviet Military's Influence on Foreign Policy" in Michael MccGwire et al., eds., *Soviet Naval Policy*, pp. 29–31; Alexander Dallin, "Domestic Factors Influencing Soviet Foreign Policy" in Michael Confino and Shimon Shamir, eds., *The U.S.S.R. and the Middle East* (Jerusalem: Israel Universities Press, 1973), pp. 49–50; Ilana Kass, *Soviet Involvement in the Middle East,* p. 219 ff; Galia Golan, *Yom Kippur and After: The Soviet Union and the Middle East Crisis* (New York: Cambridge University Press, 1977). See also Hannes Adomeit, in this volume. On Shelepin, see also Grey Hodnett, "Khrushchev and Party-State Control," in Alexander Dallin and Alan F. Westin, eds., *Politics in the Soviet Union* (New York: Harcourt, Brace, & World, Inc. 1966), pp. 113–164; and Tatu, "Decision Making in the USSR." Mackintosh implies that Egorychev was echoing a military

viewpoint that Soviet policy in the Middle East was too risky in 1967, rather than too timid. Firm evidence on this point appears to be lacking. Myers and Simes, "Soviet Decision Making," affirm that Shelepin was demoted to chairman of the trade unions "because of his criticism of Soviet policy in the Middle East which led to the Six-Day War."

In her study of the Soviet press, Ilana Kass (pp. 219–220) finds a close correlation between Shelepin's statements and that of *Trud*, the trade union newspaper. She also shows that Shelepin's skepticism regarding better relations with the United States was linked to his failure to echo Brezhnev's attacks on China and to his and his associates' criticism of Soviet policy in the Middle East as having abandoned the Communist parties there in favor of (presumably unreliable) nationalist movements.

88. On Shelest, see Grey Hodnett and Peter J. Potichnyj, *The Ukraine and the Czechoslovak Crisis* (Canberra: Occasional Paper no. 6. Australian National University, 1970); and Grey Hodnett, "Ukrainian Politics and the Purge of Shelest" (manuscript, 1977).

89. The so-called Penkovsky Papers include the statement, "Churayev says that there are many foreign policy issues on which Mikoyan disagrees with Khrushchev. When Varentsov asked Churayev one time why nothing had been heard about Mikoyan or his whereabouts recently, Churayev answered, 'They are at each other's throats again.' Incidentally, Mikoyan is against the hard policy on Berlin." (*The Penkovsky Papers* [New York: Avon Books, 1966], pp. 208–209.)

90. Connie M. Friesen, *The Political Economy of East-West Trade* (New York: Praeger Publishers, 1976), pp. 49–53; *Pravda*, 16 October and 3 November 1974. A valuable study is by Bruce Parrott, "Technological Progress and Soviet Politics," *Survey* 23, no. 3/4 (Spring 1977/78):39–60, who documents "continued disagreement within the leadership about the sufficiency of the USSR's technological performance." In a good insight, he finds that "the search for solutions to these problems is complicated not only by the intellectual difficulty of discovering an administrative pattern which can promote more rapid technological progress, but by the political difficulty of imposing such a pattern on the bureaucracy" (p. 49).

91. Rensselaer W. Lee, "Soviet Perceptions of Western Technology" (Mathtech., Inc., 1978), pp. xiv, xv ff. To date, there are no case studies of foreign policy attitudes of Soviet leaders such as Suslov and Ustinov. See also Aron Katsenelinboigen, "Conflicting Trends in Soviet Economics in the Post-Stalin Era," *The Russian Review* 35, no. 4 (October 1976):373–399. Friesen, pointing to another dispute over centralization in Soviet economic planning and the use of computers, concludes correctly that these can be viewed "simply as the latest rounds in the decade-old debate on economic reform and industrial reorganization in the Soviet Union."

See also Abraham Katz, *The Politics of Economic Reform in the Soviet Union* (New York: Praeger Publishers, 1972); Karl W. Ryavec, *Implementation of Soviet Economic Reforms* (New York: Praeger Publishers 1975); Daniel Tarschys, *The Soviet Political Agenda: Problems and Priorities, 1950–1970* (White Plains, N.Y.: M. E. Sharpe, 1979).

92. Friesen, *The Political Economy of East-West Trade*, p. 56. As she remarks, "even

within a centrally planned economy, the potential meanings of economic detente are many."

93. *Pravda*, 15 September 1978.

94. Christer Jonsson, "Soviet Foreign Policy and Domestic Politics: A Case Study," *Cooperation and Conflict*, vol. 12 (1977), pp. 129-148. See also his *The Soviet Union and the Test Ban: A Study in Soviet Negotiating Behavior* (Political Studies no. 21, Lund, Sweden: Student litteratur, 1975).

95. Ibid., p. 145. It is impossible here to examine the role of all major institutions in regard to foreign policy. The attitude and behavior of the security organs, in particular, deserve study. From time to time incidents, seemingly provoked by one of the branches of the KGB, appeared to constitute "direct action" calculated to undermine efforts at improving Soviet relations with the West. After his arrest in October 1963 in Moscow, Frederick C. Barghoorn speculated that the "incident" involving him was precisely of this nature. In September 1964 there was a bizarre mustard gas attack on a West German diplomat, and several instances of harassment of British and U.S. military attachés. Several Westerners who have close personal ties with Soviet scholars and officials were summarily expelled or denied visas to the USSR. No such incidents have been publicized in the 1970s.

96. Jiri Valenta, "The Bureaucratic Politics Paradigm and the Soviet Invasion of Czechoslovakia," *Political Science Quarterly* 94, no. 1 (Spring 1979):55-76. See also Myers and Simes, "Soviet Decision Making," p. 23. It may well be that further study would show variations related to the political sensitivity of an issue. Moreover, patronage networks continue to be of key importance. See Donald R. Kelley, "Interest Groups and Policy Formation in the USSR" (Ph.D. diss., Indiana University, 1971).

97. Ilana Kass, *Soviet Involvement in the Middle East*, p. 228.

98. See Robert Levine, *The Arms Race* (Cambridge, Mass.: Harvard University Press, 1963), pp. 28 ff.

99. See Dallin, "Domestic Factors Influencing Soviet Foreign Policy," in Confino and Shamir, *The USSR and the Middle East*, pp. 36-38.

100. Similarly other studies have found that it is easiest to articulate divergent priorities if these views can be offered in instrumental, technical, and apolitical terms. See, for example, Friedgut, "Interests and Groups in Soviet Policy Making."

101. Dallin, "Domestic Factors Influencing Soviet Foreign Policy," in Confino and Shamir, *The USSR and the Middle East*.

102. Franklyn D. Holzman and Robert Legvold, "The Economics and Politics of East-West Relations,'" *International Organization* 29, no. 1 (Winter 1975):298-310; quoted on pp. 299-300.

103. An imperfect but perhaps suggestive analogy may be made here with the identification of issues in the Sino-Soviet dispute before either the Soviet Union or China acknowledged existence of the dispute. It was possible to show a number of disputed formulae and assumptions from the verbal or written record. Later evidence showed that other issues (for instance, Soviet help with nuclear know-how) were serious but could not be deduced from the available evidence. At that, the analysis of the Sino-Soviet dispute was simpler in that the fora and channels of interaction were far more limited than the universe of Soviet domestic "inputs" into the making of foreign policy.

104. Vernon V. Aspaturian, "Internal Politics and Foreign Policy in the Soviet System," p. 252. See also Barghoorn, *Politics in the USSR*, ch. 8.

A fairly senior Soviet official has remarked privately that his and his colleagues' effort on behalf of the U.S. award of most-favored-nation status to the USSR was far more a matter of status within the Soviet establishment than of commercial importance.

105. For the earlier version of this issue, see Paul Marantz, "Soviet Foreign Policy Factionalism Under Stalin: A Case Study of the Inevitability of War Controversy" in *Soviet Union* 3, no. 1 (1976):91-107.

106. See Franklyn Griffiths, "Ideological Development and Foreign Policy," (ch. 2 in this volume). Regarding China, see also Robert M. Gates, "Soviet Sinology: An Untapped Source for Kremlin Views and Disputes Relating to Contemporary Events in China" (Ph.D. diss., Georgetown University, 1974). For comparative studies, see for example, Roy Grow, "The Politics of Industrial Development in China and the Soviet Union," (Ph.D. diss., University of Michigan, 1973); Bernard M. Frolic, "Noncomparative Communism: China and the USSR," *Journal of Comparative Administration* 4 (Fall 1972):279 ff; Thomas Bernstein, "Leadership and Mass Mobilization in the Soviet and Chinese Collectivisation Campaigns of 1929-30 and 1955-56: A Comparison," *China Quarterly*, no. 31 (July-September 1967):1-47. See also Kenneth Lieberthal, "The Impact on the USSR of Chinese Disarmament Policies, 1964-67," in Thomas Larson, *Disarmament and Soviet Policy* (Englewood Cliffs, N.J.: Prentice-Hall, 1969), pp. 261-274; William Badour, "La Chine et l'URSS: Liens entre politique interne et politique externe," *Études internationales* 3, no. 4 (December 1972):473-484; as well as various papers by Roderick MacFarqhuar, Harry Gelman, C. Thomas Fingar, and Thomas Robinson.

On the Third World, see for example, Donald S. Carlisle, "The Changing Soviet Perception of the Developmental Process in the Afro-Asian World," *Midwest Journal of Political Science* 8, no. 4 (November 1964):385-407; Morton Schwartz, "The USSR and Leftist Regimes in Less-Developed Countries," *Survey* 19, no. 2 (Spring 1973):209-244; also William Zimmerman, *Soviet Perspectives on International Relations*; and various papers and collections by Roger Kanet, David Morison, Alvin Z. Rubinstein, and Elizabeth Kridl Valkenier.

107. See, for example, Jiri Valenta, "Soviet Foreign Policy Decision-making and the Problem of Eurocommunism: The Impact of Bureaucratic and East European Politics" (manuscript, 1977). On China the evidence is scattered and thin but suggestive. See, for example, Victor Zorza, "Kremlin Split Over China Policy Glimpsed," *Christian Science Monoitor*, 7 December 1977.

108. Nikita Khrushchev, *Stroitel'stvo kommunizma v SSSR i razvitie sel'skogo khoziaistva*, vol. 8 (Moscow, 1964), p. 51.

109. K. P. Ivanov, *Leninskie osnovy vneshnei politiki SSR*, cited in Sidney I. Ploss, "Politics in the Kremlin," *Problems of Communism* 19, no. 3 (May-June 1970):8.

110. Craig Whitney, "Moscow Aide Concedes Differences in the Soviet Leadership Over Arms Pact," The *New York Times*, 7 November 1978. Needless to say, this may be a considerable oversimplification by Falin.

111. See, in addition to the Hodnett-Potichnyj monograph cited earlier, Jiri Valenta, "The Bureaucratic Politics Paradigm and the Soviet Invasion of Czechoslovakia"; Valenta, "Soviet Decisionmaking and the Czechoslovak Crisis of

1968"; and Dimitri K. Simes, "The Soviet Invasion of Czechoslovakia and the Limits of Kremlinology," both in *Studies in Comparative Communism* 8, nos. 1 and 2 (Spring/Summer 1975):147–180; David W. Paul, "Soviet Foreign Policy and the Invasion of Czechoslovakia," *International Studies Quarterly* 15, no. 2 (June 1971):159–202. See also Horelick et al., *The Study of Soviet Foreign Policy*, pp. 46–47; Mackintosh, "The Soviet Military's Influence on Foreign Policy," pp. 32–33; Boris Meissner, "Der Entscheidungsprozess in der Kreml-Fuhrung unter Stalin und seiner Nachfolgern," in Meissner and Georg Brunner, eds., *Gruppeninteressen und Entscheidungsprozess in der Sowjetunion* (Cologne: Verlag Wissenshaft und Politik, 1975).

112. See Ilana Kass, *Soviet Involvement in the Middle East: Policy Formation*; Dina Spechler, "Internal Influences on Soviet Foreign Policy: Elite Opinion and the Middle East," Research Paper no. 18 (Soviet and East European Research Centre, Hebrew University of Jerusalem, 1976). See also Galia Golan, *Yom Kippur and After*. For a rather different approach, see Hannes Adomeit, "Soviet Policy in the Middle East: Problems of Analysis," *Soviet Studies* 27, no. 2 (April 1975):288–305; as well as the standard studies of Soviet policy by Jon Glassman, Oded Eran, Robert Freedman, Uri Ra'anan, and others.

113. Soviet arms control policy offers a fruitful and important field of investigation for the study of "linkages" in Soviet politics. Among available studies, see in particular, Thomas W. Wolfe, "The SALT Experience" (RAND memorandum R-1686-PR, 1975); Lawrence T. Caldwell, "Soviet Attitudes to SALT," *Adelphi Paper*, no. 75 (London: IISS, 1971); Samuel B. Payne, Jr., "The Soviet Debate on Strategic Arms Limitations: 1969–72," *Soviet Studies* 27, no. 1 (January 1975):27–45, and his "'From Positions of Strength': Soviet Attitudes Toward Strategic Arms Limitation" (Ph.D. diss., Johns Hopkins University, 1976); John Newhouse, *Cold Dawn: The Story of SALT* (New York: Holt, Rinehart and Winston, 1973); Marshall D. Shulman, "SALT and the Soviet Union" in Mason Willrich and John B. Rhinelander, eds., *SALT: The Moscow Agreements and Beyond* (New York: Free Press, 1974), pp. 101–121; Raymond Garthoff, "SALT and the Soviet Military," *Problems of Communism* 24, no. 1 (January–February 1975):21–37; his "Mutual Deterrence and Strategic Arms Limitation in Soviet Policy," *International Security* 3, no. 1 (Summer 1978):112–147; and his "SALT I: An Evaluation," *World Politics* 31, no. 1 (October 1978):1–25; Franklyn Griffiths, "Inner Tensions in the Soviet Approach to 'Disarmament,'" *International Journal* (Toronto) 22, no. 4 (Autumn 1967):593–617; and the studies by Kolkowicz, Jonsson, and Ross, cited above. On the diversity of Soviet views and the process of decision making for SALT I, see especially Myers and Simes, "Soviet Decision Making, Strategic Policy, and SALT," pp. 32–57, an informed discussion.

114. See note 47 above for references to some of the works cited; and Robert W. Hansen, "Soviet Images of American Foreign Policy, 1960–1972" (Ph.D. diss., Princeton University, 1975) and his "Recent Conflicts in Soviet Images of American Foreign Policy" (paper delivered to the International Studies Association, annual meeting, St. Louis, Missouri, 16–20 March 1977); Donald R. Kelley, "The Soviet Debate on the Convergence of American and Soviet Systems, *Polity* 6, no. 2 (Winter 1973):174–196; Stephen P. Gilbert, *Soviet Images of America* (New York: Crane,

Russak & Co., 1977); Alayne P. Reilly, *America in Contemporary Soviet Literature* (New York: New York University Press, 1971).

Hansen finds that in the 1960s there were three policy clusters with regard to the interrelated issues of military strategy, arms control, and détente:

1. The hard line: Continued priority on military and heavy industrial production; a striving for nuclear parity and, for some advocates of the hard line, nuclear superiority over the U.S.; confrontation with imperialism in the Third World; and opposition to normalized relations with the U.S., especially as concerned arms control.

2. The moderate line: Concern about lagging Soviet economic growth and a desire to increase allocations to the consumer sector although not necessarily to agriculture; temporary heavy investment in arms production so as to achieve parity with the U.S.; interest in disarmament on the basis of parity; increased global deployment of Soviet forces but avoidance of confrontation with the U.S. in the Third World.

3. The soft line: Priority on consumer production and on increased efficiency in the Soviet economy; comprehensive detente with the West including limits on the arms race and greatly increased trade; avoidance of military conflicts with the West in the Third World and selective resolution of conflicting interests there. (p. 23.)

115. Asked to provide an example of a topic on which the editorial board of a major Soviet journal has recently had serious disagreements, a senior editor cites the nature of economic crises in the United States. This is indeed congruent with the dichotomy, posited above, between political/ideological preconceptions regarding the inevitable doom of capitalism, and the empirical/realistic approach of those who wish to expand economic ties with the United States.

116. *Samizdat Register*, Document AS 1461.

117. *Pravda*, 4 April 1971.

118. For a good discussion, see Robert C. Horn, "1969: Year of Change in Soviet Foreign Policy" (paper delivered to the Western Slavic Association, annual meeting, San Diego, California, 19–21 February 1976).

119. Hodnett, "Succession Contingencies in the Soviet Union," p. 10.

120. Michel Tatu, "Decision Making in the USSR," in Pipes, ed., *Soviet Strategy in Europe*, pp. 62–63. Tatu further draws attention to the difference between center and periphery when he suggests that disapproval of détente—and the whole policy of interaction with the outside world—"is expressed mainly by provincial Party officials, by those who are more in touch with their 'base' [rank and file] and are more aware of the dangers inherent in a general ideological relaxation for the cohesion of the system. These provincial cadres make up the bulk of the active membership of the Central Committee, and they also have some spokesmen within the Politburo."

121. Marshall Shulman, "Trends in Soviet Foreign Policy," in MccGwire et al., eds., *Soviet Naval Policy*, pp. 8–10. See also Alexander Dallin, "All Orwellian Pigs?" in *Encounter* 42, no. 6 (June 1974):83–84; Wolfgang Leonhard, "The Domestic Politics of the New Soviet Foreign Policy," p. 69; Boris Meissner, "Der Entscheidungsprozess in der Kreml-Fuhrung," pp. 49–52.

122. Aspaturian, "Internal Politics and Foreign Policy in the Soviet System," pp. 256–283. The debate regarding autarky or interdependence is alluded to by a number of studies cited in this chapter. For an attempt to systematize alternative

positions and implications, see Walter C. Clemens, Jr., *The U.S.S.R. and Global Interdependence* (Washington, D.C.: American Enterprise Institute for Public Policy Research, 1978); also Marshall I. Goldman, "Autarky or Integration—The U.S.S.R. and the World Economy," in U.S. Congress, Joint Economic Committee, *Soviet Economy in a New Perspective* (Washington, D.C.: U.S. Government Printing Office, 1976), pp. 81–96.

123. Astrid von Borcke, "Der Kreml und die Entspannungspolitik: Machkonstellation und Richtungskampfe," in *Elemente des Wandels in der ostlichen Welt* (*Moderne Welt: Jahrbuch fus Ost-West Fragen*, Cologne: Markus Verlag, 1976), p. 253.

124. Myers and Simes, "Soviet Decision Making," pp. 58–75.

125. Simes, *Detente and Conflict: Soviet Foreign Policy 1972–1977*, especially pp. 50–59.

126. Alexander Yanov, *Detente After Brezhnev: The Domestic Roots of Soviet Foreign Policy*, Policy Papers in International Affairs, no. 2 (Berkeley: Institute of International Studies, University of California, 1977), p. 67. See also his *The Russian New Right-Wing Ideologies in the Contemporary USSR*, Research Series, no. 35 (Berkeley: Institute of International Studies, University of California, 1978).

127. Boris Rabbot, "Detente: The Struggle Within the Kremlin," The *Washington Post*, 10 July 1977. See also his "One View Why Podgorny Was Ousted," *Christian Science Monitor*, 13 June 1977; and "A Letter to Brezhnev," The *New York Times Magazine*, 6 November 1977. While some of his assertions (e.g., on the Cuban operation in Angola as a compromise between Brezhnev and Shelepin) do not seem credible, others (e.g., the assertion that the idea of a preventive war against China was abandoned in 1969) appear to be corroborated by other sources.

128. Morton Schwartz, "Detente and Internal Soviet Politics," (paper delivered to the Western Slavic Association, annual meeting, San Diego, California, 19–21 February 1976). On these experts, see also Tatu, "Decision Making in the USSR," p. 60; Ronald Pope, "Soviet Foreign Affairs Specialists: An Evaluation of Their Impact . . . [1958–73]" (Ph.D. diss., University of Pennsylvania, 1975); Oded Eran, "The *Mezh-dunarodniki*: Soviet Foreign Policy Experts (An Interpretation)" (manuscript, 1976). See also Richard B. Remnek, ed., *Social Scientists and Policy Making in the USSR* (New York: Praeger Publishers, 1977).

129. A variety of adjectives are used in Russian to refer to these—especially petit bourgeois—inclinations: *zhiteiskii, bytovoi, obyvatel'skii, meshchanskii*.

130. On this aspect, see Yanov, *Detente After Brezhnev*; Alexander Dallin, "The Fruits of Interaction," *Survey* no. 3/4 (Summer/Autumn 1976):42–46; also Rabbot, "Soviet Travelling Professionals: An Inside View" (manuscript, 1977).

131. Aspaturian, "Internal Politics and Foreign Policy in the Soviet System," p. 286.

132. Donald R. Kelley, "Group and Specialist Influence in Soviet Politics: In Search of a Theory" in Remnek, ed., *Social Scientists and Policy Making in the USSR*, p. 134.

133. Such research ought to include case studies of the sort suggested at various points in this chapter, as well as work on discrete policy decisions and key individuals. Another promising avenue is the comparative exploration of the problem of "linkages" between domestic and foreign policymaking. There is a growing,

varied, and often sophisticated literature here. See, for example, Robert Axelrod, ed., *Structure of Decision: The Cognitive Maps of Political Elites* (Princeton, N.J.: Princeton University Press, 1976); Robert Burrows and Gerald DeMaio, "Domestic/External Linkages: Syria, 1961–1967," *Comparative Political Studies* 7, no. 4 (January 1975):478–507; Alan Dowty, "Foreign-Linked Factionalism as a Historical Pattern," *The Journal of Conflict Resolution* 15, no. 4 (December 1971):429–442; Ole R. Holsti, "Cognitive Dynamics and Images of the Enemy: Dulles and Russia," in David J. Finley, Ole R. Holsti and Richard R. Fagen, *Enemies in Politics* (Chicago: Rand McNally & Co., 1967), pp. 25–96; Laurence I. Radway, "Domestic Attitudes as Constraints on American Foreign Policy" in David A. Baldwin, ed., *America in an Interdependent World: Problems of United States Foreign Policy* (Hanover, N.H.: University Press of New England, 1976), pp. 294–313. Reference was made earlier to studies of linkage in Chinese and East European politics.

In regard to the effect of personality on policy in the United States, a recent study concludes, "The structural source of war and hard-line foreign policy lies in self-selection and political recruitment patterns of individuals with greater personal predispositions to threaten or use force." (Lloyd S. Etheredge, "Personality Effects on American Foreign Policy, 1898–1968.") We are still very far from undertaking anything comparable in regard to Soviet policymaking.

Finally, it may be appropriate to warn against the temptation to overanalyze and read too much into a limited body of sources. It may be more charitable not to identify some particularly outrageous examples of the misapplication of enthusiasm and imagination in reading between the lines what others do not believe is there.

134. Snyder and Diesing, *Conflict Among Nations*, p. 513.

135. Herbert S. Dinerstein, *Fifty Years of Soviet Foreign Policy* (Baltimore, Md.: Johns Hopkins University Press, 1968), p. 7.

136. Roy A. Medvedev, *On Socialist Democracy* (New York: Alfred A. Knopf, 1975), pp. 282–290.

137. Allen Kassof, review of Robert F. Byrnes, *Soviet-American Exchanges,* in the *American Historical Review* 82, no. 3 (June 1977):773.

138. Jiri Valenta, "The Bureaucratic Politics Paradigm and the Soviet Invasion of Czechoslovakia," p. 30.

139. Robert W. Hansen, "Soviet Images of American Foreign Policy," p. 220.

140. Snyder and Diesing, *Conflict Among Nations*, pp. 514–515.

141. Among those who have dealt with it in their writings are Urie Bronfenbrenner, Bernard S. Morris, and Jan F. Triska.

142. Colin S. Gray, "The Urge to Compete: Rationales for Arms Racing," *World Politics* 26, no. 2 (January 1974):207–233. I owe this reference to Dan Caldwell (Ph.D. diss., Stanford University, 1978), pp. 4–29. See also Edward L. Warner III, "The Bureaucratic Politics of Weapons Procurement" in MccGwire et al., *Soviet Naval Policy*, p. 67. He writes on the basis of personal experience:

The interactive U.S.-Soviet competition is complicated by the extreme secrecy that surrounds the major weapons development programs in both countries. Largely denied information about the early stages of the opponent's research and design efforts, the political-military leaderships on both sides are prone to fear the worst. In the name of prudence, they frequently employ worst-case analysis, which attributes to the adversary maximal weapons development efforts and optimum operational performance for a wide variety of weapons. Initial development efforts for off-setting systems are often undertaken based upon anticipated or vaguely perceived activities rather than the directly observed programs of the opponent. As a practical matter, the efforts attributed to the enemy are likely to be those that one's own weapons system researchers have conceived and proposed. As a result, programs undertaken in response to such anticipated developments are often the product of an "arms race against oneself" in which one's own offense is pitted against one's defense in a manner that fortifies the claims of each. This process can easily produce an action-overreaction pattern, where, although the anticipated threat fails to materialize, the "response" nevertheless results in the procurement of a major weapons system.

143. Boris Rabbot, who was still in Moscow at the time, writes: "In the end, political diehards in Washington who supported the Jackson[-Vanik] Amendment were unconsciously helping their conservative counterparts in Moscow by giving them a cause around which to unite to defeat the Brezhnev doves." (The *Washington Post*, 10 July 1977.) Alexander Yanov, in his *Detente After Brezhnev*, makes the same point strongly, arguing for a more skillful, sensitive, and differentiated U.S. policy.

15

Soviet Foreign Policy: Sources, Perceptions, Trends

Seweryn Bialer

The Brezhnev era is coming to an end. The approaching succession will go well beyond replacement of the top leader to involve, inevitably, change of the core leadership group and, in the not too distant future, a major generational turnover within the Soviet elite. The coming vast realignment of personnel, however unpredictable its consequences, will in all probability interrupt the visible drift and inertia of Soviet internal and external policies. Disputes over central policy issues that apparently already divide the leadership, even if their outlines are as yet unclear, will come to the fore; and it is around these central issues that the succession struggle will be fought and the new alignment of leadership and elites will emerge.

The most important issues will undoubtedly concern the internal Soviet policy line and especially economic policy. Yet foreign policy issues will also figure prominently in the disputes and policy realignments if for no other reason than their interconnection with domestic Soviet problems. In this situation, it behooves us to take seriously Richard Lowenthal's warning that "possible major Soviet decisions are being prepared in a situation in which the Soviets have the impression that they have nothing to hope and nothing to fear from the United States, and indeed from the West in general."[1]

It is not the purpose of this chapter to address directly the question of what U.S. policy toward the Soviet Union should be during this critical period, to define that policy that will maximize for Soviet policymakers those options that are least dangerous and most conducive to the promotion of U.S. international interests. The chapter will concentrate rather on the necessary preparatory steps in the process of devising such a policy — on an attempt to understand some of the sources of the conduct of Soviet foreign policy and the contradictory pressures that shape its formation.

Domestic Factors that Shape Soviet Foreign Policy

The domestic factors shaping Soviet foreign policy can be summarized succinctly as capabilities, politics, and beliefs.[2] The first group of factors (capabilities) includes the assessment of Soviet economic strength, the level of technological development, the overall military potential and the actual noncivilian expenditures, the allocations for foreign assistance and its utilization, the contribution of Soviet allies to actual Soviet strength, the degree of Soviet dependence on international cooperative arrangements and on foreign trade, etc.

The second group of factors (politics) is concerned with the institutions and process of Soviet foreign policymaking; with the nature and quality of the information inputs that go into this process; with the power and personality of the key actors who participate in this process; with the identification of major pressure groups that have vested interests in foreign policy decisions, the degree of their access to the foreign policymaking process and the degree of their influence; with the identification of the agenda of foreign policymaking and the changing orders of priority on the agenda; and with the more or less pronounced divisions within the Soviet leadership and elites regarding the main foreign policy line as well as separate foreign policy issues.

The third group of factors (beliefs) deals with the basic outlook on international affairs of Soviet decision makers; with the basic beliefs that they share in common and that were shaped by their common tradition, experience, and value system; with the basic assumptions about themselves and other international actors with which they approach their activities in the international arena; with the process of learning by which these assumptions are slowly adjusted; with their capital concerns about foreign relations; and with their fears and hopes.

The first group of factors is probably the best known and most studied. It deals with measurable, physical facts and more or less testable projections. It is the purview of the economist and the military specialist. It constitutes the main focus of the great debate in which the West is presently engaged. Our knowledge of the second group of factors is very severely limited, in part because few serious attempts have been made to study these factors, but primarily because the available data for their study are scarce and unreliable. Discussion depends more on imagination and speculation than on hard, testable conclusions.

If our lack of knowledge about the second group of factors is at least in large part understandable and excusable given the nature of the data at our disposal, there is no such excuse for the poverty of our knowledge and effort to learn and understand the third group of factors, although there is an explanation. For decades we have studied the Soviet leadership and system, its continuity and change, the diverse influences on the "Soviet mind," and the perception of the "Soviet mind." Yet now when so much in our own policy depends on understanding the "Soviet mind," we more often than not, under the influence of the "totalitarian" approach, either draw simplistic parallels with Nazi Germany; rely on overarching generalizations — or rather generalities — about the centuries of Russian imperial history; or seek understanding in the holy writ of the Bolshevik Revolution. It is precisely this third group of factors determining Soviet foreign policy that, if not the least known, is the least understood in the great debate that now sweeps the West; and it is this third group of factors that, it seems, generates the basic differences of views expressed in this debate.[3]

A number of reasons explain the difficulty in comprehending the third group of factors and the extraordinary divergence of views in evaluating them. It is an area in which one deals with the least calculable element in policy formation, namely, leadership intentions. It is an area where even if the data available were more complete, there would be numerous ambiguities and contradictions that do not result from the analysts' indecisiveness but reflect the ambiguities and contradictions of reality. It is a subject that must be dealt with on different levels of analysis and where it is very easy to move unconsciously from one level to another; to confuse values, beliefs, and attitudes that are held with different intensity and are not equidistant from actual policy decisions, short- and long-range views, strategies, and tactics.

In our opinion, however, the most important reason has to do with the difficulty of an empathetic approach in which the analyst must transcend the values, beliefs, and attitudes of his own society which he considers self-evident and adopt for the purpose of analysis those of the society that he attempts to analyze.[4] My concern in this chapter is overwhelmingly with this third group of factors of Soviet foreign policymaking. Before proceeding to their discussion, however, a short review of what we know about the first two groups of factors is in order.

Capabilities

Just what is known and characteristic of the first group of factors shaping Soviet foreign policy in the late Brezhnev era? Some important elements of those "capabilities" factors can be presented as follows.

- By far the most impressive achievement of the Brezhnev era and the greatest swing in Soviet capabilities has occurred in the military sphere. The Soviet Union achieved strategic parity with the United States; built up a numerical conventional preponderance in the European theater; increased immensely both its strategic and conventional strength in the Far Eastern theater; developed for the first time serious capabilities of global intervention, including the ability and the willingness to deploy large-scale surrogate interventionist forces far from its own borders; increased significantly the level of its military assistance in terms of arms sales, arms grants, and advisory personnel to friendly nations; and is engaged in as yet marginally successful efforts to integrate more tightly the Warsaw Pact armed forces.

- The accomplishments of the Brezhnev era in building up the economic potential of the Soviet Union should not be minimized. The Soviet Union has solidified and improved its status as a major industrial power, second only to the United States in the size of its overall production. It became in this period the largest nation-state producer of oil, coal, steel, cement, machine tools, and other traditional heavy-industry items. While it was unable to overcome the chronic shortcomings of its rural sector, despite enormous investments in agriculture, it was able to increase substantially its production, that is to say, to stabilize the agricultural crisis at a much higher level of foodstuffs consumption than in any previous period in Soviet history. The Soviet Union clearly entered the era of mass-consumption society, underwent a virtual income revolution, and achieved a standard of living comparable to that of other highly industrialized nations in the early phase of the mass-consumption era.

- Yet, as important as these achievements are, the fact is that the relative size of the Soviet economy in comparison to those of the United States and other key industrial democracies has not changed significantly and the overall technological gap between the West and the Soviet Union has not closed at all. Indeed, for a number of reasons the technological gap is probably even more important today—in fact and in the perception of Soviet leaders—than it was in the past. The Soviet Union exhibits an increased tendency toward a slowdown in quantitative overall growth. It may be unable to develop energy resources at a ratio adequate for its planned economic development. It is in the throes of a serious demographic problem where the curve of the increments of its working population is declining to a point where labor resources cannot be considered a substitute for an increase in productivity and where the productivity factor itself shows a clear declining tendency (i.e., where even expansion of capital investment has a declining influence on production growth). [5]

- In this situation, strong expansion of trade with and technological infusion from the West must be considered major changes in Soviet economic life in the late Brezhnev era. Economic ties with the West, still quite modest when expressed in the percentage of national income, already play a highly significant role in assuring the fulfillment of key aspects of Soviet economic plans and in arresting the downward trend in the growth of Soviet productivity in key areas.[6]

This evaluation of the Soviet economic and socioeconomic situation leads to a number of propositions. First, the level of Soviet economic development and Soviet achievement in the last decade provide a sufficient base for the maintenance of a strong military posture, strategic and conventional, highly competitive with the present levels of Western military expenditures.

Second, if Soviet economic growth in the 1980s falls in the upper range of the projection of probable development, then for the foreseeable future the Soviet Union can continue to increase the level of its military expenditures at a ratio similar to that of the last decade without incurring additional major difficulties in its economic programs. (The upper level rate of projected Soviet growth in the 1980s is of the same magnitude as the rate of increase of its military expenditures in the last decade and the projected increase in the coming decade.) In this case, the new Soviet position of strength in the area of military capabilities will persist in the 1980s, even if the Western allies increase their military expenditures.[7]

Third, an increase in military expenditures that is rapid or much above the present levels would be very difficult for the Soviet leadership to sustain, more so than at any time in the past. This situation derives on the one hand from the slowdown in Soviet economic growth and the decline of the productivity factor and on the other hand from the increase in the consumption level and rising popular expectations, the satisfaction of which constitutes for the first time in Soviet history a condition of sociopolitical stability. Assuming that this proposition is correct, for the Soviet side there is a significant disincentive for an unrestricted arms race apart from—or rather in addition to—the dangers that such a race would constitute for the fate of war and peace between the superpowers.[8]

Fourth, the expansion of foreign trade and the infusion of advanced foreign technology and the attendant questions of credits, foreign indebtedness, and cooperative arrangements acquire an importance for the Soviet leadership comparable to that in the initial industrialization effort of the late 1920s and early 1930s. The significance of this question has already brought appreciable changes in Soviet foreign policy. The important question whether the infusion of foreign technology and economic cooperation with the advanced Western nations is regarded by Soviet leaders as a one-shot affair or a long-range arrangement is unanswerable a priori. It depends partly on their ability to find domestic resources to arrest the decline in their productive growth—which even with very major economic reform is very unlikely—and partly on the consistency and the costs to the Soviet Union of Western policies and cooperative arrangements.

Politics

Turning to the second group, some important elements of the "political" factors shaping Soviet foreign policy of the late Brezhnev era can be presented as follows. First, the role and weight of foreign policy as a factor in general Soviet top level policymaking has increased in the Brezhnev era. It finds its visible expression in the greater stress on foreign policy issues in deliberations of top policymaking and symbolic bodies, in the much greater interconnectedness of key domestic issues with foreign policy concerns, as well as in the expanding recognition of this fact in ideological and theoretical literature.

Second, parallel with the increased Soviet activity on the international arena, the foreign policy of the Soviet Union and its successes abroad are used to an increased degree and probably play a greater role in the legitimation of the position of the leader and leadership among the elites and legitimation of the regime in society at large.[9]

Third, the making of foreign policy has become more institutionalized and regularized than in any previous time in Soviet history. The foreign policy apparatus of both the party and the government has been greatly expanded and upgraded. The foreign policy process is no longer an ad hoc, highly improvised activity as it was during the Khrushchev era.[10]

Fourth, the input of information into the foreign policymaking process has greatly expanded in the last decade and the quality of information has vastly improved. Aside from the expansion of foreign policymaking institutions and the improved training and employment of their cadres the Brezhnev era witnessed the creation and maturation of the academic discipline of international relations and the employment in a supportive and advisory role of a large group of specialized and well-informed outside experts.

Fifth, despite the key role of the top leader, Brezhnev, in formulating Soviet foreign policy, the policymaking process has become more consensual than at any time in the past. An attempt is made to achieve unanimity in policymaking at the top level and to take into consideration the institutional interest of various elite groups.[11]

Sixth, the indisputable decline in the compartmentalization of foreign and domestic policy issues and the attendant tendency toward greater participation and greater access of diverse political groups in foreign policymaking seems to have resulted in a situation in which no one institutional group, for example the defense complex, achieves or carries a preponderant influence. It seems also that while the Soviet leadership still possesses greater freedom of action in the foreign policy field than, let us say, the U.S. executive, its freedom of action is more limited than in the past (and, incidentally, will be more limited in a time of succession with no strong leader at the top). Because of its need for compromise solutions at home, Soviet flexibility abroad becomes somewhat restricted, its ability to arrive at compromises in its dealing with foreign powers somewhat more limited.

Seventh, there is sufficient evidence to suggest the existence within the leadership and among top elite groups of significant differences of opinion, if not about the general course of Soviet foreign policy then about its particular steps. Some differences can be traced to the particularistic interests of bureaucratic groups and some to predispositions of orientation that cut across functional and organizational lines. The evidence, however, is insufficient to identify particular leaders with specific long-range foreign views or to posit the existence of long-range foreign policy orientations among various bureaucratic complexes.[12]

Finally, the streamlining of the Soviet foreign policy process has not led to the establishment of a Soviet foreign policy line that is clear-cut and highly consistent. As a matter of fact the policies of the late Brezhnev period are characterized by inconsistencies, ambiguities, and drift. (While the Soviet foreign policy offensive of recent years is very often seen as the execution of a long-range master plan, my impression is rather that of a case-by-case response to opportunities that arise.) These policies are partly a result of the feedback into the Soviet foreign policymaking process of the unintended consequences of Soviet foreign policy plans and actions. But partly they probably reflect the nature of the policymaking of the Brezhnev era with its sensitivity to diverse internal pressures and its stress on compromise solutions.

The domestic factors that we have discussed propel Soviet foreign policy in diverse directions. The economic situation of the Soviet Union, the partial loss of the political system's immunity to social pressures, and the concern for internal stability, together with the leadership's preoccupation with Soviet security and its recognition and fear of dangers inherent in great power confrontations all argue strongly against an unrestricted arms race and for the development of increased elements of control in strategic arms employment and development.

The attainment of strategic parity with the United States and the acquisition and expansion of elements of global capacity push strongly toward the development of a policy that would permit the translation of these eagerly awaited and newly acquired capabilities into a broadly ranging influence in world affairs.

Domestic economic difficulties, present and projected, in conjunction with the unwillingness of the leadership to engage in a basic restructuring of the Soviet economic system of management, controls, and incentives, push strongly toward the development of cooperative arrangements with democratic industrial societies, especially those that secure the infusion of advanced technology (and grain) on advantageous terms.[13]

The intensity of these pressures is uneven; it varies with changes in the domestic Soviet situation and its international environment. In the final analysis it depends on the perception of the international environment by Soviet leaders and on the options that our own policies create, that is to say on the opportunities and costs that are associated with different policies.

The main policy line adopted by the Soviet leadership in the late Brezhnev era reflects these diverse pressures and contains the ambiguities and contradictions inherent in their multidirectional thrust. The result is a policy of détente in which the relative weighting of constituent parts constantly changes, a policy that combines commitment to SALT and to the avoidance of direct confrontation with the United States and an eagerness to engage in cooperative economic arrangements with a strong competitive military and political impulse toward expanding the sphere and magnitude of Soviet influence in the international arena.

From this brief consideration of the first two groups of factors that shape Soviet foreign policy we turn to the third group, which is primarily cultural in nature and can be construed to a large extent as ideological factors broadly understood.[14]

Beliefs

The question of the relationship of ideology to Soviet foreign policy has never been resolved and probably never will be. The lack of resolution and clarity on this subject is due not only to the lack of available and testable data but primarily to the fact that no clear-cut answer is possible: The influence of ideology on human affairs in general and on foreign policy in particular is highly ambiguous. It seems, therefore, that any general answer to the question is of very limited importance, except to provide a framework within which one can discuss the nuances and specifics of the influence of ideology on Soviet foreign policy and discern any secular trends in the influence of ideology in particular periods. In doing so, one should avoid the hazard of supposing the influence of ideology on foreign policy to be predetermined in the past and preordained for the future, that is, to be inherent in the nature of the Soviet system itself and not dependent on external realities, action, and feedback.

I should like to address myself to three sets of issues. First, I should like to ask what questions are involved in the subject of ideology and Soviet foreign policy. In some respects, this is the most difficult part of the inquiry, because how one formulates the questions largely determines the answers one gets. Second, I should like to discuss why questions about the influence of ideology on Soviet foreign policy are again being asked with some urgency; why a subject that has been discussed so frequently before is being raised anew; and what is new in the way it is being raised. And third, I want to suggest some elements of the answers to questions concerning the influence of ideology on Soviet foreign policy, especially those elements that I consider particularly pertinent today or distorted in the past.

Questions usually raised regarding Soviet foreign policy are of two types. The first involves Soviet capabilities — that is, the resources the Soviet Union has at its disposal in conducting its foreign policy and the projection of those capabilities into the future. One would like to know how Soviet capabilities are developed, how fast they are increasing, in what areas, and in what specific aspects. Ideology may have an influence on both the perception and the development of capabilties. But I would argue that when we consider the relationship of ideology to foreign policy we are not so much concerned with Soviet foreign policy resources and capabilities per se as with the purposes to which these capabilities may be applied. As John Strachey has remarked, "It is a military maxim that in framing a country's defense policy, the capabilities alone never the intentions of other nations must be taken into account. But this is one of those maxims, which however dutifully they are preached in the staff colleges, can never be adhered to in the cabinet rooms."[15]

Evidently, the United States and the Western alliance as a whole think and worry about Soviet capabilities today because they are worried about Soviet intentions. If we did not worry about intentions, we obviously would not be so concerned about the pronounced expansion of Soviet foreign policy resources. It seems clear to me, therefore, that when we raise questions about the relationships between ideology and Soviet foreign policy we are primarily interested in the second type of questions, those involving Soviet intentions rather than their capabilities and foreign policy resources.

Three questions concerning Soviet foreign policy intentions are particularly important. First is the straightforward question: How does the Soviet Union intend to use its existing and developing foreign policy capabilities? To ask this question it is not at all necessary to posit some kind of master plan or long-range strategy imposed by ideology on Soviet foreign policy, for it is doubtful that any such plan or strategy exists now or ever existed. But what one can or should ask is whether there is a long- or intermediate-term predisposition among Soviet policymakers, whether there are some preferences and predilections in Soviet foreign policy planning that can be referred to as long-range intentions. Here the analysis of the ideological orientation of the policymakers can tell us a great deal. Such an analysis cannot tell us whether the Soviets will use the foreign policy capabilities that they have in any particular way, but it can provide clues as to how they are *inclined* to use those capabilities.

The second question that arises concerns the sources of these intentions, and here again the ideological orientation of Soviet policymakers is relevant not only analytically but for our own policy as well. Analytically, the issue is whether the Soviet predisposition toward a specific type of behavior is connected with the characteristics of a particular generation of leaders or with the politics of an oligarchy, or whether the predisposition is primarily structural, rooted in a system of institutions and beliefs. In other words, the analytical problem involves determining how deeply a particular pattern of Soviet behavior is ingrained in the structure of a political society or in the political leadership. Clearly, our evaluation of this problem will have important policy implications because it will provide clues as to how to react to particular Soviet actions.

These considerations bring us to the third and broadest question concerning the impact of ideology on Soviet foreign policy intentions. This question involves the nature of the Soviet nation-state. The Soviet nation-state, as we know, was created to fulfill a mission. It was founded to be a refuge, a bastion, a base of revolution for the whole world. Historical experience suggests that nation-states with missions are apt to be even more self-assertive and aggressive than are nation-states that do not place high values on any particular ideological and international ties, duties, or responsibilities. It seems unquestionable that what the Soviet Union has in fact been during most of its existence is a nation-state with a mission. I would argue that in the past, even when its leaders most ruthlessly sacrificed the direct interest of Communist parties in the rest of the world — and they doubtless did sacrifice those interests — they often did so in the belief that by preserving and strengthening the Soviet Union at all costs they were in the long run furthering the interests of world Communism. Now, however, the question is to what extent the Soviet Union is, or will be in the future, a nation-state of such special character.

In sum, the central issues in the relationship between ideology and Soviet foreign policy involve the nature of Soviet foreign policy intentions, the sources of these intentions, and the nature of the Soviet state. From this perspective, it is not at all difficult to understand the renewed interest in this relationship. The reasons for this reawakened interest and for the sense of urgency that underlies it are numerous and interconnected. Some of the reasons are old, some are new, but in their combination and intensity, they are unique to the contemporary period. Some of the most important ones are listed below.

1. The first and most obvious reason is the level of Soviet international capabilities already achieved. It is one thing to discuss the influence of ideology, however expansionist and self-assertive, on the foreign policy of a

weak or at least clearly inferior Soviet state and quite another to consider the intentions of a Soviet Union that has attained strategic parity with the United States and is achieving the position of a global power. Under such circumstances, when one is inquiring into the influence of ideology on Soviet foreign policy, one is asking whether the achievement by the Soviet Union of global great power status parallels the development of more responsible and responsive Soviet behavior in the international arena or whether that achievement can be described as a Soviet dream come true, an opportunity at last to push long-held and long-unfulfilled ambitions. The influence of ideology alone on Soviet foreign policy clearly can suggest only a part of the answer, but just as clearly it is highly relevant to the whole answer.

2. A closely related reason and the key explanation for the sense of urgency that has lately become almost an obsession with Western policy-makers is the question: Why is the Soviet Union arming at a pace that by any standard has to be considered extremely high? Overshadowing all disagreements about the level of Soviet capabilities already achieved and its projected military strength vis-à-vis the West is the question "Why?" In attempting to answer this question the evaluation of Soviet intentions looms as absolutely crucial. The unprecedented Soviet armament effort may be in part a response to past nightmares, to traumas of past insecurities that push the Soviets relentlessly toward the unattainable and often counterproductive goal of total and complete security, or what one can call "oversecurity." It may be an attempt to overcompensate, in the only area of real Soviet competence and achievement, for political and economic weaknesses at home and abroad. But it can also be explained as an attempt to achieve global military superiority, reflecting the belief of the Soviet leadership that such superiority is not only attainable but can be translated into political power and influence. Again, consideration of the question of ideology may help to explain Soviet goals in the arms race and Soviet perceptions of its possible and desirable payoffs.

3. Another reason for the urgent interest in Soviet foreign policy intentions and their ideological underpinnings involves recent Soviet actions, particularly their Angolan and Ethiopian adventures. Their use of surrogate Cuban troops in a local civil war and in a war between two neighbors so far from their own shores is an unprecedented action for the Soviet Union — the first example of this kind of Soviet behavior in the international arena. Soviet policy in Angola and Ethiopia could turn out to be no more than an episode, a very limited action taken because of the very low risk involved in an intervention at that particular time (for example, the state of U.S. foreign policy and of the U.S. polity in general and the South African intervention in Angola that made Soviet intervention accep-

table to other African states) and because of the internal pressures of Soviet politics. Yet there is the probability that the Angolan action is not an exception but rather the beginning of a new pattern of behavior, reflecting growing Soviet capabilities and deeply seated predilections that will push Soviet action in this interventionist direction.

4. The search for explanations of Soviet international behavior and foreign policy intentions is also related to the discernible change in the Soviet attitude toward détente. This is not to say that there is evidence that the Soviet leadership does not want détente to continue but first that their initial expectations of the benefits of *cooperation* with the Western powers and especially with the United States have clearly been lowered and remain largely unfulfilled, especially in the economic sphere, and second that a shift has occurred in Soviet expectations about détente from defensive to offensive, that is, the Soviets now stress less the benefits that can be derived from cooperation than the benefits that can accrue from competition with the West. As a result, the general level of cooperation within the framework of détente is being lowered vis-à-vis early Soviet intentions and Western expectations. Such a change may be connected with the Soviet perception of the crisis in industrial democracies (which the Soviet leadership did not envisage when détente was being shaped), with the resulting revitalization of their own ideological expectations about the decline of the West and the temptation that this offers for an activist, interventionist Soviet foreign policy.

The entire set of circumstances in which the question of Soviet foreign policy intentions and their ideological underpinnings again looms so large is related not only to Western perceptions of the present but even more to those of the future. A forceful argument can be made that current international trends point to an almost inescapable increase in global tension, turmoil, conflict, and uncertainty. If this proves to be the case, global cooperation and the gradual institutionalization of cooperation among big powers will become more urgent than ever before. Here again the question of the impact of ideology on Soviet foreign policy is asked with some urgency because that impact is relevant to how the Soviet leadership will react to those global tensions and turmoil. Will they—aware of the dangers to them as well as to us—respond constructively and act to defuse tensions and dampen conflict and thus effectively commit themselves to the maintenance of order in the international system (even if it is an order that they cannot dominate)? Or will they see international instability as a dream come true, as a vindication of long-held hopes and a balm for long-felt frustrations? That is, will the Soviets perceive global disorder as a danger or as an opportunity—an opportunity to be used in attempting to replace the United States as the pivot of the international system?

Clearly, ideology alone will not answer these questions. One can repeat that ideological influences on Soviet foreign policy are highly ambiguous. On the one hand they make the Soviets extraordinarily conscious of their own security and hence hesitant to take risks; on the other hand they prompt them to see their global expansion in terms of a mission legitimized by history, therefore reinforcing the desire to capitalize on their growing international capabilities and power.

But it is equally clear that the global situation now differs qualitatively from what we have known in the past and will differ increasingly in the future. Not only will the Soviet Union be presented with unprecedented opportunities to exploit global anarchy and turmoil, but its available and developing foreign policy resources—both absolutely and relative to the West—will provide it with unprecedented means to do so. Under such circumstances—marked by a vivid U.S. sense of the limitations of the power of the United States, by the decline of West European influence in world affairs, and by the rapid growth of Soviet capabilities to intervene, directly or through surrogates, in areas far away from the Soviet borders—we cannot rely entirely on past Soviet international behavior either to divine Soviet intentions in the present or to predict them for the future. The circumstances that prevail underscore the importance of taking a new look at the relationship between ideology and Soviet foreign policy.

There is another major reason why the question of the relationship of ideology and Soviet foreign policy is so important today. This reason has to do with the incongruity between our image of the Soviet internal system and our anxieties about present and future Soviet international behavior. When we speak about the Soviet Union internally, the picture that we have—and I think correctly—is of a system in which Communist doctrine has lost its operational importance. Communist doctrine remains one of the legitimizing principles of the Soviet internal system, particularly for the elites, but it is hardly an operational principle that still exercises a major influence on Soviet internal policies. Domestically, the Soviet Union is one of the most status-quo–oriented countries in the world. Of all industrial countries it is undoubtedly the most frozen, conservative, and Victorian in its political, socioeconomic, and cultural relations. Its oppressiveness is no longer oriented toward reshaping society but toward preserving the mold into which the society has been shaped. And yet when one discusses Soviet foreign policy intentions and asks about the impact of ideology on Soviet international behavior, one tends to think in terms of a revolutionary ideology, in particular Communist doctrine. Thus the incongruity that emerges between the two images of the Soviet Union—the internal and the external—seems to be pronounced.

One other phenomenon invests the paradox posed above with an additional dimension that makes it even more complex. The Soviet system as an emulative revolutionary model belongs basically to the past; in the present it is for all practical purposes dead. Even those major Communist or radical parties that still declare some allegiance to the Soviet Union do not consider the Soviet model applicable to their own societies. Most crucially, the process of radicalization, the growth of militancy in the world, is not at all proceeding in a pro-Soviet direction; it does not have a pro-Soviet effect. In a growing number of cases — as specific strata, movements, and even nation-states become more and more militant — they tend to evolve as much in an anti-Soviet as in an anti-American, anti-West, and anticapitalist direction. Therefore, the dilemma of how a nation and a system can be reactionary internally and have revolutionary goals externally is supplemented by another dilemma: Can it be sufficiently revolutionary externally to satisfy the new world militancy without endangering its own stability and its internal reactionism? Of course we can still hypothesize that the Soviet Union remains a nation-state with a mission, but the question then becomes: What is the mission? The paradox described is real; it reflects one of the built-in dilemmas of Soviet international behavior and intentions.

I shall now suggest partial answers to some of the questions that I have raised. The issue of the influence of ideology on the perceptions and outlook of the Soviet leadership and political elite raises the entire complex of problems expressed by the concept of the "erosion" and even the "end" of ideology.[16] The "end of ideology" theme is misleading insofar as it implies that the political realism dominant in the thinking of the contemporary Soviet elite is devoid of ideology because it is not associated with serious theorizing and is even averse to it. It is as nonsensical to view the contemporary Soviet political elite as revolutionary fanatics whose every major policy or act is colored by the ultimate ends prescribed by Marxist and Leninist holy writ as it is to see them only as cynical manipulators who simply drift toward undefined goals and whose response to reality is not influenced by their intellectual and political revolutionary origins.[17] The question is not whether their beliefs have changed but which beliefs, how much, and in what direction; not whether they have an ideology but to what ideology they subscribe; not whether ideology makes any difference but what kind of difference it makes for the shaping of their intentions, policies, and behavior.

This is not the place to get bogged down in a discussion of the meaning of "ideology." I prefer to understand ideology in its broad meaning and it seems to me that most students of belief systems would agree that the concept includes much more than purely doctrinal elements.[18] One may distinguish various dimensions and levels of ideology, the most basic of which is doctrinal — what is termed "pure ideology."[19] Whatever distortions of selectivity, interpretation, or addition were introduced by the Soviet elaboration of Marxian theory and of Bolshevism, Marxism-Leninism is still the core of this pure ideology. On this ideological level, the basic tendency of the last ten to fifteen years has been that of ideological retrenchment and increasing ritualization.

The retrenchment finds its expression in the disappearence of ideological innovations. Instead the emphasis has been on resistance to and defense against "alien ideas." The increasing ritualization finds its most important expression in the fact that the doctrinal position on policy issues is ambiguous, nonauthoritative, and ill defined. Policy discussions, therefore, are conducted neither for nor against a doctrinal prescription but parallel to doctrine. Direct doctrinal intervention in expert deliberations is limited, and thereby the urge to issue binding verdicts on policy questions that are unresolved or unclear is curtailed. Thus the doctrine can retain a semblance of consistency, and disagreements about its meaning and consequences for action are minimized by keeping it increasingly aloof from social practice — that is, by the increased ritualization of doctrine.

With respect to foreign policy questions and to the analysis of international relations, attacks from both the left and the right in the Communist movement and from the radical community have brought about a revitalization of Soviet doctrinal writings. Angered and concerned about these attacks, the Soviet leaders have responded by reaffirming their international "revolutionary" doctrine and their commitment to the "world revolutionary process." The form and substance of this reaffirmation is aptly described by Alexander Dallin:

> What the thrust of reformations and reformulations amounts to in practice is a persistent widening of options; it brings the substitution of vaguer, weaker, broader terms and categories, the elimination of compelling cause-and-effect relationships, and a withering of the fundamental optimism about the future which animated the movement at the start. "The world revolutionary process becomes ever more complex and multiform," declares a recent Soviet study of the problem. In substance, the belief system now sanctions the view that anything is possible. Any one thing may or may not occur; revolutions may or may not take place; force may or may not be needed; Communists may or may not be in control of "bourgeois" or "mass democratic" movements; nonwestern countries may or may not opt for a non-capitalist path, which in turn may or may not lead to socialist revolution. . . . The multiplicity of labels, options, forms, alliances, and combinations continues to grow. Given such a broad range, which in advance foresees and justifies all success and all failure, Soviet doctrine (which thus cannot be falsified) becomes useless as an analytical or predictive tool. It is rather a distorted reflection of a political system trying to come to terms with the present without betraying its past.[20]

In sum, the process of ritualization regarding doctrinal inputs in foreign policy is well advanced. The doctrine as such scarcely acts as a guide for actions and policies. There is no evidence whatsoever that revolutionary prospects abroad constitute a controlling factor in Soviet foreign policy decisions and in Soviet leadership intentions in the international arena.

Yet an examination of the influence of ideology on policy should concern itself primarily not with "pure" but with "practical" ideology — with the ideas, principles, and preferences that provide the dominant conceptual *framework* of elite intentions and actions, the mind-set of the leadership, the matrix of its collective conscience. When one conceptualizes ideology in this broader way, one stresses the experiential and cultural factors that shape the world outlook of the leadership and elite — the most potent and the most constant assimilated assumptions about fundamental issues of domestic and world affairs. Ideology, whether narrowly or broadly understood, performs a number of functions; all of these functions relate the ideological influence to actual patterns of behavior. In our case, the stress is on the conscious cognitive function, the analytical framework that the Soviet leadership applies to its evaluation of world events and trends, and on the unconscious *motivating* function that defines the a priori images, biases, and beliefs that the leadership brings to its perception of international reality and that are almost never spelled out and enunciated in analytical terms.[21]

"Practical" ideology continues to be influenced by doctrine not only in its symbolic expressions (language, terminology, emotive meanings) but also in substance. Increasingly, however, the influence is mainly negative: Doctrine rules out certain options in decision making and reinforces or weakens the arguments against others. For instance, it reinforces Soviet resistance to change in Eastern Europe; ideologically based conceptions of the state have a great deal to do with Soviet insistence on regimes that are not merely friendly but Communist. But doctrinal influence is only one influence on practical ideology, the dominant source of which is the tradition of the Soviet system — the historical experience of the political elite itself. This is especially true of those elements of practical ideology that are directly relevant to the political process. I shall mention some of the most important elements that form the perceptions and basic political outlook of the practical ideology that constitutes the "collective conscience" of the Soviet leadership and political elite, stressing whenever possible the direction of its evolution in the post-Stalin and the post-Khrushchev era and indicating, if at all pertinent, the foreign policy manifestations of such an evolution.

First, the withering away of utopianism in the thought and practice of the ~al elite has been accelerated. This Soviet utopianism, the strongest ~sest derivative of the doctrinal tradition, continued to constitute under Khrushchev one part of the vision of the future within which the elite operated. The present Soviet leadership, however, dislikes and discourages the futuristic "Communist" fantasy. Realism and businesslike behavior have become their ubiquitous slogans and the leadership qualities that are most praised.

Second, the elite impulse to reshape society has radically declined. For the ruling elite, Soviet social structure has found its permanent shape—at least for the foreseeable future. What the party proposes to the Soviet population is the indefinite continuation of the basic existing social relations plus material progress.

Third, generations of Soviet leaders have assimilated from the Marxian tradition the dimension that it shared with Western rationalism: the belief in progress. Although the idea of progress has suffered a decline in the West, it has not done so in the Soviet Union. True, the optimism of the Khrushchev era has been replaced by a more somber assessment and by a much greater realism about what can be achieved in the short and intermediate terms. The future looks less like unilinear, unbridled progress, but the deeply entrenched belief in and commitment to continuous economic growth and to the all-pervading technological ethos has changed little.

Fourth, the persistent centrality of the belief in progress and its almost total equation with material growth are associated with and supplemented by the deeply rooted attitude of evaluating one's performance in "progressing to progress" by the standards of Western industrial nations. The sources of this "comparative" mentality are many—justification of the past history of sacrifice and denial, ultimate legitimation of the superiority of the system, and the felt need to ensure the security of the system from alien and hostile external forces. Regardless of the specific sources of this mentality, however, the important point to note is that it has taken hold in all segments of the Soviet elite and thus has acquired an existence of its own. This mentality infuses into the political elite a sense of urgency and a stress on mobilization that persist even in times of notable achievement, let alone when a growing lag in comparison with the performance of Western industrial societies is discernible.

Fifth, the thinking and behavior of the Soviet leadership and political elite is still dominated by a set of beliefs and attitudes that expresses deepseated fear and mistrust of spontaneity in political and social behavior, which induces an interventionist psychology and places a premium on strong central government, organization, and order.

Last (and crucial from the point of view of foreign policy), the mainstay of the Soviet political elite's sense of common purpose is provided more than ever by nationalism. Partly in its superpower Soviet variety and partly in its cultural, traditional Russian variety, this nationalism constitutes the major effective, long-lasting bond within the political elite and between the elite and the masses. The old conservative theme — the cult of national unity and the condemnation of individuals and groups who threaten to impair it — provides the emotional base for an authoritarian political outlook and is in turn reinforced by it.

The above elements of the dominant practical ideology have numerous implications for Soviet thinking, intentions, and behavior in international relations. The decisive decline in Soviet utopianism is reflected in foreign policy behavior that stresses pragmatism, gradualism, and deliberateness; puts a premium on a strict realistic evaluation of the attractiveness of specific goals in terms of available resources; and shuns shortcuts and grandstanding.

Despite the fact that the paranoic isolationism and insecurities of the Stalinist era belong largely to the past, the reactionary Soviet attitude toward changes in their internal sociopolitical structure makes for a pronounced and apparently growing sensitivity and sense of vulnerability to possible deleterious and destabilizing external influences on the Soviet domestic scene. This seems especially the case now, when contacts with the outside world are being extended, when many of the barriers to international communication are being lowered, when internal pressures for changes and improvements at home are increasing, and when the existence of dissident movements has become a permanent feature of Soviet life. One of the major expressions of this sensitivity is the fear and the strong reaction against attempts, real or imagined, to influence Soviet domestic policies with regard to human rights.

The centrality of the goal of material and technological progress as the raison d'être of the Soviet system is paralleled, as mentioned above, by the continuing Soviet tendency to assess their achievements by the measuring rod of Western material and technological standards (accompanied by a disdain and contempt for Western spiritual achievements and sociopolitical organization). The effects of such a combination are twofold: on the one hand, in view of a lack of commitment to internal reforms that may improve technoeconomic performance, it pushes the Soviet leadership to seek highly expanded and improved economic relations with the industrialized West; on the other hand, it leads the Soviet political elite to push in the one area of development in which they have real strength and, *nolens volens*, to rely inordinately on those foreign policy resources that are available and solid — that is, military resources. Military development is no longer the sole goal of Soviet economic expansion as it was in Stalin's time. Despite Khrushchev's hopes to catch up with the West on a broad economic front, however, the military sector remains the only internationally competitive sector, the most visible and measurable achievement of the Soviet system, and the key competitive international resource at the Soviet leadership's disposal.

The deep-seated conservatism shared by the Soviet leadership and elites is intertwined with and feeds a sense of great national pride. In international relations it is exemplified by the yearning for a recognition of Soviet accomplishments, by an extraordinarily developed feeling of the importance of Soviet national status and prestige. It is a feeling that makes the Soviets acutely sensitive to real and imaginary slights, sharply defensive about the equity of their treatment, especially by the United States, the only power they consider an equal and by whom they will insist on being treated as an equal. On the other hand, it makes them more responsive to pressures of international public opinion than in the past.[22]

When we speak about Soviet sensitivities we are speaking about the *style* of relations with the Soviet Union, about the *forms* and externalities of the policies of the West and especially the United States vis-à-vis the Soviet Union. But for the Soviet Union this question of style and form acquires an emotive meaning far beyond the importance attached to it by the West; it represents a substantive attitude of the West — the recognition of Soviet equality with the West and of Soviet political parity, or lack of it, with the United States.

While all the above factors are important in themselves, the absolutely crucial relation of practical ideology to Soviet foreign policy intentions and behavior has to do with the nature and influence of Soviet nationalism. But when stressing the importance of nationalism as the central component of the practical ideology that informs the attitudes, intentions, and actions of the Soviet political elite, it is not sufficient to speak about it in a general way. What is required is the identification of its specifically Soviet character.

There are four major components that in their mutual interaction constitute the determining characteristics of Soviet nationalism today. First, it is a nationalism shaped by the past experiences of the Soviet Union and Russia that can best be characterized as defensive in nature. It is a nationalism that grew out of the traumatic experiences of being so often invaded, of being weak, of being beaten or even nearly destroyed. It is a nationalism for which the next disaster and crisis always looms large on the horizon. It is a nationalism that stresses the separateness of Russia from other nations and the unbridgeability of the "we-they" syndrome in international relations, one that shapes the total and unusually intense preoccupation to repulse a world that is axiomatically assumed to be at least potentially hostile.

It is also an as yet undiminished imperial nationalism — in all probability the last one left on the globe. It is a nationalism committed to an empire that Stalin built in Eastern Europe, the existence and integrity of which his successors have continued to defend at all costs. In this dimension it is a nationalism that expands the basically defensive preoccupation with security to include not only the Soviet Union proper but the entire East European area of uncontested Soviet influence. It is as if the slogan "socialism in one country," under which Stalinism was established in the Soviet Union, was expanded by Stalin himself after the Second World War into "socialism in one empire" and is accepted with no sign of diminished commitment by his successors.

Furthermore, and most important for the future of international relations, it is to an increasing degree the nationalism of a great power that is attaining global stature. It is the nationalism of a power that is still young, growing, ambitious, and assertive, and that still entertains hopes and illusions about what the application of great power in the international arena can accomplish. It is a nationalism of the older generation of Soviet leaders who worked so hard, waited so long, and hoped so much for the Soviet Union to achieve a dominant international position; who only now are starting to see the complications and limitations of their newly acquired status; and who still do not want to face the difficulties of translating their real power into tangible international recognition and rewards. It is the nationalism of the younger post–World War generation of Soviet leaders, who share the ambitions of their elders but not the lingering insecurities and memories of past weaknesses, and who lack the maturing influence of knowing what past sacrifices meant and at what cost Soviet power was created.

It is, fourth, a nationalism that is still fused to a higher degree than "normal" ascending great-power nationalisms are with universalism, with a perception of a universal mission. This universalist attitude discernible in Soviet nationalism and explicable in terms of a Soviet international mission was present in Russia long before the Revolution. It took a while for this dimension of Russian nationalism to take root in Soviet soil and to fuse with the Communist world outlook, but the symbiosis of the two was not a difficult one. Its operational validity was muted for a very long time by the natural Soviet preoccupation with its internal problems and with the primarily defensive aspects of its internal relations. But as an ingrained attitude, it was there even at the height of Stalin's isolationism.

In the post-Stalin era, and especially today, its most visible expression is the domestic legitimizing function of Soviet pure ideology on the one hand and the legitimization of Soviet international activities among its foreign sympathizers on the other hand. Yet it seems to me that it is more than merely a legitimizing device. Within the outlook of the Soviet leadership and elites it represents a supportive element, however limited in its direct influence on Soviet actions and motivations—an element of historical justification.

In my opinion, the interaction of the dimensions of Soviet nationalism—Russian in substance, Soviet in form—constitutes a crucially important explanatory factor in Soviet international behavior. But what about the explanatory value of other constituent elements of Soviet practical ideology as a means to analyze the intentions and actions of Soviet foreign policy? How important in particular is the doctrinal component in such an analysis? This problem—the question of the relative importance of separate determinants of Soviet foreign policy, of their relative causal influence on the shape and direction of Soviet international behavior—is of course the most difficult one. No clear-cut answer is possible; some general remarks will have to suffice.

The crucial point to be made here is that the distinction among the various elements of Soviet practical ideology discussed above (the doctrinal inputs, nationalism in its many dimensions, the authoritarian impulse, the reactionary attitude toward the Soviet sociopolitical organization, Soviet conservativism, etc.) are in essence analytical distinctions that in real life are not necessarily separate, distinct, or counterposed to one another. Under certain conditions, these analytically separate elements—for example the doctrine and the nationalism—are inseparable. One can put them in separate chapters in a textbook on the sources of Soviet international behavior, but in reality they are entwined. They are blended in the minds of the people who make policy, they are fused in the perceptions and feelings of the Soviet elite, and they cannot be separated when analyzing the elite's intentions and actions. Of course, particular groups and individuals within the Soviet political elite will differ in their devotion to particular doctrinal principles or pronouncements or in the intensity of their nationalistic feelings and commitments. I do not believe, however, that these differences are as clear-cut as they are sometimes made out to be. It is a vast oversimplification, to take an extreme example, to counterpose a doctrinaire group of ideologues whose devotion to doctrinal ideology is supreme to a military group composed of pure and simple nationalists. The differences among groups and individuals who make Soviet foreign policy are seldom of an either-or nature; rather, they are distinctions of degree.

The fundamental difficulty, then, is that the relative weight of the various elements and components of Soviet practical ideology can only be evaluated when these elements create tensions in the actual conduct of Soviet policy and policymaking, that is, when they conflict with each other. Often, however, the various components of Soviet practical ideology supplement and reinforce each other. In such cases the distinctions we draw among them are primarily analytical; we are separating factors that in reality are intertwined.

One such case is the Sino-Soviet conflict. In evaluating the sources that have influenced this conflict, how can we separate the doctrinal elements from divergencies of national interest? The elements reinforce each other. Doctrinal differences and commitments — the belief of each side that it represents the truth — reinforce nationalism and the dislike and fear of one another. Indeed, it is this reinforcement that makes the conflict so intractable and its solution so particularly difficult.

Another example concerns the Soviet quest for absolute security. Here again nationalism and ideology in the narrow, doctrinal sense reinforce each other. As indicated before, the *defensive* dimension of Soviet nationalism provides a basis for the extraordinary Soviet preoccupation with security. But so does the ideology, with its view of the world as divided into hostile, irreconcilable camps and its view of the Soviet state as the "bastion of progress," the base of a system to which the future belongs. As Thomas Wolfe suggests, the main impact of the Marxist-Leninist doctrine on Soviet foreign policymakers is expresesed in two tendencies — to see the world in terms of systemic struggle that cannot be "annulled" by intergovernmental agreements and to see that the security of the Soviet Union, as the principal Communist state, must be preserved at all costs. He continues,

> The common denominator in both instances seems to lie in seeking to eliminate or reduce potential sources of threat to the Soviet Union. What might be called, in strategic parlance, a "damage limiting" philosophy, thus seems to permeate Soviet behavior. . . . This philosophy finds expression in Soviet military doctrine and policy, as well as in Soviet diplomacy. Whether at bottom such a philosophy owes more to ideological imperatives than to those of Soviet national interest remains a moot question. For that matter, the impulse to limit damage to one's interests is not peculiar to the Soviet leaders; they simply seem to carry it farther than most, as if satisfied only with absolute security. Thus, the really relevant point seems to be that to the extent that negation of potential military and political threats to the Soviet Union involves measures that other states find inimical to their own vital interests, the Soviet proclivity to seek absolute security tends neither to promote global stability nor a fundamental relaxation of tensions within the international order. [23]

Still another example is the Soviet commitment to its East European empire. Soviet imperial nationalism by itself does not, in my opinion, explain the strength of this commitment and its successful defense. Rather, one of the very important long-range functions of doctrinal orthodoxy is tied to the Soviet imperial position in Eastern Europe and to the Brezhnev doctrine of limited sovereignty that safeguards it ideologically. Doctrinal orthodoxy provides the sole possible legitimization of the empire in the eyes of the Soviet political elite, among some segments of the East European party elites, and in some Communist parties outside the Soviet bloc. Of course Soviet dominance of Eastern Europe rests primarily on Soviet military power. But for the Soviet elite to contemplate the use of that power, let alone actually to use it, requires the evocation of the doctrinal right that makes it "just."

Supplementation and reinforcement are, however, not the only existing or possible relations among the component elements of Soviet practical ideology. And when the various elements do not supplement and reinforce each other, their analytical separation can become a reality in which the various inputs into the belief system may conflict and create tensions and major cross-pressures on Soviet foreign policymakers. These major cross-pressures, conflicts, and tensions sometimes lead to greater militancy in Soviet foreign policy and sometimes to greater restraint. But they always create an ambiguity that does not exist when the component elements of the Soviet practical ideology supplement and reinforce each other.

The conflicts, tensions, and ambiguities to which Soviet policymakers are exposed are at bottom tensions between what the Soviet leadership and political elite want and what they fear; between the rewards that they hope for or expect and the risks that they must take to get them; between what Alex Dallin so aptly termed the impulse to enjoy and the impulse to destroy. Again, many examples can be provided for such tensions, conflicts, and ambiguities.

One of the areas in which the tensions and cross-pressures on Soviet foreign policymakers are especially clear now concerns a major issue in European foreign policy, the question of Eurocommunism. The tensions and ambiguities intertwine on many levels. On one level, there is a tension between the opportunity implied in Eurocommunism to destabilize Western Europe and the Western alliance and to strengthen Communist influence in the major industrial countries of the West, and the fear of what successful Eurocommunism may do to détente. One aspect of this fear is that détente may be so undermined that the key Soviet economic interests motivating the pursuit of that policy as well as the quest for the control of nuclear armaments will be severely damaged. An even greater fear is the possibility of a miscalculation on the part of the European Left so that, instead of leading to the establishment of Left or Left-centered regimes in Western Europe, Eurocommunism could lead to a powerful and successful reaction by the Right and the recurrence, at least in part, of past Soviet nightmares about national security. On another level, it is the tension between the potential rewards to be reaped from, let us say, the success of the Italian Communist party and the potentially dangerous repercussions that a successful Italian party, authentically and continuously committed to democratic procedures, may create in Eastern Europe—an area, after all, much more important to the Soviet Union than is Italy.[24]

In such situations—those in which Soviet policymakers are subject to severe tensions, conflicts, ambiguities, and cross-pressures—the relationship between ideology and Soviet foreign policy is both problematical and crucial. When there are tensions between rewards and risks or conflicts between different components of the practical ideology, then the ways in which the Soviet leadership and political elite assign priorities to particular goals, rewards, or expectations take on special importance.

One may infer the order of priorities that becomes discernible in the long run from the conduct of Soviet foreign policy. I would divide these priorities basically into two groups. First, there are *absolute* priorities—the priorities that are almost constant attributes of Soviet international behavior at the highest order of importance. They have not changed perceptibly in the past and can be considered the minimal, irreducible requirements of Soviet foreign policymaking. One such priority concerns the security of the Soviet home base—the security of the homeland and of Soviet rule within the homeland. The second such absolute priority concerns the security of the Soviet empire. I would suggest that in the perception of the Soviet leadership, the question of Communist rule and Soviet dominance in Eastern Europe is now considered basically an internal Soviet problem. The Soviet commitment is total, approaching in intensity its commitment to the defense and security of its own homeland. Until now, to a degree greater than is the case with any other major power, no step in Soviet foreign policymaking was envisaged that could be thought to endanger the security of the Soviet homeland, the basic stability of the Soviet political elites' rule, or the stability of Soviet dominance in Eastern Europe. (This of course does not mean that some Soviet foreign policy actions did not in fact bring about such dangers as their unintended consequences; it means only that in the calculus of Soviet foreign policymaking, leadership sensitivity to such dangers is extraordinarily developed.)

The second group of priorities I would describe as *relative*—the priorities that carry variable weight in Soviet foreign policymaking and whose importance as determinants of Soviet international behavior changes sometimes very quickly and perceptibly. Here I would include first the goal of enhancing Soviet political influence in the international arena. This goal is reflected particularly in attempts to establish through bilateral relations strong ties of dependence with individual strategically located countries and to foster, support, and encourage governments friendly to the Soviet Union and to its international positions. Efforts to attain such goals may focus in different periods on diverse areas of the world. But in this regard the most important characteristic of Soviet policy in the last decade, reflecting its developing global power status, is that it is not limited to any specific area. These efforts are partly defensive in nature, directed at achieving the retreat and isolation of recognized hostile powers or unfriendly competitors for influence (for example, China and the United States), and partly offensive, directed at establishing a solid base of support in particular areas of the world. The major policy forms through which these goals are pursued are primarily political (for example, a quid pro quo of Soviet support for the solution of a specific grievance of a country for that country's support of Soviet positions in a particular area of the world); partly economic (for example, economic aid); and indirectly to a very large extent military (for example, supply of weapons including weapons systems and licensing, military instruction teams).

Another such relative priority would include the economic goals of developing the inflow of technology from industrialized capitalist countries, of securing sources of agricultural imports, and of obtaining credits from and cooperative economic arrangements with the West. In the last decade this Soviet goal has acquired a great deal of importance, becoming a necessary prerequisite of maintaining the desirable rate of growth of economic and particularly of industrial productivity without resorting to major internal economic reforms.

The priority, if the term is applicable at all, of revolutions abroad, of fostering and helping Communist takeovers, ranks probably rather low on the list. Here of course the degree of control that the Soviets hope or expect to have over the regimes that would emerge from such takeovers and the strategic importance of the countries themselves make an important difference in the extent of Soviet interest generated and the type and scope of Soviet resources devoted to the enterprise. The above must be distinguished from the goal of helping to sustain foreign Communist movements and the goal of trying to keep actual or at least symbolic control of these movements, a goal that still retains an important place among the relative priorities of Soviet international behavior.

The order of importance of the priorities described above is quite flexible; it is not set once and for all. The different weight attached to the various relative priorities depends on a number of factors. The key factors are the connections associated with the influence exerted on absolute priorities. If, for example, a situation were to evolve in the Soviet Union in which the spread of consumerist attitudes among the working class reached a level where it seriously impaired economic performance, then the leadership — afraid of unrest that might endanger the internal stability of the regime — would probably elevate economic progress through relations abroad to the top of the list of relative priorities, assigning it an importance close to that of absolute priorities.

It is clear, then, that ideology provides neither a blueprint for Soviet decision makers nor a guide for Western scholars. It has served to create Soviet perceptions, inclinations, and predispositions that are frequently inconsistent among themselves and that rarely have unambiguous implications for action. Its impact has varied with time, place, and issue, and cannot be assessed independently of numerous other factors that shape the character and direction of Soviet international behavior. However strong the influence of ideology in general and doctrine in particular has been on Soviet foreign policy in the past, both the policy and the ideology have always been conditioned by external realities, feedback, and actions. Throughout its history, the Soviet Union has adapted its international behavior to the changing circumstances of world politics and to its own domestic conditions and requirements.

The terminology applied and the imagery evoked in the American discourse on Soviet foreign policy more often than not duplicate the terminology and imagery of the Nazi expansion in the pre–World War II period. On the whole, such a terminology and imagery are misleading, especially when the matter concerns the place of foreign policies in Soviet policymaking and the role of international concerns on the agenda of the Soviet leadership.

First (and in this respect the late Brezhnev era is not an exception) domestic concerns and internal policy issues — political, economic, and social — traditionally are a matter of primary concern for the Soviet leadership; they still have clear priority on the leadership's agenda. Second, in foreign policymaking, considerations of the security of the Soviet state and, to a virtually similar degree, of its East European sphere of interest (its satellite empire) and thus questions of the defensive posture of the Soviet Union, are their most preoccupying concern. Third, in its activities and initiatives abroad the managers of Soviet foreign policy display an attitude that assigns the highest value to low-risk and relatively low-cost operations and especially to actions that will have only marginal disruptive influence on the process and plans of maximal domestic development. There is no evidence as yet to indicate that the achievement by the Soviet Union of strategic parity and the activization of the Soviet Union in the international arena has changed this state of affairs, although of course it cannot be excluded that this will happen in the future.

The Soviet Union is obviously not a "sated power." Even when measured only from the point of view of great-power competition, it is a new, still dynamic great power that only now is reaching a global status; a great power in its ascendency phase, looking for a "place in the sun" commen-

surate with what it feels to be its due. This in itself would make any relations with the Soviet Union now and for the foreseeable future difficult,
highly competitive, complex, and unstable. It would preclude realization of
the exaggerated hopes of the early Kissinger détente, construed as a long-
range balance-of-power and sphere-of-interest agreement.

But the Soviet Union is not simply a great or global power. It is a power
the leadership of which holds a view of a world divided into opposing
systems of competing values, a view that is inherently contrary to the acceptance of a long-range status quo. It is this combination of the traditional
dynamic of an ascending power with the dynamic of a power that
represents the world outlook different from and competitive with the other
powers that makes the balance-of-power policies unlikely to succeed, limits
the scope of bilateral U.S.-Soviet agreements, and makes long-range solutions inherently unstable.

The difficulties in U.S.-Soviet relations do not have as their source
mutual misperceptions of the two powers by each other. At the heart of the
conflict is the real diversity of their interests, a real difference in their
evaluation and perception of the international situation, a real diversity of
their priorities in approaching the world system, and a real asymmetry in
the development of their international appetites and their consciousness of
what is possible and obtainable for their respective countries in the international arena.[25]

Notes

This chapter is part of a larger work by this author that will be published
separately.

1. Richard Lowenthal, "Dealing with Soviet Global Power," *Encounter*, June
1978, p. 90.

2. Writing on the domestic sources of Soviet foreign policy is very limited. The
most important works are: Alexander Dallin, "Soviet Foreign Policy and Domestic
Politics: A Framework for Analysis," *Journal of International Affairs* 23, no. 2
(1969):250–265; Alexander Dallin, "Domestic Factors Influencing Soviet Foreign
Policy," in Michael Confino and Shimon Shamir, eds., *The USSR and the Middle East*
(Jerusalem: Israeli Universities Press/John Wiley, 1973), pp. 31–58; Alexander
Dallin, "Soviet Conduct at Home and Abroad: In Search of Patterns" (Paper, April
1976, for conference sponsored by the American Association for the Advancement
of Slavic Studies R&D Committee, Ann Arbor, Michigan); Morton Schwartz, *The
Foreign Policy of the USSR: Domestic Factors* (Encino, Calif.: Dickenson Publishing
Company, 1975); William Zimmerman, "The Sources of Soviet Conduct: A Recon-
sideration" (paper presented to the annual meeting of the American Political Science
Association, Washington, D.C., 5–9 September 1972). A useful compilation of

various sources and viewpoints is the selection of readings edited by Alexander Dallin, *Soviet Conduct in World Affairs* (New York: Columbia University Press, 1960) and that in Erik P. Hoffmann and Frederic J. Fleron, Jr., eds., *The Conduct of Soviet Foreign Policy* (Chicago: Aldine-Atherton, 1971), pp. 31–212. See also Wolfgang Leonhard, "The Domestic Politics of the New Soviet Foreign Policy," in *Foreign Affairs* 52 no. 1 (October 1973) and Boris Meissner, "Wesen und Eigenart der sowjetischen Aussenpolitik Triebkräfte und Faktoren der sowjerischen Aussenpolitik," *Europa-Archiv* 18 (25 September 1969).

In the general literature of political science the question of domestic determinants of foreign policy is treated quite extensively. For a representative overview of existing sources see: James N. Rosenau, *The Domestic Sources of Foreign Policy* (Princeton, N.J.: Princeton University Press, 1965); Howard Lentner, *Foreign Policy Analysis: A Comparative and Conceptual Approach* (Columbus, Ohio: Charles E. Merrill Co. 1974), pp. 155–170; Michael P. Sullivan, *International Relations: Theories and Evidence* (Prentice-Hall, N.J.: 1976), pp. 102–143; William Wallace, *Foreign Policy and the Political Process* (London: Macmillan Press, 1971), ch. 4; Henry A. Kissinger, "Domestic Structure and Foreign Policy," in Harold K. Jacobson and William Zimmerman, *The Shaping of Foreign Policy* (New York: Atherton Press, 1969); James N. Rosenau, ed., *Comparing Foreign Policies: Theories, Findings, and Methods* (New York: John Wiley & Sons, 1974), chapters by Harf, Hoover and James, and Moore; Dina Zinnes, "Some Evidence Relevant to the Man-Milieu Hypothesis," in Rosenau, Davis, and East, eds., *The Analysis of International Politics* (New York: Free Press, 1972), pp. 209–251; G. H. Ramsey, "External vs. Internal Sources of Foreign Policy Behavior: Testing the Stability of an Intriguing Set of Findings" (paper presented at annual meeting of International Political Science Association, Montreal, 1973); Barry B. Hughes, *The Domestic Context of American Foreign Policy* (San Francisco: W. H. Freeman and Co., 1978).

3. The most recent and vituperative round of this debate began with the publication of George Kennan's book, *The Cloud of Danger* (Boston: Little, Brown and Co., 1977), and his article in *Encounter* (March 1978) and continued in *Encounter* (April–July). I sympathize neither with the views of Mr. Kennan nor with those of his most extreme opponents such as Richard Pipes and Leopold Labedz. Mr. Kennan makes an unwarranted leap when he deduces from internal changes in the Soviet polity the changes in the direction and nature of its international activity. To use Richard H. Ullman's expression, he "avoids coming to grips with hard problems by soaring over them." In contrast, Messrs. Pipes and Labedz have a totally static view of Soviet internal reality and foreign policy. Their view of the Soviet Union froze into a set mold decades ago. They do not soar over the hard problems but approach them from an extremely narrow and one-sided perspective. Mr. Kennan wants us to turn away from the realities of the past even when they are present today; Messrs. Pipes and Labedz want us to turn from the realities of the present to the past.

4. On the empathetic approach and the perceptual difficulties in analyzing interactions with other states, see the brilliant work by Robert Jervis, *Perception and Misperception in International Politics* (Princeton, N.J.: Princeton University Press, 1976). See also Richard W. Cottam, *Foreign Policy Motivation, a General Theory and a Case Study* (Pittsburgh, Pa.: University of Pittsburgh Press, 1977).

5. According to some calculations the total factor productivity growth in the years

1970–1975 was negative — minus 0.2. See: U.S. Congress, Joint Economic Committee, *Soviet Economy in a New Perspective* (Washington, D.C.: U.S. Government Printing Office, 1976), p. 279.

6. The Soviet minister of foreign trade makes this point very clearly when he says, "Today it would perhaps be difficult to find an economic sector in the USSR that is not connected with foreign trade to some extent or does not receive effective practical aid in its further development. To put it figuratively, foreign trade has become an important artery in the blood circulation of the Soviet Union's economic organism." (*Vneshnaia torgovlia*, 1978, no. 6, p. 3.) A good compendium of Soviet views on the present stage of their economic relations abroad is V. A. Brykin and B. S. Baganov, eds., *Vneshneekonomicheskie sviazi Sovetskogo Soiuza na novom etape* (Moscow, 1977). For a more theoretical approach see the important article by O. Bogomolov, "Material'naia osnova prochnogo mira," *Kommunist*, no. 2 (January 1978).

7. For a discussion on this subject see Hans Bergendorff and Per Strangert, "Projections of Soviet Economic Growth and Defense Spending," in JEC, *Soviet Economy in a New Perspective*.

8. For a discussion on this subject see Lars Calmfors and Jan Rylander, "Economic Restrictions on Soviet Defense Expenditure," in ibid.

9. The view that external expansion has become today the key Soviet domestic legitimizing device is strongly advocated by Adam Ulam who writes:

> National greatness vindicates ideology; ideological expansion is both a proof and an essential condition of national greatness. . . . For the Communist Establishment, constant even if prudent "extension of our power" remains the only practical course for demonstrating the viability and vitality of the doctrine on which the Soviet system bases its legitimacy. Domestically this doctrine has become discredited or irrelevant insofar as the majority of the Soviet people are concerned. Communism can be vindicated as the wave of the future, and the average citizen induced to acquiesce in the system under which he lives, *only* if it can be convincingly and repeatedly shown that under it the Soviet Union — Russia — advances in power and world-wide influence, while the West, for all its vaunted freedom and riches, has been on the defensive and will continue to decline. (Italics mine — S. B.) (Adam Ulam, "Soviet National Security" [paper presented at the Lehrman Institute, New York City, 27 September 1977], pp. 6, 23).

I do not question the proposition that Soviet external expansion performs a domestic legitimizing role for the system. I do, however, object to assigning to "legitimization by expansion" such extraordinary weight, as does Ulam, partly because there is little evidence to support the view that the Soviet public is really supportive or entranced by foreign adventures. But moreover, because I believe that the Soviet domestic system still displays important sources of legitimization and support.

10. One basic Soviet source on Soviet foreign policymaking that stresses the enhanced role of the party organs and institutions is D. A. Kerimov et al., *Mezhdunarodnaia politika KPSS i vneshnye funktsii sovetskogo gosudarstva* (Moscow:1976). Interesting insight into the working of the Soviet policymaking apparatus is provided by Alain Jacob, "The Soviet System," *The Guardian*, 2 March 1974.

11. One may formulate a "law" of Soviet bureaucratic politics as follows: "The higher the level at which a decision is taken, the more consensual is the nature of this decision." The higher the level at which a decision is adopted the greater the diversity of inputs into the decision and the larger the number of groups and individuals that participate in it and have a partial veto over its final shape. Soviet foreign policy decisions are highly consensual precisely because as a rule they are adopted at the highest level of decision making.

12. Differences of opinion with regard to foreign policy on the Soviet leadership level can be ascertained basically in two ways: first, when there is a purge and a leader is ousted; second, by a comparison of statements from different leaders on the same issues. With regard to the first there is no doubt that in some of the major changes in the Politburo in the post-Stalin era foreign policy differences played a substantial role. In the 1955 demotion and subsequent ouster of Molotov and Malenkov, foreign policy issues played a crucial role. (See Seweryn Bialer, "The Three Schools of Kremlin Policy," *The New Leader*, 29 July 1957.) In Khrushchev's ouster in 1964, questions of foreign policymaking were an important consideration. Evidence for this view comes not only from Western researchers but also from Zhores A. Medvedev, *Khrushchev: The Years in Power* (New York: Columbia University Press, 1976), and from an important Soviet "Samizdat" publication close to elite sources. See *Politicheskii dnevnik* (Amsterdam: The Alexander Herzen Foundation, 1972). It is also well documented that the ouster of Shelest in 1972 was at least partly attributable to foreign policy concerns. See Grey Hodnett, "Ukrainian Politics and the Purge of Shelest" (paper prepared for the annual meeting of the Midwest Slavic Conference, Ann Arbor, 5–7 May 1977). According to at least one source (the highest politically ranking recent emigré, Boris Rabbot), the dismissal of Podgorny in 1977 is explained primarily by foreign policy differences. See his article in the *Christian Science Monitor*, 29 June 1977. See also Rabbot's "Detente: The Struggle Within the Kremlin," the *Washington Post*, 10 July 1977.

With regard to the second method of ascertaining differences, the most recent study to suggest visible differences among such leaders as Brezhnev, Suslov, Andropov, and Shcherbitsky is Christian Duevel's "Similarities and Differences in the Soviet Leaders' Recent Approach to Some Issues of Foreign Policy," Radio Liberty Research, RL 211/78, 28 September 1978. Most convincing evidence exists with regard to sometimes sharp and profound differences of view and policy preferences both at the apex of the hierarchy and at the level of various bureaucratic complexes concerning the importance and the extent of infusion of technology from the West. See Bruce Parrott, "Soviet Technological Progress and Western Technology Transfer to the USSR: An Analysis of Soviet Attitudes" (paper prepared for the Office of External Research, U.S. Department of State, July 1978).

13. The very important role of Western technology import in arresting the declining trends of Soviet productivity growth is analyzed extensively in D. W. Green and H. S. Levine, "Macroeconometric Evidence of the Value of Machinery Imports to the Soviet Union" (SRI-WEFA Soviet Econometric Model, Working Paper no. 51, prepared for the National Science Foundation Workshop on Soviet Science and Technology, 18–21 November 1976). See also the earlier paper: Green and Levine, "Implications of Technology Transfers for the U.S.S.R.," *East-West*

Technological Co-operation (Brussels: NATO, 1976). See also J. Hardt and G. Holliday, "Implications of Commercial Technology Transfer Between the Soviet Union and the United States," in U.S. Congressional Research Service, *Technology Transfer and Scientific Cooperation Between the United States and the Soviet Union: A Review* (Washington, D.C.: U.S. Government Printing Office, 1977), pp. 55-103.

14. At various points in the following discussion on the role of ideology in Soviet foreign policy I use formulations and ideas expressed by me in an earlier paper: "Ideology and Soviet Foreign Policy," in George Schwab, ed., *Ideology and Foreign Policy, A Global Perspective* (N.Y. and London: Dyrco Press, Inc., 1978), pp. 76-102.

15. John Strachey, "Communist Intentions," *Partisan Review* 29, no. 2 (Spring 1962):215.

16. For a discussion on this subject initiated by the well-known article of Daniel Bell in his *The End of Ideology* (New York: Free Press, 1960), see Chaim I. Waxman, *The End of Ideology Debate* (New York: Simon and Schuster, 1968).

17. In a paper prepared for the U.S. State Department, William Taubman writes, "The question of whether and to what extent Soviet writers really believe the ideological formulations which they speak and write must be taken seriously. My own impression, based in part on interviews with Soviet scholars and journalists, both in Moscow and emigration, supports Solzhenitsyn's conclusion that ideology is both dead and as influential as ever; few in the top elite really believe in much of it anymore, but all must act as if they do." ("Soviet and Western Views of Each Other's Future in an Interdependent World," paper prepared by U.S. State Department for the Office of External Research, June 1977, p. 49.) This kind of formulation, however, does *not* treat seriously the question of the role of Soviet ideology. First, if people act as if they do believe in the ideology, then what is the significance, if any, of their alleged lack of belief? Second, it conflicts with the experience of human behavior and the findings of social psychology, and especially the tested idea of "cognitive dissonance," to argue that for prolonged periods people will act out ideas without coming to believe them. (See, for example, one of the most interesting and relevant case studies of the tendency to reduce dissonance by Leon Festinger et al., *When Prophecy Fails* [Minneapolis: University of Minnesota Press, 1956]). Third, Taubman does not differentiate between doctrine and ideology understood broadly and does not stress the main cognitive function of ideology and the main effect of ideology or even doctrine in shaping the mind-set of individuals who are exposed to it and influenced by it.

18. My views on ideology and the distinction between doctrine and ideology broadly understood are influenced by the brilliant work of Clifford Geertz, "Ideology as a Cultural System," in David A. Apter, ed., *Ideology and Discontent* (New York: Free Press, 1964) and by Franz Schurmann, *Ideology and Organization in Communist China*, 2d. ed. (Berkeley: University of California Press, 1970). For a perspective that in substance, in its stress on mind-sets of the political actors, does not differ from my own yet uses a different conceptual apparatus and terminology, see Ole R. Holsti, "Foreign Policy Decision Makers Viewed Psychologically: 'Cognitive Process' Approaches," in James N. Rosenau, ed., *In Search of Global Patterns* (New York: Free Press, 1976); Holsti writes, "Belief systems and cognitive processes should be distinguished from ideology or mere policy preferences" (p. 122). See also a valuable

summary of various views on ideology in L. B. Brown, *Ideology* (London: Penguin, 1973).

19. The distinction between "doctrine" and "ideology" seems to me absolutely crucial in evaluating the perceptual sources of Soviet foreign policy. Among the broad range of views expressed with regard to these sources two seem of special importance. One, expressed by William Zimmerman, sees not only a decline in the role of ideology in Soviet foreign policymaking but also its limited relevance in understanding Soviet international perceptions, let alone behavior. The second, held by Hannes Adomeit, is best expressed in the subtitle of a chapter of his work: "L'idéologie est morte! Vive l'idéologie!" Yet the weakness of both positions is that neither makes the distinction between "doctrine" and "ideology." For Zimmerman the "doctrine" is the "ideology." Adomeit's argument moves back and forth from one dimension of the belief system to the other. See William Zimmerman, *Soviet Perspectives on International Relations 1956–1967* (Princeton, N.J.: Princeton University Press, 1969), especially pp. 275–294; Hannes J. Adomeit, *Soviet Risk Taking and Crisis Behavior: From Confrontation to Coexistence?* Adelphi Paper, no. 101 (London: International Institute for Strategic Studies, 1973) and "Soviet Risk Taking and Crisis Behavior: A Theoretical and Empirical Analysis" (Ph.D. diss., Columbia University, 1977).

20. Alexander Dallin, "Retreat from Optimism: On Marxian Models of Revolution," in Seweryn Bialer, ed., *Radicalism in the Contemporary Age*, vol. 3: *Strategies and Impact of Contemporary Radicalism* (Boulder, Colorado: Westview Press, 1977), p. 146.

21. The two volumes of Khrushchev's memoirs and the additional unpublished hundreds of pages of his testimony deposited in Columbia University archives provide a unique and unparalleled source for the study of the Soviet leadership's perceptions. Their value can only be enhanced by the fact that they were made under conditions so unlike the usual memoirs of great leaders. They contain a chaotic, lively, uncontrolled free flow of reminiscences, impressions, and reflections. Moreover, Khrushchev belonged to the same generation of leadership that presently composes the apex of Soviet policymaking, and undoubtedly his views and perceptions have a validity that encompasses to a large extent the entire generation of Soviet leaders who will shortly pass from the scene. It is, therefore, unfortunate that no serious effort has yet been made to map out the shape of Soviet leadership beliefs and perspectives on international relations on the basis of these memoirs. My own impression from reading the memoirs, the unpublished testimony, and listening to the tapes is of an astounding similarity of Khrushchev's public and private views and of an extraordinary proximity of his basic orientation, biases, and assumptions on international relations to those espoused in Soviet published materials. The memoirs are reassuring about what we can extract from Soviet leaders' and experts' public statements and writings.

22. A very interesting discussion on the role in Soviet thinking of prestige and status, its connection with Soviet conservatism, and the Soviets' exaggerated sensitivity to real and alleged slights can be found in Stephen F. Cohen, "Why Detente Can Work," *Inquiry*, 19 December 1977. It is my opinion that the weaknesses of the policy of the present U.S. administration with regard to the Soviet Union have primarily to do not with the question of substantive policies but rather with style and

form of policies and their lack of perception of Soviet psychology and sensitivities. In the case of the Soviet Union more than with any other country the question of style and form easily becomes a question of substance.

23. Thomas W. Wolfe, "Military Power and Soviet Policy," in William E. Griffith, ed., *The Soviet Empire: Expansion and Detente* (Lexington, Mass.: D. C. Heath and Co., 1976), p. 149.

24. For a discussion of Eurocommunism and the dilemmas it poses for Soviet policymakers see Robert Legvold, "The Soviet Union and West European Communism," in Rudolf L. Tökés, ed., *Eurocommunism and Détente* (New York: New York University Press, 1978) and Bogdan D. Denitch, "Eurocommunism: A Threat to Soviet Hegemony," in Grayson Kirk and Nils H. Wessell, eds., *The Soviet Threat: Myths and Realities*, Proceedings of the Academy of Political Science, 33, no. 1 (New York: Praeger Publishers, 1978).

25. Yet misperceptions do intrude powerfully into the policymaking process of both countries. The arrangement of relations, which would be in any case difficult enough, are complicated all the more when misunderstanding accompanies disagreement and competition. This is why it is so important for us to understand Soviet perceptions of the key issues in the international arena. Without such understanding, the policies that we adopt might unnecessarily aggravate existing tensions, minimize the potential for agreements, compromise any steps in the direction of partial solutions, and, most important, have fewer chances to succeed.